A HISTORY
OF THE CHURCH
IN LATIN AMERICA

A HISTORY
OF THE CHURCH
IN LATIN AMERICA

Colonialism to Liberation
(1492 – 1979)

by
Enrique Dussel

Translated and Revised
by Alan Neely

WILLIAM B. EERDMANS PUBLISHING COMPANY
GRAND RAPIDS, MICHIGAN

Translated from the third edición of *Historia de la Iglesìa en América Latina*.

Library of Congress Cataloging in Publication Data

Dussel, Enrique D.
  A history of the church in Latin America.

  Translation of: Historia de la Iglesia en América
Latina. 3rd ed. 1974.
  Includes bibliographical references.
  1. Latin America — Church history. I. Title.
BR600.D8713 1981   278   81-17483
ISBN 0-8028-3548-1   AACR2

PSALM 5—A Paraphrase

HEAR MY PROTEST
Hear my words, Oh Lord, give ear to my groanings.
Listen to my protest.
For you are not a God who is friendly with oppressors,
nor do you support their devious ways,
nor are you influenced by their propaganda,
nor are you a cohort with gangsters.
One cannot believe anything they say,
nor have any confidence in their official pronouncements.
They talk of peace while they increase their production of arms.
They make gestures toward understanding at the Peace Conferences,
but in secret they prepare for war.

. . . .

Punish them, Oh God,
bring to naught their machinations.

— Ernesto Cardenal (Managua)

"Then I saw a new heaven and a new earth. . . ."
— *Revelation 21:1.*

Dedication

To the Christs of Latin America:

To the martyred Bishop of Nicaragua,
Monseñor Antonio de Valdivieso (d. 1550),
assassinated by the oppressive violence of
the sixteenth century.

To the martyred priest of Recife,
Padre Antonio Pereira Neto (d. 1969),
assassinated by the coercive violence of
the twentieth century.

"Nations on the road to progress, like those recently made independent, desire to participate in the goods of modern civilization not only in the political field but also economically, and to play their part freely on the world scene. Still they continually fall behind while very often their dependence on wealthier nations deepens more rapidly, even in the economic sphere. People hounded by hunger call upon those better off. Where they have not won it, women claim for themselves an equity with men before the law and in fact. Laborers and farmers seek not only to provide for the necessities of life but to develop the gifts of their personality by their labors. . . . Man is becoming aware that it is his responsibility to guide aright the forces which he has unleashed and which can enslave him or minister to him. That is why he is putting questions to himself." (*Pastoral Constitution Gadium et Spes,* 9, Second Vatican Council)

"*Growing distortion of international commerce.* Because of the relative depreciation of the terms of exchange, the value of raw materials is increasingly less in relation to the cost of manufactured products. . . . This injustice clearly denounced by *Populorum Progressio* (n. 56 – 61) . . . constitutes a permanent menace against peace. . . . *International monopolies and international imperialism of money.* We wish to emphasize that the principal guilt for economic dependence of our countries rests with powers, inspired by an uncontrolled desire for gain, which leads to economic dictatorship and the "international imperialism of money" condemned by Pope Pius XI in *Quadragesimo Anno* and by Pope Paul VI in *Populorum Progressio.*" (2. Peace, n. 9, "Conclusions" of the Second General Conference of Latin American Bishops in Medellín)

Preface to the English Edition

This English edition of *History of the Church in Latin America* is a translation of the third Spanish edition completed in 1971. It is for this reason that I have added a section describing the period of 1972—1979 (from Sucre to Puebla), which brings the work up to date. Also, some of the Spanish appendices that are not of interest to the English-speaking readers have been eliminated. This English edition is, nonetheless, substantially the same as the Spanish one.

It is anticipated that the reader, in addition to learning of what has taken place in and to the Latin American Church, will comprehend more fully the suffering of this continent and the appearance of our own creations such as the Theology of Liberation — which is the product of the lives and the suffering of our oppressed people.

ENRIQUE DUSSEL

Mexico City
July 1979

Contents

PART THREE
THE AGONY OF COLONIAL CHRISTENDOM
(1808–1962)

PART FOUR
THE CHURCH AND LATIN AMERICAN
LIBERATION (1962–1979)

Translator's Preface

The prophets of Latin American liberation theology have been said to be Rubem Alves of Brazil, the systematic theologian Gustavo Gutiérrez of Peru, and the apologist Hugo Assmann of Uruguay. Were it possible to limit the circle of spokesmen to these three, which it is not, the group would have to be enlarged to include the Argentine Enrique Dussel who is liberation theology's principal historian and ethicist.

During the early days of the liberation theology movement Assmann wrote, "The greatest merit of the 'theology of liberation' probably lies in its insistence on the historical starting point of its reflection: the dominated situation of Latin America."[1] Professor Dussel has ably verified this fact in this his major work, *A History of the Church in Latin America.*

To the reader familiar with the writings of the Latin Americans, the intensity and passion with which Dussel writes will come as no surprise. But for one who has read little or nothing of the theology of liberation, this work will be unsettling not only because of the substance of the indictment against Christians' complicity in oppression, but also because of our North American and European insensitivity to such oppression. For this is not a cool, dispassionate retelling of events in the style of the "objective" historian, but a disquieting, painful, and sometimes glorious narrative written by one who is a careful observer and a meticulous investigator, as well as a competent theologian and a committed participant.

A half-century ago John Millington Synge wrote: "A translation is no translation . . . unless it will give you the music of a poem along with the words of it." I have tried to render faithfully and accurately not only Professor Dussel's thoughts and the results of his exhaustive research, but also the anguish and poignancy of his descriptions. The story is a moving example of what Robert McAfee Brown has aptly called "theology in a new key."[2]

The value of this work is threefold: it recounts concisely and lucidly the complex and tumultuous history of Latin American Christianity; it recreates the religious and secular context from which emerged an abundance of saints and sinners — some well known, others obscure or long forgotten; and it forces a rereading of a history not known by most of us North Americans and Europeans — and by relatively few Latin Americans — a history in which all of us are inextricably involved.

It has been my good fortune to have had the encouragement of many to undertake this task of translation, including Orlando E. Costas, recently elected Professor of Missions at Eastern Baptist Theological Seminary in Philadelphia, who first suggested it, and many of my colleagues both here in the United States and in Latin America. In addition, Professor Dussel has been able to read the entire manuscript and to point out the occasions when another word or phrase would better express his thoughts.

John E. Steely, Professor of Historical Theology here at Southeastern Baptist Theological Seminary and translator of numerous works, has been particularly helpful in checking references and bibliographical materials in German and Dutch. The careful and competent assistance of my wife, Virginia, both in the translation and in the preparation of the manuscript has been invaluable. I could not have completed this nor much else without her.

ALAN NEELY

Southeastern Baptist Theological Seminary
Wake Forest, North Carolina
October 1, 1979
The Day of Panama's Liberation

Preface to the First
Spanish Edition

We should like, in the first place, to make clear our purpose in writing this book, so the reader will understand what we have attempted to do.

This is a study centering on a limited area between the *philosophy of culture* and *history*, but it is basically *theology*. We believe, as we will demonstrate, that we must place ourselves within the contiguous boundaries of diverse sciences if we are to help the history of the Latin American Church to emerge from the crisis in which it has recently been born.

It should be evident even to one who has only begun historical studies that the history of the Church in Latin America has just begun. During the period of the conquest, soldiers, rulers, missionaries, and clergy — those gifted in the art of writing — left us many interesting stories, chronicles, and descriptions of the events and activities in which they participated. But their chronicles and anecdotes are not history in a scientific sense. Little more than these was written during the colonial period, and one will look in vain for any significant historical work prior to the third decade of the nineteenth century. In fact, it was not until the latter part of this century that important historical works began to appear. We would refer the reader, for example, to the writings of Icazbalceta in Mexico or of Groot in Colombia. One must wait until the twentieth century before a Cuevas appears in Mexico, or a Furlong or a Carbia in Argentina, an Eizaguirre in Chile, a Vargas Ugarte in Peru, a Leturia in Spain, a Ricard in France, or a Konetzke in Germany. The fact is that Latin American church history as a science is very recent, and works like those of Valencia on Toribio de Mogrovejo, or that of Juan Friede on the life of Juan del Valle are very rare.

We have already noted that the birth of the history of the Latin American Church was intimately related to a crisis. We believe that this can be affirmed by observing that until recently it has not been possible to distinguish clearly in what way the history of the Church differs from secular history. We believe there is a radical difference. None of the historians we have mentioned has published a "problematization" of his method of recounting the history of the Church which could be referred to as scientific history and which at the same time could be regarded as theology. We believe, furthermore, that the development of history as a science will necessitate our working together as interdisciplinary teams composed of historians, theologians, sociologists, and philosophers. Otherwise we will continue to produce merely secular history — as we have already indicated — or apologetic history.

In this brief essay, we attempt to initiate a dialogue regarding certain fundamental *hypotheses* that must be discussed if we are to open the history of the Church in Latin

America to the issues currently debated in theology, philosophy, and sociology, as well as in the economic and political sciences.

A *hypothesis*[1] in science is a proposition considered to be a possible explanation for the occurrence of a certain phenomenon that must be tested by additional investigation. But a hypothesis can also result from previous scientific investigations. A hypothesis can be, therefore, either a beginning or a terminal point. As the former, it involves a certain risk in that it may prove to be unfounded. But as the result of investigations already done, a hypothesis can be accepted as an established fact.

What we propose is a beginning hypothesis of the periodification of *all* the history of the Latin American Church. As a hypothesis, we are obligated to sketch briefly the contents and the meaning of what we propose to include. Each period is described in a few short pages because we are not attempting to recount all the historical events of each era — even if we knew them — but rather to demonstrate the validity of establishing limits for each of these periods. In the second place, only certain characteristics of these periods are noted, characteristics that appear to us as essential and related and for which sufficient data are available to describe them.

This work is not, therefore, a finished history of the Church, but rather a "problematization" of a method and a periodification which can be completed later by other historical and theological scientists working together.

At the same time, as will be observed, a certain "interpretation" is implicit in this study, and it is here that the dialogue begins regarding the ultimate meaning of history, especially of the history of the Church, and how one should understand this history in the light of faith. If *our* history has ultimate meaning, then all who are Christians in Latin America — and even those who are not — can begin to search for a source of contemporary understanding of their Christian existence. What began therefore as our hypothesis for a scientific endeavor is transformed into a particular *reading* of our history and is, or can be, beneficial to the common citizen, to the trade unionist, and even to the politician. Herein we see an essential point, namely, that history constitutes the cultural comprehension of a people when it is given "meaning," and even more so in the Christian understanding when history is viewed as an eschatological teleology — the meaning of history that moves towards Christ who will come because he has come — for the people of the continent. In this way history can become our teacher.

One major problem is that the history of the Latin American Church is cloistered within the circle of scientific publications, and the public at large, Christian or otherwise, is never exposed to it. This leaves the Latin American bereft of one of the essential dimensions of his own cultural development.

When a Latin American Christian — or even one who is not Christian — becomes aware of the importance of discovering his role on this continent that is moving toward liberation, it becomes evident that as never before he needs to understand the function and continuity of *his* own tradition. When he is equipped with a new understanding of himself, he will be able to read basic and diverse works on the origins of Christianity and its development during the Patristic and medieval periods, the Reformation, and the modern era. Even so, all of these movements are European. And when he asks, "What has been the history of the Church in Latin America?" or "What is the background of my own Christianity?" a vacuum is immediately created because an authentic history of Latin American Christianity has not been written. Moreover, when one sets out to write such a history, it is possible to find only isolated anecdotes, while the central thread of development, the nucleus around which this history has moved, remains obscure. When a Latin American, therefore, wishes to understand himself as a Christian in the written histories of the Church, he becomes hopelessly confused by the ambiguity of the historical accounts since their real meaning has not yet been explained. This is the situation in all dependent cultures deprived of their own histories.

We attempt to set forth therefore a historical hypothesis and a periodification with its essential elements so that we may begin discussing the method that should be utilized in the understanding of the history of the Church in Latin America. We also address ourselves to the militant in Latin America who is demanding a reasonable and understandable exposition of the present Christian phenomenon on which the future of our people evidently depends.

E.D.

Institut für europäische Geschichte (Maguncia),
March 1964.

Preface to the Second Spanish Edition

In 1963, during a trip that I made from Maguncia to Paris, I wrote the outline that forms the basis of this work as published in Spanish in 1964. This second edition, rewritten in 1971, is the product of a more comprehensive knowledge of Latin America acquired from journeys through Mexico, Central America, the Caribbean, Greater Colombia, the Andean Zone, and the River Plate to Brazil — knowledge I did not have when I was studying in Europe.

During these last eight years Latin America has moved to a new and crucial level in her history, one unforeseen a decade ago. Today in Europe as well as in Latin America there exists abundant information regarding our continent, but, to my knowledge, there does not exist a comprehensive description and interpretation of our history from the beginning in the fifteenth century until the present, one that includes the later developments of Vatican Council II and of the 1968 Latin American Bishops Conference in Medellín. Paradoxically, only by seeing the total picture is it possible to have an adequate understanding of what is now taking place. Recent events, especially those since 1962, are in themselves incomprehensible unless they are placed within a framework that explains them.

Latin America, situated on the outer and forgotten fringes of the Church, is now being transformed into an authentic laboratory of a new ecclesiastical experience, one with worldwide ramifications because the present confrontation and precariousness, as well as contradictions of a condition of dependence and of structural oppression is beginning to be recognized. Theological, ecclesiastical, or pastoral experiences of people in the oppressive cultures (in the United States or Europe, for example) are irrelevant for Latin Americans who now are reflecting on their own experiences. The cultural and theological awakening of Latin America as oppressed and dependent, forces us to rethink our situation in the light of faith as a means of escaping the apparent dead-end with its perpetual underdevelopment. But it brings the Christian face to face with the possibility of having to choose the ay of revolution as an expedient for liberation and as a means of transforming the oppressed into free persons and at the same time liberating the oppressor who alienated himself by regarding the oppressed as nothing more than "things."

If the youth of the world have taken "Che" Guevara as their model and if many Christians admire the Colombian priest Camilo Torres, it is because these two men gave their lives to liberate the oppressed. The meaning of their lives and deaths is not, however, readily apparent. It is necessary to reflect on the meaning and theological significance within the history of the world and particularly within the history of the Latin American Church. What will emerge then will not be an historical oddity, but rather a new theology. Europeans are not even aware of this, and the time is coming when Latin American Christians will no longer depend on European theologians, but, struggling for liberation, will turn on them as the oppressed against their oppressors.

In this second edition we have modified our original periodification. Basically we have regarded the colonial period (1492– 1808) as the time of the Christianizing of the Indies, which adapted Byzantine, medieval Latin, and principally the Spanish Christianity of the Catholic rulers and their descendents. The period that I call the agony of Christendom (from 1808 until 1962) has been subjected to a major revision. Finally, the period from 1850 to 1930 has been given new limits, especially the years from 1930 to 1962, which stand out as the time when consideration was given to the organization of a New Christendom; that is, to replacing the medieval and colonial "model" with a new one. The attempt was frustrated, however, because of the new attitude that Vatican Council II generated. The new spirit proceeding from the Council encountered the force of popular revolution that was slowly developing. The Church, therefore, came to a crucial time in her history, and Medellín (1968) was merely the beginning. Behind the superficial events, the military coups, terrorism by extremists, repression, and so forth, a profound movement developed in Latin America that now needs to be understood and described. In the introductory reflections and in those which conclude Part Four, we attempt to suggest solutions that will enable us to discover the *import* of these developments in the light of faith. In this way the history of the Church in Latin America acquires adequate form for being one moment in the unique history of salvation which is the history of liberation.

E.D.

National University of Cuyo (Mendoza, Argentina)
Latin American Pastoral Institute (Quito),
January, 1971.

Preface to the Third Spanish Edition

This third edition appears only one year after the second and is a reprinting of it. The only changes we have made are in a few details; for example, the inclusion of some references to "Chicanos" (Mexican-Americans) and to "Latinos." We have postponed a major revision until the fourth edition because such a modification would take several months, and the editors are asking that we fill the growing number of orders already on hand.

During the latter months of 1973, it became necessary to explain several important events in the Latin American Church that resulted from the November 1972 meeting in Sucre of CELAM,[1] and the changes that came about in the Southern Cone because the military coups in Uruguay and Bolivia, the fall of Allende in Chile, and the triumph of Peronism in Argentina. All these changes as well as an amplification of the treatment of the colonial period and of the events of the nineteenth century will have to be dealt with in a subsequent edition.

Finally, I have been personally affected in a concrete way by the reality of the struggle for liberation on our continent, for during the night of October 2 a large bomb destroyed part of my home — an experience that only reconfirmed my deepest convictions.

This written history is a lived history, day by day, step by step, which we have wanted to interpret in the light of the risk of faith and with a legitimate historical method.

E. D.

Mexican American Cultural Center (San Antonio, Texas),
November, 1973.

Abbreviations

ACO	Workers' Catholic Action
APRA	American Popular Revolutionary Alliance (International political party founded in 1924 by Peruvian leader, Victor Raul Haya de la Torre.)
ASO	Catholic Action in Cuba
BID	Inter-American Development Bank
CAL	Pontifical Commission for Latin America
CASC	Autonomous Confederation of Catholic Trade Unions
CEAS	Center for Studies and Social Action (Ecuador)
CECLA	Special Commission of Latin American Coordination
CEHILA	Commission for Latin American Church History
CELAM	Conference of the Latin American Episcopate
CEPAL	(U.N.) Economic Commission for Latin America
CESA	Ecuadorian Education Center of Agricultural Services
CGT	General Confederation of Labor (Argentina)
CIA	Central Intelligence Agency (USA)
CIASC	Inter-American Confederation of Catholic Social Action
CICOP	Catholic Interamerican Cooperation Program
CIDOC	Inter-Cultural Center for Documentation (Cuernavaca, Mexico) (Founded and directed for fifteen years by Ivan Illich. Closed in 1976.)
CIEC	Interamerican Confederation of Catholic Education
CLAR	Latin American Confederation of Religious Orders
CLASC	Latin American Confederation of Trade Unionists
CNBB	National Conference of Brazilian Bishops
COGECAL	General Council of the Pontifical Commission for Latin America
COMIBOL	National Corporation of Mines (Bolivia)
CONFREGUA	Confederation of Guatemalan Religious Orders
COPEI	Christian Democratic Party (Venezuela)
COSDEGUA	Confederation of Diocesan Priests of Guatemala
DAS	Administrative Department of Security (Colombia)
DEOPS	Brazilian National Security Police
DESAL	Center for Economic and Social Development

ECLA	Economic Commission for Latin America
FCLA	Latin American Peasant Federation
FERES	Federation for Religious and Sociological Studies
FEUC	Federation of Students of the Catholic Universities (Chile)
ICLA	Latin American Catechetical Institute
ILADES	Latin American Institute of Doctrine and Social Studies
ILPES	Latin American Institute for Economic and Social Planning (An organ of the U.N. for educating economists for entire continent)
INCORA	Colombian Agrarian Reform Institute
INPROA	Institute for Agrarian Promotion (Chile)
IPLA	Latin America Pastoral Institute
ISAL	Church and Society in Latin America (An entity of the World Council of Churches)
ISPLA	See IPLA. Became IPLA (Pastoral Institute of Latin America) in 1968
JAC	Young Catholic Action
JAC	Young Catholic Agrarian Movement
JEC	Young Catholic Students
JECI	Young International Catholic Student Movement
JOC	Young Catholic Workers
JUC	Young Catholic University Students
JUDCA	Christian Democratic Youth of America
LADOC	Latin American Bureau Documentary Service, U.S. Catholic Conference
LAFTA	Latin American Free Trade Association
MAPU	Movement of United Popular Action (Chile). A coalition political party formed by Jacques Chonchol in 1970 to attract left-leaning members of the PDC (Christian Democrats).
MEB	Brazilian Educational Movement of Paulo Freire
MIEC-JECI	MIEC — International Movement of Catholic Students JECI — International Catholic Student Youth
MNR	National Revolutionary Movement (Bolivia)
MURO	University Movement for Renewed Orientation (Mexico)
NADOC	Latin American Service of Documentation for Development (Lima, Peru)
OAS	Organization of American States
OCSHA	Spanish Organization for Collaboration
ODECA	Organization of Central American States
ODUCAL	Organization of Latin American Catholic Universities
OLAS	Organization of Latin America Solidarity (Castro's counterpart to the OAS)
ONIS	National Office for Sociological Investigation (Peru)
ORMEU	Office of Relations of University Student Movements
OSLAM	Organization of Latin American Seminaries
PRSC	Christian Democratic Party (Colombia and Ecuador)

PSDC	Christian Democratic Party (Dominican Republic)
SAL	Priests for Latin America or Priests for Liberation (Colombia)
SIAC	Interamerican Secretariat of Catholic Action
SUDENE	Superintendency of the Development of the Northeast (Brazil)
TFP	The Society for the Defense of Tradition, Family and Property (Brazil, Argentina, Chile)
UECA	Union of American Christian Educators
ULAPC	Latin American Union of Catholic Press
UMAS	United Mexican American Students
UNELAM	Latin American Evangelical Pro-Unity Movement (An entity of the World Council of Churches)
UNESCO	United Nations Educational, Scientific, and Cultural Organization
UNIAPAC	Union of Catholic Professionals (Doctors, lawyers, engineers, etc.)
UNIP	Interamerican Union of Parents
UPI	United Press International

Part One
A Hermeneutical Introduction

Part One of this study proposes to clarify certain methodological norms and to enter fully into the current debate over the theology of liberation by giving the bases necessary for a constructive dialogue.[1] Frequently nowadays, references are made to liberation, faith, culture, praxis, and history, but the meaning of these terms is not always clear. In this limited study of Latin American culture and the history of the Latin American Church we cannot possibly deal in minutiae, but we do hope to address enough detail to provide the reader with an adequate outline. The reader who is not interested in the methodological questions may wish to proceed directly to Part Two, where the synthesis of the history and thinking of the Church in Spanish America actually begins.

Chapter I

Domination-Liberation: A Different Kind Of Theological Discussion

In this section the theological discussion proceeds on two levels. In the first place, there is a *methodical* discussion regarding some of the themes of theology as it is presently being done in Latin America. In the second place, there is a *methodological* discussion regarding contemporary theological development in Latin America to show that it applies not only to our sociocultural continent, but to all "peripheral" cultures; that is, it applies to *world* theology, the theology beyond the limited horizon of the Europeans.

I. DOMINATION-LIBERATION

This first section includes a summary exposition of the direction that theological discussion in Latin America is taking, proceeding not from the *theological* status but rather from the *real* status of the situation. Our point of departure is not, therefore, what the theologians have said about the real situation, but rather what reality itself shows us. As we attempt to indicate some of the possible issues, we will address three of the more serious ones, those suggested to us by tradition. In ancient Semite thinking Hammurabi clearly enunciated in his *Code*: "I have defended them with wisdom, therefore the strong shall not oppress the weak, and justice shall be accorded the orphan and the widow."[2] In Judeo-Christian revelation *political, erotical,* and *pedagogical* levels are indicated by Isaiah's words: "Pursue justice and champion the oppressed; give the orphan his rights, plead the widow's cause" (1:17 NEB). The same three levels are suggested by Jesus when he declares: "I tell you this: There is no one who has given up home, or wife, brothers, parents, or children . . . " (Luke 18:29 NEB).

In the middle of the sixteenth century, in 1552, Bartolomé de las Casas accused European Christian colonizers in the Americas of injustice because these "respected gentlemen . . . imposed upon the indigenous peoples the most arduous, horrible, and bitter slavery."[3] The relationship of brother to brother (man, oppressed, weak) is the *political* level; the relationship of man to woman (home, wife, widow) is the *erotical* level; and the relationship of parents to children (orphan, child) is the *pedagogical* level. In looking at these three levels, we will see how a discussion proceeding from *reality* originates and develops.

1. A Genetic-Political Beginning

The present world reality manifests in its structure a lack of equilibrium that has existed for five hundred years. As a result of Portugal's experiences in North Africa, and after the European nations' failure to expand to the East by means of the Crusades (whereby in the Middle Ages they dreamed of arriving in the East by crossing the Arab world), Western Christian nations began their expansion in the North Atlantic, which eventually became and remains until now the geopolitical center of world history. First Spain, then Holland and England, and later France and other European countries constituted the real ecumenical world, for until the fifteenth century the Latin, Byzantine, and Arab oecumenes, the world of India, of China, of the Aztec, and of the Inca were all regional. This new oecumene, which had Europe as its "center," expanded during the end of the nineteenth century and the beginning of the twentieth to include the United States and then Japan. An enormous "periphery," therefore, remains: Latin America, the Arab world, Black Africa, India, Southeast Asia, and China.

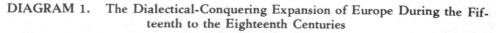

DIAGRAM 1.   The Dialectical-Conquering Expansion of Europe During the Fifteenth to the Eighteenth Centuries

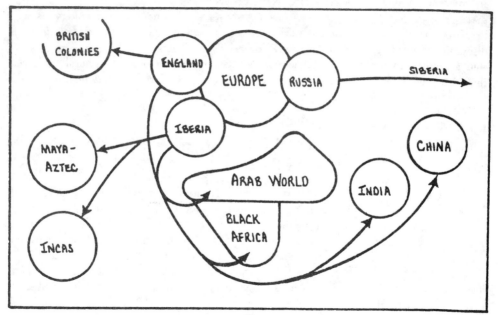

Europeans said—first it was Spain and Portugal through Pizarro and Cortéz—"I conquered the Indian." Then Thomas Hobbs enunciated even more clearly: "*Homo homini lupus.*" And then Nietzsche revealed man's insatiable "will to power." The politico-economic structure of the world continues to be unified by a single international system of domination. Two examples can be offered to show the profound ethical injustice of this dehumanizing system.

This colonial system of dependency and unjustice continued uninterrupted from the sixteenth until the twentieth century, and according to Raúl Prebisch, the Argentine economist, between 1950 and 1961 the total investments of foreign capital in Latin America amounted to some 9.6 billion dollars while during the same period the amount expatriated from Latin America amounted to at least 13.4 billion dollars, meaning a net loss to the continent of nearly 4 billion dollars.[5]

On the political level (brother to brother), the domination today is of the "periphery" by the "center"; that is, the interior or provinces are exploited by the capital

**Exportation of Precious Metals from the Private Sector
and the Importations from Europe of Finished Products
(In *maravedís*, Spanish currency of the period)[4]**

Period	Exports from the Private Sector	Imports in Finished Products	Differece in Spain's Favor
1561— 1570	8,785,000,000	1,565,000,000	7,220,000,000
1581— 1590	16,926,000,000	3,915,000,000	13,011,000,000
1621— 1630	19,104,000,000	5,300,000,000	13,804,000,000

cities,[6] the working classes are dominated by the oligarchies, and the masses are directed by the bureaucrats. It is on this political level that our history of the Church is developed.

2. A Genetic-Erotic Point of Departure

The contemporary interpersonal situation perpetuates the injustices of the ancient male-female relationship that has existed for millennia but is still practiced by European moderns. If it is true, as Freud suggested, that in our male-oriented society "the *libido* is commonly masculine in nature (*mannlicher Natur*),"[7] has it not been clearly demonstrated in Latin America that the conqueror was a man of respectability, while the most alienated was the Indian woman? Bishop Juan Ramírez of Guatemala wrote on March 10, 1603, that the worst "forms of violence never before heard of in other nations were being practiced against the Indian women, and they were compelled against their will by order of the authorities to serve in the houses of the *encomenderos*,[8] on their plantations and in their shops; they were kept as concubines by the owners along with the mestizos, mulattoes, and blacks —those soulless ones."[9] The conqueror who cohabitated illegally with an Indian woman was the father of the mestizo while the Indian woman was the mother. The conqueror, the *encomendero* —first a colonial bureaucrat, afterwards a Creole oligarch, and finally a subordinate bourgeois — is the one who oppressed and sexually alienated the Indian, the mestiza, the poor woman of the society. The man of the subordinate national oligarchy continues to seduce and otherwise take advantage of the girl from the poor working section on the periphery of the large cities —the theme of the tango "Margot" written by Celedonio Flores in 1918 —while at the same time demanding that his aristocratic lady remain pure and chaste —a form of hypocrisy described by W. Reich but which may be studied much more radically from the perspective of the Third World.

The practical "I conquered," the ontological *ego cogito*, is that of the male oppressor and can be psychoanalytically observed in Descartes' denying his mother, his mistress, and his daughter. In the words of Maryse Choisy y de Lacan, we could say that the phallocracy of today is the concomitant of the plutocracy of yesterday. In our history of the Church, however, we will not consider this aspect.

3. A Genetic-Pedagogical Point of Departure

Political or erotic oppression is personified in the *pedagogical* domination of a child domesticated and made submissive by his parent(s), or the young person "massified" and manipulated in society by the communications media. Political oppression is seen primarily in government and economic structures, while erotic domination is manifested primarily in various forms of sexual discrimination. Since the time of Aristotle[10] the pedagogy of domination has insisted that parents "love their children as themselves (for their issue are by virtue of their separate existence a sort of other selves) ... [and] are, therefore, in a sense the same thing, though in separate individuals" (*Nic. Ethics*, VIII, 12, 1161 b 27 – 34). The cultural conquest of other peoples has likewise been represented as the extension of "the Self." The conqueror or the pedagogical dominator controls by force of arms, and then by violence imposes upon another human being (such as the Indian, the African, the Asian, the masses, the worker, or the defenseless) the conqueror's civilization, religion, and deified cultural system in its ideological Totality. Pedagogical domination is dialectical (from the Greek *diá-*, i.e., by means of), for it is the means by which the cultural Totality of the father, the empire, or the oligarchy establishes dominion over another by controlling his or her analytical horizon.

The conquest and colonization of America, of Africa, and of Asia, the education of the child in knowing himself — as Socrates proposed by his dialectical method — is a kind of negative celebration of oppression. The ideological dialectic *continually* conceals oppression from the oppressed, and dominates completely by permeating the total being of individuals and societies. Paradoxically, the time comes when the oppressed child or culture begins to sing the praises of the oppressor. At one time there were in Latin America two distinct civilizations, one indigenous and the other alien, that is, European.[11] In Argentina, Domingo F. Sarmeinto — to cite but one example — depreciated the dependent national culture of the *gaucho* and of the economically impoverished "periphery" while at the same time glorifying the oligarchic, elitist, oppressive culture of the "center."

4. "Face to Face": Totality and Exteriority

The point of departure in the discussion thus far has been "reality" as seen on three anthropological levels. Reality, however, can have two very different meanings. The real can be something intraworldly, that is, a physical entity.[12] In this sense the Indian was real as an *encomendado* and the Negro was real as a slave. But the real can also be something otherworldly,[13] that is, an entity whose reality is constituted by non-physical categories.[14] The political, erotic, and pedagogical conditions that have been cited thus far are merely aspects of the structures of diverse totalities in which beings function in different internal roles — such as dependent, underdeveloped nations or as dependent women and children. These dependent roles are, nonetheless, distortions and sometimes obliterations of their original and intended roles as "face to face" beings. In oppressive systems, the metaphysical reality of a human being as exteriority is denied; and it is this exteriority that conveys the metaphysical meaning of reality.

"Face to face" is a repetition in Hebrew and Greek signifying the ultimate, supreme confrontation. It represents a proximity, an immediacy of two mysteries confronting each other as exteriority. An example can be seen in Exodus 33:11, "Yahweh would speak with Moses face to face (Hebrew *pním el-pním*), as a man speaks with his friend," and in I Corinthians 13:12, "For now we are seeing a dim reflection in a mirror; but then we shall be seeing face to face (*prósopon pros prósopon*)." On the erotic level, "face to face" can represent a gentle or passionate touching of the lips, an example of which is found in Song of Solomon 1:1, "Let him kiss me with the kisses of his mouth." It is a primary experience, *veritas prima*: the experience of being confronted by the face of Someone as someone, of an Other as other, a mystery that opens an incomprehensible and sacred *beyond* which I see not with my eyes and which sees me in my innermost being.

"Face to face" is the Conqueror standing before the Indian, the African, or the Asian. It is the *patrón* standing before the peasant who comes begging for work. It is the man standing before his abandoned and pleading wife. It is the father standing before his newborn, totally dependent child. But "face to face" can also be the man who "speaks with his friend." And from the Totality of the world, this ontological world, Europe, the man and father opens to the Exteriority, the metaphysical exteriority (if the *physis* represents a being that constitutes the horizon of the world) of peripheral cultures, of women and children, or better said, of the peripheral "foreigner, widow, and orphan" proclaimed by the Prophets.

The Other is the first, the progenitor of the child, the society that maintains us in its tradition. The Other is the Creator who confers upon us real being. A person, however, is exposed to another person before establishing a relationship with nature — in this case with the economic order. We are conceived in the womb of another, our mother's. We originally are fed by another, that is, we nurse from another's breasts. And we long to remain in this "face to face" relationship. But the proximity of this "face to face" and the remoteness of the economic order entails a painful detour.

A: the Dominator; a: the project of the dominating group; b: the project *a*: imposed on Totality; c: in the conquest the project *a* is imposed on Other human beings; 1a: Totality dominated by A; 1b: the new order, the conquered empire; B: the dominated without their own established project; d: the project of liberation; 2: the *new* country or the "new" order emerging as service to the Other; arrow X: domination; arrow S: "service."

DIAGRAM 2.   The Different Moments in the Process of Total Alienation and of Alternative Liberation

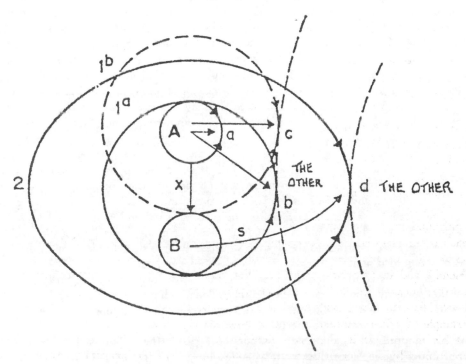

5. The Dominating Praxis: Sin and the "Poor"

Permit me to diagram the movement of the discussion in order that we not lose in the resumé the exposition that we have begun. The following diagram represents the different areas in the process of a complete alienation and of an alternative liberation.

The biblical symbolism set forth in the prophetic tradition can be outlined very briefly. First, "Cain set on his brother Abel and killed him" (Gen. 4:8). Jesus indicated that Abel was the first of many innocent people who have been slain (Matt. 23:35). This No-to-the-Other is the worst possible sin; it is the "sin of the world," that is, the original sin. The no-to-Abel as Other was likewise the offense of the priest and Levite in the parable of "the good Samaritan" (Luke 10:31– 32). In his discussion of original sin, Augustine clearly asserted that Cain "built a city, while Abel, as though he were merely a pilgrim on earth, built none"[15] (*The City of God*, XV, 1). Historically as well as actually, beginning in the fifteenth century, sin reappeared in concrete form as the *No* of the North Atlantic "center" to the marginalized Indian, African, Asian, laborer, and peasant. It has been and is the *No* to the women in a patriarchally controlled household and the *No* to the child made compliant by a pedagogy of domination.

This No-to-the-anthropologically-Other (fratricide) is the epitome of the totalization of the "flesh" (*basar* in Hebrew and *sarx* in Greek). The appeal of this structured temptation, however, is not that of a Prometheus chained to the *anángke* but rather the promise of the Totality or the "system" that "you will be like gods" (Gen. 3:5). Sin, which begins as a No-to-the-Other, a self-deification, and an autofetishism, culminates in idolatry, in a No-to-the-creative-Other. Thus, in order for the North Atlantic conqueror to be able to say with Nietzsche that "God is dead," it was necessary to slay God's epiphany, namely, the Indian, the African, and the Asian.

This absolute idolatry of the *flesh* as seen in the modern European system of Christendom produced within the Totality (circle 1a in Diagram 2) a schism between the one who dominated the "world" (a new manifestation of the *flesh* that was totally deified) and the one dominated. "You know that among the pagans the rulers (*árkhontes*) lord (*katakyrieuoúsin*) it over them, and their great men make their authority felt" (Matt. 20:25). In Diagram 2 these "rulers" are symbolized by A. They are the "angels" or emissaries of "the Prince of this world." They are the Pilates who ask for water to wash their hands and disclaim all responsibility for wrongdoing (Matt. 27:24). They are the current economical, cultural, sexual, and aesthetic "systems" of the world within the specific structure of sin that now oppress the poor. The "principalities" (A) are an element in the plan of the group (a) which is objectified as part of the total system (b) which in turn expands as an imperialist project for the domination (c) of Latin America, Africa, and Asia. It is the "Self" (1a) continuing as "Self" (1b). The "praxis of domination" in a system that usurps the place of God and proceeds to deify itself is sin in the most blatant and contemporary sense. It is the "praxis" of a No-to-Abel, to the oppressed brother, to the woman valued only as a sexual object, or to the child who is regarded as nothing more than a servile dependent.

The "oppressed *as oppressed*" is like Job. He suffers because of the sin (the "praxis of the powerful who dominate him") that alienates him while the wise men of the "system" (Bildad and Zofar) attempt to convince him that he, Job, is the sinner — and in so doing, they exonerate the real oppressors.

The "oppressed as oppressed" is not the "poor" (the "oppressed *as Exteriority*"). The "poor" as in "How happy are you who are poor" (*ptokhoi*) (Luke 6:20) or "you have the poor with you always" (Matt. 26:11), is the Other. In Diagram 2 they are symbolized by the Other in that they represent the supreme value in any sociopolitical, economic or cultural system. The "poor" are reality and at the same time a "category." They are the nation, class, or person, the oppressed woman, or the domesticated child controlled by the structures of domination. The "poor" in the biblical sense are not identified as the "oppressed *alienated*" by the system, but, nevertheless, they possess many of the characteristics of the poor, socioeconomically speaking.

6. The Liberating Praxis: Redemption and the "Prophet"

Regarding the "logic of sin" described above (Section 5), we propose the "logic of liberation," the antisin or the negation of the negation of the Other.[16] Instead of a No-to-the-Other, we propose the biblical symbol of Moses in Exodus 3 or of the Samaritan in the parable of Jesus. Both represent an explicit *Yes-to-the-Other* as Other while still being nothing more than oppressed as oppressed *within* the system. The prophetic insight of faith allows us to see, behind the mask of oppression and alienation, the *face* of the Other, — to see, for example, a free person in the Egyptian slave or the Exteriority of a human being in the stripped, beaten, and half-dead victim by the side of the road. What we propose then is not aversion (*aversio*) to the Other, but rather conversion (*conversio*) to the Other as a citizen of the City of God. Bartolomé de las Casas, the seventeenth-century evangelizing anticolonialist who strenuously and over a prolonged period opposed the enslavement of the Indians in the Caribbean and in Central and South America, discovered the Other as other. He wrote that "God created these simple people, the Indians, free from the iniquities and duplicities ... without the resentments and treacheries and contentiousness, the animosities, hatreds and vindictiveness so characteristic of the civilized world."[17]

Before affirming a Yes-to-the-Other, however, it is first necessary to deabsolutize the system, to expose its underside; it is necessary to be atheistic regarding the system. The Virgin of Nazareth while in the flesh opened herself to the Spirit (to Otherness). Jesus himself said that it is necessary "to give back to Caesar what belongs to Caesar — and to God what belongs to God" (Matt. 22:21), thereby standing with the Prophets in the refusal to acknowledge Caesar as God of the flesh or of the Totality. When Feuerbach and Marx declared themselves atheists in regard to the "god" of Hegel and of the European bourgeoisie — which was the only god Feuerbach and Marx knew — they introduced a needed corrective into Christian theology.[18]

To deabsolutize the Totality of sin, one must — subversively — break into the absolute Otherness. The analectic — that which is beyond the system — the absolute Other (the Other in Diagram 2), the Word (the Hebrew *dabár*, which is unrelated to the Greek *lógos*), becomes en-Totalized, incarnate. Christ Jesus' "state was divine, ... but [he] emptied (*ekénosen*) himself to assume the condition of a slave (*doúlou*)" (Phil. 2:6– 7). Christ, the Church, and the prophet must therefore assume within the system the place of the oppressed as oppressed (position B in Diagram 2). The servant (*hebed* in Hebrew and *doulos* or *pais* in Greek) actually assumes the sociopolitical, cultural, and economic condition of the alienated, emulating and experiencing the alienation of the Indian, the African, the Asian, the exploited woman, and the pedagogically oppressed child, and becomes incarcerated in the prison of sin — the system.

The servant, the prophet, and the "poor in Spirit"[19] will, with the oppressed, fulfill the liberating praxis (in Hebrew *habodáh*, in Greek *diakonía*) that not only is a labor of justice but at the same time is a liturgy to God the Savior. This act of service (represented by the arrow *S* in Diagram 2) of the Samaritan or Moses in behalf of the poor and the enslaved as Exteriority is a kind of subversive historical praxis and is, therefore, sociopolitical, cultural, economic, sexual, and eschatological. For this reason the servant is dedicated (Luke 4:18 and Isa. 61:1) to subvert the system, to redirect history,[20] and to liberate the poor as in the sabbatical year or the year of Jubilee.[21]

The liberator, this prophetic servant, by responding to the cry of the poor as Exteriority exposes the system of sin as an empire of international, national, economic, political, cultural, and sexual oppression, and announces the advent of a *new system* (represented by circle 2 in Diagram 2), proclaiming the dispossession of the powerful and the end of their domination. In response, the system, the Totality or the *flesh*, converts what was before simple domination (represented by the arrow *X* in Diagram 2) into systematic repression, violence, and persecution, and the liberating servant is its first victim, that is, the first to die. Our Lord cries out, "Jerusalem, Jerusalem, you that kill the prophets and stone those who are sent to you!" (Matt. 23:37). Yet by his death the liberator is transformed into the redeemer, the authentic sacrifice of atonement (from the Hebrew *kipper* of Leviticus 16), purchasing with his own flesh the freedom of the Other. Again Jesus says:

Anyone who wants to be great among you must be your servant (*diákonos*), and anyone who wants to be first among you must be your slave (*doulos*), just as the Son of Man came not to be served but to serve (*diakonesai*), and to give his life as a ransom for many (*lútron anti pollon*, the Hebrew eschatological *rabim*) (Matt. 20:26–28).

It is easy to grasp the significance of the *praxis of liberation* if one studies with care the lives of the prophets and Jesus, of the harried and persecuted Christians in the Roman Empire, of Bishop Antonio de Valdivieso who — because of his defense of the Indians in Nicaragua — was assassinated at the behest of the governor in 1550, of Father Antonio Pereira Neto in Brazil in 1969, or of Mahatma Gandhi and Patrice Lumumba in the non-Christian Third World. The deaths of all these indicate that by announcing the end of the system the liberator is himself violently eliminated by the "angels" of the "Prince of this world," that is, by the conquerors, the imperialistic forces, the capitalist bankers, and the unscrupulous Herodian politicians of the dependent nations. The system as Totality is tautological, repetitious death. The death of the liberator, however, signals the death of death and of a people being born anew (John 3:5–8).[22]

7. Toward an Ecclesiology of Redemptive Liberation

All that has been described exists concretely and historically as a part of the experience of the community or the people of God, the Church, or simply as a part of world history.

In effect, since the liberating and redemptive death of Christ, world history has a new *royal* protocol, namely, that all people of good will are recipients of grace sufficient for their salvation. Because of sin, the historical, sociopolitical, economic, sexual, and pedagogical systems tend to become closed, fixed, and eternalized. The task of the servant is, therefore, to redirect, to deabsolutize, and to make these systems more dialectically flexible and self-correcting, and to move them toward the Parousia. God, from the Exteriority of creation, called out the Church from the very heart of the flesh and of the world, from the Totality or *kenotic* environment of "alienation." The Church as God's gift is the incarnation, the en-Totalization of the Spirit. Through baptism the believer is received into the Christian community and consecrated for the service of liberation in the world. The visible Church, the institutionalized Christian community, began geopolitically in the eastern Mediterranean world. It spread to the West and to the North, and flourished in Latin-Germanic Christendom, which subsequently with that of the United States and Russia became the geopolitical center of the world. Ironically, the Church began among the sociopolitically oppressed of the Roman Empire, but today it is part and parcel of the nations that oppress the dependent, "peripheral" countries. Frequently the Church is allied with the dominating culture, especially on the national level.

The Church that was incarnated in the world as the seed in Jesus' parable of the Sower (Matt. 13:1-9) became identified with the flesh or the Totality of the system; that is, the Church adopted position A in Diagram 2. This identification with the "Prince of this world" is the sin in the Church today. The sanctioning and even the sacralizing of the sociopolitical and economic system has continued from the time of the Holy Roman Empire until the present as a part of the Christian civilization of the West.

Now if the Church is to realize its true purpose and mission in the world as a liberating community and institution, it will have to identify with the oppressed, that is, move to position B in Diagram 2, in order to "break down the wall" (arrow S) of the system that has been absolutized by national and international, economic, and social, cultural and sexual sin and injustice. The "sign" (the *semeion* of John's Gospel) of the Church and its mission of evangelization can only be realized by means of a historical commitment to the process and the pilgrimage of liberation. In Hebrew *pesah* signifies "pilgrimage," "march," or "flight" (arrow S). Liberation involves the movement from a system that attempts to oppress (b in Diagram 2) toward a new system that attempts to liberate (d in Diagram 2). Liberation is for the Church the "sign" of the eschatological mission of the Kingdom. The Eucharist anticipates this "pilgrimage" of the Kingdom and celebrates the complete liberation from sin (from Egyptian slavery). The liberation of Latin America, therefore, is for the Church in Latin America (as part of the dependent, oppressed Church in the world) the arena of her evangelization. And evangelization in this case implies the liberation of the oppressed classes, of women, of children, and of today's poor.

II. THE PROTOCOL OF THEOLOGICAL DISCOURSE

In this second section we want to return to the discussion of theology itself, first to a consideration of European and North American theology or what may be called "White Theology," in order to define subsequently the theology that will be developed as a discourse on oppression, namely, the theology of the Third World: on a world level from the peripheral nations, on a national level from the oppressed classes, on an erotic level from the exploited woman, and on a pedagogical level from the coming generations, the young people, and the children.

1. The Conditioning of Theological Thinking

Contemporary critical Latin American thinkers recognize that all geopolitical expansion is based on an "ontology of domination," either philosophical or theological depending on the case being considered. Modern European expansion, for example, had its ontological formulation in the *ego cogito*,[23] which had as its historical antecedent the "I conquered." In Spinoza's *Ethics*, the *ego* was an extension of the unique substance of God, a conclusion later accepted by Schelling in his youth and by Hegel who deified the European "I." Fichte believed the "I" in the declaration "I am I" to be absolute and unconditioned.[24] For Fichte it was ultimate, undetermined, infinite, absolute, and natural, while for Hegel the "I" was divine. With Nietzsche this "I" was transformed into creative power (the "I" became the "will to power"). For Husserl this "I" became the most discreet *ego cogito cogitatum* of phenomenology.[25] The travesty in all this reasoning was that the Other such as the Indian, the African, the Asian, or the woman was reduced to nothing more than an idea, an object whose meaning was determined by the "originally constituted 'I'," and the Other was thereby designated, classified, and alienated as a mere *cogitatum*.

European theology, however, this theology of the "center," could not escape this same kind of reductionism. The dominating expansion of Latin-Germanic Christianity was followed by an equally "dominating theology." The Semitic-Christian thinking of the Old and New Testaments was therefore reduced to a process of Indoeuropeanized Hellenization beginning as early as the second century. Medieval European theologians justified the feudal world and the *ius dominativum* of the feudal lord over the serf. And neither the Roman Catholic nor Protestant theologians gave the slightest consideration to the Indian (with the exception of the School of Salamanca for a few decades), the African, or the Asian. Finally, the expansion of capitalism and neocapitalism allowed the Christians of the "center" to develop a theology of the *status quo* and an ecumenism of peaceful coexistence between the Soviet Union, Europe, and the United States so that together they could dominate more effectively the "periphery." The *Other,* the poor, were thus newly constituted from the perspective of the European "I": *Ego cogito theologatum.* Reducing the subject of theological thought also reduces the scope of "the theological," and sin is seen from a single perspective of intranational injustice. Sin is thereby privatized, depoliticized, and asexualized (or supersexualized at other levels). Even more serious, this reduces the meaning and scope of redemption and salvation to the narrow limits of the "Christian experience of the *center.*" Emphasis is given to individual salvation and interiorized, defleshed spirituality whose goal frequently is masochistic pain, which chooses its own time and place to suffer while avoiding the real Cross of authentic history which calls for unimagined sacrifices.

This theology of the "center" has been conditioned in multiple ways of which the European and North American theologians show little or no awareness. It has been conditioned by the religiosity of Mediterranean and Latin-Germanic Christianity, which assumed that to be Latin was to be Christian. It has been conditioned liturgically by the insistence that the forms of worship elaborated in the Mediterranean Church were the only genuinely Christian forms, while other cultures were prohibited from developing their own liturgies. It has been conditioned culturally by the fact that it has been developed by an intellectual elite, primarily university and seminary professors who are well paid and who enjoy a measure of security unknown by Tertullian or Augustine. It has been conditioned politically by accommodating itself to and being a part of the metropolitan seat of world power. It has been conditioned economically by the fact that for the most part it represents the value system of the oligarchy and the bourgeoisie of the neocapitalist world — though admittedly at times it has been produced by poor monks from rich orders. Finally, it is conditioned erotically by these monks or celibates who lacked the experience to fashion an authentic theology of sexuality, marriage, and family.

In short, modern European and North American theology is inadvertently implicated in the praxis of world political, pedagogical, and sexual domination. And it would not be an exaggeration to say that to a large degree this theology is really a "theological ideology," one as incapable of seeing its own biases as the inhabitants of the earth are incapable of seeing the other side of the moon. What is worse, there are in Latin America numerous so-called progressive theologians who simply repeat this theology of the "center," and in so doing they become more culpable ideologists of oppression.

2. Faith and Christian Praxis

Existence as viewed from a pre-Christian perspective has many shades of meaning. Basically, it refers to the comprehension or understanding of being. This comprehension (from "capture" something next to something else [cumprendere], or "to grasp" something completely or in its totality, i.e., circum-prendere) is the primary way by which the world is opened to us.[26] If there is pre-Christian human existence, there is a correlative world; and if there is this perceived world, it is because there is a fundamental opening to it. This intellectual-practical opening is the basic experience of life. It has many philosophical ramifications that, because of limited space, cannot be elaborated here.[27] Concurrently, if there is such a thing as Christian existence, it is because there is a new world in which Christian transcendence can be experienced. Both pre-Christian and Christian existence depend ontologically upon an opening to the world in its totality, that is, it depends upon a supernatural comprehension of being, and this comprehension is gratuitously revealed by God and perceived by faith.

Moreover, this comprehension of being is initially and continually an ontic comprehension of things as they are in the world, though not necessarily comprehension that attempts to understand the world or being as such. An attempt to comprehend the world or being is an ontological endeavor. But we are referring to a day-to-day ontic, noumenal, and existential comprehension. Faith understood theologically can best be described as *supernatural* and *existential comprehension*.

Faith is not *essentially* a belief or blind trust. A psychological belief, opinion, or submission to the will of something or somebody, a lack of clarity or an uncertainty about something are all secondary elements of the intellectual-practical act of faith. Faith is a comprehensive act of intelligence, not intelligence functioning theoretically as theory divorced from praxis or deduced from praxis.[28] Faith is a practical act not learned theoretically as we sometimes assume in imparting oral or audiovisual catechism. Faith is learned existentially in the Christian community by the continual utilization of the tools of the Christian experience and by establishing a relationship with the Other. Faith in a practical sense is discovering in everything around us the *new* world, the world of Christian comprehension. The ultimate horizon that faith opens to us is necessarily nonobjective and nonobjectifiable. I should not make the light which permits me to see the object of my theorectical consideration. Moses did not see God in the theophany at Horeb. He only heard God's voice, and faith resulted from the hearing.[29] The Hebrew-Christian understanding of being is not theoretical comprehension; the Greeks thought of being as something permanent or eternal. Rather, being in the biblical sense is the hearing of the word spoken from the mystery of the Other as freedom. God as Three in One manifests himself through the revealed Word to those who know how to hear. But they cannot see God. If we can see God's economy manifested in human history, from this horizon of nonobjectified hearing, from this light that illumines, it will be by discerning, practically speaking, the signs of God in history. Moses did not see God, but he saw what God revealed to him, namely, "the miserable state" of his people in Egypt (Exod. 3:7). This existential, ontical seeing is essentially the historical function of faith. It is not credulity nor fidelity in spite of uncertainty. It is enlightened intelligence, informed interpretation, prophetic insight. For faith sets forth a new horizon for the pre-Christian event, illuminating it with new light and comprehending it in a radically new way. For this reason one can employ a new hermeneutic or interpretation in order to understand pre-Christian historical events. It is the *meaning* of these events that changes, and this existential change of meaning is learned only from another Christian who is committed concretely day by day. This is not theory. It is the foundation of the practical order.

Faith, then, as nonobjectified existential comprehension, is *concrete*. It is not abstract nor reducible. Rather, it is fulfilled in the historical worldly order and is a part of the ambiguities and complexities of human life.

Faith is the practical understanding of what it means to be Christian, of divine Being, of being a part of the mystery of salvation that establishes a relationship between creation and history. It is the comprehension of the interpersonal Mystery of God that establishes a new order between human beings and history through the Covenant, the Church, and the Kingdom. This Christian being is not an abstraction. It is *my* being Christian and *our* being Christian in this age. It is not a universal command that applies to everyone. It is *my* being Christian or *our* being Christian. We will not, of course, be completely Christian, for our being as such is never totally complete. There is always the possibility of being that lies before us. History has not stopped and will never stop until God wills it. Faith, therefore, is the concrete, existential comprehension of the Christian being and of the possibility of being. This possibility of being, moreover, is what opens the future, a future that is moving toward us and which draws us expectantly toward it. We move toward that which is coming. We journey on in the hope that Christ is coming (the *Parousia*, the Advent). This understanding of Christian being as that which is coming indicates that our being is always out there before us. Its essence precedes us as the horizon of the pampa precedes the *gaucho* galloping toward it. There is always an "eschatological remainder" before us, a kind of projected future. This is, therefore, analectic comprehension (*aná*: beyond + *logos*, horizon or comprehension),[30] comprehension that is revealed from beyond the horizon.

In summary, then, faith is the fundamental, supernatural, ontological comprehension of history operating in an existential, concrete, analectical, and progressive way. It opens to us the meaning of historical events so that they become Sacred History, *Heilsgeschichte*.

Faith reveals to us a concrete historical yet supernatural project that allows us to discover the environment (Sartre would call it a *nothingness*) of worldly possibilities. Between what we actually are and what we understand by the light of faith that we can become there opens before us, like a fissure, a world of freedom, responsibility, and choice that is essentially and fundamentally a world of *praxis*. This praxis or human action is the same thing as being in the world. Or to put it another way, it is Christian praxis in a world — a Christian world — which has been opened to us by faith in contrast to praxis in a closed pre-Christian world. I am in the world as a Christian to the degree that I act. Praxis is humanity's worldly present. I act because I am not yet what I understand that I can become. If I were ultimate being (God), I would not act practically; pure actuality needs no mode of expression for it is in itself sufficient. But because I am not everything I can be eschatologically, I must act. Praxis is, therefore, based ontologically, not coincidentally, on what I am and on what I can be. What impels me to act, to move toward the coincidence (which alone is total and irreversible in Christ and in the Kingdom) is the same Being which calls me to be unequivocally involved in my Christian project. Christian praxis, therefore, is the medium, the bridge, that unites the sinful situation of humanity with the Christian project yet to be completed. It links the inherently unjust conditions of the present with the eschatological possibilities of the future.

Praxis is based on faith in two ways. First, faith opens to us the possibility of being Christian, of moving toward what we can become, and of being involved in the Christian project that is founded on and wrapped in praxis. Second, praxis is based on faith in that faith is the interpretative light that enables us to discover here and now the meaning of historical events and their possibilities. Praxis is, in reality, the grasping of a possibility. It permits us to utilize a hermeneutic that reveals a hidden meaning of what was previously obscure in the history of the pre-Christian world and which now by the light of faith becomes clear. This kind of understanding or interpretation is not scientific, universal, or theoretical. It is concrete, historical, and adapted to everyday living. It is what the classicists would call "judicious."

Faith is rooted in praxis. It is comprehension functioning by, being nourished by, and constantly reoriented by praxis. Egoistic or self-serving praxis inhibits faith, while a self-giving or heroic praxis allows faith to open even greater horizons of understanding. Faith, therefore, is the integral foundation of Christian praxis. And praxis is Christian (as contrasted with pre-Christian or anti-Christian) to the degree that a new world is actually opened to us by faith.[31]

3. Revelation and Faith:
The Anthropological Epiphany

Western theology has for centuries accepted a certain kind of philosophy: the ontology of Kant which postulates faith as something rational, that of Hegel which includes faith within the scope of reason, or that of Heidegger which sees faith as the understanding of Being. Each of these ontologies prescribes the Totality of being as the only limit to thinking. "Being-in-the-world," however, is the fundamental, primary, original fact,[32] and existential theology parts company with rationalists who view the world as a Totality. A more objectionable feature of Western philosophy, however, is the assumption that Totality is mine, ours, the Europeans' — Totality which belongs to the "center." The unrecognized conclusion of this kind of thinking is that I negate other Christian worlds or totalities and other equally valid experiences, and I negate the anthropological Other as my point of departure for thinking theologically.[33]

For F. W. J. Schelling in his *Philosophie der Offenbarung* (*Philosophy of Revelation,* 1858), faith in the word of the Other is beyond ontological reasoning. It is equivalent to Hegel's *Sein* (Being), a definition with which Kierkegaard takes issue in his *Concluding Unscientific Postscript*. Faith comes from the revelation of the Other, and revelation is nothing more than God's altering or disturbing pronouncement, existential or worldly pronouncement, which sets forth the hermeneutical norms or categories of Christanity. In existential history God reveals what is obscure, such as the fact of world redemption and salvation in Christ, by means of an interpretative or normative light which is accessible to all human beings and valid for all history. God does not merely reveal something as a concrete event. Rather, he reveals the categories or norms by which I can interpret the event.[35] In a sense revelation was completed with the Incarnation of Jesus Christ, but the potentialities of the Incarnation unfold throughout all of history. What is significant in this context is the recognition that revelation is not manifested only *in* history by means of human pronouncements, but also by means of human beings as flesh and blood exteriority. Revelation comes through the poor, the Christ-person.

Faith is the acceptance of the word of the Other as other. And faith is Christian when it accepts the divine Word in Christ as it is mediated through the historical, the concrete, the real poor. The authentic epiphany of the Word of God is that word spoken by the poor man who says, "I am hungry!" And only the person who hears this cry of the poor and who is in effect a nonbeliever, a negator of the system, can hear the genuine Word of God. God has not died, but God's epiphany has been assassinated in the Indian, the African, and the Asian. Therefore God can no longer reveal himself. Abel died in the deification of Europe, of the "center," and God is now hidden. The norm of interpretation that has been revealed is: "I was hungry and you never gave me food. . . . Then it will be their turn to ask, 'Lord, when did we see you hungry . . . ?' " (Matt. 25:42 – 44).[36] Now by the death of the deification of Europe faith can be born in the breast of the "peripheral" poor. Faith in God mediated by the poor is the new manifestation of God in history, and faith becomes reality not by the writing of theological or theoretical treatises on "the death of God," but by means of applied justice.[37]

4. Theology and History

Theology is not faith. Theology is theoretical thinking that emerges from praxis grounded in existential, supernatural comprehension, that is, in faith. At this level of existential comprehension the Christian being, who has real validity as light that illumines, has not been discerned explicitly. The ontic is interpreted, but the ontological actuality is not systematized. The practical function of theology is the systematization and elucidation of what is already validated in existential, day-by-day faith. Theology is the epistemological conceptualization of what is revealed in the empirical experiences of the Christian life. This passage from factual, historical, daily experience of Christian living to conceptualization cannot, however, be achieved without risk. In fact, theology develops in stages, and perceiving this development is of utmost importance for understanding our present Latin American situation.

Semitic thinking in general and Hebrew thinking in particular had a certain way of categorizing historical experience theoretically. It was expressed not only by poetry such as the Psalms, and by historical interpretation such as the narrative passages in Genesis 12 – 50, but also by mythical expressions such as Genesis 1 – 11, and the Wisdom literature such as the book of Job. One can affirm, nevertheless, that this incipient theology of the Old and New Testaments is intrinsically and fundamentally *historical*. The prehistorical myths of Adam, Cain, and the Tower of Babel are historicized, that is, they are set forth by Israel as a means of counteracting the nonhistorical myths that circulated continually among Israel's neighbors. But history as an event (*Geschehen* or *Ereignis*) is the basis, the point of departure in the preaching of the Prophets, Jesus, Paul, and the Apostle John.[38] Their reasoning is always the same: it is in Abraham, an historical person, that we are saved by the Covenant and the Promise. And as our fathers crossed the desert, so today we are pilgrims. The structure of the Gospels and of the Acts of the Apostles — that is, from Bethlehem through Galilee, Jerusalem, Samaria, Antioch, Greece, and culminating in Rome in John's Apocalypse — is that of a "theology of history," for all of these represent an historical interpretation of the experience of salvation completed in Christ Jesus. Historical-interpretation is the foundation of Judeo-Christian theology (as Jean Daniélou asserts), and other postapostolic writings, including Augustine's *City of God.*

Nevertheless, soon after the apostles — beginning with the apologists in the second century — the epistemological and syllogistic conceptualization of the Hellenists was superimposed upon Christian history as can be seen clearly in the works of Clement and Origen of Alexandria toward the close of the second century, of Iraneus of Lyon, and of those who were slowly developing theology — first the Greek then the Latin Fathers, and finally the Scholastics of the twelfth through the fourteenth centuries. This syllogistic reasoning was superimposed on theology by a second wave of Spanish and Trentine Scholastics and again by the third Scholastic wave toward the end of the nineteenth century. In its theological conceptualization, that is, in the transition from the historical experience of the Christian life to an explicitly scientific-thematic expression, Western theologians abandoned the original historical method of the Old and New Testament writers.

It is now common knowledge that through the influence of the Tübingen School — as much by the Protestant faculty who were indebted to Hegel as by the Roman Catholic faculty who were influenced by the work of Moehler — there began a rethinking of Christian reality as a history of salvation (*Heilsgeschehen* or *Heilsgeschichte*). This theological schematization slowly continues to recover a clear historical character. Today, a century after the initial efforts at Tübingen, it is possible to affirm that theology and the systematized history of salvation are identical. Furthermore, one can also affirm that the history of the Church is but one indivisible moment or segment of this unique theology.

The history of salvation as an existential event (*geschehen*) should, however, be distinguished from systematized history (*Historie*), but this methodical and scientific systematizing has as its only theme the Trinitarian God who is manifesting himself in the one historically unfolding salvation. Existential history, then, is not only *a* locus but is the *unique* locus of all Christian theology. Other areas of theological reflection such as the Scriptures rest as it were on history as their foundation.

This issue, which appears to be merely a question of methodology, is of crucial importance for Latin American theology. Having utilized the syllogistic-scientific method of Aristotle's *Organon*, and having considered the structure developed in the Mediterranean world as unique and universal — the environment not only of Greek philosophy but also of Patristic Christianity and of the three periods of Scholasticism — the European experience was assumed to be universally applicable, and the whole system was transplanted in Latin America as the only valid historical exerience.

We now know that history cannot be retold by a single method, that in Latin America the diversities in history were not noted, and that the non-Europeans proceeded to copy and repeat the only theology they knew, namely, the Hellenistic-Christian theology that was essentially the conceptualization of the European historical experience. Upon discovering the history of salvation as the locus of theology and the same history as an indivisible segment of the one theology, the differences between European and Latin American histories became evident, and Latin American theologians could not help but take these differences into account. It was then that a new theology began to emerge. The differences in the two histories had been sensed for decades; by 1964 they became evident, and after 1968 they were undeniable.

Temporality, as the understanding of being, is an existential part of the ontological nature of humanity. A human being is never complete in a closed present, past, or future. One's existence includes a uniquely historical-traditional past that opens the future from which spring the possibilities of the present. This having-been posits the power-to-be in which being itself is grounded — all indicating the *factum* of temporality. One of its modes is historicity. The historical is written evidence for having-been in a has-been-world, inscribed by the hand of a person in-the-world.[39] If a human being can be historical, then a Christian human being can also be historical, and he or she can be historical as a part of salvation history. The theological method which begins by interpreting history is the best interpretation of the implicit on the existential level. If the historical significance of the Christian human being is not considered, then history becomes an abstraction and dissolves into the universal. Failure to take into account the historical importance of the Christian human being in Latin America allows the uniqueness of our salvation history to evaporate into insignificance.

It is because Latin America was not taken into account by European ecclesiastical historians from the sixteenth century until the latter half of the twentieth century that Latin Americans felt cut off from themselves. They felt they were alienated, nonauthentic beings, for they had been annihilated by the process of Europeanization. In order to recover their being, therefore, it is essential that the Christian history of Latin America be interpreted — this moment in salvation history that proceeds toward completion on our continent, this indivisible moment of our unique theology — if we are to think of ourselves as being a part of Christian history.

Theological thinking emerges from praxis, and our praxis is Latin American. As the theology of history (not one theology among many but *our* theology) methodically proposes a sacrament or an institution in history as a key for seeing its essential structure (for example, from the Old to the New Testament, and within primitive, conciliar, and European traditions), it is necessary in all matters — even in the discussions of such dogmas as the Trinity, the Church, or the sacraments — to continue this dialectical movement in our Latin American ecclesial history: in the missionary praxis of the sixteenth century, in the councils and synods, in the concrete decisions, in the institutional traditions, and even in "folk Catholicism." All should proceed by receiving in this moment in our Latin American salvation history its own tonality, which Latin American Christian praxis has been impressing upon it little by little.

We want to make it clear, therefore, from a hermeneutical or methodological perspective, that the history of the Latin American Church constitutes an essential part of the one authentic theology developed for Latin Americans. Because of this fact, our history is no longer a pre-Christian history (which is discussed in Chapters 4, 7, and 10, and especially in the final reflections appearing in Chapters 6, 9, and 12). This unique Latin American theology posits an ontological structure (dogmatics) completed in Christian praxis (moral) and historically concretized (exegesis in the first moment and history after the Church). The metaphysical structure of the Trinity is manifested prefiguratively in the history of the community of Israel and in Christ and the Church until the final completion in the Parousia.

5. The Praxis of Liberation and Theology

Using the data of revelation and the mediation of a practiced faith, theology can be said to be simply a reflection on reality. In recent years various theologies have arisen: "secular theology," the "theology of questioning," the "theology of revolution,"[40] and the "theology of development."[41] In Europe, however, only "political theology"[42] has attracted much attention. Contemporary Latin American theology regards European "political theology" as too limited, in that the impact of the critical and prophetic is reduced to a narrow national perspective. Consequently, the injustices of international imperialism continue unperceived and unexposed. Critical eschatological deprivatization should correct not only the internal inequities of a system but should also affect the entire world system.[43]

In the same sense, the more influential "theology of hope"[44] suffers from the same kind of limitation as the "critical theory" of the Frankfurt School, which influenced Johannes Metz, and the thought of Ernst Bloch, which inspired Jürgen Moltmann.

Neither of these philosophical hypotheses moves beyond the ontology and dialectic that considers the future as the unfolding of "the Self." And though Moltmann believes the future to be absolutely other, he nonetheless has difficulty in proposing something more or beyond the present system but less than eschatological potential; that is, he is reticent to suggest an historical plan of political, economic, cultural, or sexual liberation. Moltmann's hope envisions an "historic transformation of life,"[45] but not a radical change of the present system nor an historical project of liberation as the authentic sign of the eschatological possibility. Without this concrete mediation, however, hope merely reinforces the *status quo* and acts as an opiate.

On the other hand, a genuine European theology of liberation would address the real issue of "Christianity and the class struggle"[46] within the limits of a national Marxism and preceded by a "theory of dependence." Thus far it has not been made clear that the struggle of the proletariat of the North Atlantic "center" can be oppressive for the proletariat on the "periphery" or in the colony. The working classes have become equivocal and frequently undermine their own interests at the international level. The national liberation of the dominated countries is therefore necessary for the social liberation of the oppressed classes. And for this reason the term "masses" or "people" has a special significance today which the word "class" does not convey.[47]

Latin American theology is, therefore, a reflection on the praxis of the liberation of the oppressed by Christians who are politically committed. It is a theological ethic developed from the perspective of those on the periphery, the marginalized, the outcasts of the world. The praxis that undergirds this theological ethic is not merely a praxis meeting necessities (the ontic actuality of the system of present needs), but rather a praxis of liberation (in Hebrew *habodá* and in Greek *diakonía*). It is a liberating trans-ontological ministry. It is a reflection not only on political praxis, but likewise on sexual and pedagogical praxis. In a word, it is the theology of the *poor*, the *woman* as a sexual object, and the alienated *child*.

6. *Toward a Theology of the Liberation of the Oppressed*

Following the great "theology of Christendom" (from the fourth to the fifteenth century) and "modern European theology" (from the sixteenth to the twentieth century), the "theology of the liberation" of the periphery and of the oppressed is all of traditional theology put in motion from the perspective of the poor. The "theology of Christendom" (past model) virtually identified the Christian faith with the Mediterranean (Latin-Byzantine) culture, establishing later the process (as the crisis regarding the use of Latin in the Second Vatican Council recently indicated). Modern privatized and imperial European theology was reproduced in the colonies as "progressive theology, but it was nothing more than an imitation by the national colonial oppressed oligarchy who benefitted from the system and took as a last resource a theology which in the final analysis is abstract and uncritical and which supports the *status quo*. In contrast, the "theology of liberation" (of which the "theology of revolution" merely concentrates on a point of departure, "political theology" concentrates on its scope and characteristics, and the "theology of hope" concerns itself with the future) reflects on praxis, or better said, it reflects on the praxis of liberation, that is, on the "pilgrimage" (*pascua*) or way through the desert of human history, from sin as systemic political, sexual, and pedagogical domination toward the irreversible salvation in Jesus Christ and his Kingdom. This "pilgrimage" is made by every person, every people, every epoch, by all of human history. There are, however, certain crucial times (*kairós*) in history, and Latin America[48] is experiencing one of those periods now in that complete eschatological liberation as clearly indicated by the prophets, the apostles, and the Church. Furthermore, this "theology of liberation" is emerging among the North American Blacks, Mexican-Americans, black Africans, and even among some Asians;[49] it is destined to become the universal theology of the oppressed.

The "theology of liberation" began in Latin America[50] when the dependence of our theology was discovered along with our economic and cultural dependence. This new theology has proceeded to develop its own method and analysis which I define as "analectical" and not merely dialectical.[51] The trans-ontological voice of the Other (*aná-*) is heard, and the interpretation of its content by "similarity" leaves aside the "distinction" of the Other as other inasmuch as the liberation practice does not permit us to invade the *other* world. This is a new anthropological dimension from the perspective of analogy.

For its part, the "theology of liberation" tends toward an interpretation of the voice of *the oppressed* in order, on the basis of praxis, to stake their liberation. This is no special moment of the univocal Total of universal abstract theology. Neither is it an equivocal or self-explanatory moment as such. From the unique distinction each Latin American theologian and theology reassumes the "appearance" of theology which the history of the discipline gives it but within the hermeneutical circle from the distinct *nothingness* of its freedom. The theology of the true theologian, the theology of the people such as the Latin Americans, is analogically similar and at the same time dissimilar. For this reason it is unique, original, and inimitable. When the "appearance" becomes univocal, the history of theology can only be European. When the "distinct" in a theology is absolutized, it becomes equivocal. It is not Hegelian identity nor Jasperinian equivocalness. It is analogy.

The theology of liberation, however, is a new moment in the history of theology, an analogical moment which emerged after European, Russia, and North American modernity, and which appeared first in Latin American, then in African and Asian, theology. The theology of the poor, the theology of the liberation of universal humankind, is not easily accepted in Europe. Europe is too proud of her univocal universality. Europe does not desire to hear *the voice of the Other,* of the "barbarians," the "nonpersons," if they do their own thinking. Consequently, the theology stemming from Latin America or from the Arab world, from the black African, the Indian, the Southeast Asian, or the Chinese is disregarded if not rejected outright. The voice of Latin American theology is not merely a repetition of European theology. It is a "barbaric theology" in the same sense that the apologists were barbarians in regard to the Greek intelligentsia. But we know that we are situated beyond the modern, dominating, European Totality and that we are struggling for the liberation of the poor toward a future, postmodern, liberated universal humanity.

Chapter II
The Latin American Culture

One of the fundamental aspects of the human ontological structure is that of corporality. There is nothing about the human being that is unrelated to his body — not to his actual physical body, but to his corporal existential condition in regard to everything in the world that confronts him. Theology includes this level of being when it speaks of *sacramentality*. The corporal human condition always demands concrete mediations. Man is not an angel; all that he understands, hopes for, loves, and works for is measured corporally. The totality of these mediations at the level of corporality, such as the physical transformation of the cosmos, we call "culture." Latin American culture is still in a pre-Christian stage — although it has been affected in many respects by Christianity — and yet it will be the means by which Christian faith and praxis become authentic. Faith can never be equated with culture, but the meaning of the Incarnation (which is fundamentally a Christian belief and affirmation of corporality) is that faith is authenticated to the degree that it affects a culture. Culture is the necessary, inevitable avenue for the outworking of the Christian faith.

I. UNIVERSAL CIVILIZATION AND REGIONAL CULTURE

When we speak of culture, especially our Latin American culture, we want to make explicit those principles that are guiding our exposition. Culture is one of the dimensions — and we will specify which — of our historical existence. It is a complexity of elements that radically constitute our *world*. This *world*, which is a concrete system with its own particular meaning, can be studied, and it is the responsibility of the social sciences to do so. "Man," declares Paul Ricoeur, "is a being capable of realizing his desires and wishes in the mode of disguise, regression, and stereotyped symbolization."[1] All these intentional efforts, these "idols that incumber our false cults . . . as the 'daydreams of mankind' — could well be the subtitle of the hermeneutics of culture."[2] Hermeneutics and exegesis — designed to reveal the hidden meaning of culture — is the aim of this discussion, and we will indicate in this brief section some of the steps necessary to begin the study of culture, especially the culture of Latin America.

"Mankind as a whole is on the brink of a single world civilization representing at once a gigantic progress for everyone and an overwhelming task of survival and adapting our cultural heritage to this new setting."[3] It would appear that a world civilization already exists in contrast to individual traditional cultures. Before continuing and in order to apply these ideas to the Latin American situation and national cultures, we should clarify the terms that we are using.

I have already explained in some of my previous writings the meaning of civilization and culture.[4] What follows is a summary with some additional considerations.

1. Civilization

Civilization[5] is the system of instruments invented by man, accumulated and transmitted progressively through the history of the species, that is, through humanity in its entirety. Primitive man, let us say, for example, the *Pithecantropus* who lived a half-million years ago, possessed the ability to distinguish between a mere "thing" and a "means." Likewise he was able to distinguish between *this* thing and *that* thing and to adapt a thing as a means to achieve some end. From his beginning man surrounded himself with a world of "instruments" with which he lived, and having these at hand he developed the context of his being-in-the-world.[6] The "instrument," that is, the means, ceased to be simply a thing of the present, and became something nontemporal, impersonal, abstract, transmissible, accumulative, and capable of being systematized according to its varied uses. The so-called high civilizations are instrumentally super-systems that mankind has been able to organize since the Neolithic age after a million years of innumerable experiences and additions stemming from technical discoveries. Nonetheless, from the primitive's use of a rough stone to the modern satellite which dispatches to earth photos of the surface of the moon, there is only a quantitative difference of technification. But there is no qualitative distinction, for both spheres are useful to the degree that they produce the effect which is something apart from the "thing" as such. Both are elements of the human world.[7]

The system of instruments that we call civilization has different levels of complexity ranging from the most simple and evident to the most complex and intentional. This is a part of civilization as the instrumental totality available for mankind's use: the climate, vegetation, and topography. Human achievements such as roads, houses, cities, and all the rest, including tools and machines, are a part of civilization. By discovering their multiple uses, new inventions and the systematic accumulation of other instruments are possible through technology and the sciences. All these levels and the elements that constitute them are a cosmos, a system — more or less perfect — with different degrees of complexity. To affirm that something possesses structure or is a system is the same as indicating that it possesses meaning.

2. The Ethos

Before indicating the direction of the meaning of the system that develops the values, we should first analyze the role of the transmitter of civilization with respect to the instruments that constitute it. "In everything that is done and accomplished there is a hidden important and peculiar factor: life always moves according to a determined attitude — the attitude in which and from which the work is done."[8]

Every social group develops a means to manipulate the instruments of civilization, a means of utilizing the tools. Between the pure objectivity of a civilization and the pure subjectivity of freedom there exists an intermediate plane, namely, the *modes,* those fundamental attitudes and experiences of every person or people which make them what they are and which predetermine as an *a priori* inclination their behavior.[9]

We would therefore define the *ethos* of a group or a person as the total network of attitudes that predetermines behavior and that constitutes an habitual or systematic pattern of action, the spontaneity of which in certain instances is limited. A weapon (as a simple instrument) was highly prized by the Aztec and was readily used in battle to defeat the enemy, to capture, and even to offer him in sacrifice to the gods. For the Aztec, the weapon was a means of survival. In contrast, the Buddhist monk eschews weapons because he sees war as a source of intensifying desire, the human appetite, the source of all evil. We see, therefore, two distinct attitudes in regard to the same instrument. To one it can be a means of survival while to the other it can be the source of all that is evil. The *ethos* is that which makes a civilization different and is to a large degree incommunicable. It remains always just below the level of subjectivity or within what may be called regional or partial intersubjectivity. The modes which together form the individual character of a group are acquired by ancestral education in the family, the social class, or the larger social configurations, but within the scope of all those with whom a people live. These modes constitute what a group recognizes as a *we*. An element or an instrument of civilization can be transmitted by written information, by journals or documents; and learning to use it may require no more time than comprehending it intellectually or technologically. An African can leave his tribe in Kenya, for example, pursue studies in one of the highly technological countries, and later return to his native land and build a bridge, drive an automobile, operate sophisticated electronic equipment, and dress as a Westerner. His fundamental attitude, however, will remain virtually unchanged — although civilization obviously will have an effect on him to a greater or lesser degree — as one can readily observe in the case of Gandhi.[10]

The *ethos*, therefore, is the world of experiences, that existential and habitual disposition that is transmitted unconsciously by the group without being analyzed or criticized either by the person on the street or even by the scientist, as Edmund Husserl clearly demonstrated. These systems of guiding principles, as distinct from civilization that is essentially universal or at least capable of being universalized, are experienced by the participants of a group and can be assimilated but not transmitted. In order to experience them it is necessary that one first become adapted to and assimilated by the group that determines one's behavior.

For this reason civilization is universal, and its progress is continual — although with some secondary ups and downs — in world history. Meanwhile the attitudes that constitute what may be correctly called culture are by definition distinct whether they are the attitudes of a region, nation, family, tribe, or group. Furthermore, they are in the most radical sense individual (the personal *So-sein*).[11]

3. The Project

In the final analysis the whole system of instruments as a network of attitudes is ultimately a veritable kingdom of aims and values which justify all action.[12] These values are disguised in symbols, myths, and structures with double meanings and purposes, and as a part of their content they include the ultimate ends of the intentional system to which we referred at the beginning as *world*. To refer to them as world, however, we are following Paul Ricoeur who was influenced in part by the German thinkers:[13] world refers to the ethico-mythical nucleus, to the symbolic concretion of the fundamental existential understanding, that is, to the system of values that a group consciously or unconsciously possesses and that it accepts but does not analyze. "According to this morphology of culture, we should force ourselves to investigate which is the central ethical and religious ideal"[14] of a culture. For as Rothacker declares, "Culture is the culmination of values, and these prevailing or ideal values form a coherent kingdom in themselves which one must discover and fulfill."[15]

To discover these values, however — to become aware of their origin, evolution, and hierarchy — it is necessary to know the history of culture and the phenomenology of religion, for until a few centuries ago it was the divine values that sustained and nourished and gave meaning to all human systems. Following Ernst Cassirer and Sigmund Freud, Ricoeur declares:

Images and symbols constitute what might be called the awakened dream of a historical group. It is in this sense that I speak of the ethical-mythical nucleus which constitutes the cultural resources of a nation. One may, therefore, think that the riddle of human diversity lies in the structure of the subconscious or unconscious. The strange thing, in fact, is that there are many cultures and not a single humanity.[16]

The concrete effects of this methodological distinction we will discuss later.

4. What is Culture?

One may attempt a definition of culture — and this is of course important — but what is more important is comprehending adequately the constituent elements of culture. Values are the contents or the teleological center of attitudes. According to our previous definition, it will be remembered that the *ethos* depends on the objective nucleus of values. And one's values determine his or her daily behavior within the social institutions and functions. The individual manner of human conduct as a totality, as a complex structural organism with a unity of meaning, we call *life-style*. The life-style or temperament of a group is the coherent behavior that results from their system of values, which in turn is determined by certain attitudes with regard to the instruments of civilization.[17] One's life-style is systematically and simultaneously all of these things.

The objectification of life-styles in cultural objects, in specific observable ways, constitutes a new element in culture which we are analyzing, namely, in works of art such as literature, sculpture, architecture, music, dance, dress, food, and behavior in general. But also life-style is objectified in the so-called social sciences of history, psychology, sociology, and jurisprudence. Language itself objectifies the system of values of a people. All this network of cultural realities — which is not the same as the integral comprehension of the culture — is referred to by the German philosophers as the *objective spirit*, if one follows the direction of Hegel and more recently of Hartmann. It is easy to confuse these cultural objects with the tools of civilization. A house, for example, is both an object of civilization and an instrument developed through the technique of construction. Yet at the same time it is a work of art as much as if it had been produced by a sculptor. In this same sense the architect is an artist. We can affirm, therefore, that every object created by a civilization is transfromed into a mode and an object of culture. For this reason, in the last analysis, the whole human world is a world of culture that expresses a life-style reflecting the technology or impersonal, neutral, objective instrumentality of a cultural point of view.

Culture may be defined, therefore, as the organic accumulation of behaviors pre-determined by the attitudes manifested toward the instruments of civilization whose teleological content is composed of the values and symbols of the group and based ultimately on their ontological understanding. Culture is the composition of life-styles that are manifested in the works of those who transform the physical environment of the human world, the world of culture.[18]

We are aware that this description is confined to the structural level and that it is founded on the ontological level. In the philosophy of culture one speaks of the values, structures, contents, and *ethos*. All these notions can be absolutized and assume a metaphysical connotation, thereby opening to us the ontological level. A discussion of the ontological foundation of culture is not, however, within the scope of this chapter.

5. Latin American Culture?

Some insist that a Latin American or national culture does not exist. It may be confidently affirmed — and we could readily justify it but for the fact that it is in part evident — that no people or group of people can avoid having a culture. Latin America not only has a culture, it has its *own* culture. And as no human group can avoid having a culture, Latin Americans cannot truly possess a culture which is not theirs. The problem in regard to our culture stems from the confusion of two questions. First, do we Latin Americans have a culture? And second, is our culture a great original one? As will be evident, these are two separate issues.

It can be said that not every group of people has a great culture; neither has every group created an original culture. But every group of people unavoidably has a culture, be it contemptuous, inorganic, imported, unintegrated, superficial, or heterogeneous. And paradoxically there has been no great culture which from its beginning had its own original classical culture. It would be nonsense to expect a child to be an adult, although many times people who are culturally children pass to an anemic cultural adulthood without ever developing a noteworthy culture. When the Achaeans, Dorians, and Ionians invaded Hellas (Greece) more than a thousand years B.C., they did not possess a great culture. Rather, they appropriated and copied from the beginning the culture of the Cretans. The same can be said of the Romans in respect to the Etruscans; of the Accadians in respect to the Sumerians; and of the Aztecs in respect to the infrastructure of Teotihuacán. Certain cultures become great cultures because together with their vigorous civilizations they

create a literature, sculpture, and philosophy as a means of organizing their life. And this is accomplished by a continual stream of human beings and represents a human self-interpretation ... Life then manifests an advanced stage because the art, poetry, and philosophy are created as a mirror of self-formation and self-interpretation. The word culture comes from *colere*, to take care of or to refine. It is the means of self-interpretation.[19]

What has been said in another way can be expressed thusly: a people that attains the level of self-expression, self-consciousness, the awareness of its cultural structures and ultimate values by the cultivation and development of its tradition possesses identity in itself.

When a people rises to a superior culture the most adequate expression of their own structures is manifested by those who are most aware of the total complexity of the elements. There will always be a group, an elite, that is responsible for objectifying the culture of the community in material achievements. In this elite the whole community views what it spontaneously lives as a result of its culture. Phidias in the Parthenon and Plato in *The Republic* were cultured members of the elite of their times who were able to manifest to the Athenians the hidden structures of their own culture. Netzahualcoyotl, the Aztec king of Texcoco, and José Hernández with his Argentine classic *Martín Fierro*[20] served the same function in their cultures. The cultured individual is, therefore, one who possesses the cultural conscience of his people, the self-consciousness of the structures and values, who "is completely prepared, ready, and quickly moves in any concrete situation of life; for whom it is second nature to understand a concrete or a specific problem and what is demanded at the time. . . . In the course of experience, regardless of the class from which one comes, the situation demands for the man of culture a cosmic totality, articulated according to the meaning [of his own culture]."[21] "A cultural consciousness is fundamentally an awareness which is totally spontaneous. . . . Cultural consciousness . . . produces a radical structure fundamentally pre-ontological" according to Ernesto Mayz Vallenilla in his *Problema de América*.[22]

We will see that there is a synergy between a great culture and a cultured person. The greatest cultures have had legions of cultured individuals, and even the masses manifested a style of life which made them aware of their past tradition and the possibilities of their future. This awareness was transmitted by education in the family, the tribe, the city, and the institutions, because "education always signifies the rejection of methodical development having in mind the vital structures earlier accepted."[23] No education is possible apart from a fixed custom previously established.

II. LATIN AMERICAN CULTURE AND NATIONAL CULTURE

The individual accounts or narratives of our Latin American nations in their neocolonial configurations have a rather short history. In most cases their bodies of fundamental laws were developed hardly more than a century ago. The cry of independence, sounded at the beginning of our nations' struggle for political freedom, incited a response not because of our strength but primarily because of the Hispanic weakness. The old viceroyalties — at times only courts (*Audiencias*) or military headquarters (*Capitanías generales*) — were economically and culturally autonomous principally because of the distances that separated them from Spain rather than because of their intrinsic importance or the number of their inhabitants. Following an historical analogy, these peoples began organizing themselves into nations in 1822, thus completing the dual process of revolution. Only three of our nations, however, had in their prehistory a cultural foundation sufficiently established so as to justify a national personality and adequate history. We refer specifically to Mexico, Peru, and Colombia, which incidentally were the geographical centers of the only three advanced Latin American cultures. Colonial life allowed for the birth and development of two, or at the most, three nations: Mexico in the sixteenth century, Lima in the seventeenth, and Buenos Aires in the eighteenth century. Yet today we see more than twenty different nations, none of them with an "intelligible field of historical study" as Toynbee would say. In other words, none of these nations is able to give an adequate account of its culture, not even of its national institutions, which were unified during the Christian colonial epoch, and which were really the seed beds of the revolutions. Attempting to explain our national cultures in themselves is an impossible task because they represent a nationalism that should be surpassed. But the challenge is to overcome not only the national boundaries and divisions but also the historical limits produced by a periodization far too restricted. We cannot explain our national cultures if we only go back to certain recent revolutions, if we begin for example in the nineteenth century or even in the sixteenth century. And even the Amerindian cultures provide only the context of certain residual elements of the succeeding Latin American culture. If we are to comprehend the meaning of our culture, we must see it from the perspective of universal history.[24]

1. Prehistory

To discuss adequately the profound and universal meaning of our Amerindian culture, we must include a discussion of mankind from the time of his origin, moving progressively from the African and Euroasiatic Paleolithic peoples, in order to see the later development of the indigenous people in America — those beings who, while so frequently ignored were yet the most Asiatic of the Asiatics, the most Oriental of the Orientals — not only in race but also in culture. The fact is that Columbus discovered Asiatic peoples. And to comprehend the advanced American cultures we must begin with the civilizations organized four millennia before Christ in the Nile valley and in Mesopotamia. For it was from these cultures that mankind moved through the Orient, and it is in them that we catch glimpses of the great Neolithic American cultures that began after the initiation of the Christian era. In these Paleolithic and Neolithic cultures we find our *prehistory*. There is no evidence to indicate that all of these advanced cultures had direct contact, but if there was social intercourse between them it was through the Polynesians. And these cultures were the results of structures already configurated in the Paleolithic peoples when the ancestors of the Americans were migrating through east Asia and the islands of the Pacific.

2. Protohistory

The most important aspect of our background is our protohistory — our "first" constitution or the formation of the most radical elements of our culture — which began in Mesopotamia and not in the arid Euroasiatic wastelands of the Indo-Europeans. The protohistory of our culture, namely, the Semitic-Christian beginnings, originated in the fourth millennium before Christ when, by successive invasions, Semitic tribes infiltrated the whole Middle East: Accadians, Assyrians, Babylonians, Phoenicians, Aramaeans, Hebrews, and Arabs who from a cultural point of view and together with Christians all form the same family.

This Semitic-Christian man dominated the Roman and Hellenistic Mediterranean and later evangelized the Germans and Slavs as well as the Indo-Europeans such as the Hittites, Iranians, Hindus, Greeks, and Romans. Finally, the Semite conquered and controlled the Iberian peninsula both in the Calif of Córdoba as well as during the reign of Castile and Aragon. The fundamental attitudes and supreme values of the conquistador of the Americas are to be found — if one desires a full explanation — in the Syrian-Arabic deserts four millennia before Jesus Christ. From this cultural womb came Byzantine, Latin, and Russian Christianity.

3. History

Our Latin American *history* began with the arrival of a handful of Hispanics who possessed, in addition to a national messianism, an immense superiority over the Indians not only in regard to the instruments of civilization but also in the coherence of their cultural structures. Our Latin American history began then in 1492 with the incontrovertible domination by the Hispanic — who was a product of late medieval Christianity — over tens of millions of Asiatics or of Asiatics and Australoids who for thousands of years had inhabited an enormous land area, but one terribly deficient because of its ahistoricity. The Indian possessed no history because his world was one of atemporal, primitive mythology with its eternal archetypes.[25] The conquistador began, therefore, an American history and in the process forgot his European history. Hispanic America began at point zero in the distressing situation of being a dependent culture.

4. The Latin American Nation

There are nations in the world that are distinguished by their totality or unity of culture such as Russia, China, and India. There are others that possess a perfect coherence in regard to their past, and still others that were constituted by an original culture such as France, Germany, and England. Conversely, there are nations that are absolutely artificial in that they possess neither a linguistic, religious, nor ethnic unity, such as South Africa. What of the Latin American nations? The truth is, we are more or less in the middle of the road. We have our nation-states with their century and a half of autonomous histories, and we manifest certain distinctive modalities of the same life-style and common culture. We even boast of our own poets and literary movements, our architecture, sculpture, philosophers, historians, essayists, and sociologists. What is more, we maintain certain attitudes in regard to civilization and hold certain values. But are the differences between one Latin American country and another so pronounced as to allow us to think in terms of distinct cultures? There are obviously significant differences between Honduras and Chile, between Argentina and Mexico, and between Venezuela and Uruguay. But is there not greater similarity between the residents of Caracas, Buenos Aires, Lima, and Guatemala City than there is between those of the Latin American urban culture and the *gaucho* of the Argentine Pampas or the Orinoco, or between the Indian in the Peruvian jungles and the Indian of modern Mexico?

Our national cultures can only be said to possess distinct personalities within a limited scope manifesting a certain consistency which could be legitimately designated by the name "culture." That is, our individual national cultures are constituent parts of the overall Latin American culture. Furthermore, these same regional cultures have for four centuries in one way or another — as all germinal cultures have — manifested secondary and marginal characteristics of European culture, and at the same time they have become consistently more autonomous. Despite the sociopolitical, economic, and technical underdevelopment, Latin America has become aware of its life-style and has tended to separate itself from European culture. Our hypothesis is, therefore, the following: to comprehend fully the individual national cultures, one must consider the structures of Latin American culture as a whole. It is a serious mistake to postpone an analysis of Latin America until the study of our national cultures has been completed, for the structures of the *whole* can be explained by the morphology of the individual parts. Physiology begins with a study of the body as a functional totality so that one can analyze and understand the complementary activities of the individual organs and systems.

Regional, national, or local studies of culture add to our understanding of the multiple forms of life and formation of common human values as well as helping to explain the attitudes of the larger group and the life-styles of Latin Americans. If one is to understand historical development on a national or international level, it is necessary to have some knowledge of history at a more restricted level. The same applies to an understanding of cultural structures. To understand the common cultural structures, one needs to comprehend the essential components of individual cultures. From these common structures, then, the national particularities will be clearly evident. Otherwise one is likely to confuse as something national that which is a part of the total Latin American heritage, and miss altogether that which can be correctly distinguished as national. In Argentina, for example, there does not exist a single institution which is dedicated to the study of Latin American culture as a whole. Paradoxically, entities such as Berlin's *Iberoamerikanische Institut* or the Latin American Library in Austin, Texas, do not exist in Latin America. Latin America has yet to find its place in the world history of culture, and our national cultures are like fruit without a tree. They are like something which sprang up by spontaneous generation. There does exist a kind of cultural "nationalism" in our countries; but if we are to preserve these national cultures we must move beyond nationalism as such and discover for ourselves that which is truly Latin American.

Moreover, we must be aware of the existence of multiple similarities between the countries of Latin America, especially at a regional level. For example, there exists a Latin America of the Caribbean, another of the Andes (including Colombia and Chile), still another of the Amazon region, and a fourth of the River Plate area. These subgroups cannot be ignored in the study of individual national cultures. To put it even more simply, it is possible to speak of a Latin America of the Pacific — which takes into consideration a prehistoric past — and another of the Atlantic, which was far more susceptible to foreign and European influences.

5. The Different Levels

How can we develop and possess a cultural knowledge, a conscious reflection on the organic structures of our Latin American and national culture? It will come only by a careful and patient analysis of each of the levels and each of the constituent elements of our culture.

The symbolic or mythical nucleus of our culture, the values on which the whole edifice of attitudes and life-styles are founded, forms an intentional complex that has its own structure, content, and history. To do a complete historical and morphological analysis would at this point be impossible,[26] but we can indicate some fundamental hypotheses and conclusions.

There have been several important studies of the history of ideas in Latin America.[27] I do not minimize the value and importance of these works, but what is needed is a concrete understanding of the ideas of the man on the street in his daily life. And we will find the ultimate values of our pre- and protohistory as well as our current history — at least until the beginning of the nineteenth century — in the symbols, myths, and religious structures. To discover these values we should use principally the tools of the historians and phenomonologists of religion, because until the recent secularization of culture, fundamental values and primary symbols of a group were always a part of their teleological structures, that is, a *logos* of what they perceive to be divine.

In America the study of the values of a cultural group should begin with an analysis of the primitive awareness of the Amerindian mythical structure in whose rites and legends are found the intentional contents and values for which we are searching[28] — as Karl Jaspers and Paul Ricoeur have both indicated.[29] Philosophy is nothing more than the rational expression (at least until the seventeenth century) of the theological structures accepted and adhered to consciously by the group.[30]

In the second place, one should observe the clash between the value systems of the Amerindian and the Hispanic not only during the period of conquest but also during the time of the evangelization. The domination of the Semitic-Christian values are colored by the medieval and Renaissance Hispanic messianism, which did not avoid a syncretism with the surviving Amerindian myths in the popular conscience. One can discern the configuration of these two values systems in the history of colonial Christianity in Latin America. After the revolutions a crisis developed as a result of the conflicting currents of thought proceeding from Europe beginning in 1830, which ultimately produced a generation of positivists in Latin America beginning about 1870.

The most significant phenomenon that developed was that of the secularization of a society which was in part culturally Christian — certain values were common among Latin Americans, and there was a relative intolerance for alien values — and Latin America became a kind of pluralistic and secularized society. Nevertheless, the basic content of the mythical nucleus, though secularized, continued unchanged. The view of man, history, the cosmos, the transcendental, and liberty, continued — with minor exceptions — to be the ancestral. Positivism completely disappeared, and the models which were inspired by the North Americans, French, and English came to be regarded as alien to the Latin American culture, that is, Latin America rejected them as foreign.

For our part we believe that it is necessary to analyze consciously the world of ancestral values — to discover their basic contents and to differentiate between the permanent and essential and the transient — in order to move toward the development of our own culture and civilization.[31]

One can say precisely the same thing about our *ethos*, this organism of fundamental attitudes that constitute our values.[32] Here the situation is even more delicate: Latin Americans do not possess the same tragic *ethos* of the Indian upon whom an inevitable destiny is quietly forced. Neither does the Latin American have the same *ethos* of the Spaniard about whom Ortega y Gasset clairvoyantly wrote as follows:

The Spaniard is that person who has no ultimate or real needs, and who can accept life and face it with a positive attitude of not needing anything. The Spaniard needs nothing to live. In fact, he does not even need to live for he has no great stake in living. This is precisely what frees him to live and what permits him to be the master of his life.[33]

Latin Americans, in contrast, have another *ethos*, which Mayz Vallenilla describes saying that "facing the pure Present — here is our primordial affirmation — we feel on the margin of history, and we function with a mood of radical precariousness,"[34] and this "only after a prolonged familiarity and adjustment within our world by means of a spirit of a constant and reiterated *expectation* in regard to the future."[35] Another has put it even more succinctly when he says,

Latin America is immature. Perhaps the fact that a Latin American — and I am speaking of more than one — tolerates this immaturity without embarrassment is an indication that he has taken the first step toward maturity. What is more important in my way of thinking, if one is to move toward maturity, one must be conscious of one's immaturity. In our case, unless we are aware of our condition, we are ignorant of the real situation on our continent, and we are unable to progress a single step.[36]

Ortega y Gasset lamented: "The Creole soul is full of broken promises; it feels pain in members which it does not have and which it has never had."[37]

We should not, however, think of our *ethos* as a collection of deficiencies simply because "Latin America does not appear to be tranquil in regard to her judgments."[38] Our *ethos* possesses without doubt a fundamental attitude of "hope," and as a result of this revolutionaries for example are sometimes victorious because they are infected with doses of vitality stemming from their anticipation of something better.

We are not attempting in this work to undertake an exposition of the network of attitudes that constitute the Latin American *ethos*. To do so it would be necessary to include a study of the phenomenological method, for it is in the particular modality of our people that the human conscience in general is determined by a world view distinctly our own, the product of circumstances that are irreducibly the components of communication.[39] Besides a structural investigation, one should always consider the evolution of the phenomena, which involves, of course, an historical investigation.

Finally, we should see the third aspect of the constituent elements of culture, namely, the total life-style together with its objectifications in artistic and cultural works.[40] It is this level that has already been studied most and about which we possess the majority of recorded investigation. This includes the histories of art, literature, folklore, architecture, painting, music, and the cinema, and there is a concerted attempt to understand the originality of these expressions of our way of life. Evidently a clear comprehension of this life-style can only be achieved by the analysis of the nucleus of values and organic attitudes of the *ethos*, a work which we have barely outlined in the two preceding paragraphs. What is lacking to the present is a perspective of the whole, in a coherent and evolutionary manner, of all the levels of the cultural objectifications, that is, a work that will bring together all the Latin American arts and cultural movements and that will show their interrelations and the values on which they are founded, the attitudes by which they are determined, and the historical circumstances that modify them. As of yet, we do not have an exposition of our own cultural world, that is, a history of Latin American culture.

6. Is National History Particular?

If we could undertake in this context the study of the development of our *national* culture, and if we could examine individually every nation, it would be possible to apply analogically what we find in all the rest of the Latin American nations and affirm analogically that there are shades, grades, and levels of diverse applicability.

First, however, we must reject the understanding of our separate cultural extremes such as *nationalism* and the ideas of those who maintain utopian positions, whether of the right or of the left, be they conservatives or liberals. The absolutization of the nation is a fallacy which in one way or another goes back to the French ideologists of the eighteenth century or to Hegel in the beginning of the nineteenth century. Likewise we should move beyond any form of racism, even that of those who, longing for a pure indigenization, speak "of the race. ... " For all forms of racism, be they German or Amerindian, propose the primacy of the biological over the spiritual and tend to define the human being at the zoological level. At the same time we should leave aside any facile Europeanism which simply postpones our taking the responsibility for our own culture and continues the ancestral transatlantic alienation.[41]

We should, therefore, place each of our nations *in* Latin America, our smaller country in our larger country, not only so that we might understand ourselves as a people, but also so that we can participate with some influence and meaning in the world dialogue of cultures and in the integral development of our civilization. What is needed is the ability to discern, separate, and distinguish the nations to enable us to unite and integrate them. We should know which of the levels of our culture are historically and structurally dependent on other peoples and at which levels one encounters individual styles and individual temperaments. If we attempt to make everything autochthonous, we will appear to be ridiculous — much like the well known Argentine anthropologist who declared his desire to objectify Argentine originality even to the level of physical anthropology, proposing in the process an "autochthonous race of the Pampas." This is the height of myth carried to its zoological extreme. We should know where and how to look for our originality not only as Latin Americans but as national cultures.

Chapter III

Relations Between the Church and Culture

When we study the relation of the Church to a human group, we have to understand clearly the level on which we are moving.

I. THE LEVEL OF CIVILIZATION

The Church or Christianity cannot be related as one instrument to another, because the Church does not possess the instruments of civilization, neither is it a civilization as such. Only when two civilizations meet can there be a clash of the instruments between them. The continual temptation of Israel with its temporal messianism, of the Christian Empire of Constantine, of the Hispanic world, and of contemporary Catholic integralism is precisely at the point of confusing Judeo-Christianity with a particular culture, race, people, or nation. Christianity can become slave to the *instruments* of a philosophy, a group, a party, a Christian institution, or to Western culture; but Christian institutions are by nature supplementary and transitory. In many cases, of course, they are beneficial, but we fall into serious error when we attempt to eternalize them. All of this relates to the problem of the creation, growth, and death of Christian institutions. A case in point would be the Pontifical States in the mid-nineteenth century, or the Spanish *Patronato* beginning in the seventeenth century. Each of these is an example of an institution that could have been beneficial at one time but that became injurious to the cause of Christianity when it was no longer needed for the transcendental ends of the gospel.

It is clear that there are other extreme positions, such as that of angelism, fideism, or Monophysitism, which claim that the Kingdom of God is unrelated to any institution and does not need a single instrument of civilization nor the support of any culture. The Manichaeans depreciated the *corporal,* and at times Protestantism has tended to deny the value of the *natural.* The millenarian sects, Jansenism, and certain forms of progressivism are equally deficient at this point.

Between the extreme of identifying Christianity with a human institution and that of denying any relationship between the Kingdom of God and all institutions is the affirmation or the doctrine of the Incarnation of Jesus Christ who was both God and man. Knowing that no concrete instrument of civilization is necessary for the Church — because it transcends them — we know that the Church must always employ the instruments of civilization. Being aware that "corporality" is not the only feature that constitutes the human condition, we can be sure that everything related to the human being is of necessity "carnal" in the biblical sense of "human totality" or "sacramentality." *Ecclesiastical institutions* divinely established are not the instruments of civilization, and civilization should clearly distinguish them from the innumerable "Christian" institutions not divinely established. The latter are transitory and depend upon a given culture. Even in divine institutions we should distinguish the accidental, dependent elements such as language from the essential elements. It is understood that the supreme element of a divine institution is the Trinity, which assumes in the person of Jesus Christ historical humanity by means of sacramentality — essentially in the Eucharistic mystery — of the living Church, that is, the Kingdom of God. In this sense Christianity can "exist" in different cultures and can utilize any instrument without necessarily becoming a slave to it.

II. THE LEVEL ON WHICH "RELATIONS" ARE ESTABLISHED

The Church and Christianity can have a twofold relationship with groups and cultures: on the level of understanding and on the level of "ethos." We shall examine these two aspects separately.

1. The "Ethico-mythical Nucleus" of a Culture and Christian Understanding

If we could grasp, for example, the significance of the work of the apologists in the primitive Church, we would immediately see that they concentrated on criticizing the basis of the total Greco-Roman culture. In light of their Christian understanding of the dogmas of the faith and revealed truth, the apologists utilized the intentional instruments of the Greco-Roman culture, namely, the sciences and philosophies of the era, to critique the "ethico-mythical nucleus" of the culture, such as man as a soul, the body as evil, the universe as eternal, the gods as intraworldly, and history as an eternal cycle of events. Slowly but surely the Judeo-Christian world view filled the vacuum in the ancient culture and began to transform it completely. Evangelization involved not only personal or individual conversion, but also social and community transformation. As a result a new "ethico-mythical nucleus" was created with a clear Christian orientation. It would be incorrect to refer to the new culture as a "Christian civilization" because no such civilization has ever existed. Neither can we assume that a single civilization resulted. Civilizations with a Christian orientation have been multiple, and furthermore, paganism in one form or another has always existed. A primitive or syncretic civilization is monist, that is, it allows for only one "ethico-mythical nucleus," while a superior civilization such as contemporary Europe, North America, or Russia is pluralistic, or at least it can be. There can exist in a civilization — a system of instruments — different movements, intentional groups, and centers of interpretation. Thus from medieval civilization with its Christian orientation there resulted the neopagan movements of which Marxism and secularism are the logical consequences. These are distinct world views within the same limits of the prevailing universal civilization.

2. Christian Charity and the Pagan Ethos

The fundamental Greco-Roman attitude in regard to the various instruments of civilization was primarily, on the one hand, obedience to the system established by law, both political and cosmic, because the citizen belonged to the *polis* or the Empire. On the other hand, perfection was achieved by a certain sufficiency of instruments and by the leisure and solitude which the wise man achieved through contemplation apart from his duty to the city. This was classical culture.

Meanwhile, the primary attitude of the Christian in regard to the instruments of civilization was expressed in love for one's neighbor motivated by the love for God. Herein did one participate in the same interpersonal love of God. Charity was not regarded as mere philanthropy; rather it was seen as interpersonal divine love. This was the foundation of the *Christian ethos*. Obviously such love was and is impossible without faith, without the fundamental experience, without understanding. This love for a person as a person, this respect for another's present and future in God, this created and redeemed understanding, produced innumerable effects in the field of civilization and of the *ethos* — for example, the improvement of the situation for women, the recogition of the equality of people of all races, and the abolition of the institution of slavery. All these things were not achieved in a day, but rather in centuries — results of the fundamental Christian attitude and understanding that faith produces in the conscience, and the awareness of another's inalienable dignity. The people of Israel, and later the Church, entered into dialogue with different peoples, nations, and civilizations, and from this interchange Judeo-Christianity emerged enriched and aware of its universality.

In order to understand the development of culture in Latin America and its mutual relation with the Church, one should distinguish between the pre-Hispanic American civilization and *ethos* and the Hispanic civilization and culture, which clashed with each other. Furthermore, the dialogue that Christianity began with the pre-Hispanic communities was complicated by its apparent identity with the Hispanic culture. Also, the clash between the two civilizations as well as the dialogue between Christianity and American paganism is totally *sui generis*. A description of the actual differences in these two peoples will constitute the objective of the remaining chapters.

Prior to the birth of Christ, Judaism dialogued with the Canaanites, Egyptians, Babylonians, and Greeks. The Primitive Church dialogued with the Roman Empire. In all these cases the Hebrew or Christian community was situated within the *interior* of a superior culture which in one sense had been permeated by the Semitic spirit in the course of three millennia. The individual conversion of a minority and the subsequent conversion of the masses came by the transformation of the "ethico-mythical nucleus" of the Greco-Roman culture and resulted in the development of Constantinian Christendom. The Germanic tribes — representing external inferior civilizations — invaded the Christian empire, but in the last analysis the invaders were assimilated into the civilization and religion of the invaded, namely, into Latin Christendom. Islam, on the other hand — representing an external superior culture historically — coexisted with Christianity without Europe's ever discovering a means by which to transform the Muslim "ethico-mythical nucleus."

Finally, as a result of the naval expeditions of Portugal beginning in the fourteenth century and of Spain in the following century, Europe entered for the first time into a program of expansion. Also for the first time Europeans were confronted by superior and inferior cultures which were absolutely external. Like the Germans who invaded the Christian empire, Christians invaded the territory of these external civilizations and cultures. The Scandinavian peoples, for example, resided in a territory outside that of Constantinian Christendom but were, nonetheless, adjacent to the Empire. Their conversion was achieved within the scope of normal terrestrial continental expansion, and the inroads achieved politically and economically influenced the Scandinavians to adopt what they perceived in the medieval civilization as a superior culture. Theirs was a marginal area within the Christian orbit. Conversely, in Africa and on the Atlantic coast of America, Portugal and Spain encountered inferior cultures in an environment totally pagan. In Asia and on the Pacific side of Latin America superior cultures did exist. The great civilizations of India and China, for example, were comparable and even superior to that of the pagan Roman Empire. It is now apparent that Christianity should have entered into dialogue with the Indian and Chinese cultures — and could have done so, as the experience of Matteo Ricci clearly demonstrates — had they followed the example of Francisco Xavier.

We can also say that without doubt the Hispanic civilization virtually annihilated the Amerindian civilizations in America. The indigenous political and military organizations were obliterated, and the Amerindian elites and their institutions of education and culture were destroyed. What was left of the Indian community after being decimated in part by epidemics, wars, and inhumane treatment was totally unhinged from the ancient context which the norms and the organization of the Amerindian cultures provided. Christianity, therefore, encountered an enormous difficulty in attempting to begin a dialogue on the level of existential understanding, in that the Christian faith did not encounter an adequate interlocutor, and the defenders of the Indians would not have served. Moreover, encountering a pagan environment, half of which the Spanish invaders were inclined to accept and the other half to change, certain ancestral practices continued from the time of the conquest. Consider, for example, the important influence on the Latin American *ethos* of the cohabitation between Spanish and Indians that took place during the first years of the sixteenth century, together with the wholesale lack of respect for the laws pouring forth from the Spanish court. All of this produced an *ethos* of habitual antilegalism. It is certain that the Hispanic culture contributed to or provided a Latin Americanized Christendom, and in the Indian communities a catechetical process was begun that has not yet been completed.

Part Two

The Christendom of the West Indies (1492–1808)

Three aspects of Latin American history will be examined briefly in this part: the Amerindian cultures prior to the arrival of the Spanish, the Hispanic culture itself, and the conditions in the Church during the colonial period.

1. The Amerindian Cultures

In America the European conquistadores and colonists encountered two highly developed cultures: the Mayan-Aztec in Mexico and Central America, and the Inca in Peru. At the time of the arrival of the Spanish each of these indigenous cultures had reached a stage of development more or less on the level of the Egyptians during their first dynasty. The "cultural distance" therefore between the Spanish and the Indians of these two superior cultures was more than five thousand years. The rest of America was secondary and in an absolutely primitive state.

The "ethico-mythical nucleus" of these cultures has been carefully examined by students of the philosophy of religion. These indigenous communities were by and large agricultural — or, as in the case of the Aztecs, warriors — highly syncretistic in which the *chtónicos* gods, such as Mother Earth and the Moon, were combined with the *uránicos* gods. Basically, the Indian mentality was antihistorical, that is, a ritualistic rhythm and a transcendental reality of the divine archetypes controlled and sacramentalized all daily activity. The Inca and Aztec empires originated in the fifteenth century, and by the beginning of the sixteenth century when the Spanish were arriving in America, these civilizations were still relatively young. Their pantheons had not as yet been codified nor adequately organized, their theogonies and beliefs were still heterogeneous, and their philosophical reflection had hardly begun.

2. Hispanic Christendom

The Hispanic people — a segment of European medieval Christendom — were the descendants of the Caucasoid tribes who originally inhabited the Iberian peninsula. During the early Christian era the area — present-day Spain and Portugal — was a province of Rome that subsequently converted to Christianity. In the seventh century the peninsula was invaded by the Arabs, and the Spaniards entered the eighth century locked in a desperate struggle against Islam, a conflict that continued for eight centuries and which produced in the Spanish people a spirit of the "crusades." They were able to reconquer their territory by advancing slowly toward the southern part of the peninsula. But it was not until 1492, the same year that Columbus discovered some of the islands of the Caribbean, that the Moors were finally expelled from Granada.[1]

The structure of the Hispanic world was therefore essentially that of medieval Europe together with certain elements of the Arab world. One of these elements was the tendency to unify indissolubly the aims and purposes of the state and of the Church. This tendency can be traced from the Constantinian period through the Visigoths and the Pontifical States. It should be observed, however, that the Islamic doctrine of the caliphate demanded this same kind of unity, a religio-political monism which was also promoted by various royalist schools such as that of Marsilio de Padua and all the other jurists who supported the absolute primacy of the monarchy. The absolutism of Henry VIII of England and of some of the Danish monarchs was an expression of the same philosophy but was obviously carried to an extreme.

In Spain there existed, therefore, something akin to a "temporal messianism" in which the destiny of the nation and the destiny of the Church were believed to be united. Hispanic Christianity, it was believed, was unique in that the nation had been elected by God to be the instrument for the salvation of the world. This idea among the Spanish that they had been elected by God — which, incidentally, was the perennial stumbling block for Israel — constituted the foundation of the religio-politics of Isabella, Charles, and Philip.

3. The *Patronato* System as an Institution of Christendom

The Catholic Church in Spain and Portugal during the twelfth to the sixteenth centuries was subservient to the Portuguese and Spanish governments not only because of the absolutist policies of the Hispanic kings, but also because of the weakness of the Roman pontiffs during the period. Portugal was the first to obtain significant concessions from Rome beginning in the thirteenth century. These "rights" were followed by others.

The Holy See first recognized the *possessio* of Portugal over lands already discovered and those yet to be discovered. Then the Pope awarded to the Portuguese Crown exclusive authority over all of Africa. Third, anyone who proceeded contrary to this absolute right of Portugal would be, according to the Pontiff, subject to excommunication. The rights and powers of the Portuguese Crown were declared to be not only spiritual, but also political and economic, and these rights became the basis of a slowly developing colonialism.[2] Moreover, the Papacy ceded to the Portuguese kings the *right* and responsibility, the *jus patronatus*,[3] of "propagating the faith"[4] among the peoples in the newly discovered lands and in those retaken from the Sarracen power. This was the first time in history that the Papacy gave to a nation the twofold authority to colonize and evangelize, that is, temporal and eternal, political and ecclesiastical, economic and evangelistic authority. This consolidation of power by Portugal and Spain produced two military and imperial theocracies more Islamic than Christian but not unique for the Middle Ages. There also developed within the Portuguese and Spanish endeavors a fundamental ambiguity between colonizing and evangelizing. Only the Jesuits were able to constitute as *territorium nullius Diocesis* the newly discovered lands under direct protection of the Holy See, and for a long time this Order enjoyed a greater freedom than other churchmen in Latin America.[5]

Spain, especially Castile and Aragon, hypertrophied the Gothic tradition and gained unlimited power over the Church — an understandable and justifiable phenomenon in view of the chaos that existed in Rome. The Hispanic system of the *Patronato* had its antecedents in the Middle Ages, but more proximate causes were the conquest and evangelization of the Canary Islands that began in 1418 when the Roman pontiffs gave to Spain not only jurisdiction over the peoples of the Islands but also the responsibility of defending them and of sending missionaries to them. A Franciscan convent was founded in Ondarra for the sole purpose of preparing missionaries for the Canaries. The *Patronato* was of even greater significance in regard to the territory of Granada after it was retaken from the Arabs in 1492. Two crucial concessions had already been awarded to Spain by the papal bulls — *Provisionis Nostrae*, promulgated on May 15, 1486, and *Dum ad illam*, which followed on August 4. According to the terms of these pronouncements, the kings of Spain reserved the right to nominate all bishops, tantamount to naming them, and also to participate in the benefices and tithes of the Church. Granada had been the ultimate goal of the Spanish "crusade," but it signaled in reality the beginning of Spanish expansion. The newly discovered lands and inhabitants of the Americas were placed under the authority of the Spanish Crown by two additional papal bulls, *Inter coetera* and *Eximiae devotionis* of May 3 – 4, 1493, on the principle that as subjects of the Catholic kings and as members of the Church these people could thereby partake of the benefits of the gospel.

The astute Ferdinand of Aragon was able to wrest from the popes one concession after another: the nomination of all bishops, the establishment of new dioceses together with determining their geographical boundaries, as well as the sending of all missionaries and religious, that is, monks, friars, and nuns. But the culmination was the right granted to the Spanish Crown to the tithes of all the dioceses and parishes. On the one hand it would appear that the popes were unaware of all that they were ceding, while on the other hand Rome hardly possessed the power to deny the demands of the Spanish and Portuguese kings. It is significant, nonetheless, that in Burgos in 1512 the first three bishops named for the Americas accepted their posts under these conditions and with the royal privileges.[6]

The executive organism of the *Patronato* developed slowly until the creation in 1524 of the *Supreme Council of the Indies*, which consolidated and exercised authority in all matters related to the Spanish colonies: religious, economic, administrative, political, and military. The American Church in turn was denied any right to communicate directly with Rome or with any other European prelate. Furthermore, the Council was empowered to send missionaries to Spanish American colonies without advising their superiors, to nominate all bishops, to organize new dioceses and to divide others. The representatives of the *Patronato* in the American provinces were the viceroys, the governors, and the courts (*Audiencias*). The episcopacy in the colonies was organized by these representatives of the Crown, which deemed the Church as a necessity. But the royal authority became the basis of a clash between the Church and the state when the episcopacy attempted to gain freedom in its work of evangelization. For example, Toribio de Mogrovejo, Archbishop of Lima, is a key to understanding the reaction of the Church to the absolute authority of the Council.

According to the laws and decrees emanating from the Spanish Crown and from the Supreme Council of the Indies, the purpose of the conquest of the Americas was essentially missionary. But in actuality this missionary or evangelistic purpose was often negated by the actions of those who engaged in the conquest, actions which in reality were contrary to the laws. Latin America was characterized by a "perfect legalism" in theory, and a shameful illegality and an inadequate application of the laws in fact.

Chapter IV

The Clash Between Two Cultures
and the Condition of the Church

The Hispanic civilization arrived in America during the apogee of her cultural, military, and even religious power, especially since the reform of Cisneros, and encountered other cultures that from virtually any point of view were substantially inferior. Spain, with the generous help of her people, of her unoccupied military forces, of her noblemen passionate for new titles, of the multitudes of poverty-stricken individuals thirsting for riches, and of religious and priests, among whom there were many saints, doctors, and others not quite as impressive — as is normal in all of history — initiated the political, economic, and spiritual conquest.

I. THE INSTRUMENTS OF ONE CIVILIZATION VERSUS THE INSTRUMENTS OF ANOTHER

In this unequal struggle Spain triumphed rapidly over the indigenous peoples. The Aztec and Inca empires succumbed in holy terror before the power of the Spanish harquebuses, cannons, horses, bloodthirsty dogs, and weapons of iron and invincible armor. A mere handful of men conquered a continent with millions of inhabitants, thereby signaling the supremacy of the Mediterranean over the pre-Hispanic American civilization. This entire indigenous civilization was defeated by the Spanish and then exploited to the ultimate degree possible. Europe benefited greatly from the multiple agricultural products of the American civilization, from her gold and silver mines, and at least in part from her ancient cultures. We will observe from a demographic perspective — and as an example — what the clash between these civilizations produced.

In the royal commissions (*Cédulas Reales*) the Supreme Council of the Indies and the Crown continually sought information in regard to the growth or the decrease in the number of Indians. The Laws of the Indies were created specifically for their defense. Bishops were horrified by the disappearance of the indigenous peoples, which was attributed to bad administration, inhumane treatment, injustices, as well as the impact of European diseases, plagues, and the "pestilences" as they were called.

The following table (p. 42) indicates the rapid decrease of the indigenous peoples in Mexico during the period from 1532 until 1608.

These statistics appear to be accurate from the investigations I have made, and they explain the repeated complaints voiced during the sixteenth century regarding the alarming decline in the Indian population.

II. THE INDIAN WORLD VIEW VERSUS THE HISPANIC WORLD VIEW

The Spanish invasion and conquest led to the total disintegration of the Indian world. Nonetheless, as always, the intentional elements of the Indian world view tended to

Regional Populations in Various Periods in Mexico[1]

Upper Regions	1532	1568	1580	1595	1608
I — Central Macizo	7,999,307	1,707,758	1,233,032	770,649	
II — Central Vera Cruz	171,984	32,340	21,560	20,200	
IV — Oaxaca Misteca	1,560,931	222,165	150,620	146,740	
VIII — Michoacán	1,038,668	188,398	161,299	96,913	
IX — Guadalajara -Zacatecas	462,446	80,515	64,618	90,670	
Subtotal	11,233,336	2,231,176	1,631,129	1,125,172	852,244
Lower Regions					
II — Panuco-Vallés	1,532,860	74,087	42,370	45,690	
III — Alvarado Coat- zacoalcos	710,230	37,682	32,207	17,876	
V — Oaxacas-Zapo- tecas	681,372	68,076	56,076	37,119	
VI — Oaxaca Coast	862,687	63,545	43,885	33,729	
VII — Michoacán -Tlaxcala Coasts	243,163	113,531	64,264	71,158	
X — Guadalajara Coast	614,760	61,476	21,336	41,484	
Subtotal	5,645,072	418,397	260,138	247,056	217,011
TOTAL	16,871,408	2,649,573	1,891,267	1,372,228	1,069,255

be retained for a much longer period of time than the instruments of the indigenous civilization. The Hispanic concept of life destroyed the basic foundations of the indigenous cosmology. The Indian elites — not only the Aztecs but also the Incas and other Indian peoples conquered by the Spanish — adopted the Hispanic world view or were relegated to an inferior level in the society, that is, they ceased being a part of the ruling elite and became members of the marginal elements of the new society.

Even to the present the Indian lacks the normal institutions necessary for the development of a world view, and it appears that the indigenous peoples as a nation and as a culture have been virtually destroyed. The Spaniard was scandalized, for example, by the Aztec offering of human sacrifice — one of the pre-Hispanic instruments — and failed to see any theological significance in this practice. Human sacrifice, however, was the essential rite understood by the Indian to assure any cosmic renewal in view of the fact that the gods needed blood to live and to give life to the universe. The Spaniard, unable to understand the ultimate bases of the Indian culture and civilization, sought to obliterate every vestige of the pre-Hispanic American civilization. Tragically, there was no adult interlocutor such as Matteo Ricci encountered in China or as Roberto de Nobili found in India. The indigenous American peoples lacked the philosophers and theologians who could have acted as bridges between the Hispanic and the American "ethico-mythical nucleus." Moreover, the multiplicity of languages and cultures impeded the conquerors from absorbing the cultural wealth of the conquered tribes and peoples.

The result of this clash of cultures can be seen in the emergence of the Hispanic world view as the predominant one in the new American civilization. The key posts politically, culturally, and economically were occupied by Spaniards. The Indian civilization, on the other hand, as a vital system and organism with the possibility of development, simply disappeared, and the Indian peoples became an inferior social class which the Spanish attempted to isolate and prevent from becoming a part of the controlling elite in any sense. This was a very real but tragic fact. Perhaps in a sense it was inevitable — but the pre-Hispanic existential understanding was eradicated.

III. THE WORK OF THE MISSIONARY

In the organization of the Hispanic empire, the Church became the primary organism responsible for and committed to the perpetuation of the Hispanic world view primarily because the ecclesiastics controlled the universities, the secondary and primary schools, and the printing and distribution of literature. The vast majority of the intellectual elites in Latin America were priests. Also, virtually no member of the intellectual elite in Spain, with the exception of the missionaries, came to America with the idea of making a cultural contribution. Noblemen and soldiers as well as colonizers came to the New World with the understanding that they were responsible for the defense of the interests of the Crown and of the *Patronato*. The Church, on the other hand, was responsible for the work of evangelization and acculturation of the newly discovered peoples.

The Christian existential understanding — the faith and tradition that essentially transcended all human culture and civilization — became inextricably bound to the "ethico-mythical nucleus" of the Hispanic culture, which in time was superimposed upon the indigenous peoples of the Americas. Christianity became identified with the Spanish, and this identification was virtually absolute, especially in the mind of the conquistador. For him, to be a Spaniard and to be a Christian were identical, just as being a Mohammedan and a member of the *umma* were for the Arab one and the same. The Indian, therefore, deduced logically that to be a Spaniard or to belong to his civilization and to be a Christian were equivalent, especially in view of the fact that submitting to the authority of the Inca meant respecting and worshiping his gods. It was only the missionaries — and not all of them — who discovered the necessity of distinguishing clearly between "Hispanism" and "Christianity," that is, between the understanding of the Christian faith and the "ethico-mythical nucleus" of the Hispanic civilization.

Missionary work should have involved the conversion of each member of the Indian culture to the Church. But it should have also involved the massive conversion of the Indian culture by a century of dialogue between the Christian apologists born in the Indian culture who could critique the "ethico-mythical nucleus" of these indigenous cultures from the perspective of Christian understanding. This, however, was not possible. Having failed to understand the basic organisms of the Indian civilization, the missionary encountered a culture of disintegrating and diverse elements. And though the baptism of these people proved to be fairly simple — because there was little effort to catechize the "ethico-mythical nucleus" — there remained a pagan atmosphere diffused and uncontrolled and almost impossible to discern and evangelize.

Spanish expansion was achieved in the same manner as that of the Roman Empire, the Medieval Crusades, and the Arab caliphates, that is, a region was occupied militarily, then pacified, a government formed, and the people of the area converted to the religion of the invaders — although in the Roman empire the local gods were simply placed in the pantheon. This was the *modus operandi* of a worldly empire. But if this empire claimed to be Christian, the missionaries and the prophets could only rise up and cry to heaven as Antonio de Montesinos did in December of 1511 on the island of Hispaniola. The cry of this Spanish priest continues to be heard throughout the history of the Latin American Church. To know how to hear it, to understand it, and to repeat it is the work of the Church historian.

One often hears of the missionary meaning or purpose involved in the conquest — a phrase which can conceal a basic misunderstanding. For to speak of the missionary purpose would seem to signify above everything else its importance. But was the missionary purpose the principal one, or a secondary, marginal one? Was it the only purpose, or, on the contrary, was it merely an apparent one?

I would prefer to speak of the integral meaning of the conquest as seen in the *modus operandi* of a Christian nation still living in the Middle Ages. The conquest signified the expansion of the Hispanic type of Christianity, including all the ambiguity that such a formula indicates. By understanding the structure of the Hispanic national Christianity one can immediately comprehend the diverse elements of which that Christianity was constituted, and the spurious contradictions will disappear.

It was not possible for Spain to be a national Christendom of a Medieval type — where there was a confusion between the spiritual and the temporal and the certain Caesarian tapestry *sui generis* — and at the same time an economic power inspired by a growing capitalism. It is absurd to claim that Spain attempted to exploit her American colonies for her own economic benefit. Was Spain a state organized to defend the interest of private companies such as was Venice, Holland, and later England? Or was Spain a state organized according to the imperial model as was the Byzantine Empire in the East or the Holy Roman Empire in the West? During the Crusades the spiritual and political goals of the Franks and the Anglo-Saxons were completely distinct from the economic objectives of the Venetians and the Genovese. On the other hand, the objectives of the Franks were not exclusively spiritual. They were also very much political as the organization of the Christian kingdoms of the East clearly indicate. We are speaking here of the Christianity of these kingdoms.

In the same sense Spain by her expansion as a Christian kingdom mixed ambitiously two indissoluble objectives: the *domination* of the lands and inhabitants newly discovered under the temporal power of the Crown, and the *evangelization* of these peoples by incorporating them into the Church, the spiritual arm of the kingdom. The political objectives of Spain, however, should be clearly distinguished from those merely economic as well as from later capitalistic exploitation such as one sees practiced by the German company in Venezuela or according to the familiar organization of colonies as parts of a Commonwealth. Isabella and Ferdinand, Charles, and Philip did have political objectives not only in Europe but also in America, and because of these objectives it was necessary for the monarchs to invest large sums of capital. But the reason was not merely economic, and to criticize them as capitalists is an unfounded anachronism.

The religious or missionary aims of the Spanish rulers are easily understood. They were an integral and necessary part of the effort to expand — and thus were mixed essentially with the political aims of Spain as a Christian kingdom. Freed from any admixture or ambiguity the missionary aim would not be a part of the expansion of a Christian kingdom, but it would be only that of the Roman Catholic Church. The history of Christian missions in Hispanic America, however, is the account of a continual crisis between the state which included the aims of the Church as a means of expansion — a position clearly accepted by many members of the Church but certainly not by everyone—and those of a Church which recognized very slowly the necessity for freedom, the problems of poverty, charity, as well as the separation of the political aims of the state from the missionary objectives of the Church.

Bartolomé de Las Casas was the first to propose a peaceful evangelization, that is, that the missionaries should go to the Indians before the military. And it was the Jesuits in particular who, under the direct authority of the Pope and with a relative independence from the Crown, were able to demonstrate clearly an exclusively missionary purpose.

How has this colonial period been judged as a civilizing effort in relation to the Church?

Some support the Black Legend—they refuse to give any value to the work of Spain and Portugal, calling them rather intolerant because of the method of the *tabula rasa;* exploiters because of the extraction of gold and silver from Latin America; supporters of slavery because of their treatment of the Indians; and religiously superficial because the Christianity implanted in America was inadequate and in many respects pagan.

Others support the Hispanic Legend recently proposed. To support their position they cite innumerable documents and testimonies from the colonial era which portray Spain as a great missionary nation closely identified with the Catholic Church. The work of Spain in the Americas is seen as being almost perfect, and as evidence for this the letter of the laws are cited instead of the events of history.

The truth is that the Catholic kings and the Austrians had a politic of military expansion, economic mercantilism, and of evangelization by which they proposed to unify Europe and the world within the Roman Catholic Church under the sign of the cross. But this noble objective demanded certain means, and these means were purchased with the gold and the silver of the Indians who were organized into the *mita,* and by other systems extracted from the American mines.[2] The exploitation of these precious metals along with the agricultural production of the colonies instituted an economic-social system with artificial and monopolistic privileges that impeded the work of evangelization.

The missionary Church opposed this state of affairs from the beginning, and nearly everything positive that was done for the benefit of the indigenous peoples resulted from the call and clamor of the missionaries. The fact remained, however, that widespread injustice was extremely difficult to uproot.

The Church should have established its independence with respect to three poles: the Crown to which it was tied by the system of the *Patronato,* the Hispanic-Creole society with which it was unified naturally by its ethnic and cultural solidarity, and the Indian communities to which it was sent for the purpose of evangelization and protection, for the bishops were the logical and most conspicuous protectors of the Indians. Although the missionary orders for the most part made heroic sacrifices in their initial attempts to evangelize the indigenous peoples, the missionary spirit waned and this original purpose became incidental.

As to the civilization itself, the major error of the Spanish beginning in the sixteenth century was the organization of a mercantile system by which the gold and silver were purchased at low costs with the products of raw or manufactured materials from Europe. Because of this system Spain did not industrialize its colonies. Rather, it impeded industrialization and agricultural exploitation in Latin America. The British, on the other hand, based their colonial system in the eighteenth century on the industrialization of the mother country, and thereby surpassed Spain as modern industrial capitalism displaced the agrarian Medieval mercantilism. Latin America and her Church, however, were equally united in this process of civilization.

Alexander von Humboldt wrote toward the end of the eighteenth century regarding the Latin American civilization:

I have had the advantage, which few Spaniards can dispute, of having visited successively Caracas, Havana, Santa Fe de Bogotá, Quito, Lima, and Mexico. ... It appears to me that there is an intense interest in Mexico and Santa Fe de Bogotá in the profound studies of the sciences; more interest in Letters and in developing a passionate and fickle imagination for flattery in Quito and Lima; more light regarding political relations among the nations and a greater understanding of the state of the colonies and of the metropolis in Havana and Caracas. The multiple communications with European commerce, and this sea of the Antilles which we have characterized before as a Mediterranean, have powerfully influenced social progress in Cuba and in the magnificent provinces of Venezuela.[3]

These words are cited as evidence that there existed in Latin America an authentic culture, the product of the Hispanic effort, from its origin until today, although it was profoundly *dependent* on the Empire.

Chapter V

Important Stages in the History of the Church During the Colonial Period

The basis for the division that we have adopted is simple, and at the same time it permits an understanding of the progress as well as the difficulties encountered in the mission and organization of the Church. We are able to discern five stages which parallel the conquest and the history of Spain in general.

I. THE FIRST STAGE (1492–1519)

No priest accompanied Columbus on his first voyage in 1492. Friar Bernard Boyl, confidant of the Catholic kings, was the first priest to arrive in America. Boyl was empowered with enormous authority by the papal bull *Piis fidelium* of June 25, 1493. Unfortunately, his authority — as was to recur frequently — clashed with that of Columbus who represented the Crown, and Boyl was obliged to return to Spain in 1494. Two other friars whom he had left in the Americas returned to Spain in 1499. Consequently, the evangelization of the island of Santo Domingo did not really begin until 1500 with the coming of a Franciscan mission, which was augmented in 1502 by the arrival of an additional seventeen religious. In 1505 the Franciscans created the Mission of the West Indies.

On November 15, 1504, Pope Julian II, without consulting the Spanish king, established the dioceses of Bayunense, Maguence, and Ayuguance. Ferdinand protested this action on the basis that the Pope had violated the terms of the *Patronato*. And much to the Pope's chagrin, the dioceses were never effective. Julian was therefore obliged to accede to the claims of the Spanish king. In 1511, then, the first three Latin American Episcopal Sees were established: Santo Domingo (which became an archbishopric in 1546), Concepción de la Vega (abolished in 1528), and Puerto Rico. The See of Santa María of old Darién (Panama) was created in 1513, Cuba in 1517, and Florida in 1520.

In 1510 three religious from Salamanca arrived on the island of Hispaniola under the guidance of Pedro de Córdoba, OP. One of them, Father Antonio de Montesinos, was designated as the preacher for the Sundays of Advent in 1511. Montesinos seized on the occasion to excoriate the colonists for their exploitation and oppression of the Indians. "*Vox clamantis in deserto*," began the preacher, using as his text John 1:23. "You are all living in mortal sin, and you will live and die in sin because of the cruelty and tyranny with which you abuse these innocent people." The Dominicans subsequently were able to talk with King Ferdinand, and as a result the Spanish Crown promulgated the laws of Burgo in 1512 in favor of the Indians.

Bartolomé de Las Casas, priest and *encomendero*, arrived in Santo Domingo in April

1514. Reading the biblical text from Sirach 34:22, "A man murders his neighbor if he robs him of his livelihood, sheds blood if he withholds an employee's wages," Las Casas recognized the injustices that he himself was inflicting upon the Indians and consequently turned those in his charge over to Governor Velázquez on August 15, 1514. Almost a year later Las Casas preached his famous sermon in the Church of Sancti Spiritus, then journeyed to Baracoa, and left Cuba for Spain in July 1515, thereby setting his course in a direction from which he would not deviate until his death in 1566.

Las Casas had become convinced that it was useless to attempt to defend the Indians by trying to work from Santo Domingo. Thus, accompanied by other Dominicans, he departed for Sevilla in order to present the matter before King Ferdinand himself. Las Casas and his party arrived in the royal city on October 6, 1515, but to his dismay he found the king dying and the Court indifferent to the cause that Las Casas had come to represent. He soon departed for Flanders, hoping to gain a hearing from Prince Charles. Passing through Madrid, Las Casas felt himself fortunate to be able to present his case before Adrian, the future Pope, and Cisneros, the Archbishop of Toledo and future regent of Spain. The latter declared to Las Casas, "You have no need to proceed further because it is here that you will find the remedy for which you are searching." It was, therefore, in Madrid that the *Plan for the Reformation of the Indies* was developed. Las Casas was named "priest procurator of the Indians" on September 17, 1516. Two months later, on November 11, Las Casas returned to America accompanied by some Hieronymite fathers. Little is known about the work of his companions with the exception that they were all failures. When Las Casas realized that their labor was in vain, he returned to Spain in 1517 and settled in Valladolid, where he began serious studies of the juridical questions regarding the Indies. Subsequently he had contact with the court of Charles V and there presented his *Petition in Defense of the Indian* before the Supreme Council of the Indies itself on December 11 of that same year. Step by step Las Casas developed a plan whereby he would be allowed to attempt a peaceful colonization of the Indies without the use of any arms and accompanied only by peasants. On December 12, 1519, Las Casas was granted the privilege of defending the Indian cause in the court of Barcelona, presided over by Charles V. Arguing against Father Bartolomé was Juan de Quevedo, OFM, Bishop of Panama. The king was greatly impressed by the spirit and reasoning of Las Casas and granted him the right to begin "villages of free Indians," communities of Spanish and Indian peasants that were proposed as the initiation of a new civilization in America. The place selected for this ambitious undertaking was the north coast of Venezuela in the region of Cumaná. Las Casas sailed for the area along with several peasants on December 14, 1520. But the project was doomed from the beginning for several reasons: the questionable selection of colonists who accompanied Las Casas, his own concessions in the *capitulación,* the disaster which befell the Franciscan mission sent to Cumaná, the interests created by the *encomenderos* of Santo Domingo, and finally an attack by the Indians themselves on the settlement. The disaster was complete by January 1522, and Las Casas, together with a few remaining settlers, was obliged to withdraw.

In summary, during these first stages of the Christian mission in the Americas, efforts to evangelize the Indians were made on some of the smaller islands of the Caribbean and in various places on the mainland, but the Indians were subdued by force of arms. Subsequently the missionary and the *encomendero* arrived, the former attempting the enormous task of evangelization, and the latter proceeding in the agrarian exploitation of the indigenous peoples.

II. THE SECOND STAGE: CHRISTIAN MISSIONS IN NEW SPAIN AND PERU (1519–1551)

Hernán Cortés began the conquest of Mexico from Cuba in 1519. Accompanying Cortés was the Mercedarian friar Bartolomé de Olmedo and the secular priest Juan Díaz, who together attempted to present the Christian message to the Indians. It was not until 1524, however, with the arrival of twelve Franciscan missionaries, that the systematic evangelization of Mexico began — the Indians having been subdued by force of arms.[1] These "Twelve Apostles of New Spain" were exceptional in their courage, determination, and ability, and they were later joined by twelve Dominicans who arrived in 1526. Almost seven years passed before seven Augustinian fathers arrived (May 22, 1533) as reinforcements. The Christian beginnings were at best modest, but each year after 1533 new missionaries arrived, and soon the Creoles themselves responded to the missionary calling. In 1559 the Franciscans had eighty houses and 380 religious; the Dominicans had forty houses and 210 religious; and the Augustinians boasted of forty houses with 212 religious.[2]

These early missionaries traveled by foot from the coasts and lowlands to the 2,200-meter altitude of present-day Mexico City. They crossed innumerable rivers — one missionary wrote of having forded twenty-five different rivers in a distance of only ten kilometers or six miles. They moved through dense jungles, parched deserts, and mountain areas covered with snow and ice. They survived innumerable fevers and insects by the millions, moving without the benefit of maps and oftentimes without guides. And as if these impediments were not sufficient to discourage them, they encountered innumerable peoples of different races, languages, and religions, all of which tested their determination to continue their work of evangelization. The Aztec Empire, as great as it was, had not been able to unify the indigenous peoples of Mexico. In fact, it was the missionaries who extended the area in which *Nahuatl*, the language of Mexico, was used, so they could avoid having to preach in Spanish. From gestures and mimicry the missionaries progressed to utilizing interpreters. But seeing the imprecision of the translations, the missionaries began a serious study of the languages and thus produced dictionaries, grammars, catechisms, confessionals, and sermons in *Nahuatl, Tarasca,* and other indigenous languages. The Diocese of Carolense was created in 1519, which from 1526 was known as *Tlaxcala*. There followed the Diocese of Mexico in 1530 (made an archbishopric in 1546), Comayagua (1531), Nicaragua (1531), Coro, Venezuela (1531), Santa Marta and Cartagena (1534), Guatemala and Antequera (1535), Michoacán (1536), Chiapas (1539), Guadalajara (1548), Vera Paz and Yucatán (1561), and Durango (1620). Thus in a single century the hierarchy of Mexico was established and progressively assumed responsibility for the Church as well as assuring the continuation of the missionary efforts. During this same period the Church was blessed with several notable bishops: Zumárraga in Mexico, Quiroga in Michoacán, Fuenleal in Santo Domingo, and Maraver in Guadalajara.

Francisco Pizarro arrived in Peru, according to the *Capitulación de Toledo* (July 26, 1529), with a group of Dominicans among whom was Friar Vicente de Valverde, Licenciate in Theology from the University of Salamanca. By 1531 the missionaries had begun to penetrate the Inca Empire, and on November 15, 1533, a Christian cross was raised in the plaza of Cuzco. Four years later, January 8, 1537, Pope Paul III created the Diocese of Cuzco and named Valverde as the first bishop. He arrived at his new See along with twenty other Dominicans on September 5, 1538. The Diocese of Lima was created in 1541, as well as Quito (1546), Asunción (1547), Charcas (1552), Santiago, Chile (1561), Bogotá (1562, an archbishopric in 1564), Concepción,

Chile (1564), Córdoba del Tucumán (1570), Arequipa and Trujillo (1577), then La Paz, Santa Cruz, and Guamanga, and finally Buenos Aires in 1620. All these dioceses were dependent upon Lima, which became an archdiocese in 1546. Two Colombian dioceses — Santa Marta-Cartagena and Popayán (1546) — were subject to Bogotá beginning in 1564.

The Dominicans were the first to initiate missionary work in Peru after Paul III declared in 1539 that the Peruvian province was the responsibility of the Preaching Order. By 1544 the Dominicans numbered more than fifty religious. Shortly thereafter a group of Franciscans began missionary work in the province, as did the Augustinians. The diffusion of these missionary priests throughout this region of South America was remarkable: from Quito to the River Plate. The Mercedarians, for example, had at least sixteen urban monasteries and nineteen Indian parishes in the province of Cuzco as early as the sixteenth century.

The missionary methods utilized by these representatives of the Church were similar to those employed in Mexico, and Francisco Solano was a typical missionary evangelist. He would walk from village to village, baptizing the Indians, preaching first through interpreters and later in the Indian dialect, following a pattern of mass Christianization. Every effort was made to eradicate idolatry and ancient cults, at least those most evident to the Christian missionaries. Friar Bertrán who labored faithfully in Colombia is another paradigmatic example of this era.

The general approach was that of assuming the Indian mind to be a *tabula rasa* — even though the preaching was done as often as possible in the indigenous languages. The reason is easily understandable: the Inca Empire did not provide a structure sufficiently advanced and organized on which the missionaries could build. Pizarro, in becoming the head of the Peruvian Empire, not only disrupted the political unity that existed under the Incas, but also undermined the spiritual unity that prevailed. As a result, the missionaries encountered diverse peoples who were separated from each other, introverted, and without benefit of a common language.

On the Day of the Epiphany, January 6, 1536, a school for the children of Indian noblemen, Tlatelolco, was begun in the suburbs of Mexico City. Bishop Zumárraga applauded its creation and strongly supported it during its early years. One would have thought that from this attempt indigenous missionaries would have come forth to work among their own people. Unfortunately, the Spanish lack of understanding in this regard made such a venture impossible.

Herein lies the second plateau of Christian mission work in the Spanish colonies. At times it involved the use of arms, that is, forced conversion. But primarily it was by missionaries who pacified the Indians through preaching, persuasion, and direct involvement. Nonetheless, one observes the growing influence of the Spanish civilization, and the newly baptized Indians became the integral components of the *encomiendas*. Many of them simply submitted to the system. Others, however, fled to the mountains, to the jungles, to the desert regions, or to the *sertão* — the Brazilian backlands — adopting anew their ancient paganism. The missionaries, nevertheless, followed them and in so doing inaugurated a new stage of missionary work which would serve as an example for future centuries.

One of the most beautiful but obscured stages in the history of Latin American missions was the struggle in behalf of the Indians led by a group of Spanish bishops during the period of 1544 to 1568.[3] Americans should be as familiar with Latin American "Fathers of the Church" such as Las Casas, Juan del Valle, and Antonio de

Valdivieso who was Bishop of Nicaragua from 1544 to 1550, as they are with the Byzantine or Latin Church Fathers such as Basil, Gregory, or Augustine.

Bartolomé de Las Casas, for example, was invited by Bishop Marroquín of Guatemala (1533– 1563) to attempt the evangelization of the feared Indians in that area. Las Casas had written in his *De único modo,* "The only way to win people to the true faith" is not by force of arms but by the power of the gospel. Las Casas was remarkably successful in evangelizing these feared aborigines whose territory became known as "Vera Paz," that is, the land of true peace. In 1540 he returned to Spain where Vitoria had read Las Casas' outstanding work, *De indis recenter inventis relectio prior* (1538), in the University of Salamanca. The King, doubtless influenced by a wave of interest in Spain in the indigenous peoples of America, promulgated in 1542 the famous *New Laws.* Meanwhile, Pope Paul III had proclaimed in his encyclical *Sublimis Deus* on June 9, 1537, that "in virtue of our apostolic authority we declare ... that the said Indians and other peoples should be converted to the religion of Jesus by evangelization and by the example of edifying customs." *Law 35* of Charles V's *New Laws* ordered that Indians could not be maintained within the *encomienda* in perpetuity, nor could the rights of *encomienda* be inherited, and that within the course of a generation all the indigenous peoples should be set free. The Crown attempted to undergird the new law by naming bishops who supported the spirit of the new legislation. They were Bartolomé de Las Casas as Bishop of Chiapas (1544– 1547), Antonio de Valdivieso of Nicaragua (1544– 1550), Cristóbal de Pedraza for Honduras (1545– 1583), Pablo de Torres for Panama (1547– 1554), Juan del Valle for Popayán (1548– 1560), Fernando de Uranga for Cuba (1552– 1556), Tomás Casillas for Chiapas (1552– 1597), Bernardo de Alburquerque for Oaxaca (1559– 1579), Pedro de Angulo for Vera Paz (1560– 1562), Pedro de Agreda for Coro (1560– 1580), Juan de Simancas for Cartagena (1560– 1570), Domingo de Santo Tomás for La Plata (1563– 1570), Pedro de la Peña for Quito (1566– 1583), and Agustín de la Coruña for Popayán (1565– 1590).

A study of the lives of these heroic bishops reveals that they risked everything, committing themselves without reservation, suffering expulsion from their dioceses, imprisonment, deportation, and even death in behalf of the Indians who were being violently oppressed and exploited by the Spanish colonists. The lives of these pastors should serve as an example for bishops of our era where the majority of violence is inflicted—as in the time of the conquistadores—by "men of arms." Because of this situation Las Casas advocated "evangelism without arms," which signifies today liberation not as a struggle against subversion but in favor of the humanization of those unjustly treated: the Indian, the mestizo, the peasant, the laborer, the simple people, the poor, and the uneducated.

Ironically, the Mexican bishops who have been outstanding in their defense of the Indians, such as Zumárraga, Juan de Zárate of Oaxaca, the *Tata* Vasco de Quiroga of Michoacán, and even Marroquín of Guatemala became more conciliatory, and because of their attitudes the *New Laws* were never enforced in Mexico. They were "pre-Lascasian" bishops, if I might use this expression. Las Casas and other bishops like him struggled for the integral freedom of the Indian not only in fact but also on the principle of their natural rights. A generation earlier bishops such as Loaisa in Lima defended the cause of the Indians in certain cases, but their defense did not touch the basic issue of the Indians' rights. The ideologues who promoted liberation for the Indian were primarily theologians from the Dominican convent of Santiesteban in Salamanca, for only three of the above-named bishops were of other orders. It was the Dominicans — from Montesinos and Pedro de Córdoba on the island of Hispaniola in 1511 until Bartolomé de Las Casas — who began the struggle for justice and liberation in Latin America.

In Central America the position of the bishops continued to be paradigmatic. The violence of the Conquest — no different in the region of Nueva Granada, present-day Colombia — was immense.[4] Las Casas was named bishop of Chiapas in 1543 by the papal bull of December 10.[5] He departed from Sevilla for his new See on July 4, 1544, and arrived at his new post during Lent of 1545. He was cooly received in the royal city of Chiapas, and he waited until the Sunday of Holy Week to preach in favor of the Indians. He followed this by canceling the power of the priests and religious to hear confessions and offer pardon, reserving for himself the power to forgive certain sins, especially that of maintaining Indians in *encomienda* — which for Las Casas was nothing more than enslavement. The three secular priests and the Fathers of Mercy opposed their bishop. Only the Dominicans supported Las Casas. The *encomenderos,* along with the Spanish colonists, retaliated by withholding financial support from the convent, and Las Casas and his supporters were forced to abandon the city and live among the Indians. Thus isolated, Las Casas journeyed to Guatemala in 1545 where he met with Bishops Marroquín and Valdivieso in the well-known Commission of Thanksgiving to God. Together these representatives of the Central American episcopacy attempted to draw up ways and means whereby the Indians could be defended against further exploitation. The presence of Las Casas in Guatemala so infuriated the Spanish population that they attempted to seize the prelate before he was able to leave the country. He returned to Chiapas but remained there for only two or three months before being expelled by the Spanish members of his congregation. In fact, Las Casas was able to remain in his bishopric for a total of only six months. Defeated by the *encomenderos,* Las Casas departed for Spain never again to return to his diocese, from which he resigned in 1550. He wrote in his testament as a sign of his unyielding fidelity to the struggle for liberation:

[It was] by the goodness and mercy of God that I was called into His ministry which I did not merit, that I might attempt to protect those multitudes of peoples who are called Indians . . . from the unimaginable and unthinkable wrongs, evils, and injustices which we Spaniards inflicted upon them against all reason and justice.[6]

Even more important than Bartolomé de Las Casas was the Bishop of Nicaragua, Antonio de Valdivieso, who ultimately suffered martyrdom for his defense of the Indian. From the moment he arrived in Central America in 1544 he began correspondence describing the tragic situation suffered by the Indians.[7] They were brutally abused and killed, he wrote, by Contreras, the governor, his brother, and the governor's wife and sons, who according to Valdivieso had under their control more than a third of the principal villages in Nicaragua. The governor's wife alone, declared the bishop, had charge of Nicoya, a village of Indians in which there were ten or eleven *repartimientos.*[8] Valdivieso gave himself unstintingly to the Indians, but he eventually lost all hope of any improvement in their situation given the violent opposition of the governor.[9]

Valdivieso did not limit his efforts to Nicaragua, however. In addition, he sought to inform the King of the injustices which were being committed and of the danger which he felt for his own life. The president of the court (*Audiencia*) reported that the Nicaraguan bishop "feared each day that he would be killed."[10] Valdivieso wrote that he suspected that the letters which he was sending to the court were being intercepted and destroyed, and that he feared that there would soon be persecution against him as well as against the Indians. "I write these letters hurriedly in order that Your Majesty might be aware ... of the great need that exists in these parts for justice."[11] And although Valdivieso labored continually for the welfare of the Indians, he reported that each day they were more oppressed.[12] He also noted that the situation was growing more critical each day as the climate of opinion turned steadily against him, and that he recognized the possibility that his congregation would force him to leave (as had already occurred in the case of Las Casas in Chiapas).[13] Valdivieso indicated that he had sought to know personally all of his parishoners,[14] and he continued to preach in favor of the liberation of the Indians and strongly reproached the Spanish community, including the conquistadores and governors, for the horrible treatment that they were inflicting upon the indigenous peoples. The latter in turn were so infuriated by the words and actions of their bishop that they determined to eliminate him by one means or another. A number of soldiers who had been part of Pizarro's conquest of the Inca Empire had come to Nicaragua from Peru. Among them was one Juan Bermejo, a "man of evil intent." He was soon recognized as one of the henchmen of the Contreras brothers and was often seen with them. One evening Bermejo, along with several others, went to the bishop's house, and, finding him alone except for a single colleague, they proceeded to stab him to death.[15] Thus died Antonio de Valdivieso on February 26, 1550, in León, Nicaragua, martyred because of his love for and struggle in behalf of the liberation of the Indians in Spanish America.

Another hero in the cause for the indigenous peoples of Central America was Cristóbal de Pedraza, Bishop of Honduras. In him and his ministry one sees the enormous difference between European and American bishops. Those of Castilla, for example, could travel from Medina del Campo to Valladolid sleeping each night in a populated area in a bed with four mattresses beneath silk and satin. But a bishop of Central America who cared for his flock traveled by foot from mountain to mountain, sierra to sierra, through narrow ravines and gorges, fording rivers and streams, and struggling through swamp lands infested with millions of insects.

Honduras was a bishopric composed of seven Christian towns and four villages of twenty-five to thirty families each plus the city of Trujillo in which there were some fifty families. It required a full year to visit the various areas of population given the difficulties of travel.[16] But the major problem for Pedraza was establishing contact and communicating with the Indians, for as he approached their villages they would flee. He soon learned that the reason for their fear was that the encomenderos had warned them that they would "be strangled, decapitated, and thrown to the dogs" if they spoke a word to the bishop of the treatment they were receiving from the Spanish. Pedraza, nonetheless, interceded for the Indians who had been enslaved, humiliated, and tormented. He wrote: "Is it not a disgraceful injustice that these indigenous peoples should be forced against their will to serve the Spaniards who in turn kick them, beat them, tie them to trees and posts as if they were slaves, and even kill them" when by terms of the law the colonists are responsible to protect them? Pedraza concluded his letter declaring, "I am the Father of the Indians."[17] The worst aspect of this scandal was that the Spaniards were considered by the Indians to be Christians, and not a few of the indigenous men as well as the women committed suicide rather than submit themselves to the system of brutality and injustice.[18] It is to Pedraza's credit that he labored for and spoke out against this violence on which Latin America was built.

The conquest of Nueva Granada (Colombia and Venezuela) involved violence of unequaled proportions in that the Indians suffered indignities and physical abuse from the *encomenderos,* and subsequently it was in Colombia that the peasant endured the pain and injustices of a social and economic system controlled by the Conservative and Liberal oligarchy. Against the violence of the *encomenderos* arose one of the great bishops of the Latin American Church, Juan del Valle. Professor of Arts in the University of Salamanca and a colleague of Vitoria, Valle abandoned his post of security and prestige to become involved in the vibrant history of Latin America. As Bishop of Popayán, an area stained with the blood of the Indians by a former lieutenant under Pizarro, Captain Sebastián Belalcázar, Valle had his first contact with his congregation in Cali in 1548, and from Cali he wrote his first pastoral letter on November 20. He soon became painfully aware of the terrible conditions in which the Indians were forced to live, and he began a program for their defense, traveling from village to village carrying with him a lance for his own defense, which on certain occasions he was known to use against the colonists. Three years later he wrote that the Indians were being treated even more terribly than when he had arrived in Colombia, especially in the city of Cali, where he reported that the Indians were more abused than in any other region of the Indies. As a result, he said, "I am, in the opinion of the conquistadores, the worst bishop of the Indies."[19] Valle struggled valiantly and continually in defense of the Indians, risking his own life in the process.[20] He was responsible for calling, in 1555 and in 1558, the only diocesan synods in which the rights of the Indians to their own lands and their freedom were defended doctrinally. It should be noted in this regard that the Supreme Council of the Indies thereafter prohibited the celebration of this type of synod.[21] In 1559, after eleven years of continual and debilitating labor during which time he was constantly harassed by the colonists, Juan del Valle left Cali and Popayán with a mule loaded with papers and dossiers with which he hoped to prove to the King himself the crimes being perpetrated against the Indians in Southern Colombia. Valle reached Santa Fe de Bogotá in 1560 and attempted to present his case before the court (*Audiencia*) who refused to hear his accusations against the *encomenderos*. In August of the following year (1561) he was in Spain for the purpose of laying his case before the Supreme Council of the Indies. To his dismay the Council did not receive Valle's protests warmly. Consequently he decided to present the matter before the Council of Trent, and with his mule burdened with the documentary evidence he crossed the border into France where he died without ever reaching his destination. Neither the Council of Trent nor that of Vatican I heard Valle's cry of injustice, and if they had, it would have been incomprehensible to them. His words would have to wait four hundred years before his protest would again be heard. Valle died in 1561 — a valiant Segovian and staunch defender of the American Indian and of Christian doctrine — and was buried far from his chosen country and people.[22]

Valle's successor, Agustín de la Coruña (1565– 1590), took up the struggle immediately on behalf of the indigenous people because "for thirty-three years the Spaniards had been drinking the blood of the Indians."[23] Coruña was unable to govern his bishopric peacefully, and because of difficulties he was suspended from the post by the King during the years from 1570 to 1575. But the bishop did not accept his fate quietly. "Have I been banished because I have served and preached so as to uphold your just laws?" Coruña wrote. "Am I to return to my bishopric? I fear that I have been condemned because the colonists are so inured to the cruelties that they are inflicting upon the Indians that they are unaware of their sin, and they claim that in other areas there are bishops, courts, governors, preachers, and religious orders who see what I see but remain silent, while *I am the only one who protests.*"[24] Thus did Coruña follow in the steps of his predecessor who declared, "If this situation is not remedied, I will continue to cry out even though they stone me."[25] Coruña was allowed to return to Popayán in 1575, and he continued his campaign aginst the cruelty of the colonists. Seven years later, however, in 1582, while he was celebrating the Eucharist, a group of conquistadores on horseback entered the cathedral, took the bishop prisoner, and transported him to Quito where he was forced to remain until 1587. In the Provincial Council of Lima in 1583, Coruña was an example of simplicity, poverty, and holiness. He died three years later while visiting some Indian villages in Timaná. When his body was returned to Popayán, it was said to have been in a state of "incorruption."[26] Coruña is another example of those who struggled against the violence of the ancient oligarchy who still oppress, intimidate, and kill the poor and defenseless whose ultimate relief will be postponed, it appears, until the Parousia.

In Panama Bishop Pablo de Torres also attempted to enforce the *New Laws,* but he soon clashed with the *encomenderos* by defending the Indian to the ultimate degree of his authority, even to excommunicating the offenders when it was necessary. But the local governor as well as the Supreme Council of the Indies nullified Torres' actions. The saddest aspect of the situation in Panama was that the Archbishop himself, Loaysa, condemned Torres, a judgment confirmed by the Supreme Council. Pablo de Torres left his bishopric in 1554 not only saddened by his inability to defend the Indian, but also because after his return to Spain he was accused of treason and never permitted to return to Panama.

These few examples should be sufficient to provide a measure of understanding regarding the present era. The bishops herein cited were heroically committed not only to the gospel but also against the violence perpetrated by the civilized oppressors upon the defenseless natives of the Americas.

III. THE THIRD STAGE: THE STRENGTHENING AND THE ORGANIZATION OF THE CHURCH (1551–1620)

The events herein discussed begin with the first Provincial Council of Lima in 1551 and lead to the creation in 1620 of the Diocese of Buenos Aires in the South and of Durango in the North. During this time the Latin American Church proceeded to develop a functioning organizational structure. There were no councils on dogma such as Trent, but there were pastoral and missionary convocations. From the council convened by Jerónimo de Loaysa in 1551 to the Diocesan Synod of Comayaguen in 1631, the Latin American Church manifested a profound desire to organize itself as a new Church, "the new Christendom of the Indies," as Toribio de Mogrovejo expressed it. To achieve this end the bishops met in various places on the continent and after prolonged discussions promulgated the ecclesiastical laws by which the Church was governed until the nineteenth century. Yet one must wait until the Latin American Council of 1899 in order to see the norms adopted in the sixteenth century effectively applied to the Latin American situation.

Only fourteen days after their arrival in Mexico in 1524, the first twelve Franciscan missionaries met together to plan their strategy and work for the evangelization of Mexico.[27] During that same year, 1524–1525, the First Apostolic Commission met under the direction of the Franciscan friar, Martín de Valencia. Nineteen religious, five seculars, and several lawyers met for the purpose of discussing openly the problems related to the dispensing of the sacraments, especially Confirmation, Penance, the Eucharist, Marriage, and Extreme Unction.[28] At first these were denied the indigenous peoples but later were permitted at the discretion of the confessors.[29] It was not until 1532[30] and again in 1536[31] that a Church commission met with a bishop present.

After his return from Spain, Juan de Zumárraga consecrated the bishops of Guatemala, Michoacán, and Oaxaca, and met with two of these, Juan López de Zárate of Oaxaca and Francisco de Marroquín of Guatemala on November 30, 1537. The purpose of the meeting was to petition the King for permission to participate in the Council of Trent.[32]

On April 27, 1559, Zumárraga met in Mexico City with Juan de Zárate, Bishop of Antequera, and Vasco de Quiroga, Bishop of Michoacán, along with the provincials or representatives of various religious orders. Together they reached the conclusions that have come to be known as the *Chapters of the Ecclesiastical Commission of 1539*.[33]

The last public act of this first Bishop of Mexico was the convening of the Commission of 1546 in which Zumárraga, Marroquín of Guatemala, Alburquerque of Oaxaca, Quiroga of Michoacán, and Las Casas of Chiapas met together and adopted five points which bear the unmistakable influence of Las Casas.[34]

The First Provincial Council of Mexico was convened on June 29, 1555, by Alonso de Montúfar, OP, Archbishop of Mexico.[35] Present were the bishops of Tlaxcala, Michoacán, Chiapas, and Oaxaca. (During the meeting of the council, Bishop Juan de Zárate died.) A reading of the Constitutions will reveal the crucial Mexican issues with which the prelates dealt.[36] They produced ninety-three chapters, each of which was laden with teachings. Montúfar convened the Second Provincial Council on November 8, 1565, but it was of lesser significance than the first.[37]

Of all the councils which took place in Mexico, by far the most important was that convened by the third Archbishop of Mexico, Pedro Moya de Contreras. This "Mexican Trent" met from January 20 until October 16, 1585. All the bishops were present with the exception of the prelate of Comayagua who was in Spain. The council was approved by Pope Sixtus V on October 27, 1589, and by the King of Spain on September 18, 1591. Though there was formidable opposition to the conclusions reached by the council, they were finally published in 1622. The basic problem that the bishops encountered was related to their plea for the reduction of the privileges of the religious.[38]

In South America, in the Inca territory, the first Provincial Council of the new kingdom was convened by Archbishop Jerónimo de Loaysa in the city of the kings, Cuzco, in the year 1551. The texts of this council — as was the case of Councils I and II of Mexico — were originally written in Spanish and not in Latin.[39] The constitutions of the council were of two types: the first forty were entitled the *Constitutions of the Natives* (Indians), and they proposed the organization of a "new Church of the Indies" in the ancient Inca Empire. The parishes were to occupy the same territory or region of the ancient tribes (*ayllu*) with their regional capitals. A catechumenate, that is, a period for instruction in doctrine and discipline for a convert to Christianity, was required before baptism for all adults, and instruction had to be given in the indigenous language (*Const*. 4, p. 9).[40] The second part of the constitutions dealt specifically with matters related to the Spanish colonists, and it contained eighty separate constitutions dealing with the steps for organizing Hispanic-Creole Christianity in the cities. The division of colonial Peruvian society into two communities is clearly evident: the white Hispanic urban dwellers and the rural Indian population living in mission territories.

Archbishop Contreras convened the Second Provincial Council, which met in 1567 and 1568.[41] The pronouncements were, however, inverted. The first 132 chapters dealt with Christianity for the Spaniards in which by a thousand details everything related to the life in the colonies, the culture, public morals, and so forth was discussed.

The second part of the council's declarations consisted of 122 constitutions — *Pro indorum et eorum sacerdotorum constitutionibus* — and reaffirmed the power of the episcopacy over the privileges of the religious in regard to the Peruvian mission to the Indians. Priests working with the Indians were to be chosen with great care (*Const.* 1);[42] they would be responsible for the organization of the catechism and the parishes (*Const.* 75 – 97); and they were to be especially diligent in rooting out idolatry and superstition (*Const.* 98ff.).

The most important of the American provincial councils was without doubt the one convened by Archbishop Toribio of Lima. This council met during 1582 and 1583 and was the Third Council of Lima.[43] As the Council of Mexico had proposed in 1585, the Lima Council declared: *In nomine Sanctae et individuae Trinitatis ... ad fidei exaltationem et novae Indorum Ecclesiae utilitatem, clerique ac populi christiani ecclesiasticae disciplinae congruentem reformationem rite ac legitime congregata....*[44] The first issue with which the council dealt was that of the catechism (*proprium Cathecismum huic Universae Provinciae edere*, Act II, cap. III, p. 266) and was written both in Quechua and Aymara, the ancient languages of the Inca Empire (*quam in cathecisme in linguam Cuzquensem, vel in aymaraycam aliam traductionem*, ibid). The love which Toribio manifested for the poor, the Indians, the Negroes, and children is especially evident in the declarations of the council (*maxime rudiores Indi, Aethiopes, pueri ...*, ibid., cap. IV, p. 267).

Also clearly evident is the importance which the Council gave to religious instruction: *ut intelligat, Hispanicus hispanice, Indus alioquim quantumvis bene dicat ... multoque melius sit, suo idomate pronunciare ...* (ibid., VI, p. 268). Matters related to communion were left to the judgment of the parish priest.[45] The Sacrament of Orders was to be dispensed with discretion in view of the fact that it was better to have few worthy priests than many unworthy ones.[46] The bishops reaffirmed their title as "protectors of the Indians."[47]

Archbishop Toribio dispatched José de Acosta, editor of the Conciliar texts and of the Catechism, to Rome for the purpose of obtaining papal approval of the acts of the council. They were approved by Pope Sixtus V in 1588, and were published on September 18, 1591. Toribio convened two other provincial councils[48] in Lima of lesser importance, and multiple diocesan councils.[49] The complete list of the provincial councils convened during the colonial period are as follows:

Provincial Councils of Christendom in the Indies

Year	See	No.	Name of the Metropolitan
1551 – 1552	Lima	I	Jerónimo de Loaysa
1555	Mexico	I	Alonso de Montúfar
1565	Mexico	II	Alonso de Montúfar
1567 – 1568	Lima	II	Jerónimo de Loaysa
1582 – 1583	Lima	III	Toribio de Mogrovejo
1585	Mexico	III	Pedro Moya de Contreras
1591	Lima	IV	Toribio de Mogrovejo
1601	Lima	V	Toribio de Mogrovejo
1622	Santo Domingo	I	Pedro de Oviedo
1625	Santa Fe	I	Hernando Arias de Ugarte
1629	La Plata	I	Hernando Arias de Ugarte
1771	Mexico	IV	Francisco de Lorenzana
1772	Lima	VI	Diego de Parada
1774	La Plata	II	Pedro Argandoña
1774	Santa Fe	II	Agustín Camacho y Rojas

Some of the diocesan synods of the sixteenth and early seventeenth centuries were Popayán I (1555) and II (1558), convened by Juan del Valle; Santa Fe de Bogotá I (1556), convened by Juan de los Barrios, Santa Fe II (1576), convened by Luís Zapata Cárdenas, and Santa Fe II, convened by Lobo Guerreo (1606); and Quito I (1570), convened by Pedro de Peña. Also one should note Quito II (1594), those of Lima beginning with Lima I (1582), Imperial I (1584), Yucután I (1585), Santiago de Chile I (1586), Tucumán I (1597),II (1606), III (1607), Coro I (1609), Santiago de Chile II (1612), Puerto Rico II (1624), Concepción II (1625), Trujillo I (1623), Santiago de Chile III (1626), Guamanga I (1629), and Comayagua I (1631).

IV. THE FOURTH STAGE: CONFLICT BETWEEN THE MISSIONARY CHURCH AND THE HISPANIC CIVILIZATION (1620–1700)

This period began when those who saw the urgency of evangelization faced up to the deficiencies and aspirations of the *Patronato*. The white community and the Hispanic civilization whose representatives were determined not to lose a single one of their privileges became serious impediments for the missionary endeavor. The *Patronato* system had financed the mission work even while reserving for itself the ties of Spain and America, and the mendicant religious orders had cornered and cultivated much of the arable land, which they continued to control well into the eighteenth century in California. But the defenders of the *Patronato* and the mendicant orders jealously held on to the rights and privileges they had acquired. Two new factors, nevertheless, became very decisive during the seventeenth and eighteenth centuries: the bishops and secular priests along with the powerful Company of Jesus. In addition, the *Propaganda Fide*, which proceeded to limit greatly the power of the Spanish and Portuguese *Patronatos*, was created in 1622.

An interesting example can be seen in the case of the University of Lima. The Dominicans decided to begin a university in 1548, and on May 12, 1552, the institution was created by royal decree. According to the proposal of the Dominicans, it was to function within the walls of the monastery.[50] The University was considered by the Dominicans to be their personal fiefdom.[51] Archbishop Jerónimo de Loaysa, however, petitioned the King to place the University under the authority of the cathedral in order that it be the common charge of the diocese as well as the other religious orders. The Pope responded on April 25, 1571, giving the Universities of Mexico, Santo Domingo, and Lima the same rights and privileges enjoyed by the Universities of Valladolid and Salamanca, but he placed the University of Lima under the exclusive authority of the Dominicans. The Jesuits meanwhile declined an invitation to accept the responsibility for the schools of Arts and Grammar and continued striving for equivalent recognition and rights for their own schools in the University and in the School of San Pablo.[52]

The Jesuits were already famous for their educational   ligious, and benevolent endeavors, but they were never able to be integrated into the Church organization and the episcopacy as were the other religious orders. In a sense this was their greatest strength and possibly their greatest weakness. Because of their fourth vow and the universal vision of Ignatius Loyola, the Jesuits regarded themselves as under the exclusive authority of the Pope and therefore not under the kings.[53] The struggle between the representatives of the Company of Jesus and those of the *Patronato* was intense and without respite. The attitude and *modus operandi* of the Jesuits was regarded by many bishops as fully justified, and for this reason they invited them to be a part of their dioceses.

The first Jesuits came to Brazil under the direction of Father Manuel de Nóbrega who arrived in Bahía on March 29, 1549, as members of the expedition of Tomé de Sousa. They soon began a school for Portuguese and Indian children. Nóbrega, along with several other Jesuits, moved toward the South, and in 1551 arrived in Espíritu Santo and proceeded to Reritiba where the celebrated Father Anchieta died. In 1553 and 1554 they participated in the founding of São Paulo and later of Río de Janeiro. They advanced as far south as Santa Catarina and the territories of the Guaraní. As the Jesuits had done in Mexico, those in Brazil organized the Indians into villages or *reducciones*. Following the example of the work of the Jesuit Father Roque González in Asunción, the *reducciones* began to flourish also in Brazil. The method used by the Jesuits was that of the *tabula rasa*, for in Brazil no vestige of civilization existed. Studying the *Tupí* language, Juan de Azpilcuera Navarro produced a dictionary, and Father Anchieta developed the first grammar. The Jesuits also provided the first Christian martyr in Brazil, Father Ignacio Azevedo.

Later they labored in Florida,[54] and on October 11, 1567, the San Francisco de Borja Jesuits were asked by Royal Letter to begin a school in Lima, Peru.[55] Five years later they began missionary work in Mexico.[56] From there they spread throughout the entire continent, maintaining exemplary missions in the colonies of Nueva Granada — present-day Colombia and Venezuela — and in Paraguay.

The consolidation of the ecclesiastical structures was strengthened by the creation of the Inquisition in Peru in 1570, in Mexico in 1571, and later in Cartagena. Unfortunately, however, the hierarchy chafed under the old order of things but was impotent to free itself from the yoke of the *Patronato*, even though on several occasions there were concerted attempts to nullify it. In these cases the voice of the Pope would have been far more influential in liberating the Church, but it must be remembered that the Papacy, by virtue of the terms of the *Patronato*, had no direct contact with the Latin American Church — a situation that prompted Toribio de Mogrovejo to complain that the bishops sent to America were "elected" but not "consecrated." He was severely reprimanded by Philip II who warned the good Archbishop that further outbursts of this nature would not be tolerated. The Spanish King had disallowed any correspondence between the bishops and Rome, instructing that nothing should go to the Holy See except what "His Majesty allowed."[57] Indirectly, of course, the complaints of the American hierarchy reached Rome, and by the same token instructions from the Pope found their way surreptitiously back to the American Church despite the rigorous effort to prevent such interchanges. The Viceroy in turn denounced the American episcopates, allowing that the churchmen were guilty of gross ingratitude in regard to their Sovereign to whom they were all greatly indebted.[58]

The seventeenth century was characterized by prolific and widespread missionary work, and the methods represented an improvement over the previous century, doubtless the result of experience. This was the period of the famous Franciscan *reducción* in Mexico and of the Jesuits not only in Paraguay but also in Brazil, Peru, Colombia, and Venezuela, among the Chiquitos and Moxos in Bolivia, as well as with indigenous tribes in Ecuador and the Amazon valley. It would be a mistake to conclude that the missions slowed their pace of labor during this time. The curates organized the best possible defense of the Indians. The Franciscans, for example, had eighty convents in the region of Mexico, fifty-four in Michoacán, twenty-two in Guatemala, twenty-two in the Yucatán, and twelve in Nicaragua, while the Dominicans had forty-one in

Mexico and twenty-one in Oaxaca—all by the end of the seventeenth century. The Jesuits could boast of 345 priests in Mexico alone in 1603, and they were already known for their dedication and efficiency. Also for the first time the Church was able to maintain exclusive contact with many areas without the presence of Spanish soldiers or the interference of commerce and economic exploitation. During this fourth stage of the Christian mission the dreams of Las Casas were being realized in many parts, and this period was by far the most impressive.

V. THE FIFTH STAGE: THE BOURBON DECADENCE (1700–1808)

The last of the Hapsburgs had lived in the glories of the past, and the end of the seventeenth century marked the termination of the reign of Charles II (1665–1700). France triumphed over Spain and imposed a Bourbon, Philip V, who reigned from 1700 until 1746. The Spanish decadence spelled isolation for the American colonies, a spirit of separatism in every region, and a severe decline in new missionaries. The English took Jamaica in 1655, and Holland and England soon replaced Portugal and Spain as the major world powers. By the Treaty of Utrecht in 1713, Spain and Portugal resigned their control over the seas. Latin America suffered tremendously because of this Hispanic decline, for it also brought about the deterioration of the Latin American colonies. The Church especially suffered the European missionary crisis,[59] and the history of the Church in Latin America should be studied with these eighteenth-century developments in mind and not from that of assumed mistakes in the evangelization of the area. Historians have now come to recognize that evangelization did occur where Christians have remained until the present day.[60]

Christian missions continued during the eighteenth century. A good example can be seen in northern Mexico. In 1607, for example, the Jesuits moved into California, but it was the genial Friar Junípero Serra (1713–1784) who promoted missionary work like that of the days of the Primitive Church. The Franciscans replaced the Jesuits in 1768 and did outstanding work in their missions and *reducciones* from San Diego—which Friar Junípero founded in 1769—to San Francisco, founded in 1776. The Dominicans also maintained *reducciones* in many areas of present-day California.

The most decisive event of the eighteenth century in the history of the Latin American Church was the expulsion of the Jesuits in 1767. They were suppressed by the Bourbons in France on November 26, 1764, replaced by the Jansenists, and suffered the same fate under the Bourbons in Spain on March 31, 1767. More than 2,200 Jesuit priests were obliged to leave Latin America that same year, and they represented the most capable, educated, and committed of the missionary force. Their *reducciones* were immediately grabbed by the colonists, and the work with the Indians was left in shambles. For the most part it soon disappeared. It is impossible to calculate the effects of the Jesuit expulsion on the destiny of Latin America although it is obvious that the congregation of *Propaganda Fide* was never able to fill the gap left by their departure.[61]

The Latin American Church, still young and undeveloped, had to face a number of difficult changes: the politico-economic depression in Spain, the risks involved in attempting to sail from Spain to America through seas controlled by the English, the lack of support from the Papacy, the conversion of an economy previously based on gold and precious metals to an undeveloped agricultural system, and the increasing resistance by the Indians—especially those who populated the jungles of the Amazon basin and Peru as well as the Araucanos in southern Chile. Furthermore, the colonial

Spanish society had degenerated into a state of lethargy, which was as spiritual as it was social and emotional.

The work of the Church continued, however, and in some respects was strengthened in that Hispanic America at the time was composed of certain cities united by roads across immense deserts, pampas, and territories yet to be colonized. From the capitals of the viceroyalties toward the interior there moved a growing stream of colonists who settled and began new cities, towns, and villages which became parishes manned by diocesan clergy that was totally Creole, mestizo, and in some cases Indian.[62]

Another aspect of colonial life should be mentioned, namely, the daily life of the Christian laity.[63] It has been stated at times, without reason, that the Christianity of the Indies was composed almost exclusively of clerics. The very opposite is the case, for the Christian layperson — conquistador, Spanish, and Creole — participated actively in the life of the Church. One should not overlook the many flourishing Christian organizations and activities in which Spaniards, Creoles, mestizos, Indians, and Negroes participated without regard to office, sex, age, or social classes in the cities, in the countryside, in the parishes, and in the reducciones through which these laypeople exercised an authentic apostolate.

An aspect of ecclesiastical history often unrecognized was the access the people had to the Holy Scriptures in the Spanish language and at times even in Amerindian dialects — if one takes into account the number of Bibles in Hebrew, Greek, Latin, and Spanish that were sold and distributed in the capitals and the Indian villages.[64] The Church Fathers were also widely read,[65] and there were numerous books written and distributed on spiritual growth for laypersons. Outstanding were the Regla Christiana Breve written by Bishop Zumárraga and published in Mexico in 1547; a translation from Latin by the Príncipe de Esquilache, the Viceroy of Peru; the works of Thomas á Kempis such as Prayers and Meditations of Jesus Christ (1660); and the profoundly mystical work of the Bishop of Puebla, Palafox y Mendoza, Varón de deseos, en que se declaran las tres vías de la vida espiritual, published in Mexico in 1641. All of these were read and valued by the Catholic laity.[66] To a limited degree, all the people — including the discoverers, conquerors, colonists, men, women, and even children — were responsible to live uprightly and thereby promote the work of evangelization. School teachers, government auditors, fathers of families, and every member of society was to manifest by word and deed a certain apostolic intention. Even the most crude and violent of the conquistadores faced their hour of death with a certain Christian piety. It is said that even Pizarro "though suffering intensely from the attack of his assassins, took time to pardon them, and made his profession of faith with sufficient lucidness to give it solemnity. Few scenes are more dramatic than the agony of the fallen conqueror, making a large cross with his right hand and placing it upon his mouth and kissing it until he died."[67] In his will he recognizes that "because of the malice, ignorance, and persuasion of the Devil, I have often offended God my creator and redeemer. I have broken his commandments and failed to do the works of mercy using neither my common sense nor performing those deeds which our Holy Catholic Faith commands. I repent of all these sins which I now acknowledge and confess and for which I now beg forgiveness."[68] There is no better document to demonstrate the culpability of the sin of the conquest about which Bartolomé de Las Casas so passionately preached and wrote.

Chapter VI

An Analysis of the Evangelistic Work Continued by the Church In Latin America

We believe that the major difficulty in this type of value judgment is the lack of a comprehensive method that permits the consideration of the phenomenon in its totality and not merely in a single aspect. It is necessary, therefore, to review briefly certain elements outlined in the Introduction regarding methodology.

All human communities have at certain times instruments that we regard as indicators of civilization. The same is true of a religion, especially the Roman Catholic faith. Religions maintain analogically a system of *mediations,* which we have designated as sacramentality, ecclesial corporality, the organizing instruments instituted by Jesus Christ in time, and the presence of his universal, salvific grace. At the intentional level, that is, the level of understanding, civilization has a structure or an "ethico-mythical nucleus" contained or revealed finally in the actions of the group. Meanwhile, the Church possesses an existential understanding which in the last analysis is faith in the person of Jesus Christ and in the Trinity functioning by divine economy in sacred history.

In order to evaluate the level of the evangelization of a community, it is necessary to know at which level one is now situated and to what point the evangelization has been achieved. Otherwise one can confuse the secondary for the essential, and vice versa.

I. THE "MEDIATIONS" OF THE PRE-HISPANIC RELIGIONS AND THE CLASH WITH THE "MEDIATIONS" OF THE HISPANIC CATHOLIC CHURCH

We designate as "mediations" the institutions, writings, rites, liturgies, and sacraments, that is, the corporality of a religion. This stratum, although essentially constituting the Catholic religion, is situated at the level of communication, comprehension, and symbolism. It is necessary to speak a truth or transmit a grace to the conscience, and the conscience should in turn understand the proposed sign. The sign or symbol should be introduced through a catechetical process designed to enhance understanding, that is, initiation is requisite. Not unlike the people of Israel, the Church in the cultural Greco-Roman environment adopted many symbols of the world in order to communicate the content of the Christian faith, and thus was born the sacramental mediation of the Oriental, Latin, and much later the Mozarabic liturgies.

The evangelists of Latin America were in the same manner required to select — among the means of expression of the lower or higher pre-Hispanic civilizations —

certain expressive elements or symbols that permitted communication with the Indian and allowed him to comprehend and learn the content of the faith that was presented.

Indigenous religion in the Americas was basically agrarian. All the rites and gods as well as the cosmovision of the Indians had the earth as the primary point of reference. One should recall, however, that the Hebraic religion, being an expression of a people essentially nomadic, incorporated many agrarian elements such as the great feast days of the Jewish calendar, Pentecost being especially significant in sacred history. Conversely, because of having lost completely the profound and real sense of the liturgy, the missionaries attempted to superimpose or at best adapt the liturgical cycle from the European hemisphere to America. Even more regrettable, they did so without any consideration of the relation of man to nature. The Indian, as a result, felt devoid of support and of the sacredness which his ancient religion provided. The rebound of idolatry among the neophytes may be explained in part by the inflexibility of the Spanish religious system that ignored the roots of the Indian existence in its most intimate originality.

The Church — organized to counteract the Reformation — possibly became more rigid in its missionary approach, though it must be admitted that this rigidity appeared early in the Middle Ages, in the Crusades, in the struggle against Islam, and above all, in the *Patronato* itself, which limited freedom in missionary activity. The missionary, unable to reorganize the liturgical year in Latin America, created innumerable *para-liturgies*. These secondary manifestations offend the European, but he should recognize that his own Christianity was profoundly affected by pre-Christian liturgies.

An example of the liturgical innovations that took place in the Americas can be seen in the custom of the Indians of Tlaxomulci who celebrated each year in their village the Day of the Epiphany. The following is a description by a nineteenth-century historian.

They construct a facsimile of the entrance to Bethlehem in the patio of the Church and place against the bell tower the stable of the Christ Child along with Mary and Joseph. On a hill high above the village the Kings descend ever so slowly on horseback, their pace indicative of the seriousness with which they portray the Magi, and also because the road is very rough. . . .In the interim before they arrive, there is a dance of angels who as they perform sing various stanzas in the Indian dialect with many bowings and genuflections to the Child. . . .This is followed by the participants fighting with each other, and when some are knocked down, they roll around in the dirt frenetically embracing each other with such agility that it is shocking. If someone wants to stop those who are rolling on the ground, he merely places his shepherd's crook in the dirt in order that the participants go no farther. They in turn begin rolling in the other direction, embracing each other all the while. . . .Present for these ceremonies are the friars as well as many secular Spanish priests along with five thousand Indians. Thus is the Day of Epiphany celebrated in Tlaxomulci as well as in other villages.[1]

This dancing, leaping, and juggling were evidently forms of expression, mediations, or symbols that the Indians utilized in order to communicate to their god their reverence, devotion, and submission. A contemporary European spectator would have been shocked by these proceedings, as doubtless a primitive Jewish Christian would be scandalized at seeing the Basilica of St. Peter. One must understand, however, that the same motive that prompted the primitive Christian to select certain elements intrinsically neutral, that is, neither good nor bad in themselves, from the Greco-Roman civilization is the same motive that prompted the missionaries to Latin America to accept many Indian forms which were neither illicit nor immoral for expressing their devotion to God.

Moreover, it should be noted that the post-Tridentine Roman Church prohibited the development of a liturgy adapted to the American reality. Consider, for example, the fact that in the Southern hemisphere, Easter, the commemoration of the resurrection of Christ, is celebrated at the beginning of the Fall season when everything in nature is dying. This is a liturgical contradiction that has remained unchanged even today.

The responsibility for the lack of adaptation cannot be ascribed exclusively to Spain; rather, it was the fault of the whole European Catholic Church, not unlike the French position in regard to the question of the rites in China during the time of Matteo Ricci. Conversely, the often-heard criticism that the failure to adapt the liturgy and doctrine to the indigenous situation by the use of the *tabula rasa* method confirms the deep fear that the missionaries had of any kind of syncretism. The Inquisition in the Latin American Church pursued with a vengeance any admixture of paganism, magic, or sorcery.

Unfortunately, as can be seen, every missionary method has its drawbacks and intrinsic dangers.

If certain elements of the primitive rituals are admitted — as they were in Latin America — one runs the risk of developing syncretistic religion; which in fact has existed in Latin America, but only at the level of the "mediations."

If the *tabula rasa* method is utilized in order to avoid syncretism, one runs the risk of impeding a genuinely profound evangelization simply because the symbols of the culture that permit the transmission of the message are destroyed.

The Latin American missionaries did not adopt either of these methods exclusively. Rather, knowing the situation, they moved in a very prudent manner. On the level of the "mediations" we can say that the Christian mission in Latin America essentially involved the introduction of Catholic sacramentalism of a Hispanic type that accepted, on the level of the paraliturgies and popular devotion, a wide margin for the incorporation and mixture of the pre-Hispanic "mediations." This does not in itself negate the value of the evangelization. Rather, it demands of the spectator or critic a great deal of circumspection and care before making a value judgment.

II. THE "COMPREHENSIONS" OF THE PRE-HISPANIC RELIGION AND OF THE CATHOLIC MISSIONARY RELIGION

What we call the "existential comprehension" of the pre-Hispanic religion should be identified as the "ethico-mythical nucleus" of the Indian cultures in that the religion of these primitive cultures, whether superior or inferior, had its own nucleus. To transform this nucleus, the missionaries would have been required to engage in extensive dialogue with the culture just as the Apologists and Church Fathers did in respect to the Greco-Roman civilization. It would have been necessary for the Latin American missionaries to have known firsthand the elements that constituted the Indian mind and conscience. But this was extremely difficult. First, it was difficult because studies of the collective indigenous conscience became increasingly scarce with the passing of time. We can divide the whole process into four stages. During the first stage the missionaries attempted to obliterate the mythical conscience of the primitives, thinking that it was intrinsically and absolutely perverse. The second and third generation of missionaries — among them José de Acosta and Bernardino Sahagún — understood that in order to be effective it was necessary to have a thorough understanding of the

Indian system of thought. By this time, however, it was too late. The ancient traditions had already been recast in new molds. The Indian rites had been virtually obliterated, the ancient "wise men" had for the most part died, and the "mimicry of protection" of the Indian conscience was virtually impossible to investigate. The third stage extended from the seventeenth to the nineteenth centuries, but the authentic Indian conscience was ignored by the Spaniard, the Creole, and the urban dweller. The final stage began in this century with the indigenous movements, especially those related to the study of the phenomenology of religion. Perhaps in these developments the Indian conscience will be recovered, at least as an organic, living, dynamic system with its own intrinsic value.[2]

Our sources of information are threefold: the reports sent to or requested by the kings of Spain, the judgments and written works of the colonists and governmental authorities, and the studies done by the missionaries for the purpose of knowing the Indians in order to evangelize them more effectively. For the most part these aforementioned studies dealt with only certain aspects of Indian mentality and overlooked some of the more crucial issues. The Crown, for example, was interested in the intellectual, moral, and manual capacity of the Indians, as were the colonists. There are very few descriptions of the Indian mentality as such or of the mythical structures, the systems of thought, or the reasons and ultimate causes of their theogonies. Few of the colonists had the ability to make these kinds of investigations, and the missionaries — because of their scholastic orientation — were ill-prepared for this kind of analysis. It was asked, for example, if the Indian were really a human being, but it was never asked what kind of human being the Indian was. This vast ignorance in regard to the indigenous people led to a minimizing and devaluation of the importance of the primitive mythical element. As a rule the missionary did not bother to refute the Indian beliefs; rather, missions concentrated on teaching directly the exposition of Christian doctrine.

The second and third generation of missionaries, as has already been pointed out, attempted a serious investigation of what can be called the "soul of the American Indian." Cristóbal de Molina in his *Fábula y ritos de los Incas*,[3] Juan de Tovar,[4] José de Acosta,[5] and especially Bernardino Sahagún[6] were very diligent in their studies of the Indian religions and cultures. Sahagún, for example, spent two years with the Indian tribes in his area dialoguing with the elders who had been designated as the most knowledgeable, and with interpreters and other helpers he was able to gain a working knowledge of the hieroglyphics and of the Nahuatl language. Sahagún, with the help of these Indian elders, spent more than a year editing the first draft of his *Historia general* (*General History*), which is a significant scientific contribution to our knowledge of the indigenous peoples.[7]

The truth is, however, that the great mass of missionaries — even those who knew the Indian languages — neither made this kind of investigation nor availed themselves of the works of those who did. Sahagún's *History*, because of the persistent opposition of his Franciscan brothers and of the Crown, was not published until the nineteenth century. The missionaries proceeded in their evangelization with the knowledge that they themselves gained from the contact they had with the Indians. The basis of this attitude should be well understood. Spain in general — because of the long struggle with Islam, the contact with Judaism, and its unbending opposition to Protestantism — had developed an integralist mindset that was intransigently antisyncretistic. The accusation that the Church in Latin America promoted or permitted syncretism, that is, the admixture of primitive Indian mythology and rites with Christianity, is an ill-founded assumption, although a kind of syncretism did result for other reasons. The Church was, conversely, uncompromisingly opposed to all forms of syncretism. The knowledge of and the publication of books that contained descriptions and expositions of the ancient rites and myths, in the judgment of the kings and many members of the Church, risked the possibility that certain responsible elites would retrieve these myths and ceremonies. In their passion for Christian purity — poorly understood to be sure, but explicable in view of the times — studies of the Indian "ethico-mythical nucleus" were not encouraged.

Because of ignorance and the rapidity with which the conquistadores destroyed the structures of the Indian civilization and the "ethico-mythical nucleus" of the pre-Hispanic cultures, a slow passage (pesach) or transition from the pagan "ethico-mythical nucleus" to the acceptance of the Christian faith and understanding — as occurred, for example, in the Greco-Roman empire — was not achieved. Rather, what occurred was a rupture, a severing, and an annihilation of the heart of the ancient cultures. This lamentable turn of events impeded a normal and authentic evangelization.

The situation, however, should be closely examined. One must admit that the Indian communities, deprived of the basic contents of their cultures, should have by all logic disappeared as cultural groups and should have been progressively assimilated into the superior civilization that invaded the Americas.

Uninterrupted evangelization of the Indians took place almost as a necessity from the sixteenth till the nineteenth century. Little by little the Indian communities, deprived of the ultimate bases of their culture, began to adopt the culture of the Spanish. Some Indians accepted the Christian existential understanding at the cultural level possible for them to comprehend. This is to say that at the most profound level of the group — that of the ultimate intentional structures — the missionaries arrived too late and with limited success were able to implant within the Indian mind the great truths or elements of Christian understanding: the creation, the Person of Jesus Christ as Redeemer, and the contingency of things. There were, therefore, great areas in which paganism continued in a pure state and broad zones in which many of the intentional pagan structures were not completely purified. We can say, nevertheless, that where the early evangelization took place — that of the sixteenth century — Christianity has remained firmly established. "The spiritual geography of contemporary Mexico, to the degree that it can be measured, corresponds to the map of the primitive missionary expansion."[8]

The Spanish or missionary culture worked at the fundamental level of comprehension that, when the tabula rasa method was applied, rejected the pre-Hispanic "ethico-mythical nucleus" without discussion, thereby initiating the slow formation of a Latin American Christian conscience.

III. WHAT HAS CONSTITUTED A MIXED RELIGION?

Writers in the past and in our own time have adopted differing positions in regard to the encounter of Christianity with the primitive pagan religions in Latin America. Some believe that the Indians only accepted Christianity externally. This is the position of Jiménez Rueda who says, "The Indian was able to capture only the external aspects of worship — the plastic art of the ceremonies, the choral music, and the organ."[9] Mariátegui insists that the "missionaries did not impose the Gospel on the Indians; rather what was imposed was the cult, the liturgy. . . .Aboriginal paganism meanwhile continued to survive below the surface of Catholic worship."[10] This same position has been adopted by many other thinkers in France, Germany, and even in North America.

George Kubler, for example, also believes that the Christianity of the Indian is only external and superficial.[11]

Others contend that the Indians are *essentially* Christians, although they manifest, according to geographical region and the attention given to them by the missionaries, major or minor deficiencies. This is the position of Constantino Bayle and of Fernando de Armas Medina in their work, *Cristianización del Perú (The Christianization of Peru).*[12]

Finally, there are some who believe that the indigenous religion that developed after the arrival of the missionaries was a mixture of or the juxtapositioning of the two religious traditions, although these two points of view are obviously distinct. Borges justifiably says that there was no mixture or fusion of religion. Rather, he contends there was a "coexistence of two juxtapositioned religions by which the Indians attempted to combine Christianity with paganism."[13]

It appears to me that one cannot evaluate correctly the Christianity of the Indian by separating the two religions — the pre-Hispanic paganism and Christianity — as if they existed independently from the *subject*. For the Christianity of the Indian is not exclusively exterior, nor can one know directly the essence of the Indian soul. Neither is Indian Christianity a mixture or a juxtapositioning of religions.

We should begin with the individual and collective conscience of the Indian, the mythical conscience, and observe the slow conversion that has taken place by degrees and after great effort and difficulty. Our point of departure, therefore, should be the mythical cosmovision of the Indian where the *sacred* invaded his whole existence, where every act was regulated by examples that were located in the original time of the living gods who dwelt alongside men. We should, therefore, understand this ahistorical existence where the world view did not include the abstract and where everything had theological significance.

In this mythical world, pregnant with significance and value, there appeared the Spaniard with his astonishing instruments of civilization — his ships, harquebuses, dogs, horses, and armor. Into this mythical world came the missionary with his purity, benevolence, and magnificent services of worship. The Indian accepted all this as a *theological novelty*. The gods who protected the Spaniards had to be great, thought the Indian, much more powerful than our own, for the power of a people is nothing more than the expression of the power of their gods. Many times the Indian sought to become a Christian in order to ingratiate himself with the Christian gods, to participate in and receive the benefits of their power, and finally to make a peaceful alliance with them.

It was, therefore, by necessity that the Indian was attracted to Christianity. It was the logical result of his primitive and mythical cosmovision. It could not have been otherwise. Christianity as a religion was, it must be admitted, accepted by the Indian for reasons which were essentially pagan.

The demythification, the "atheization" of all that existed in the Indian mind, was a process that could not be hurried. The Greco-Roman culture, for example, needed no less than six centuries of contact with Christianity before any significant transformation of the basic theological outlook of that world occurred.

There existed in the Indian mind, therefore, gradations of lightness and darkness, a chiaoscuro which at one extreme could be considered as purely pagan while at the other it could be regarded as purely Christian. The transition from paganism to Christianity, if it is achieved *en masse* without excluding major segments of people, will of necessity require many centuries. To accelerate the process, the missionaries and the bishops adopted the practice of isolating the Indian community that had accepted

Christianity. The *reducciones* were specifically for this purpose, namely, for developing a Christian mentality within the space of a generation.

The Indian made sacrifices to his gods because he feared them, and his fears stemmed from his belief in their existence. Now the fact that the Indian believed in the gods did not mean that he believed any less in Jesus Christ, at least insofar as it was possible for him to understand with his semipagan awareness of the significance of Jesus Christ. Simultaneously, as the Indian discovered the demands of Christianity, there was created for him a deep conflict of obligations. Such a conflict, nevertheless, was not absent in his primitive religion. As a matter of fact, all primitive religions are marked by a sense of tragedy, but the contradiction and the conflict are accepted as inevitable. The tragedy in the Indian soul would, however, remain for a long time. When the conscience was not sufficiently enlightened or strengthened by Christian practice or living, it was only in the *reducciones* that this sense of the tragic would be uprooted for a brief time.

May we conclude, therefore, that the religion which resulted in Latin America among the Indians was superficial, mixed, or juxtapositioned? This does not appear to be the case. The problem was much more complicated. On the level of the "mediations," as has already been said, there was an accumulation of Hispanic Catholic liturgy with its many gestures, symbols, and attitudes that were rooted in the pre-Hispanic religions. At this level one can see not so much a *mixed* religion as an *eclectic* accumulation, that is, the missionaries simply selected those aspects of the rites, dances, arts, and symbols which they deemed acceptable in the paraliturgies for the architecture, catechism, and the Eucharistic mystery plays. In this sense one can say that the missionaries consciously and officially attempted a transformation of the basis of the primitive ritual while at the same time they accepted many secondary forms of the primitive religions. This was, in fact, inevitable. The Indian people were, therefore, able to follow for a longer or shorter period, depending upon the geographical regions, their ancient cults in an Americanized Christian form. There resulted slowly, nonetheless, a substantial change, a progressive catechumenization.

On the level of fundamental comprehension, that is, of faith itself where authentic evangelization takes place, a chiaoscuro resulted which is almost impossible to discern but which avoids two obvious extremes:

1. The extreme of confusing *religious ignorance* with *paganism*. Many Indian people lived on a very primitive level culturally, and their faith, if one can put it thusly, was on the same incipient, primitive, undeveloped level.

2. The extreme of concluding too readily that the Catholicism of the Indian was valid simply by his having received baptism and by possessing various notions regarding Christian dogma.

Between these two extremes one should attempt a realistic evaluation. The Indian is more or less at the stage — as much in the eighteenth century as in the twentieth — of an initial but unfinished catechumenate. Every community or person is somewhere between these two extremes: that of simple catechumenal initiation or that of mature Christianity. At times the Indian appears to be at the point of "recent catechumenal initiation" with the pagan elements of his consciousness strongly evident. Is his religion therefore a mixed faith? It does not appear to be so, for a truly syncretistic religion should express in the form of dogmas or doctrines its "mixtures," such as the case of Spiritism in Brazil where oftentimes individuals from the middle class manifest characteristics of an undeniably mixed religion.

IV. THE TYPOLOGY OF THE INHABITANTS OF THE CONTINENT WITH RESPECT TO THE CHRISTIAN FAITH AS DISCERNED IN THE COLONIAL ERA

We will outline in six groups the various positions that the conquerors, missionaries, and Indians adopted with respect to the person of Jesus Christ, which was, as has been said, the proper objective and essence of the faith and of Christian existence.

1. A few nourished a clear and conscious faith. This group has always been a minority in the history of the Church and will be until the end of time. It includes the great individuals in whom we are able to discern clearly in the quality of their virtues the liberty of Christianity regarding civilization. We refer here to the saints, certain great theologians or missionaries, some bishops, and some Indians.

2. Some leaders of the Church, principally the bishops, missionaries, and priests, along with a few laypeople, attempted to evangelize, but in their efforts they unconsciously mixed Hispanic and Christian elements as if they were identical. This group includes the great majority of missionaries to the Indians as well as some laypeople and Indians themselves.

3. The great majority of conquistadores, colonists, and Spaniards — who along with the Creoles and later the mestizos — united completely the goals of the Spanish Empire with those of the Catholic Church to the point of possessing a narrow *Hispanic messianism*. One was a Christian by virtue of being a Spaniard, of being baptized, and by observing certain precepts of the Church, but without any existential linking of conduct and the gospel.

4. The great majority of the Indians were baptized without being thoroughly catechized or genuinely converted — much less being part of the life of a Christian community — the exception being evidently the Indians who were organized into villages, curacies, missions, or *reducciones*. Their existential attitude on a moral or cultural plane, their faith and comprehension, were not sufficiently developed to allow them adequate understanding of Christian doctrine and its demands. Thus moral degeneration, drunkenness, and concubinage could coexist with the belief in the existence of *huacas* (spirits that resided in various places) along with sorcery, magic, and the belief in Jesus Christ as Savior.

5. There were also areas wherein the Indians were only indirectly touched by Hispanic civilization or by Christian missions and which remain until today substantially pagan.

6. Some Indians continued to be essentially pagans without any contact with Christianity and by the end of the eighteenth century represented a marginal group isolated from the pre-Hispanic as well as from the Latin American civilization.

What conclusions, then, can be drawn from this summary?

1. One should keep in mind the fact that at the end of the sixteenth century there were only 120,000 Spaniards living in Latin America surrounded by at least 12,000,000 Indians. The Spanish population constituted barely one percent of the total population. Moreover, the Spanish were dispersed over an area of more than 12,000,000 square miles (20,000,000 square kilometers). The conquistadores were not theologians — even though for the glory of Spain they were faithful in religious observances — neither were they saints, although they did not lack for saints (images). The majority of the Spaniards who came to the New World were from the rural areas of Spain and Europe where some paganism remained. Furthermore, one should remember the enormous influence of Islam on Spanish culture. The Christian conscience was already contam-

inated with paganism from its own culture as well as from humanity in general when the conquistadores came to the New World, and it grew in America in an environment essentially pagan. The result was the release of a pent-up paganism in the Hispanic population. The immigrant, having broken the sociological mold of the Christianity which he knew — this phenomenon is easily observed in every immigrant from Italy, France, or Germany, if the immigrant came from areas deeply Christian — lost the empirical supports of his faith and experienced the sensation of having lost his faith altogether. This weakening of religious experience together with the impact of an overwhelmingly pagan environment led to the development of a new Hispanic and mestizo urban society which is now referred to as "Latin American Christianity."

The Spaniards, Creoles, and mestizos were the foundation of the Latin American culture. They were the most astute of the elites who have in fact been the major protagonists in the history of Latin America. Until the eighteenth century they remained for the most part Christians, and at times they even moved to the second level of Christian understanding. The ideological monopoly that the Latin American metropolis enjoyed in the colonies, especially through the power and influence of the Tribunal of the Inquisition, impeded the efforts of Protestants to penetrate the society and also retarded the influence of the French and English philosophies of the sixteenth and eighteenth centuries. (In the University of Córdoba, nevertheless, Descartes' philosophy was being taught as early as the eighteenth century.)

The Spanish and Creole citizens, each in his own way and in his own time, were truly Christians. Consider, for example, the illustrious testimony of Francisco de Miranda, the precursor of the American emancipation, written in 1805:

To the University of Caracas send in my name the Greek classics from my library as an indication of gratitude for the sound principles of literature and Christian morals with which I was nourished during my youth and which became the basis for my ability to overcome the great dangers and difficulties of these present times.[14]

2. The great mass of Indians proceeded to incorporate features of the Hispanic-Creole urban culture and thus developed their own forms of Christianity. But they continued their semiprimitive lives remaining at a level of catechumenates more or less aware of their faith and to a greater or lesser degree utilizing the instruments of sacramental Christian structures along with those essentially pagan. This phenomenon we have chosen to designate as the *eclectic accumulation* at the level of the "mediations."

We repeat, therefore, the question: Can we rightly speak of the Indian religion as being superficial, mixed, juxtapositioned, or substantially Christian simply on the basis of the outward appearance? It would seem that the matter is much more complex, and that univocal and global judgments are really impossible. In summary: (1) On a deeper, more comprehensive, and existential level the Indian masses have adopted Christianity neither superficially nor otherwise. Rather, they have begun to adopt Christianity radically, substantially, and authentically. But this adoption is neither essentially a juxtapositioning nor a mixing of religions. It is rather a chiaoscuro faith in which no one is able to determine where Christianity begins and where paganism ends. (2) Lamentably, the great masses do not participate in the Catholic liturgy because of the lack of priests and missionaries or because of the great distances and other impediments. What expressions do exist, therefore, are surrogate paraliturgies: professions, cults to the saints, and local shrines built on the ruins of ancient religious rites and ceremonies, as occurred also in the Greco-Roman and Canaanite worlds. Thus the elements, expressions, and symbols — that is, the "vehicles" and "mediations" of the ancient religions — are still very much present. But can these supplementary forms be rightly called *mixed* religions? This does not appear to be the case. What all this may be called is the creation or mixture at the popular level of that which was inevitable in view of the vacuum left by the *tabula rasa* missionary method, and these substitutionary creations will disappear with the finalization of the period of rudimentary Christian instruction, that is, at the conclusion of the catechumenal stage. The so-called folk Catholicism is not, therefore, a mixed religion. Rather, it is a temporary, supplementary manifestation by a people who long for the completion of evangelization. This popular form of faith can hardly be said to be unvarnished paganism. No, it more rightly can be considered the manifestation of an awareness of conscience not yet entirely Christian.

Part III
The Agony of Colonial Christendom (1808–1962)

In the course of a century and a half Latin America has been confronted with a growing number of problems which Europe earlier had encountered and was able to resolve during almost six centuries. Relatively young communities have had to face successively the crises of being new nation-states with growing nationalism, secularization, the injustices of the colonial system imposed by the great industrialized powers, and the development of a pluralistic society. On the other hand, the diverse social groups have had to attempt to recover their coherence, equilibrium, inspiration, and means of government. The Church has been situated amidst these conflicts attempting all the while to defend her ancient privileges to the point of having almost lost them altogether, and has had to begin a vigorous renovation of which the first fruits are only now apparent, and far from complete.

The beginning of this period in the history of the Church witnessed the transition from the *Patronato* system, in which the Spanish State and government officials actually had charge of the church and its mission, to a secular system in which the Church recovered its freedom of action and is now able to address itself to the modification of the unjust structures and thereby recuperate the support and confidence of the masses. At the same time one can observe the transition from a Christendom in which the Church enjoyed the support of the political system — and where all other religious expressions were excluded from the body — to a pluralistic system in which the Church is required to depend upon its own resources and means in an environment of religious freedom. In this second stage the Church can no longer pull legal strings by its relationship to the State but must work by means of *Christian institutions*. And the birth of these *institutions* allows us to see the beginning of the renovation that we are contemplating in our day.

This also means that the Latin American Church began a direct relationship with Rome, contact that was interrupted by the *Patronato* system, which in turn allowed for an opening not only to Europe but to the whole world as the vestiges of the Spanish Empire were abandoned.

Chapter VII
The Crisis in the Neocolonial States

The political independence of Latin America from Spain produced a series of demands upon the new fledgling countries. The organization of the new nations absorbed the energies of the first generations, and later the struggle was with universalization, and finally with secularization.

I. THE CRISIS OF THE BOURGEOIS REVOLUTION AND OF THE CREOLE OLIGARCHY

The independence of the Spanish American colonies did not signify merely the separation from the mother country; rather, it signaled a profound change in the level of civilization, of political technology, and of economic systems. Understandably, at the time of independence there was an enormous disorientation that required time for reorganization and consolidation into a new Latin American order. The latter did not actually begin until the twentieth century. The crisis produced by the revolution and independence seemed to run the gamut from one extreme to another. In time, however, the situation began to stabilize and to assume definite and discernible positions. Throughout the whole process the Church has been deeply involved, for throughout Latin American history the Church has been one of the basic institutions of the social order.

Colonial society was composed of several social classes that were distinguished as much by their functions as by the degree of their culture, economic power, or race. These classes were as follows: (1) The *peninsulares* (colonists born in Spain) who occupied all the chief posts in the government and in the Church, in the viceroyalty as in the courts, and for the most part in the episcopacy. (2) The Creoles (children born in America of Spanish parents) who controlled the town councils and at times gained responsible positions as government administrators. Among these were many who were quite rich, and some were even ennobled by the Crown. As in Europe, the most prestigious profession among this group was that of the law or jurisprudence. (3) The mestizos who little by little became the great urban masses. (4) The Indians who were and who remained principally the rural masses. (5) The Negroes and mulattoes who were able to gain their independence after the revolution. Prior to independence, however, the Spanish Crown controlled completely her American colonies, and after the revolution the Creoles gained power and replaced the Spaniards or *peninsulares* in the administrative and episcopal posts — a truly French-type revolution in which the Creole bourgeois gained control of the instruments of power.

This oligarchical elite, inspired by a liberal or physiocratic economic philosophy, began the legal and cultural organization of the new nations. They discarded all the trappings of the monarchy in order to establish a type of representative democracy, and there ensued a bitter and in some cases a prolonged struggle between the federalists and the unitarians, the latter in the majority of cases gaining control of the national political systems.

In one sense the first revolutionary generation, constituted by men born in the colonies and integrated into the vital functions and professions of the Spanish, failed to implement their federalist ideology, as did Bolívar in the Panamanian Assembly of 1826. The powerful territorial body united by Bolívar, which could have been the heart of a future South American confederation, divided into three nations: Colombia, Venezuela, and Ecuador. In 1839 the Central American Confederation had virtually dissolved, and during 1837 and 1838 Chile withdrew from a proposed union with Bolivia and Peru. This continental tendency toward proliferation into separate nation-states not only divided governments but also tended to divide the Church into separate national entities. The Hispanic colonial empire disappeared — and with it "Latin American Christendom."

One should remember, as was indicated above, that at the time of independence only twenty percent of the people in Latin America were white, twenty-six percent were mestizo, forty-six percent were Indian, and eight percent were Negro. The vast majority of whites resided in the cities. The emancipation movement to free the slaves, essentially an urban movement, was fostered and directed exclusively by Creole whites. Bourbon centralism — as in France during the same period — produced a decrease in municipal life and the prevalent discontent. The per capita taxes decreed by Charles III benefited the wealthy and set them apart even more from the poor. By the end of the eighteenth century a classist society composed of whites and "the others," urban and rural, rich and poor — a society profoundly divided — was already evident. The Creole elite was not reluctant to ally themselves with a foreign power in order to achieve their objectives. They became, however, the suboppressive class.

By the end of the eighteenth and beginning with the nineteenth century, England became the focal point of revolution in the West: political revolution in its parliamentarianism, economic revolution in its capitalistic liberalism, technical revolution in its mechanization, and intellectual revolution in its scientific empiricism and political theory of the social contract. The growing British Empire supported in principle what has been called the neocolonial system. The Anglo-Saxon metropolis sold manufactured products to its colonies while at the same time purchasing from these colonies agricultural products and raw materials for use in the metropolitan community and industry. This system in itself created and promoted a disequilibrium of industrial development; at least the imbalance was real and not fictitious as in the Spanish mercantile economy, which depended on the exploitation of American gold and silver. The English nation, whose origin and tradition can be traced to the type of commercial government of Phoenicia, Carthage, Venice, and Genoa (and because of the economic technology and mechanized development that served as its base of industrialization), imposed on all the people an economic system which Adam Smith set forth in his *The Wealth of the Nations*. This system proposed that the regions that produced the raw materials open themselves to the markets of the more recently industralized countries, and the result was a process of moving away from Spanish mercantilism. The Spaniard sold raw materials and agricultural products *which the colonies produced* in order to buy precious metals. The English produced manufactured goods in order to buy in turn agricultural products and raw materials for British industries. The British system pressured the buyers of its manufactured goods to increase their agricultural and mineral production. Spain, on the other hand, opposed agriculture, cattle, and mineral production or organized it in such a way as to have a complete monopoly over it. This system impeded any real development of the economy of the colonies. The English system was superior, but in time, when the politics and economics of the colonies prompted attempts to begin industrial development, the Latin Americans encountered a twofold problem. First, there was the direct and indirect opposition of the oligarchies in the already industrialized and developed countries who enlisted the ready support of the neocolonial oligarchies in the Latin American countries. Second, goods could not be manufactured as cheaply in the colonies as they could in the already industrialized countries. Thus there was the impediment of unequal or unfair competition, which stemmed from the ability of the British to manufacture and sell goods in Latin America cheaper than the same goods could be produced and sold here.

Liberated from Spain politically and from its artifical economic monopoly, the new Latin American countries, for lack of other possibilities, became a part of the British and later the continental European and North American neocolonial system. The underdeveloped countries, from an industrial point of view, would see the prices of their raw materials controlled by the highly industrialized countries who could sell to these underdeveloped nations manufactured goods at constantly increasing prices. This system has dominated capitalistic liberalism on the international plane and is a type of economic colonialism based on industrial primacy. The Church, which was linked hand in glove with the monarchy during the colonial period, became closely tied to the new Creole and later bourgeois oligarchies of the new Latin American countries.

The nineteenth and twentieth centuries were for these new republics periods of struggle to develop their agricultural, cattle, and mineral production to the degree that they could enter the free market as equal participants. But the world market was dominated by the industralized countries, especially Great Britain and later the United States, while the exploitation of the raw materials was directed by Creole or foreign capital, first British, but also North American in Central America, the Caribbean, and the northern countries of South America. Our countries in turn depended for their protection on these industrialized powers. But when we attempted to become a part of the community of nations as industrialized countries, that is, when we attempted to liberate ourselves from the *neocolonial system,* there began a struggle with two solidly entrenched and unified entities: the capital of the industrialized nations which saw their sources of cheap raw materials threatened, and the liberal Creole oligarchies who had been the beneficiaries of this system, working in perfect harmony with the foreign industrialized capital.

Many revolutions would be attempted to destroy the neocolonial system, and efforts would be made to prevent the industrialized countries from fixing the prices of the raw materials and thereby increasing the prices of the manufactured products. Efforts would also be made by the Latin American nations to overcome their internal crises by a very simple tax system that completely disorganized these industrially undeveloped countries. Furthermore, these revolutions attempted to displace the power of the Creole oligarchies who were so fond of foreign products and who possessed all the economic and political power that permitted them to maintain the Latin American republics in this state of being producers of raw materials at low cost for the highly industrialized countries.

All of this began in the colonial period as a part of the Spanish system that based its fictitious economic progress on the fluctuating resources of the precious metals and not on the technical efforts of the people. Spain chose the easy way: exploiting the American mines with the Indians rather than taking the narrow road that England chose, namely, the hard work of an industrious people. The Spanish lack of economic vision was catastrophic for Spain and also for the Latin American countries. Spain could easily have had coal and steel in Europe, but this would have signified an austere, simple, daily industrial effort. Spain preferred to mine only gold and silver, which in the short run produced an ephemeral splendor, but in the long run produced economic catastrophe from which Spain as well as Latin America has never recovered.

The Church, more or less implicated with the conservative governments — in view of the fact that the *Patronato* system had been maintained and was closely tied to the Conservatives by family and social relations — represented, at least for a time, interests foreign to those of the more humble people, namely, the Indians, the workers, and the poor. Insofar as the liberal or semisocialist governments have liberated the Church, it can be a crucial factor in the reorganization of Latin American society.

II. THE CRISIS OF THE UNIVERSALIZATION OF THE NATIONAL COMMUNITIES

Organization was achieved at the level of *civilization*, and universalization at the level of *culture* and of the Latin American "ethico-mythical nucleus." The Spanish Empire maintained a formidable barrier to all foreign ideological meddling: the Tribunal of the Holy Inquisition. Latin America failed, therefore, to permit the entrance of any new world views and thereby began the crisis of universalization. At times the Church followed a traditional course, and at other times it was supposed that it would do so, all of which indicated the opposition of the reforming elites.

From a social point of view, at least in principle, immediate liberty was granted to Negro slaves (in Argentina in 1813 and in Brazil in 1888). The Indian was considered an integral part of the new society, but neither the emancipated Black nor the native American was permitted by the Creole elite to rise to any place of importance. The mestizos, on the other hand, achieved rapid social advancement. Racial universalization was, therefore, relative.

The Scholastics disappeared from the universities, that is, from those that had not closed their doors after independence, and the Church degenerated toward the end of the nineteenth century into a state of complete disorientation. "The nineteenth century was, therefore, for Spain as well as for Spanish America a century of philosophical decadence."

Philosophical and political ideas were imported from Europe and mixed with those already existent in Latin America, producing foreign systems and at times a kind of Latin American mythology. These movements clashed with the Church in that European philosophical systems were anti-Catholic and anti-Christian. Encountering a situation already in total disarray and without any possibility of marshaling a satisfactory response, the Church during the entire nineteenth century assumed a negative or defensive posture.

We are able to compare in this opening process different levels that we will describe in the following manner:

1. The movement for emancipation was under the influence of Spanish and French liberalism but was basically conservative. The new nations discovered later alternative forms of government at the level of the instruments of civilization and eventually became aware of the new physiognomy of the marrow of their culture and the "ethico-mythical nucleus." Civilization was easily transmissible, but the fundamental structures required more time to develop.

For example, an Argentine, Manuel Belgrano, graduated in 1789 from Salamanca with his bachelor's degree, and in 1793 with a degree in law. He was clearly a Physiocrat in his philosophy. "Cattle raising," he said, "will produce far more than all the gold in Peru." Another indication can be seen in the "French party" that arose in Brazil as a result of influences from Portugal in Porto Bello in 1791 and in Bahía in 1797.[1] The truth is that French and English influence entered Latin America more by way of Spain than directly, and the basis of all these ideologies was an ambiguous *liberalism*. In Central America Pedro Molina declared, "The Supreme Creator created all men equal ... political liberty is absolute.... I was born free, therefore, I should govern myself."[2] The famous priest, Hidalgo, in his proclamation from Guadalajara on December 6, 1810, demanded equality for the Indians in the Mexican society.[3]

Equally influential in Latin America were the encyclopedist movements, the sensualism of Condillac (Mont'Alverne y Gonçalves de Magalhaes in Brazil), the eclecticism of Víctor Cousin, the economics of John Stuart Mill and Jeremy Bentham, and the slow growth of technology as seen in Thomas Falkner of Argentina who was a student of Newton. The Masonic lodges functioned among the Scotch and Yorkshires in Mexico and were supported by Lucas Alamán and José María Mora. Slowly these movements began to take shape in an ideological environment strictly Latin American, and although they were still floating on colonial structures, they signified an authentic era of transition.

The Church was totally disoriented and could only oppose or support existing situations. Many members of the clergy and even one bishop became deeply involved in the movements of ideological emancipation, but the ecclesial body as a whole could not offer any coherent solution.

2. The constitutive moment of the new national forms took place in approximately 1850, when the most profound "revolution," "renovation," or "rupture" in the history of Latin America occurred. The Mexican Constitution of 1857 is a clear example, as is that of Colombia in 1853. The romanticism of Echeverría, the work of Alberdi and later of Sarmiento in Argentina, Lastarría and Esteban Bilbao in Chile, Sacco and José de la Luz y Caballero in Cuba began a preparatory movement. With them one can observe a clear separation from the past and the formation of new bases of national consciousness. The Church was always present, but in the majority of the cases only as a critic or combatant, a residue of the colonial era and of the disintegrating Christendom.

But the true ideological rupture by the bourgeois minorities who formed the Creole oligarchy — not yet aristocracy but really from the middle class — was first Krausism as is seen in the work of Arthur Roig and later in the positivist movement. F. Brandâo wrote in 1865 his *Escravatura no Brasil*, but it was M. Lemos with his *Comte-Philosophie Positive* (1874) who really introduced positivism into Brazil. His disciple, Teixeira Mendes, continued Lemos' work. Positivism, especially in Brazil but also in all of Latin America, was really a religious philosophy, at least as it had been developed by Comte. Gabino Barreda was a student of Comte in Paris and in 1870 introduced positivism into Mexico. P. Scalabrini was the first from the River Plate area to teach the positivist philosophy, and it became very popular in Uruguay between 1873 and 1880. Porfirio Díaz decreed positivism as the ideological underpinning for his government (1876 – 1880, 1884 – 1911). Together with positivism the doctrines of Littré were universally espoused by the liberal bourgeois who governed in Latin America, which resulted in a laicised teaching toward the end of the nineteenth century in virtually the whole continent. Opposition to the Church was as widespread as it was intense, but only a few writers made any attempt to defend Christian institutions. For the most part, as we indicated above, few were concerned with the lamentable state of the Church, and those who could have risen to the Church's defense remained outside the political or cultural arena.

3. A slow but radical change began in the twentieth century as a result of the influence of Bergson, Bretano, Husserl, Neo-Thomism, and later Ortega y Gasset. Positivism was subjected to ample criticism, and a position generically "spiritual" was defended in the university chairs, if not by the political parties that continued to be liberal. Slowly, however, new contemporary positions developed: socialism and Marxism along with the birth of Christian political parties. José E. Rodó in Uruguay and Jackson Figueiredo in Brazil both represented this transition from positivism to neospiritualism. The *conciencialismo* of Alexander Korn in Argentina was also a reaction against the doctrines of the nineteenth century. The work of Trinidad Sánchez Santos in the social arena was a position unknown in the previous century. The Church at this time was slowly receiving support from the experiences of certain "prophets" of the nineteenth century, and with the renovation of European Christianity the Church began to exercise a more prominent role. The stage of defending the faith began to give way to the discovery of new forms for diffusing the faith.

Latin America, because of the crisis that we call "universalization," can at the present time and in a global manner (through its elites, especially university, labor, and political leaders) begin a dialogue with the contemporary ideologies of the world, knowing their methods as well as the consequences. The "opening" from the Hispanic colonial to the total world and to humanity produced — during a century and a half, doubtless through much suffering, struggle, opposition, and lives — visible fruit that may be imperceptible to the foreigner who is not able to understand this secular revolution "from within."

Protestantism is, with respect to the "universalization," the only significant religious movement representing foreign influence in Latin America, especially North American influence. As one can see, the orientation at the level of *civilization* — technology, economic, and political philosophies — stemmed from the Anglo-Saxon world, first from England and later from the United States. The orientation at the level of culture and of the "ethico-mythical nucleus" stemmed primarily from France, namely, from the romantic, positivist, and antipositivist movements. The influence of Protestantism resulted from the expansion into Latin America of the North American civilization as well as the Anglo-Saxon and German immigration extending over a long period of time and affecting the development of the Latin American conscience, although it is one of the new elements of the contemporary conscience. Yet this did not prevent the Latin American culture from being alienated by a culture of domination for the benefit of the metropolitan powers.

III. INSTITUTIONAL SECULARIZATION

This phrase, institutional secularization, covers two different concepts. In the first place, secularization can signify a movement *contrary to the Church,* that is, an attempt to confiscate the property or restrict the rights of the Church. This usage is incorrect, or at least inappropriate. In the second place, secularization can signify the awareness of the *autonomy of the State* with respect to the Church and the effective means by which this autonomy can be achieved. It is evident that many times the State can achieve autonomy by a defective or imprudent process such as the Church's refusing to allow such a process or postponing its realization. In both cases secularization is antiecclesial. One should understand that the process of secularization is not, however, necessarily anti-Christian. Rather, it is the fruit of sound Christian theology. The anti-Christianity of many efforts toward secularization is more the effect of an irregularity on the part of the State or the Church than it is the product of the secularization process itself. In Latin America secularization has been achieved by every means possible — from extreme violence, as in Colombia in 1861 and in Mexico from 1917 onward, or peacefully, as in Chile in 1925. We are speaking at this point of the level of the relations between the Church and the various nation-states. Secularization has been operative on various levels.

1. The first step was the transition from the *Patronato* exercised by the Spanish Crown to the *Patronato* subject to the authority of the new national governments. In some cases the Church was at the mercy of the political leaders who at times were less than scrupulous and who in the majority of the cases lacked experience and prudence. The liberal governments and even the positivists did not renounce their political power over the Church; rather they pursued it in every area. The movement toward secularization, nevertheless, was intrinsically opposed to the *Patronato* and was eventually abandoned by the national governments in Latin America. In Chile the Church was separated from the State in 1925. More recently, in 1961, the Bolivian government renounced the right of the *Patronato*. But until the Church was separated from the State, the governments of the nineteenth century were able to prevent anything in the Church deemed undesirable and thus could impede any significant reform of the Church itself. The Latin American Church, nevertheless, did not become a "national Church" as many political and some ecclesiastical leaders attempted in the history of Europe. This in itself indicated a relative maturity and fidelity to Catholicity.

2. The Church was deprived of all the economic advantages it enjoyed during the colonial era. The new national governments, desperate for funds, were able to achieve a complete restructuring and seized many of the ecclesiastical properties, as did the Germans during the Reformation or as occurred after the French Revolution. Not only were diocesan properties seized, but also those of the religious orders. In Argentina, Bernardino Rivadavia is a good example of a leader in the movement toward secularization. Not only did Rivadavia attempt to create a national Church, he also confiscated the properties of the Church and attempted to reorganize the religious orders in 1824. Anticlericalism took a more violent form in Bolivia in 1826 with the plundering of the convents, and in Nicaragua with their confiscation in 1830. Much later, in 1861, Colombia expropriated the Church properties, as did Mexico after 1917. In most of Latin America the Church lost virtually all its agricultural properties as well as other lands and buildings which it would have inherited from the colony. In fact, one can say that the Church was reduced to real poverty in view of the fact that it depended and now depends in a majority of cases on only the financial contributions of the faithful. Bishops and priests no longer enjoy the income from rentals or salaries from the State in the majority of Latin American countries, but this allows the Church as an institution much greater liberty than it enjoyed during the colonial era.

3. Following the revolution the Church progressively lost its legal and political power and influence. During the struggle for independence the Church intervened actively, even to the point of helping frame the constitutions in many countries during the first half of the nineteenth century. Yet from 1850 onward the Church lost almost completely its political power, except in those cases where the government in a kind of trade-off allowed the Church certain rights in exchange for concessions in other areas. The Liberal parties were the most consistent opponents of the Church while generally the Conservatives supported the Church in its political and legal struggles.

There appeared at times confessional political parties such as the Catholic Party in Mexico in 1911. None of these parties, however, gained any effective power for themselves or for the Church. It has only been those political parties of Christian inspiration, not confession, organized at the beginning of the Second World War, that have had any real impact on Latin American politics. They have, however, signified the presence of the Christian conscience in Latin American society not only in the political parties themselves, but also in the trade union movements, among worker elites, and among Christian university students. This latter group has been very active, and on numerous occasions controlled student elections in the universities of Chile, Argentina, Brazil, Bolvia, and Peru. Thus one can say that the Church has become involved positively in secular society, and that the Christian conscience has begun to manifest a confidence in the new "mode of being."

The first occasion of the separation of Church and State occurred in Colombia in 1853 along with the government's approval of divorce. Colombia has been an especially sensitive country in regard to the religious question, and in all its history one sees a dialectical struggle between Catholic and anti-Catholic governments, between Liberals and Conservatives, each gaining power and proceeding to change the total structure of the country. In fact, Colombia is a kind of paradigm of the Latin American soul. In 1886 Rafael Núñez, elected as a Liberal president, reestablished the union of Church and State in Colombia, thus ending a period of separation that began during the regime of José Hilario López in 1849.

4. Finally, as a result of the influence of Littré, *secular teaching* was imposed in almost all of Latin America, although there were changes beginning in 1884 in Argentina and Costa Rica. There has been, however, a tendency to transplant Scholasticism and in certain countries to make religious teaching optional in the state schools. Catholic universities have grown alongside state and national universities, but theology is not accepted as a legitimate member of the sciences.

In some countries the Church has recognized the importance of working within the doctrine of the freedom of conscience but has insisted that this not be solely secularism. In these cases the tendency has been to avoid the utilization of the organisms of the State for achieving the goals of the Church. In contrast, the Church has supported freedom for the formation of a religious awareness within its educational structures, advocating a pluralistic system as a part of secular civilization, albeit a system that advocates respect for religion and is not antireligious as in the case of secularism. In the field of teaching, the Church has discovered several new media such as radio, television, newspapers, books, and other publications.

Secularization has slowly produced the freedom of conscience that signifies for the Church the discovery and creation of new ways and means by which to do its work in a pluralistic society. Protestantism, on the other hand, has recognized the possibility not only of its existence but of its growth within this system of secularization. At first this complicated and even worsened the relations between Protestants and Catholics in that liberal governments, secularists, positivists, and others who were struggling against the Church saw in Protestants ready allies. In time, Protestants and Protestantism have acquired a structure more nationalized, and the Church in turn has slowly adapted itself to reality and has been able to begin an ecumenical dialogue.

IV. THE CRISIS WITHIN "POPULAR CATHOLICISM"

In the conclusion of Chapter 6 we indicated that *folk Catholicism* does not represent a mixture of religion; rather, it is simply a religiosity or piety of a people in Christendom. With the disappearance of Christendom, piety of this *cultural* form no longer has the freedom to function and also disappears. The militant Latin American Christian today who has lived within the experience of the ideal of a "new Christendom" (1930– 1962) suffers in his own soul a painful transition from a type of piety supported in Christendom — at least as a future ideal — to a type of piety that can only be exercised in a pluralistic, secular society. This is a crisis in the transition to the level of spirituality, of pastoral theology, of ecclesiastical institutions, and of the ways of carrying out the mission of the laity, priests, and bishops. In general, although the question is intensely debated today by Latin American theologians — for example, as a result of the investigations in Argentina regarding "folk Catholicism" and also in Ecuador in the IPLA, in Mexico City, in Cuernavaca, in Peru, and among university groups in many other countries — there is lacking a universal and historical perspective which in summary form we could propose immediately.[4]

The nineteenth century represents the agony of colonial Christianity. A poetic composition very popular during the period clearly indicates the end of an era.

> Religion is done for; it is gone —
>   Along with virtue and devotion.
> All one can hear now are the cries of passion,
>   The raising of the capricious sword.
> There is now no Holy Father in Rome,
>   No one to bless us.
> O, what a terrible disgrace!
>   There is no King, no Crown.
> Only the sound of war is heard.
>   There are no virtues, not a single one.
> This, in a word, is the situation.
>   There are now no bishops, no priests.
> No one can deny this fact.
>   Religion here is done for. . . .[5]

Beginning with the war of independence, one can see the state of colonial Christianity becoming progressively more precarious. The war was continued as a war of national organization. The Church and the believing masses in "folk Catholicism" began to drift. In a real sense, the war represented the end of an era, the termination of "folk Catholicism" as an adequate expression of the faith for the masses and of the Christian culture that had moved so far from the Christendom that began with Constantine in the fourth century A.D., and which, after a lengthy period of development, expanded into medieval Latin and Hispanic Christianity. The latter subsequently flourished in Latin America and entered an irreversible crisis beginning with the nineteenth century.

What was the origin of the piety of this "popular Catholicism"? Folk Catholicism is well known but has been studied very little, even in Europe where the phenomenon originated and was later brought to America. The Europeans of today are ignorant of the origin of this religious legacy. Israel had its "folk Judaism," the religion practiced by the Jewish people during the kingdoms founded by Samuel and David. Moreover, the Jewish people drifted and deviated from the official cult of the Temple and of the demands of the Law into idolatry, magic, and witchcraft. The prophets in turn threw the cult to foreign idols into the face of the Jewish people. See, for example, Judith 8:18.

Pre-Constantinian Christianity, in contrast, possessed a liturgical vitality adapted to the demands of the diverse communities and did not insist on a *pia devotio* with which the masses were dissatisfied and would in consequence go in search of a substitute. Before Constantine, Christianity had no "popular Catholic" manifestation, rather only a living "Christian piety" that differed from community to community, from diocese to diocese, from church to church, and from East to West.

Under Constantine, the liturgies and rites became unified, and the masses of the empire began to stream into the Church. The market places and the house churches became basilicas. Together with a liturgy no longer understood by the larger community, there appeared supplementary devotions among the masses of people in Christendom, namely Byzantine and Latin "folk Catholicism." Thus the pagan celebration of *Natalis Invicti* of the sun came to signify the birth of Jesus, Sun of Justice, the 25th of December when in the northern hemisphere the sun has just passed an equinoctial point and the days become longer as Spring approaches. Latinized European "folk Catholicism" assumed special characteristics in Spain given the influence of the Visigoths, Arabs, and the local idiosyncrasies of the primitive Hispanic Roman province.

The Amerindian, meanwhile, developed his own primitive piety, which persists in vivid forms even until today. Note, for example, the Inca prayer:

> Pachamamá Santa tierra
> caita cocata regalaskaiki
> ¡Amas apihuaspa!
> Pacha Santa Tierra,
> Amas apihuaspa,
> Ucui orco maicha.[6]

> Pacha mamá, Santa tierra
> de esta coca te regalo.
> ¡No me hagas mal!
> Madre Santa Tierra,
> ¡No me hagas mal!
> por todo el cerro.

> Mother Earth, Holy land,
> to thee I dedicate this plant.
> Do me no wrong or evil!
> Holy Mother Earth,
> Do me no wrong or evil,
> on any part of this hill.

When the devotion of Christendom through the Virgin clashed with this preHispanic piety or religiosity, a certain mixture resulted, as can be seen in this invocation:

> Pachamamita, Santa Tierra,
> Virgen, ayúdanos![7]

> Mother Earth, Holy Land,
> Virgin, help us.

Thus were born the popular devotions to the virgins of Guadalupe, Copacabana, Luján, and others — devotions that manifested the same characteristics of the great cathedrals of Constantinople, Poland, Germany, France, or Santiago de Compostela in Spain. Along with the disappearance of Christendom there occurred the depopulation of the rural areas and a constantly increasing migration of people to the cities. "Folk Catholicism" of the rural type and colonial origin found refuge first in the cities, a visible survivor of the previous era, only to appear later in the secularized functional substitutes in religion. To understand better the total process, we propose the following diagram:

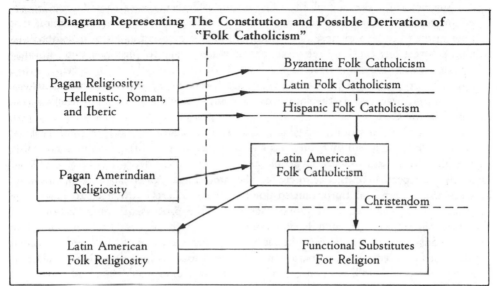

Diagram Representing The Constitution and Possible Derivation of "Folk Catholicism"

In the Latin American culture of the twentieth century, the secular city has progressively deprived our society of the ambiguous unification between values merely cultural and profane with those religious. This deprivation of Christendom's unity is a process that has intensified since the 1960s. "Folk Catholicism" thus drifts at times into a mere popular religiosity as seen in the adoration given to various saints who signify the deification of certain unusual deaths or the apparent miraculous incorruption of corpses. Due to the technological media of communication through magazines, newspapers, and television, there are other widespread substitutes for religion such as horoscopes. Few people in Latin America, nevertheless, are completely devoid of religious inclinations. Moreover, at times, as can be seen in certain urban devotions, carry-overs from Christendom — such as the devotion to St. Cayetano in Buenos Aires — enjoy a very fervent following. This last example represents the final stage of "folk Catholicism," the remains of Christendom — especially among the Spanish and Italian immigrants not yet influenced by the impact of the secular city. The new era, however, has not resolved its contradictions. The solitary individual in the cities, a product of secularized and universal civilization, feels uprooted, devoid of any foundation. Existence appears absurd and without meaning. Having left behind the security of Christendom, and — as a result of the influence of the scientific spirit — having cast aside all superficial piety, the modern urban dweller is unable to confront resolutely the "absence of meaning." Thus recur the functional substitutes for religion, which are, as their name indicates, nothing more than substitutes, crutches for a crippled religious inclination. Underlying the horoscope one reads daily — believing that his or her destiny is somehow predetermined — there is an antihistorical, mythical attitude that attempts to free one from all commitments and that sets forth a secure prototype of physical-natural necessity of primitive man.

The disappearance of "folk Catholicism" is not only a religious and pastoral fact, it is a secular fact. The secularization not only of institutions but also of the intimate life of every human being proceeds along an irreversible course and direction. This situation sets forth globally the entire question of the missionary and prophetic guidance of a Christian congregation in the secular, post-Constantinian, post-Tridentine and, in Latin America, the postcolonial city. The events of recent years should provide sufficient material to allow reflection in the light of faith and also an interpretation that will permit us to catch a glimpse of the meaning of the apparent chaos of developments. Within a forest one can only see trees, and it is necessary to withdraw some distance to enable one to see the forest as a whole. History, even the most recent, is this analogically prophetic perspective that searches for meaning, especially in the history of the Church practiced as theology from a living faith, the search for meaning that history has for God.

At the present, pastorally speaking, one should adopt a balanced and realistic position. Folk Catholicism by nature was and is an expression of the daily understanding of the life of the Latin American people and should not be depreciated nor evaluated from the perspective of the aristocratic, alienated Latin American elite or from an ahistorical, abstract, and Europeanized point of view. There is the need to know how to divest all the inauthentic structures that retard the process of evangelization from folk Catholicism as such, and having done so, begin a process of liberation. The popular consciousness will be reclothed in various manners; one of those — depreciated by the Europeanized Catholic liberal minorities — is folk Catholicism. One should not, however, accept this folk religion casually, as Frantz Fanon would say, and leave it as it is. What is needed is a prophetic critique in order that popular piety or religiosity will begin to move toward a new type of humanity.

Chapter VIII

The Principal Stages in the History of the Church In Politically Neocolonial Latin America

Following independence, the Church in Latin America was absolutely isolated and forced to give up many of its previous advantages and privileges. During this process the Church passed through a veritable "dark night of her history," but later emerged profoundly purified, poor, and adapted to the new situation.

I. THE SIXTH STAGE: THE CRISIS OF THE WARS FOR INDEPENDENCE (1808–1825)

In the struggle for independence the secular and religious clergy played a significant role, even though the hierarchy for the most part adopted an ambiguous position. In view of the fact that the clergy were the most educated people in Latin America at the end of the eighteenth century, their attitude toward Spain and the question of independence was crucial for the success of the struggle for freedom. This explains the fact that immediately following the revolutions, all the governments did not move toward the secularization of society. Very soon, however, the lack of members, the disorganization, the divisions, and the weariness brought about by the wars for independence began to take their toll. As early as 1815 the Paraguayan dictator, José Gaspar Rodríguez de Francia (1816– 1840), abolished the tithe, suppressed religious orders as well as the Inquisition, and established civil marriage. Francia's efforts to make the Church subservient to his will probably stemmed more from his determination to control the ambitious Creoles and Spaniards in the colonial oligarchy than from any theological or anticlerical convictions. By 1820, however, several new national governments had begun to suppress the Church. The discussion of this period will be enlarged not only because new nations arose in Latin America during this time, but also because the period signified for the Church enormous and irretrievable losses, especially of its professors of theology, religious communities, seminaries, churches, and ecclesiastical projects in general. This crisis, together with the missionary crisis in France and in all of Europe, helps to explain the history of Latin America until the beginning of the twentieth century.

1. The Attitude of the Episcopacy

Though it is not possible to examine the position of the higher clergy in every nation, several of the more outstanding examples can be noted. In Mexico, for example, Bishop Friar Antonio de San Miguel of Michoacán brought together a group of legal economists, some of whom were known supporters of the revolution. Other bishops, however, such as Lizana of Mexico City, Primo Feliciano Marín of Monterrey, Llanos of Chiapas, Estévez in the Yucatán, and especially Manuel Ignacio González del Campillo of Pubela, were either indifferent or openly opposed to the revolution. During the second war for independence, however, and primarily as a result of the liberal posture of the Spanish government of 1820 and the action of Canon Monteagudo in 1821, the Mexican episcopacy tended to support the patriots.

In Peru the movement for independence began in 1809, and the first rebellion or uprising occurred in Pumacagua. Bishop José Pérez y Armendáriz in Cuzco did not oppose the insurgents, and when the rebellion was crushed, Pérez was deposed by Ferdinand VII. The other Peruvian bishops supported the royalists against the independence movement, although Silva y Olave, Carrión, and Goyeneche maintained cordial relations with the victorious patriots. It was clear to the Church in Peru, however, that with the end of the colony there would be the loss of the Church's predominance in South America. Furthermore, because of the rich and powerful Spanish organization, the patriots saw the opposition as highly structured. It was the charisma of San Martín that instilled confidence in the Southern struggle for independence. "I cite the importance of what took place in the attainment of freedom and independence of Peru. ... I cite the prodigious triumph of a small group of men coming from such a long distance, half-starved, half-naked, led by a half-dozen generals who were simple, peaceful men, without any more artillery than a cannon, fighting against an army double or triple in number, and situated in its own territory." Thus did Bishop Orihela, in his "Pastoral to the People and Clergy" in February, 1825, eulogize the army of San Martín that originally had been recruited in Mendoza, Argentina.

In the area of the River Plate the situation was quite different. Bishop Lué y Reiga of Buenos Aires opposed the organization of the First Junta, but once it was constituted his opposition ceased. The bishop died, however, in 1812. Bishop Orellana of Córdoba, in contrast, allied himself with the counterrevolutionary movement headed by Liniers and was banished from the country in 1818. Bishop Videla del Pino of Salta was expelled by Belgrano because of support given to a group of royalists. As early as 1812, therefore, the episcopacy began to disappear from Argentina. Uruguay had no bishops. In Bolivia, Bishop Moxó y Francolí of Charcas adopted a more moderate and conciliatory position and even received the triumphant troops who came from Buenos Aires. Unfortunately, however, he also was banished in 1816. Meanwhile, Bishop Remigio de La Santa y Ortega of La Paz, a convinced royalist, returned to Spain in 1814. Bishop Javier de Aldazábal of Santa Cruz did not oppose the revolution, but he died in 1812, and his position remained vacant until 1821. Bishop Roque Antonio de Céspedes of Paraguay was alleged to be insane by the dictator Francia and was thus deposed.

In Chile, the Capitular Vicar, José Santiago Rodríquez Zorilla, was an unalterable royalist, as was Bishop Diego Antonio Martín de Villodres of Concepción, who supported the counterrevolution in 1813. The latter left Chile in 1815 when the victory of the patriots was evident.

The situation was quite distinct in Ecuador, however, where the president of the Second Junta was Bishop Cuero y Caicedo, who also presided over the First Constitutional Congress.

The Reverend Bishop, Don Juan José Caicedo, was one of the most implacable enemies of the royal cause. His pastorals and revolutionary preachings attracted a great number of the clergy, and many religious were extended indulgences by the prelate when they left their offices to defend the country and the cause of liberty. The Bishop also provided arms for many of these roving bands who were dedicated to harassing the royalists and thus strengthened the forces of those who supported the movement for independence.[1]

Andrés Quintián, Bishop of Cuenca, was conversely a convinced royalist and fought consistently against independence.

In Colombia, the Bishop of Santa Fe de Bogotá, Juan Bautista Sacristán, was reluctant to endorse the revolution at first but later adopted a more conciliatory position and was permitted to continue governing his diocese until he died in 1817. The Bishop of Santa Marta, Sánchez Serrudo, followed the example of Sacristán, but Sánchez died in 1813. The Bishop of Cartagena, Carrillo, was expelled from Colombia in 1812 because he refused to accept the revolutionary Junta. Salvador Jiménez de Enciso Padilla became Bishop of Popayán in 1818, and he became one of the major supporters of the revolutionary cause. His explicit support of the new governments can be seen in a letter written to Pius VII in April 1823. Bolívar in turn never ceased to be political, and he always manifested an attitude of prudence and respect toward the Church.

The Bishop of Caracas, Coll y Prat, accepted independence as inevitable and served as an intermediary between the revolutionaries and the Venezuelan Church. He was promptly recalled to Spain, however, and Venezuela was without a bishop for an extended period of time. It was not until 1829 that the Bishop of Guyana was finally consecrated. The acting bishop, Santiago Hernández Milanés, also accepted independence as a foregone conclusion, but he died in 1812.

Finally, the Bishop of Guatemala, Casaus y Torres, attacked the independence movement with an intransigent pastoral but succeeded only in alienating the episcopacy from the revolutionary effort.

It is evident that those bishops who had been named by the *Patronato* system remained for the most part strong supporters of the Crown rather than of the new revolutionary governments. But important for this study is the fact that as a result of their proroyalist sentiments or ambiguity, the disorganization of the hierarchy was virtually complete. There followed a severe decline and even absence of ordinations of priests and monks, the closing of seminaries, the vandalizing and destruction of archives, and the isolation of churches and parishes in every country. And as "medieval Christendom" suffered disunification with the constitution of the new European nation-states — over a period of four or five centuries — in Latin America the "new Christendom," as it was called by Toribio de Mogrovejo, lost its unity in the space of a single decade. Latin American bishops during the colonial era had a sense of belonging to a nation, a feeling reinforced by the fact that a bishop in Peru could be named for Mexico, or one from the area of the River Plate could be appointed to an episcopal post in the North. After independence, however, the Church became an island, and for nearly a century there was virtually no communication between the various national hierarchies. The crisis for the Latin American Church was, therefore, much greater than that suffered by   Church in France after the French revolution, not only because of France's proximity to Rome, but also because of the presence of many other "Christendoms" not affected by the events in France. This allowed the French Church to regroup and reorganize in a relatively short period of time. Latin America, on the other hand, had "suckled at the breast of Spain," and now liberated, it was forced to attempt its reconstruction alone. The whole ecclesiastical structure was in ruins, and rebuilding would have been difficult enough in an environment of peace and order. But the century that followed was one of fratricidal wars and ideological struggles inspired by anti-Christian doctrines. The disorganized Church became in time, therefore, even more anemic. It could not have been otherwise.

2. The Attitude of the Clergy

The priests, who had played a vital role in the colonies, maintained direct contact with the people, not only with the aristocracy, but with the lower classes and Indians as well. These clerics were without doubt the most significant supporters of the revolution. In the beginning the Creole revolutionaries were really an insignificant minority without widespread support. It was only the priests who possessed the twofold advantage of being sufficiently educated and cultured and who also maintained a wide range of contact. The support of the lower clergy proved to be indispensable, therefore, to the liberation movement.

There were at least eight thousand priests in Mexico, but only six of these appear to have supported the revolution initially.[2] The valor and exploits of Fathers Miguel Hidalgo and José María Morelos, both parish priests, are well known. These two clerics incited the uprising of the Indians, as did also Fathers Izquierdo and Magos. In 1815 some 125 priests were executed in Mexico by the Spanish royalists, and the Augustinian convent in Mexico City became one of the primary centers of revolutionary activity during the first period of the struggle for independence. When their sedition was discovered, the entire group was banished. The Presbyter, José María Mercado, who was known for his virtue and was in charge of the army barracks in Guadalajara, determinedly embraced the cause of independence. No less significant was the support given to the initial efforts for revolution by Fathers Monteagudo, Pimentel, and Arcediano de Valladolid.

In Peru many of the religious were involved in the uprising in Pumacagua. In the viceroyalty, however, the clergy were less fervent in their support of the revolution.

In Argentina, in contrast, the participation of the clergy was decisive not only in their support of the revolutionary cause, but also in their individual involvement. Friar Ignacio Grela was one of the first who protested the election of Cisneros as President of the Junta, and seventeen priests signed the petition presented to the City Council requesting the naming of a new Junta. Father Funes, Dean of the Cathedral in Córdoba, helped to abort the counterrevolution of Liniers, which was, as mentioned earlier, supported by Bishop Orellana. The Chaplain of the Army of San Martín, Friar Luís Beltrán, expropriated the bells from various convents and directed the construction of the cannons that were used in the liberation of Chile. Beltrán is referred to as "the first engineer of the army of liberation." Of the twenty-nine representatives commissioned by the provinces to sign the Act of Independence on July 9, 1816, in the Assembly of Tucumán, sixteen were Roman Catholic priests.

In Uruguay, Vigodet wrote to Bishop Lué y Reiga of Buenos Aires that it would be futile to attempt to restore order and tranquility on the Eastern border for, he asserted, it was the pastors and priests who were bent on sowing discord, a clear reference to the incipient revolutionary movement. Vigodet   led that virtually all the secular and regular clergy were involved in the revolutionary ferment.[3] The fact is that the Uruguayan clergy manifested the same attitude toward revolution as did those in Argentina as well as in Bolivia.

On the night in 1809 that the decision was made in Ecuador to raise the "first shout" of revolution, three priests were involved. They concluded their meeting by singing the Salve Regina. Father Rodríguez, Professor of theology in the seminary, was the author of the Ecuadorian Constitution, a document that manifests the most recent philosophical and political concepts of the nineteenth century. The royalists responded, however, by expelling many of the clergy involved in the independence movement.

Three members of the Metropolitan Chapter, along with a group of presbyters, took part in the Colombian uprising of July 1810. The royalist Morillo promptly imprisoned several of the priests for their revolutionary activities. In "El Calí" Friar Joaquín Escobar served as president. The Dominican covent of Chiquinquirá — as hundreds of others in Latin America — decided to turn over to the revolutionary government all their properties, those held in common and individually, as well as the money and other objects of gold in order to aid the new State.

The clergy was much more divided in Venezuela. Canon José Cortés de Madariaga and nine other priests played an important role in the 1811 Congress in Caracas which declared the independence of Venezuela.

In Central America the clergy was also divided. The patriotic *tertulia* of Guatemala met in the house of Father José Castilla, and the group became an integral part of the revolutionary movement. Secret revolutionary meetings also took place in Belén. When the Capitan General learned of these clandestine meetings, the participants were severely punished. Father José Matías Delgado inspired the revolutionary movements in El Salvador. In the meeting of the Assembly of Guatemala in 1821, Canon Dr. José María Castilla cast the first vote for the declaration of independence, which was subsequently signed by twenty-eight individuals, thirteen of whom were priests. Not the least significant of these events was the insistence by Dr. Simón Cañas, himself a priest, who included the rights of citizenship for the Negroes, "our brother slaves" as they were called.

It is obvious that the participation of the clergy in the revolutionary movements in Latin America was crucial. The fact is, however, that the revolution itself had in various areas two stages, and that in all of Latin America there developed afterwards two opposing governments which succeeded in harassing the clergy, the most influential persons of the society. Expulsion, death, imprisonment, disorientation, activism, and unchecked anxiety separated the priests for many decades from their pastoral responsibility. The tragic situation resulted in the priests' adopting a very compromising position. But their compromise stemmed from the fatigue, annihilation, disorganization, and lack of continuity in their priestly endeavors. Also, guerrilla or political priests found it difficult to return to their previous life of the apostolate. It was inevitable that the Church, virtually having burned itself out, should complete its mission by sacrificing itself to the point of exhaustion.

3. The Attitude of the New Governments

The general position of the new governments was as follows: in view of the fact that the revolutionaries were a minority and not the entire population, the new governments were more or less liberal, but initially they were profoundly Catholic — even to the point of being intolerant toward other religions. They nevertheless proceeded to adopt disciplinary and economic measures in keeping with the conditions of the *Patronato*, which almost ruined the already disorganized Church that had barely survived the crisis of the independence. Throughout this period as well as during the following one (1825—1850), the governments were more conservative than liberal. It is impossible to imagine a more radical change in so short a period of time.

The general policy followed by the new governments was to initiate direct relations with Rome. But Rome was deeply committed to Madrid and the Holy Alliance. Even so, little by little the Holy See regained its independence and began to pursue two ends. The first was an attempt to gain indirect recognition of the independence of Latin America, the moral value of which was essential. Then there was the effort to free the Church from the actual and official subordination resulting from the national *Patronato* system. But the new national governments could hardly have imagined themselves as having less power than that exercised by Spain. It was as much a question of prestige, however, as it was of power.

In Mexico the popular religious character of the revolution can be seen in the Constitution of Apatzingan of 1814, which declared, "The Roman, Apostolic, Catholic religion is the only faith which should be professed by the State" (Chapter One) and that "heresy, apostasy, or high treason would result in the loss of citizenship. Temporary residents or transients would be protected by the state ... if they acknowledge the sovereignty and independence of the nation and respect the Roman, Apostolic, and Catholic religion" (Chapter Three). When Agustín de Iturbide was able to take advantage of a chaotic situation produced by the Spanish revolution of 1821 to unite the ruling class of Creoles and Spanish under an independent, limited monarchy, he retained the established Church. The liberalism of the Spanish Court inclined the Church toward the support of the cause of Independence. The Guadalajara government's *Gaceta (Gazette)* of July 11, 1821, reported, "It would be impossible for us to propose a better defense for the cause of Independence than to affirm that this government will retain the Roman, Apostolic, Catholic religion, so violated and slandered in the parliamentary reports of the States General of 1820" (the Spanish parliament).[4] Father Pradt, who desired to direct the Mexican Church (the only example of this type in Latin America), proposed to free the Church of Mexico from all obedience to Rome. The measures taken in 1821, such as the suppression of the convents and the confiscation of Church properties, appeared to have been greatly influenced by him. José María Luis Mora proposed the complete separation of Church and State, but during the decade of 1820—1830 the two most important religious parties were the ecclesiastics who considered the *Patronato* null and void, thus allowing the Church to recover its freedom, and the politicians who attempted to maintain intact the conditions of the *Patronato* system.

In Peru, San Martín assumed all the powers of the *Patronato* to the point of being abusive, and the procedures of Monteagudo were even more negative. The aged Bishop Las Heras decided to retire. The Church in turn was deprived of all ecclesiastical ties, the Spanish priests were suspended, the novitiates of the religious were closed, and the taking of vows was prohibited for those under the age of thirty years. Furthermore, the government imposed upon all religious orders a special tax designed to assist the fledgling nation. In 1826 the government stripped the Church of all it convents but a short time later returned them primarily because of the poor results that came from the operation. The *Patronato* was, nevertheless, integrally exercised by the government of Peru.

In Argentina the piety of Belgrano, San Martín, and Pueyrredon — somewhat less political — contrasted with the liberalism of Castelli and later of Bernardino Rivadavia. At least seventeen priests lost the right to hear confessions because of their continued support for the royalist cause. Seventeen other clerics along with thirty-two religious were expelled from the country for the same reason. The constant interference by the Argentine government in the life of the convents began to undermine an already undisciplined religious life. In the Assembly of 1813 the government assumed all the rights of the *Patronato*, the religious hospitals were expropriated, the Inquisition was suspended, the administration of the tithes was regulated, the religious were declared to be independent of all foreign authority, all concessions to the Church were abolished, and the bishop was declared to be the only ecclesiastical authority in the country. These and other steps were taken to control the Church despite the fact that twelve priests were present as members of the Assembly and that Article 19 stated that "the Roman and Apostolic Catholic religion is the only religion of the State." In October 1822 a more comprehensive project for the reform of the clergy was presentd with the endorsement of Bernardino Rivadavia. It called for the abolition of the personal code of laws for the clergy, the abolition of the tithes, and the closing of all convents with less than sixteen members. This wave of liberalism dominated Argentina for a time and ultimately caused the failure of the Muzi mission in the country.

In Paraguay, the dictator Francia was in complete control. He had received his doctorate in Canonical Law from the University of Córdoba del Tucumán, but he never received major orders.

In Chile, the Catholic religion was declared to be the official religion of the State in 1812 as well as in 1818, even though the government was more liberal in 1812 and more conservative in 1818. It was during the latter period that O'Higgins, and above all Cienfuegos, made possible the Muzi mission. As early as 1823, however, the climate was changing, primarily because of the influence of events in Buenos Aires, and the process of secularization began with the confiscation of the religious properties and the closing of convents with less than eight members or where there were two or more convents in a single city. The political situation in Chile continued to be influenced by events in Argentina until 1827, even though on January 3, 1820, the Congress of Antofagasta manifested a desire to establish relations with the Holy See.

In Bolivia the reform of the religious was initiated in August 1825. Both Bolívar and Sucre desired to establish relations with the Holy See.

In Ecuador, Bolívar was unusually cautious in his relations with the Church. The First Article of the Constitution of the Province of Cuenca declared that "The Catholic, Roman, and Apostolic religion will be the only religion adopted by the Republic, and in the future no other religion will be tolerated for any reason whatsoever." During this early period of independence, there is no indication that the Liberals in Quito exercised the slightest influence.

In Colombia and Venezuela, the geographical area where Bolívar worked so strenuously, the religious issue became one of the primary causes for the separation of the area into two nations. In 1811 all the leaders of independence vowed "to defend with their lives and with all their power the states of the Venezuelan Confederation and to conserve and to maintain pure and unscathed the Holy Roman Apostolic religion, the unique and only religion of these countries." Bolívar himself had vowed on the *Monte Sacro* after meeting personally with Pius VII in 1805, "I swear by the God of my fathers ... and I swear by my country that I will never rest until the chains of the Spanish will to power which bind us are broken." In 1814 Antonio Nariño ordered the expropriation of the jewels of certain convents to defray the costs of the revolutionary armies. On the other hand, Bolívar manifested a desire in 1817 to fill the vacant bishoprics as "in the most illustrious centuries of the Church."

As early as 1820 the Masonic lodges began to organize in Venezuela, and in Mexico the Bishop of Mérida, Monseñor Lasso, stated that the Church would benefit if separated from the State. In the Congress of Cúcuta in 1821 Bolívar reaffirmed the *Patronato* powers of the state. Colombian representatives were sent to the Holy See in 1822 and 1823 for the purpose of dealing with the question of the Concordat, and also to arrange for the resumption of the missions to the Indians. Unfortunately, these attempts were all unsuccessful. The Law of the *Patronato* was signed in Bogotá on July 28, 1824. Two years later matrimony was declared to be legal only if performed by the courts or civil tribunals, and on July 26, 1826, all convents with less than eight members were closed.

Guatemala is an example of the spirit of fidelity to the Church in all of Central America, for in June of 1823 the government declared, "The religion of the United Provinces is Catholic, Roman, and Apostolic, with the exclusion of all others."

It should be noted, however, that the crisis of neocolonial emancipation that prevailed throughout Spanish America did not have the same impact in the Caribbean or in Brazil. Cuba, for example, did not gain independence from Spain until 1898. The Dominican Republic was occupied by Haiti from 1822 until 1844 and thereafter became an independent country. Puerto Rico gained its independence from Spain in 1898 but became a protectorate of the United States. The relationship of the Church to the governments of these islands continued relatively unchanged.

In Brazil, the political sagacity of the King of Portugal led to the creation of the Brazilian Empire under Pedro I, thus allowing the great Lusitanian colony to gain independence without crisis or war. The benevolent rule of Pedro II in Brazil from 1841 until 1889 explains the institutional continuity of the country, its coherent foreign policy, and its progress toward the conquest of the no-man's-land of the Amazon basin during the nineteenth century. While its neighbors — Venezuela, Colombia, Ecuador, Peru, Bolivia, Paraguay, Argentina, and Uruguay — were being exhausted by the internecine struggles for national organization, Brazil was moving toward becoming the primary power in South America. The transition from Empire to Republic in the latter decades of the nineteenth century was for Brazil a logical and mature step in its progress.

During this initial period of nation building, the Church suffered its greatest crisis, and at the same time the new nation-states began their search for a new mode of being. The governments, although inspired by liberalism, were basically conservative, and the anticlerical measures were not in the nature of a persecution, but rather a reform — as it was called in that period — which the governments were able to achieve by their use of the *Patronato*. The phrase "the Catholic, Roman, and Apostolic Church" repeatedly appears in the national constitutions, an indication of the fact that a thorough transformation was not achieved and that all the new governments desired to be recognized by the Papacy, which was seen by the Latin Americans as the major European spiritual power.

II. THE SEVENTH STAGE AND THE DEEPENING CRISIS (1825–1850)

Although there were exceptions, this period was less liberal than the preceding one, especially in regard to the measures taken by Rome. At the same time, however, a movement for true institutional and ideological revolution began. The period actually represents a time of pacification and deliberate organization of the new groups that would be in control for the succeeding fifty years.

1. The Antecedents of the Attitude of the Holy See[5]

From Europe the phases of emancipation were fourfold:

(1) Bayona resigned in 1808, and Ferdinand VII was restored to the Spanish throne in 1814. Meanwhile, Miranda began his revolutionary movement in 1808 and quickly discovered that the patriots needed direct contact with Rome. Such contact was,

however, extremely difficult in view of the impediments Spain could interpose. In 1813 Pius VII proposed an encyclical to the Latin American clergy favoring the revolution, but the Papacy had no direct knowledge of the American situation.

(2) The restoration of Ferdinand VII (1814– 1817) produced a regression in the emancipation movement to the point that only Argentina could maintain independence after the expedition of Morillo against Nueva Granda. Güemes, a *caudillo* of Salta, Argentina, permitted the reorganization of the liberation effort. The Holy See named twenty-eight new bishops for thirty-eight posts between 1814 and 1820, although many of them never were able to assume their responsibilities. On January 30, 1816, Pius VII issued an encyclical to the archbishops and bishops of Spanish America entreating them to attempt to persuade their followers to submit to the authority of King Ferdinand.

You can easily accomplish the suppression of disorders and sedition if each one of you is willing to expose zealously the dangers and grave evils of defections and will expound the noble and exceptional qualities and virtues of our dear Son and your King, Ferdinand, Catholic King of Spain, to whom nothing is more important than religion and the happiness of his subjects; and finally, let us cite the illustrious example, which should never perish, of the Spanish people who did not hesitate to sacrifice goods and life in showing their adherence to religion and fidelity to the King.[6]

The Pope was obviously committed to the Holy Alliance and acted accordingly.

(3) The inability and disaster of Ferdinand VII (1818– 1823) in his attempt to suppress the translantic revolutions is evident, as is the failure of his attempts in Aquisgrán. Moreover, in 1820 the revolution of Riego began, and the troops that were destined to leave Cádiz to quell the uprising in Buenos Aires were suddenly involved in a civil conflict in Spain. The result was that the insurrection in Argentina spread to Chile and finally to Peru. Meanwhile, the Bourbon absolutism collasped in Spain, and the government was taken over by the Liberals, producing a situation that allowed the American patriots to pressure the Latin American Church to support the emancipation from Spain. At the same time reports arrived in Rome from Bishop Orellana of Córdoba del Tucumán, from Father Pacheco, and from the Archbishops of Caracas and Lima, but it was the communications from Bishop Lasso de la Vega which prompted Pius VII to decree in 1823 a pontifical neutrality in regard to the situation in Latin America.

(4) King Ferdinand was liberated anew by the Holy Alliance (Verona, 1823), and France began to consider Latin America as the locale for the ideal monarchy — even though America was republican because of French inspiration! The Monroe Doctrine, however, declared "America for the Americans." Bolívar and his forces arrived in Peru, and following the battles of Junín and Ayacucho on December 9, 1824, the Spanish forces were finally defeated. Great Britain's foreign minister, George Canning, formally recognized Grand Colombia, Argentina, and Mexico on December 16, 1824. During this same period Monseñor José Ignacio Cienfuegos was appointed Chief of Mission to Rome by the Chilean dictator Bernardo O'Higgins. Cienfuegos was instructed to declare the loyalty of the Chilean people to the Holy See as well as to request from the Pope an apostolic nuncio and to send to Chile auxiliary bishops to fill the vacancies. As a temporary measure, Cienfuegos proposed that an apostolic vicar be sent to Chile, and after prolonged discussion, Monseñor Juan Muzi was appointed. When Friar Pacheco insisted that La Plata was in greater need than Chile, Muzi's jurisdiction was enlarged to include all of America. Muzi wrote his famous *Cartas apologéticas (Letters of Defense)* and proceeded to organize the diocese of Mon-

tevideo. When Spain protested the Pope's appointment of an apostolic vicar, Cardinal Consalvi persuaded Leo XI to recognize the importance of the Latin American question and insisted that "Spanish legitimacy no longer implied any authority whatsoever."[7]

Rome seemed to take a step backward, however, with the encyclical *Etsi iam diu*, issued on September 24, 1824, the existence of which is definitively demonstrated:[8] "We have received the ill-fated news of the deplorable situation in which discord and rebellion are being sown in the Church as well as in the State" (the original text says: *"superseminata est hic zizaniz homine inimico"*).[9] The most "interesting paragraph," as it is called by Vargas Laguna, addresses ". . . our very dear son Ferdinand, Catholic King of Spain, whose sublime and solid virtues cause him to place before the splendor of his greatness the luster of religion and the happiness of his subjects."[10]

Obviously the patriots could not accept this encyclical, and they responded to it by insisting that it was apocryphal or was falsified by the Spanish. The fact was that the pressure by Ferdinand on Leo XI was so intense that the Pope almost acquiesced but finally decided against the Spanish cause.

2. The Constructive Attitude of the Holy See since 1825

The Tejada delegation, which Bolívar sent to the Vatican and which first recommended that the bishops communicate directly with Rome, helped considerably the cause of Nueva Granada. Rome proposed the naming of bishops *in partibus* so as not to offend further the Spanish king. On November 22, 1825, France, Russia, Austria, and Spain opposed all "concessions of a spiritual nature, because they believed that they were a de facto recognition."[11] Tejada warned of the danger of a religious schism in Spanish America (1826)[12] and offered a list of candidates for the various bishoprics. On January 18, 1827, Cardinal Capelari presented to Leo XII the bishops for Grand Colombia, not *in partibus*, but rather "proprietary." This decision, together with the attached brief, was the culmination of the religious policy of Bolívar, and it produced an instantaneous change of opinion that persisted for many decades. And Rome, after seventeen years, had spoken clearly for the first time. On October 28, 1827, Bolívar declared in a public discourse: "The greatest cause that brings us together today is the wellbeing of the Church and the wellbeing of Colombia. . . . The descendants of St. Peter have always been our fathers, but the war has left us orphans, as a . . . lamb that bleats in vain for its lost mother."[13]

The Vásquez mission from Mexico failed in 1829, and the same year Joaquín Pérez, Bishop of Puebla, died and left Mexico without a single bishop.

Ferdinand VII briefly broke relations with Rome, and Leo XII was obliged to retreat anew (1828–1829); nevertheless, thinking above all of Argentina where there was not a single bishop, and of Chile, he was reported to have exclaimed, "I will give my blood for my king, but I will not give my soul." And "his soul" was the responsibility of providing bishops for the vacant sees in Latin America. After prolonged and painful negotiations, Vicuña y Larraín Salas was named for Santiago and Cienfuegos for Concepción. Pius VII, well aware of the American problems, named Friar Justo Santa María de Oro as the first Bishop of Cuyo—Mendoza, San Juan, and San Luis, Argentina—who had been presented on January 11, 1828, elevated on December 15 of the same year, and finally consecrated by Cienfuegos on his trip to Chile on December 21, 1830. Thus in a matter of a few years the Argentine episcopacy was reorganized. Pius VIII, however, failed in his negotiations with the Mexican government.

Gregory XVI (1831–1835), in his first consistory of February 28, 1831, named residential bishops for Mexico. Pablo Vázquez was consecrated as Bishop of Puebla, and he proceeded to ordain the other five. Madrid was not in a position to prevent what was an accomplished fact, and Mexico in turn was ecstatic because of the naming of the six new prelates.[14]

Several other residential bishops were also named, those who had been before consecrated *in partibus:* Medrano for Buenos Aires on March 20, 1832, and Vicuña on July 2, 1832, Cienfuegos on December 17, 1832, de Oro on September 3, 1834, Lazcano for Córdoba on December 30, 1834. Gregory XVI also established the Apostolic Vicariate of Montevideo on August 2, 1832, naming Larrañaga as the first vicar on August 14 of the same year. Because of the political instability and the lack of clergy, Montevideo continued for several decades as only a diocese.

On three occasions (1821, 1825, and 1828) reports and lists of priests were sent from Peru to Rome for the purpose of their being named as bishops. Luís José Orbegaso began negotiations with Rome, and Jorge Benavente was named Bishop of Lima on June 23, 1834. Francisco Javier Luna Pizarro was consecrated as Archbishop of Lima in 1846 in the category of *in partibus infidelium.*

On August 5, 1831, Gregory XVI issued his encyclical *Sollicitudo Ecclesiarum,* which served to prepare for the recognition of the new American republics, "more respectful of the Holy See than the current Spanish government" (of María Cristina). On November 26, 1835, Gregory XVI formally recognized the independence of the republic of Nueva Granada, that is, Colombia, and on December 5, 1836, he recognized the independence of Mexico. Other formal recognitions of national independence were to follow, but the question of political recognition for the new American nations was settled.

Finally, O'Leary of Venezuela exclaimed in Rome on April 9, 1839, "It is said (by the Pope) that we change ministers too frequently, and that revolutions in Latin America are eternal, et cetera. I said to him that France has had more revolutionary movements in these past eight years than Venezuela, and ten times more changes of ministers. . . . It is very difficult to work with these people!"

The insistence by the new governments — against Spain, and at times against Europe as a whole, and even against Rome — that they establish direct relations with the successor of Peter, clearly indicates that the Catholicism of the ancient Spanish American colonies was far from being superficial. In reality, it was an essential element of the collective consciousness. That this was true speaks of the positive and profound character of Spanish evangelization.

3. The Church and the Conservative State

In each country the Church had to conform to the demands of concrete events and to develop a means of relating to the new and inexperienced governments.

In Brazil, this era was dominated by Pedro II who came to power in 1831 at the age of six, when Pedro I abdicated. Pedro II governed as emperor from 1841 to 1889. Though Catholic in his faith, Pedro II was profoundly monarchical and absolutist in the exercise of power, and the Church was obliged to subordinate itself to the State. In addition, many outstanding members of the Church belonged to the Masonic lodges. Thus, Pius IX's condemnation of Masonry resulted in a wave of negative reaction in Brazil against the Papacy. The Church was situated between three poles: the State, which exercised the *Padroado* of Portugal, the Liberal parties, and Masonry. The *Irmandades* began in 1872 with a widespread anticlerical campaign. Despite these social and political convulsions, the entire period was basically conservative, as it was in all the countries to be considered.

In Mexico this period (1824– 1857) terminated with the coming to power of the Liberals and the proclamation of the Juárez law, the Lerdo law, and the Iglesias law, which confiscated the properities of the Church, prohibited any financial subsidies from the government to the parishes, made matrimony a civil act, and declared that Roman Catholicism was no longer the religion of the State. Herein began the first great rupture between Church and State, which would be augmented and structured under the dictatorship of Porfirio Díaz. The Masons were well organized beginning in 1825 and slowly became the primary power group in Mexican politics. Santa Ana, first a Liberal and then a Conservative, is an example of the instability of this era (which progressed from the *puros* to the *moderados*). There was, however, no significant change for the Church. In 1827 Dominique de Pradt enumerated the personnel of the Mexican Church as one archbishop, nine bishops, 1,194 parishes, 3,483 secular priests, 1,240 of whom were dedicated to the *cura animarum*, six monastic orders, 151 convents, 969 religious — 323 of whom were members of the *Propaganda*, 101 were missionaries, and forty were in parishes — and a total Mexican population of eight million.[15]

From the time of its discovery by Alvar Núñez Cabeza de Vaca until the founding of Santa Fe in 1610, the area known as the Southwest was slowly developed in the north of New Spain with the regions of New California, New Mexico, and San Luís de Potosí, which included the present North American states of Texas, New Mexico, Arizona, California, Utah, Nevada, and Colorado. In 1803 Napoleon ceded Louisiana to the United States, giving birth to the doctrine of Manifest Destiny — which ultimately legitimized for the North Americans their expansion to the Pacific Coast. The occupation of the Mexican territory was slow and deliberate. The Mexican federalists, including those from the Yucatán to those north of the Río Grande, were strongly opposed to Santa Ana. The North Americans meanwhile encouraged the federalist spirit until the Texas revolution in 1835– 1836. Santa Ana crushed the weak resistance of the Texans at the Battle of the Alamo in San Antonio, which prompted Sam Houston to declare war and gain the independence of Texas, which remained an independent nation until 1845. Mexico finally ceded the entire region including California to the United States in 1848. Thus there exists in the United States a large number of Latin Americans, a nation of Spanish-speaking people who are virtually without the Church and relegated to their "folk Catholicism."[16]

Central America was unified in the Confederation from 1824 to 1839, but its relations with the Holy See were tenuous and difficult primarily because of the presence of the semischismatic Bishop Delgado of San Salvador. The Conservative governments of Rafael Carrera (1839– 1865), Francisco Ferrer (1840– 1853), and of the "Conservative Regime" in San Salvador (1839– 1871) did not, however, produce any significant change. The confiscation of ecclesiastical properties began in 1822, and the Dominicans, known for their wealth, lost more than the other religious orders. They had founded, for example, five cities around Lake Amatitlán. In 1818 the Archbishopric of Guatemala had seventeen vicariates, 131 parishes, 424 churches, 85 missions in the valleys, 914 in the haciendas, and 910 in the sugar plantations, and a total of 1,720 brothers and 505,000 parishioners.[17]

In 1824 the Republic of Colombia declared the *Patronato* in force, which resulted in innumerable and lamentable abuses on the part of the government and its continual interference in ecclesiastical issues and problems. The instability resulting from the resignation of Bolívar in 1830 continued indefinitely in Colombia. The government of Santander (1832– 1837) is another example of tyranny. José Ignacio Márquez clashed openly with the Church, and José Hilario López's Liberal government (1849– 1886) in 1849 produced the first open schism between the Church and the State in Latin America. The conflict between the Conservatives and Liberals has always been exceedingly violent in Colombia and apparently has been detrimental for both parties.

In Venezuela there were 200 fewer priests in 1837 than there had been in 1810. There was only one priest in Guyana, and in the plains of Apuré the people had only auxiliary priests. Some had died, others had emigrated, still others had been exiled not only by the royalists but also by the patriots. If the situation was difficult for the Church during the war years, it worsened as a result of the enforcement of the new laws. The government of José Antonio Páez (1829–1846) attempted to normalize relations and manifested some concern for the deterioration of the missions.

In Ecuador the government of Juan José Flores (1829–1834) and of Vicente Rocafuerte (1835–1839) proclaimed that the "Roman and Apostolic Catholic Religion" was the official religion of the State to the exclusion of all others. Despite this fact, Rocafuerte allowed the introduction of Protestantism into Ecuador. The anticlerical reaction was stemmed by the government of Gabriel García Moreno (1860–1875).

Peru experienced a prolonged period of instability from 1823 to 1845, with nine different presidents or dictators. The governments of Ramón Castilla and of José Rufino Echenique (1845–1862) established some equilibrium in public affairs. Roman Catholicism was declared to be the official religion of the State with the exclusion of all others. Thus in 1915, when Protestant groups attempted to organize missions among the Indians, they were forbidden on the basis that it was contrary to the Constitution.

The ecclesiastical reform of Rivadavia (1826) in Argentina almost resulted in the disappearance of the religious orders. The dictator Juan Manuel de Rosas (1835–1852) achieved a significant measure of national unity, even though his means for doing so were despotic, such as the lamentable *mazorcas*.[18] Rosas was in reality a Conservative and manifested respect for the Church. He even invited the Jesuits to return to Argentina. The party slogan during his rule became "religion or death." The *caudillos* were still in control of various provinces, however, and one of them, Justo José de Urquiza of Entre Ríos, together with other opponents of Rosas, were able to overthrow him. But the Constitution of 1853 maintained "the Roman and Apostolic Catholic religion" as the religion of the Argentine nation. It was with the triumph of Buenos Aires, thanks to Bartolomé Mitre in 1861, that the break with the past became clearly evident.

In Uruguay the conflict between the *Blancos* and the *Colorados* (1830–1852) divided the country for three decades. Once Monseñor Larrañaga died, his successors were unable to halt the deterioration in the Church that followed the war. Free commerce between England, France, and Uruguay introduced early the European ideologies, and eventually a liberal elite developed that has governed the country until the present.

In Chile the Conservatives, the *pelucones* or "bigwigs," were in control from 1831 until 1861, while Ramón Freire and other Liberals, the *pipiolos* or "novices," were exiled. The Constitution of 1833 declared that the State would exercise the *Patronato* but simultaneously indicated that Roman Catholicism was the official religion of the State and that all other religions were excluded. The true religious state of affairs, however, can be seen in the fact that in 1831 there were only 147 priests for the 60,000 inhabitants in Santiago, a ratio of only one to four thousand.

Dean Friar Matías de Terrazas wrote to the Pope from Bolivia: "There are eighty parishes which are vacant in this country ... which have not been attended because of the disruptions of the war. In all of the Bolivian Republic there is not a single bishop. ... We must turn to the Republic of Bajo Perú where there are only two bishops, in Cuzco and in Arequipa, who are 1,500 kilometers away."[19] When Andrés de Santa Cruz (1829– 1839) began his dictatorial government, peace was imposed by force, but from 1840 until 1864 there was political chaos. The Church was unable to develop in this climate.

4. The European Missionary Crisis

Another factor which should not be overlooked is that Spanish America had depended upon the assistance of the *Patronato* for its missionaries. Once the countries were independent, the *Patronato* ceased to exist as an institution, and at the same time there was a severe decline in the number of European missionaries,[20] all of which left the new American republics in a state of religious abandonment. The Secretary of the Congregation of Propaganda expounded on the painful situation in 1773, saying that the expulsion of the Jesuits, the French Revolution, and the struggles between royalists and republicans in Europe simply aggravated an already critical situation.

As a result of the wars for independence in Latin America, virtually all the missions were in a terrible state of disorganization. In Chile, for example, with the closing of the Seminary of Chillán (1811) and with the expulsion of the last thirty-one missionaries in 1817, the missions among the Indians ceased to function. The Franciscans who had replaced the Jesuits in the *reducciones* of Paraguay were likewise expelled in 1810, and the 106,000 Guaraní dispersed into the jungles while their church buildings and villages were looted by Bolivian, Paraguayan, and Portuguese colonists. Some advances, however, were achieved in Peru with the creation of the mission stations of Conibos and Sendis in 1812.

During the pontificacy of Gregory XVI, the Franciscans were expelled from Texas, New Mexico, and California (1833– 1834). By not reinforcing these missions, Mexico in effect invited the United States to take over these territories. The 30,000 Indians whom the Franciscans had evangelized and civilized were dispersed, and in 1908 only 3,000 of them remained. They became no more than vagabonds and beggars.

One can observe, however, a slow reawakening. Andrés Herrero, a Franciscan who was Commissioner General of the Missions in Spanish America, in 1834 commissioned a group of twelve Franciscans to evangelize the Indians of Bolivia. The Indians, incidentally, constituted the majority of the population. A short time later eighty-three other Franciscans were commissioned for Bolivia. Catholic schools reopened in Peru, Chile, and Bolivia, and in 1843 the Dominicans returned to Peru. In 1849 feminine congregations (nuns) began to arrive in Brazil and continued to come in significant numbers until 1872, even though the government closed the novitiates of all the religious orders from 1854 until 1891 when the Church was separated from the State. Pius IX, as a young canon, was in Chile in 1825. The flourishing missionary activity in Latin America in the nineteenth century began with him.

During this entire period, however, the Church was further weakened. The economic, political, and intellectual climate reminds one of those times in history that represent the end of an era, in this case the end of the colonial empire and of Latin American Christendom. It was an agonizing period not unlike the barbarian invasion of Europe, and at the same time a little hope for the future was slowly being generated. Subsequently the deepening crisis appeared to erase all possibilities of a solution. If Christianity continued it was more because of inertia and the valor and generosity of a few rather than the faithfulness and commitment of the many. The people maintained the testimony of colonial Chistianity, but the new elite governments, who were in fact the nucleus of a new civilization, turned their backs on the past and likewise on the Church.

The conditions in the universities, the few that existed, worsened along with the reorganized seminaries; neither one nor the other was able to stimulate any widespread intellectual activity. Theological and philosophical texts did not arrive from Spain, and the Church lacked the means of publication. The stimuli for a renaissance simply were exhausted, and all hope was lost for a future renovation.

III. THE EIGHTH STAGE: THE FINAL RUPTURE (1850–1930)

At the level of *civilization* the Latin American nations began to feel the enormous Anglo-Saxon impact from Great Britain and North America, an impact which was in reality neocolonialist with its commerce, technology, and schools of engineering. On the level of *culture* and of the *mythical-nucleus*, liberalism for the first time made an impact on the opinion of the political-cultural elite. This resulted in a veritable transformation of the elements of the collective Latin American conscience, first at the level of the institutions and subsequently among the populace as a whole. A pluralistic society, a secular civilization developed in Latin America and is a twentieth-century fact — especially in the large cities, the universities, the labor unions, and among the ruling minorities.

1. The Church and the Liberal State

The schism was at times imperceptible, but in general it began in 1850. The separation of Church and State in Brazil was delayed until the formation of the Republic in 1889, even though the Liberals had been in control for many years. Positivism had a growing influence in Brazil beginning in 1870, and it was in fact an ideological element in the Constitution that formalized the separation of Church and State on an institutional level.

In Argentina Liberalism burst forth with Mitre and Sarmiento, but an open clash between the Church and the government did not ensue. The Law of Lay Teaching (1884) signified at the popular level a severe blow to the collective conscience of the type of colonial "New Christendom."

In Chile the Liberals (1861–1891), beginning with José Joaquín Pérez, produced a period of political and religious peace. President Aníbal Pinto (1876–1881), however, attempted to decree the freedom of religion and civil matrimony. The latter was accepted and put into effect beginning in 1884. Nevertheless, reaction of José Manuel Balmaceda (1886–1891) and his tragic fall from power impeded the separation of Church and State, which was finally promulgated by the Constitution of 1925.

The *Colorados* were in control in Uruguay during this entire period (1852–1903). The separation of Church and State came, however, in 1917, together with a veiled religious persecution and a wave of antireligious sectarianism. The laws of secularization and laicism were decreed during this period. In 1856 José Benito Lamas was named the first Bishop of Montevideo, and in 1897 the Uruguayan capital became an Archbishopric.

In Paraguay, under the governments of both Carlos Antonio López (1841–1862) and his son, Francisco Solano López (1862–1870), the *Patronato* was exercised, and the Church remained under government control. The war with the combined forces of Argentina, Uruguay, and Brazil, which continued from 1864–1870 — surely the most inexplicable and savage war in Latin American history—left the Paraguayan society in a state of unequaled decadence. The Church did not escape the consequences of this internal crisis.

An attempt by Bolivia to establish a Concordat with the Vatican failed in 1851 and again in 1884. There was political chaos from 1864 until 1870 during the government of Mariano Melgarejo. With the election of Narciso Campero in 1880 the Conservative government maintained cooperative relations with the Church. When the Liberal party regained control in 1898, however, the situation changed. Freedom of religion was decreed in 1906, officially permitting the diffusion of Protestantism.

There was a prolonged period of instability in Peru until the election of the government of Nicolás Piérola (1895–1899). No fundamental changes occurred at the institutional level, but at the cultural level positivism began to exercise significant influence within the society. This was followed by several indigenous and socialistic movements that signified the various currents of thinking, and by individuals who were developing an authentic pluralism of thought in the country.

In Ecuador the militant Catholic Christian, Gabriel García Moreno (1860–1875), reinforced the union of Church and State established by the Concordat of 1862. The first Provincial Council convened in 1863, but when the Liberals again came to power in 1897 the Concordat was abolished. The antagonism between the Conservatives and Liberals, between the Catholics and the anticlerics, has produced only misfortune for this small country.

In Colombia the Liberals were in power from 1849 until 1886. Religious persecution began under the regime of José Hilario López (1849–1853), and the Jesuits who had returned to the country were again expelled. The separation of Church and State was effected in 1853, the first such separation in Latin America, and was accompanied by a great deal of violence. Freedom of speech, universal suffrage, as well as civil marriage and divorce were instituted. In 1861 the State confiscated all ecclesiastical properties together with the schools and centers of charity. Many bishops were exiled along with the Apostolic Delegate. In 1863 when the legal status (*personería jurídica*) of the Church was nullified, a new wave of persecution ensued, and a number of priests and bishops were exiled. With the triumph of the Conservatives in 1886, the Church was reunited with the State; it was not until 1930 when the Liberals finally regained power that freedom of religion was proclaimed. This last governmental act allowed the diffusion of Protestantism throughout the country.

In Venezuela, following the fall of the Monagas brothers in 1858, there was a series of revolutions, sometimes instigated by the unitarians and other times by the federalists. Antonio Guzmán Blanco (1870–1888), a Liberal with dictorial propensities, clashed with the Archbishop of Caracas, Monseñor Guevara y Lira, who in turn was obliged to seek refuge in Trinidad. In 1872 seminary courses in theology were transferred to the national university, convents were closed, and ecclesiastical properties were confiscated. Two years later civil marriage was instituted and the religious were expelled from the country. Guzmán Blanco, a Grand Master in the Masonic Order, promoted Protestantism, and even went so far as to offer Protestants one of the confiscated church buildings for their services. He further antagonized Catholic ecclesiastical leaders by naming a bishop on the basis of the *Patronato*.

In Central America the situation was very similar. The Liberal presidents of Guatemala, Justo Rufino Barrios (1881–1885) and Manuel Estrado Cabrera (1898–1923), promulgated laws of laicised teaching, instituted the Napoleonic Code, separated the Church from the State, confiscated the properties of the religious orders and priests, and opened the country not only to Protestants but also to North American capitalists such as the International Railways of Central America. President Jorge Ubico (1931– 1944) opened the country to United Fruit. The Liberals came to power in Honduras in 1880 and that same year separated the Church from the State, imposed taxes on Church properties, and thereby reduced the number of clerical residences as well as church buildings. In Nicaragua the Conservative regime (1857– 1893) permitted the creation of the "Conservative Catholic Party," but with the Liberal revolt in 1893 and the coming to power of José Santos Zelaya (1893– 1909) the Church was separated from the State, religious orders suppressed, and bishops and priests exiled. These events occurred between 1893 and 1904. The Liberal party controlled El Salvador from 1871 to 1945. The federal Constitution separated Church and State, instituted civil marriage and divorce, promulgated laicised teaching, and proscribed religious orders. In Costa Rica, in contrast, the Conservatives imposed order and stability in the country beginning in 1870, even though freedom of religion existed from 1864. A Liberal government, however, expelled the Jesuits as well as the Bishop of San José in 1884 and instituted laicised teaching as well as other reforms. These laws were repealed in 1942.

In Mexico the break with the past has been most radical, to the point that all the struggles of the period are referred to as La Reforma, in opposition to the Continuistas or Conservatives. "The Reform consummated the struggle for independence and gave it its true significance by setting forth an examination of the bases of Mexican society and of the philosophical and historical presuppositions which supported it. This examination concluded with a threefold negation of the Spanish heritage, the indigenous past, and of Roman Catholicism, the first two being reconciled by a previous affirmation."[21] A study of the general history of Latin America, however, reveals that these three "negated" constituents survived the Reform and continued pleading for authentic validity in the adult Latin American conscience. The Constitution of 1857 produced a breach with the Church, and even more so with the triumph of the Liberal forces of Benito Juárez in the following decade. The Church was separated from the State, and the ecclesiastical properties were confiscated.

During the presidency and subsequent dictatorship of Porfirio Díaz (1876– 1910), the government promulgated positivism as a national doctrine, instituted civil marriage and burial, nationalized the properties that still remained under the control of the Church, and expelled the religious (1873– 1875). The government claimed to be one of the cientificos (scientists), as they were called, and manifested a capitalistic, industrial, and urban propensity. In the rural areas, however, the Indians—under the direction of various caudillos, especially Emilio Zapata and Pancho Villa—brought about the downfall of the government in 1910. The revolution of Mexican socialism in 1910 turned in part against the Church and initiated the greatest persecution of modern times in Latin America.

From 1848 until the end of the Second World War the Chicanos or Mexican Americans survived a history of lamentable oppression without help from either Latin America or the Church. In reality they have been more oppressed than the Negroes in the United States. The number of original inhabitants also has been greatly augmented by immigrations of Mexican braceros, agricultural migrant workers in the southwest United States. Slowly the leagues, federations, and trade unions for Spanish-speaking workers have arisen, but not without major repercussions.

After gaining independence from Spain, Puerto Rico was incorporated into the

United States as a protectorate[22] and Puerto Rican immigration into the United States, minimal before the Second World War, increased appreciably afterwards.

In the nineteenth century opinions were polarized between the Conservatives and Liberals, the former composed generally of those who supported the continuation of the Catholic Church (although within a *patronato* system) and represented the oligarchy and the Creole aristocracy. The latter group, influenced by the French and other foreigners, proposed a complete break with the past. They were anticlerical, primarily middle class intellectuals — lawyers, doctors, and teachers. Obviously each country had its differences and peculiarities, but the basic patterns were comparable.

Early in the twentieth century these two factions divided. The Conservatives were made up of a right wing — many times a Catholic right, a populist right, or military dictatorship — and a central wing composed of the old oligarchy newly become capitalist and somewhat fond of anything foreign. These groups formed the real Conservative parties. The Liberals also had their right wing, which was sometimes confused with the central wing of the Conservatives. These right-wing Liberals represented certain members of the new bourgeois oligarchy. The popular wing of the Liberal parties was constituted many times by the so-called radicals or by those of analogous persuasion who continued to be dedicated to the old causes but with popular support from regional *caudillos*. All of these groups, nevertheless, suffered a loss of influence for lack of doctrines to support their actions, and also because of the residue of a narrow nineteenth-century nationalism.

Two new forces then appeared: first came the socialists, Marxists, and the Communist parties, which attracted the most active of the old Liberals, and then there appeared the Christian parties, organized in all the Latin American countries.[23] These two forces have been the only ones consciously opposed to each other in every part of the continent, and because of this they have had not only a nationalistic hue, but also a continental hue.

These historical parties, consisting of all those named above, have for the most part retired their candidates — one example among many of the new situation that exists in Latin America and of the function that Christianity is beginning to have in the new civilization. The time of the *Patronato* has ended, as well as that of colonial Christendom.

2. Inorganic Development

The Church is clearly an integral part of the global situation of the existing civilization. And if Latin America is an oppressed, underdeveloped continent, the Church cannot be otherwise. The continual political, social, and economic movements, the instability, the poverty, and even the misery, the struggles and persecutions simply have not allowed for the restructuring of the Church since the wars for independence. Moreover, since 1880 there has come a second wave of emigration of Spaniards and Italians in large numbers, as well as lesser numbers of Germans, English, eastern Europeans, and even Asians. The result has been a demographic growth without precedence. The present crisis for the Church is that it is surrounded by a growing number of baptized but not catechized constitutents.

The European who arrived in Latin America during the last century was forced to live without the sociological support of a regional or national Christianity which he had enjoyed on the continent. His faith, whether he was Spanish, Italian, French, or German, was engendered in an environment that had been Catholic for more than a thousand years. In Latin America, however, the Church was persecuted, and with the indifference that characterized the middle class, the Church had no possibility of caring

Demographic Growth In Latin America 1650–1950[24]

1650	12 million inhabitants	(80% Indians	6.4% White)
1700	" " " "		
1750	11 " " "		
1800	19 " " "	(35% "	18.8% "
1850	33 " " "		
1900	63 " " "		
1950	163 " " "	(8.8% "	44.5% "
2000	592 " " "		

for the newcomers. These emigrants, who for the most part were Catholics, lost their faith or at least ceased to practice it. Those who lived in the rural areas, which had been more or less Christianized during the colonial era, migrated to the large cities in search of employment. The lack of parishes, of clergy, and of Christian organizations produced a general disorientation. Slowly in all the larger cities — which are the heart of Latin American civilization — a process of profound de-Christianization took place. The working classes lived in this environment of the semi-industrial, semipagan, pluralistic, and secularized city. The old pastoral of the colonial "New Christendom" was impotent before this invasion of foreigners who emigrated into Latin America and who subsequently, migrated within the various countries. The universities were controlled by the positivists and the political arena by the Liberals. The end of the nineteenth century was truly agonizing for the Church, and the twentieth century began with a sense of tragic hopelessness.

3. The Missionary Renaissance

Under Pius IX the *Colegio Pio Latino Americano* was founded in Rome in 1858, and concordats were signed with several Latin American nations: with Bolivia in 1851, Guatemala and Costa Rica in 1860, Honduras and Nicaragua in 1861, Venezuela and Ecuador in 1862. The Church, however, failed to obtain any financial support from the Latin American governments for the missions of the *Propaganda Fide*. In 1848 twelve Capuchins began evangelizing the Araucanian Indians in Chile. Today there are more than 340,000 Araucanians, and at least 327,000 of these are professing Christians. In 1855 twenty-four Franciscans began work in Argentina followed by fourteen others in 1856. In 1850 the island of Guadalupe was made the Suffragan of Bordeaux. Evangelistic work among the Indians of the Amazon basin of Brazil was begun in 1860 by the Franciscans and Capuchins. They were reinforced by the Domincans beginning in 1880 and by the Salesians in 1895. Pope Leo XIII exhorted the Peruvian episcopacy in 1895 to increase its missionary efforts among the Indians who at the time represented 57 percent of the Peruvian population. The first group of Augustinian missionaries arrived in Peru in 1900. The Salesians of Don Bosco initiated a successful evangelization among the Araucanians in the Argentine Patagonia and among the Fuegians of Tierra del Fuego beginning in 1879. The reorganization of Catholic missions began in Colombia in 1840, but the Augustinians did not arrive until 1890, the Montfortists in 1903, the Lazarists in 1905, the Clarentians in 1908, and the Carmelites and Jesuits in 1918. Between 1928 and 1953 Colombia had missions in twenty different areas ("mission territories"). These missions among the Indians, though important, did not, however, constitute the major challenge that the Church faced in the twentieth century, except in Bolivia and Peru.

The nineteenth century closed with the Church maintaining the structures of the old colonial "New Christendom," though it was a part of a secularized and pluralistic civilization. Even more lamentable, the Church—dreaming of a civilization that no longer existed—continued to struggle to protect its rights and privileges and to recover the ones long lost. One cannot help but think in this regard of the First Vatican Council, which expended so much energy in defending the territories of the Holy See. Advocating the preservation of traditions already lost is a kind of anachronism that too often has characterized the struggles of the Church, although, as we will see, there were prophets who had begun even before the end of the nineteenth century to lay the foundations for a broad and profound renaissance for the Church in the succeeding century.

4. The Plenary Latin American Council of 1899

On December 25, 1898, as a result of the Apostolic Letters *Cum Diuturnum*, the First Continental Council of the Latin American Roman Catholic Church was convened. Leo XIII had already issued his encyclical *Quarto abeunte saeculo* on July 16, 1892 to the Latin American episcopacies, an encyclical that celebrated the fourth centennial of the discovery of the Americas. The Council was held in Rome in 1899 for the expressed purpose of reiterating the conciliar decrees of the sixteenth century, and it became the basis for the Code of Canonical Law of 1917.[25] Thirteen archbishops and forty-one bishops were present. This Council of 1899 was preceded by a meeting promoted by Monseñor Casanova in 1890 in Rome, the Plenary Latin American Council.

The Latin American bishops (*Nos, Patres huius Concilii Plenarii Latinoamericani*, Chap. I, *tit.* 1) dealt with the problems of paganism, superstition, religious ignorance, socialism, Masonry, and the press, and attempted to develop a strategy whereby the advance of these as well as other anti-Christian movements could be checked. The Council issued 998 canons or articles that proposed the reorganization of the Church in Latin America. Obviously these articles were inspired by the "School of Rome" as well as by current theology and Canonical Law. The thrust of the articles was, however, designed more to conserve or defend the faith than to be a strategy by which the faith could be spread. The importance of the meeting, nonetheless, was that it represented the reawakening of the collegial consciousness of the Latin American episcopacy and became the foundation for all the initiatives that would be taken in the future.[26]

IV. THE NINTH STAGE: THE RENAISSANCE OF THE LATIN AMERICAN ELITES AND THE MODEL OF A "NEW CHRISTENDOM" (1930–1962)

The world economic crisis of 1929 had profound repercussions for the history of the Church in Latin America. In reality it represented the end of an era, for by that time the neocolonial pact between the Latin American bourgeois oligarchy and the United States and England had run its course. The Liberals came to power in Brazil in 1930, and in Argentina a military takeover toppled the regime of Hipólito Irigoyen. The oil boom began in Venezuela, Velasco Ibarra was elected president of Ecuador, and Rafael Trujillo initiated his rise to absolute power as president of the Dominican Republic (1930–1961). The "Socialist Republic" in Chile came to an end in 1932 with a military takeover, and the Chaco War errupted between Bolivia and Paraguay. In Mexico, Plutarco Elías Calles lost control of the government, while in Peru the military was the government. The ruthless Cuban dictator Gerardo Machado fell in 1933, and an army sergeant, Fulgencio Batista, seized control (1952–1958).

During the 1930s the Church was forced to adopt a different posture in regard to economic and political structures. From Europe the influence of Jacques Maritain began to excite the dream of a "New Christendom" for Latin America, and partially as a result of Maritain's philosophy, Catholic Action emerged as a significant force. Christian Democracy was a reaction to the rightist propensity of the Spanish Fascist government of Francisco Franco, who came to power in 1936, the year when the Christian spirits divided in a germinal way, a division that would be accentuated during the time of the Second Vatican Council. The following stage in the historical development of the Church will demonstrate the limitations of experience and the difficulties of finding one's way in a totally new, unpredictable situation.

1. The Intellectual Renewal

The Catholic intellectual in Latin America during the nineteenth century was a "loner," a kind of theological sniper. But the beginning of the twentieth century saw the emergence of several important national groups dedicated to theological and philosophical issues. It was only after 1955, however, that these groups began to organize and make their presence felt on a continental scale.

An important antecedent of the contemporary awakening can be seen in the work of José Manuel Estrada (1842—1894) in Argentina. Estrada was greatly influenced by the Spanish traditionalism of Jaime L. Balmes and Juan Donosco Cortés. Earlier, Friar Mamerto Esquiú (1826—1883) and Jacinto Ríos (1842—1892) were challenging the dominance of positivism. A neo-Thomist school began to emerge with Martínez Villada (1886—1959) as a prototype of the new direction. Martínez was especially influenced by Augustine, Pascal, and the French traditionalist Joseph de Maistre. Martínez also devoted himself to the study of the *Summas* of Aquinas as well as to the thought of Maurice Blondel and Jacques Maritain. A whole generation of Martínez's disciples followed: the Thomist, Nimio de Anquín (a specialist in German thought), Manuel Río, Rodolfo Martínez Espinosa, Guido Soaje Ramos (who has greatly influenced this writer), Alfredo Fraguerio (a specialist in the work of Francisco Suárez), Ismael Quiles, Octavio Derisi, Juan Sepich, and Alberto Caturelli. The philosophical journal *Sapientia*, clearly Thomist, has been published for several years in Argentina.

These distinctly Argentine developments can be said to have occurred in all of Latin America. Brazil owes a great deal to Jackson de Figueiredo who was educated in the Protestant *Colegio Americano* in Salvador, Bahía, studied law there, and in 1916 wrote *Algunas Reflexões sobre la Filosofia de Farias Brito: Profissão de fé espiritualista* (*Reflections on the Philosophy of Farias Brito: A Spiritualist Profession of Faith*). Sergio Buarque of Holland wrote that Figueiredo belonged to "that caste of men, captains of a noble heroism who by nature are designated to stimulate, orient, direct and combat" (*In Memoriam*, p. 148). Figueiredo is reported to have said one day to V. de Mello Franco, "Dissolvent socialism and iconoclastic bolshevism are nibbling away at the European organism like leprosy. But Europe is prepared to defend herself. What will happen to us, I wonder, when we have to defend our poor bones against these evil assaults?" Buarque's eulogy continued: "The entrance into the Church was for Figueiredo a struggle, a conquest, a peaceful victory. . . . His encounter with Catholicism was for his great intelligence a revelation, the discovery of something new. It was an unexpected vision into truth . . . of peace, and of the complete appreciation of mankind" (*In Memoriam*, pp. 298, 336). Alceu Amoroso Lima, who wrote under the pen name of Tristão de Ataíde, came later. He was a friend of Maritain, a founder of the Catholic student movement in Brazil, and a guiding light for Brazilian youth. Figueiredo died in 1930 at the age of thirty-seven, but Lima continued as a leader among the Brazilian intelligencia. A legion of Christian thinkers in Brazil has followed these men.[27]

The Catholic universities, although deficient in some respects, have made a significant contribution to Latin American Christian thought. For example, the old University of Santiago, Chile, founded in 1869 and now with a student body of some five thousand, has provided an environment conducive to the revival of Christian reflection. The same can be said of the Javeriana University of Bogotá, founded in 1937, and of the Catholic universities of Lima (1942), Medellín (1945), Río de Janeiro and Sâu Paulo (1947), Porto Alegre (1950), Campinas and Quito (1956), Buenos Aires and Córdoba (1960), and Valparaíso and Centroamericana (Guatemala) in 1961. As can be seen, all of these Catholic universities, with the exception of Santiago and Bogotá, were founded after the Second World War, and all are part of the ODUCAL (Organization of Latin American Catholic Universities) and the student movements organized through the ORMEU (Office of Relations of University Student Movements) of Santiago. One should observe that in a recent meeting of Latin American university syndicates in Natal, Brazil, the Christian representatives constituted the majority of the executive committee as opposed to large numbers of Marxists who defended their position, even including the use of arms. Friar Sanhueza, Secretary General of ODUCAL, said, "We face the future with confidence."[28]

2. Catholic Action

In Latin America the beginning of Catholic Action as conceived by Pius XI was preceded by many individual and collective developments in nearly all the countries. In Argentina, for example, Félix Frías founded the Catholic Association in 1867. In Mexico the first Mexican Catholic Congress met in 1903 and decided to begin "workers' clubs" and to commend them to the parish priests. Refugio Galinda began the publication of *Restauración y Democracia Cristiana (Restoration and Christian Democracy)* in 1905 as an organ of the *Asociación Operarios Guadalupanos* (Association of Workers of Guadalupe). By 1908 there were at least twenty thousand members of the Catholic Workers' Union, from which was born in 1911 the Catholic party. The Confederation of Catholic Workers' Clubs was functioning by 1912 in conformity with the principles enunciated in the encyclical *Rerum Novarum*. In the first *Jornada Social Obrera* (Workers' Social Organization), which met in Zapotlán el Grande, Jalisco, in January 1923, it was decided to begin agricultural syndicates to provide loans for farmers. Many other movements sprang up during these years. The persecution that began in 1910 was not directed against the colonial Church, but rather against the Church that had begun to comprehend its function in contemporary society. Consequently the revolutionaries were determined to suppress their only real opposition. It should be understood, however, that the large majority of those Catholics who were awakening to their social responsibility were *Conservatives*. It was necessary to wait until the Second World War, nevertheless, before the Catholic laity became sufficiently detached from the Conservatives so that they could adopt their own position and overcome the long-standing Conservative-Liberal conflict and consciously face up to and dialogue with Marxism.

Catholic Action was organized in Cuba in 1929, in Argentina in 1930, in Uruguay in 1934, in Costa Rica and Peru in 1935, and in Bolivia in 1938. These few examples indicate the beginning dates of this important phenomenon in the history of the Latin American Church. Originally, Catholic Action followed the Italian pattern, but after the Second World War the French influence became evident. In Latin America the movement adapted rapidly to the national situations in Argentina, Uruguay, Venezuela, Peru, Cuba, Bolivia, Brazil, Paraguay, and Colombia, and in reality it became a unique Latin American institution. It filled a need and role uncharacteristic of the organization in Europe and other continents. Laymen assumed responsiblity for problems that the Church faced to the degree that when Latin American lay leaders traveled to Europe they were shocked at the amount of "clericalism" in the Church there as well as the secondary and passive role of the laymen in European ecclesiastical communities.[29]

In 1934, for example, 600 young people attended the national assembly of Argentine Youth for Catholic Action (JAC), and in 1943 there were 8,000 present in Mendoza. These youth movements have afforded not only broad opportunities for involvement but also reasons for hope. The Brazilian JAC had some 15,000 members in 1953, and by 1961 it had grown to 120,000 members in more than 500 chapters. The JUC (Catholic University Youth) have inspired a spate of movements that progressively exercised increasing influence in Chile, Argentina, Brazil, Peru, and even Bolivia. The fact is that in Latin American history the university movements have signaled the most significant historical changes. The European observer does not discern clearly these "signs of the times."

Obviously, the elites in Latin America also fulfilled an essential function, and Catholic Action has certainly formed, although with varied success, a small but responsible elite group. Furthermore, it can be affirmed that no other elite group of such number, coordination, and formation existed on the Latin American continent.. Consider, for example, the Chilean Agrarian Youth Movement (JAC), which in less than ten years did an incredible amount of work. In fact, in many respects the Chilean movement has been the most outstanding Catholic youth movement in the world.

3. The Social Struggle

The Church, after having been allied with the regal power of the colony, with the Creole aristocracy during the period of independence, and with the Conservatives during the nineteenth century, slowly began to be aware of its freedom, of its prophetic function, and of its renewing and even revolutionary responsibility — as the bishops of Northeast Brazil have expressed it. The collective Pastoral of the Chilean espiscopacy, *El deber social y político en la hora presente (The Present Social and Political Duty)*, citing Pius XII, declared:

Peace is not equivalent to a tenacious, infantile, obstinate clinging to what no longer exists. . . . For a Christian aware of his responsibility, even for the most humble of brothers, indolent tranquility does not exist, neither is there escape. Rather there is struggle against all inaction and uninvolvement in the great spiritual conflict which now endangers the formation, even the soul itself, of future society.[30]

In a sense history has forced the Latin American Church to adopt positions that the European Church eventually will be obliged to follow. The situation has been extremely difficult, and the Latin American Church found it necessary to make unanticipated commitments. For this reason, the European Christian parties, more conservative in their orientation, and the Latin American parties, which have been clearly more revolutionary, have almost experienced a break in their relationship.

At the political level this attitude is seen in the trade union movements in Latin America. In 1954, for example, trade unionism had only four national organizations in the whole continent, whereas today only Costa Rica, Guatemala, and Cuba are without these organizations. (Trade unionism existed in Cuba prior to Castro's revolution but was then dissolved.) There are now at least twenty-three national organizations with a total membership surpassing one million. One should note in this regard, however, that membership includes the elites and not the masses. Also, in order to reach the ninety million workers, the Latin American Confederation of Christian Trade Unions has a budget no larger than most North American parishes.[31] Schools for training in trade unionism exist in Argentina, Ecuador, Peru, and Venezuela. There have been four continental seminars that brought together ninety delegates from fifteen different countries. These seminars have received financial and technical assistance from OIT, UNESCO, and CEPAL. In 1961 the Christian Confederation sponsored the Seminar on Rural Issues, the first meeting in Latin American history for the purpose of organizing rural workers. "The amount of money, however, expended by Cuba for the diffusion of Marxism in Latin America has been at least fifty times more than the budget of the Confederation. In Latin America Christian trade unionism could save the continent from the implantation of Marxism."[32] But the Marxist challenge is bearing fruit.

Numerous other examples of social experiments and efforts could be cited, such as Sutatenza Radio in Colombia, Integral Reform of Northeast Brazil begun by the Bishop of Natal, the Radio Schools of Mexico and Brazil, the Fómeque Cooperative, and others. The number and creativity of these efforts are indisputable, and the Christian parties, although completely autonomous, represent a new reality that must be taken into account.

The social investigations being done by various groups should also be noted. Among them has been an organization known as Human Economy, the Institute for Political Studies in Latin America (I.E.P.A.L. of Montevideo), and the Belarmino Center in Santiago, Chile. There have been others in Peru, Mexico, and Colombia.

4. Sources of Renewal

Since the Second World War Latin America has experienced not only a change of spirit but also a change of direction. Little has been written about this phenomenon, primarily because Christians as well as others in Latin America work without giving sufficient time for reflection and writing, which would enable others to know what is being done. This lack of information has caused observers to assume that little is happening. The following are indicative of the events, movements, and changes that have taken place.

(1) The contemplative life

We cite the words of a Christian brother:

The history of the first centuries of the Latin American Church is virtually unknown not only by Europeans, but also by Latin Americans. . . . The chapters of the *Historie de l'Eglise* by Augustin Fliche and Victor Martin dealing with this period are not only insufficient but laced with negative judgments which oftentimes one author copies from another when attempting to write of the work of the Spanish in America.[33] The evangelization of Hispanic America and the Christian life in those countries during the colonial era is without doubt one of the most impressive pages in the history of Christianity. This is true not only of the missionary effort, . . . nor merely because of the adaptation of the Gospel to the primitive people, . . . nor only because there has emerged in a short time a large number of Creoles who wanted to become priests and nuns — so much so that the abundance of secular and religious clergy constituted a problem for the authorities and inhabitants of Spanish America,[34] but also *because of the existence of a contemplative element.*[35]

In Peru and Ecuador, Santa Rosa de Lima (1586– 1617) and Mariana de Jesús Paredes (1619– 1645) promoted the contemplative life. Such a large number of hermits existed in Peru that the Council of Lima in 1583 had to decree that the religious habit must be black. There was, among others, the edifying example of the hermit Juan de Corz who lived near the City of Guatemala in the seventeenth century. These recluses sprang up almost by spontaneous generation, as did the Augustinian nuns in Santiago, Chile, in 1574. Also, in the southern Chilean town of Osorno a community of contemplatives was founded in 1571. The town itself lived under an almost constant stage of seige by the Araucano Indians, so much so that between 1600 and 1604 the nuns almost perished from hunger and fatigue, and the town was finally abandoned.

At the time the Spanish nuns and brothers left the city, the majority on foot, without any food, the women carried the children. Some were forced to give up the journey because of exhaustion, and others because of hunger. ... The saintly nuns, who for reasons of decency and modesty traveled apart from the other members of the party, moved together, barefoot but joyful because of the hardships they were suffering for God, recited their offices during the journey and sang praises to God, so much so that they inspired devotion and courage in everyone.[36]

This is but one example among many.

In the nineteenth century "one could almost conclude that the Spanish American Church had ceased to exist ... but this is precisely the period of liberal indifference when the first monasteries for men were founded in Latin America." The Brothers of Melloc founded the Abbey of the Infant Jesus in Entre Ríos, Argentina, in 1899. The Brothers of Samos, Spain, founded the Priory of Viña del Mar, Chile, in 1920, and the Brothers of Santo Domingo de Silos, Spain, founded San Benito in 1919. The Benedictines of Sainte-Odile founded a monastery in Caracas in 1923, and the Solesmes founded a monastery in Las Condes, Chile, in 1938. The Benedictines also founded the Abbey Santa Escolástica in Buenos Aires in 1943, and the Abbey of Einsiedeln founded Los Toldos in Argentina in 1947.

Beuron continued the work of Las Condes while the Argentine Abbey of the Christ Child (Niño Dios) founded another abbey in Tucumán, Argentina. The Cistercians began their work in Brazil, and the Trappists in Azul, Argentina, and in Orval, Brazil. The Community of the Niño Dios Pauvres of Landes, France, founded a community on Isla del Rey (King's Island), Chile, and the Petits Frères and Petites Soeurs of Charles de Foucauld began work in Buenos Aires, Santiago, and Lima. These examples are indicative of the reawakening that was taking place.

One should not conclude, however, that the contemplative life has been limited to the monasteries. The opposite has been the case, for the life of prayer has been emphasized among dedicated lay groups — minorities to be sure — as well as in the Christian family movements and among priests and religious. Father Alberto Hurtado of Chile wrote the book ¿Es Chile un País Católico? (Is Chile a Catholic Country?) long before Godin thought of writing France, pays de mission? Father Hurtado died a saint, and his prayers were certainly contemplative. As a matter of fact, it was Hurtado who persuaded the Petits Frères to see the importance of their contemplative presence in Latin America.

(2) The theological, biblical, liturgical, catechetical, and parochial reawakening

The bibliography in regard to the comprehensive religious awakening in Latin America is fragmentary because it is so recent. We will, nevertheless, outline the general direction of what has transpired. Although Latin America has not produced up to the present time a great theologian as such, a progressive theological reawakening has occurred because of the availability of European theological works in translations and because of the studies done in various centers such as the Catholic University of Santiago, the older seminaries such as Villa Devoto of Buenos Aires, and because of the theologians of the various religious orders such as Máximo de San Miguel of the Argentine Jesuits. The theological journals like the *Revista Eclesiástica Brasileira* published in Petrópolis, *Teología y Vida* published in Santiago, and *Stromata* published in Buenos Aires all have indicated that there began, although timidly, a study and reflection adapted to the existential reality of the Latin American Church. In the past, in Rome — because of the *Pio Latinoamericano* and the *Pio Brasileiro* more recently — and in Spain, the Latin American theological student received a doctrinally sound formation, but he was left with the task of adapting his universal and scholastic dogmatic to the concrete reality of a continent in profound change. This deficiency produced a schism between the theologian, life, and spirituality. The influence of Louvain, Innsbruck, and Paris have permitted — thanks to a more existential theology — a somewhat slow but effective beginning of a scientific and theological reflection on the Latin American reality. But this reflection has hardly begun.

In the biblical field, although there are two or three relatively good translations of the Bible that can be secured at a modest price, the Church is unable to compete with the North American and British Bible societies, especially if one considers the innumerable Indian languages into which the Bible has been translated by Protestant groups. Their work, nevertheless, has prompted Catholic ecclesiastical leaders to do something specific in regard to biblical studies. In a meeting in Rome in 1958, CELAM decided to begin the biblical institutes, and various scholars with their doctorates or licentiates in biblical sciences who had studied in Rome or Jerusalem began to publish their first works. The parochial biblical centers were then organized in various Latin American countries. There is, however, a lack of a dynamic organization and the hierarchical authority to supervise the interest in biblical studies in Latin America. In regard to the exegetical reawakening, a certain static and anachronistic concept still exists, which has tended to smother important groups that are attempting to do relevant Catholic exegesis such as certain teams in Buenos Aires.

Preconciliar liturgy has passed through two stages. During the first period the practicing faithful were reached, beginning in 1930, by the bilingual translations of the Catholic Missal, a work of the Benedictines. This allowed the already practicing Catholics to understand the liturgy and to participate in it personally. During the second period there has been an emphasis on community renewal inspired principally by French groups. These have been centered primarily in parish churches such as *Todos los Santos* in Buenos Aires, but the movement is now slowly and somewhat unevenly spreading through all the dioceses and countries.

The official editions of the sacraments and other liturgical acts — some directed by CELAM for the whole continent while others are of a national character — have continued to produce a profound change in the life of the community at the level of the "mediations." On the catechetical plane the advances have been more impressive, primarily as a result of the Latin American Institute of Catechesis, which has strong parish, diocesan, and national support. Given the fact that in many countries teaching is laicized in the schools, the Church must develop some means for reaching the children. Until the present, no such means have been forthcoming. Catechetical teaching is, therefore, very deficient if one believes that the masses in all of Latin America should be reached and Christianity perpetuated. On this level, nevertheless, theological, biblical, and liturgical renewal is producing its first fruits, leaving aside the traditional scholastic catechism in order to concentrate on the religious education of the child in the life of the Christian community.

All of this is clearly dependent on parish renewal. Everywhere one feels the necessity for a profound reform, and partial initiatives are many, especially with respect to the economic problems and the freeing of the priests from handling finances, the liturgical life celebrated and lived in common, parish services, Catholic Action, the parish itself, and the missionary community. Many negative factors are, nonetheless, encountered: the great distances, the lack of priestly teams, the strength of traditionalism, and the opposition to the overall Pastoral.

Religious sociology has provoked a profound desire to know the parochial, diocesan, and national reality. The reforms are proposed and are accepted slowly primarily because of the gradual awakening to the reality that is taking place. Various institutes of religious sociology now exist, such as the Center of Social and Religious Investigations of Buenos Aires, the Center of Investigation and Social Action of Santiago, Chile, the Center of Social Investigations of Bogotá, and the Center of Socio-Religious Investigations of Mexico, as well as others in Brazil and other Latin American countries. Slowly the CIAS are being founded by the Jesuits in all the countries.

5. The Attitude of the Episcopacy

In line with the episcopal collegiality and as a step toward reawakening, one must consider the General Conference of the Latin American Episcopacy (CELAM), which met in Río from July 25 until August 4, 1955.[37] Its historical importance cannot be exaggerated. Europe, for example, after having lost its medieval unity, never recovered it on the ecclesial level. Latin America, on the contrary, in a century and a half regained the unity that it enjoyed during the period of colonial Christianity. The recovery, however, involved innumerable difficulties. At the present, the Church is gradually coordinating its work without depending on any *Patronato* at a continental level. In this sense the Church has moved beyond many Latin American political, economic, and cultural organizations, and in one sense — at the level of civilization — represents a prophetic achievement. Evidence of this can be seen in the conclusions adopted by this historic General Conference, conclusions that continue to determine all the action of the 1955 Latin American Episcopal Conference.

Cardinal Adeodato Piazza gave an address on July 30, 1955, from which we have taken certain significant texts.[38] He said,

To be able to go back to the origins of the apostolic mandate is always a great source of encouragement for us. We know that the mission of the Church is the continuation and the gradual development of the mission of Jesus Christ in the world. In Nazareth Jesus himself defined his mission by appropriating unhesitatingly the passage from the Prophet Isaiah:
The Spirit of the Lord has been given to me,
For he has annointed me.
He has sent me to bring the good news to the poor,
to proclaim liberty to captives
and to the blind new sight.
To set the downtrodden free,
to proclaim the Lord's year of favor. (Luke 4:18)
It is especially moving for us to observe the mission of Christ, formulated in its multiple aspects, in the history of the evangelization of the peoples of this immense continent. But

how was the mission of Christ converted into the "apostolic mission"? You will well remember how the transmission of power occurred on the same night as the Resurrection when Jesus said to his Apostles

As the Father sent me,

so am I sending you. (John 20:21)

This is the central event of our lives and the most moving experience in our memories, namely, the episcopal consecration. . . . The history of the evangelization of this new continent constitutes one of the most prodigious chapters in the history of the Universal Church in the modern era which began with what is called the "discovery of America.". . . This historical account reminds us of the prophetic announcement:

The people that walked in darkness

have seen a great light. (Isa. 9:1)

. . . The question is, however, Has this light shone in all of Latin America? . . . Has this preaching of the Gospel reached "every creature"? Have all the children of Latin America been transformed into children of God and of the Church? . . . Obviously, the evangelization is still being done. . . . I believe at this point it is well to note a serious problem which exists in all our countries, namely, the question of the conversion and Christian formation of the Indians and simultaneously of the colored peoples. In the urban centers, where local wealth contributes to a prosperity "whose appearance is materialistic, hedonistic, and almost pagan," Christianity has been reduced to a formalism of good customs rather than something deeply felt (p. 99).

Cardinal Piazza saw the problem of a secular civilization with its "almost pagan appearance" and the necessity to continue the work of missions on every level — "the evangelization is still being done." With a clear theology one can see that all ecclesiastical efforts should be founded on and should originate from the episcopal consecration and from its adherence to the example of Jesus of Nazareth who, annointed by the Holy Spirit, evangelized the poor.

Pope Pius XII, also speaking to the Conference, declared,

It is necessary that precious energies not be wasted, but rather multiplied by proper coordination. If the circumstances so indicate, new methods of the apostolate should be adopted, and new ways of evangelism should be tried (*nova exercendi apostolatus general novague carpantur tinera*) in order that, while remaining faithful to ecclesiastical tradition, we will be more in tune with the demands of the times and take advantage of the advances of civilization.[39]

The conclusions of the Conference were arranged under eleven headings. The first three headings were dedicated to the serious problems of vocations and the formation of foreign as well as autochthonous seminarians, priests, and religious. There was already a Subsecretariat for the Clergy, Religious Institutes, the Care of Souls, Vocations, and Seminaries (see further *Estatutos y reglamentos del CELAM, Estatuto*, c. III, art. 13, 2; *Reglamento*, c. I, art. 2, 2) besides the *Latin American Confederation of Religious* (CLAR, Río de Janeiro, 1958[40]), the *Latin American Organization of Seminaries* (OSLAM, Tlalpam, Mexico, 1958), *Spanish Organization for Collaboration* (OCSHA, Madrid, 1947), *Collegium pro America Latina*, Louvain, 1957), and *The Missionary Society of St. James the Apostle* (Boston, 1958).

Section IV deals with lay involvement in Catholic Action. There also existed a Subsecretariat (ibid., 4), as well as the Interamerican Secretariate of Catholic Action (SIAC, Santiago, Chile, 1946), the Regional Conference of the International Federation of Catholic Youth (Buenos Aires, 1953), the Information Center of the JOC (Río de Janeiro, 1959), the General Delegation for Latin America (UNIAPAC, Santiago, 1958), and the Christian Family Movement (Montevideo, 1951).

Section VI dealt with the special means of propaganda. A Subsecretariat already existed for the Defense of the Faith, Preaching and Catechesis, the Press, Radio, Cine, and Television. Also created were the Latin American Headquarters of FERES (Religious Sociology, Bogotá), and the Latin American Union of the Catholic Press (ULAPC, Montevideo, 1959). In addition, there was the third meeting of CELAM in Rome in 1958, which projected the founding of biblical, liturgical, and other institutes.

Section VII dealt with Protestantism and other non— Roman Catholic movements. As far as can be determined, a subsecretariat or institute has not yet been organized to deal specifically with this issue.

The social problems that CELAM had indicated as being especially serious or significant were dealt with in Section VIII. A subsecretariat that already existed (ibid., V) was the subject of the fourth meeting of CELAM in Fómeque, Colombia. There was also the CIASC, founded in Mexico City in 1942, the Latin American Christian Penitentiary Movement (Santiago, 1958), and the Latin American Confederation of Christian Trade Unionists (CLASC, Santiago, 1954).[41]

Section IX dealt with the questions of missions, especially to the Indians and colored peoples, which already had its own organization as a part of the Subsecretariat of the Propagation of the Faith. The Conference proposed the additional founding of an "Intermissional Seminary for the Formation of Native Clergy" (Section IX, 86b), and of an "Institute of Ethnological and Indigenous Character" (89b). Unfortunately, however, neither of these organizations has been created. In Mexico there is a seminary for foreign missions, and several missionaries have already been sent out to East Asia.

Section X dealt with the issue of immigrants and seamen throughout the continent.

As to culture, there already existed the Interamerican Confederation of Catholic Education (CIEC, Bogotá, 1945) with three subsecretariats: The Interamerican Secretariat for Pedagogy (Santiago), and the Interamerican Secretariat for Freedom in Teaching (Río de Janeiro). There also existed the Interamerican Union of Parents of Families (UNIP, Lima, 1952), the Organization of Catholic Universities in Latin America (ODUCAL, Santiago, 1953), the Union of American Christian Educators (Buenos Aires), and the International Catholic Center of Coordination of Work with UNESCO (Santiago).[42]

Two other factors should be noted. First, all of these organizations are of relatively recent origin, which can be explained by the fact that the awakening of Catholic laity began about 1930 in most of the countries of Latin America, and it has taken almost a full generation for these movements to develop continental organizations. The second factor that should be noted is the importance of Chile in the coordination of all these movements. The Chilean Church, because of certain priests such as Father Hurtado and bishops such as Monseñor Manuel Larrain of Talca, together with certain progressive lay groups, was a prime mover in CELAM as well as in the other organizations already cited.

We have reviewed rapidly the factors that have preponderantly affected the contemporary situation in Latin America. The new elites have neither a sense of solidarity nor culpability in regard to the actual situation; neither do they attempt to relive the agony of colonial Christendom. Rather, they are attempting with intelligence and enthusiasm to consolidate a vibrant, mature, unified Catholicism within a secular and pluralistic society. At the same time they are aware of being the only group able to assume responsibility for all of Latin American history and to give it at this crucial stage its fullest meaning.

Demographic growth as well as the revolutionary nature of the present situation forces the Latin American Church to initiate completely new avenues in the field of the Pastoral. The "diaconal" function, one of the most profound concepts of the priesthood (that is, collaboration with the laity), is awaiting a total restructuring which is possible for the elites who have been emerging. The experiences in Natal, Brazil, among others, demonstrate that "Latin American Catholicism can fulfill a decisive role which will have repercussions beyond its own borders, in that the crucial problems faced here will sooner or later be faced in the entire world."[43]

All the above indicates that on the level of the elites there has been a profound renewal, the ultimate fruits of which are impossible to determine at this time.

Chapter IX

An Evaluation of Latin American Catholicism Until 1962

In order to judge catholicism in Latin America until 1962, it is necessary to understand the word *catholicism*. The reality of the Latin American Catholic Church is often misunderstood because of the ambiguity of the word "catholic."

The Church has been called *Catholic* since antiquity for reason of its being universal (*Kata-ólon*), that is, without borders.[1] The universality of this *catholicity* is not so much geographical as it is the Christ-like grace that surpasses all limits, even those of the visible Church, by means of the Universal Spirit. Moreover, it is *catholic* to the degree that it is not circumscribed within any given limits but transcends all boundaries and confines. The Catholic Church is, in contrast, a *sectarian* community. It is an assembly of the "few" (*olichoi*), of the predestined, the religion of the minority, of the "saints." Conversely, catholicism is the religion of the "many (*polloi* or the *rabim*), of the "multitude" of which only a small group, a minority, is fully aware of the demands of the faith, and only a minority truly fulfills the precept of charity, only a few await passionately the Advent of the Lord and believe that we are living in "eschatological times" and that the Parousia is imminent. Sectarian religion is by nature "closed." It is the faith of the "pure" (*Katharoi*). The catholic religion is by nature "open." It is the faith of the "sinners" who have heard the call of the Lord and have followed him step by step. As he said, "Many are called, but few are chosen" (Matt. 22:14). It is the faith of those who have not heard or who have disregarded the call.

Sectarian religion is the religion of the "just." The catholic religion meanwhile is that of the "sick" who need a savior. Therefore, within catholicity there is a dialectic between the elite and the masses, between those who maturely and conscientiously live their faith and those who participate in religion as an expression of the popular understanding.

In Latin America this dialectic has a paradigmatic characteristic and *sui generis*. For the masses, the Catholic religion exists as a residue of colonial Christendom as in the case of the Indians, mestizos, and Creoles, or as a residue of European Christianity as in the case of the European immigrants. The Christian elite who began to appear in the twentieth century after the dark night of the preceding era have their own characteristics and are without any direct antecedents from the colonial period or from Europe. Hence the typical Latin Americans call themselves "Catholics" because they were baptized and they possess something of the structure of thought of the Latin American people — the "ethico-mythical nucleus" of the civilization — rather than their faith being truly Christian, that is, based on the Person of Jesus Christ and his Church. This majority (*polloi*) should not be ignored. To do so would be a mistake, theologically as well as pragmatically. Their "catholicity" should be analyzed and brought to light.

The new responsible *elite*, the university, trade union, political and religious leaders — as well as the writers and artists — do not ordinarily sense any relationship with the colonial past or with Christendom, and on the other hand they view the future with a certain optimism as they note the lack of power in other elites. This is to say that this new elite is aware of the historical task that should be fulfilled within a brief period of time.

In general, when "Latin American Catholicism" is evaluated, sufficient differentiation is not made between these two types of Catholicism. There is the desire to unify the faith and to assume that the religion of the minority is the same as that of the masses who are not yet sufficiently evangelized. There is an attempt to unify the Catholicism of the new anticonservatives and even revolutionaries with the colonial past that this newly aware elite, more than anyone else, is attempting to overcome. Thus it is sometimes assumed that the great problems of "Latin American Catholicism" are the lack of priests, or the spread of Protestantism, spiritism, Marxism, Masonry, and secularism. All of these are issues, but they do not explain the Latin American reality nor do they point us in the direction of a solution that could be applied with success.

History, if it attempts to be a science, cannot be the manifestation of negative and incoherent aspects. Rather, it must attempt to offer an explanation of the present and ascertain its causes. It is necessary, therefore, to discover in the first place the *origins* of the actual situation and the current events that we have outlined in the description of the crisis of the nineteenth century and the reawakening in the twentieth at the level of the elites. In the second place it is essential to discover in the past the "prophetic" groups who, ahead of their time, began to see in all of their profundity the difficulties of the immediate future, and who led others to the same kind of awareness. Likewise, it is the work of the historian to discover in the present those groups who will become the foundation of the immediate future, the evolution of the apparent phenomena, and the direction of the development of these phenomena and their structures. Investigations regarding Latin America should concentrate first of all on the evolution of the elites because they will determine the immediate future. Of much greater historical importance, however, for a scientific historical work, are the Christian student movements in such educational centers as the universities of Buenos Aires, Lima, or Santiago, those student groups that can win the elections and that represent twelve to twenty-five percent of the people in these cities. The percentage of those who practice their religion is merely the "residue" of the Christendom of the past and represents a negative phenomenon. The results of student elections in the above universities, on the other hand, represent the foundation of the secular and pluralistic civilization of the immediate future. What religious practice is in fact essential? It will obviously be for those aware of their faith, for those of the living Christian community, the means by which the masses are evangelized if in the divine providential economy such evangelization is possible or necessary. We say "if" because never in history has conscious faith and efficacious charity been practiced by the majority, and probably it never will be.

I. CATHOLICISM AND THE MASSES

The Latin American masses can be schematically divided into four groups: the inhabitants of the rural areas, the inhabitants of the cities, the Indians, and the foreigners. In each of these groups the causes of Christianization and de-Christianization and the means of evangelizing them are different. Note the examples of Argentina, Mexico, and Brazil.

Percentages of Urban and Rural Populations in Three Countries[2]

Nation	Years	% of Urban Population	% of Rural Population
Argentina	1895	38%	62%
	1914	56%	44%
	1955	67%	33%
Mexico	1921	31%	69%
	1930	33%	67%
	1950	42%	58%
Brazil	1920	28%	72%
	1940	31%	69%
	1950	36%	64%

As a whole, the Latin American countries are economically and technologically underdeveloped. The rural "world" remains in a quasicolonial stage while the great cities, the urban "world," benefits from the advances in industry that have slowly been achieved or that have resulted from the machines and technology bought from the developed countries. These two "worlds" coexist in the same geographical territory but live in different eras. There is no contemporaneousness. The rural world represents the agony of colonial Christianity — that of the Indians, mestizos, and Creoles who today are less than sixty percent of the population of Latin America.[3]

The urban world developed very rapidly. Note the following three examples.

Number of Inhabitants By Parishes in Three Cities

City	Years	Population	No. of Parishes	Inhabitants By Parishes
Havana	1898	125,000	12	10,420
	1919	400,000	14	28,640
	1954	1,000,000	16	61,535
Buenos Aires	1911	1,200,000	24	56,680
	1954	3,497,000	121	28,900
São Paulo	1890	60,000	10	6,000
	1920	579,000	23	25,175
	1954	3,100,000	115	22,692

The population of these cities is exclusively from the third group, that is, the Creoles, mestizos, and foreigners. From 1821 to 1932 at least fourteen immigrant missions came to Latin America. The inhabitants of the great cities were, and are, doubly uprooted: the Europeans lost the Christian structures in their respective mother countries, and the Creoles lost the rhythm of rural life. Neither group encountered an ecclesiastical structure that would permit them to rechannel their faith. One can see that the number of the faithful in the parishes tends to diminish. This is another of the signs of renewal already discussed. It is possible that by the year 2,000 as many as ninety percent of the inhabitants of Latin America will live in the cities. If the third level (see above, pages 55ff.) was essential for the new national, independent society, the urban sector will be essential for the future secular and pluralistic civilization.

The census of 1947 in Argentina revealed the following official data: of the 16.5 million inhabitants, 93.6 percent said they were Catholic, and 1.5 percent claimed to be without any religion.[4] There were 66,099 members of Catholic Action in 1945, and 3,500 priests.[5]

Thus, the situation in Latin American can be depicted clearly. The masses who call themselves Catholic, who have been baptized and in most cases married by the Church, and who in lesser numbers receive the sacrament of extreme unction, constitute the majority of the Latin American people both in the rural areas and in the cities. The *practicing* Catholics, however, fluctuate between 12 percent and 25 percent. No country has the general practice of religion such as one finds in Germany or in the "Christianities" of the French Bretons. Neither does one find the conscious and traditional de-Christianization that has characterized the French province of Creuse. The Catholic elite is but a small minority in Latin America, yet it is growing in awareness, responsibility, and numbers.

The rural population is weighed down by the traditions of the "mediations" instilled by the practice of Catholicism — the "fiestas," the "prayers," the "devotions," and the pilgrimages to holy places — many times associated with the superstition and magic of folk Catholicism. In Brazil this takes on the character of spiritism, and in the Caribbean it resembles the African religions: it is the "chiaoscuro" that we mentioned in the conclusions of Chapter VI. Certainly faith exists, but it is an incipient, inchoate faith. Evangelization, therefore, should be continued.

Among the urban population, the ecological, economic, and social disorganization has produced a neopaganism easily recognized in Paris, Hamburg, Rome, Madrid, London, or Buenos Aires. The problem in Latin America, however, is aggravated by the lack of current missionary structures.

Surely all those who have been baptized — although questions should be raised regarding the advisability of baptizing everyone who requests it and who calls himself or herself Catholic — belong to the people whom the Church embraces in its universality, but there is a twofold defect evident. The essential defect consists of the fact that Latin American faith and charity are distorted, insufficient, or, we might say underdeveloped. In the second place, Latin America is unaware of the distance that separates it from Jesus Christ and of being ineffective participants in the Church. This in turn impedes the masses from offering themselves for evangelization, and they are not prepared "to be missionized."

We are opposed to two extreme positions. One premise is that Latin America be considered as a continent absolutely in need of mission simply because a developed faith does not yet exist among the masses. This evaluation is not only somewhat immoderate and self-serving, but it is also frequently based on insufficient knowledge of the Latin American people and on technical, erudite, European criteria. The other extreme position that we oppose is that Latin America is a Catholic continent simply because more than ninety percent of the people are baptized. This judgment confuses the value of one's freely and consciously accepting the grace offered by Jesus Christ in the sacraments and substitutes a medieval or colonial manifestation of Christendom.

We believe that the truth is otherwise, namely, that Latin America is a continent partially evangelized — Indians, mestizos, and Creoles — and de-Christianized by the perplexity that exists among the foreigners or immigrants. This is to say, Latin America is initially Catholic but is equally a *continent for mission.* The masses, whether they are ignorant or learned, possess only an incipient faith. A *minority* should begin to evangelize with the signs that the times clearly demand.

II. THE CHURCH AND FAITH

Let us consider the same problem from another point of view but entering into the essential aspects of the question.

The de-Christianization is far too rapid among the masses, and it is necessary to make a decision. That is, we need to know who is truly Christian and those who are susceptible to being authentic Christians in these countries. In a certain sense we need to begin anew constructing a Christianity deeply rooted in the Christian structure. In order to do this it will be necessary to decide if we will continue to occupy ourselves with the masses with the same intensity. Also we need to decide if priests should continue to maintain superficial contacts with people in order that they come from time to time to the Church. . . . This would mean that the pastoral of the Church would renounce the choice between a Christianity which would subsist as those structures of Christendom subsisted, even though these are very few in Latin America . . . . Christendom should not be evangelized. Neither should Latin America as a whole be evangelized! . . . For the basic preoccupation in Latin America is to protect the *Christian institutions* by all possible means. This has comprised Christianity much more so than in Europe. It has corrupted the *words* by which Christianity should be proclaimed and which should be employed in evangelism. And now we have no words.[6]

The writer of the preceding paragraph poses with valor and clarity the pastoral decision which will decide the future of the Church in Latin America.

In 1961 there were in Latin America 186,623,042 Roman Catholics, 18,783 diocesan priest, and 20,013 religious brothers, for a total of 38,796 priests. That is, there was one priest for every 4,810 faithful.[7] In contrast, there were in the United States 38,600,000 Roman Catholics with 55,006 priests, or a total of one priest for every 701 faithful. The ratio between priests and communicants in Latin America indicates the importance of the decision that was discussed above. Can the Latin American priest do the normal work of a priest in Christendom, or should his work be clearly defined allowing him to do only the essential functions, as was the case in the primitive Church? Furthermore, would this not be even more justifiable if one takes into account the number of Protestant pastors in Latin America (20,660 in 1957)?[8]

Nevertheless, one should not ignore the dialectic between the Christian minority and the masses. If we take, for example, the case of the Brazilian Northeast, of the trade union minorities, of Catholic Action in the parish, or even of the priestly life, these are the means by which the minorities become aware of and work with the masses, and their faith is developed and their charity universalized. It is evident that what should be left aside are the Christian institutions that are the ballast, or the dead weight, of Christianity — institutions such as the private school, the sacrament of baptism performed without any condition or commitment, or the time lost in administrative work. But *the contact* with the masses, those who "call themselves Catholics," should not be set aside, in view of the fact that this contact is a means of evangelism.

With respect to demographic growth, the number of priests has stabilized,[9] but the ratio is not likely to diminish between the number of priests and faithful. To increase the contacts between those who have a living faith and those who practice an effective charity, to whom we have referred as the elite, it is necessary to augment the pastoral staff, that is, allow the members of this elite to participate in functions that before have been reserved exclusively for priests. There is a great need for catechists, teachers of the rosary, deacons, deaconesses, and nuns who can distribute the sacraments, a need that has been met in Brazil. Surely the dialectic between the elite and the masses calls for new methods, new ways of relating or "mediations," created by the hierarchies as a solution to the problems outlined in this book.

In order to evangelize effectively the incipient faith of the *masses*, it is necessary to decide resolutely the means or the ways of involving the minorities who are already active Catholics, creating at the same time as a means of expression of these communities — as the beginning of the reevangelization — the hierarchial missionary structures that are now constituted exclusively by celibate priests.

Protestantism should be seen by Latin American Catholics as "a providential gesture" that demands that the Chruch be involved in the formation of authentic Christian and missionary communities in order to bring together the "elect" with the "called," that is, the elite with the masses.

Is the goal of evangelistic work the constitution of a new Christendom analogous to medieval Christendom? No, the goal of evangelism is the conversion of those who will discover the message and who will actively cooperate and participate in the work of universal salvation. The elite will always be a minority, that is, a group within a pluralistic society. Even when Catholics are authentic and are in the majority, they will be a part of a secular civilization. The religious community should always be autonomous in relation to the political community. It will not be the *umma* of Islam or Christendom where legally, intellectually, and sociologically Christianity becomes an exclusive and excluding faith. Rather, it will be a secular civilization in which the elite accepts pluralism and the majority is tolerant. This is, of course, in contrast to what the rightists or "integralists" (members of a late nineteenth-century Spanish political party that advocated the preservation of national traditions) proposed, namely, to develop a "natural Christian society." The latter is not only a *contradictio in terminis*, it is also a theological error, for it presumes to universalize as essential and nontemporal a concrete and archaic system. Catholics in many countries in Europe as well as in the United States continue to live within certain structures of Christendom. In this sense, one can say that Latin America is confronting a problem at the present that these other countries will have to face in the future.

III. FAITH AND SIGNS

The "message" of Jesus Christ is directed toward human existence, that is, it represents an understanding of humankind. The human being, however, can understand this message only by means of signs: "This was the first of the signs (*sémeion*) given by Jesus " (John 2:11). But in order for a sign to be understood, it must signify something to the one to whom it is directed. To be comprehensible there must be a relation between the "sign" and the "people" to whom this sign is given.[10] The one giving the sign should have in mind the situation in which the people live. Otherwise, the supposed sign signifies nothing. The Church is the "sign" of Jesus Christ in Latin America. But the "sign" that is understandable by this ignorant, starving people is *justice*. To appreciate the sign one must be aware of the suffering and injustice on a national and international level.

Karl Marx judged the European Church as the workers judged it in their time: "Religion is the opiate of the people";[11] and Catholicism was allied with conservatism, monarchism, and in the final analysis with the bourgeois. Support for agrarian reform was accompanied by turning over lands that were previously held by the diocese or religious orders — as in Chile — and began to produce in the people, at least in a small number of them, and in the working classes, a reaction unknown until the present: "Perhaps we can count on the Church in our struggle for justice." It is obvious that the bourgeois, oligarchical, urban, and liberal minorities have been discredited in the eyes of the Latin American people, and even more so the conservatives. The Church, however, has been liberated not only from its old enemies, but also from many of its previous allies. Do not believe, however, that the concepts outlined thus far have been accepted in all of Latin America. On the contrary, there are still bastions of conservativism together with a false traditionalism or desire for a *new Christendom*.

CELAM in particular, and Christian groups in general, have begun to take a position in regard to social conditions by calling for a thorough reform of the structures. The committed laymen in the trade unions, guilds, and political parties represent the real dynamic in these movements.

At the level of *civilization* — in that the problems of faith and of pluralism remain at the level of the "ethico-mythical nucleus" — the Latin American Church, much more so than the European Church, is committed to the struggle for justice.

It is certain that, beginning with the wars for independence, that is, from 1808 until 1962, Latin America passed through a crisis that we have called the "agony of Christendom." It was not, however, an agony of Christianity; rather, to a certain degree it was Christianity's *modus vivendi*. Two phases of agony were endured. The first was the growing and inevitable decadence during which time all the institutions of colonial Christendom were virtually annihilated (1808– 1930). Gradually, however, from this agony sprang new efforts for "reconstruction." We would say that if one desires to view this second phase against a medieval or colonial "model," it would be the model of a "new Christendom." Catholic Action began with the "participation of the laity in the apostolate of the hierarchy of the Church," forgetting that the laity as such have their own ecclesial apostolate because of their baptism without needing special participation. The Christian political parties, such as Christian Democracy, that arose raised several difficulties, for these parties assumed in the name of Christianity a responsibility that every citizen already had. Both institutions — the lay apostolate and Christian Democracy — attempted the conversion or a return to the past culture and to a new type of Constantinian Christianity, even though the issue was not set forth in this way. The attempt to institute a "new Christendom" resulted in a temporal renaissance between 1930 and 1962. It is possible, however, that the way chosen was not definitive, yet on the other hand it is also possible that the way chosen was the most adequate for the phase that we have begun. Only an unanticipated fact, the greatest in the history of salvation, began to end the agony of Christendom, not because there was no one still struggling for a reestablishment of the old order of things, but because of the appearance of a new horizon, a new theological, pastoral, and existential way of living Christianity as it was lived before the advent of Christendom. This unanticipated fact was Vatican Council II which signified a new stage in the history of the universal Church, but was even more decisive for the history of the Church in Latin America. The events of sacred history experienced by the Christians in Latin America since 1962 to the present will be the subject of the last part of this work.

In 1962 we wrote that in Latin America there had been created a twofold attitude. On the one hand, many Christians — insufficiently developed theoretically and existentially — had become victims of the disorientation, the anarchy of a progressivism that ignored tradition and the institution. Others, in contrast, were equally unprepared to face the changing reality and suffered a kind of vertigo, opposing any kind of reform or change. The preconciliar Christian attitude should have been what Christ indicated when he said, "Follow me, and leave the dead to bury their dead" (Matt. 8:22).

Part Four

The Church and Latin American Liberation (1962–1979)

In this last section we will undertake an analysis of the most recent era, which is pregnant with meaning and significant events. About a decade ago Latin America entered a new period of revolutionary change. Furthermore, the Church began to move into a new stage of its history. The converging of these two situations prefigures a new state of being in the panorama of the universal Church and of the cultural history of our world. Following the oligarchical revolution led by the Latin American Creoles at the beginning of the nineteenth century, this same oligarchy retained the political and social power well into the twentieth century in nearly all the countries of our geographical-cultural area. The Mexican revolution that began in 1910, however, signaled a new political, economic, and cultural reality, namely, the emergence of a new proprietor of power, that is, the *people* composed of a technocratic minority in their two essential elements: the proletariat created by industrialization and the rural workers together with the student population and some from the middle class. This *popular revolution,* which possibly will conclude by the end of the twentieth century, produces a profound uneasiness in the oligarchy, in the liberal bourgeois State, and in the institutions that they founded — including the Church and the military class. This popular revolution stems from the Church's experience of trying for three decades the pastoral solutions offered by the theology of the "new Christendom" such as Catholic Action and Christian Democracy. The oligarchy and liberal bourgeois have been even more disturbed by the directions signaled by the Second Vatican Council. Following the period of colonial Christendom and of the nationalism of the Creole oligarchy, the popular revolution signifies, in contrast, the integration of Latin America into one great country for Latin Americans.

The primitive Church, following a period of disorientation resulting from its Judaizing tendencies, began a second stage by being open to the conversion of the gentiles and eventually of the entire Roman empire, primarily as a result of the experience of the Christian community in Antioch and in conformity with the decisions of the Jerusalem Council of A.D. 50. From that first century of the pre-Constantinian Church and of Byzantine Constantinian Christendom, the second stage culminated with the evangelization of the Roman empire and its *colonies.* This period comprised the evangelization of the Byzantine empire, of Europe, and of Latin America, including the Christendom of the Indies. Only with the Second Vatican Council was the framework of the Roman empire — Latin and Hellenistic — surpassed in a real cultural sense, allowing the Church to engage universally in the evangelization of all cultures and of all people. The third stage in the history of the Church, which began in 1962, was climaxed in Latin America by a profound cultural phenomenon, namely, the popular antioligarchical and antiimperialistic revolution. These two converging developments explain the events in the history of the Latin American Church during recent years. We will attempt to synthesize this history in a few words, describing first the general conditions of the culture, the "tenth" moment in the history of the Church, and the "theological significance" of this brief but fertile period.

To designate 1962 as the beginning of this new period in history may appear at the outset unjustified, for any periodification is an attempt to simplify what is really very complex. A new stage in the history of the Church in Latin America is clearly seen beginning in 1955 and terminating in 1968, that is, from the meeting of CELAM in Río de Janeiro in 1955 when, at the first General Conference of Latin American Bishops, Dom Hélder Câmara was consecrated Bishop of Recife and Olinda through the slow but irreversible conversion that the Second Vatican Council signified from 1962 until 1965, until in various national ways the conclusions and implications of the Council began to be implemented. In the second General Conference of Latin American Bishops, which met in Medellín in 1968, those conclusions and implications were spelled out even more stringently. In these thirteen years a new attitude was formed, and since Medellín a new ecclesiastical situation has developed.

Chapter X

The Latin American Crises
of Liberation

The nature of this crisis of liberation could be discussed on numerous levels. We prefer to limit our analysis to the crisis of the popular revolution, of the Latin American integration, and of the discovery of the cultural autonomy of our sociocultural group.

I. THE CRISIS OF THE POPULAR REVOLUTION

If the crisis of the national revolutions that began in the nineteenth century against the Spanish monarchy represented a prolonged struggle for national organization by a minority, first of all conservative and then liberal — the latter being profoundly influenced by foreigners — then the present revolution signifies an even greater and more violent crisis in that it involves the change in the exercise of power from an oligarchy to a people educated, cultured, and committed to authentic democracy. It further signifies the suppression of many privileges, not from a nihilistic desire for destruction, but rather from the humanitarian desire that everyone should have the right to benefit from the values of contemporary universal civilization. This crisis is even more painful when, with the confrontation between the oligarchy, so influenced and dominated by foreign power, and the people in the process of liberation imposes the dialectic of the dominating, developed, and superdeveloped countries upon the oppressed and underdeveloped countries which oftentimes are experiencing a deteriorating political process and an economic disintegration. The cultural and economic gap between the oppressive colonial oligarchy and the oppressed peoples becomes even more intolerable. The gap between the per capita GNP of the developed countries (such as the United States, Western Europe, and the Soviet Union) and the Third World is abysmal. This creates a progressive dialectical movement of humanity moving toward a convergence that cannot be achieved unless contradictions are overcome. It is too late, however, for an impoverished people to follow the direction characterized by the individualism of the Creole oligarchy. It is equally late for these countries to attempt to imitate the development of Western Europe, North America, or even of the Soviet Union. Possibly the countries of the Third World should attempt a "shortcut" and try to bypass those stages and diverse models followed by the developed countries if these underdeveloped countries are to be united on a level of equality with the rest of the world during the twenty-first century.

"The dialectic of the master and the slave" perhaps has never been more clearly illustrated than in Latin America. During the period of the conquest, the conquistador (and later the *encomendero*) pressed the Indian into service. Indigenous America became the servant of Europe. And if it is true that there was no racism in Latin America, there was certainly the total domination of the Indian. Furthermore, the Indian con tinued to subsist in history not as an Indian but as a mestizo. And the mestizo is the first conciliation, the true fellow inhabitant of Latin America.

During the period of the contradictory and weak, independent nation-states, the master was the Creole oligarch — the landholder who for the most part lived in the great cities — who controlled the people from the provincial capitals and from the land of the rural worker, the *campesino, gaucho,* and *peón*. At the same time the powerful landowners allowed the birth of the industrial, neocolonial bourgeois, and a new relationship of domination developed between the national or foreign capitalist and the proletariat. The nineteenth-century national revolutions displaced the Spanish minority, and the control of the countries passed to the Creole oligarchy; but it appears that the economic crisis of 1929 dealt a mortal blow to the political power of this oligarchy. There followed the development of the military class as a political force, but their ideals and life-style differed little from those of the oligarchy. The Liberal was then transformed into a Conservative and began to defend strenuously Latin American *Christendom* under the guise of "Western Christian Civilization." This loss of power by the oligarchy, formerly Liberal, explains why conflicts between them and a large part of the Church ceased to occur: for the most part the ecclesiastical leadership came from this social class. Meanwhile, the bearer of the new political power continued to gestate, namely, the popular classes who were slowly being conscienticized and who began to enter the struggle for power. At the same time, the Church was passing through a new experience in history as there was developing within her own precincts a parallel polarization to that taking place within Latin American culture. All of this manifested the characteristics of the inevitable, and the meaning of this process will become evident. One other clarification should be noted. If we are speaking of a popular revolution, one should not assume that it will take place in a uniform way or even simultaneously. This slow gestation will probably continue throughout the twentieth century as it acquires sometimes national and at other times Latin American characteristics. Many times the development will signify progress, but, at other times regression as when the people as a community fail to exercise their power and when a new class, neither the bourgeois oligarchy nor the military, but the technocrats of our modern, universal civilization, gain control. This new class will be supported by the people because they represent a means of wresting the power from the current minorities. But the time will come when the technocrats will also be the objects of the liberating criticism of future Christian prophets. Meanwhile it is necessary to discern correctly the situation in order to discover who are the actual prophets in the Latin American Church.

In the nineteenth century, as we have said in the preceding pages, a *pact* was established between Latin America and the industrialized countries, namely, with England and the United States, wherein Latin America was placed in a neocolonial relationship, no longer Iberic but rather Anglo-Saxon. At the end of the century Latin America had clearly structured its economy within its dependence on the new economic capitals of London, New York, sometimes California, and other times New Orleans. The landholding Creole oligarchy, rarely creatively bourgeois, received, however, the full impact of the economic collapse of 1929.

From 1930 until the decade of the 1960s, a stage in the political and economic history of Latin America ended. The Second World War began to modify and even to accentuate the traditional international division of labor. "The international demand for raw materials lost its dynamism as reflected in the evolution of structures in the industrialized countries."[1] The decline in the prices of exportable raw materials to the developed countries produced an incipient industrialization that allowed a simultaneous reduction in importation.

The Evolution of the Coefficients of Industrialization in Some Latin American Countries[2]

	Argentina	Mexico	Brazil	Chile	Colombia
1929	22.8	14.2	11.7	7.9	6.2
1937	25.6	16.7	13.1	11.3	7.5
1947	31.1	19.8	17.3	17.3	11.5
1957	32.4	21.7	23.1	9.7	16.2

This industrial production resulted in a sudden growth of the proletariat class and the simultaneous loss of power by the oligarchy. The governments were able to promote industrialization by a process of accelerated inflation. This of course meant a widespread and profound social instability, which in turn led to the appearance of numerous dictatorships or reformist governments of a military type. In 1945, for example, the military overthrew the government in Brazil. That same year Juan Perón assumed power in Argentina. Three years later (1948) Manuel Odría established his dictatorship in Peru. In 1952 Batista took over in Cuba and Pérez Jiménez in Venezuela. General Gustavo Rojas Pinilla became dictator of Colombia in 1953, and in the following year Castillo Armas in Guatemala and Alfredo Stroessner in Paraguay took control of their respective countries. Before this, Trujillo in the Dominican Republic and Anastasio Somoza in Nicaragua had become dictators. During this time the Church generally maintained a working if not cordial relationship with the dictators. It was only after 1954, when the Church became critical of the Perón regime, that the situation began to change. There followed a new cycle of events in the toppling of one dictator after another and the attempt at civil reform by a neocolonial bourgeois. Perón fell in 1955, Odría in 1956, and Batista, Rojas Pinilla, and Pérez Jiménez in 1958. In Uruguay the *Blancos* replaced the *Colorados* who had governed since 1865. Jorge Alessandri replaced Carlos Ibáñez in Chile, and Adolfo López Mateos replaced Adolfo Ruiz Cortínez in Mexico. Somoza was assassinated in Nicaragua as was Trujillo in the Dominican Republic in 1961. Paz Estensoro returned to power in Bolivia in 1968, and Janio Quadros succeeded Juscelino Kubitschek in Brazil. Thus began the decade that we are analyzing in this section.

The dictatorships had produced ordinarily reformist governments of force but not really revolutionary governments. Consequently they did not effect any significant change in the governmental structures. But in the decade that followed, the governments adopted some rather radical positions as a result of two contradictory experiences. The first was the Cuban revolution of 1959 wherein Fidel Castro established a socialist state despite the opposition and intransigence of the United States. A short time later — primarily because of the failure of the political parties of Goulart in Brazil, Illía in Argentina, and Belaunde in Peru — there was another round of military takeovers. The *golpe militar* occurred in Brazil in March and April 1964, led by General Castello Branco and continued by Artur da Costa e Silva in 1967. In Argentina the Illía government fell to the military takeover of Onganía in 1966, and Belaunde was sent into exile by the Peruvian military in 1968. In Brazil the government followed a "hard" line defending the order of the bourgeois state and of "Western Christian Civilization" by the ruthless suppression of "subversion." "Western Christian Civilization" was a formula that approximately expressed the ideal of Byzantine Christianity in which the Caesar was over the Church, and to the Church in turn there was attributed a cultural function. Christians, as we will see, adopted different attitudes in regard to these events that demonstrate the diverse types of temporal, political, and cultural commitments.

Between Cuba with its socialist state (1959) and Brazil with its military dictatorship (1964) — highly organized and controlled from the Pentagon in coordination with the Latin American military — are situated the other Latin American governments. On the one hand is the old and now institutionalized oligarchy as seen in the party of the Mexican revolution (Institutional Revolutionary Party), which has been in perpetual crisis since the government of López Mateos in 1964. On the other hand is the more recent example of the Christian Democratic party of Eduardo Frei in Chile with its "revolution with freedom" (1964– 1970), and the even more radical "Popular Front" of Salvador Allende (1970– 1973).

It is obvious that by means of these political epiphenomena a slow *popular revolution* is developing. At times there is advance and at other times regression, but the direction is irreversible — as can be seen in the example of the Peruvian military revolution that began in 1968 — for all governments now set forth as the basis of their political task the will and well-being of the people. Agrarian reform, whether in Mexico, Bolivia, Chile, or Cuba, signals the progressive loss of power by the traditional landholding classes. The growing number and power of the trade unionists also indicate that the incipient industrial bourgeois faces a growing force that will not be dominated indefinitely.

The success of the *popular revolution* in Latin America of course depends on the degree to which Latin American politics and economics can be freed from the domination of the United States. In this regard, with the exception of Cuba, Latin American countries remain very much within the economic orbit of the North Americans. An indication of this fact can be seen in the slow growth of steel production in Latin America.

Production of Steel Ingots in Latin American Countries (in Thousands of Tons)[3]

	1958	1960	1962	1963	1964	1965	1966	1967
Brazil	1,362	1,843	2,396	2,604	2,983	2,923	3,713	3,667
Mexico	1,038	1,503	1,851	1,974	2,279	2,455	2,763	3,023
Argentina	244	277	658	913	1,265	1,368	1,267	1,326
Venezuela	40	37	225	364	441	625	537	703
Chile	348	422	495	409	544	477	577	638
Colombia	149	172	157	222	230	242	216	256

Industrial progress, no matter now impressive, will never allow Latin American countries to overtake the development of the United States or Western Europe, especially if one keeps in mind that fact that since 1965 "the United States has been unwilling to finance social revolution for Latin America as was proposed by various professors of economics of CEPAL. The United States has preferred to support the forces of the established order, that of the bourgeois state, which in turn has resulted in a growing disequilibrium which is continually becoming more violent."[4] It is not surprising, therefore, that since 1960 the amount of violence has dramatically increased, on the one hand by the military governments supported by the Pentagon and the national police (with their methods of torture often taught by the United States experts in counterinsurgency), and on the other hand by the rural and urban guerrillas. With the death of John Kennedy and the failure of the heralded Alliance for Progress program, the United States began to support all the forces in Latin America that called themselves "anti-Communists," a euphemism for counterrevolution, that is, those governments that directed their efforts against the popular revolution through neo-colonial militarism. This confrontation between the military and the popular revolution can, however, modify the whole situation. It has been more than eighty years since the troops of the *caudillos* were educated and trained by the French and German military. These troops were professionalized, but not fighting any wars, they lost their historical reason for being. The combination of professionalism and frustration has obliged them to look for new fields of action. With the decrease in the political power of the oligarchy, the military has moved in to fill the political vacuum. These new political leaders are concerned, however, not with the external defense of their countries but with maintaining the internal order and the security of the bourgeois and "democratic" State.[5] The Rockefeller Report of "The Security of the Western Hemisphere" declared, "Unfortunately, freedom and respect are denied too many people in the hemisphere," a reference to certain military governments.

The forces of anarchy and subversion are rampant in the Americas. . . . Our dilemma is how to respond to the legitimate desires for modern equipment without encouraging the diversion of scarce resources for the development of weapons which, in some cases, can be totally unrelated to real needs for security. . . . The military leaders of the Latin American hemisphere are frequently criticized in the United States. . . . There is a tendency in the United States to identify the police of the other American republics with acts of political repression more than with security.[6]

The solution was simply to arm the military, and the enemy of the military became the popular revolution. It is unfortunate that those who possess the weapons, namely, the military, do not understand that the real problem in Latin America — the problem that should be dealt with violently — is not subversion, but rather, it is the domination and economic, political, and cultural imperialism, and the suppression of all human potential of the Latin American that impede development.

It is possible that the time will come when the military will be the means of liberation. Perhaps the Peruvian case is the first hesitant, indecisive step in that direction. One should not think *a priori* that the army is unable to transform itself from a repressive to a constructive force or from a dominating to a liberating power. It does of course appear to be very difficult for this transformation to take place.

Few documents are as farsighted as the study prepared by Monseñor Cándido Padim, Bishop of Lorena, Brazil, which he presented to the ninth General Conference of Brazilian Bishops in July 1968, and in which he said that the "political crisis that Brazil endured during the decade from 1950 to 1960 terminated with the military overthrow of 1964." The ideological justification for the military takeover, according to Padim, was that "there are two blocks of nations in the world irreducibly opposed: the democratic and Christian West and the Communist and materialistic East. Between them there is a permanent and omnipresent antagonism, a total war."[7] The most serious defect of this twofold oversimplification is, he said, that Christianity is confused with Christendom and with Western Culture. Christendom could disappear while at the same time Christianity could flourish. But in the second place, Padim declared, this kind of reasoning makes a messiah of the military and permits the continuation of Christendom, which by being confused with Christianity pretends to defend by arms the Kingdom of God, which is eschatological. Thus under the banner of the most sublime values the will to power and power itself are orchestrated for the disguised end of economic domination by the national and international oligarchies. Christianity is confused with Western Christendom, and the bourgeois world is identified with law and order. As a consequence, all forms of subversion are suppressed, and the revolution and struggle for liberation by the oppressed people are immobilized. The people continue to be exploited as much as was the Indian in the colonial *encomienda,* the *mitra,* or in the "personal service" required by the *encomendero.* The rural *peón* and urban worker continue to be as oppressed as they were in the eithteenth- and nine-teenth-century colonies. In defense of security and order the violence and repression of the unjust system are obscured. Yahweh said to Moses, "I have seen the miserable state of my people in Egypt. I have heard their appeal to be free of their slave drivers. Yes, I am well aware of their sufferings. I mean to deliver them out of the hands of the Egyptians" (Exod. 3:7 – 8). And Bishop Juan del Valle of Popayán, in a letter of August 1, 1551, wrote of the sufferings of the Indians in colonial Colombia, "It would seem that this land is more like that of Babylon than of Carlos I. ... What is certain is that the Indians are more exhausted than were the Israelites in Egypt."[8] Time passes but injustice continues.

II. THE CRISIS OF INTEGRATION AND THE DISCOVERY OF LATIN AMERICA

The process of national independence began in various countries in Latin America when Ferdinand VII fell to the army of Napoleon in 1808. This resulted in a division of the small American communities that were eventully parceled out amicably among the neocolonial powers. Only Brazil, because of the prudence of the King of Portugal, managed to maintain its unity while the artificial and lamentable division of the vice-royalties of Mexico, Peru, and the River Plate was being effected. But this movement of division or dispersion is today changing to a convergence, a coming together, despite the fact that in the past the neocolonial powers — today the United States — prevented Latin American integration as a means of perpetuating their indisputable domination. If from a political and economic point of view the reunification of Latin America is essential, this integration parallels the discovery of Latin America as an autonomous horizon of creative cultural life. It is now common knowledge that the Vikings were the first to arrive in America. In the year 985 or 986 Bjarni Herjolfsson apparently saw the coast of North America when his ship was driven off course while attempting to sail from Iceland to Greenland. Leif Ericson came in 1002 or 1003, followed by this brother Thorvald. Leif named one section of the coast *Helluland* or Land of Desolation. To discover a continent, however, is not merely to see it or walk on it. It is rather to incorporate it and introduce it into the world as a whole. The geo-graphical discovery of America was the achievement of Columbus and Castille. But it has only been in the twentieth century, in the present stage of our history, that the cultural discovery of Latin America has taken place.[9]

1. The Movement toward Integration

One should not confuse contemporary Latin American integration with the disinte-gration that is taking place in the Americanism of the Organization of American States (OAS). The Monroe Doctrine insisted on "America for the Americans," a position that has been variously modified from the time of Thomas Mann to the Rockefeller

Report that opposed all forms of Latin Americanism. I am not referring to the Pan American meetings in Washington in 1889, nor to the others in 1890, 1901—1902, 1906, 1910, 1923, 1928, etc., until their culmination in the foundation of the Organization of the American States in Bogotá in 1948. Nor am I depreciating the Pan American conferences that preceded Bogotá, namely, those of Montevideo in 1933, Buenos Aires in 1936, Havana in 1940, Mexico in 1945, and Río de Janeiro in 1947. Curiously this integration of the Americas was taking place at the same time that the Latin American struggle for economic, political, and cultural liberation was being attempted. The neocolonial powers — England in the nineteenth century and the United States in the twentieth — have, however, opposed all Latin American reunification. The net result, therefore, has been that the wars for independence divided the continent into small countries that are dominated and oppressed by the neocolonial pact and without any fixed destiny in universal history.[10]

The first notable example of the Latin American of the future was Simón Bolívar, who attempted as early as 1821 to bring together the new governments in a conference wherein a kind of unity would be discussed. The Confederation that Bolívar proposed did not include Spain or the United States. Immediately, England reacted negatively to the projected meeting that was to take place in Panama. The ambassador of Gran Colombia, Joaquín Mosquera, journeyed south through Chile, arriving in Buenos Aires in 1823 with the mission of promoting the Panama conference. The British Foreign Secretary, George Canning, pulled all possible strings in order to assure the presence of England in the meeting so they could wreck it. Lucas Alamán in Mexico openly supported a Confederation as early as 1823. But when the conference was finally held in 1826, there were two delegates present from Colombia, two from Central America, two from Peru, and two from Mexico, as well as representatives from Great Britain and the Netherlands. The British and Dutch representatives, however, did not take part in the deliberations, and the United States representatives did not reach Panama until after the Congress had adjourned. The sessions concluded on July 15 with little of practical or lasting significance coming from them. The dissolution of the new Latin American states was inevitable, and the centers of power of the neocolonial pact proceeded to oppose in every way any real Latin American unity. All attempts to achieve unity, even the most modest, were opposed by the United States. On December 17, 1830, when Bolívar died in a borrowed bed, financially destitute, Gran Colombia had already divided into five nation-states. Subsequently, Panama was detached by the machinations of representatives from the United States who wanted to continue the construction of the canal begun earlier by the French.

The Confederation composed of Peru and Bolivia divided into two separate nations. The River Plate area separated into four sections: Paraguay, Uruguay, Buenos Aires, and the United Provinces. In 1823 the United Provinces of Central America, with their capital in Guatemala, separated from Mexico and Spain. The Honduran, Francisco Morazán, became president of these United Provinces of Central America in 1829, but by 1838 the federation was disintegrating and subsequently became five separate nations. There was a renewed effort in 1849 to reunite these Central American republics, but it failed. Perhaps the strangest attempt to promote a kind of unity can be seen in the filibustering invasion of Nicaragua in 1855 by the American soldier of fortune, William Walker. But his "glorious" escapade concluded in 1860 with his being executed by a firing squad. Guatemala's most impressive political leader of the nineteenth century was General Justo Rufino Barrios who declared, "We shall never be a great country until we are a united country," and he sought to impose federation upon the four neighboring republics. Barrios and his army got as far as El Salvador, but unfortunately the General himself was one of the first to fall in battle. The United States, meanwhile, in its session of March 19, 1885, declared that "every attempt at Union by force with the other republics of Central America will be considered as unfriendly and hostile intervention in their rights, in view of the pending treaty regarding the interoceanic canal."[11]

With the termination of the Second World War in 1945, European nations began to talk of unity, and as a result of this influence different currents of opinion began to surface in Latin America in regard to more cooperation. Leaving aside the influence of the Church in this Latin American convergence — especially that of CELAM, which has been the only effective entity operating as a united force in Latin America, promoting integration in the programs of the political parties and diverse lay movements in general — it has been the United Nations Economic Commission for Latin America (ECLA or CEPAL), presided over by the Argentine economist Raúl Prebisch, Keynesian in tendency but not uncritically so, that has led numerous studies that demonstrated the advisability of economic integration. In the CEPAL meeting in Mexico in 1951 the five Central American governments — Costa Rica, El Salvador, Guatemala, Honduras, and Nicaragua — agreed to form the Central American Economic Council and the Organization of Central American States (ODECA). The General Treaty of Economic Integration was signed in Managua in 1960, which allowed for the creation of the Central American Common Market. This effort toward integrating the small Central American nations in a plan of economic cooperation "and with a coefficient of relatively high importation (approximately seventeen percent in 1960) created conditions conducive to industrialization."[12] Unfortunately, however, this Central American experiment in unity was vulnerable to domination by the United States.

Representatives from other Latin American nations — Argentina, Uruguay, Paraguay, Brazil, Chile, Peru, and Mexico — met in Uruguay in February 1960 and signed the Treaty of Montevideo, creating a Latin American Free Trade Association (LAFTA). It aimed at the development of a Latin American Common Market, and the original signers were later augmented to include Bolivia, Colombia, Ecuador, and Venezuela. Though there has been an active program of trade liberalization and tariff reductions, the treaty did not envision a completely free trade area such as that of the European Economic Community. In reality little has been achieved, and full economic, political, and cultural integration will apparently have to come in stages. Significant in this regard was the first Latin American Parliamentary Assembly, which met in Lima in December 1964, as well as the meeting of the presidents of all the American republics in Punta del Este, Uruguay, in April 1967, when, after three days of discussions, there was proposed the inauguration of a Latin American Common Market by 1970. The failure of the Alliance for Progress, however, together with the triumph of the "hard line" military governments and the increase in violence at various levels, have severely damaged the progress toward integration. "National security" has been deemed more important by the United States and the Latin American governments than the need for economic integration. Meanwhile, these political entities are apparently unaware that the dialectic of domination and oppression makes integration impossible.

Bolívar wrote prophetically in the invitations he sent to the governments regarding the Panama conference of 1826 that if the various governments did not condescend to participate, and if they refused to face the fact of the accelerating tendency toward unity in the world, independence and isolation could work to their own detriment. In effect, the whole nineteenth century worked against Latin America, given the closed nationalistic egoism of the national governments who were occupied almost exclusively with internal issues. The net result was that the national oligarchies shortsightedly began to establish preferential relations with the neocolonial powers and were uninterested in any popular Latin American revolution. It is only now that some movement in that direction has begun to take place.

2. Toward Cultural Liberation

Possibly more important is the cultural awareness that is developing in Latin America, the discovery that our continent can be culturally autonomous and liberated from cultural dependence on the developed countries.

We must understand how to separate ourselves from monotonous routine in order to develop a reflective awareness of the colonial structures of our culture. And when this awareness of our dependence is effected by an entire intellectual generation, we will then see that we can have confidence in this cultural group and anticipate a liberated future. Surely there is a generation on our continent that agonizes to be Latin American.

The first to set forth with clarity the profound reason for this preeminent Ibero-American preoccupation was Alfonso Reyes in a discourse given in 1936 to the seventh meeting of the International Institute of Intellectual Cooperation, a discourse that later he incorporated into his book, *Notas sobre la inteligencia americana (Notes on American Knowledge)*. Speaking of the generation previous to his own, the positivist generation that had been Europeanized, Reyes said,

The previous generation is believed to have arisen within the prison of various concentric fatalities.[13] ... Having arrived tardy at the banquet of European civilization, America lives trying to leap over stages, hurrying its pace and running in one direction or another without taking time to carry through on all it is attempting. At times the leap is daring and the new form has the appearance of a meal withdrawn from the oven before it is thoroughly cooked. ... Such is the secret of our politics, of our lives, presided over by an office of improvisation.[14]

It is tragic that our cultural past has been so dependent and heterogeneous, at times so incoherent and disparate that we are a marginal or secondary phase of European culture. But even more tragic is that we have been unaware of this fact. It is of major importance, therefore, that we recognize that there is a culture in Latin America, and, even though some deny it, that our cultural originality is evidenced in our art and in our whole way of life. It is the responsibility of the intellectuals to uncover the structures of our culture, test its origins, indicate the deviations, and point us in the direction of liberation.

This is our mission: to make Latin Americans aware of the dependency of our culture, and not only aware, but also to be transformed into shapers of an autonomous way of life. And this is even more urgent when we recognize that "mankind as a whole is on the brink of a single world civilization representing at once a gigantic progress for everyone and an overwhelming task of survival and adapting our cultural heritage to this new setting. To some extent and in varying ways, everyone experiences the tension between the necessity for the free access to progress and, on the other hand, the exigency of safeguarding our heritage."[15] As we become more Latin American this problem will be seen to lie at the very heart of our contemporary reflection. Shall we give emphasis to originality and cultural autonomy or to technological development? And how will we survive as a Latin American culture in the universalization taking place at the level of contemporary technology? This problem is central to the most committed thinkers from Mexico to Argentina.

The Peruvian philosopher Augusto Salazar Bondy in his work *Existe una filosofía de nuestra América? (Does a Philosophy Exist in Our America?)* poses precisely this question when he declares that

Hispano-Indian America was subjected first to Spanish power only to pass from this state of political servitude to being the economic colonies of the factories and markets of the British Empire, completely under its economic and even political control, an empire which was later inherited along with a network of power more efficient and closed by the United States of America. We have been dependent and are underdeveloped for this reason, and consequently we are countries with a culture of domination.[16]

Because of this fact the oligarchical national elites, especially those who are a part of the intelligentsia, are charged with the responsibility of oppressing the masses in the name of the international imperial powers. Culturally a population is oppressed when the people are simply and directly taught the science and the culture of the oppressors without this knowledge passing through the filter of a self-conscious awareness of domination that is being exercised by means of the same imported cultural structures.

The problem of our philosophy is inauthenticity. And inauthenticity is rooted in our historical condition of being dominated and underdeveloped countries. The development of our own philosophy is initimately related to our being able to overcome this domination and underdevelopment. If, therefore, we have an authentic philosophy, it will be the result of a transcendental historical change. And authenticity will be a part of the effort to overcome our historical backwardness by recognizing it and making an effort to remedy it.[17]

Furthermore, "the nations of the Third World such as the Spanish American countries will have to forge their own philosophy in contrast to the concepts assumed and defended by the current centers of power by making themselves felt in the history of our time thus assuring their independence and their survival."[18]

This awareness of our cultural dependence and of our determination to reflect on it will lead to the discovery of a new, independent, liberated person and will signify a new beginning: the declaration of the cultural independence of Latin America in a revolution that will take time, but one that has already begun.[19]

Chapter XI

A Description of Recent Events

The preceding summary indicates that in recent years we have reached a new stage in the history of the Church in Latin America. This experience has affected the empirical and personal life of all Christians who were already adults in 1961 and who were involved in some Christian endeavor. All asked, "What has happened? What do these events mean?" Some of course were against any change, while others supported change wholeheartedly. But virtually no one has had a comprehensive idea as to the meaning of what has taken place. And it is the search for the meaning of these developments that has prompted us to give this lengthy description of the history of the Latin American Church. *The past has no value whatsoever if it does not illuminate and help us to discover some meaning for the present.* Obviously, to find some meaning for the present by reflecting on the past involves both the past and present in an understanding of the future. We cannot avoid the question of the future, for it is a hope against all hopelessness that supports our interpretation, and it is hope in the last analysis that is the foundation of the history of salvation as an eschatological event.

THE TENTH STAGE: A NEW BEGINNING (1962–1979)

We have thus arrived at the crucial issue, namely, the *why* of the present. Our interpretation is really archeological (*arjé* signifies origin: an understanding of the origin of the events and of their meaning). We are all acquainted with the many partial descriptions of what is occurring in the contemporary Latin American Church, but none of these descriptions fulfills the twofold condition of explaining all of what took place throughout the continent from 1962 until 1970, nor do they represent the actual events in the light of all the history of the Latin American Church. Apart from this dual approach it is impossible to have an adequate understanding of what has occurred or to integrate the events into the history of salvation, which is the basis of our present commitment. Therefore, as we attempted in Chapter VIII, the Sixth Stage (1808–1825), we will set forth a description of each of the various levels. The economic and political events were most important during the period of 1808 to 1825. But since 1962 the decisive events in Latin America have occurred on the ecclesiastical level. If a single person symbolized paradigmatically colonial Christendom, it would be Toribio de Mogrovejo, the heroic Archbishop of Lima during the sixteenth century. And if we had to select a symbol of the era of the crisis of Christendom, two archbishops would come to mind, Monseñor Valdivieso (1845–1878) and Monseñor Casanova (1887–1911), both archbishops of Santiago, Chile. Likewise it would be a Chilean, Monseñor Manuel Larraín, who in the twentieth century serves as an example of the attempt to establish a new Christendom. But in regard to the current epoch, contemporary attitudes are very much akin to those of a previous era, and it would appear that our historical moment has as its best antecedent the events of the sixteenth century. The most exemplary of that period was the indefatigable combatant, the

expelled Bishop of Chiapas, Bartholomé de Las Casas, defender and universal procurator of the Indian, who prefigures certain bishops of the twentieth century, Dom
Hélder Câmara, for example. For this reason we want to describe briefly an unknown
exploit that liberated from their origins the outstanding American bishops of the
sixteenth century in order to compare them with the most committed bishops of the
present century. Though history does not repeat itself, it does offer us perspectives
for understanding the present. Likewise one can make a comparison between the
involvement of the clergy in the revolution of 1808— 1825 and the commitment of
many of the clergy to the national and oligarchical liberation of the popular Latin
American revolution. Many overlook the fact, for example, that the instructor and
constructor of the artillery for the Army of the Andes, the person who manufactured
the cannons from the bells of the Church in Mendoza, was Friar Luís Beltrán, OFM.
Beltrán is a national hero who is honored today by monuments in villages and by
avenues named for him because he fought against the Spanish despite his cultural
heritage and ecclesiastical orientation, both of which condemned the revolution. How
will yet-to-be-written history judge the Colombian priest Camilo Torres, Licentiate in
sociology from Louvain, university chaplain, and finally a guerrilla who gave his life
in opposition to violence?

I. THE CHURCH AND ITS GREAT CHALLENGES

1. Fundamental Collegial Moments

We have already dealt with the first moments of collegiality in Chapter V, section 3,
the Third Stage, in the discussion of the Apostolic Commission of 1524, the various
commissions of bishops in Mexico, the provincial councils in the sixteenth and seventeenth centuries, and the councils in the eighteenth century, the last of which was
the second Council of Santa Fe de Bogotá, which was called by Archbishop Augustín
Camacho y Rojas in 1774. There were other councils and numerous diocesan synods
in the nineteenth century, as well as the first Latin American Plenary Council in 1899.
During the present century there has been a growing number of general conferences
as well as provincial meetings of the Latin American episcopacy.

Had it not been for the provincial or continental councils and the diocesan synods,
few if any would have participated in the ecumenical councils of the Church. Alejandro
de Geraldini, for example, was named Bishop of Santo Domingo on November 23,
1516. Less than a month later, December 15, Geraldini attended the eleventh Session
of the Ecumenical Council of Letrán in Rome.[1] He was the first American bishop to
participate in an ecumenical gathering. It is noteworthy however, that Geraldini had
never been to America at the time and did not arrive in Santo Domingo until 1519.

The Council of Trent was called on June 2, 1536, but the papal bull announcing
it did not reach Mexico until early in 1537.[2] The Commission of Bishops finally met
in November of the same year and decided to attend the General Council. Zumárraga
wanted to participate and wrote to the King stating that "if His Majesty will permit
me to go, neither the sea nor my advanced age will deter me. But if it is better that
I work here with what little strength I have that these souls continue in the right
direction, will you direct me in such a way that I may be excused from the Holy
Council."[3] The Monarchy requested that Rome issue an Apostolic Brief permitting
the absence of the bishops given their obligations in America and the long distance.
The fact is that no such Brief has yet been discovered — if indeed it ever existed —
but the King proceeded as if he had obtained it and indicated to the bishops that they
were excused from the Council. Vasco de Quiroga had made plans to attend the

Council in 1542, but a royal warrant forbidding it reached him at the port of Vera Cruz. Years later the courageous Juan del Valle attempted to present the issue of the Indians to the Council of Trent, but unfortunately he died in France in 1561 before reaching his destination. The King of Spain, therefore, was able to prevent any contact by the Spanish American episcopacy with Rome or with any European Council.

A small number of Latin American prelates was permitted to attend the First Vatican Council called by Pius IX on June 29, 1868, which began on December 8, 1869. Because of the nature of the matters treated by the Council, the presence or absence of the Latin Americans was of little consequence. Vatican I dealt exclusively with European dogmatic issues and gave no consideration to the Latin American pastoral experience. More than a thousand prelates were given permission to attend the sessions of 1870, but only seven hundred and two were present. Of these, two hundred and twenty-three were from the Americas, and sixty-five of these were from Latin America, that is, barely nine percent of the total. The Latin Americans did participate in the votes that defined papal infallibility, participation which gained them the reproach of the "old Catholics." For their part, these traditional Catholics erred in thinking that the Church in Latin America was as recent a Church as those of Africa or Asia "whose testimony lacks any significance for Catholic tradition."[4] The truth is that the Latin American bishops supported Rome against the great European churches: the Roman universality was a guarantee of the survival of a *catholic* Church.

Meanwhile the Second Vatican Council, unexpected in Europe and in Latin America, had an effect that no one could have imagined when John XXIII announced the possibility of such a meeting to Cardinal Tardini in December 1958. By January 19 the idea had begun to take form, and on the 25th of that month the Pope announced in St. Paul's Basilica that he had thought of convening a council for "the spiritual well-being of the people of God and the search for unity." The extended process of planning for the Council began. On July 15, 1961, the encyclical *Mater et Magistra* was issued, and on June 30, 1962, there appeared the *monitum* regarding Teilhard de Chardin, which seemed to indicate that the process was moving rather timorously. The announcement of a convocation was received with little enthusiasm in Latin America except by certain enlightened bishops.[5] Only three collective episcopal letters were written, and these by the bishops of Chile, Brazil, and Colombia. Some twenty bishops in Peru, Argentina, Colombia, Mexico, and Venezuela wrote pastoral letters to their faithful. It would appear that the almost single theme of these communications was the danger of Communism. Nothing was mentioned in regard to the serious theological questions that were approaching, nor of the possibility of pastoral or administrative collaboration with laymen. There was very little stated regarding theologians and presbyters. It was as if we were again in Trent.

When the Council began, however, on October 1, 1962, the Latin American Church was numerically present as follows:

Number of Latin American Bishops and Experts
Present at Vatican Council II

	Latin America	Europe	Rome
Participating Bishops	601 (22.33%)	849 (31.6%)	65
Members of Commissions	52	219	318
Percent of World Catholic Population	35%	33%	
Percent of World Population	7%	11%	

A Latin American cardinal, Monseñor Antonio Caggiano, was a part of the presidential committee whose participation approximated that of a prelate committed to the ideal of Christendom. It was, however, Cardinal Achilles Lienart who on October 3, 1962, declared: *Mihi non placet*, which opened Vatican II.

It would be impossible to name each of the various bishops who participated in the deliberations. Some supported the inclinations of their conscience and the Curia while others labored independently and placed before the Council issues to be discussed. One figure, however, stands out for the historian, that of Don Manuel Larraín who in 1963 was elected president of CELAM. In a sense the Council had been predicted by Don Manuel in his now dated pastoral letter of 1946: "We are now in the middle of the road reviewing the errors of one era while looking toward the future."[6]

It was not so much the contributions of the Latin American bishops as it was the immense numbers of contacts, discoveries, coordination, personal knowledge, institutions, and theological reflection — when the era and theology already studied allowed for this. The Council signaled a global conversion, although as is currently demonstrated, in the majority of cases there was not a personal change of orientation.

Meanwhile the encyclical *Pacem in Terris* ("To All Men of Good Will") appeared. John XXIII died on June 3, 1963, and Paul VI was elected Pope on June 21 by the College of Cardinals in which twelve Latin Americans participated. From 1963 to 1965, CELAM had three regular meetings — the seventh, eighth, and ninth. National conferences of bishops met in Rome as well as in their respective countries.[7] These meetings had occurred primarily because the bishops believed that a new era was beginning. But it was soon obvious that the situation in Latin America was not the same as in Europe, and that our bishops, who were more pastors than they were theologians, had voted many decrees and constitutions whose application would involve a prolonged process and not a few struggles. But the direction initiated by Pope John even for Latin America was effective and irreversible. "John XXIII, it was said, would be a transitional Pope. But in fact, he opened consciously a passageway."[8]

When the Council closed on December 8, 1965, an encyclical dealing with social questions, *Populorum Progressio*, was already being discussed and has continued to have profound repercussions in Latin America. We are in the dawn of a new age; the Church has become conscious of the fact that "the human race has passed from a rather static concept of reality to a more dynamic, evolutionary one. In consequence, there has arisen a new series of problems, a series as important as any and which calls for new efforts of analysis and synthesis."[9] Paul VI had written directly to the Latin American bishops on November 23, 1965, at the tenth anniversary of the formation of CELAM, and he referred "to the responsibilities of the sacred pastors in the postconciliar period."[10] We will discuss this period which is of major importance on various levels, beginning by repeating what was said above in the sense that the Council was the place of encounter. If it had not been called, the ideas and concepts of the seventeen bishops from the three underdeveloped continents, Asia, Africa, and Latin America, that is, from the Third World, would not have been exchanged nor would they have signed a document that expressed one of the basic teachings of the Council. The document appeared for the first time in *Témoignage Chrétien* and was published in Paris on July 31, 1966. The first bishop to sign the declaration was Dom Hélder Câmara who, although he did not speak during the sessions of the Council itself, was actively involved in the question of "the Church and the poor." The bishops declared: "The peoples of the Third World constitute the proletariat of the contemporary world."

The document further stated that the Church does not condemn revolution in principle, that revolution is acceptable when it serves the cause of justice, and that frequently it is the rich and not the poor who begin class struggle and violence.[11] We will see the importance of this postconciliar interpretation.

Returning to Latin America, each bishop began a program of action. Monseñor Mendiharat, Bishop of Salto, Uruguay, manifested an exemplary spirit by stating, "I believe that each baptized person in this postconciliar era will find himself in the position of being awakened from a long and profound sleep in a strange place and will ask himself sincerely and with a spirit of openness and generosity, 'Where am I? Why am I here? What should I do?' "

Almost immediately consideration was given to ways and means of applying the findings and implications of the Council on a national level. In Brazil, for example, the bishops launched the "Joint Pastoral Plan" in January 1966, which was to continue until 1970, replacing the "Emergency Plan of 1962–1966." It was said that those baptized in Brazil had only an "implicit faith." Also ways whereby Catholic unity could be manifested were outlined, and missionary and catechetical programs were promoted, as well as the renewal of the liturgy and ecumenical efforts.

In Argentina the bishops met on May 3, 1966, to study ways to apply the conclusions of the Council, and on May 15 they issued a "Declaration" affirming their desire to put into practice the findings of Vatican II. They spoke of a new spirit, a new language, of what community implied, and of the necessity for dialogue and for Christian service. The pronouncement was, however, couched in very general terms. Then on November 25, following nine days of work, the Argentine episcopacy published a "National Plan for Joint Pastoral Action."

In Uruguay the bishops began preparation in May 1966 for a synod in Montevideo for the same purpose, namely, the application of Vatican II, and in Colombia the bishops met during June and July to discuss how the conclusions of the Council could be carried out in their country. In Ecuador 418 delegates, including bishops, priests, religious, and laymen, met from July 31 until August 6 for the purpose of studying a plan for applying the teachings of the Council. Priests and laymen met together in Lima from August 1 to 11 to reflect on the same question. Liturgical reform was initiated in Bolivia in 1966, and two years later, from January 28 to February 3, 1968, sessions designed to actualize the changes were held in Cochabamba. All of these meetings indicate the profound change of spirit that Vatican II had produced. It would be possible to continue with examples from every country in Latin America, but suffice it to say, the attempt at application was universal. Unfortunately, however, the application proceeded along lines of the "new Christendom." Hardly anyone had an inkling of the meaning of what was to come. The first session of the synod, held in Santiago, Chile, from September 8 to 18, demonstrated a much greater insight and maturity. To put it simply, there was a different attitude among the 419 priests, religious, and lay people who attended.

A thorough understanding and application of Vatican II on a collegial level did not take place nationally, but rather continentally with the second General Conference of Latin American Bishops held in Medellín in August, 1968.

In Chapter VIII we touched on the beginnings of CELAM. From the first General Conference in 1955 until the second in 1968, there were eleven regular meetings, which we will sketch briefly. The first preconciliar assemblies followed the direction and ideal of the "new Christendom." The first regular meeting took place in Bogotá in 1956 and basically was devoted to the initial organization of CELAM.[12] The second regular meeting, in Fómeque, Colombia, in 1957, continued the process of organization especially in relationship to the religious orders. Also at the Fómeque meeting the bishops publicly gave their support to the work of UNESCO.[13] The third regular meeting took place in Rome in 1958 where the prelates insisted on the need to "preserve and defend the faith." Discussions centered on the activities of the three organizations: OSLAM (seminaries), CLAR (religious), and CAL (Commission for Latin America located in Rome).[14] The following year (1959) the fourth regular meeting convened again in Fómeque and dealt with a theme characteristic of the period: "An apostolic plan of action for the Church in regard to the problem of Communist infiltration in Latin America."[15] The fifth regular meeting in 1960 in Buenos Aires portended a new direction, reluctant to be sure, but indicative of a new interest.[16] Primarily because of the instigation of Monseñor Larraín, the Buenos Aires meeting dealt with the pastoral question. Religious sociology was freely utilized by the bishops, but not a theology, a history, or a hermeneutical investigation of culture. The meeting resulted in the organization of the Latin American Pastoral Institute (IPLA), at first itinerant as we will see, and also of the Latin American Catechetical Institute (ICLA). In the sixth regular assembly in Mexico in 1961 the bishops gave themselves to the development of an adequate pastoral for the Latin American family. Again socioeconomic data were utilized but with a hermeneutical bias.[17] There was no indication of support for rapid or radical change, neither was there any apparent awareness of the presence and power of neocolonialism in Latin America. The Mexico meeting represented a new departure, but one within the scope of a "new Christendom," including even Dom Hélder Câmara at that time.[18]

In 1962 the Latin American bishops met for the first time in Rome, occasioned by the Second Vatican Council. There was no regular meeting of CELAM that year, but given the assembly of the episcopacy in its totality, together with the import of the Council, a new era began for CELAM. The seventh, eighth, and ninth regular assemblies of the Latin American bishops took place in Rome between 1963 and 1965, and Monseñor Larraín was able to state that "CELAM is the first group in the history of the Church to develop the concept of episcopal collegiality"[19] in a permanent and organic way. During these meetings the total reorganization of CELAM resulted, basically because of the experiences stemming from Vatican II.

The whole panorama changed completely, and the Church began to move with a different rhythm in Latin America. For this reason the tenth regular meeting of CELAM and the extraordinary assembly in Mar del Plata in 1966 were a kind of Medellín somewhat aborted by the prevailing conditions in Argentina and because of the lingering presence of the ideal of a new Christendom stemming primarily from the economic interpretations of CEPAL and from the political philosophy of Christian Democracy. The document representing the work of the Mar del Plata meeting, nevertheless, was a "theology of the temporal" together with "a Christian anthropology" — published under the title of "Theological Reflection on Development" — and was indicative of the new spirit.[20] CELAM was unquestionably moving in the direction of "developmentalism." The meeting continued from October 9 to 16, and Dom Hélder Câmara acted as the coordinator of the studies. He had said on September 19, "I have my own method of fighting against Communism, namely, by fighting against underdevelopment" because "a greater danger than Communism threatens the world. It is the capitalist system." The Bishop of Santo André, Jorge Marcos de Oliveira, had recently declared to university students, "Do not be intimidated. The current cruel repression reveals simply that the military is afraid of you. .... Remain united and strengthen your presence in the political arena. ... The men who today are directing Brazil have never been the true leaders, and it is because of the desire of certain foreign powers that these men are in power today." But the attitudes of Câmara and Oliveira are not evident in any way in the Declaration of Mar del Plata. There were too many compromises, too many half-tones. Also, Monseñor Larraín had died on June 22, 1966, and his absence was severely felt in CELAM.[21] The influence of Larraín's pastorals affected the meeting, however, even though theologically they reflected much of the spirit of the "new Christendom."[22] If the Mar del Plata assembly represented a short step forward rather than a leap, the eleventh regular meeting in Lima, which took place November 19– 26, 1967, was of even lesser significance. A transition was in the offing, nevertheless, as the emphasis began to shift from that of "development" to one of "liberation." The following year at Medellín was of imponderable importance for Latin America. It was not only the moment of the "application" of the Second Vatican Council but also of the discovery of the real Latin America and the transition to a clear commitment to liberation. Liberation had been supported for several years by a small number of priests and bishops, and Medellín evidenced that the number had grown to significant proportions.

In the Medellín meeting, because of the presence of a large number of journalists, Europe as well as the rest of the world was informed as to what was taking place in Latin America.

Early in 1968 when Pope Paul VI indicated that he would travel to Bogotá for the International Eucharistic Congress and for the meeting of the Second General Conference of Latin American Bishops in Medellín, a feeling of universality began to circulate. The events had repercussions far beyond what anyone imagined at the time.[23] Prior to the meeting in Medellín, hundreds of letters were sent by groups of lay persons, trade unionists, and priests to the bishops, to the national conferences, to CELAM, to the Pope, and to the Church in general. Many of these letters are included in the works of Gheerbrant, Laurentin, and in other documents related to the Medellín Conference. All of them contained the leaven of what was taking place among the masses. In preparation for the meeting, CELAM prepared a "Basic Document" in which the Latin American reality together with theological reflection and possible pastoral projections were included. Monseñor Aníbal Muñoz Duque, Apostolic Administrator in Bogotá regarded the document as far too negative, while Bishop Botero Salazar of Medellín stated that it had to be negative in view of the fact that a true diagnosis of the Latin American situation could hardly have been positive. The president of CELAM, Bishop Brandâo Vilela, also believed that "a false optimism would be even more dangerous." The Argentine episcopacy regarded the document as too advanced, negative, and even dangerous, but the theological judgment of Father Joseph Comblin began a ground swell. On June 14, 1968, the Brazilian *O Jornal* of Río published an article written by a group of theologians in Recife which Dom Hélder Câmara would later utilize personally in the second General Conference. *O Jornal*, however, branded Comblin as a "Leninist theologian," and this label was repeated in other Latin American newspapers, especially in *La República* of Bogotá. Comblin responded by circulating the Recife document in its entirety. In it one can see a theological interpretation based not on sociological statistics, but rather on an historical and political foundation in which the question of the gaining and wielding of power is analyzed. The "Basic Document," he asserted, was really quite general and deductive, and though it has value as a sociocultural analysis, it avoids dealing with the question of imperialism and with what is even more serious, the issue of autocolonialism.[24]

In Brazil, Monseñor Padim, Bishop of Lorena, published an article describing the meaning of what is usually referred to as "national security" in which he expounded on the contemporary militarist ideology and contended that in many respects it was comparable to what one might imagine existed in Nazi Germany.[25] In contrast, Monseñor Sigaud, Bishop of Diamantina, Bishop Moraes of Niteroi, and Bishop Castro Mayer of Campos circulated a violent denunciation of Father Comblin that included the accusation that "the Communists have infiltrated the ecclesiastical hierarchy." These bishops, twelve in all, were supported by the "Brazilian Association for the Defense of Tradition, Family, and Property," which a short time later opened branches in Argentina and Chile. In the meantime, Dom Hélder Câmara along with thirty-two other Brazilian bishops founded the "Movement for Moral and Liberating Influence."

Preparations continued for the second General Conference in Medellín. In Rome the Commission for Latin America, whose president was Monseñor Samoré, had in 1964 begun a new organism, the General Council of the Pontifical Commission for Latin America (COGECAL) composed of delegates from CELAM together with certain European bishops. The design of the Commission was to provide help for Latin America from Spain, France, Germany, and Belgium as well as from other European countries. This Roman superstructure named the president for the Commission for Latin America (CAL) as well as the copresident for the second General Conference in Medellín. The Commission even considered various concrete details such as expositions, themes, and internal regulations, and insisted that the last word in regard to all the questions dealt with in Medellín would be that of Rome. It was announced that the conference would be held in Medellín from August 26 to September 6, 1968, following the International Eucharistic Congress, which was to take place in Bogotá from August 20 to 24.

On the opening day of the Eucharistic Congress, Monseñor Lercano, representing the Pope, stated that "the Congress concludes an era which began with the colonization of Latin America with its fierce and radical Catholic religiosity and opens a new era nurtured by the spirit of the Second Vatican Council which was singularly mindful of the most profound exigencies of the Gospel." On August 22 Pope Paul VI arrived in Bogotá, the first Pope in history to come to America. During the three days that he was in the Colombian capital, he read four discourses that should be seen from the perspective of the previously issued encyclicals. "The bishops did not deviate from papal thought, but they did extract from it more profound and lasting dimensions. Medellín demonstrated that the discourses of Paul VI in Bogotá did not exhaust his understanding regarding the Latin American situation. But this regional situation had already been judged by the bishops themselves and not only by the Bishop of Rome."[26]

On his first day in Bogotá the Pope spoke to the priests and urged them to have "the clarity and the courage of the Spirit in promoting social justice and in loving and defending the poor."[27] On August 23 he spoke to the Colombian peasants and concluded by exhorting them "not to put their confidence in violence nor in revolution; such an attitude is contrary to the Christian spirit and can also retard and not promote social progress."[28] These words produced diverse reactions depending on the attitudes already manifested regarding the Latin American historical commitment. For certain observers they appeared to indicate that Medellín would be merely another meeting such as that of Mar del Plata. That same day, already proclaimed as the "Day of Development," the Pontiff declared that "some conclude that the basic problem of Latin America cannot be resolved without violence. . . . We must say and reaffirm that violence is neither evangelical nor Christian."[29]

Then on August 24, the Second General Conference of Latin American Bishops symbolically began with the Pope addressing the bishops and calling attention to the theologians and Christian thinkers who in abandoning the *philosophia perennis* "introduce into the field of faith a spirit of subversive criticism,"[30] exhorting the prelates to be obedient to the encyclical *Humanae Vitae*,[31] that together they might achieve "the formation of a new modern and Christian civilization."[32] In general the discourses of the Pope sounded in the ears of the Latin American people, with all respect that His Holiness deserves, as a call to patience on the part of the poor — which doubtless produced an immediate sigh of relief for the rich and the oppressors. It was as if the Pope had said, "We should now resign ourselves to suffer violence and injustice in peace." But he said nothing regarding the extent of the first kind of violence, "violence number 1," as Hélder Câmara expressed it. "You will find that everywhere injustices are a form of violence. One can and must say that they are everywhere the basic violence, violence number 1."[33]

Two days later, August 26, 146 cardinals, archbishops and bishops, 14 brothers, 6 nuns, and 15 laypersons, only four of whom were women, together with the various consultants met in Medellín. The theme of the Conference was "The Church in Present-Day Transformation of Latin America in the Light of the Council." There were numerous position papers reacting to the "Basic Document" given by Bishops Marcos McGrath of Panama; Eduardo F. Pironio, President of CELAM; Eugenio de Araújo Sales of Brazil who spoke on "The Church in Latin America and Human Promotion" in which the question of revolution and violence was debated; Samuel Ruiz García of Mexico; Pablo Muñoz Vegas of Ecuador; Luís E. Henríquez of Venezuela; and Leonidas E. Proaño of Ecuador. The four original issues dealt with by the position papers were augmented by order of Rome to include four others. Some of the proposed consultants such as François Houtart, Michael Schooyans, Augusto Vanistendael, Gonzalo Arroyo, and Manuel Velásquez were rejected by Rome.

The "Basic Document," which had been proposed for the first time in December 1966, took form between January 19 and 26, 1968, in a meeting of CELAM, and was submitted to Rome and to various episcopal conferences. It was revised considerably by the nine commissions that finally issued it as a part of sixteen fundamental documents.

Three little-known incidents characterized the Medellín Conference. The first was the intercommunion experienced on September 5 with the "separated brethren" from other Christian Churches and observers at the Conference. The second was the meeting of 200 university students and workers that took place each evening in the café La Castilla to discuss the same issues and problems that the bishops were debating, meetings that night after night were broken up by the police. The third incident was that the text of the conclusions was published and distributed before it was given final approval by Rome. Each of these events had its consequences.

The conclusions themselves centered on questions of varying importance. We will discuss only the essentials here. In general they manifested an awareness "that we are on the threshold of a new epoch in the history of our continent. It appears to be a time full of zeal for full emancipation, of liberation from every form of servitude, of personal maturity and of collective integration. In these signs we perceive the first indications of the painful birth of a new civilization" (Introduction).

In the section "Human Promotion," the issue of *justice* clearly resounds in the "doctrinal bases," surpassing the partial focus of the theology of development (McGrath) or of revolution (promoted in Protestant circles by Richard Shaull) and opting for a "theology of liberation" which, as we shall see, has primarily a biblical and political foundation. "It is the same God who, in the fullness of time, sent his son in the flesh so that He might come to *liberate* all men from the slavery to which sin has subjected them: hunger, misery, oppression, and ignorance, in a word, that injustice and hatred which have their origin in human selfishness."[34] The discussion of justice also included the observation that "in the economy of salvation the divine work is an action of integral human development and liberation which has love for its sole motive."[35]

In the discussion on *Peace* a new language resounded: the "power unjustly exercised by certain dominant sectors," "international tensions and external neocolonialism," "the growing distortion of international commerce," the "rapid flight of economic and human capital," the "international monopolies and international imperialism of money," and an "exacerbated nationalism" in some countries. In view of all these problems the bishops recognized

that in many instances Latin America finds itself faced with a situation of injustice that can be called *institutionalized violence*. . . . We should not be surprised therefore that the 'temptation to violence' is surfacing in Latin America. One should not abuse the patience of a people that for years has borne a situation that would not be acceptable to anyone with any degree of awareness of human rights.[36]

Addressing the question of the *Family and Demography*, the bishops gave a sociopolitical interpretation to the encyclical *Humanae Vitae*, and it was viewed not merely in an individual moral sense, but historically and within the perspectives of the "vicious cycle of underdevelopment." The bishops insisted, however, that in view of the fact that the majority of the Latin American countries were underpopulated, demographic growth was a prerequisite to development, but not at so pronounced a rate, because uncontrolled population growth impeded the so-called socioeconomic takeoff.[37]

Regarding *Education* the Conference proposed

a vision of education more in conformity with the integral development which we are seeking on our continent. We could call it "liberating education," that is, that which converts the student into the subject of his own development. Furthermore, "because all liberation is in anticipation of the complete redemption of Christ, the Church in Latin America is particularly in favor of all educational efforts which tend to free our people.[38]

All of the section "Evangelization and Growth in the Faith" reflects a new spirit and a more realistic analysis. We will refer especially to this in the final reflections in the next chapter.

In the third section of the conclusions, "The Visible Church and its Structures," the discussion of *Lay Movements* makes no reference whatever to Catholic Action but rather permits and even encourages the creation of new lay institutions, remembering that "the lay apostolate will have greater sign value and greater ecclesial weight when promoted through teams or communities of faith, to whom Christ specifically promised his cohesive presence."[39]

The conclusions regarding *Priests* allowed great latitude for new commitments and new styles more in keeping with the ideal of service, but lacked perhaps at this point a deeper and more comprehensive interpretation of the ecclesial institution and the way in which it should endure the blow and the transformation from an agonizing Christendom to a missionary Christianity in a universal, secular, and pluralistic civilization. The Conference reached no conclusion in regard to the conferring of holy orders on the faithful who are married, which, incidentally, has nothing to do with the debate on the marriage of priests, for the Church has always ordained faithful who are married, but never have priests been allowed to marry and continue in their office. Married deacons do not resolve the pastoral question that the Latin American Church faces, and the day will come in the not-too-distant future when the married adult, together with the natural leaders in the basic Christian communities, will be ordained, as was always the case in the oldest of Catholic traditions, namely, in the Oriental Church.[40]

The *Conclusions* of the Conference represent the most important document in the history of the Church in Latin America, and they manifest the same spirit which prompted and animated the Third Provincial Council of Lima, which Toribio de Mogrovejo celebrated in 1582—1583. The major difference is that the Second General Conference of Latin American Bishops was continental, and the Council of Lima was only for the immense archdiocese of Mogrovejo. Further, the third Council of Lima was the "American Trent" with a Tridentine theology and pastoral, while the second General Conference of Medellín was the "Vatican II of Latin America" with a theology of liberation and a missionary pastoral. Medellín has had and will continue to have enormous influence in Latin America. In the twelfth regular assembly of CELAM, held November 24—28, 1969, in São Paulo, it was declared that the agreements and resolutions of the second General Conference would be "the norm for inspiration and action in the coming years."[41] Other reactions were, however, discordant but unanimous in judging the Conference as the most significant event in the history of the Latin American Church and perhaps in the continent as a whole during the twentieth century.[42] The Chilean episcopacy meeting as a synod[43] on October 4, 1968, called laypersons, priests, and members of the Church to practice reconciliation and peace and cited Medellín as the authoritative basis.[44] The document issued from this synod spoke of the necessity of overcoming the opposition that existed between the so-called churches of the poor, the young Church, the clandestine Church, and the rebel Church. Various episcopacies followed in their attempts to apply the conclusions of the Medellín Conference. The Argentine bishops issued their "Declaration of the Argentine Episcopacy" in San Miguel where they met from April 21 to 26, 1969.[45] On July 2 of the same year a meeting of the Colombian episcopacy was held. In August the Mexican bishops met together with laypersons and religious in an open spirit of fraternity and dialogue.[46] The bishops of Paraguay met from August 11 to 14, and the Venezuelan episcopacy met during the same month. In Guatemala a meeting of the Episcopal Council of Central America and Panama met on August 17—22 with the same purpose of applying the conclusions of Medellín.[47] The Brazilian episcopacy was one of the first to meet.

It is evident, therefore, that within a year of Medellín all the Latin American episcopacies had reaffirmed the *Conclusions* of the second General Conference. The new spirit prompted a joint meeting between CELAM and the National Catholic Conference of Bishops of the United States, which took place June 3—5, 1969, in Caracas. In the final communique of this interamerican meeting the bishops declared their support of "the principal outline of the pastoral contained in the Conclusions of the II General Conference of Latin American Bishops." A second meeting followed in Miami in February 1970.

The fourteenth regular assembly of CELAM convened in Sucre in November 1972, in what appeared to be a new epoch for the organization. These collegial meetings of the bishops represent only a single facet of a phenomenon that we will consider in the following sections.

2. The Church and the Militarist, Bourgeois, or Reformist State

During the period from 1962 to 1972 the Church passed through a momentous, precarious stage of its history. At times it was a history of torturous zigzags wherein the testimony that could have been expected from her was totally discredited. The situation was quite dissimilar from country to country depending of the foresight of the bishops — frequently there were Church leaders who adopted prophetic positions — of the priests, and of the laity. In this section we will outline the attitude of the Church in regard to certain bourgeois states and the prevailing social situation. Then in the following two sections we will see the change in attitude regarding violence, socialism, and agrarian reform.

The Church received blows from the "Herodians," just as Herod the Great attempted to eliminate Jesus Christ, the Child of Bethlehem.[48] We will discuss the situation by countries and by areas but will give more attention to the regions where reaction to the political pressure applied by the military helped to shape the developing attitude of the Church.

(1) The coup d'etat in Brazil in 1964

Following the government of Juscelino Kubitschek (1955– 1961), Jânio da Silva Quadros was elected President. He resigned unexpectedly on August 25, 1961, leaving the presidency to João Goulart, the Vice-President who lacked genuine national support and who was unanimously opposed by the military as well as by a majority of Brazil's governors. Goulart promised reforms but did not deliver. Earlier, in 1961, the Brazilian episcopacy had founded the Basic Education Movement utilizing the methodology of Paulo Freire.[49] By 1963 there were some 7,353 schools using 15,000 radio receivers with 180,000 pupils and 7,500 teachers. The motto was "To Live is to Struggle," the title of one of the primers that, after the military takeover, was condemned by Carlos Lacerda, the Governor of Guanabara (State of Río), who ordered 3,000 copies confiscated on the basis that they were subversive. The governor also ordered the police, according to the *Jornal do Brasil* of February 24, 1964, to enter the publishing office of the bishops and to seize their alphabet charts. Monseñor Tavora, Bishop of Aracaju and Director of the Basic Education Movement, objected to the accusations by asking, "Are the papal encyclicals also subversive?" In the Northeast, Monseñor Eugenio Sales, founder of the "Natal Movement," proposed a cultural and social reform for urban dwellers and peasants that was a forerunner to the work of the government agency SUDENE (Superintendency of the Development of the Northeast), which since 1959 was responsible for stimulating and planning development for that area of Brazil. Sales also suggested beginning a rural workers union akin to the peasant leagues that had been organized earlier by Francisco Julião, and cooperatives for colonization. Only a small minority involved in these movements was pro-Communist or even pro-Cuban, and Monseñor Padim, Auxiliary Bishop of Río, declined to condemn them. In 1963, Cardinal Motta of São Paulo blessed a group of cement workers who for nine months had been on strike. There followed a Message issued by the Brazilian Bishops Conference regarding the situation in the country that, they said, indicated the need for a thoroughgoing agrarian, banking, fiscal, administrative, and electoral reform.[50] This episcopal message was published on April 30 under the title *"Pacem in Terris* and the Brazilian Reality." It condemned the *status quo* and declared that "expropriation in the people's interest is not contrary to the social teachings of the Church." Almost immediately there appeared the "Association for Tradition, Family, and Property," composed in part of many conservative Catholics who with rosaries in hand met in a rally under the aegis of Monseñor Sigaud, Bishop of Diamantina, to oppose the plans for agrarian reform. Monseñor Sales, in contrast, described "a pastoral experience in the underdeveloped region" of Northeast Brazil that indicated the new way in which the Church was facing up to its pastoral responsibilities.[51]

The weakness and ineptitude of Goulart together with the renewed aspirations of the military to be involved in the political situation prompted a coup d'etat on the night of March 31, 1964, led by General Castello Branco who on April 15 officially inaugurated the seventh Brazilian Republic. Rapidly there followed imprisonments, expulsions from the country, censure, withdrawal of citizenship, and the beginning of political tortures. These were the most important events in the decade of the 1960s in regard to the politics of the oligarchy that supported the military in conjunction with the North American strategy, all together forming a perfectly organized system of oppression.

The reaction of the Church was anything but unanimous. Monseñor Warmeling, Bishop of Joinville, wrote in O Luzeiro Mariano that "the vast majority of the Brazilian people are Christians, and for this reason we support the courageous members of the Congregation of Mariana against Catholic Action in this diocese" (of Belo Horizonte). "It is common knowledge," stated the Bishop, "that Catholic Action has been infiltrated by Communists." "The social doctrine of the revolution led by Castello Branco," asserted the Prelate, "coincides with the social doctrine of the Church."

A few days before this declaration of April 2 by Monseñor Warmeling, the Secretary General of the Brazilian Bishops Conference, Dom Hélder Câmara, had been named to and had occupied the Archdiocese of Olinda and Recife in the state of Pernambuco. He indicated that he took advantage of the occasion to set forth with clarity his thinking because he knew that if God did not give him the courage to speak out in that moment of entering the diocese, later he would possibly lack it.[52] In prophetic as well as poetic words, Dom Hélder began his oration stating,

I am a native of the Northeast who speaks to other natives of the Northeast with our eyes on Brazil. . . . I am a human being who is regarded as human with the same weaknesses and sin as all men of all races and in all areas of the world. I am a Christian who is speaking to Christians but with an ecumenically open heart to all men of all creeds and all ideologies. I am a Bishop of the Catholic Church who attempting to imitate Christ comes not to be served but to serve. Catholics and non-Catholics, believers and unbelievers, hear my fraternal greeting: Praise to our Lord Jesus Christ.[53]

Thus the Bishop of Recife began his prophetic path: "It would be an error to assume that because we struggle against atheistic Communism that we are defenders of liberal capitalism. And it would be incorrect to conclude that we are Communists simply because we criticize with Christian courage the egoistic position of economic liberalism." Câmara continued by condemning the imprisonments of the directors of the MEB, of the JUC, of the Popular Action movement of laymen, and of the Fraternal Confederation of Rural Workers.

Fathers Senna, Alméry, and others were already living in exile, and hundreds of other priests had been imprisoned. The Marplan Company, similar to the Gallup organization in the United States, reported that some sixty-three percent of the Brazilian population were against the military takeover but virtually no one, not even the bishops, desired the return of Goulart.

On May 7, 1964, Tristâo de Atayde (Amoroso Lima) wrote in the Fohla de São Paulo,

When men of world renown in the field of education such as Anisio Teixeira, in the field of sociology as Josué de Castro, in the field of economics as Celso Furtado are suspect simply beause their thinking is different from that of the new dominant theology, we face a plan of cultural terrorism. When philosophers and pure metaphysicians such as Ubaldo Puppi or young intellectual leaders such as Luis Alberto Gommes de Souza and others are thrown into prison without being charged, or simply because their methods of literacy training are considered to be subversive, we face a plan of cultural terrorism. When the police of the country distribute instructions to clean up the nation and prescribe the following: "We warn the groups of Catholic Action ... that they separate themselves from and abstain from activities incompatible not only with their own program, but also with the permanent interest of the Nation and of the people," as Mussolini attempted to do in regard to Italian Catholic Action, as if the Church in Brazil were under the tutelage of a totalitarian State, we face a plan of cultural terrorism.

All this prompted the Brazilian episcopacy to reach a decision, somewhat ambiguous, and to make a statement or declaration entitled "Regarding the Events which Took Place as a Consequence of the Fall of Goulart."[54] More courageous was the document of the bishops of the Northeast, which stated, "It is essential to establish Christian order in the country."[55]

The position of the bishops, however, was not unanimous. Cardinal Rossi of Sâo Paulo, who replaced Monseñor Motta who had voluntarily retired, celebrated a mass stating that by "the mercy of God and the courage, piety, and strength of his children, the imminent Communist plot had been thwarted," apparently a reference to Goulart, "which proposed to change this Christian nation to a zone of silence." Meanwhile Monseñor Scherer, Bishop of Porto Alegre, protested the persecution of Professor Erani Fiori, an intellectual leader in Río Grande who was a well-known disciple of Jacques Maritain, ... tended toward existential and Hegelian thinking. The clash between the military government and the Church, however, was not public. Only in 1965 did the tension and disagreement become known, and it has continued to ebb and flow since that time. These have been some of the major events in the relations between the Church and state in this century, and they have prophetic significance for the history of the Latin American Church whose antecedents can be seen in the struggle of the bishops in the sixteenth century in defense of the Indians, as well as in that of the Mexican *Cristeros* within a doctrine of Christendom in the early years of the twentieth century, though this last example is highly equivocal and certainly not prophetic except as a conservative sign.

On May 11, 1965, Dom Jorge Marcos de Oliveira, Bishop of Santo André, wrote an open letter to Castello Branco stating,

We love Brazil and its people, but how long will it be before the widespread hunger will unleash a civil war? We are against war. We condemn it, and we fear it as contrary to our Christian training and to the nature of the Brazilian people. How happy we would be if, when we look up into the skies of our country, rather than seeing planes carrying our armed soldiers to a neighboring country (Santo Domingo) we could see the most diligent means being employed for the solution of the very serious Brazilian crisis![56]

This did not, however, prevent Cardinal Rossi's declaring in New York that "Brazil is moving in the right direction" and that the government desired what the Church desired. Ironically, when Rossi returned to Sâo Paulo he was faced with the problems of staggering unemployment and lack of food, contradictions that resulted in the loss of much of his authority. In the meantime, Dom Hélder was harassed by a breaking and entering into the episcopal palace in Recife, but he continued to preach. In March

1965 he spoke on the subject of "A Dialogue Between the Developed World and the World in Development,"[57] Then on March 31, 1966, he refused to celebrate a mass commemorating the military coup d'etat of 1964. He wrote the Commandant of the Fourth Army that the mass would signify a "civic-military reunion with political overtones."[58] Between July 12 and 14 when, as a result of reports by the ACO (Workers Catholic Action of the Northeast) and of the JAC (Catholic Agrarian Youth), which had met in February, the bishops of the area met in Recife and issued their "Manifesto of the Bishops of the Northeast."[59] This courageous declaration sparked a serious conflict between the Church and the state.

"The ambition and the uncontrolled egoism of some," stated the bishops, "has created the current situation in which the poor are sacrificed for the benefit of the privileged." Immediately Dom Hélder was accused of organizing a plot against the government. On July 27 the Diario da Noite of São Paulo announced that the military government had prohibited the circulation of the "Manifesto." Friar Chico, a French Dominican in São Paulo, had declared a few days earlier that the government was torturing student leaders and that there existed in Brazil "a police state which showed no respect for the sacred principle of basic freedom." Then General Gouveia do Amaral, Commandant of the Fourth Army, without discussion with or securing the authorization of the bishops, ordered the distribution of, among the parish priests and other Church leaders of the Northeast, a vilifying circular against Dom Hélder. The campaign to discredit him expanded throughout the country. In an article published in the Jornal de Comercio of Recife on August 21 written by the famous Gilberto Freyre and Gustavo Corçao — prestige-wise their position in Brazil was analogous to Maritain and von Hildebrand in Europe — along with Bishop Castro Mayer of Campos in the State of São Paulo, criticized the "Manifesto" because it impeded a country that "desires to repel Communism in a decisive way."

In an editorial published in the Estado de São Paulo on August 6, the position of Bishop Castro Mayer was supported. Meanwhile, Castello Branco changed commandants for the Fourth Army, naming General Souza Aguiar, which was interpreted by some as a triumph for Dom Hélder. Dom Fragoso, Bishop of Crateus, Valdir Calheiros, Auxiliary Bishop of Río, and Vicente Scherer of Porto Alegre, together with many others, came out publicly in defense of Dom Hélder.

Cardinal Rossi issued a statement on August 18 deploring those who were "pitting the Church against the government," obviously a veiled defense of the status quo. The same day, however, Alceu Amoroso Lima published in A Folha de São Paulo an article comparing Dom Hélder with Dom Vital who during the time of the Empire defended the Church against the state. "Now," wrote Amoroso, "Dom Hélder represents a change from a polemical Church to a missionary Church." It should be noted that during this period — the tenth stage in the history of the Church in Latin America, 1962 to the present — the Church was not attempting to defend its privileges or rights acquired during the period of Christendom, but rather to risk and sacrifice itself in service to the oppressed and ravaged peoples. Brazil is, therefore, a key, a paradigmatic country.

The National Union of Students had scheduled its twenty-eighth Congress for Belo Horizonte, but a police order prohibited the meeting and warned everyone against allowing the students to use their premises. The Congress was held secretly, however, in the Franciscan convent.[60] On August 4, Franciscan Friar Guido Vlasman of Río stated the reason why asylum was being given to the students. "The government desires to maintain the Church in a subservient position while attempting to impose upon the country a type of liberal Christianity wherein there will be a divorce between the Christian and the secular life." Father Corazza, adviser to the JUC, was threatened with imprisonment. On August 1, Friar Chico, OP, defended the students, and the following day he was jailed. Catholic Action, the JEC, JUC, and JAC became virtually clandestine organizations. In September student demonstrations were brutally broken up by the police, which in turn prompted an immediate reaction on the part of bishops, priests, and laypersons. Dom Angier led a student demonstration in Piracicaba on September 22, and in October Dom José Newton, Archbishop of Brasilia, was accused of subversion.

The following year (1967) brought new tensions between the Church and the state in Brazil. When the bishops attempted to apply the teachings of the papal encyclical *Populorum Progressio,* and when Friar Chico, inaugurating the "Movement for Peace" in the Church of Santo Domingo on June 11, appealed to the faithful (who were standing), "Those who are in favor of protesting against the war, please remain standing," no one sat down. No less unsettling for the government and the defenders of public order were the declarations of some of the Brazilian bishops in regard to Cuba, as well as the Manifesto of the ACO of the Northeast issued on May 1 under the title, "The Northeast: Development Without Justice," which declared that "a capitalist structure" had been substituted for the feudal structure in that area of Brazil. On November 6 an ex—government minister, Raimundo de Brito, accused the priests of the Northeast of sowing seeds of subversion. These events, of course, brought the conflict out into the open and are only examples of many that could be cited. During 1967 Costa e Silva succeeded Castello Branco as head of the government, and on July 3 the police violently entered the joint student residences of the University of São Paulo, expelled the students, injured some of them, and arrested a priest. Cardinal Rossi, along with 127 professors and 50 priests, issued a strong protest against the police violence. A month later the National Union of Students secretly met again in the Benedictine convent of Campinas, São Paulo. On August 2 the police (SNI) jailed eleven North American Benedictines who were working in Vinhedo and Campinas, as well as the Dominican Friar Chico. The reaction of the Church was again unanimous. Cardinal Rossi issued a protest the same day to the governor. Two days later the newspaper *O Estado de São Paulo* published an editorial entitled "Religious Orders and National Security," in which the Cardinal was personally attacked. The clergy of the Archdiocese responded by defending the Bishop on August 6: "His Eminence, Cardinal Motta, was many times called a Communist by the press. His Excellency Dom Hélder Câmara has been accused of heresy . . . and now, this same newspaper begins to accuse His Eminence Cardinal Rossi." A group of women members of Catholic Action in São Paulo, and later Monseñor Scherer of Porto Alegre criticized priests whom they said were utilizing the prestige of the Cardinal for the promotion of personal ideas.

A second important conflict developed in the diocese of São Luis regarding the "Educational Radio of Maranhão," which operated under the authority of Bishop de Motta e Albuquerque. The station was shut down for eight days for having broadcast on September 6, the Day of Independence, a text that began by stating: "Is this truly independence that we are celebrating? Is a country that has more than thirty millions of undernourished people independent? . . . Brazil is a rich country, but what is happening to our riches?" The Bishop also protested against the police by exclaiming, "In a region of death it is necessary to work in order that people might live."

A new conflict developed as a result of a discourse given by Dom Hélder before the Legislative Assembly of Pernambuco on the occasion of his being declared an honorary citizen. Even though General Souza Aguiar was present, Câmara asked, "If tomorrow Joaquín Nabuco were to come to Recife and were to visit, for example, our sugar production zone, would he not feel impelled to renew the abolitionist campaign? ... Without an effective understanding in the Third World we will never be able to pass from being beggars to equals." When on November 30 the General was accorded the same honor, he responded quite obviously to Câmara's earlier statement by saying, "It is necessary to fight against the Communist invaders and against their allies including their cretin tools."

On November 5 four Catholic young people were arrested and jailed by the police on orders from the military for distributing pamphlets produced by the Catholic Diocesan Youth (JUDICA) in Volta Redonda. Six days later, November 11, the episcopal palace of Dom Valdir Calheiros was surreptitiously entered. The bishop gave a statement to the *Jornal do Brazil,* copies of which were seized by the army on November 14. Calheiros responded by issuing a public document that was read in the churches on November 19 and that stated: "Colonel Armenio is worried about ferreting out subversives. I am worred about: (1) the wage negotiations which have dragged on for five months; (2) the difference the increase in cost of living means for many." The same newspaper, *Jornal do Brasil,* published on November 23 an editorial entitled "Red Vestments." General Aragâo, a representative of the hard-liners, declared on November 27 that "the Church has become an asylum of the enemies of God and of men. ... Popular Action is confused with Catholic Action" — both of which, he said, were led by subversives. The same day Representative Moreira Alves presented in the House of Deputies a list of fifty-two priests who were then either prisoners or who had been expelled from the country, indicted, or prosecuted in Brazil since March 1964. On November 29 the Central Commission of the Brazilian Bishops Conference, composed of twenty-two bishops representing the entire country, examined the case of Dom Valdir and issued a declaration on December 1 entitled "The Mission of the Hierarchy in Today's World." The declaration stated that

it is our responsibility to explain more fully what is our mission, a mission unknown to some, misunderstood by others, and deliberately falsified by certain groups who pretend to serve the Church by promoting their own interests. Neither misunderstanding nor distortion will prevent us from continuing the function given us by divine command and which has marked the presence of the Church in our history.... Their assertion that they are defending *Christian civilization,* while at the same time they deny the Church's mission of defending human values, is nothing more than the defense of a disguised paganism. We are surprised by the miraculous transformation of violent liberals and agnostics into defenders of an other-worldly Christianity far removed from the gospel.[61]

In 1968, the year of the Medellín Conference, an authentic "silent Church" existed dramatically in Brazil. Dom Antonio Batista Fragoso, Bishop of Crateus, stated in a report given in Belo Horizonte in January on "The Gospel and Social Justice":

Christ did not come merely to liberate man from his sins. Christ came to liberate him from the consequences of sin. These consequences are seen in our houses, in our streets, in our cities, in the interior of our country, and they are called prostitution, racial discrimination, marginalization of the peasants, the lack of roads and highways, and the scarcity and inad-equacy of housing. ... To those who accuse the defenders of justice as being Communists, as struggling to superimpose a subversive regime on Brazil, we raise the question, Why? For the poor do not expect anything from those who illegally wield the economic power.[62]

In July, Bishop Batista issued his courageous document entitled "The Doctrine of National Security," mentioned above, in which he demonstrated that the basic ideology of the Brazilian military could be compared with the doctrine of Adolf Hitler and his predecessors by way of Hegel, Fichte, and Gobineau. The Brazilian military, however, had — according to Batista — substituted Christ either "for the myth of blood and race" or for a paganized view of " Western Christian civilization."

Dom Hélder, meanwhile, having returned from Europe, began his crusade for nonviolence in Río on July 19, the "Movement of Liberating Moral Persuasion," which was supported by many bishops and which prepared the way for Medellín. There followed a new intensive campaign to persuade Rome to remove Dom Hélder from office, as had occurred earlier with Monseñor Podestá, Bishop of Avellaneda in Argentina. The campaign against Father Comblin was more "grist for the mill." But the Brazilian episcopacy issued a declaration on July 20 entitled "Evangelical Imperatives for Integral Development in our Country."[63] Then in August, shortly before the Medellín Conference, a letter from 350 priests was sent to their bishops, many of whom would be going to Medellín,[64] in which the Brazilian people were described as an "assassinated people."

The year 1969 was one of violence. Police tortures of political prisoners multiplied. Priests, religious, and laypersons became the objects of brutal and inhumane treatment. Father Juan Talpe testified after fleeing to Chile that he had on several occasions "seen a cadaver with the nails of both the hands and the feet pulled out, the eyes punched out, and the body shamefully and horribly mutilated. This [Talpe declared] was what had happened to Juan Lucas Alvez of Río de Janeiro.[65] Thirty-nine priests of Belo Horizonte sent to the Medellín Conference a document describing the tortures perpetrated against the Brazilian people, and accused three of the cardinals of having consented to the government's imposition of the death penalty. Because of the illness of Costa e Silva, a Junta took charge of the government and decreed the death penalty for subversion. The episcopacy responded publicly on November 21, 1968, when Dom Valdir of Volta Redonda accused the government of using torture against political prisoners. The government responded by opening a new investigation of Valdir. Cardinal Sales then denounced the abuses and violence, especially those of the "Death Squadron" — a body of anonymous vigilantes who were responsible for more than one thousand assassinations in Brazil. Paul VI spoke on March 25, 1970, regarding the tortures in Brazil, but the government appeared to be insensitive to all of his criticisms. Later, the Pope refused to receive a special envoy to the Vatican, Colonel Manso Neto, and as a result of these international repercussions the Brazilian government accused the bishops of national treason and of discrediting the country. Finally, there was some consideration given by the government to trying seventeen bishops of the Northeast before a military tribunal on the basis that their activity was contrary to the "security of the State," a plan that, according to the Dutch news agency KNP, originated with the CIA. The tortures continued,[66] but the Church did not abandon its opposition. The death of a priest in Recife, as we will subsequently note, gave the Brazilian Church an authentic Christian and priestly martyr.

(2) The coup d'etat in Argentina in 1966

In Brazil the determined attitude of the Church was manifested primarily by the bishops, while in *Argentina* the prophetic position in regard to social and political questions was adopted by the laity and the priests. The Argentine episcopacy simply lacked the foresight. The revolution of Onganía in 1966 was analogous to the military overthrow of Brazil in 1964.[67] The opposition of Argentine Catholics therein began from below, that is, with the laity. With Perón, Catholicism was rightist, nationalistic, and integrist in theology; but beginning in 1954 there was a social Catholicism — democratic in policy — that opposed Perón and that was alert to social problems but at the same time espoused the ideal of a "new Christendom," that is, Christian Democracy, philosophically Maritainian, which was concretized in the political party by the same name, in university "humanism," and in Catholic Action of 1955. This form of Catholicism was suppressed by Perón and therefore became *antiperonista*. Thus, an autonomy of the temporal and an almost dualistic relationship between the Church and the State developed during this period. Only in 1960 did there appear a force with a new awareness, the JUC, in the meeting of Lavallol. The later meetings in Santa Fe (1961), in Embalse (1962), and in Tandil (1963) indicated that the experiences of university "humanism" and of Christian Democracy were a kind of social Christianity, but the Christian left was an "integrism of the left" and was a continuation of "the myth of a new Christendom." By 1962 it became evident that new directions were demanded. The Peronists won the national elections on March 18. John XXIII injected a new spirit into world Catholicism, and in October the Second Vatican Council began. The Argentine bishops had published a declaration "On the National Situation" on June 29 describing the institutional chaos in the country.[68]

In 1963 the "Social Christianity" of Christian Democracy became open to populism and to Peronism, the group known as "Human Economy" was organized, and many of the followers of Perón became involved in leftist groups. Meanwhile Cardinal Antonio Caggiano acted as conciliator between sectors of the army, and José María Guido — a puppet of the military — exercised the presidential functions.

In 1964 the CGT (General Federation of Labor) launched its "Plan of Struggle," which was preceded by a very unusual act for that time when Father José Ruperto led the "March of the Unemployed" of the meatpackers guild of Berisso who worked for Swift and Armour. The demonstration was dispersed by a police order, and Father Ruperto continued alone walking the six miles from Berisso to La Plata where he presented to the Legislature a memorial that declared, "The time has come to work."

The renewal of Peronism in Argentina produced the first serious conflict among priests in Latin America. Father Viscovich, Dean of the Faculty of Economic Sciences, Nelson Dellaferrera, and José Gaido y Vaudagna issued two public statements entitled "New Pharisees See the Church as an Industrial Company" and "Between the Church of the Stock Market and the Church of the CGT, I Remain with the Latter." Archbishop Ramón Castellanos reacted negatively, and the conflict between the two opposing sides became widespread. The younger clergy had become politically and socially aware, as we will describe in a special section on the evolution of this basic question for the Latin American Church. The Cardinal again became a mediator between President-elect Arturo Illía and the CGT, which was supported by 1,900,000 workers on strike in some 4,000 industries. The Catholic attitude became more radicalized between integrism on the right and progressive reformism on the left.[69]

From June 28 until July 9, 1965, eighty priests, together with Monseñor Podestá, Bishop of Avellaneda and Quarracino, met in Quilmes. A new image of the Church began to emerge.[70] On June 28, 1966, the Brazilian situation was repeated. The inept government of Illía was deposed by a military takeover led by General Juan Carlos Onganía. There followed the rise of the traditional groups, especially those Catholics who represented the old leaders of "Humanism" and Christian Democracy who together with the political and economic liberals were willing to work with the new government. The purpose of the "Revolution of 1966" was to unite the Church and the military as the foundation for the defense of the "Western Christian civilization." The relations between the government and the Church, therefore, were very close, and on October 10 the government renounced its opportunity to present candidates for various bishoprics. The old system of the *Patronato* thereby ended in Argentina.

On July 28, however, Monseñor Devoto, Bishop of Goya, manifested his anxiety in what he regarded as the appearance of a "compromise" between the hierarchy and the government. Monseñor Podestá declared that "identification with any political regime would be prejudicial to the Church" (August 16). Conflicts immediately resulted. First, there was the confrontation over the editing of the periodical *Tierra Nueva* (*New World*), that is, between the previous directors of the JUC and Cardinal Caggiano who was the founder of Catholic Action in Argentina and who demanded unconditional obedience on the part of priests and parishoners. The editors of *Tierra Nueva* desired to rethink the theological and historical foundations of Christians praxis, and the Cardinal objected, saying that the periodical "used a language half historical and half prophetic."[71]

More important was the conflict in the Córdoba parish Cristo Obrero (Christ the Worker), where seventy university students went on a fast protesting the situation in the country. The two parish priests, José Gaido and Nelson Dellaferrera, supported the students and were thus forced to resign. In their farewell letter of October 1966, Gaido and Dellaferrera declared that their "pastoral experience in Cristo Obrero had been violently aborted."[72]

The third conflict developed around Monseñor Podestá who was the object of continual criticism by the government, the hierarchy, and the Apostolic Nuncio. On December 4, 1967, Podestá was relieved of the post that he had assumed in 1962, and since that time he has known how to create a populist response. On November 2, 1967, he declared publicly, "I am personally responsible to the Apostolic Nuncio for the deterioration which has been produced." He even said, "Contrary to all that I could have believed or thought, the defamation and calumny have become public including that from high ecclesiastical circles."[73] The Bishop of San Luis, Carlos Cafferata, condemned the government on May 8, 1968. On January 7, Monseñor Víctor Gómes Aragón, Bishop of Tucumán, came out in defense of the priest, Father Sánchez, and thereby clashed with the governor. Monseñor Iriarte, Bishop of Reconquista, issued a pastoral letter regarding the "shameful exploitation" of the inhabitants of the northeast region of Argentina.[74] In Mendoza, Córdoba, Tucumán, San Isidro, and Rosario the conflict between the priests and the government created a climate of confrontation, and on July 17, 1968, the parishoners prevented the new priest named by Archbishop Bolatti from assuming pastoral responsibilities. An escort of seventy uniformed police clashed with the persons who were protesting the appointment of the new pastor, and five persons from Canãda Gómez were wounded, all of them shot with .45 caliber bullets.

Finally, there was the event that brought about the downfall of Onganía: the *Cordobazo* (the Córdoba event). On May 29, 1969, workers who were out on strike from the industrial plants in Córdoba were demonstrating in the central part of the city. There were barricades, shootings, and demonstrations that reproduced in Argentina the veritable "May" of Paris. Committed Christians united in expressing their opposition to the government. Workers and students alike violently protested what was taking place in the country. The Bishop of President R. Sáenz Pena, Monseñor Italo Di Stefano, came out in defense of the youth. "I can attest to the fact," stated the bishop, "that their motives are pure, authentic, renewed and renewing. ... A great deal of the spirit of the Gospel resides in them." Meanwhile, seventeen priests in Mendoza stated that "the attitude of our students cannot be taken lightly. ... Our comfortable attachment to tranquility ... is what condemns us to successive military regimes. In no way should our reflection encourage the old professional politicians. ... It is the people and only the people who are mobilized."[75] The government, nevertheless, continued to present itself as Catholic.

The difficulties that the workers were having in Chocón-Río Colorado prompted the Bishop of Neuquén, Monseñor Francisco de Nevares, to issue a statement regarding "the socioeconomic situation in northern Neuquén"[76] and to say in a news conference[77] that what appeared to be "the greatest Argentine work of the twentieth century could become the greatest Argentine disgrace of the twentieth century."

Finally, the government proposed to consecrate Argentina to the Virgin of Luján. The president made the announcement on November 12, 1969, stating that "as President of the Nation" he would offer the country to the Virgin. The "Priests for the Third World" publicly replied, saying that "we expect that the people will not respond to such an invitation in which religion is used in this way," that is, to smother opposition. The episcopacy, however, met between November 18 and 26, and the consecration took place on December 8.

The year 1970 witnessed the beginnings of urban guerrilla extremism. The kidnapping of former President Pedro Eugenio Aramburu and his subsequent execution have not been clarified, nor has the attempt to involve the Third World priest Alberto Carbone in the incident. Suffice it to say, Carbone was accused of being implicated, and following a prolonged trial he was released. The government attempted in every way to discredit the priests of the Third World movement. During the period that the excommunication of the *Correntino* priest Marturet was announced in Rome, the Argentine episcopacy issued a declaration that was exhortive and critical but not condemnatory. The disagreement between the government and the priests continued.[78] To mark the beginning of the new year, 1971, Monseñor Zazpe, Archbishop of Santa Fe and President of the Department of the Pastoral of CELAM, wrote a courageous pastoral regarding conditions in the country, the injustices, and the position of the Church. The Bishop of Paraná, Monseñor Tórtolo, President of the Bishops Conference, noted that the prelates should not refrain from offering guidance by expressing their "personal opinion" regarding events. All of this tends to point up the fact that in Argentina it has been the priests who have given testimony to the people of the Christian faith.

"Recent history shows us that until the end of the II Vatican Council the Church was conservative; in the period immediately following the Council, a liberal and progressive spirit of modernization and renewal prevailed. Ultimately, currents of sociopolitical, revolutionary, and popular orientation have begun to increase."[79]

The overwhelming triumph of Peronism on March 11 and on September 23, 1973, provided a *raison d'être* for the "Priests for the Third World."

(3) The 1968 coup d'etat in Peru

From all indications Peru would have witnessed in 1962 the election to the presidency of Raul Haya de la Torre, but the military aborted the electoral process. When a new election was held the government was under the control of a coalition headed by Fernando Belaunde Terry. The episcopacy had issued a pastoral letter entitled "Politics: a Social Responsibility," which emphasized the need for Christians to participate in the elections of 1963. That same year guerrilla centers began to spring up and later were confused with a process of expropriation of land, which was accelerated in 1964.

Belaunde decreed the death penalty and launched a bloody repression in the Amazon areas of the Sierra against the mountain strongholds of the peasants. The loss of confidence in and the deterioration of the government, however, brought about a military takeover on the night of October 2, 1968 — similar to the Brazilian and Argentine coups — but with characteristics far more nationalistic and with tendencies more and more popular. Cardinal Landázuri Ricketts stated that he rejoiced in the "affirmation of national sovereignty and economic independence which the complete recovery of the petroleum complex at Talara represented. ...." At the same time he expressed his "sincere desire that the nation return as soon as possible to the sound exercise of democratic suffrage and constitutional normality."[80]

The Peruvian military has avoided for the most part any confrontation with either the laity or the clergy. The episcopacy approved in 1970 the "Law of Industrial Communities," an important plan for development. This did not signify, however, that Peru had become the best of all possible worlds. On the contrary, already in March 1968 an important group of priests met in Cieneguilla, and later with the support of the Cardinal they issued a "Declaration of Peruvian Priests," which stated that "Peru is a proletarian nation in the world," and "the majority of Peruvians are proletarians in Peru."[81] This sociopolitical interpretation apparently upset some people in the country, and, according to the priests, their statements were distorted and condemned. But they insisted that "the history of the Church and the history of the world are mutually influential."

The Peruvian bishops concluded a meeting of the National Conference on January 25, 1969, with a declaration entitled "The Church Denounces this Sinful Situation." Church buildings were occupied by workers, especially the Cathedral of Trujillo, and the increasing sociopolitical awareness of the Peruvian Church became evident. The National Office of Social Investigation (ONIS), directed by Peruvian clergy, issued a statement supporting the workers who had been discharged by the Triumph Metallurgical Industries. The ONIS statement was strongly worded: "We do not want industries nor industrial parks if they are to serve no other purpose than making the rich richer and poor poorer."[82] It is noteworthy that on June 24, 1969, when President (General) Velasco Alvarado publicly decreed the law of agrarian reform, he cited a paragraph from a declaration of June 20 by ONIS on the subject of agrarian reform.

(4) The situation in Paraguay

General Alfredo Stroessner has governed Paraguay since September 1954. He has been able to dominate the Church and to avoid any direct conflict, although a courageous priest, Father Ramón Talavera, once incited a reaction from the government because of his declarations, sermons, hunger strikes, and mobilizations. Talavera was finally expelled from Paraguay. In 1958 there was a general workers strike, but it was broken up by government police. The bishops have remained silent with few exceptions. On June 28, 1963, a pastoral was issued regarding development and the problem of the "flight of national capital which constitutes a grave sin of egoism," according to the bishops.[83] The following year (1964) a collective pastoral was circulated stating that fifty percent of the couples in Paraguay lived in common-law relationships, and that at least fifty percent of the children were illegitimate. It is necessary, declared the bishops, to give the family a vital, physical, economic, juridical, moral, and religious place in the life of the country. In 1969, however, a direct conflict developed between the Church and the Stroessner government. Monseñor Felipe Santiago Benítez, Bishop of Villarica, gave his public support to the workers of the Rosado Company who had witnessed their houses reduced to rubble. This as well as other activities of the Bishop prompted the government to launch an orchestrated campaign against him. The Jesuits were also harassed, and an official periodical published a "slanderous accusation against three of the bishops of Paraguay of being implicated in the plans of the guerillas."[84]

On April 23 the priests of Villarica, seventy-five in all, issued a carefully worded but prophetic declaration. Student unrest increased, and there were strikes and demonstrations. The bishops meanwhile interceded for the nearly one hundred men and women who were being held in solitary confinement by the Stroessner government, people who had been neither formally charged nor tried. The culmination of the growing tension came when the bishops protested angrily against the projected law of "defense of democracy and the political and social order," a law that in one form or another emanated from the CIA and that inspired some measures taken by the Brazilian and Argentine military governments.[85]

On October 22 the government began a series of repressive measures. First, the Jesuit Father Francisco de Paulo Oliva, professor at the Catholic University, together with the members of a religious procession of The Way of the Cross were attacked and brutally beaten, and the priests, religious, and laity were subjected to numerous insults. The Archbishop of Asunción, Monseñor Aníbal Mena Porta, excommunicated the authorities responsible for this atrocity in a *Message* given on October 26.[86] A short time later the police seized copies of *Comunidad (Community)*, an official publication of the Paraguayan bishops. The General Secretariat of the episcopacy protested in an open letter of October 31 to the Ministry of Education and Worship. On December 7 the bishops denounced the Stroessner plan to form a national Church.

(5) The Caribbean area

Conflicts between the Church and the state have increased in this area since 1962. François Duvalier, dictator of *Haiti* from 1957 to 1971, provided other republics in the Caribbean with a vivid example of repression against the Church. Several priests in Gonaïves were expelled from the country in November 1962.[87] A short time later Father Milán was jailed in Port-au-Prince for subversive activities, and the episcopacy responded by excommunicating Duvalier. In 1964 the Jesuits, twelve in all, were expelled from the country. Duvalier would not allow the Church to function as a parallel power but used all his force to eliminate the Church's influence, even though the Church as such had little influence in view of the fact that ninety percent of the people in Haiti are illiterate. The years passed but the situation remained the same. In 1969 ten priests were expelled from the country. The government claimed to be fighting Communism by following the line of the Department of State of the United States. Another nine priests were expelled, others tortured, and some were imprisoned. Duvalier, nevertheless, was supported as a champion of the Christian faith, and his "revolution" was described as a "human and Christian revolution."[88]

In neighboring Dominican Republic, since the fall of Trujillo in 1961 and the overthrow of Juan Bosch in September of 1963, the people lived under a military Junta that was supported by the direct intervention of the United States in 1965. The Church has continued to function very close to this institutional and political chaos. In 1963 Monseñor Beras stated the need for urgent social reform in a pastoral that was read in all the churches and in which the directives of the encyclical *Mater et*

Magistra were applied to Santo Domingo. Following the military intervention by the United States, the bishops insisted that Christians had a responsiblity in regard to political issues, but in the elections of June 1, 1966, the episcopacy declared itself politically neutral.

There followed expulsions of priests in 1969, but the conflict became extremely serious when the government denied Father Sergio Figueredo, SJ, and Father Gratiniano Varona, OP, the right to reenter the country on June 13. The bishops and the superiors of the two religious orders appealed to the government. Figueredo, speaking to his superiors in Rome, declared that "while our TV programs were limited to religious issues or sexual guidance, as is the case ordinarily, we had no problem. But from the moment when we began to publicize the social documents of the Church and to reflect on our concrete reality . . ." we were refused reentrance into the country.[89] On June 29, 1970, two religious of La Salle were expelled from the Republic. The following Sunday all the churches in the country were closed as a sign of protest.

In Puerto Rico the Church at times has assumed a political-prophetic responsibility for the Latin American cause. In 1963, for example, Bishop Aponte, Auxiliary Bishop of Ponce, spoke against the teaching of English in the schools. There has never resounded in the Island, however, a voice as clear as that of Monseñor Parrilla Bonilla, a bishop without a diocese, who was leader in the public demonstrations favoring independence. On the day of the "Shout of Lares," September 23, 1970, Bishop Parrilla publicly burned the draft cards of five thousand Puerto Rican young men. He declared, "It is Christ whom we should see behind all the movements for liberation. . . . How can we understand such compromises on the part of an institution [the Church] called by vocation to be prophetic?" He added,

To achieve political and socioeconomic liberation is to achieve what Moses and Jesus achieved. It is the ministers of the Lord who should commit themselves to liberation. In the next few years there will be a growing number of priests, religious, and lay persons in prisons and in torture chambers. . . . It would be a disgrace for the Church of Jesus Christ not to offer its testimony in the immense work of liberating the world from slavery in all its forms.[90]

In March 1969 Bishop Parrilla issued a call to all the clergy of the Island, concluding, "The capitalist system with its characteristic of unlimited profit, its distressing compromising of spiritual values, and its absolutist character of property without social content must step aside for a popular socialist system of democratic making in which man and society will be primordial."[91]

As one can readily see, the attitude of the Church regarding repressive regimes — we could also mention at this point those of Nicaragua, Panama, Guatemala, and others — is not that of the mere defense of privileges that it has enjoyed since the time of colonial Christendom. The Church now creates conflicts because it comes forth in the defense of humanity, because it is moving forward prophetically in the process of liberation. "We ask also for the abandonment of reprehensible methods such as torture, illegal imprisonment, exile, and the suppression of human life. . . . We want to indicate that the most profound cause — according to the declaration of Nicaraguan priests headed by Ernesto Cardenal, the Rubén Darío of Latin American Christian liberation — of all social unrest is the lack of justice."[92]

3. The Church, the Socialist Movement, and Violence

If Brazil is an example of a military government, Cuba may be seen as the opposite where the people have elected the way of socialism.

(1) The Situation in Cuba

Cuba's history is distinct from that of the other Caribbean islands. It was discovered on October 27, 1492, and was a colony of Spain until 1898 when, after thirty years of fighting for independence, the Liberals constituted the Republic. In the twentieth century the Church has had a very active role in national life. Catholic Action began early in Cuba, and in 1933 Father Manuel Arteaga — who would be Cardinal at the time of the confrontation with Castro — presented to President Ramón Grau the social encyclicals of the Church, and their influence is evident in the Constitution of 1940. In 1941 Christian Social Democracy emerged. The Catholic University of Santo Tomás of Villanueva became a prestigious institution in the Cuban culture. In 1954 Fulgencio Batista was elected President and continued to govern the island directly and indirectly until 1956 when Fidel Castro, lawyer and former university student leader and activist in Latin American guerrilla movements, began the struggle against Batista from the Sierra Maestra. With Castro was the Argentine medical doctor, Ernesto "Che" Guevara, a very active "reformer" in the university movement in Argentina and a declared Marxist.

In July 1953 Monseñor Pérez Serantes, Archbishop of Santiago, sent a letter to Colonel Del Río interceding for the fugitives who had attacked the Moncada Barracks. Fidel Castro was among those attackers, and he owes his life to the prelate (who later opposed Castro) about whom, at the time of his death, he said, "All that is now taking place is providential. . . . We believe more in our schools than in Jesus Christ."[93] On January 2, 1959, Castro entered Santiago, and on January 8 marched triumphantly into Havana.

The achievements of Castro in 1959 could be regarded as "democratic and humanist" despite that fact that the Archbishop of Santiago on January 29 issued a strongly worded circular "against the executions."[94] The episcopacy openly intervened again between January 13 and 18, defending the private schools. The agrarian reform law of May 17, 1959, alerted the bishops to the fact that there was an incipient Communism within the new government. The "Catholic Congress" of November 1959 — attended by Castro — brought together a large number of Cubans who declared, "We want Cuba Catholic." "Cuba Yes, Russia No."

From December 1959 — with the condemnation of Commandant Húber Matos — until April 1961 there was a progressive move in Cuba towards Marxism. A trade treaty was signed between Cuba and Russia in February of 1960, and on June 27 Castro declared in an address, "Whoever is anticommunist is antirevolutionary."

On April 17, 1961, Cuban exiles invaded the island at the Bay of Pigs. Though supported by the United States, the invaders were crushed, and Castro was more firmly entrenched than ever.

The Church had no other recourse during this time than to oppose openly the regime. On August 7, 1960, the Cuban episcopacy declared that "it has not occurred to anyone to come and ask Catholics, in the name of a misunderstood patriotism, that we desist in our opposition to these doctrines, because we could never accede to them without betraying our most profound principles against materialistic and atheistic Communism. The absolute majority of the Cuban people, who are Catholic, could only by deception be led by a Communist regime."[95] During the Fiesta of Our Lady of Charity, the patron saint of Cuba, on September 8, 1960, a Catholic demonstration was violently suppressed and the government unleashed a series of persecutions, expulsions of priests, nuns, and influential laypersons from the country. Then in March

1961 Castro accused the Cuban clergy of being "allies of theft, crime, and deception." "They are today," he said, "the fifth column of the counterrevolution."[96]

Consequently, between 1961 and 1968 the Church was transformed from a cultic institution to "a silent Church." Even in this period, however, there were signs of change. First, there was the paternal attitude manifested by John XXIII in November 1961, when he wished for the Cuban people "Christian prosperity" and allowed Cuba to name Dr. Amado Blanco as Ambassador to the Vatican. In 1960 there were 745 diocesan priests in Cuba and 2,225 religious. By 1970 the numbers had been reduced to 230 and 200, respectively. In 1962 Monseñor César Zacchi came as Papal Nuncio to the island. Zacchi had extensive experience in socialist countries, and as a result the relations between Rome and Havana began to improve. Castro declared in an address in 1963 that "the imperialists have wanted to turn the Church against the revolution, but they have failed." That same year the Premier requested the Nuncio to send Belgian or Canadian missionaries. In the meantime Vatican II had begun, and the Cuban bishops were allowed to attend. In 1968 the Latin American bishops met in Medellín, and the Catholic clergy evidenced some revolutionary attitudes themselves.

A new era began in Cuba in 1968. Castro, speaking to the Intellectual Congress meeting in Havana, said to the more than five hundred in attendance, "We find ourselves undeniably facing new situations. . . . These are the paradoxes of history. How is it that we see sectors of the clergy becoming revolutionary forces? Are we going to resign ourselves to seeing sectors of Marxism becoming ecclesiastical forces?"[97] When the Canadian Nuncio conferred upon Cuba the episcopal order on December 14, Castro was present in the Nunciature to indicate publicly a new governmental attitude. The Brazilian Bishop, Monseñor Eugenio Sales, made a visit to Cuba in 1967 which, as will be noted, was an important step in improving relations. The Cuban Nuncio stated to the Inter-Press Service of Christian Democracy that "the Church should begin to consider the place it should occupy in the new society (socialist)."[98]

All these events helped to explain the communique issued by the Cuban episcopacy on April 10, 1969.[99] The bishops, in the light of Medellín, proposed to reflect on the new situation. The originality of the situation in Cuba, according to the bishops, "resided in the renewed vision" of their moral and social responsibilities in regard to "the problem of development." With this perspective they affirmed that it was then possible for the Cuban Church to move in a different direction by defending the Cuban people against the economic blockade imposed by the United States. "Seeking the well-being of our people and faithful to the service of the poor, in conformity to the command of Jesus Christ and the commitment proclaimed again in Medellín, we denounce this unjust situation of the blockade which contributes to the unnecessary and increased sufferings and makes more difficult the program of development." The communique was not accepted unanimously by all Catholics in Cuba, but the ASO (the new Cuban form of Catholic Action) in its annual meeting of August 16 and 17, 1969, recognized the communique "as a valid point of departure for undertaking pastoral renewal."[100]

On September 3, 1969, the bishops issued another communique in regard to the problem and growth of the faith, in which they called attention to the fact that in contemporary atheism "in promoting all people and the whole person there is an enormous area of common involvement among all people of good will, be they atheists or believers."[101] The communique continued, "This is the time in which, as in all times, we need to discover the presence of the kingdom of God in the midst of those positive aspects of the crisis through which our world is now passing in this time of its history."[102]

The Church had obviously changed its attitude toward Cuban socialism. The government of the Socialist Republic of Cuba also changed in its response and attitude toward the Church. In the early 1960s the Church in all of Latin America condemned Communism in every form. The Peruvian episcopacy, for example, in 1960 spoke of Communism as "the negation of society."[103] The Venezuelan bishops spoke in 1962 regarding the difficult social situation in their country and of the "fateful Communist infiltration and atheism which are one and the same."[104] The episcopacy of Central America and Panama issued a joint pastoral "On Communism,"[105] an issue that was also stressed by the bishops of Guatemala in their pastoral "On Social Problems and the Communist Menace."[106] During these years, nevertheless, there was one discordant voice, the Bishop of Guinea, Monseñor Tchidimbo, who stated that it was possible for "African socialism to have God as its center." The issue was addressed in the Second Vatican Council only by very small groups and in conversations in the halls.

During February 1964 the "Week of Marxist Intellectuals" was held in Paris with the presence of Yves Jolif, and the dialogue was continued in Barcelona later in the year. In Latin America Dom Hélder Câmara began to talk of the possibility of a "personalistic socialism." But the change was very slow. Monseñor Raul Silva Henríquez, the leading Chilean cardinal, declared that "it is necessary to change the structures without capitalism or Communism.... What we desire is a Christian solution." The same spirit was manifested in Peru when a minister, Miró Quesada, wanted to begin classes in Marxism in a secondary school.

It was not until 1967, however, that the issue of socialism became generally prominent in Latin America, and the way was effectively prepared by the commitment of university students in Brazil, Chile, Argentina, Peru, and Mexico. Monseñor Eugenio Fragoso, Bishop of Crateus, in an address given on October 9, 1967, explained the reasons for his making a trip to Cuba and his reactions after returning.[107] "Why has the Bishop of Crateus said that Cuba, that the courage of little Cuba was a symbol and a call for Latin America...?" He gave four reasons: first, because Castro fought against the military dictatorship of Batista and against the imposition of the United States, and because when plans were made for agrarian reform "forty percent of the land belonged to North Americans." They protested, and the Department of State said, "This will not happen." Therefore, in the name of a small island of six million inhabitants, Fidel Castro said to the richest and best-armed giant in the world with two hundred million inhabitants, "We will not give in. We will not retreat. The reform will proceed. ... Who was guilty? I am not the one to respond." Rather, it was John Fitzgerald Kennedy who explicitly declared in the course of his electoral campaign that the reason for and the responsibility of Cuba's abandoning the continental unity and entering the Soviet orbit is that of the United States who did not know how to support the aspirations of the Cuban people in their struggle to liberate that small island. The Bishop continued by speaking of the situation in Brazil saying, "Why has the government not had the courage to close the universities and the secondary schools here and lead a million professors to teach and conscienticize in four months the forty million Brazilians who have absolutely no education? Why has Brazil not done what Castro has done in Cuba?" A short time later—March 11, 1968—Dom Hélder, in an address given at the Catholic Institute of Recife, stated that the Christian need not fear that the world is moving toward socialism in view of the fact that Christians "can offer a mystique of universal fraternity and incomparable hope far more comprehensive than the narrow mystique of historic materialism. . . . The Marxists, conversely, feel the need of revising their concept of religion."[108]

The year 1969 brought new surprises. The Venezuelan bishops, for example, according to Cardinal José Quintero of Caracas, were ready to serve as intermediaries between the government and the guerrillas. At that time the government was led by the COPEI party, the Venezuelan form of Christian Democracy, which had been in power since December 1968. In Colombia, Monseñor Botero Salazar of Medellín raised the question as to whether collaboration between Marxists and Christians was possible in the pastoral and social apostolate.[109] The successor of Monseñor Larraín, Carlos González of Talca, declared in a pastoral "Constructing in Hope" that it would be permissible to support a certain kind of socialism. "It is not possible at the present time," he said, "to ignore that right of Christian laity to search for a form of modified socialism, a socialism whose goal would be to construct a society based on mankind, human values, and with the clear aim of transforming people as human beings and children of God."[110] The situation in regard to the Chilean Christian Democratic Youth, which separated itself from the Christian Democrats — Christian Democracy had separated from the Conservative party (the Falange) — motivated the Bishop of Talca to face this serious question. It is certain that socialism was being viewed by many Christians as a possiblity within their political, economic, and humanistic options.

(2) The revolutions in Mexico and Chile

An interesting comparison can be made in the attitude of the Church in two Latin American revolutions. A half century before Castro, Mexico began the revolution of 1910. But only in 1964 did the Church there recognize the positive aspects of that revolution in the "Document of San Luis de Potosí" emanating from the organs of Catholic Action. Monseñor Méndez Arceo, Bishop of Cuernavaca, had anticipated the notice in an interview with a representative of *Life* magazine on April 13. The Mexican Church should have faced the crisis during the time of the agony of colonial Christendom, for by 1964 it did not have the possibility of responding creatively or prophetically as it was able to do later in Cuba. And the life of Mexican Catholicism in 1970 conditioned the way in which the Church could respond to the revolution. In effect, in the time of President Calles (1924– 1934) a kind of social Catholicism began to develop[111] that made possible the National Catholic Workers Congress, the National Catholic Peasant League, and the Middle Class National Catholic League. But all these organizations disappeared during the time of the religious conflict of 1926 to 1929 when the "critiques" continued to incarnate the ideals of a nonexistent Christendom. The "revolution" in Mexico was not Marxist, but it was a real revolution. The structures of Mexico changed. It was not a proletarian revolution, for there was no industry; nor was it a peasant revolution. Rather, it was a revolution of a small bourgeois against the high bourgeois oligarchy of the nineteenth century, reformist in regard to agrarian questions, liberal and anticlerical culturally, and socialistic in spirit. The Church, however, received a staggering blow and remained basically enclosed within the temples. Freedom of worship was permitted within the buildings, but religious demonstrations in the street were prohibited. The Church has not yet recuperated a social, cultural, decisive, liberating presence, although it appears that this is possible in the future.

"In certain circles, unfortunately limited, the Council and the encyclicals have awakened interest, but much less than they deserve, because the hierarchy in general has not put a great emphasis on these," according to Father Alberto de Ezcurdia. He adds, alluding to the ecclesial documents regarding social issues and responding to the question as to whether hierarchy deals with concrete issues, "No, they always remain in the area of the abstract."[112]

In Chile the change was quite different. The triumph of Eduardo Frei in 1964, candidate of the Christian Democratic Party, was an important time in the history of the temporal commitment of the Church in Latin America and was the result of thirty long years of social action in Chile, a lesson that was later utilized by COPEI in Venezuela. But more important was the fact that Frei's election allowed for the surpassing of the ideal of a "new Christendom," which Christian Democracy had proposed in its beginning.

In 1962 the Chilean bishops issued a collective pastoral regarding the "Social and Political Responsiblity at Present," which was widely circulated and had significant impact in all of Latin America. The pastoral insisted that collaboration between Christians and Communists was an impossibility.[113] Earlier Monseñor Larraín, Bishop of Talca, published his "Economic Development in the Light of *Mater et Magistra*."[114] That same year the famous issue — one dedicated to revolution — of the periodical *Mensaje* (*Message*) appeared. (*Mensaje* was founded by Father Alberto Hurtado and edited by the Bellarmino Center.) In October 1963 a second issue dedicated to the Christian perspective on the "Revolutionary Reforms in Latin America" appeared. The Christian Democratic Party, however, which had only thirteen percent of the votes in Chile in the 1957 elections, won fifty-four percent on September 4, 1964, when Frei's party with its motto of "Revolution in Freedom" came to power. Immediately, however, the proposals of the Christian Democrats were frustrated by Conservative forces on the right and the Radicals on the left. Monseñor Larraín wrote another pastoral in October 1965 on "Development: Success or Failure in Latin America."[115] "The most serious problem for us Latin Americans," stated Don Manuel, "more than the atomic bomb, is the material and spiritual underdevelopment of the people who form the Third World. . . . Underdevelopment is an evil. It should be condemned as an enemy of humanity. . . . Furthermore, wasteful spending should be halted. The greatest waste is in armaments which absorb incredible sums of money. The problem of development, therefore, and the problem of disarmament are interrelated."

Other indications of the change in Chile were evident in the ecclesial agrarian reform program that began in 1961, the "Social Weeks" that began in 1963, the crisis in the Catholic universities from 1967, and the actions of the synod beginning in 1967, all of which indicated the vitality of the Church in that country. The deterioration that the Christian Democratic Party suffered in Chile, however, led to the election of Dr. Salvador Allende, candidate of the Popular Front, as the President of the nation on September 4, 1970. The Church reacted favorably to the situation and demonstrated a positive attitude toward the socialist government. Cardinal Silva Henríquez said in 1970 that the Church was partially responsible for the unjust order that existed in Latin America,[116] a statement that indicated the high level of awareness among the bishops. Also, the Cardinal was one of the first public figures in Chile to congratulate Allende on his election, and the Popular Front had within its ranks aggressive groups of Christian youth, socialist in principle and revolutionary in concrete attitudes.

(3) The Church and subversive violence in Colombia, Bolivia, and other regions

We will describe the environments in which there has existed violence of both kinds: subversive violence that reacts to oppressive violence, and, following the dialectic, the renewed coercive violence that is of greater importance and significance.[117]

Colombia has been a land of violence since its colonization in the sixteenth century.

One should remember that on February 7, 1948, when the Panamerican Conference met in Bogotá, hundreds of thousands of Colombians marched through the streets of downtown Bogotá decrying and repudiating the Conservative Party. During the Conference, the popular Liberal leader, Jorge E. Gaitán, was assassinated on the street, and within hours a decade of violence erupted. From the time of Gaitán's assassination until June 1953 when General Gustavo Rojas Pinilla came to power in a military overthrow of the government, there were some 200,000 deaths in the country. The Liberals were killing in reaction to the murder of Gaitán, while the Conservatives were slaughtering in the name of Jesus Christ. A general strike paralyzed the country in May 1957, and Rojas was forced to leave the country. The Conservatives and Liberals proceeded to sign a treaty instituting the National Front and agreed to alternate the presidency and the power for periods of four years until 1974. The first president elected under this arrangement was Alberto Lleras Camargo in 1958; Guillermo León Valencia followed in 1962 and Carlos Lleras Restrepo in 1966. The oligarchy, therefore, continued to govern the country under the cloak of a popular majority and violently suppressed any opposition. Taking Castro as a model, some Colombians defended subversive revolution and were able to organize a guerrilla movement with the armed bands dispersed throughout the rural areas of Colombia. Several "socialist republics" sprang up, but by 1964 they had been reduced to the areas of Marquetalia and Pato.

A work by Germán Guzmán, Orlando Fals Borda, and Eduardo Umaña Luna, *La violencia en Colombia (Violence in Colombia)*,[118] traced the history and the extent of internecine conflict in the nation. In 1961 the Colombian episcopacy issued a condemnation of violence and urged peace.[119] But the document was in fact the Church's approval of the Conservative-Liberal pact forming the National Front government which at the time was attempting to suppress subversive violence. This subversive violence was, however, the fruit of the oppressive violence of the institutionalized injustice of the oligarchy. In a study on "Violence and Sociocultural Changes in the Rural Areas of Colombia," Father Camilo Torres, Licentiate in political science from the University of Louvain (1958), and at the time Professor of Sociology in the National University in Bogotá,[120] insisted that the peasant violence was the result of the "lack of divergent work, social isolation, conflicts with entities outside the group, feelings of inferiority, lack of vertical social mobility, latent hostility, and political sectarianism." Torres analyzed each of these factors, employing the techniques of the sociology of European education and frequently citing Durkheim, Weber, Parsons, Redfield, and Wiese. He manifested a reflective, scientific, and intellectual bent, and concluded saying, "Violence has forced all these changes through pathological canals and without any harmony in respect to the process of economic development in the country."[121] Torres' study was published in 1963 in the *Minutes* of the First National Congress of Sociology, which had been organized by the Colombian Association of Sociology.

Camilo Torres Restrepo, besides belonging to one of the traditional families of Colombia, was part of a cultural elite, a scientist whose university career was guaranteed. Three years later, February 15, 1966, his body was found in rural area near Bucaramanga. Camilo's subversive violence was crushed by the coercive military violence. In his last "Proclamation to the Colombian People" he had written, "When the people sought a leader and found him in Jorge Eliécer Gaitán, the oligarchy killed him. When the people sought peace, the oligarchy sowed violence in the country. When the people could no longer resist this violence and organized themselves into guerrillas in order to take power, the oligarcy fabricated a military coup d'etat in order to entice the guerrillas to surrender. When the people asked for democracy, they were deceived again with a plebiscite [December 1957], and the National Front imposed a dictatorship of the oligarchy." Torres concluded saying, "The people know that the only way left to them is that of armed insurrection."[122] How did he arrive at this decision? As historians it is our task to understand more than to defend. For this reason we will return briefly to some of his previous writings.

From Louvain, Torres had sent in 1956 a report to the First Seminar of University Chaplains[123] on "The Social Problems in the Contemporary University." The paper revealed Camilo's character in its totality. The entire analysis was written not only from a scientific but also from an ethical perspective. He stated that it is by divine revelation that we know the supreme commandment is that of charity — agape love for our neighbor — but that we also know that even Christ was tempted to utilize inappropriate means in order to manifest this charity. Already he was laying the foundation for his ultimate commitment in his search for an "efficacious charity." He advocated no abstract love; not an ideal, but a real, concrete love that would grasp the opportunity. For his Licentiate in political science at Louvain, Camilo wrote a thesis entitled "Approximations of the Socioeconomic Reality in the City of Bogotá," and he had several papers published in the Cuadernos latinoamericanos de economía humana (Latin American Notebooks in Human Economy) of Montevideo on "The Problem of Structuring an Authentic Latin American Sociology," "The Social Disintegration in Colombia," and "The Revolution: A Christian Imperative"; the latter also was published in French in Pro mundi vita (1965). These writings reveal a person who desired to understand the real, the concrete, namely, the grass roots situation. As a scientist he warned of the danger of "Latin American cultural colonialism,"[124] and as a priest he cautioned against counterfeit, uncommitted spiritualism. He said that although the mission of a priest was specifically supernatural, there existed for him the imperative of charity. Charity, he said, "is that which motivates us, and charity can be measured by our response to the needs of our neighbor." "For this reason," he declared, "many priests must assume temporal functions."[125] Moreover, "as a sociologist I have desired that this love be effectively expressed." The theme of "efficacious love" was the foundation of Camilo's Christian ethic, and it was implemented by technology and science. "By analyzing the Colombian society," he wrote, "I have realized the necessity of a revolution in order to give food to the hungry, drink to the thirsty, clothing to the naked, and assure the well-being of the majority of our people.... The supreme measure of human decisions should be charity, it should be supernatural love. I will take all the risks that this measure demands of me."[126]

It is difficult to conceive of a choice or a decision more responsible, preceded by study and analysis during almost ten years of investigation and commitment. Camilo's final decision was really a priestly choice.

I opted for Christianity because I consider it the purest form of loving my neighbor. I was chosen by Christ to be a priest eternally, and I was motivated by the desire to give myself in full-time love for my fellow man. ... The Mass, which is the final objective of priestly activity, is fundamentally an act of the community. But the Christian community is unable to offer in an authentic way the sacrifice if in an effective way the precept of love has not been expressed for one's neighbor.[127]

It is important to note that for Camilo the possible means of changing the structure were gradual. There was the status quo in Uruguay, repression in Venezuela, the rightist coup d'etat in Brazil, reformism in Colombia, violent revolution in Cuba, and peaceful revolution in Chile. For Camilo the best of all these options without doubt was the ideal of a "peaceful revolution" with a maximum of desire, foresight, and social pressure.[128] He considered subversive violence an evil, but the time came when he viewed it as a lesser, necessary evil. It is clear that at the beginning he gave no thought to violence as a political option, for in the "Platform" of the United Front, the political party that he founded, it was declared: "At the present time the *necessary* decisions for Colombian politics to be oriented for the benefit of the majority ... must originate with those who hold the power."[129] The power, it was said, was held by three trustees: "Military power in our country serves basically to support the present structure. ... Ecclesiastical power in our country is united with economic and political power in order to pursue common interests."[130] This conclusion stirred Camilo to enter politics as a Christian. He was immediately accused of being a Communist, to which he responded in his "Message to the Communists" saying that although they search sincerely for the truth and love their "neighbor in an efficacious way..., they should clearly understand that I am not allying myself with them. I am not nor can I ever be a Communist neither as a Colombian, as a sociologist, as a Christian, nor as a priest." He said this on September 2, 1965. He added, however, "I am disposed to join in the struggle with those who have the same objectives as I: against the oligarchy and the domination by the United States. ... John XXIII authorized me to work with those who attempt to improve our world. And the example of Poland shows us that a socialist system is possible without destroying what is essential in Christianity."[131]

Shortly before Camilo made the preceding statement, Cardinal Luis Concha on August 10 had publicly condemned violent revolution. Five days earlier he had issued a pastoral in which he said, "An attack against a legitimate government is to be condemned on the basis of natural law, and if one doubts the natural law, the authority of Sacred Scripture adhered to by the Church will demonstrate — as the Holy Fathers have constantly taught — that an assault against the legitimate government is illicit because it signifies disobedience, rebellion, or the overthrow of legitimately constituted power."[132]

It is lamentable that in this major event in the history of the Latin American Church there was a lack of theological understanding which could have guided Camilo to a commitment within the bounds of prophetic but not armed violence. Even so, the position of the Cardinal can hardly be defended in view of the fact that the government in Colombia at the time resulted from a pact between the Conservatives and Liberals and was less than legitimate. For analogous reasons Rome had condemned the revolutions of independence in the beginning of the nineteenth century but soon recognized them as legitimate.

The year 1965 was decisive. On April 19, Cardinal Concha, Archbishop of Bogotá, issued a declaration regarding social instability and the Communist danger in the country. President Guillermo Valencia meanwhile accused the Church of concealing Communists — evidently hoping to discredit Camilo Torres who at the time was organizing the Popular Front in opposition to the government. Concha also said, "The Church exercises its influence in the temporal order for the personal transformation of the man who freely accepts the message of the gospel," clearly an individualistic and privatized understanding of the Christian faith. The Cardinal continued, "The influence of the Church in the temporal order is the direct responsibility of the laity," an apparent reference to a theology of Christendom.

On June 9, Camilo was prohibited from taking part in any political activity. He responded by renouncing his priestly office and asking the Cardinal to reduce him to lay status. The Cardinal responded on June 18 by issuing a statement to the effect that "Father Camilo Torres has deliberately rejected the doctrines and ordinances of the Catholic Church." Father Efraín Gaitán then resigned from a Catholic publication in order to support Camilo. When Gaitán organized a demonstration in Medellín for the Popular Front, Bishop Botero Salazar publicly condemned subversive violence. On September 7, Cardinal Concha in a interview with a group of Catholic intellectuals in Bogotá passionately defended the right of private property. One of the delegation sharpened the issue by stating:

Since, as Your Eminence has stated, the Church is the defender of private property, I would like to know exactly which type of property ownership is defended by the Church. For example, is it land acquired by expropriation? Or is it money earned in shady deals, or by devaluation which forces the poor to sell and leave the land piling up in the hands of a few? After all, these are the most common forms of acquiring land in Colombia.[133]

The Cardinal was awestruck and visibly agitated. He stood up and said, "I am not disposed to continue this conversation." In less than six months Camilo Torres was dead and soon was transformed into a universal symbol.

Tension within the Church increased, and on September 9, 1966, Mario Bravo and Hernán Jiménez were dismissed from their posts at the diocesan newspaper *El Catolicismo* because the Cardinal believed that they were sowing seeds of dissension. In an editorial entitled "The Church and Development," Bravo and Jiménez had indicated that "a vast reform of the institutions is necessary."[134] More than a hundred Colombian priests protested the dismissal of the editors, and the Cardinal responded by saying, "The prescriptions of the Council do not obligate the Cardinal nor the Colombian Church to begin immediate action in the social field, but only in regard to the liturgy."[135] Clearly it was the "cultural Church" that Camilo had wanted to surpass, as can be seen in a letter that he wrote to Monseñor Rubén Isaza in 1965: "If the pastoral is one of conservation, it will be difficult for me to collaborate in an effective way. . . . If the priority of love is accepted above everything else, and preaching above worship activities, then the hierarchy has to come to a pastoral of mission. . . . By pastoral, I understand the total activity which should be exercised in order to plant and increase the kingdom of God in society and in a specific historical epoch."[136] What alienated Camilo Torres from Cardinal Concha was that the latter was dedicated to the defense of Christendom while the former, because of his studies, saw a new era and stage in the history of the Church that had already begun and for which ultimately he gave his life. Although subversive violence is not as evangelical as prophetic violence, Camilo offered his life, and this is the supreme indication of love — effectual love — which was the motto of his life, and it is in effectual love that all Christian perfection is expressed.

Shortly before the Medellín Bishops Conference, a group of priests met together in a rural *hacienda* called "Golconda." They were closely watched by the DAS (Administrative Department of Security). Father René García revived the idea again in 1970 of a "Popular Front of Opposition," and Father Laín joined the guerrillas in the Colombian Sierra.[137] The impact of these events has not subsided and is clearly material for future theological reflection.

Bolivia is the land from which the first resident bishop of La Plata wrote a letter to the Spanish king dated July 1, 1550, which read: "Four years ago when Spain was ready to abandon this area, a mouth of hell was discovered in which there enters every year a great number of people (Indians) sacrificed to the god of greed by the Spaniards. It is a silver mine that is called Potosí."[138] Short of a detailed history of the violences which the Bolivian people have been forced to endure, one should note that the year 1964 brought the end to the MNR (National Revolutionary Movement) and the exile of President Paz Estensoro, when a military coup overthrew the government. Two years earlier the Bolivian bishops had asked the government to take measures to reduce Communist influence among the miners, and on November 15, 1964, the Committee for Christian Democracy was organized for the purpose of uniting all Christian political forces.[139] On October 6, 1965, the Archbishop of La Paz, Monseñor Abel Antezana, along with 126 Bolivian priests, sent a communication to the Military Junta defending the miners of COMIBOL (the national organization that administered the state mines). The communique demonstrated the ways in which the Bolivian miner was exploited: his daily salary was less than the equivalent of one United States dollar, and this salary was controlled by the state in order to maintain an unjust price for tin. Bolivia sold its products for ten cents (U.S.) per work-hour and bought products from the United States for three dollars per work-hour.

General René Barrientos was elected president in 1966, and on September 14 he proposed a new Constitution in which "the State recognizes and supports the Catholic, Apostolic, and Roman religion." The southeast part of the country was declared a "military zone" on April 11, 1967, because of the activity of various guerrilla groups there.

The Argentine medical doctor, Ernesto "Che" Guevara, had begun his *Diary* on November 7, 1966, writing, "A new state began today."[140] Subversive violence clashed with coercive violence. Meanwhile, Monseñor Gutiérrez Granier, Bishop of Cochabamba, condemned the guerrilla activity in a pastoral saying, "The Church has always condemned hatred and violence in human and social relations and equally repudiates in our time the guerrillas who represent a new kind of war." Gutiérrez also indicated that the Bolivian government had the responsibility and the right to "repel force with force."[141] The subversive violence was, however, the result of the widespread injustices in the country. The situation in Bolivia was not unlike that in Peru, and it reminds one of the protests of Monseñor Dammert, Peruvian Bishop of the Sierra, who in 1965 censured the upper classes for having bought bonds to support antiguerrilla activity — that is, the occupying of land by armed peasants — but who refused to finance the rural infrastructure that would have eliminated the injustices and made peasant violence unnecessary.[142]

On October 8, 1967, "Che" Guevara was captured and executed. Don Antonio Fragoso said on October 27, "We pray for our brother Guevara who has tragically died in Bolivia," and *Le Poty*, the Natal, Brazil daily newspaper, carried the statement: "The courage of little Cuba can be a symbol and a call for the liberation of Latin America. . . . If one is not capable of seeing the good in one's enemies there is a question as to whether that one is Christian. . . . We are not, however, in accord with the dictatorship in Cuba . . . nor in Brazil." Alceu Amoroso Lima, philosopher and member of the pontifical Commission for Justice and Peace, wrote in the *Jornal do Brasil*:

I am able to reverence without fear the heroism of three men who had little in common, the priest (Camilo Torres), the philosopher (Régis Debray), and the doctor ("Che" Guevara), because the more I see violence (subversive) the more I repudiate and detest it as a means of social change and progress. But I cannot deny the fact that these victims of violence (coercive) represent in our epoch of technological pragmatism an example of what is most pure in human nature, namely, the capacity to sacrifice oneself for a just cause, a desperate protest in behalf of human dignity and against pessimism, against a false contentment, against the injustice of civilization, and against prosperity founded on injustice. . . . The meaning of the death of saints and heroes resides precisely in the fact that suffering and death have meaning. To die for a just cause, although by means of condemnable violent methods, has more value than agreements made with the defenders of the worst kinds of violence, those which hide behind the mask of peace, of legality and democracy, but who in fact are the very causes of the unjust social order.[143]

The injustices, however, continued in Bolivia, and the guerrilla groups reorganized. In August 1970, the Archbishop of La Paz, Jorge Manrique, issued a pastoral pleading for a radical transformation of the country and charging the government with "economic strangulation" and social oppression which, he insisted, made possible and stimulated the existence of guerrilla centers. In September four clergymen who were serving as professors in the National University were dismissed. The students went on strike September 16 and "took to the streets." The government retaliated by expelling the four former professors from the country for "subversive political activity." One of the four was a member of the Oblate Order, and another was a Protestant pastor. Priests in the mining region of Llallagua called for a thoroughgoing study of the revolutionary process. Shortly thereafter the government of General Alfredo Ovando fell when on October 6 General Juan José Torres took charge. On December 24 the French guerrilla Régis Debray was released and celebrated Christmas in Santiago, Chile. This history has not yet concluded.[144]

Before continuing to examine other Christians who have chosen the way of subversive violence, even armed violence, we need to make a very important clarification. On January 1, 1971, the French newspaper *La Croix* (Paris) published a declaration by Monseñor Brandão Vilela, President of CELAM, indicating that "the Church maintains its position against violence" — although the Monseñor did not specify against which kind of violence — "in the necessary transformation of the structures in Latin America. . . . It is necessary, however, to distinguish the case of Camilo Torres from that of 'Che' Guevara and Régis Debray. Camilo Torres, although he was wrong in regard to the methods, was a Christian. The other two, in contrast, were Marxists." We would not want the examples we will give to be considered on the same level as the "olive green revolution" launched by the OLAS.[145] There is a basic difference in the motivation of a "Che" and the Maryknoll Fathers, which we will attempt to describe.

During the week of June 18, 1954, Guatemala suffered a bombing by North American planes. That same week Colonel Castillo Armas crossed the border and presided over a Military Junta that deposed the elected President, Jacobo Arbenz, whom they accused of being a Communist.[146] This military takeover of the Guatemalan government had the complete support of the United States. Consequently, the United Fruit Company was able to continue its exploitation of the workers without further difficulty. In light of these events, the conflict resulting from the work of three North American Maryknoll priests and a Maryknoll sister dedicated to help the Indians in the northern part of Guatemala is of special significance. One of them, Thomas Melville, published in the *National Catholic Reporter* (Kansas City) of January 31, 1968, an article that described the nature of the violence in Guatemala.

The National Liberation Movement was initiated by General and later President Castillo Armas who was assassinated in July 1957, and the movement was continued by his successor who makes no move to control the rightist terrorists called the *Mano Blanca* [the White Hand]. Another rightist terrorist band is the NOA [New Anticommunist Organization] directed by an army colonel, Máximo Zepeda Martínez. . . . A Third group of rightist terrorists, the CADEG, is composed of ruffians. . . . During the last eighteen months these three groups together have assassinated more than 2,800 intellectuals, students, union leaders, and peasants who in one form or another have attempted to organize and combat the evils of the Guatemalan society.[147]

Speaking of his own personal experience, Melville continued,

I know personally a good friend and benefactor of the Maryknoll Fathers who receives communion daily and who accused a Christian guild leader of being a Communist because he was trying to organize a union on a large sugar plantation. As a result of the accusation the organizer was executed by the army. ... When the cooperative that I began among the destitute Indians in Quezaltenango was finally able to buy its own truck, the rich attempted to bribe the chauffeur to drive the vehicle off a cliff. When he refused to cooperate, they made at least four attempts to force the truck off the road, and the last one of these was successful. In the parish of San Antonio Huista where my brother, who is also a Maryknoll priest, was pastor, the president of an agrarian cooperative was assassinated by some of the town's wealthy leaders — a group that included the mayor. When the case reached the capital of Huehuetenango, the judge had already been bribed, and we could do nothing. The three leaders of the parish cooperative in La Libertad, Huehuetenango, were accused of being Communists and were threatened with death as a consequence of their attempts to raise the economic level of their neighbors. The American government has sent jets, helicopters, arms, money, and military advisers to the Guatemalan government, which only gives them more power to control the peasant masses. Last year, 1967, the salaries, uniforms, arms and vehicles for two thousand new police were paid for by the Alliance for Progress.[148]

On December 23, 1967, Thomas and Arthur Melville, along with Father Blase Bonpane and Sister Marian Peter Bradford, were suspended and a short time later expelled from the congregation and the country. The Vice-president of Guatemala, Marroquí Rojas, accused the Church of "fomenting Communist activities," an accusation that was printed in the capital city newspaper *Impacto*. Thomas Melville responded to the charge by saying, "It is not the hungry who initiate the violence, rather it is the rich and the powerful who are not content to live with their excessive and ill-gotten wealth, but who always want to have more."[149] Melville added, "I with two other priests and a sister were accused of helping the guerrillas in Guatemala, and we were expelled from the country without being given any opportunity to defend ourselves." "As Christians we only desire peaceful change. ... It is the rich, together with those who have the same interests, who have the power to decide if the process will be peaceful or violent." John F. Kennedy said, declared Melville, that "those who make peaceful revolution impossible, make violent revolution inevitable." Apparently this small group of clergy desired to join the guerillas in the northern part of Guatemala, but they returned to the United States and began a crusade against North American militarism in the Third World.[150]

There are many others who, because of their Christian faith, have decided to become actively involved in subversive violence. The case of Father Antonio Soligo is well known in Brazil. He was imprisoned for six months and tortured by the police without ever being charged with a crime. Upon leaving the prison, Soligo joined a clandestine group and never returned to his order nor to his parish. Father Tito de Alencar attempted suicide by slashing his wrists after being tortured with an electric goad and having to observe the torture of nuns in "obscene parodies" perpetrated by police dressed in sacred vestments.[151] Sister Maurina Borges de Silveira, Superior in the Santa Ana Home, tells how she was tortured on October 24, 1969, in the Ribeirão Preto Prison, how she was beaten, insulted, blasphemed, and finally how one of the eight agents of the civil police said to her, "Dear Sister — I can call you Sister, can

I not? — I love you very much." He then said to her, "It pains me to have to leave you here all night nude before everyone. . . ." Then he "took me by the neck and attempted to caress me."[152] Together with the Dominicans of São Paulo there were several prisoners who were peasants. They declared, "We workers from the rural area belong to the most exploited class in our country. . . . We see Christ as a man who has died on the Cross to liberate us from tyrannical regimes. . . . And, behind these bars, we vividly sense his presence."

Those who practice coercive violence want to involve the Church in the chaos. In Uruguay, for example, two ecclesiastics attempted to mediate between the government and the Tupamaros and were ultimately accused of being members of the urban guerrilla group. In Argentina the government did everything possible to link the two priests Alberto Carbone and Fulgencio Rojas to the assassination of ex-President Aramburu. The defense attorney showed that the entire maneuver was a scheme to create confusion and a means by which the movement of the Priests for the Third World could be implicated in the case. A body assumed to be that of Aramburu was found on July 16, 1970.[153]

The situation at present is as follows: the great powers, the developed and dominating countries, have ended their "Cold War" and embarked upon a relationship of peaceful coexistence. Premier Khrushchev sent to John XXIII on his eightieth birthday a message of congratulations wishing for the pontiff "success in the nobel aspiration of contributing to the consolidation of peace in the world."[154] But while the powerful enjoy peace, the Bishop of Tacuarembo, Uruguay, said in a pastoral letter of 1961, "The animals here are treated better than the children. . . . These people, [speaking of the farm workers] suffer in their flesh injustice. . . . We should remember that those responsible for the evils endured in those countries that have become Communist are the same ones who maintain the social system that forces the people to choose either bread without liberty or liberty without bread."[155]

Dom Hélder Câmara, in a address given in the Mutulaité of Paris on April 25, 1968, stated that as Asia has its Bangkok and Africa its Algiers, Latin America has its Tequendama. The entire Third World suffers violence. The violence of oppression exists in the developed countries and in the underdeveloped countries (with the difference being that in the latter the oligarchies are at the service of the dominator). Moreover, the developed countries live off the underdeveloped, oppressed, and dominated countries. In a document presented to Nelson Rockefeller when he visited Bolivia, a group of Bolivian priests and nuns stated:

According to CEPAL in its last report to the Special Commission of Latin American Coordination (CECLA), the United States earned more than three billion dollars between 1965 and 1967, but it has reinvested only two hundred million annually, and what is worse, this aid is always tied to a series of economic and political conditions. We are a country not poor but exploited. The United States buys our raw materials — tin, for example — at the price of ten cents U.S. per man-hour of work. We in turn must buy their manufactured articles at a price of between two dollars and three dollars U.S. per man-hour of work.[156]

This is the violence of the dominator.

The Church has spoken with greater frequency on the question of violence, but it appears that there is no awareness of the fact that violence is *equivocal* and not analogical.[157] Dom Hélder Câmara together with Pastor Ralph David Abernathy signed the "Declaration of Recife"[158] in which nonviolence such as that practiced by Mahatma Gandhi was defended. Personally, however, I do not believe that nonviolence is a viable option for Latin Americans who want to effect change. The ontological and even theological basis of nonviolence is well expressed in the *Bhagavad-Gita* (the *Song of the Blessed*), chapter 18, 2: "The wise call exterior renunciation the abandonment of actions engendered by desire, and call interior renunciation the abandonment of the interest in the fruit of one's labors." In the ontological understanding of the Indo-European world, especially that of India, positive action, and much more violent action, is intrinsically evil because it is directed toward the fulfilling of a desire, and it is desire that enslaves us to the plurality and that impedes our returning to the Brahman unity. Nonviolence is psychologically a masochistic movement that voluntarily has for its objective the enduring of pain through discipline, suffering, and oppression in order to call attention to those who control the political power. In the Judeo-Christian ontology and theology the question has always been faced in another way.[159]

It should be clearly stated that neither in the Old nor the New Testament, neither by the Church nor tradition has violence as such been condemned. What has been condemned is the *unjust* use of violence. Violence as passion, for example, is a meditative attitude that is justified by its purpose. When a father, let us say, violently snatches a knife from his son who is about to injure his small sister, no one would say that the father did wrong. "Violence" comes from the Latin word *vis*, that is, force. The question is, therefore, what is the reason for force being used, and what kind of force is used? The seed germ, when in search of light, pushes up through the ground thus employing violence. In the same way, "Since John the Baptist came, up to this present time, the kingdom of heaven has been subjected to violence and the violent are taking it by storm" (Matt. 11:12).[160] The New Testament does not condemn violence, but rather proposes "prophetic violence" as the supreme way of being a person.[161] This violence is a subversive type, but it has its own character. Subversion — from the Latin *subvertere*, to put below what is above and vice versa — is exactly what Jesus was referring to when he said, "How happy are you who are poor. ... But alas for you who are rich" (Luke 6:10, 14); and Mary sang in the *Magnificat*, "He has pulled down princes from their thrones and exalted the lowly" (Luke 1:52), that is, he pulls down (*sub-*) those who are above (*-vertere*). To say before the people, before the powerful, before the Romans, and before the Empire that God will put down the mighty, are examples of prophetic force, courage, valor, and even audacity. And the prophet pledged this by his life, by his unmasking of injustice, unto death, but without the use of arms, without killing, although he himself was killed. "Jerusalem, Jerusalem, you that kill the prophets and stone those who are sent to you!" (Matt. 23:37). Jesus had no desire to enter into the dialectic of mutual annihilation: "Put your sword back, for all who draw the sword will die by the sword" (Matt. 26:52). These two passages, however, should be examined individually.

The first and most inhuman violence that exists is that which destroys millions of people, whole generations: the violence of the oppressors, of the dominators, of the empires which is objectified in the unjust and oppressive structures that do not allow a human being to be human. And, what is worse, it makes the oppressed, because of their desperation, into oppressors themselves — as is seen in the foreman over the worker, the police over the people, and the middle class over the lower classes. Those historically responsible before God — in a universal humanity as represented in the history of salvation — are the dominating powers, that is, the developed countries that live off the exploitation of the underdeveloped countries.

Reacting to this oppressive violence is the violence of a small number who coura-geously challenge egoistic conformity, risk their own well-being and even their lives in order to transform the oppressor-oppressed dialectic into a relationship of brother-with-brother. Some are desperate or ideologically convinced that there is no other way but to take up arms (*subversive armed violence*). The Christian does have in this regard the example of such saints as Bernard of Clairvaux who in the twelfth century preached in favor of a Crusade to wrest the holy places from the Arabs, and heroes such as Friar Luís Beltrán, OFM, who manufactured the cannons for the army of San Martín in the nineteenth century. The situation in which armed subversive violence is justified was enunciated by Paul VI and by the Medellín bishops who said that "revolutionary insurrection can be legitimate in the case of evident and prolonged tyranny that seriously works against the fundamental rights of man, and which damages the common good of the country!"[162] And Father Thomas Melville was correct when he said, "If this situation does not exist today in Guatemala, Nicaragua, Bolivia, Brazil, Panama, and probably in all the Latin American countries, then the possiblity that it exists anywhere is purely theoretical."[163] It would be difficult to find a single Catholic moral theologian who would deny that in this case even armed violence is justified. But in the growth of the Kingdom of God violence is an equivocal sign, and there exists a sign that is unequivocal, but it is a sign based upon certain conditions.

In response to the oppressive violence of the bourgeois-militarists, neocolonial state — the worst kind of violence — there exists the *prophetic subversive violence,* which utilizes neither offensive nor defensive arms. It is the violence of the "Word of God" that is directed to those who hurl insults at the Cross, and that raises oppressed people to an awareness of their value and initiates the process of liberation. Jesus died on the Cross with neither the support nor the defense of the Zealots, those armed subversives, those anti-Roman Jews. Jesus died despite the "good will" of Pilate whom the Empire allowed the luxury of appearing to his victims as one having compassion but who in reality represented the real cause of the injustices suffered by the oppressed. Jesus died after having been arraigned before the Herodians or priests who internally oppressed the humble people in the name of the Empire, and it was these internal oppressors who utilized the means of oppressive violence and who made possible the coercive violence against Jesus and the people. But Jesus, as did the prophets, proposed a subversive prophetic violence without the use of arms. His method was that of the "pedagogy of the oppressed."[164] Subversive armed violence prepares one for domination. The dominator, however, is always eliminated, and his place is occupied by a new dominator. Subversive prophetic violence, conversely, prepares one for liberation: the dominator will be humanized in the liberation of the dominated.

The conditions for subversive prophetic violence are distinct from those advocated by the proponents of nonviolence as well as being different from those advocated by the supporters of armed violence. Subversive *prophetic* violence is "violent," and this distinguishes it from nonviolence in that it confronts, shocks, and harasses those who live as part of the oppressive structures. The intent is to destroy these structures, not to eliminate the oppressor; it is to humanize him in order that he will be transformed. Subversive prophetic violence will, furthermore, reveal the evil of the manufacture of arms and the wrong which the lowering of international prices of raw materials entails. It will denounce the "good conscience" of those who steal millions and who later return crumbs as "aid to the Third World." Moreover, this violence is *subversive* because it puts down the universally held values such as money, prestige, and "having more," and exalts the basic values of equality among people, justice, and liberty for all. But the means advocated are not guns, grenades, and bombs, but rather the pen and the committed life. Both commitments, armed subversive violence and prophetic subversive violence, often result in death. Jesus went to the Cross for having utilized prophetic subversive violence as did Antonio de Valdivieso, Bishop of Nicaragua, and Father Pereira Neto of Recife. Their deaths, however, are intrinsically different from a victim of the Crusades against the Arabs in the Middle Ages, or of Camilo Torres against the Colombian army. These latter examples are heroes of subversive armed violence involved in a "holy war." The death of the prophet is martyrdom — unequivocal "testimony" that liberates the oppressor, the police, or the army that assassinates him. The death of the hero for a cause, even a just cause, is not the death of a saint. Between the hero and the saint lies the distance of the equivocal sign of the struggle that attempts to annihilate the dominator and the unequivocal sign of the struggle to liberate the dominator and the dominated in a historical process which in the last analysis is eschatological because no stage of history is absolute, ultimate, or the Kingdom of God on earth.

Finally, we would say, the prophet should be *poor* in order to be completely free from the oppressive structures of violence. The prophet should be *wise*, aware of the possible scope and depth of the sin of oppression. He should be *courageous* and not fear being violent. He should be *astute* in order to show authentically what he uncovers and what the oppressors desire to hide. He should be *ready to die* because life (*vis*, force and violence, both are derived from the word *life*) and liberation grow and are watered with "the blood of the martyrs." Jesus did not stain his hands with Roman blood, neither did his blood stain the Romans. He saved them; he liberated them because "the Son of man came not to be served but to serve, and to *give his life* as a ransom for *many*" (Matt. 20:28). Our Lord had a "populist" vocation.

4. The Church and Racial Minorities

A minority of the African race live in Latin America, primarily in certain countries such as Brazil, Haiti, and other areas of the Caribbean. Latin Americans, on the other hand — Chicanos, Latinos, and Hispanic Americans — represent a large minority living in the United States.

(1) The Latin American Black

Negroes were brought in increasingly large numbers to the Americas beginning in the sixteenth century. They were sold as slaves by the English and Portuguese. (The Spaniards, incidentally, never sold slaves; they merely bought them). Toward the end of the sixteenth century there were certain regions of the Caribbean that had no Indian population, and the land was worked exclusively by Negro slaves. In the Synod of 1610, for example, Bishop Cristóbal y Rodríguez y Suárez spoke only of Negro slaves, and there were no constitutions written regarding the Indians. During the colonial era at least six to twelve million Negro slaves were brought to the Americas. The *Negro Year Book* of 1931 – 1932 gives the following figures for two epochs:

1666 – 1776	Slaves sold only by the English in the British, Spanish, and Portuguese colonies	3,000,000
1776 – 1800	An average of 74,000 slaves per year brought to the Americas: 38,000 by the English, 20,000 by the French, 10,000 by the Portuguese, and 6,000 by others, for a total of	1,850,000

The slaves who were brought to the Hispanic American colonies came primarily from the Congo and Angola,[165] although the Guinea Coast provided the majority of slaves for Bahía, Brazil, during the sixteenth century, Angola during the seventeenth century, and the Gold Coast in the eighteenth century. The Africans were consequently from multiple tribes such as the Wolof, Mandingo, Bambara, Yoruba, and Ashanti. The most recent arrivals were called *Bossales*; those born in America were called *Creoles*; and fugitives and runaways were called *Cimarrones*. The blacks were organized into "nations" or councils with their own kings and governments. From their meetings, dances, and deformed religious services there sprang up their *santarias,* their *candomblés* (dances), and their voodoo. In Brazil "the division by nations appeared at diverse institutional levels: in the army where the colored soldiers formed four separate batallions, the Minas, Ardras, Angolas, and Criollos, and in the Catholic religious confraternities. In Bahía, for example, the confraternity of Our Lady of Rosario attracted primarily the Angolas while the Yorubas grouped themselves in a Church in the lower part of the city."[166] In Haiti the different "nations" transformed themselves symbolically into gods or "mysteries": thus the Congo gods Mayombe, Madrague, Ibo, and Maki were mixed with those of the Dahomy region and became subordinated to the Fon culture. In Central America a highly syncretized Afro-American cultural zone existed. The Yoruba civilization predominated in Cuba, Trinidad, and Northeast Brazil while the Dahomey and Fon cultures prevailed in Haiti and North Brazil. The Kromanti culture was predominant in Jamaica, Barbados, and Santa Lucía.

In 1840 there were more Negroes in Cuba than whites, but today only twenty-four percent of the population is black. Haiti is almost totally black. Some sixty-eight percent of the population in the Dominican Republic are mulattoes, and nineteen percent are pure Negro. Puerto Rico has a twenty-three percent population of mulattoes and four percent pure Negro. Panama is predominantly black. In North Brazil — in Acre, the Amazonas, and Pará — more than sixty percent of the population is Negro, while in the Northeast — in Maranhão and Alagoas — forty-eight percent of the people are black. In the East — from Sergipe to the Federal District — forty-six percent of the people are black, while in the South — from São Paulo to Río Grande do Sul — only eleven percent are Negroes. In the West Central states of Mato Grosso and Goiás, thirty-five percent of the people are black.

Christianity has deeply penetrated the consciousness of the black worship services but primarily as a syncretistic element from their previous traditions, which were very deformed because of the oppression that the Negroes suffered. In reality their cults and traditions were preserved through their dances, which their owners naively permitted.

Thus there grew up, for example, the *macumba* of Río de Janeiro — a mixture of *Fon* gege, *Yoruba* nago, the musulmi of *Islam*, Bantú, the *Indian* cambocle together with Catholic elements and spiritism — a syncretistic cult very powerful in the rural areas as well as the slums of the urban centers.

The Negro culture has also had a political dimension. There were numerous slave revolts — they could be numbered in the hundreds; for example, in Santo Domingo in the early years of the sixteenth century there were slave revolts in 1523, 1537, 1548, etc. — but only in Haiti, beginning on the night of August 14, 1791, were the Negroes successful in gaining their political independence. The revolution began with a voodoo ceremony presided over by Boukman in a clearing in the Caimán forest during a severe rainstorm. Negritude as a movement — analogical to indigeneity — has only begun in Latin America with a reflection on the meaning of voodoo itself. The intellectuals of the Antilles have manifested a special interest in this question, not for

The Black and Mulatto Population In Latin America (1940)

	Negroes	Percent	Mulattoes	Percent
Mexico	80,000	0.41	40,000	2.04
Antilles	5,500,000	39.29	3,000,000	21.43
Guatemala	4,011	0.12	2,000	0.06
British Honduras	15,000	25.55	20,000	34.03
Honduras	55,275	4.99	10,000	0.90
El Salvador	100	0.0001	100	0.0001
Nicaragua	90,000	6.52	40,000	2.88
Costa Rica	26,900	4.09	20,000	0.14
Colombia	405,076	4.50	2,205,382	24.32
Venezuela	100,000	2.79	1,000,000	27.93
British Guiana	100,000	29.30	80,000	23.44
Dutch Guiana	17,000	9.55	20,000	11.23
French Guiana	1,000	0.25	1,000	0.25
Ecuador	50,000	2.00	150,000	6.00
Peru	29,054	0.41	80,000	0.71
Bolivia	7,800	0.26	5,000	0.15
Brazil	5,789,924	14.00	8,276,321	20.01
Paraguay	5,000	0.52	5,000	0.52
Uruguay	10,000	0.46	50,000	2.30
Chile	1,000	0.02	3,000	0.06
Argentina	5,000	0.038	10,000	0.076

the purpose of "returning to Africa" or recreating the African culture, but rather to emphasize the honor of being black and of conserving their cultural traditions and discovering their political commitments. The Church in Latin America has done little in the way of the black pastoral.

(2) Latin America in North American Catholicism

More than fifteen million *Chicanos* or Mexican Americans, to which we must add the *Latinos* (Puerto Ricans, Dominicans, Cubans and recently people from virtually every country in Latin America) constitute already thirty percent of North American Roman Catholics.

Since 1973 pastoral letters in the United States have been bilingual, that is, written in both English and Spanish. By the year 2000, fifty percent of all North American Catholics will be of Latin American origin if the demographic growth by birth and immigration continues.

Since the end of the Second World War and especially since 1962, the Chicanos have become aware of conditions in which they live, as evidenced by this poem:

I am Joaquín,
lost in a world of confusion,
caught up in the whirl of a gringo society,
confused by the rules,
scorned by attitudes,
suppressed by manipulation.[167]

The year that the Second Vatican Council began, César Chávez, leader of the United Farm Workers Organizing Committee (UFWOC), began his work among rural farm workers in California. In 1963 Reyes López Tijeirina began the *Alianza Federal de*

Mercedes (Federal Alliance of Mercy) in New Mexico. Thus began the confrontation between the Chicanos and the established economic powers which resulted in the police repression, the jailing, and the assassination of the Chicano leaders. In 1965 the "long *huelga*" (long strike) in California began in the San Joaquín Valley with the dramatic march of three hundred thousand workers and sympathizers from Delano to Sacramento. Other movements followed such as Rodolfo "Corky" González's Denver Crusade for Justice, the political party *La Raza Unida* (The United Race) which began in Texas in 1967 under the leadership of José Angel Gutiérrez and other activists, and an effort to mobilize Hispanic Americans in schools, communites, and universities which led to the founding of the United Mexican American Students (UMAS). These activities grew, and with the naming of Monseñor Patrick Flores as Auxiliary Bishop of San Antonio, Texas, the Chicanos had their first Hispanic American bishop. The imbalance can yet be seen, however, in the fact that even though Spanish Americans represented nearly thirty percent of North American Roman Catholics, they had only one bishop of their race. In contrast, fifty percent of North American bishops are of Irish descent despite the fact that Irish represent no more than twelve percent of the Catholics in the country. In 1971 the Mexican-American Cultural Center was founded in San Antonio, Texas, where apostles are being prepared to work with Spanish American people in the United States. Shortly before, a group of priests and sisters — Chicano priests and nuns — organized to begin to unify their pastoral. The Latin American clergy in North America are becoming aware of their mission.

5. Support for Agrarian Reform

The issue of agrarian reform is of supreme theological and historical importance in Latin America. One should not forget that as a part of the conquest the lands were divided among the conquerors. The Indians in turn were "given" to the conquerors and colonists to work the land. The land owners, the *terratenientes* (those who "have" the land), constituted the oligarcy that was in power until 1929, the date which, according to our analysis, can be cited as the time when the incipient industrial bourgeois originated. To change the system of land tenure was in effect to eliminate the power of the oligarchic-agrarian class, and this became a major political, economic, cultural, and religious issue.

One may take a more recent date as a point of departure. In 1961, for example, Father Antonio Melo, twenty-eight years of age, led two thousand peasants assisted by some Catholic university students from the Brazilian region of Pernambuco to occupy some land. When the government of Goulart ceded the land to the new occupants, the military deposed the president.[168] Dom Hélder Câmara, at that time Secretary of the Brazilian episcopacy, as a member of a special commission signed the approval of the agrarian reform project that was to be discussed in the parliament. The Archbishop of São Paulo, Cardinal C. C. de Vasconcelos Motta, proposed to President Goulart a meeting in the Catholic Institute *Frente Agrario* (Agrarian Front) in order to discuss the distribution of land to those who had none. The episcopacy in its "The Agrarian Reform Faces Communism"[169] indicated that the proposed reform was a dike erected against the Communist infiltration in that it represented an advance in and shaping of the movement around generalized property questions but not at the state level. At the same time the episcopacy was critical of the Communism of those who were invading the land because "their abuses constitute a suicidal attitude."

Monseñor Geraldo de Proença Sigaud, Archbishop of Diamantina in Minas Gerais, and Monseñor Antonio de Castro Mayer disagreed with Cardinal Motta and declared that "the expropriations of lands are illegal." Dom Sigaud then published his "Anti-communist Catechism" at the same time that the Bishop of Santo André, Monseñor Jorge Marcos de Oliveira, was defending a group of strikers. The episcopacy, the clergy, and the laity — in fact all of the Church — adopted differing points of view to the point of being antithetical in regard to the question of agrarian reform, which remains a sign. The Brazilian episcopacy, nevertheless, issued a message on April 3, 1963, on the necessity of a threefold reform — agrarian, fiscal, and electoral — as a way of applying the teachings of the encyclical *Pacem in Terris*. The message was signed by the three Brazilian cardinals.

Northeast Brazil has suffered periodic and devastating droughts, and the *sertâo* has been progressively abandoned by a growing number of peasants. In 1955 the Peasant Leagues of Juliâo adopted the motto, "The land for the peasants." (Some seventy percent of the inhabitants of the Northeast are illiterate, and their annual income per capita is less than one hundred dollars U.S.)

The Catholic right, however, influenced by French groups such as "Verbe" and "La cité catholique," has become more influential all over Latin America. In Mexico the periodical *Puño (Fist)* of the University Movement for Renewed Orientation (MURO), following the ideological direction of Víctor Manuel Sánchez, published an ultra-integrist article by Father Castellanos. A response was writtin by Father Allaz, OP, who was supported by his own Dominican Order as well as by the Archbishop of Mexico, Monseñor Miranda. These events took place in 1963. Articles were published in *El Día* by González Pedrero on "John XXIII and Primo de Rivera" and by López Cámara, Professor of Political Science in the Autonomous University, on "The Two Churches." The reactions to the article by Allaz were favorable, and Father Castellanos was obliged to leave the country. Monseñor Miranda prohibited the MURO in the religious schools in 1964. The position of the Archbishop was reaffirmed by the "Committee of Catholic Organizations," which issued a communique in 1964 in which for the first time the Mexican revolution of 1910 was referred to in positive terms.

Meanwhile, Brazil had experienced its military takeover, and Monseñor Padim protested when Catholic Action was accused of being infiltrated by Communists. "In a time when even Pope John XXIII has been called a Communist," wrote Padim, "we should not be surprised that faithful Catholics, true to their spiritual leader, receive the same treatment." In Belo Horizonte, however, numerous Catholics, rosary in hand, staged a public march in opposition to the agrarian reform program, a march that was organized by Lionel Brizzola. Catholic Action manifested its disapproval of the march.

In Chile, Christians had adopted a much more positive attitude, but there existed also in this Andean country a group of laypersons closely tied to the rightists in Brazil, and who called themselves the *Fiducia* (Trustees). They accused President Frei of being a Chilean Kerensky[170] because the Christian Democratic government, according to these critics, proposed a system in which private property would be eliminated. Following the same line, the periodical *Cruzada (Crusade)*, published in Argentina by the "Organization for the Defense of Tradition, Family, and Property," began in 1965 a vigorous campaign against the CGT stating, "We want to know if they are Christians and anti-Communists or anti-Christians and Marxists," an interrogatory that, according to the article, stemmed from the fact that the reforms proposed by the CGT coincided with the Marxist view of private property and opposition to Catholicism and Western civilization.[171] The periodical *Mensaje (Message)* stated, "A few days ago we read in *El Mercurio* an advertisement placed by the *Fiducia* group which contained eight hundered sixty signatures of 'peasants and workers of Curaví,' " which purported to be a protest against "the agrarian reform" and asserted that the reform program was of "no advantage to the working class." The origin of the advertisement can be traced to the fact that a country estate belonging to the President of the *Fiducia* had just been expropriated by the government. The *Mensaje* article concluded, "We pray that Our Lady will liberate Chile from socialism which is the bane of Christian civilization."[172]

One cannot say *indiscriminately*, however, that the Church always defends private property. The right to property that has been stolen, for example, cannot be defended. But what of an inheritance that was previously stolen? Are the lands that have been taken by armed violence now Spanish lands, asked the theologians of Salamanca in the sixteenth century, those lands wrested from the American Indians? When General Roca in his expedition into the Argentine Pampas in the nineteenth century gave to his lieutenants the Indian lands that the Spanish were pillaging, did they by right belong more to the Spanish than to the primitive inhabitants who were violently expelled? Furthermore, one should remember that there is more than one type of property. In the secular doctrine of the Church, in the Scriptures, in the writings of the Fathers, and in tradition, property is analogous. In the first place, "common ownership and universal liberty are said to be of natural law, because private property and slavery exist by human contrivance for the convenience of social life, and not by natural law."[173] The "distinction of possessions," [174] therefore, is a secondary natural right which is traditionally referred to as one of the "human rights," that is, the right of private property.[175] The Cenobite monk, Saint Basil of Caesarea, said that "the community of goods [practiced by his order] is a norm of existence more appropriate than private property, and it only conforms to nature,"[176] Today we are shocked by such a statement, and if we are, it is because of our ignorance of "tradition," even when we think we are following tradition. Furthermore, this is not all that can be said, for not all ownership of private property is a natural right. In the first place, private or exclusive property can be that belonging to a person or to a group. A corporation or a jointly owned company is an example. But also, property can belong to the citizens of a country who have for their use the resources or goods of that country to the exclusion of other countries.

Furthermore, private property can be a positive right. In the example given above, the Indians — that is, the tribe — possessed the land as their private property, and though Roca's lieutenants took the land by force, their possession of it was merely positive, that is, "by means of the determination" of General Roca.[177] Two other clarifications need to be made. First, natural property rights are a *necessary* means for the organization of human life materially, culturally, and religiously. But the natural right to property cannot be absolute if by the exclusive use of that property my being human is frustrated. *I have no natural right* over any property that is not absolutely necessary for my perfection. I have only a positive right. Furthermore, one of the oldest Christian traditions — and this is the second clarification — is that "in case of extreme necessity, everything is common."[178]

Besides referring to these traditional principles in Catholicism, one can also affirm the following: private property is not illegitimate in principle, that is, by nature, but it can be illegitimate *in fact*. For example, property obtained by armed violence is illegitimate — such as the lands taken from the Indians either at the time of the Conquest or later by the national armies in behalf of the oligarchies. Property that is bought too cheaply or obtained through fraud is illegitimate. And even in cases where property is gained legitimately, one cannot assert that all such property is one's natural right. Only that which is necessary for the development of the person can be defended as property by natural right. United Fruit, therefore, does not have a natural right to the thousands of acres that it possesses in Central America, nor does the land owner who lives in the city have any natural right to the hundreds of acres worked by someone else for him. He possesses by *natural* right only what is necessary for him and his family to live honestly and decently. All the rest he has by *positive* right, and *the remainder* is the *natural* right of those who work the land even though they do not possess the positive right over it. Moreover, in virtually all the countries in Latin America, one encounters "the case of extreme necessity, where all is common." It was on these traditional principles of Catholic Scholastic theology that Chile began to be aware of the need for "agrarian reform."

The appeals of the Bishop of Matanzas, who opposed the agrarian reform program in Cuba in 1959, really belonged to another stage in history,[179] as did the opinions of the Cardinal of Bogotá, Monseñor Luís Concha, when he asked in 1961, "Why talk about an agrarian reform?"[180] The Chilean episcopacy, guided by the foresight of Monseñor Manuel Larraín, issued a pastoral letter on March 11, 1962, regarding the Chilean peasants who struggled under the yoke of Liberalism and for whom the Church committed itself to develop a plan of agrarian reform of those properties belonging to the Church.[181] The letter declared: "Conscious of the situation of the peasant and desirous to collaborate not only with the fundamental doctrine, but also as an example of concrete acts, we in the Plenary Assembly agree this year to begin a study of an eventual colonization of the agricultural properties which belong to the hierarchy."[182] Monseñor Larraín had begun in 1961 a division of some 342 hectares of irrigated lands of the "Alto Las Cruces" property by dividing them among 12 families. Cardinal Silva Henríquez of Santiago almost simultaneously followed the same procedure by dividing over 1200 hectares of "Las Pataguas" among 80 families.[183] The Church then created the Institute for Agrarian Promotion (INPROA) because it wanted not only to provide land but also to educate the farmers in the establishment of cooperatives, in the accumulation of capital, in the technology needed for the exploitation of the land, and in the sale of their products. *Misereor*, a West German Catholic aid foundation, and the Taizé Community made possible the formation of the initial capital of INPROA. In 1965 the Chilean Jesuits offered to the Institute farms of 1,128 and 5,256 hectares. When the Christian Democratic government of Eduardo Frei came to power a more extensive agrarian reform program was proposed, and the lands belonging to the Church were confiscated in order to continue the program already begun.[184] As late as 1967 Monseñor Sánchez Beguiristain, Bishop of Concepción, ceded to the Agrarian Reform Institute an estate of 2,700 hectares.

Other Latin American bishops have also supported agrarian reform. Monseñor Domingo Roa, Bishop of Maracaibo, spoke out in defense of the Indians of the Yupa tribe whose chief, Abel Ramírez, was killed on December 21, 1961, by hired gunmen of the land owners. The bishop defended the Indians and their "right to possess their land." We would add that they had the *natural* right, but they were assassinated in the name of *positive* right. In Peru Bishops Pineda of Huánuco, Valdivia of Huancayo, and Ortiz y Coronado of Huancavélica began distributing their ecclesial lands among the peasants in 1962. Doubtless these acts by the bishops prompted many landless peasants to invade other lands, incidents which occurred later in Peru and Bolivia. In June 1962 the land owners accused two priests who were working with the Indians in Huancavélica of theft and also of having violated minors. The priests were jailed, and when the bishops came to their defense and demonstrated that they were being falsely accused in order to discredit their social work among the Indians, the Lima newspaper *El Comercio* published the story, and the two priests were freed — much to the dismay of the land owners. In 1963 the Bishop of Cuzco, Monseñor Jurgens Byrne, distributed the lands belonging to the Church among the peasants. When they began to occupy those lands, Father Pardo, Vicar General of the Diocese of Huacho, defended the agrarian reform program that was violently being criticized by the Lima newspaper *La Prensa* during December 1963. The Indians continued to occupy the lands around Cuzco and in other areas. After observing the results of this program, Monseñor Byrne distributed the last 15,000 hectares of the archdiocese to the colonists in 1964. When the Belaunde government fell — in large part because of the brutal repression of the peasants — and the military Junta came to power, a group of priests working with ONIS sent a declaration regarding the agrarian reform program to General Velasco Alvarado, President of the Junta. The declaration was dated June 20, 1969,[185] and cited the Pastoral Constitution of the Second Vatican Council, *Gaudium et Spes*, which stated: "God intended the earth and all that it contains for the use of every human being and people" (n. 69). Four days later when General Velasco decreed the Agrarian Reform Law he cited this document from ONIS. But as late as 1970 Father Neptali Liceta, a priest in Cajatambo, was accused of having incited the peasants to rebellion. He responded to the accusation saying, "I am the son of peasants. I know this system of oppression. To liberate my neighbor is part of my vocation as a priest."[186]

In Ecuador the Church has been more indifferent to the agrarian reform question, as can be seen in the pastoral letter of the episcopacy written in 1963.[187] It was not until 1969 that Monseñor Leonidas Proaño, Bishop of Riobamba, signed an agreement with the Ecuadorian Education Center of Agricultural Services (CESA) on March 13 giving to the Reform Institute the 3,000-hectare Hacienda "Tepeyac." This project was also financed by *Misereor* of West Germany. The Center for Studies and Social Action (CEAS) began to work in close coordination with CESA, the former having a strong program of education by radio as well as the Institute for the Formation of Peasant Leaders. As one might expect, Monseñor Proaño has had a great deal of opposition in view of the fact that nearly one-third of all the land in Ecuador belongs to the Church, that is, to the dioceses, religious orders, and congregations rooted in colonial traditions.

In Argentina Monseñor Iriarte and his priests of Reconquista signed a declaration in defense of the peasants illustrating that the poverty of those in the Northeast, and especially of the wood-gatherers in the Chaco of Santa Fe, was a result of agrarian injustices. Monseñor Cafferata of San Luis, after a pastoral visit of eighteen months, stated that "the people of the rural area were prevented from gaining property rights over the land which they worked, and no one had any interest in their cause whatsoever. ... Social and economic liberalism," the Bishop declared, "has created an unjust order."[188] But this did not impede Monseñor Buteler, Archbishop of Mendoza, from celebrating a Mass for the Association for Tradition, Family, and Property, which encouraged these self-styled defenders of Catholic tradition.

In Colombia the Church gave to the Agrarian Reform Institute (INCORA) 800 hectares shortly before they were to be expropriated by the government. And the Bishop of Honduras, Marcelo Gerin Boulax, spoke disparagingly of the invasion of land, criticizing those involved for their violent methods,[189] and forgetting the violence and oppression of those whose use of the land was founded on positive property rights while the exploited had the *natural* rights over the lands they worked in all of Honduras.

II. THE MINISTRIES AT PRESENT

1. The Attitude of the Bishops

The work of the sociologist and of the historian is difficult when the effort is made to discover meaning in recent phenomena. There is the risk of overlooking important facts and of failing to recognize persons who have played essential roles. In this section, however, I will describe only a few bishops about whom much is already known through public articles and through their own books and pastorals. Only God truly knows who is working in the history of salvation. There are many who occupy humble posts on the frontier of the advance of the Kingdom, and there are many more than those who are apparent. It would be well if we could indicate the different attitudes of the Latin American episcopacy, and in an earlier work we did examine the perspective of the bishops of the sixteenth century — the century of great renewal within Christendom, especially in Spain.[190] There was an ideal as to what a bishop should be: poor (although not in Europe), one who visited his diocese, wise, saintly, and in Spanish America, a missionary — though in the latter role there was a certain kind of paternalism in regard to the Indian whom the bishops wanted to incorporate into Christendom. In the twentieth century, since the time of Vatican II and the Medellín Conference, the ideal regarding the bishop has changed dramatically. *Some* continue with the idea of a Christendom wherein the bishop is a Father who demands obedience, who is a doctor in Latin Scholastic theology, who defends above all else the good relations with the state, and who defends the rights of the Church in regard to teaching, the *Patronato*, divorce, and good customs. In general he is a canonist, and he thinks of Communism as the antithesis of Christianity, often confusing Christianity with Western civilization. Many of the Latin American bishops have this attitude, but few of them are as consistent theologically as Monseñor Geraldo Sigaud, Bishop of Diamantina, Brazil, who defended this point of view by his acts and in his writings — though in fairness to him, it should be recognized that in July 1970 while in Rome, he condemned the injustices such as torture being perpetrated by his government.[191] Many of these traditionalist bishops have had serious conflicts with their priests, bishops such as Monseñor Buteler of Mendoza, Bishop Bolatti of Rosario, Cardinal Caggiano of Buenos Aires, Cardinal Concha of Bogotá, and Archbishop Casariego of Guatemala.

There are others, however, who have adopted the attitude of desiring to do away altogether with the idea of Christendom and who are looking for new ways for the Church to be missionary and to become more knowledgeable in regard to the changes that are taking place in the world. In Latin America this implies the discovery of the commitment of the Church in political, economic, and cultural structures of our underdeveloped and oppressed continent in the struggle for the liberation of the poor. These bishops, like Bartolomé de Las Casas who desired obedience to the *New Laws*, are intent on applying the teachings of the Constitutions and Decrees of the Second Vatican Council and of the resolutions of the Second General Conference of Latin American Bishops in Medellín. Besides these major documents, the bishops have other authoritative statements to which they can appeal in the development of a new episcopal ideal. One is the address Paul VI gave to the Latin American episcopacy on November 23, 1965, in which he said, "There is no lack, unfortunately, of those who remain closed to the renewing winds of the times,"[192] or, "The Church has always used its goods for the community, and if not, it has been weighed down with unproductive temporal goods, especially of lands, which today do not have the importance as in other times and which it would be wise now to employ in a better way."[193] The bishops could also appeal to the Decree on the Bishops Pastoral Office in the Church, *Christus Dominus*, in which the bishops are urged to respond to "the difficulties and problems by which people are most vexatiously burdened and troubled ... with a special concern ... [for] the poor and the lower classes to whom the Lord sent them to preach the gospel"[194] and "welcome priests with a special love ... and thus by his readiness to listen to them and by his trusting familiarity, a bishop can work to promote the whole pastoral work of the entire diocese."[195] Also available is the supremely important Decree on the Church's Missionary Activity (*Ad Gentes*), which reminds the bishops that mission is not only exterior but also interior and reminds them that "the pilgrim Church is missionary by her very nature. For it is from the mission of the Son and the mission of the Holy Spirit that she takes her origin, in accordance with the decree of God the Father."[196] Furthermore, "this mission is a continuing one. In the course of history it unfolds as the mission of Christ Himself who was sent to preach the gospel to the poor. Hence, prompted by the Holy Spirit, the Church must walk the same road which Christ walked: a road of poverty and obedience, of service and self-sacrifice. ... This duty must be fulfilled by the order of bishops ... and is one and the same everywhere and in every situation, even though the variety of situations keeps it from being exercised in the same way."[197] "If this goal is to be achieved, theological investigation must necessarily be stirred up in each major socio-cultural area [as in Latin America, we would add]. ... Thus it will be more clearly seen in what ways faith can seek for understanding in the philosophy and wisdom of these peoples."[198]

In Latin America, where one can observe generally a certain partiality in the exercise of the episcopal functions — each bishop is bishop in his diocese, and no one can interfere with his manner or function — it should be remembered that "as members of the body of bishops which succeeds the College of Apostles, all bishops are consecrated not just for some one diocese, but for the salvation of the entire world."[199] This is the theological foundation of CELAM, a providential institution in Latin America. Finally, the bishops could appeal to the Pastoral Constitution on the Church in the Modern World (*Gaudium et Spes*), which stresses an "intimate bond between the Church and mankind ... especially those who are poor or are in any way afflicted."[200]

The opening address of Paul VI to the General Conference in Medellín as well as the final document entitled "The Church in the Present-Day Transformation of Latin America in the Light of the Council" have been studied in a dialogical way by bishops, priests, and laity in very few dioceses. Everything, however, could be summarized in the Pastoral Conclusions of the Medellín Conference, which state: "To us, the Pastors of the Church, belong the duty to educate the Christian conscience, to inspire, stimulate, and help orient all the initiatives that contribute to the formation of man. It is also up to us to denounce everything which, opposing justice, destroys peace."[201] These are the principles by which an historian may judge the action of the bishops, and we will select a few examples, according to the information available, which indicate the direction of commitment.

Without doubt there is today in Brazil a group of bishops who know how to witness in this difficult period through which they must live. Among them are Dom José

Távora of Aracaju, Waldir Calheiros of Volta Redonda, Antonio Fragoso of Crateus, Cándido Padim of Lorena, Hélder Câmara of Olinda and Recife, Jorge Marcos de Oliveira of Santo André, Joâo da Mota e Alburquerque of Sâo Luís do Maranhâo, Avelar Brandâo Vilela of Teresina, José Pires of Joâo Pessoa, Aloisio Lorscheider of Santo Angelo, and David Picâo of Santos. Outstanding among these is the Archbishop of Recife and Olinda, Dom Hélder Câmara, of whom Amoroso Lima has written, in response to the attempt to defame him, "I see a *sign* much greater than his personal greatness and his destiny which is of international renown currently acquired."[202] In reality, Dom Hélder has been marked from his childhood, from his formation, from his first priestly commitments and even earlier by a certain vocation which at this time is a sufficient *sign* for our time. His conduct approaches the ecclesial praxis that Christians and the world demand of the Latin American Church, namely, *prophetic commitment* to the oppressed people who are beginning a process of liberation. Dom Hélder has written a poem in which he says:

> When I was a youngster
> I wanted to go out running
>   Among the mountain peaks.
>
> And when, between two summits
> A gap appeared,
>   Why not leap
>   Across the chasm?
>
> Led by the angel's hand,
> All my life long
> This is what happened,
>   This, exactly.[203]

He tells us, "I was born February 7, 1909, in a primary school of Fortaleza, the capital of Cerá, in Brazil, where my mother was a government teacher."[204] Câmara was born into a world of simple poverty, in an educational environment, in a position open to the world, for to be a teacher in a government school is quite distinct from serving in this capacity in a religious institution. He entered the seminary, but his classical scholastic training did not prepare him for theological renewal. Dom Hélder was not to be, however, a theologian, but a pastor. He was ordained on August 15, 1931, at the age of twenty-two. He was sent to Fortaleza, the provincial capital, and shortly thereafter became involved with the *Legion of October*, a rightist movement inspired by the Portuguese leader Antonio Salazar. By order of his bishop, Câmara accepted the responsibility of Secretary of Education in the *Legion* movement in Ceará. In 1934 when the Archbishop founded the "Electoral League," a pressure group to promote the political candidates who were responsive to the desires of the Brazilian Church, Dom Hélder was transformed into a very active propagandist. A short time later he was named Secretary of Education for the State of Ceará and was later transferred to the Secretariat of Federal Education in Río. He learned ry early, therefore, to work directly with political and administrative functionaries totally outside the Church. Since 1933, therefore, Dom Hélder has learned personally something of the Church-world relation about which Vatican II and the Medellín Conference had so much to say. In 1936 Câmara was appointed to the task of Technical Assistant for the Ministry of Education of the municipality of Río de Janeiro, then the capital of Brazil. He subsequently was asked to work in the Institute for Educational Research as head of a department that was developing programs and tests for pupils in the public schools of Río which at the time had approximately 120,000 students.[205] While in Río he led in the organization of the National Conference of the Bishops of Brazil (CNBB), and he was named Secretary General, a post he held for twelve years. He was also responsible for preparing for and organizing the International Eucharistic Congress in Río as well as the First General Conference of Latin American Bishops. Both of these meetings took place in Río in 1955.

Following the Eucharistic Congress, Cardinal Gerlier of Lyons called on Câmara. The purpose for the visit was not social, for Gerlier said to him,

I have had some experience in organization, and since taking part in this Eucharistic Congress I must tell you that you have exceptional capacities as an organizer. This is not a compliment I am paying you. I say it instead to awaken you to a sense of responsibility. Now I ask you, why do you not put those capacities of yours to work at solving the problems of the slums, what you call the *favelas*?[206]

This was probably one of the most important incidents in the history of the Church in Latin America. A committed European prophet who had long been concerned with social problems passed the torch to his Latin America brother. "Thus," says Câmara, "Cardinal Gerlier was the one who gave me the push that plunged me into this action. Formerly I had felt the problem but had not been involved in the battle."[207] But the path of protest and social work eventually alienated Dom Hélder from his Cardinal, and the day came when the Cardinal himself indicated that they must separate. It was the time of Vatican II, and after some consideration was given to sending Câmara to the diocese of São Luis de Maranhâo, he was named instead as Archbishop of Olinda and Recife in March 1964, the same month of the military takeover of the government in Brazil. "On April 12," he says, "I took possession of the diocesan center of Recife."[208] This multifaceted personality is difficult to describe in a few sentences. He "sees far beyond the limits of his own experience. He has the eyes of a poet, of a prophet who reads the analysis of a Father Lebret with the eyes of a Teilhard de Chardin and who interprets the pontifical encyclicals in the firey language of a Saint James." "I am not an expert," he says, "either in economics or sociology or politics. I am a pastor and I see my people suffering."[209]

Dom Hélder is not a politician, and he has rejected all suggestions that he accept a political appointment, though on one occasion he was even offered the vice-presidency of the country. His commitment is to be a "prophetic politico." He of course does not refrain from speaking about political issues. In a report prepared for the CELAM meeting at Mar del Plata in October 1966, Câmara wrote: "The social revolution that the world needs is not an armed coup d'etat, nor guerrilla fighting, nor war. It is a profound and radical change which presupposes divine grace and a transformation of public opinion which can and must be aided by the Church of Latin America and of the entire world."[210] Nevertheless, he believes that "the revolution will not be fought either by the students or the priests or the artists or the intellectuals; it will be fought by the masses, the oppressed, and they will be the victims of that repressive action of power."[211]

Later Câmara confided,

I dream of a Latin American integration confronting the capitalist empire which is headed by the United States, and confronting the socialist empire which is headed by Soviet Russia, and confronting the Common Market. The nations of South America must draw together, must become integrated. But not in the way that Latin America has up to the present carried out integration. I dream of an integration that will accept neither external imperialisms nor internal imperialisms. . . . We must therefore be very careful: Latin American integration, yes; but without mini-imperialism, whether Brazilian or Argentinean or Chilean.[212]

Imperialism obviously troubles Câmara greatly, and he often speaks of it. "Let us be finished with the illusion that we can overcome underdevelopment," he contends, "by accepting aid which has proved to be deceitful and even counterproductive; let us align ourselves resolutely with those who demand a complete reform of international commerce. Let us be finished with the false dichotomy of capialism versus communism, as if the fact of being in disagreement with capitalist solutions implied adherence to communism, and as if to criticize the United States were synonymous with a liaison with Russia or Red China."[213] But though he speaks of politics and political issues, Câmara insists that he is not attempting to be a politician.

I am a man of the Church. I am here to serve the people, and what I can do as bishop I would never do if I agreed to follow a political line and accepted a government position. . . . I am persuaded that the Church in Latin America can still be of service to the people. And so, . . . I am making the most of a certain clerical advantage. There! That is what I am doing! Because, in this county today and in the present conditions, a bishop can say what a student or a workman or an intellectual — even a professor — could not risk saying.[214]

Dom Hélder is not an economist, but he understands and preaches that the "underdeveloped world takes note that its desire for a thorough and rapid renovation of the socioeconomic structures which keep it in poverty is opposed by one or the other of those two power blocs as being 'subversive and Communistic' and sees that it is being exploited by one or the other power blocs eager for new satellites." Clearly he is speaking of the United States and the Soviet Union.[215]

Câmara does not give the impression of being an intellectual, but he proposed a total program for the regional seminary in Camaragibe. At the seminary's inauguration, Dom Hélder insisted that it be an institution in which "the old theological and philosophical themes will be examined along with the new, against the background of ecumenism and the Second Vatican Council, and in the light of the Third World's experience."[216] He included as a part of the curriculum the "reexamination of the principle of subsidiarity . . . studies of the attempts at a new socialism . . . clergy and laity in the developed and developing world, and automation and its human problems."[217] Câmara believes that "we might profit by the Marxist analytical method which is still viable today.[218] If we leave aside the materialistic concept of life and history bound up with that method in the beginning, we could complete the Marxist analysis with a true vision of Christianity which presents no obstacle to human advancement, but quite the contrary."[219]

"Why not recognize that there is no such thing as a unique type of socialism?" he asks. "Why not demand, for the Christian, the free use of the word socialism? It is not necessarily linked with materialism, nor does it have to designate a system that destroys the individual or the community."[220] This becomes all the more important when one comprehends that "Latin America is the Christian portion of the underdeveloped world."[221]

As an expert in pedagogy, he asks, "Is there any other nation in the world that is so completely alienating itself in a domain as vital and sacred as education? We will never attain a harmonious and responsible civilization at the price of the spiritual annihilation of one people by another."[222] Here he is referring to the political influences and control exercised by the United States over Brazil.

As a pastor he confesses that "I believe we will always need priests with long years of formation, but in order to respond to the needs of the communities we shall also have to ordain men from those same basic communities. I will never do so without the approval of Rome, but I will try to find the means to show that there is no other solution."[223] Câmara is influenced greatly by Gandhi and Martin Luther King, and he has been the outstanding proponent of nonviolence in Latin America. In 1968 he launched a world movement that was to begin on October 2 to awaken the "Abrahamic minorities" who "hope against all hopelessness," with the purpose that these movements exercise a "moral pressure for liberation," conscienticizing not only the people but also the oligarchical oppressors. More than forty Brazilian bishops supported the movement, and in 1969 it was referred to as "Action, Justice, and Peace." Along with Ralph Abernathy, a longtime associate of Martin Luther King, Câmara issued on March 21, 1970, the "Declaration of Recife" calling for nonviolence in the struggle against injustice. Shortly thereafter he was proposed by numerous entities for the Nobel Peace Prize. He would be a worthy recipient.

All of his personality is reflected in this statement: "I accuse the true instigators of violence, all those on the right or left, who impair justice and impede peace. . . . Personally, I prefer a thousand times to be killed than to kill."[224]

Dom Hélder is not alone. In a Mass celebrated on May 8, 1968, to commemorate those lost in the Second World War, Dom Edmilson da Cruz, Auxiliary Bishop of São Luis do Maranhão, asked in a sermon, "Is there freedom in Brazil? If there is, why are we not permitted to have peaceful demonstrations?" The military representatives present were so incensed that they walked out of the service. Archbishop da Mota e Alburquerque said later, "The Church in Brazil at the present time profoundly senses her *prophetic mission* to denounce error and announce truth."[225] The Catholic periodical *Vozes* ceased publication on September 3, 1969, by order of the government because the editors had denounced the political tortures that had been going on in the country since 1968. For the same reason Monseñor Calheiros was jailed along with eleven of his priests, all of whom were accused of subversion because they had issued a pastoral letter denouncing the tortures. They were freed, however, after several days. Cardinal Rossi responded by saying, "We prefer men who will confront difficulties even when there is risk, and not those who hide behind an attitude of criminal indifference." Cardinal Barros Câmara was also critical of the "war against the Church," and by 1970 even Monseñor Sigaud, who had defended the military government, denounced on October 6 the frequent tortures. In these difficult times, therefore, the Brazilian episcopacy manifested a dramatic unity, although within the group there have been and are varying positions.

Since the nineteenth century the Chilean episcopacy has been one of the most homogeneous in Latin America. They have been blessed with great bishops who have manifested an advanced social and ecclesial awareness. Chile has given to Latin America one of the outstanding leaders, the late Bishop of Talca, Don Manuel Larraín, who was tragically killed in an automobile accident on June 22, 1966. Don Manuel (1900– 1966) together with Father Alberto Hurtado (1901– 1952) reflected all the optimism of the ideal of a New Christendom to be fashioned by Catholic Action and Christian Democracy. Don Manuel was a graduate of the Catholic University in Santiago with a degree in Law, and when he was twenty years of age he began his seminary studies. Later he was sent to the Gregorian University in Rome where he earned a doctorate in theology. He served as professor and director of the Theological Institute of Santiago and in 1938 was named Bishop of Talca. Until 1962 he was the national adviser of Catholic Action. Larraín conceived and proposed the founding of CELAM, and he was president of the Conference when he died. He was a cultured person, a theologian of his time who had a vision of the Latin American Church as no one else in his era. He had a great influence over Rome and over the Papal Nuncio, and he achieved within the Chilean episcopacy an internal unity without equal. Curiously, he never became a cardinal.

The Archbishop of Santiago, Cardinal Raul Silva Henríquez, is likewise an example in his ministry. As already noted, he began in his diocese an agrarian reform program, and he has shown a readiness to speak out regarding the most difficult questions. Silva was one of the first national leaders to congratulate Salvador Allende upon his election as President of the country. One could continue by calling attention to other Chilean bishops such as Manuel Sánchez Beguiristain of Concepción, Carlos González Cruchaga of Talca, former spiritual director of the Catholic Seminary of Santiago, and several others.

In Argentina the situation is much more complex. It would appear that the commitment of outstanding priests is altered once they are incorporated into the episcopal body. There are, however, some striking exceptions. Cardinal Caggiano, about whom comments have already been made, was a typical prelate of his time. He was founder of Catholic Action in Argentina, serving as mediator between the government and the CGT on various occasions, defender of free teaching[226] and of private property.[227] Caggiano celebrated a Mass in 1970 in honor of the founding of the Federal Police, at which time he lauded them for their defense of our civilization and as a bulwark against subversion. Bishop Ildefonso Sansierra of San Juan has experienced a serious crisis with his priests, especially those in the Catholic University. Archbishop Alfonso Buteler of Mendoza has also been opposed by many of his priests. Monseñor Vicentín of Corrientes excommunicated Father Marturet in an attempt to control the unrest in the diocese. Monseñor Guillermo Bolatti had a severe problem with twenty-seven of his priests in Rosario.

The Archbishop of Reconquista, Juan Iriarte, represents a striking contrast. Even before the Second Vatican Council, Iriarte had begun a reform in his diocese. The same is true of Monseñor Alberto Devoto of Goya who was one of the first to support the XIV Schema committing himself to the episcopal life of poverty and simplicity. Monseñor Angelelli of Rioja declared in 1970, "We are weary of hearing that every attempt to raise the level of the people from inhuman conditions is solely by leftists and subversives." His pastoral regarding the conditions in the province of Rioja is a classic.[228]

Other bishops who should be recognized for their courage and efforts are Jaime de Nevares of Neuquén for his role in the work of the Chocón-Río Colorado; Monseñor Carlos Cafferata of San Luís for his courageous stand against the governor of his province and his pastoral concern in regard to the poor; Monseñor Italo Di Stéfano of the province Presidente Roque Sáenz Peña who is a former president in the Department of the Pastoral of CELAM; Monseñor Vicente Zazpe, Archbishop of Sante Fe, for his social pastoral begun in 1971; Monseñor Podestá, former Bishop of Avellaneda; Monseñor Brasca of Rafaela; and Monseñor Quarracino of Nueve de Julio.[229]

In order to avoid prolonging this exposition, we will indicate some of the bishops who have distinguished themselves in recent years. In Mexico other than Cardinal Miguel Darío Miranda y Gómez, Archbishop of Mexico City, one thinks first of Monseñor Sergio Méndez Arceo, Bishop of Cuernavaca. A graduate of the Gregorian University in Rome with a doctorate in theology, Don Sergio served as professor in the Seminary of Mexico and at the time gave no indication of the fact that he would later become a person of prophetic renewal. But Don Sergio has been molded by contemporary history — not by books, but by the history of salvation as an event. He is not blind to reality, nor is he reluctant to speak out and express his convictions. And he knows how to wait for results. Consequently, his "Mariachis" Mass, the renovation of the Cathedral in Cuernavaca, his courageous defense of the Benedictine convent of Don Lemercier, and of Monseñor Ivan Illich and CIDOC are the results not of an *a priori* calculation nor of a theological ideology, but of an awareness of what history is teaching. Don Sergio is a prophet because he is a good historian, a historian not of the past for the past's sake, but of the past for the future, a future which he announces because he is truthful and because he says what he thinks.

In the Dominican Republic the episcopacy has known how to survive in a difficult situation. Examples can be seen in the unequivocal positions adopted by Monseñor Octavio Beras, Archbishop of Santo Domingo, and in the first pastoral letter of Monseñor Roque Adames of Santiago de Caballeros in 1966 in which he said, "The number of unemployed is serious and shocking. Hunger is the daily bread of many and anguish the permanent patrimony of all. Almost three hundred thousand children are without any schools."[230]

The Apostolic Administrator, Monseñor Polanco Brito, the continual object of reactionary pressure and accused by some as being a Communist, was announced by the Papal Nuncio as the future Archbishop of Santo Domingo in 1970.

Noteworthy in Puerto Rico has been Monseñor Antulio Parrilla Bonilla, Bishop without territorial diocese, who in March 1969 stated that the Church should "liquidate its vast land holdings and inaugurate nonpaternalistic programs of social promotion as a means by which the Church could distinguish itself as a poor Church for the poor of Yahweh. The riches of the Christian Church," Monseñor Parrilla declared, "are a stone of stumbling as much for the rich as for the poor. We must divest ourselves of power or of the appearance of power, of luxury and of the triumphalisms which remain. We must appear as a poor Church, humble and defenseless."[231] Monseñor Aponte also should be mentioned because he is the first Puerto Rican to be consecrated as Archbishop of San Juan.

In Panama the young dynamic Bishop of Santiago de Veraguas, Monseñor Marcos McGrath, has distinguished himself not only in his own diocese but in all of Latin America. He was the former Director of the Catholic Seminary in Santiago, Chile, vice-president of CELAM, directly involved in the Document of Buga in regard to universities, took a courageous position against the Panamanian government in regard to the martyrdom of Father Héctor Gallego, and has inspired many efforts in the entire continent.

The episcopacy of Colombia is one of the most traditional in all of Latin America, but even here there are contrasting positions. At one extreme has been Cardinal Luís Concha, Archbishop of Bogotá, who was personally involved in the Camilo Torres tragedy. But there is also Monseñor Tulio Botero Salazar, Archbishop of Medellín, who in 1962 abandoned the Archbishop's palace in order to live in a working-class community and who declared, "Nothing is more profoundly revolutionary than the gospel."[232] At the opposite extreme from Luís Concha was the Bishop of Buenaventura, Gerardo Valencia Cano, who was the only member of the Colombian episcopacy to sign the Declaration of Golconda in 1968. Bishop Valencia, however, was killed in 1971 when the aircraft on which he was a passenger crashed in the mountains of southwest Colombia.

In Ecuador Monseñor Leonidas Proaño Villalba, Bishop of Riobamba and former President of the Department of the Pastoral of CELAM, besides instituting an agrarian reform program in his diocese, also began the "Pastoral Plan of Riobamba," which projects the transformation of the parishes into diaconates in which the priests will work in teams in various capacities and receive voluntary donations from the faithful. The sacramental celebrations are by groups and not by individuals. This change was projected for the decade of 1970 to 1980, and in the following decade, 1980 to 1990, the parish sectors will be replaced by diaconates. According to the Plan the rural areas are to be served by itinerant apostles. Bishop Proaño has also led in the construction of the Santa Cruz Home for meetings, study, discussions, and prayer. In January 1970 he proposed that the priests leave their parishes and form communities, work alongside their neighbors, and thereby divide the parishes into smaller sectors.

In Peru Cardinal Juan Landázuri Ricketts, Archbishop of Lima, has always shown himself to be a Christian apostle from his participation in the second General Conference in Medellín, even leaving the Archbishop's palace and moving into a small house in the working-class barrio of Vitoria in Lima. The Bishop of Cajamarca, Monseñor Dammert Bellido, recognized as an expert in canon law, has likewise taken a nontraditionalist position. For example, in 1963 he issued a pastoral letter expressing his appreciation for the government donation of a million *soles* for the restoration of the colonial cathedral, but he used the money to improve the living conditions in the prison, to dig a channel for the San Lucas River, and for repairing the new hospital and modernizing the old one. The cathedral, he indicated, could wait, but the poor could not.

In Bolivia the bishops have progressively adopted attitudes more clearly prophetic. On October 5, 1965, Monseñor Manrique, Archbishop of La Paz, together with his priests and several lay persons, sent a petition to President Barrientos in behalf of the Bolivian miners. In 1968 Manrique condemned all those who contemplated depriving union workers of the right to strike after the Minister of Education had fired striking teachers in the national schools. Cardinal José Maure of Sucre supported Manrique in protesting the action of the Minister of Education to the President. Another indication of the posture of the Bolivian bishops can be seen in the fact that in 1970 the Secretariat of Social Studies of the Bolivian episcopacy approved the measures directed toward the nationalization of the Bolivian Gulf Petroleum Company. And though Monseñor Armando Gutiérrez Granier, Bishop of Cochabamba, in his pastoral of August 3, 1967, did not approve of the guerrilla activity, he was not reluctant to call attention to the causes of revolution. He said, "Our people live in misery with insufficient salaries even to pay for the basic human necessities."

In Paraguay, after years of silence, voices of protest have finally been heard. First was that of Felipe Benítez Avalos, Bishop of Villarrica, and then that of Monseñor Gerolamo Pechillo, Bishop of Coronel Oveido, who declared that "the Church cannot remain silent in the face of the continual violation of human rights" — note that he did not say "the rights of the Church" — but protested "the prohibition of priests, religious, and laity from working to relieve the misery of the people, from fulfilling the mission of the Church, and accusing the Church of being Communist."[233]

We must also mention Monseñor Carlos Parteli, Archbishop Coadjutor of Montevideo, and Monseñor Luís Henríquez Jiménez, Auxiliary Bishop of Caracas, both prelates with enormous influence in their respective countries.[234]

As there were in the sixteenth century and during the period of independence bishops who opposed the *New Laws*, and royalists in the nineteenth century who opposed the reforms, there are today bishops who have resisted the renewal advocated by Vatican II and Medellín. Their opposition is existential, that is, more in their conduct than in their words or theory. But as there were those who supported the *New Laws* in defense of the Indian and those more American than royalist, there are today bishops who took a leading part in the Council and Medellín, but who also go beyond what has been proposed in their attempts to create prophetically the image of a missionary Church that transcends the narrow limits of Christendom and extends the frontier to all persons of good will, be they Liberals or Communists, Christians or atheists. All bishops should be able to state, "My door and my heart are open to everyone, absolutely everyone. Christ died for all men, and no one should be excluded from fraternal dialogue."[235]

2. The Attitude of the Priests

No sector of the ecclesiastical institution receives as directly as the presbytery the shock of the crisis of growth that the Church is experiencing. The priests, especially when they are "involved in the key issues of the process of transformation,"[236] should live a double life: as men of the Church and, as missionaries, men of the world. Traditionally the priest has been only a "man of the Church" following the schema of the seminary and of the priesthood of Trent. In a Christendom-type society the priest has occupied a temporal "office" — as others such as the soldier, the politician, the medical doctor, the goldsmith, or the peasant — of "cura," that is, priest (*cura animarum*). With the collapse of Christendom, the priest was placed in a sociocultural situation quite distinct. In the community of believers he is pastor, prophet, and priest. But in the daily life of the world that is no longer a part of the Christendom system, he is more a Christian as was Peter, Paul, and the other apostles in the Empire. It is thus the institution of the priesthood that must bear in a more direct and difficult manner[237] the weight of the "renewal of the Church."[238] The "clergy" is a social class within Christendom. What we contemplate is the disappearance of a "clerical social class," but not in the ecclesial function of the priesthood, which is adapted to the fulfillment of a necessary function within the Christian community as pastor and priest and outside the Christian community as prophet. This prophetic function in Latin America coincides with the concept of the Council when it was stated that "a priest has the poor and the lowly entrusted to him in a special way. The Lord Himself showed that He was united with them (cf. Matt. 25:34 – 35), and the fact that the gospel was preached to them is mentioned as a sign of Messianic activity (cf. Luke 1:18)."[239]

In a sense the Medellín Conference dealt with the Latin American situation more directly because negative as well as positive aspects of the priesthood were brought to light, especially in the "discussion about the role and image of the priest in society."[240] "The Latin American world finds itself engaged in a gigantic effort of accelerating the process of continental development. ... This requires of every priest a special solidarity of human service expressed in a living missionary orientation which enables him to put his ministerial apostolate at the service of the world with its magnificent future and its humiliating sinfulness. ... In this process the priest has a specific and indispensable role."[241] The Conference assigned to the priest an *indirect* function, according to the ideal of Catholic Action and of the theology of Christendom, which was modified by the "new Christendom": "To promote the integral development of man, they will educate and encourage the laity to participate actively and with a Christian conscience in the technique and elaboration of progress. In the economic and social order, however, and especially in the political order where a variety of concrete choices is offered, the priest, as priest, should not *directly* concern himself with decisions or leadership nor with the structuring of solutions."[242] Now this theology makes it impossible for the priest to intervene prophetically in a direct way in history. The "mediation" of the laity is necessary because the priest is still thought of as "a man of the Church," as a "social class," as the clergy in Christendom or as the medical doctor. What of the medical doctor who works as a shoemaker or a clergymen who serves as a laborer or an accountant? In the present Latin American Church it would appear that the presbyterial order, especially those "younger members"[243] — those who can still change (for in many cases, in the majority of cases, it is too late) — look for a way to fulfill the spirit of the Second Vatican Council and of Medellín. But in order to do so they are obligated, at least from our Latin American sociocultural point of view, to go beyond the *letter* (and the theology) of these documents. In view of the facts as they are now revealed to us in the history of salvation as concrete events of the people of God, it will help us to rethink and restate the question of the priesthood.

One often hears of the "rebel" Church in Latin America. Commenting on the tensions, the Secretary General of CELAM, Monseñor Pironio, said in March 1969, "The issue is not so much that of rebellious priests as it is impatient priests, those who are authentic in their courage and desire to see change."[244] The fact is, it is not impatience but an openness to new experiences out of which there will arise a priestly but not clerical way of life for the Catholic priesthood in Latin America. The institution should not stifle the prophet, for if it does it will become a sclerotic structure. It is significant in this regard that the Spanish Organization for Collaboration (OCSHA) between the years 1959 and 1965 sent 1,016 Spanish priests to Latin America. And it has been these priests, in contrast with the traditional Spanish clerics, who have come to Latin America and taken places in the vanguard for liberation. It is they who in many cases have been jailed, tortured, and expelled from the countries. This is a testimony to the change in the times.

(1) The "Priests for the Third World"

Without question, the priestly issue has taken on more importance in Argentina than in any other country in Latin America, for two reasons: the high cultural level of the clergy and the lack of pastoral orientation given by the bishops. In Brazil the confrontations, with few exceptions, have been with the government. But in Argentina they have been, for the most part, with the episcopacy. This confirms something said above.[245] In the last analysis the desire of the Argentine priest is that his experience be "not a response to theoretical and pre-established schema, but rather the repercussion and experiences of God" in him,[246] and praxis — Christian existence indicating the way for reflection — which is, of course, the inversion of those factors that have been so bad for the Church and theology.

The beginning of this new sacerdotal awareness can be seen in a meeting of eighty priests together with Monseñor Podestá de Avellaneda and Antonio Quarracino of Nueve de Julio on June 28, 1965, in Buenos Aires to discuss their role in the light of the new spirit that had been generated by the Second Vatican Council. They asked: Who is God for us? What are we in the Church? What are we in the world? The responses to these questions formed the essence of a document that is of tremendous value as a Latin American view of the theology of the priesthood.[247] "The experience of God is dynamic, concrete, historical: God is life. This reality should determine our own personal commitment to creation ... by the *direct* encounter and involvement with men, be they Christians or not."[248] In the Church the priests feel "almost unanimously as orphans who lack the support of reflection and pastoral action. Consequently they have a sense of loneliness."[249] They followed with the question, "Is celibacy a sign or not? What are the biblical, theological, and historical bases which justify it?"[250] In the world the priest "discovers values such as . . . the cosmos, technology, universal fraternity, marriage, the woman, work, and socialization."[251] But the priest cannot live and function as a missionary because of "traditional theology which places no value on the world . . . ; because of the formation and bourgeois style of life of the seminary . . . ; because of the impossibility of living a common life together with the people."[252] As a part of the solution to all of these questions, the priest advanced in historical praxis hoping that the theologians would discover the *explicit* meaning of what is necessary before the historian describes the *de facto* events.

It would appear that at times conflicts help to clarify situations and facilitate decisions. Some examples can be sighted in Argentina where in 1964 Father Milán Viscovich defended the "Plan of Struggle" of the CGT and later, together with Fathers Vadagna and Dellaferra, published three articles regarding the question of private teaching. The Bishop, Monseñor Filemón Castellanos, would not approve the terms of the proceedings. Twenty-eight other priests entered into the debate along with the seminary. The dispute was settled in May 1964 with the intervention and mediation of Monseñor Angelelli.

In Mendoza, however, a major conflict developed in early 1965 between a group of twenty-seven young priests, including the director of the archdiocesan seminary, who sent a manifesto to the Papal Nuncio on August 4, and in November directly to the Vatican. The document stated, "Since the beginning of the Council we have felt the need to bare our consciences: in Mendoza a conciliar spirit does not exist."[253] Monseñor Buteler, the Archbishop, was inflexible and rejected an appeal for dialogue. "The Pope put this pectoral cross on my chest," he declared, "and no one is going to remove it."[254] A pastoral was issued to apply the Council in the Archdiocese, and a group of priests began a "sit-down" strike because, they insisted, the pastoral lacked any indication of Conciliar conversion. An Apostolic Administrator was named, and the dissension intensified. Then on January 21 a special Commission of the Argentine Episcopacy issued the following communique: "Interpreting the thinking and the will of the Argentine bishops, we deplore the conduct of these priests."[255] The priests in turn appealed to the Holy See and declared publicly that the Commission of the Episcopacy had refused to hear them, and that they had been denied a right given even to "the worst criminals."[256] The Vatican, however, did not accept the complaint of the priests, and by the expressed desire of the Archbishop, Father Viglino was expelled from his parish in Mendoza and further disciplined.

The following year a worker-priest, Paco Huidobro, originally of the "French Mission" and who had been working in an acrylic factory in Avellaneda, was elected personnel representative for the workers' union. He was immediately discharged by the factory, and there ensued a strike of eighty employees. The Church, however, gave no support either to the union or to Huidobro.[257]

Shortly after the military takeover of the Argentine government by Onganía, three bishops — Devoto, Podestá, and Quarracino — sought to disassociate the Church from the government. On August 19, 1966, seventy priests meeting in Chapadmalal supported the position of the three bishops. Then in September the periodical *Christianismo y revolución* (*Christianity and Revolution*) directed by Juan García Elorrio charted the course for several months until the December 12 issue of *Tierra Nueva* (*New Earth*) appeared, which publicized the feelings of the priests and Christian young people in regard to the revolution of 1966.

Meanwhile in Córdoba, a student, Santiago Pampillón, was killed by the police during a student demonstration. There followed a hunger strike led by Christian students and graduates in the University parish of Cristo el Obrero in September as a repudiation of the police action. Fathers Nelson Dellaferrera and José Gaido were dismissed from the parish and wrote their now-famous "Last Letter to the Christians of Cristo el Obrero."[258]

In Tucumán conditions worsened also when in January 1967 the police killed Hilda Guerrero in a demonstration by the workers in the Santa Lucía sugar refinery. On January 7, 1968, the Governor of Tucumán accused Rubén Sánchez, a priest who had led a demonstration in the San Pablo sugar refinery, of subversion against the government. The Capitular Vicar of the Archdiocese, Víctor Gómez Aragón, defended the priest and issued a strong public response to the governor. Sánchez in turn declared, "The only thing that I have done is apply the documents of the Church and the most elemental concepts of the gospel. What happens is that these documents are general, universal, and when they are recited everyone is usually in agreement. But when one attempts to apply them to reality, it is a different matter, and one is slandered with epithets and accused of subversion and inciting disorder."[259] It is significant that Gómez Aragón, who defended Sánchez, was replaced by Blas Victorio Conrero who, when he arrived at his new post, said, "I know nothing about what has happened in Tucumán."

In the diocese of San Isidro, Father Fernández Naves of OCSHA was dismissed from his parish for "ecclesiastical disobedience." Fathers Parajón and Adame resigned as an indication of solidarity and protest with Fernández and Sánchez and returned to Spain. The group had already experienced several confrontations with their bishop over the question of pastoral orientation. They had wanted to become worker-priests. The conflict reached a climax on December 8, 1967, when the Intendant, a government administrator, proposed the continuation of the annual religious procession in El Tigre. Fernández, who was the parish priest, stated that there would be no procession because of the Intendant's order to three hundred very poor families to vacate the barrio where they were living. Bishop Aguirre stated that the conflict with the families was a serious problem, but that one should not attach such importance to it. "Otherwise," declared the bishop, "the Church would never be able to celebrate."[260] Fernández refused to submit to the wishes of the bishop and ultimately was forced to abandon the parish. Eight other Argentine worker-priests left the diocese, and one of them later signed the "Document of Buenaventura" issued by the Golconda priests in Colombia.

In Rosario the dialogue between the bishops and the priests also reached a climax on October 18, 1968, when four priests gave to Archbishop Bolatti a list of conclusions reached by a renewal group. The tension between the prelate and his priests was common knowledge in Rosario, and on January 23, 1969, one of the newspapers of the city carried a response to a student enrolled in the short "Courses in Christianity" supporting Monseñor Bolatti. On March 15 thirty priests in Rosario presented their joint resignations, followed by the resignation of fifty-three others of the archdiocese on April 10. Ultimately three hundred priests from various dioceses in the country resigned. Their resignations were accepted on June 29, the same day that the laity of the Cañada de Gómez parish took possession of the Church building in support of their priest. On July 17, when the newly named priest, Friar Montevideo, came to take possession, he was accompanied by a squad of police. A riot ensued in which five persons, all laity, were wounded by police gunshots, and twenty others were arrested. This is the first event of this kind in the history of the Latin American Church, and it indicated the state of mind of many of the people.

The first case of a building being taken over in defense of the parish priest occurred in Buenos Aires on April 4, 1966, when about twenty laypersons occupied the Church of Corpus Domini in Buenos Aires in protest of the removal of the parish priest, Father Néstor García Morro.

There was also a conflict between the Bishop of Corrientes, Monseñor Vicentín, and a group of priests committed to the poor people of the city. The clash resulted in the excommunication of Father Marturet and the removal of many priests from the diocese. Also there was the later confrontation in Neuquén between the construction company of the hydroelectric project of Chocón-Río Colorado and almost five thousand workers. The worker-priest Pascual Rodríquez was elected by the union members to lead a strike, but it was crushed by the army. The Bishop of Neuquén, however, did support Rodríguez and the workers. This took place in 1970.[261] Finally, as has already been mentioned, the government attempted to involve the movement of the Priests for the Third World in the assassination of ex-President Aramburu.

Together with these conflicts within the Church, there has developed a significant presbyterial movement. Already mentioned was the meeting of priests in Quilmes in 1965. The following year there was a second meeting in Chapadmalal with the theme "The Church and the World," and on May 11, 1967, intergroups of priests met in the same place. Another meeting took place May 25 and 26 in Buenos Aires with the theme "The Third World, Socialism, and the Gospel." Then on August 15 there was published the "Message from Eighteen Bishops for the Third World," but none of these was a native Argentine. Priests and laypersons from various areas in Argentina met together in Santa Fe on November 11–12, and in January 1968 a group of priests published an addendum to the "Declaration of the Bishops for the Third World." Then, surpassing the most optimistic estimates, 320 priests from all over the country signed the addendum. Plans then began for a meeting on a national scale.

The First National Meeting took place in Córdoba May 1–2, 1968, and used as the basic document the "Declaration of the Bishops for the Third World." Study and discussion centered on the problems of the various regions in Latin America, and the group agreed to publish a letter on violence to be sent to the Second General Conference of CELAM in Medellín.[262] The letter stated: "Every day we are more aware that the cause of the tremendous problems which the Latin American continent suffers is rooted primarily in the political, economic, and social system which is operative in almost all of our countries."[263] There was a clear awareness of "the political" as the bishops had declared: "The Church is not married to any system, no system whatsoever, and even less to the 'international imperialism of money' (Populorum Progressio), as it was not married to the regalism or feudalism of the old regime, and as it will not be married tomorrow to one kind or another of socialism."[264] On September 15, 1968, the first edition of Enlace (Link) was published by the Movement. Then the Second National Meeting took place May 1–3, 1969, also in Córdoba, attended by 80 priests from 27 dioceses. The third meeting was held in Santa Fe on May 1–2, 1970, with 117 present. From March 1968 the Movement has had representatives in all the provinces and has spoken out on the most serious social and political problems of the country and of the continent.[265] Doubtless their prophetic presence has been a continual irritant to the military government in Argentina, and the attempt to implicate members of the Movement in the kidnapping and assassination of General

Aramburu finally forced the episcopacy to take a stand. The Permanent Commission of the Episcopacy issued a statement on August 12, 1970, entitled, "To the People of God." Speaking in somber tones regarding socialism, violence, and other related issues, the statement clearly rebuked the Movement. In October the "Response of the Movement for the Third World" to the Permanent Commission was published.[266] The document manifested a meticulous elaboration and careful handling of the theological question, and the bishops were clearly surprised by the precision of this response, its orthodoxy, and clear defense of the institution, which allowed for a new missionary beginning in the Latin American spirit. Never had anyone responded in such a way. The truth is, the Permanent Commission realized that they had encountered an absolutely new situation, for the theologians of the Movement had done their homework. More importantly, this response provided the Movement with a clear "Declaration of Principles," and until the present there has been no other significant confrontation between the Movement and the Argentine episcopacy.

As is obvious, the presbyterial order now has institutions that make possible a dialogue with the episocpacy, and that allow the order to declare itself in regard to world questions, which perhaps the episcopacy itself would like to emulate, but because of tradition or pressure it is unable to do so. This represents a change from below for the people of God who are guided by the Spirit. The *presbyterium* is discovering its concrete role.

(2) Heroes and martyrs in Brazil

Because of the quality and number of excellent bishops in Brazil, the priests have had someone to follow. In January 1963, for example, prior to the second session of Vatican Council II, Dom Hélder Câmara sent to hundreds of bishops a document on "The Situation of the Priest."[267] Then on May 2, 1965, at the inauguration of the Regional Seminary of Northeast Brazil in Camaragibe, Dom Hélder gave an address[268] in which he proposed *direct* involvement of the priests in temporal issues.

This institutiton will prepare priests for preaching the gospel. But you cannot evangelize abstract creatures, atemporal, existing in a void. When our seminarians get to the churches and chapels and speak of divine grace, of the presence within us of the Holy Trinity, of the grace that enables us to share in divine life, how can they forget that they are proclaiming divine life to listeners who very often live in subhuman conditions? ... To persist in a purely spiritual evangelization would soon result in giving the impression that religion is something separate from life and powerless to touch it or overcome its absurd and erroneous aspects. It would even tend to support the view that religion is a great alienating influence, the opiate of the people. ... We, the bishops of the Northeast, are convinced that we should foster rural unionism as the only practical means for the rural workers to claim their rights from their *overlords*. ... If we feel obliged not to hand over to the laity an endeavor that would normally be the domain of these Christians in temporal matters, it is because we consider it necessary to give moral support to the elementary defense of human rights, given the blind and heartless abuse of authority by some of these *overlords*. And if certain people have the audacity to pin the label of Communist even on the bishops of the Holy Church who devote themselves to the imminently Christian mission of defending abused human beings, what will become of our priests and especially our laymen if we abandon them to their fate?[269]

The reaction to Câmara's statements was immediate. The widely distributed, influential newspaper *O Estado de São Paulo* declared that many of the Archbishop's statements were alarming. In fact, each succeeding one was "more deplorable than the others." Câmara was called an "illiterate," a "demagogue," an "unconscious tool of the Communists," one who desired to "incorporate Brazil into the Third World."

We have already referred to the large number of priests and religious who have been jailed, tortured, and otherwise intimidated but who have continued in their struggle to identify with the poor. The experience of Sister Irany Bastos must, however, also be recounted, for she has in her function as deacon assumed many parish responsibilities. She says, "My experience illustrates the fact that women can have as much success in human contacts as can men."[270] It is very possible that this simple fact will open a new chapter in the history of the Church.

On October 24, 1967, the "Letter of Brazilian Priests to their Bishops" was published and carried the signatures of priests from nearly three hundred dioceses. The burden of the letter was clearly social and indicated the desire of the priests to communicate to their bishops "some of the crushing anxieties that burdened their consciences."[271] Brazil, they stated, was "an assassinated people" because of infant mortality, lack of daily bread, and miserable salaries. It was a "plundered people" of the unjust tax system and of an even worse political expenditure — six times more money was spent by the national government for military purposes than for education, and fifteen times more than for public health. The Church in turn maintained a paternalistic attitude and spectator role where faith was commercialized. We priests felt ourselves to be "prisoners," "separated from the life of the people," "far from the anxieties of the people," "prisoners of a pastoral machine" whose function was to "sacramentalize." We desired to "evangelize" and be "sensitive to the values of the people," to the "prophetic mission." And "does not the prophetic example of Christ, of fidelity to the truth not inevitably presuppose a political implication?"[272] The declaration concluded saying, "We persistently request that, in view of the eucharistic necessities of the present and future communities, married men from those communities be accepted for priestly ordination."[273]

On March 28, 1968, students demonstrated in Río demanding improvement in the university restaurant. The police attacked them, and an eighteen-year-old student, Edson Luis de Lima Soto, was killed. Masses were said in the cathedrals, but there were arrests even in the churches themselves. At times police mounted on horseback entered church buildings looking for and harassing students. Thirty priests in Sâo Paulo and thirty-seven in Belo Horizonte made public protests against the government repression. Forty Brazilian Jesuits who were studying in Europe proposed to Father Arrupe a reform of the objectives of the Jesuit Order in Brazil.

There were other conflicts in Brazil as well. In Botucatu, twenty-three priests threatened to resign by April 17, 1968, if the new bishop named for the diocese, Monseñor Zioni, Director of the Seminary in Sâo Paulo, was not revoked. The priests objected to Zioni on the basis that his pastoral manifested a "pre-Conciliar" orientation. Their protest was supported by a 2,000-automobile caravan in Sâo Paulo. The Holy See acceded to the demand, and Dom Romeu Alberti was named instead. In August 1968 a worker-priest in Sâo Paulo, Pierre Wauthiers, was deported for his participation in a strike, one of many European priests expelled from Latin American countries by right-wing governments as a part of a purging program coordinated by the CIA.[274] Monseñor Fragoso declared at that time that "the struggle for liberation is a common objective of the bishops, priests, and laity."

The Episcopal Assembly, meeting July 20– 30, 1969, refused to grant ordination to a married person, but Cardinal Rossi did announce on August 12 that the matter was not closed, that the day would possibly come when married priests could be ordained as they are in the Eastern Church, after it is evident "that lay apostles and deacons cannot resolve certain necessities."[275]

Then on the night of May 26, 1969, an unidentified group—perhaps the police—seized Father Antonio Henrique Pereira Neto, the young twenty-eight-year-old chaplain of Catholic Youth (JUC, JEC) in Recife who served also as secretary to Dom Hélder Câmara. The following day Father Antonio's body was found tied to a tree, almost nude and showing signs of being brutally dragged and beaten. The Archbishop's palace was plastered with abusive posters and messages. In the funeral mass for Father Antonio, said on May 27, Dom Hélder exclaimed, "May the holocaust of Father Antonio Henrique obtain from God the grace to continue the work for which he gave his life and the conversion of his executioners."[276] The young priesthood in Brazil had a martyr, "for he had often been threatened with death but proceeded in his normal life and work."[277] The episcopacy testified that the young priest had been tortured and tied to the tree shortly before he died. He had been shot at least three times. On September 24 the entire national executive committee of the JOC (Catholic Youth Workers) was jailed.

About a month earlier—August 25 and 26—the bishops of the Northeast issued a public denunciation of the torture that the government was using against Brazilian citizens, a protest that stemmed immediately from the arrest, imprisonment for four months, and brutal torturing of Fathers Soares da Amarai and José Antonio Monteiro, neither of whom was ever formally charged with a crime.

On January 5, 1971, a Brazilian Dominican residing in Chile, Tito de Alencar, one of seventy priests freed and expelled from Brazil, declared to the UPI that he had been in a Brazilian prison since July 1969, that he was tortured by the police, and otherwise harassed because he had sought to give spiritual help to students who were "being hounded by the military regime."[278]

(3) The "Golconda" group

The death of Father Camilo Torres in Colombia produced differing reactions. We have already referred to the suppression by the Cardinal of Colombia, Luis Concha, of the diocesan newspaper *El Catolicismo*. It was not until July 1968, however, that any formal organization of priests who desired a radical application of the social teachings of the Church could be held. Fifty of these priests met on the Golconda farm in the municipality of Viotá, Cundinamarca, to study the encyclical *Populorum Progressio*. This was hardly a month before the Second General Conference of Bishops in Medellín. The Golconda group met again in Buenaventura, December 9–13, 1968, under the aegis of Monseñor Gerardo Valencia Cano, Bishop of Buenaventura. Fifty-three priests from all over the country together with representatives from three other Latin American nations were present. From the meeting emanated the "Document of Buenaventura,"[279] based almost exclusively on the Pastoral Constitution *Gaudium et Spes* of Vatican II and the Conclusions of the Medellín Conference. The text is formal and respectful. The "analysis of the Colombian situation" was synthesized in the assertion that the tragic state "of underdevelopment which our country suffers is the historical product of economic, political, cultural, and social dependency on foreign centers of power. These foreign entities manipulate our country through our ruling classes (cf. Medellín 2, 9 a)."[280] There followed a theological reflection "in the light of the Gospel" on two levels. First, there was the inclusion of "the temporal in the salvific design," and in the second place, consequently, the priests were able to assume directly "work and attitudes which allow for collaboration in the political formation of the citizens ... the necessity of supporting and aiding all the forces of the people to create and develop their own basic organizations, and the necessity for a work of conscientization and social education."[281] The "directions for action" also manifested a dual assignment: in regard to the "social, economic, and political field," fundamentally, there is the emphasis on the necessity to "commit ourselves more and more to the different ways of revolutionary action against imperialism and bourgeois neocolonialism, avoiding attitudes that are merely contemplative and, for that reason, self-justifying," and, in "our liturgical, evangelistic, and ecclesial conducting work" fulfill the priestly function "in the exercise of the ministry of the Word ... the participation in the liturgy by its character of anticipation and of the manifestation of eschatology ... by means of the unification of forces and of initiatives which encounter their maximum expression when done collegially."[282]

As in other countries, the harassment of the Golconda priests began immediately. In 1969 one of them protested the government's badgering, and a short time later four of them were accused of subversion. When they were arrested they stated that the reason was that they had spoken of the farce of the upcoming elections in which the candidates had already been selected by the National Front, the coalition of Liberals and Conservatives, without any participation whatsoever by the people. Another Golconda priest, Father Manuel Alzate, was suspended by the Archbishop of Cali, Monseñor Uribe Urdaneta, for having "offended the hierarchy." Monseñor Valencia Cano of Buenaventura then issued his "Open Letter to the Priests,"[283] and on a trip to New York in February 1970, declared: "We cannot remain indifferent to the capitalist structure which condemns the people of Colombia and Latin America to the most agonizing frustration and injustice." "I am definitively a socialist and revolutionary," he was quoted as saying by the news agencies.[284] The Apostolic Administrator of Bogotá, later to be the Cardinal of Colombia, Monseñor Aníbal Muñoz Duque, referred to an article in the progovernment newspaper El Tiempo on January 29, 1970, in which Father Gustavo Pérez was reported to have organized a group of "rebel priests" in Usme. Monseñor Muñoz denied the report and insisted "that it was the responsibility of priests to denounce wrongdoing and to form the conscience of the faithful, and remember that those who worked with the poor in the barrios of Bogotá did so with his instructions." A short time later a group of priests and laypersons meeting in Villavicencio accused the army of genocide in the death of the Indians of Guahiba who were accused of being guerillas and who were being tortured and killed.

Government repression against the Golconda group, however, virtually eradicated it, but a new priestly organization in Colombia emerged and is now referred to as SAL. It is said to be composed of more than three hundred priests from various sectors of the country. (The name SAL is an interesting acronym. The word in Spanish means "salt" and can represent the name "Sacerdotes a favor de Latinoamérica," i.e., Priests in favor of Latin America, or "Sacerdotes a favor de la liberación," i.e., Priests in favor of Liberation.)

(4) The organization ONIS and other priestly expressions

In Peru there was organized in 1968, as in other countries, a priestly group known as ONIS (National Office of Social Investigation), which continues to operate in Lima and in other regional offices.[285] For nearly two decades now the Peruvian clergy has become increasingly involved in social and political questions. In 1964, for example, the vice-provincial of the Jesuits in Peru, Father Ricardo Durand, responding to accusations that the Peruvian clergy had been infiltrated by Communists, explained that it was being said that the clergy had accepted a materialistic and atheistic philosophy because they were "demanding more justice." In this case, insisted Durand, the gospel itself would be Communistic, and it would appear that — for the one making the accusation, a Señor Ravines — "what is not right-wing liberalism is Communism."[286] In March 1968 sixty priests signed a document later approved by the Cardinal which stated that "Peru is a proletarian nation in the world" in view of the fact that the per capita income is less than one-tenth of what it is in the United States. "But not only is Peru proletarian, the majority of Peruvians are even more proletarian" because the national income is distributed as follows: twenty-four thousand Peruvians receive forty-five percent of the national income (sixty million *soles* annually), while nearly twelve million Peruvians receive the remaining fifty-five percent (seventy-five million *soles* annually). Following an analysis of the most serious sociopolitical problems in the country, there was a petition that the hierarchy commit itself to the poor, for this would be "for us the maximum support against those who distort our attitude by referring to it as the *intromission* in the temporal."[287] There followed a plea to all "brother priests" that they "take very seriously our obligation to inculcate in the faithful, without subterfuge, that they cannot receive communion nor live an authentically Christian life when they are defrauding the salaries of the workers, evading taxes, enslaving the Indians, subjecting others to servitude and inhuman treatment, or when they are squandering ostentatiously their wealth in a world of misery."[288] The laity was asked to be in a "virtual state of war against suffering and exploitive oppression. This is an authentic second independence for Peru which will emancipate the children of God from all servitude." "This war for independence should be waged without any reference to religious confession."[289]

In January 1969, 330 priests from all the dioceses of Peru sent to the Episcopal Conference in their thirty-sixth meeting a letter in which they requested the opportunity to present to the bishops their "concerns and desires in a spirit of dialogue and collaboration."[290] The letter, although it had many suggestions applicable primarily to Peru, described the prevailing conditions in Latin America as a whole. The principal points treated were as follows: (1) Because the Church should liberate itself from compromising ties, the "separation of Church and state" is recommended. (2) At the same time, the "appearance of the Church should be simplified in dress, ornaments, titles, and military ranks." (3) Furthermore, it is urgent and necessary to integrate in some way the major superiors of the religious in the reflection and decisions regarding ecclesiastical matters." In contrast, the priests declared, "We consider that the Nunciature should have in our Church a much less preponderant role." The formation of the secular apostolate was said to be fundamental because "our Church is clerical, and for this reason it is so conspicuously absent and silent in the history of the country." A concern was manifested also that there were yet "dioceses where the isolation of the clergy is great. . . . We must find new ways for supporting the clergy . . . and secular work could be very healthy." "It is urgent that the hierarchy denounce audaciously every kind of injustice. . . . The problems which need to be attacked are multiple. . . . We should be alert to concrete events (for example, a strike). . . . We always run the risk of being identified with one or another political group, but this can be balanced if the just demands from different segments are successively supported. Let it be noted that abstention has already a political nuance." The letter concluded with the statement that the bishops should include the priests "in the preparation of the mission" because they already have them "as necessary collaborators and *counselors in the ministry*" (Presb. Ordinis, n. 7). Why not have priests and lay counselors in the episcopal conferences as in the Council? Would this not reveal a greater unity and convergence within the plenitude of the Church?[291]

(5) Priests in Chile

The question regarding priests in Chile has become increasingly serious. The scarcity of Chilean clergy and the large percentage of foreign priests greatly affect the growing number of Latin American nationals who are trained in Europe. All of this takes place in a climate of great tension and deficiency, but, nevertheless, with adaptation to a changing reality many times economically impoverished. Monseñor Gabriel Larraín Valdivieso, Auxiliary Bishop of Santiago, however, stated in a news conference in November 1966 that married men would be ordained to the priesthood in Latin America after a very long period of reflection.[292] The tension increased until the "diocesan councils of priests" were constituted, and in the second dialogue between bishops and priests in 1968 the following questions for discussion were proposed: "Doctrinal insecurity" since Vatican II, the meaning of social reform, the emotional problems stemming from isolation and insufficient priestly recourse, and the question of authority and obedience. The Bishop of Temuco, Monseñor Bernardino Piñera Carvallo, vice-president of the Chilean Conference of Bishops, declared that "probably all of my colleagues will admit that as bishops we are not geniuses, saints, talented, or endowed with unlimited resources. Really the office is much greater than our capacities, and we are the first to suffer because of the many problems that appear to be insoluble." That same year the conflict became generalized. Father Ignacio García, subsequently laicized, wrote in *La Nación* (Santiago) in August that

because of an almost global senility of the schema and norms of the Church there has resulted a tremendous crisis of authority, because in order to live, the people are functioning under their own criteria at the margin of the norms. This situation is evidently anarchical. ... Thus, the great mass has simply left the Church, and what we call the *clandestine* Church makes its own decisions and develops its own criteria. ... The imperial system of the Church proceeds undisturbed in regard to major issues. There are changes, but these are insufficient. At this rate the Church will be more and more alienated from a world that is moving at so great a velocity.

It was in regard to statements such as the preceding one, statements that came with increasing frequency during those days, that the Chilean episcopacy issued a declaration on October 4 which stated, "Much is said today of the Church of the poor, of the Church of the youth, of the traditional Church, of the official Church, of the clandestine Church, of the new Church — as if the Church of Christ were thus divided."[293] The tension continued, however, and in 1970 Cardinal Silva Henríquez excommunicated three Spanish priests who were accused of being involved in spiritist cults.[294] The meeting of "Christians for Socialism" in 1972 and the military overthrow of the Allende government in 1973 radically altered the situation in Chile.

(6) The situation in Mexico

Mexico has witnessed multiple experiences and tensions among priests and the episcopacy. The case of the Benedictine convent founded by Don Gregorio Lemercier (1912–) is well known. This Belgian bishop decided in 1961 that because of his previous experience he would introduce within his convent psychoanalysis (modifying the Freudian doctrine). In 1963–1964 the Benedictine Visitor, Don Benno Gut, approved the experiment. Yet in 1965 the Holy Office, which had already taken note of the matter, ordered Lemercier to retire to a convent in Belgium. The issue was discussed in the fourth session of the Second Vatican Council, and in 1966 a special tribunal was constituted. Long and painful dialogues followed and finally concluded on May 18, 1967, in which the tribunal passed judgment on the future of psychoanalysis among the brothers, namely, that to continue with its use would mean the closing of the monastery. On June 12 the monastery dissolved, and five days later Monseñor Méndez Arceo demonstrated his immense understanding and support for the brothers in helping them adjust to new positions as laymen or as priests in other dioceses. On August 11 the Cardinal Primate of the Benedictines closed the monastery. Lemercier, admirable and firm in his position, declared, "I am neither an apostate nor a heretic. I will remain in the Church. I have not disobeyed in any way. . . . I will always respect legitimate orders but not arbitrary ones."[295] The historian, however, will recall that on February 24, 1616, the Tribunal of the Holy Inquisition likewise condemned "astronomy" in the person of Galileo because, it was declared, the idea that the earth moves was "foolish, philosophically absurd, and formally heretical."[296] Also it will be remembered that "philology" was condemned in the person of Richard Simon when his book *Historical Criticism of the Old Testament* was put on the *Index* in 1678. In this present century "psychoanalysis" in the person of Lemercier has been condemned. Will it be necessary that every science first be condemned in order subsequently to be approved or accepted? At any rate, Latin America has entered the *condemned history* of universal science as a means for its acceptance.

In Cuernavaca the Center of Documentation (CIDOC) directed by Monseñor Ivan Illich gained worldwide notoriety for its contribution to social and ecclesiastical issues. In two articles entitled "The Seamy Side of Charity" published in the Jesuit periodical *America*, Illich took a very negative position in regard to North American help for Latin America. He followed these articles with "Religious Imperialism in Latin America?" and another on "The Vanishing Clergyman," which first appeared in *Siempre* in Mexico. This last article appeared in a revised form in the periodical *Esprit* in Paris in 1967, and in it Illich distinguished between the clergy, ministers such as priests and deacons, monks, and theological professionals. He indicated that the clergy as a sociocultural class was disappearing and should disappear.[297] The issue, according to Illich, was that in Christendom the priesthood was a temporal "profession." With the collapse of Christendom the priestly profession — which Illich correctly calls a *clericatura* — was eliminated. The contemporary priest, therefore, is aware of having multiple charisms that should be distinguished: the pastor and the liturgical eucharistic priest, the deacon or the one who serves the community, the celibate or monk, and the prophet or theologian. These four dimensions can be fulfilled by four different persons. In Latin America, nevertheless, it is more necessary each day to conserve one in whom the four dimensions are evident. This kind of person would serve as a *periepíscopos* of the primitive Eastern Church, or the itinerant of the *Didaché* ("The Teaching of the Twelve Apostles"), that is, as one in whom the plenitude of all the charisms are evident and which together are represented in the bishop as a sign of unity. As so often happens, the position of Illich was not highly regarded, and on January 8, 1969, following an ecclesiastical trial that was publicized throughout the world, a decree against CIDOC was issued. Archbishop Méndez Arceo issued a pastoral on January 26 and again on May 24 in which the stipulated restrictions of the decree of January 8 were lifted, a development without precedent in the history of the Church.

Among the Mexican experiences the "Declaration of a Team of Priests" regarding manual labor should be noted. The "Declaration" was signed by fifteen priests in Mexico City where they had studied specific possibilities for priestly commitment in the world of the laborer and the professional. They stated that "for many this means beginning with a limited schedule of work so that they will not have to abandon the ministry for which they are responsible."[298] There followed the organization of "Priests for the People."

(7) Central America and the Caribbean

A new awareness is also evident in Central America and the Caribbean. Puerto Rico has experienced the unvarnished criticism of Father S. Freixedo, SJ, adviser for the JOC for thirteen years, who is not a theologian but rather a man of action. His polemical work *My Church is Asleep!*[299] was censured immediately after it was published, but Monseñor Parrilla Bonilla stated, without approving the work as such, that it called for a "National Council." Freixedo stated that he had written the book as "a cry of pain stemming from [my] love for the Church. ... I have no desire that this book be interpreted as a rebellion against the Church. Never."[300] But his open criticism should be kept in mind. In regard to the laity he said that there are two types: some who are like sleeping children and others who are children but who are awake. "These who are awake go here and there and are seen as capable of running errands."[301] The book is somewhat satirical, but a little humor has its place. On a more serious note, the priesthood is seen as a "victim of a method, of a structure, of a concept of the Church."[302]

In Guatemala ninety-four priests formed a "Confederation of Diocesan Priests of Guatemala" (COSDEGUA), and beginning in 1969 they issued frequent pronouncements in regard to regional and national conditions and events. On March 1, 1970, Cardinal Casariego imposed censure on all these priests, secular and religious, regarding what they had written and said. The Auxiliary Bishop, Monseñor Pellecer-Samayoa, announced that Father Méndez Hidalgo, editor of *El Quijote*, had been suspended *a divinis* for evading the censure. It is evident that the dialogue between bishops and priests sometimes becomes bitter.

In El Salvador the Cardinalship of Monseñor Casariego was challenged in April 1969 by a document that reflected on the right to express one's opinion.[303]

In Nicaragua a group of priests issued a communique in which they said, "The authorities are more capable of bringing an end to the violence than anyone else,"[304] but the Somoza government obviously took no heed. Adjacent to a humble village on a very small island in Lake Managua the monk Ernesto Cardenal has written some magnificent poetry — in some respects superior to that of Rubén Darío — regarding the Church of liberation. Cardenal's "Psalms" have been translated into many languages and are a testimony of what is taking place in Latin America.

In Costa Rica when the major newspaper *La Nación* stated that the Church had no right to intervene in political and economic questions, fifty-one priests together with Ignacio Trejos, Auxiliary Bishop of San José, responded stating that "the so-called temporal order is not beyond redemption. ... The demands of a moral gospel include a social dimension. ... Following the repeated teachings of the Supreme Pontiffs we would stress that political and social questions are not strictly economic, but that they involve an issue that is above all else moral and religious."[305]

The pastoral work of Father Leo Mahon[306] in a suburb of the capital of Panama has been outstanding. Mahon began his work in San Miguelito in 1963. The combined efforts of the parishoners were so successful in revitalizing community life that various sectors were providing leaders capable of being ordained as deacons and even as priests if this had been possible. The experience of Mahon in San Miguelito is unique in Latin America and worthy of being studied as a pilot project. However, beginning in 1970

Father Leo was indirectly linked with the dictatorial government, and this produced a crisis within the directing body. There have been, as is well known, several priests who have had serious problems with the Panamanian government of General Omar Torrijos. Father Carlos Pérez Herrera was arrested and jailed on October 23, 1968, when he became a candidate of the Panamian Party of Dr. Arnulfo Arias. The Party won the elections by an overwhelming majority, but their triumph was short-lived. The overthrow of the government occurred in 1968 when the National Guard, under the leadership of Torrijos, deposed the Arias regime. Father Luis Medrano, SJ, was expelled from Panama in 1969,[307] and the Colombian priest Héctor Gallego disappeared in 1971, the result of his valiant efforts to organize cooperatives among the peasants in Panama.

(8) Other South American countries

The worker-priest, Father Francisco Wuytack, was expelled from Venezuela on June 20, 1970, for having demonstrated in front of the National Congress along with other striking workers representing the more than 600,000 poverty-stricken people of Caracas. Wuytack stated at the time of his deportation by the Christian Democratic government (COPEI), "I have attempted to live according to the principles and to preach the gospel of Jesus Christ in Venezuela."[308] A short time later, four Spanish priests were refused reentrance into the country.

In Ecuador Monseñor Proaño had already spoken in 1967 regarding the priestly commitment in his "¿Dudas? ¿Decepciones?" (Doubts? Deceptions?).[309] Then on December 24, 1968, twenty-six priests in Quito presented a letter to the Archbishop of Ecuador indicating their uneasiness because of repeated autocratic decisions made by the episcopacy. They cited the fact that as priests they had been consulted in regard to the disposition of a seminary building, but not in regard to the naming of the Auxiliary Bishop. The letter was respectful but courageous and clear.[310]

Two years later, Father Hernández, adviser to students and an activist in Riobamba, was expelled from the country by President Velasco Ibarra. Hernández was the second Spanish priest to be deported from the country, and his became a *cause célèbre*. The National Council of Priests requested that the bishops consider the suppression of the nunciatures and that relations between the Ecuadorian government and the Papacy be a matter of responsibility for the resident bishops. After the death of Rafael Espín, however, the Council was virtually dissolved.

In Bolivia the priests have become increasingly involved in economic and political questions. Six priests were jailed after the military takeover of the government on September 26, 1969, but they were later released. Four worker-priests issued a severe criticism of COMIBOL (the National Corporation of Mines formed in 1952 when the government confiscated the industry) because the main concern, according to the priests, was profit and not the welfare of the miners. In 1970 four priests, three of the OCSHA, and a Protestant pastor were expelled from the country. The students took up their cause, and there were hunger strikes and demonstrations in La Paz. In a cathedral occupied by the students there was written on the throne, "Alas for you ..." (Matt. 23:1−3). One of the Spanish priests of the OCSHA said, "There is a Church of the oppressed and another of the oppressors." Since October 1, 1965, the priests in Bolivia have issued numerous statements making their voices heard in regard to the defense of the poor.[311]

In Paraguay the Jesuits have been the object of severe criticism, but accusations of subversion have been stoutly denied by the bishops. Monseñor Aníbal Mena Porta, Archbishop of Asunción, issued a document in 1969 entitled "On the Violent Repression of Priests and Faithful in Asunción."[312] Then some seventy-five priests in the diocese of Villarrica defended their bishop saying, "We are proud to be able to refute publicly the calumny that the distinguished Bishop of Villarrica is an agitator and instigator of strikes. But neither the distinguished Bishop nor his clergy can help but view with sympathy all those who defend the rights of human beings."[313]

In Uruguay Father Juan Carlos Zaffaroni, SJ, trained in Louvain and Paris, following his experiences in 1966 and 1967, was invited as a delegate to the World Cultural Congress in Havana in January 1968. Upon returning, Zaffaroni led sugar cane cutters in a demonstration that spread throughout the country. Then after a harangue on national television, the order was given for Zaffaroni's arrest. He immediately disappeared and became a part of the clandestine movement in Uruguay. In May 1968 the priests in the northern part of the country, in Tacuarembo and Melo, along with their respective bishops issued a letter on "The Sufferings, Anguish, and Hope of the People of our Area."[314]

In regard to the above experiences and events, the words of the Brazilian priest Father Francisco Lage Pessoa, now living in Mexico, summarize the situation: "When very infrequently a true apostle appears who has the courage to remind us of what is authentic Christianity, he is considered to be a politician, a lunatic, imprudent, a Communist infiltrator, a subversive ... who must be imprisoned, condemned, and expelled from the country."[315]

Sociographically the situation is as follows:

The Number of Priests and Religious in Latin America in 1967[316]

	Nationals	Foreigners	Totals
Diocesan Priests	16,300	3,260	19,560
Religious Priests	10,908	12,121	23,029
Religious			116,102
Lay Religious			4,020

Some words are appropriate in regard to the seminaries. "The Decree on Priestly Formation" (*Optatam totius Ecclesiae*) of Vatican II, and Section 13 on the "Formation of the Clergy" of Medellín both deal with the question of the seminaries. As early as 1964 Monseñor Manuel Larraín stated that "all the Councils have urged the revival of the seminaries. ... It is necessary that the formation of future priests be more open to the world. ... The course of studies could be done in stages in the working world."[317] The Medellín Conclusions recognized the difficulty encountered by the youth of today in regard to the old molds and standards, for example, the "tensions between authority and obedience" and the "rejection of certain traditional religious values" (13, 4). Various solutions were proposed such as a "more personalized formation based on teams and small communities" (13, 6, c). Thus little by little, all the seminaries have been directed toward a fundamental reform. In 1966, for example, the Mariana Seminary with 115 seminarians was closed in order to allow time for "reflection," according to Monseñor Oscar Oliveira, indicating a thorough reform of the institution. In a survey made of seminarians, it was evident that the majority were strongly opposed to celibacy. The question was studied in the First Continental Congress of Vocations, which took place in Lima in November 1966, and was presided over by Monseñor Miguel Darío Miranda, the Archbishop of Mexico.

At times actions have been precipitous, and the confrontation has been open and fierce. The Bishop of Trujillo, Peru, closed the seminary in his diocese in May 1969, and dismissed the governing board. The move came as a result of a public declaration made by the twenty-six seminarians on March 24 in which they defended Father Shanahan of the Sagrario Parish, which had been occupied by laypersons. The seminarians declared, "We will occupy the Seminary indefinitely."[318] Then in 1970 the Franciscan Seminary of Lima organized into small communities in order to establish and maintain contact with the people. An identical attempt was made in the Seminary of San Miguel de los Padres Jesuitas in Buenos Aires, as well as in other theological institutions in Latin America. In Cochabamba the bishops gave the Major Seminary to the young Spanish priests of the OCSHA. When they organized the seminary into small communities, the bishops accused them of becoming "arrogant." In 1970 the seminary was closed and the directors assigned to the slum area of Villa Bush.

In Quito, Ecuador, forty-three of the fifty students left the seminary stating that they "had no desire to be a part of a Church which refused to change out-of-date structures and which is not committed to the defense of the poor."[319] The seminaries likewise need to face the crisis of growth and develop a course of study which will approximate the daily life of the people; to unify philosophy, exegesis, and theology; to shorten the period of study to five or six years; and to allow more latitude for priests to follow their vocation in nontraditional ways. The reform of the seminaries, however, has barely begun.

3. The Attitude of the Monks and Nuns

In this section we want to suggest some of the characteristics of the movement for renewal that is taking place among the religious in Latin America. A sociographical study published in 1971 reveals some interesting data in regard to religious institutions.

The Founding of Religious Institutions In Latin America[320]

Dates	Masculine Institutions (Percentage)	Feminine Institutions (Percentage)
15th and 16th centuries	6.51	1.34
17th and 18th centuries	3.35	4.24
19th century	19.01	16.50
1900 to 1920	13.56	13.71
1921 to 1945	10.07	20.74
1946 to 1955	18.31	17.28
1956 to 1965	13.91	22.58
1966 to 1971	5.28	3.34
	100.00	100.00

The statistics indicate the rapid growth of religious institutions beginning in the nineteenth century. During the fifteenth and sixteenth centuries there were obviously many more monasteries for monks than there were for nuns. In the nineteenth century, given the flourishing of religious congregations in Europe, the increase in institutions both for monks and nuns is understandable. The data for this century, however, are approximations. The decline at the beginning of the twentieth was reversed by 1945 largely as a result of the emphasis given to Latin America in the world Church, and also, apparently, as a result of World War II. A more detailed sociological analysis would doubtless uncover other variables that have affected this situation.[321] As far as the numbers of religious working today in Latin America, they are more numerous than ever.

The Total Number of Religious in Latin America (1970)[322]

Country	Masculine	Feminine
Argentina	4,510	14,076
Bolivia	835	1,800
Brazil	11,524	41,998
Colombia	4,412	20,780
Costa Rica	220	968
Cuba	-0-	-0-
Chile	2,343	4,924
Ecuador	1,564	4,145
El Salvador	369	818
Guatemala	650	850
Haiti	420	1,000
Honduras	116	282
Mexico	1,909	23,630
Nicaragua	265	687
Panama	249	410
Paraguay	429	751
Puerto Rico	599	1,500
Peru	2,514	4,581
Dominican Republic	486	1,285
Uruguay	693	1,592
Venezuela	1,706	4,100
TOTAL	39,813	130,187

These numbers, nevertheless, indicate little unless they are compared with the total population of the countries and the level of missionary renewal taking place in the communities. It is for this reason that the Latin American Confederation of Religious (CLAR) founded in 1958 has been of major significance, because it represents the center of self-awareness in regard to the process of renewal. The First General Assembly of CLAR took place in Lima in May 1960. Conferences of the Major Superiors have also been organized in all the countries in Latin America, the last one in Haiti in 1964. When CLAR was organized there were only 113,000 nuns and 21,000 monks in the whole continent.[323]

Because of the outstanding work of the Cuban Jesuit Father Daniel Baldor, Secretary General of CLAR, the religious of Latin America overcame much of their theological and social obsolescence, and by the time of the Second General Assembly in Río in August 1963 — the same time as Vatican II — the organization had made significant progress. Preparation for the Río Assembly was made in Cuernavaca in June 1963. That same year Father Manuel Edward was elected president of the Chilean Conference of Religious, and two years later he was selected as president of CLAR. Contacts were established with the religious in Canada, the United States, and Europe, and Father Edward represented Latin America in the January 1965 meeting of the Catholic Inter-American Cooperation Program (CICOP).

The Latin American Conference of Religious took multiple surveys for the Second Vatican Council and also sponsored meetings for reflection such as the one in Viamao, Porto Alegre, Brazil, in which both Comblin and Daniélou participated. It was in this latter retreat that discussion was held regarding a "theology of a joint pastoral."

Latin American religious participated in the Second Vatican Council, and many of their suggestions became part of the decrees signaling a new day in which "an appropriate renewal of religious life would be undertaken," and "the return to the sources of the total Christian life and of the primitive inspiration of the institutes" as well as *an adaptation of these to the diverse conditions of the present.*"[324]

As soon as the Council concluded, innumerable evidences of commitment, the apostolate, and of the organization of the religious life became apparent. Even the formation of the novitiate and studies changed. The First Latin American Congress of Vocations, held in November 1966, recognized the declining number of postualtes in Latin America, a decline that has continued in recent years. Seventy delegates met together for the Third Assembly of CLAR in December 1966, and an inclination toward Medellín was evident. A Colombian religious, Father Luis Patiño, OFM, was elected Secretary General, and Sister Agudelo, CM, also a Colombian, was chosen to head the nuns. Father Pedro Arrupe, SJ, met with CLAR, and later he began a profound revision of the Company of Jesus in Río de Janeiro concluding that the necessary "daring transformations which will radically renew the structures is the only means of promoting social peace" on the continent.[325]

Thirteen members of CLAR were present at the Medellín Conference in August 1968, and were directed by their President, Manuel Edward, SS, CC, and by Father Patiño, OFM. There were also among them three nuns.[326] The language and inspiration of the final document on the "Religious" has a "developmentalist" tone, but it represents nonetheless a profound commitment to change. The religious in Latin America must, according to the document, "penetrate into the real world with greater daring today than ever before: he cannot consider himself a stranger to social problems, to democratic awareness, or to the pluralistic mentality of the society in which he lives,"[327] principles in agreement with, for example, the Chilean experience of that time when the country was governed by the Christian Democrat, Eduardo Frei. In the section on the "Religious Life and Participation in Development," the religious were said to be obligated to "expand and deepen their knowledge of theology and spirituality of the active life,"[328] but advised that they were "not to interfere in the direction of temporal affairs."[329]

During the time of the Medellín Conference, the First Franciscan Meeting in Latin America took place in Bogotá, August 15–25, 1968. Friar Constantino Koser, the Minister General of the oldest order in Latin America, was present. There was issued a document that beautifully describes the obligations of the Franciscans and their "great influence in the life and history of the people of America from the time of its discovery and gestation."[330] The statement concluded: "We support well-planned experiments which are directed toward informing the religious and educating our youth in the proper use of liberty and of responsibility."[331] Thus after a long period of theological, pastoral stagnation the Franciscan Order began to manifest important signs of a profound renewal, but it remains to be seen whether more evidence of the prophetic example of poverty of Francis of Assisi will be sufficiently adapted to the contemporary Latin American reality.

The second oldest order in the Americas, the Dominicans, had a Meeting of the Provincials and Vicars of South America in La Paz, Bolivia, from June 30 to July 5, 1969. From the meeting came the statement that the urgency of the situation in Latin America "impels us to adapt our action to the major indications of the Second Vatican Council, to the Conclusions of the Second General Conference of Latin American Bishops in Medellín, and to the decisions of the last General Chapter of the Order expressed in the new Consitutitons *if we are to involve ourselves in the current world.*"[332] Little by little all the orders and congregations have attempted to comply to the decrees and conclusions of the Council and of Medellín.

A new note has sounded, however, during this time, namely, "the appreciation of the woman in the Church,"[333] which in time will bring about a new understanding of the meaning, liberation, consecration, and contribution of women.

A new religious life-style was already evident in the Fourth General Assembly of CLAR, which took place in Santiago, Chile, December 3–13, 1969. The return to small communities was evident all over Latin America as were a growing political commitment by young religious, a concern for the poor, and a change in traditional roles such as in schools, hospitals, and other institutions.

Another important meeting of bishops and religious leaders in Central America and Panama was held March 16–20, 1970. Reference was made not only "to the lack of national vocations for religious," but also "to the fact that the vast majority of vocations which exist are outside of Central America and Panama." Furthermore, it was noted that "most of the religious congregations do not have national superiors. This makes the integration of the religious in the national pastoral difficult."[334]

The First Course for Latin American Provincials was held in Medellín, January 25 to March 26, 1972, and the First Meeting of Religious Superiors of Central America was held in Guatemala, August 1–6, 1972.

Finally, the First Interamerican Meeting of Religious of Canada, the United States, and Latin America was held in Mexico City, February 7–12, 1971, in which the coordination of efforts for the whole hemisphere was begun.

Among the major documents that have prompted theological reflection, mention should be made of "The Life According to the Spirit," which was the result of inspiration traditionally called "spirituality" and represented the conclusion of the first stage of the study done in Buenos Aires in February 1972. A second document, "Religious Life and the Sociopolitical Situation in Latin America," was initially done in Montevideo in May 1972 and was edited and released by a group meeting in Mendoza, Argentina, in November 1973. The theme of this last document has provoked numerous commentaries, but it represents the most significant commitment of the religious to the present time.

A detailed description of the prophetic work done by many Latin American religious from those who have given their lives for Christ, as have some of the Dominicans of São Paulo, to those who have suffered the torture of electric shock and imprisonment, as have some of the Maryknoll Fathers, will be the theme of future works.

The Fifth General Assembly of CLAR elected as its new president Father Carlos Palmés, SJ, in its meeting on January 17–27, 1973, in Medellín.

4. The Attitude of the Christians

We have been hesitant to speak of the attitude of the "laity." Our Church — not only in Latin America, but also in Europe and the whole world — is still predominantly "clerical" in the sense that it is directed almost exclusively by professional clergymen. Paradoxically, in the Second Vatican Council the influence of laypersons and even their numerical presence was less than in all the history of the Church. Previously, laypersons in Christendom were equivocally but effectively represented by the emperors, kings, and government delegates. The representatives of the European states in the First Vatican Council can be seen in the fact that the editing of certain documents bore their imprint. The Church has been liberated from this kind of political influence—which is a step forward—but has reduced the laity to nothing more than a docile mass who are taught, who obey, and who collaborate. They are allowed to participate in meetings as "observers" or "auditors"—and only then is it the directors of movements such as Catholic Action—but the great Christian university intellectuals, those committed Christians in the highest levels of political life, have not become a part of the executive organisms of the Church. Neither CELAM, nor the national episcopal conferences, nor the faculties of theology accept the baptized Christian as a fraternal equal if questions of theology, philosophy, sociology, or even the interpretation of daily life in the light of the faith is being considered. We have a long way to go in regard to incorporating the layperson into the full life of the Church. The truth is that neither in Vatican II nor in Medellín were baptized Christians, that is, the laity, represented.[335]

(1) The struggle and life in the basic communities

Doubtless influenced by the prevailing spirit of the times, the contemporary Christian has lost his previous passivity in certain areas. Monseñor Raimundo Caramuru, Secretary of the Conference of Bishops of Brazil, analyzing the current situation stated that "the tension between distinguished groups of laypersons and the hierarchy is more constant today than ever before, and it is possible that this problem will not be quickly resolved. Many laypersons are frankly scandalized by certain institutional aspects of the Church."[336] Frequently there are meetings for reflection—as the one in Moreno, Argentina, the final text of which was signed August 28, 1966[337]—but many times there are direct acts of protest.

In Uruguay, for example, on June 20, 1965, there was a demonstration of Catholic students against the actions of the Apostolic Nuncio, Monseñor Forni. According to the students, Forni "prevented the Church in Uruguay from fulfilling the decrees of the Council." On April 4, 1966, at 200 Albariños Street in Buenos Aires, a young man stood at the iron gate of the Corpus Domini Church and shouted, "We will not lessen the struggle to obtain that which from the depth of our Christian consciences we ask of the Church of Christ: a Church without luxuries, without established interests, without hypocrisies, without bourgeois life-styles. We want in Argentina the *aggiornamento* called for by John XXIII."[338] At that time the church building was occupied by some twenty laypersons who were expressing their disconformity with the removal of Father Néstor García Morro. There were posters, and there was opposition to the naming of the new priest who had been designated without consulting anyone in the parish. This was the first time in the history of the Latin American Church that laymen had protested in this manner. On August 11, 1968, some 300 laypersons and a group of priests took over the Cathedral in Santiago, Chile, in the name of the movement, the "Young Church." Their demand was for more dialogue and structural flexibility in the hierarchy.[339] In Mexico the people of the Dulce Nombre de María Parish in the diocese of Tlalnepantla protested the change of their priest, and on Jaunary 5, 1970, when the new priest came to take possession of the Church, some thirty faithful dressed in mourning clothes went out to meet him.[340] In the Dominican Republic, discharged workers of the Metaldom factory peacefully occupied the Cathedral of Santo Domingo in 1969 to protest and ask for help. In Nicaragua numerous laypersons occupied churches in Managua in 1970 to protest government tortures of prisoners. In Peru strikers of the textile factory Texoro, supported by their bishop and priest, moved into the Church of San Martín de Porres in Lima in December 1969. That same month Cardinal Landázuri Ricketts abandoned his palace in order to live in a humble community in the city of Lima, and four canons in Trujillo renounced the salaries they were receiving from the government. Peaceful occupations of the churches in Lima continued in 1970: 300 workers of the Mayólica Nacional who were on strike lived in the San Sebastián Church; 250 of the Fénix employees lived for a time in the Jesús Obrero Church.[341] In Bolivia numerous Christians called for the resignation of the Archbishop and took over the cathedral in Cochabamba on April 17, 1970, in defense of the priests of the OCSHA. In Guatemala on July 4, 1970, the movement called "Christians for Renewal" staged processions in March 1968. These examples among many that could be cited indicate a new phenomenon: laypersons are beginning to express themselves, to mould public opinion, and to make themselves seen and heard either peacefully or otherwise. Also they are having to be taken into account more and more.

One should not conclude that all the movements utilizing force stem from groups that desire renewal. In the Church of Nuestra Señora del Socorro (Our Lady of Help) in La Plata, Argentina, a group of laypersons prevented the new priest from taking possession of the Church on January 4, 1971, because he was said to be a member of the "Priests for the Third World"; and even though a locksmith was called, the priest was unable to enter the building. Traditionalist groups in Colombia, meanwhile, began the anti-Golconda Movement and were directed by Father Jairo Mejía Gómez who was Secretary General of the Liturgical Commission of the Diocesis of Medellín.[342] That same year in Uruguay groups of Christians called upon the Papal Nuncio to condemn every kind of violence. Right-wing proponents also began a vicious campaign against Monseñor Parteli, and the criticisms often came from his own priests and well-known Catholics of the country. Already mentioned were the groups organized in Brazil in 1968 against the "Action, Justice, and Peace" movement of Dom Hélder. Numerous pamphlets were distributed against the Archbishop of Recife, and some believe that certain priests were involved along with a member of the town council, Vanderkok Vanderlei.

Catholic Action has also suffered a profound crisis, and like the priesthood, it has been forced to rediscover its function in the present situation. Unspecialized or parish type Catholic Action has been unable to transcend a very menial function within the Church. In 1965 some fifty consultants and forty directors of Catholic Action met together and engaged in a heated debate regarding the meaning and the future of the organization.[343] In a meeting in July of the same year in Cerro Alegre, Peru, an agreement was reached regarding the coordination of lay movements in Latin America.[344] Specialized Catholic Action, in contrast, experiencing a similar crisis, has discovered in its historical commitments a direction to follow. The Argentine ACO, for example, on March 20, 1967, publicly denounced the antisocial attitude of the government saying that "in view of the fact that the government claims to be Christian . . . we are obligated to state that its actions have nothing to do with the word of Jesus expressed in the gospel nor with the doctrine of the Church manifested recently in the Council."[345] And the ACO of Northeast Brazil continually publicizes the injustices that are committed in that part of the country.

Meanwhile, Christian trade unionism has tended toward deconfessionalization and radicalization. Criticisms are made not only against North American imperialism, but also against those who cooperate with the imperialists. In 1970, for example, the Autonomous Confederation of Catholic Trade Unions (CASC) in Santo Domingo criticized the Vatican for attempting to help the underdeveloped countries by means of the BID (Inter-American Development Bank) and the OAS (Organization of

American States), because in the judgment of the union members both organisms were instruments of North American domination which was oppressing Latin America. Along the same line one should read the "Open Letter" written by CLASC, an organization representing five million workers, to Paul VI on the occasion of his visit to Bogotá, July 18, 1968. In the language of the worker, direct and sincere, the letter states:

We know, Brother Paul, that all the bishops of Latin America are going to meet at Medellín to discuss the Church's role in the Latin America world of today. At first we thought that a few laymen who are concretely committed to and involved in the daily work of advancing and developing people, men belonging to popular organizations, might participate in this assembly of all the princes of your Church. When some union leaders went to ask that representatives of the Workers' and Peasants' organizations be invited, these same princes of the Church replied that "they did not want any 'disturbing' elements at the Medellín meeting." And you know, the princes were right. We *are* "disturbing" elements, profoundly disturbing, because for a long time we have represented action that goes further than words.[346]

The letter continued,

Do you know what laymen will be invited to this ecclesiastical gathering? Members of the liberal professions, technologists, people who have made a name for themselves, primarily either members of the ruling class, or men who, in the schools, universities, and clubs frequented by the anti-people oligarchy have picked up the same habits and reactions as they. . . . And everything will remain just as it was, for nothing in your Church has changed in this respect. . . . It seems that nowadays the studies of sociology, economics, ideology, the political and administrative sciences and psychology are once again in vogue. So much so that theology, and especially ordinary pastoral theology, is being forgotten. . . . There are today in your Church a great many "champions" of the poor who want to bring social salvation to the workers — without regard for the workers' own wishes, possibly even in spite of them.[347]

This letter should be taken very seriously because it represents a group of Christians who for more than twenty years have struggled day after day for their faith. It was written with love, clarity, and courage, and not as just another letter among many that were sent to the Pontiff.

Prior to the Medellín Conference, a group of responsible Latin Americans who were members of the Apostolic Movements of Lay Persons met for a seminar in Lima in July 1968 and subsequently sent to the president of CELAM a letter in which they criticized the "Basic Document" of the Conference. They said, "One feature seems to be wholly characteristic and basic within the economic, social, and cultural situation of Latin America. Our countries are economically, politically, and culturally dependent on the capitalist powers. . . . We feel that we simply must look for solutions outside the ideological framework of capitalism."[348]

Another indication of the attitude of the Christians in Latin America can be seen in the reaction to the papal encyclical *Humanae Vitae*. A forum was held in Peru in 1966 for the purpose of discussing the Latin American Christian position regarding birth control. One of the first Latin American prelates to declare himself in regard to the encyclical was the Chilean Cardinal, Raul Silva Henríquez.[349] His statement was followed shortly thereafter by one from the Mexican episcopacy.[350] In Bogotá, *El Catolicismo*, the major news organ of the Church, attacked the government program of birth control despite the fact that the newspapers in general openly opposed the Church on this issue. Cardinal Luis Concha exercised some prudence by waiting, but he finally condemned all forms of birth control except the rhythm method,[351] and shortly thereafter his position was supported by the other Colombian bishops.[352] In general, the attitude was that small groups of Christians with a more personal formation tended to reject the moralisms given by the Pope regarding the question — as occurred also in Europe — while the masses, lacking both instruction in enlightened Catholicism and in birth control methods, treated the whole matter with indifference. Certain groups of Catholics felt the traditional pressure imposed by the encyclical, but not being able to follow its teachings, they temporarily moved away from the Church. For the most part the hierarchy supported the encyclical for the explicit reasons outlined by the Pope. Groups of a more populist orientation tended to support the encyclical because of its historical importance and for reasons of political expediency, but a large number of people in the underdeveloped and dependent countries saw the situation as a possibility for future liberation. Demographic stabilization in these areas of the world could definitively alter the present situation.

In light of the frustration and crises of many of the pastoral experiences of the new Christendom such as the last attempt at mass evangelization by the use of urban radio,[353] which was employed in many Latin American areas, a form of Christian community living has developed during the last decade which may indicate the direction of the future. The way of life followed by the small non-Christian religions, the spiritists and African syncretistic groups in Brazil, for example, or the non-Catholic communities such as the Pentecostals, indicate that the meeting of the faithful in groups where relations are personalized provides a concrete way by which the people can live the gospel. This has been the Catholic pastoral experience in the "basic Christian communities" in Brazil. The Second Vatican Council spoke to this issue in the Dogmatic Constitution on the Church,[354] but it was in Medellín that an explicit formulation was given: "The Christian ought to find the living of the communion, in which he has been called, in his 'base community,' that is, in a community, local or environmental, which corresponds to the reality of a homogeneous group and whose size allows for personal fraternal contact among its members. ... Thus the Christian base community is the first and fundamental ecclesiastical nucleus."[355] Thus when Monseñor Antonio Fragoso states that in his diocese in Northeast Brazil there exist ten parishes, each with 150 communities, that is, a total of 1,500 in the diocese, one can understand that this experience could offer hope for the reconstruction of a mediation between the impersonal and anonymous parish community and the individual believer.[356]

In Northeast Brazil numerous experiments and experiences indicate possibilities for the future, experiences such as that of Father Gerardo in the Ponce Carvalhos Parish, that of Father Beltrán in Girardot, Colombia, and that of Father Leo Mahon in San Miguelito, Panama. There have been other movements such as the Christian Family and the Basic Education Movement initiated by Paulo Freire in Northeast Brazil, and after his exile to Chile, the BEM was utilized by many "basic Christian communities" in that country. Together, and even individually, these movements indicate a new beginning and the fact that "all is not lost." Liberating, evangelizing, or liturgical, basic communities should be a primary concern of the Pastoral Department of CELAM as well as of the churches in the respective nations and dioceses. For it is at this level that the Church will make the transition from Christendom to religious communities in a pluralistic society where existential faith will prepare the Christian for daily, practical living, and where the catechumenate will recover its full meaning as in the primitive Christian communities of the Roman Empire prior to Constantine. The

Christian leader, the deacon, and new types of pastoral activities — renewed ministries even in the priestly order — will spring up from a life that develops *from below*, that is, from the Church of the people, from the people of God who are purged of all triumphalist attitudes of Christendom.

In Río Grande da Norte, Brazil, as early as 1964, nuns — like vicars-general — could direct prayers, lead in social work, catechize, and preside at services of worship. In Chile Cardinal Silva Henríquez allowed laypersons to preach in the Sunday masses in 1964. Nevertheless, the entire ecclesio-economic system should be changed and should follow the example in Chile where in 1970 twenty-four dioceses decided that the Church should depend only on gifts received systematically and voluntarily from the faithful, and not be supported directly or indirectly by the government. All these steps represent a mere tinkering with an institution and way of life that needs to be thoroughly revamped, but only the *basic Christian communities* and the new ministerial functions can remake the Church as it ought to be.

(2) The Christian: his political and social commitment

In a very brief period, Latin American Christianity has achieved an amazing maturity. The previous stage (1930— 1961) was greatly influenced at the political level by the organization of Christian Democracy and the separation of youth groups from the Conservative political parties. Christian Democracy in Chile, for example, sprang up during the decade of the 1930s after having earlier been a part of the fascist Falange. In 1946 the Christian Social Party (COPEI) was organized in Venezuela, and the following year the Christian Democratic Organization of America was formed. In Argentina the Christian Democratic Party was founded in 1954 as was the Christian Social Party in Bolivia. Christian Democrats succeeded in organizing both in Peru and in Guatemala in 1956. Then in 1958 the Chilean Christian Democratic Party participated for the first time in national elections. The Christian Democratic Youth of America (JUDCA) was founded in 1959. In 1960 the Christian Democratic Party was created in El Salvador, Paraguay, and Panama, and during the next two years Christian Democrats organized successively in the Dominican Republic (PRSC) and in Uruguay as The Civic Union. Christian Democrats elected two senators and twenty-one deputies in Brazil in 1962. The Christian Democratic Party appeared in Costa Rica in 1963 and in Ecuador and Colombia (PSDC) in 1964. That same year two different parties united in Bolivia to form the Christian Democratic Party of that country. Then on September 4, 1964, Christian Democrats won the presidential election under the leadership of Eduardo Frei in Chile with the motto "Revolution with Freedom."

These new parties actively participated at various levels and with differing attitudes in all of Latin America. In 1968 Rafael Caldera was elected President of Venezuela with twenty-nine percent of the votes. He became the second Christian Democrat to achieve this high office in Latin America. Unfortunately, however, the previous year a group in Chile led by Rafael Agustín Gumucio gained control of the Christian Democratic Party's Directors Committee, which eventually brought about a split in the PDC. The rebellious wing constituted itself into a new political group, the MAPU, and in 1969 supported the candidacy of Salvador Allende, enabling him to gain the presidency on September 4, 1970. The appearance of Christian Democracy and Catholic Action beginning in 1930 represented a hope for a new Christendom and originated in part with Conservative groups. The organization of MAPU, however, which also originated within Christian Democracy, represents still another development in the political commitment of Latin American Christians. Finally, one must note the growing separation between the Christian Democratic parties of Latin America and those of Europe, which seemed to indicate an awareness on the part of the Latin Americans of being situated in a colonial environment while the European Christian Democrats enjoyed the advantages of being a part of the metropolitan and imperialistic center.[357]

European Christian Democracy after the Second World War really represented a common political front against the People's Democracies, that is, Christian Democracy was a kind of ecumenical unity achieved on the religious level against the atheism of the government in the Communist countries. Latin American Christian Democracy in the dependent and neocolonial countries of this continent was made possible by the presence, although agonizing, of a colonial Christendom, by the nascent force of a new middle class — an extension of the incipient industrial development after the 1930s and the Second World War — the influence of European thinkers, especially Maritain, Lebret, and Mounier, and by the example of the European Christian Democrats, especially the Italians and Germans. Christian Democracy was founded on a kind of abstract, international, and technocratic natural law — technocratic in the sense in which the Belgian Roger Vekemans is a prime example. (Vekemans began his work in Chile and now is located in Bogotá, Colombia.) Historically, Christian Democracy was first an ideology of minorities who lacked adequate understanding of the people. It was centrist (originally tending toward the right), reformist, and developmentalist — but not truly revolutionary — with a Latin American nascent internationalism insufficiently rooted in the nations as such. There were attempts to modify the positions of the parties in several Latin American countries. In Argentina, for example, there was an attempt to make the Christian Democrats a people's party, and the failure to do so indicated a structural limitation within the movement. In Chile, Christian Democracy developed into a kind of populism, but the incipient radicalism within the group eventually led to a formal schism. The same thing happened in Venezuela.

Since 1960, however, a new situation has developed which doubtless will affect the future not only of Christian Democracy but also of the political commitment of Latin American Christians in general. In the first place, the revolution in Cuba suggested to many Latin Americans a new possibility. Eduardo Frei in Chile, on the other hand, took a different tack: "Revolution with Freedom." But his rather disappointing results paved the way for a more radical approach with Allende. Europe and the United States, meanwhile, ended the Cold War with Russia and initiated a new stage in their relationship, namely, that of "peaceful coexistence." The ecumenical movement now includes the Russian Orthodox Church. Furthermore, trade agreements between the Soviet Union and Western countries have created a means of penetrating the Iron Curtain. The major conflict now appears to be between Russia and China and not between Russia and Western Europe. "Peaceful coexistence" has also permitted dialogue between Christians and Marxists. Latin America, meanwhile, has recognized the failure of the development program and has moved to a new level of sociopolitical understanding derived f   an economic analysis that reveals the dialectic of imperialism and colonialism at all levels. And though Latin America did not participate directly in the 1955 Bandung Conference, it has been greatly influenced by its findings. A move toward the left has been evident since the early 1960s. The case of Camilo Torres, a developmentalist who became a revolutionary, is paradigmatic.

The new Christian generation faces this situation with a different sense of political vocation and sees a way in which the Popular Fronts can establish a relationship with populism, not centrist as in Argentinean "Irigoyenism" or "Peronism" or as in Brazilian

"Vargism," but in a new kind of populism: revolutionary, nationalistic, but with a primary and international sense of vocation. The nationalism is not of the old nation-state type, but more Latin American with a multistate base, that is, composed of many state organisms in Mexico, Brazil, Argentina, and others, and not from a single Latin American nation as such. At times this move toward the revolutionary left and toward populism will produce a division within the existing Christian Democratic parties. Some will simply dissolve as a party, and others will be transformed into a new political movement. What is important here is the evidence of a clear shift toward radicalization and separation from the Old Conservative-Fascist line, and the assuming of a position similar to "Guevarism" — armed violence or at least militantly revolutionary — to the Popular Front in view of a national populism. All this is not merely in prospect. At all levels one can observe a real beginning and commitment that is directed first toward the conscientization of the fundamental fact that we are dependent colonies, and that we have a common adversary: the imperialism of the dollar.

All this indicates that Christians have returned to the center of the political arena in Latin America in a manner less equivocal than during either the time of colonial Christendom or of the struggle for political independence (1808–1825). Now the struggle is for economic, cultural, and human independence in Latin America, not only in respect to the United States but in regard to all the superdeveloped powers. All of this presupposes a possibility of a Latin American socialism concurrent with a Christian existential understanding (we are not speaking of Marxism) which is ideologically founded on a political process that unites the American and Asiatic people who are no longer on developmental tracks but on the way or in the process of liberation from the oppressor-oppressed structure. It presupposes the possibility of alerting the leaders of the developed-oppressing countries who do not allow the organization of counterrevolution in the name of the struggle against subversion and the defense of the Western Christian civilization to the fact that there are many Christians who desire a liberated humanity composed of neither Occidental nor Oriental, of neither Greek nor Roman, neither Jews nor pagans, since Christ "is the peace between us, and has made the two into one and broken down the barrier which used to keep us apart, actually destroying in his own person the hostility" (Eph. 2:14). This biblical text is eschatological, but for this reason it is being fulfilled in order that the Kingdom will become more real, present, and historical.

(3) The Christian university student and intellectual

Since 1962 profound changes in the orientation of the Latin American Christian university students have taken place.[358] To better understand the dramatic nature of these changes an historical resumé is necessary. The first model of higher education in Latin America was the old colonial "university of Christendom," which originated in the first *Colegio Mayor* founded in Santo Domingo in 1537 and in the Universities of San Marcos of Lima and of Mexico. Their demise bega in the early part of the nineteenth century, and they received the coup de grace in 1918 — to indicate a symbolic date — with the "University Reform" movement in Córdoba, Argentina, a movement that extended throughout Latin America and had international repercussions.[359] The second model was that of the "liberal reformist university," which stemmed from the Córdoba Manifesto that declared: "Men of a free republic, we have just broken the last chain which binds us in this twentieth centruy to the old monarchical and monastic domination."[360] Those "reformists," nevertheless, were simply liberals representing a small bourgeois with abstract internationalist ideologies and tied to an incipient industrialism. There were great Christian thinkers such as José Vasconcellos in Mexico, or positivists such as José Ingenieros in Argentina, but only Víctor Raul Haya de la Torre, Rector of the People's Universities of Peru, was able to develop a coherent formulation of doctrine into a political movement, the APRA, with Indoamerican and antiimperialistic roots, but which, unfortunately, with time lost the best of its doctrine. Following the Second World War, as Guzmán Carriquiry stated in a paper presented to the Latin American Seminar on the University Pastoral, June 15 – 25, 1967, in Mexico City,[361] there appeared a third model: the "development university." It was neocapitalist, following the line of technological development and insisting that the university should produce technicians who would fit in with the scheme of integral development. The BID and the CEPAL, for example, enthusiastically promoted this model. Christians, therefore, responded to this "reformist" model with the creation of movements of the same type: "Humanism" in Argentina, Christian Democratic Youth in Brazil, and the JUC in various countries. The work of the Chilean team led by Roger Vekemans as well as the movement known as "Economy and Humanism" were a part of this development stage.

A fourth model, however, has appeared: the "critico-liberating university" — to give it a name. It is this nascent university, benefiting from recent experiences, that is critical of the oppression and the neocolonialism from which Latin America suffers, and that has assumed that liberation is a technico-humanistic mission. The curriculum followed is that of the "pedagogy of the oppressed," a system and philosophy developed by Paulo Freire.[362] This new university in Latin America already has a beginning history. In a different setting, the Technical University of Peking has had a novel experience: first the students, and then the workers proposed a new plan of studies for the administration and university government. The movement was supported by the government and became a part of the "Cultural Revolution" in China. Earlier in Cuba there was a similar experience. Then as an indirect result of what was taking place in Latin America, the May of 1968 occurred in Paris. The article written by Paul Ricoeur in Esprit, "The Dialectic of Teaching" (teacher-pupil), provided an interesting element for reflection. At the same time, Latin American Christian university students were having a similar experience, which was a part of the common process.

In Brazil, Popular Action was founded in 1962 and began the publication of its magazine by the same name. Following the military overthrow of the government, the students began to defend certain principles, and their reaction was interpreted by the military as being subversive. Monseñor Vicente Scherer made known his position in "The National Conference of Bishops and Popular Action."[363] The university movement became committed to revolution. Shortly thereafter the JUC and the JEC abandoned the "directive" and ceased to be confessional movements, thereby accepting temporal commitments, living theologically in the Church without being a part of the ecclesial institution itself. The Brazilian episcopacy accepted their position, and the crisis extended throughout all of Catholic Action. The National Secretariat of the JEC resigned on December 4, 1966. Monseñor Scherer, who was responsible for the lay apostolate, reported the events by radio on January 9, 1967, and said that the young people not only could resign if their consciences so indicated, but they should do so. Catholic Action continued to be considered by the government as subversive, and the deconfessionalization extended to the Legion of Mary and the Apostolate of Prayer as well as to the Basic Education Movement (MEB). The Catholic university students then began to adopt very pronounced political postures. They were expelled by the police from the Catholic University of Sâo Paulo, and although Cardinal Rossi protested, he was not able to secure the freedom of the adviser to the students, Father Talp, who was held by the secret police (DEOPS). On April 1, 1965, seven hundred Brazilian intellectuals severely criticized "the revolution" promoted by the military government. These intellectuals accused the government of political persecution, violence, torture, and of being a cultural terror without exercising any discrimination. Amoroso Lima declared publicly, "With *Populorum Progressio* the Church began a new war, not against the barbarians or the Turks, but against hunger, misery, injustice, and against war itself."[364] In other Latin American countries university students had already lost confidence in the development program of the Alliance for Progress. There followed the most significant meeting and document of this period, that of Buga.

The Second Vatican Council had spoken very clearly in regard to the university question.[365] Then the Department of Education of CELAM convened a seminar of experts on "The Mission of the Catholic University in Latin America" which met in Buga, Colombia, February 12 to 18, 1967.[366] The general tone of the document issued by the seminar was "developmentalist." Nevertheless, it contained some important indications for a critico-liberating university; for example, the statement that "the Catholic university serves as a focus for conscientization regarding historical reality ... the disalienation of the generating postures of *colonialist culture*."[367] The developmental approach was clearly falling into disfavor as can be seen in the following text: "These [the social sciences] should aid in the search for integral development. Yet certain dangers are evident in the imposition of models unrelated to the Latin American reality. Although the social sciences could be, in certain official circles of Latin America, considered as correspondingly subversive, the Catholic University will assure an environment of free and open investigation."[368] The absolutely irreplaceable role of the Catholic universities should be to provide a "meeting between the Church and the world" and encourage theological and humanistic reflection whereby horizontal institutionalized dialogue between the scientific disciplines, the university and society, are open to those who want to enter, and vertical dialogue which "allow for participation by professors and students in the government of the institution, and in the election of its authorities. ... The autonomous university is an indispensable necessity ... for the study and promotion of popular culture."[369] The document, nonetheless, is limited, for although it speaks at the beginning of the "Christian view of culture" and interprets mankind in "a history which tends to liberate more and more the personal and community values," it says nothing in regard to Latin American culture. All of the observations remain at an abstract level. The most serious deficiency is that, together with the affirmation that is the responsibility of "the university to make the transition from the old to the new Latin American system and to be the molding nucleus of the intelligentsia," nothing is said as to how this intelligentsia can be effectively formed either at the university student level or at the level of the "intellectual," be he graduate or university professor. In this sense the MIIC (the International Movement of Catholic Intellectuals) has not yet discovered its role in Latin America. Some of us organized a "Latin American Week"[370] in December 1964 in which we attempted to discover a means for producing more concrete results, namely, an annual meeting of university professors and recognized Christian intellectuals to discuss and publish findings regarding the more crucial problems of the continent. Year after year a Christian interpretation — reflexive, scientific, at a high level — is needed not only to clarify but also to make history.

The Buga document provoked an immediate reaction first in Valparaíso and later in Santiago, Chile, where there were violent confrontations resulting from the election of the university authorities. Buga had called for the participation of the students in these elections. The students, therefore, called upon the officials to modify the statutes of the Catholic universities in both of these cities. The Bishop of Valparaíso rejected the student ultimatum, and on June 19, 1967, a student strike began. In Santiago the students occupied university buildings. The movement terminated on August 22 when the Vatican named as mediator Cardinal Silva Henríquez of Santiago, who together with the President of the FEUC (Federation of Students of the Catholic University) of Santiago decided that an election would be held on November 25 to constitute a Council with seventy-five percent of its membership composed of professors, twenty percent of students, and five percent named by the Permanent Committee of the Episcopacy. This solution was also adopted in Valparaíso, and the statutes of both universities were reformed. The movement extended with even more vehemence to the national universities in Chile and from there to practically all of Latin America with differences, of course, in various areas. In La Paz, Catholic students rejected the 1967 project of Monseñor Rocco for founding a Catholic university. Later, for other reasons, but certainly related to the experiences in China and Latin America—for example, the university reaction against Onganía in 1966 in Argentina—there came the impetuous interruption of May 1968 in France. Meanwhile, in Latin America the most lamentable reaction by dissatisfied students was that which occurred in Mexico between the police, the army, and the students beginning July 26, 1968. It terminated tragically with the death of more than two hundred in the historic plaza of the Tres Culturas of Tlatelolco on October 2 after many hours of crossfire into thousands of defenseless students.[371] The Mexican episcopacy should have reacted with a document spelling out in no uncertain terms that there should be "neither impetuous destruction nor criminal exploitation" of the situation.[372]

Perhaps of equal or even greater importance than the Mexican tragedy was what took place in Córdoba, now called the "Cordobazo" in Argentina. On May 29, 1969, workers from the industrial plants of Córdoba attempted to unite with the students of the city. There were conflicts as never before in the history of that country. "It is necessary to go back ten years to encounter a national strike of the magnitude which took place on May 30" according to the CGT. Barricades isolated Córdoba. There were shootings by groups from everywhere. "On the university campus the Catholics were the principal protagonists in this process, and the majority of them were leaders in the National Student Union."[373] The movement shook the Onganía regime, which fell a year later.

Christian university students are making their presence increasingly felt in Latin America. When a professor of the Catholic University was shot and killed by the police in a demonstration, the university and secondary students in Santiago de los Caballeros demonstrated, and classes were suspended.[374] A year after the tragic events of Tlatelolco, masses were celebrated in Mexico, but the only member of the episcopacy who participated was Monseñor Méndez Arceo of Cuernavaca.

The transition from a "developmentalist university" to a "critico-liberating university"[375] is a painful process in which partial ideologies are surpassed because "the ideological option," as Don Fragoso said in November 1969, is partisan. It can be beautiful and generous, but it is partial. From a global perspective the principal objective is the liberation of mankind, and it can be realized with whatever is valid in other ideological options." Final liberation is eschatological. Cultural liberation is, on the other hand, the construction of an historically new person who overcomes the alienation of oppressive colonialism.

III. FROM SUCRE TO PUEBLA (1972–1979)

1. The Situation in Sucre (1972)

(1) The sociopolitical context

The national-security dependent model of capitalism was spreading throughout Latin America. The important dates and events were the military coups in Brazil (March 31, 1964) and Bolivia (August 21, 1971), the dissolution of the congress in Uruguay (June 27, 1973), Pinochet's coup in Chile against Allende (September 11, 1973), the rise of Francisco Morales Bermúdez in Peru (August 28, 1975), the fall of the nationalistic military government in Ecuador (January 13, 1976), and the deposition of Isabel Perón (March 24, 1976). The situation was indeed grim if one also considers the continuation of the dictatorship of Somoza in Nicaragua, Stroessner in Paraguay, Duvalier in Haiti, Balanguer in the Dominican Republic, and military dictatorships with democratic trappings in Guatemala, Honduras, and El Salvador. All of this was in keeping with the counter-insurgency model of national security proposed by Henry Kissinger, Richard Nixon, and Gerald Ford.

From an economic point of view, the difficulties that began in 1967 lessened during a period of recuperation in 1972 and 1973, but then world capitalism suffered its worst crisis since 1929. Inflation along with recession produced a "stagflation" beginning in 1974. Neo-Fascist dictatorships applied the economic doctrine of Milton Friedman's Chicago School, and transnational corporations took complete control of the economies in several nations. Policies of the International Monetary Fund (IMF) caused national debts to soar to astronomic heights, and the center-periphery relationship was duplicated when certain countries designated as centers of development — Brazil, Mexico, India, and Iran for example — began economic incursions into less developed countries.

The expansion of international capital and a new technological domination required nations to adapt a compatible ideology. Augusto Pinochet expressed this sentiment in the Sixth Assembly of the OAS in Santiago, Chile, in 1976:

Western Christian civilization, of which we unquestionably form a part, is being weakened from within and attacked from without. The ideological warfare jeopardizing the sovereignty of free states and man's essential dignity leaves no room for comfortable neutrality. In the internal politics of several nations we observe the ideological and social aggression of a doctrine which under the guise of a supposed proletarian redemption aims to implant a communist tyranny.

A theory of total warfare was developed on the political, economic, psycho-social, and military levels. The doctrine of national security, which originated in the United States after the Second World War, was adopted by the Latin American military in order to insure a political structure allowing for economic expansion from capitalist centers. The economic goal, namely, profits for foreign capitalists, has determined the political policy of many Third World countries and has resulted in the systematic repression of the people.

(2) The Church context

The most important papal document of this period was the apostolic exhortation *Evangelii Nuntiandi* issued on December 8, 1975, which summarized previous statements. The troubles of capitalism seemed to cause a widespread pessimism in Italy, and the appearance of Eurocommunism and the advance of the Communist Party frightened certain ecclesiastical groups. The Pope, however, stated clearly:

The words of many bishops from all continents, especially from the Third World, in the recent Synod [1974] are well known. ... Their peoples are energetically determined to overcome whatever condemns them to marginal existence. ... The Church has the duty to announce liberation to millions of human beings, [and] to aid in bringing this liberation about.[376]

In their Thirty-second Extraordinary Meeting in Rome (1973), the Jesuits agreed to place "the Company at the service of the Church during this period of rapid change and respond to the challenge the world presents." For them justice was a decided priority.

Yet in the 1974 Synod, Latin American bishops no longer spoke as in the previous one. They arrived at no conclusion, but rather contented themselves with issuing a "message" of commitment. In the fifth Synod in Rome (1977) it was obvious that the CELAM Assembly in Sucre had produced some fruits, for a bishop from El Salvador declared to the Synod that "in my country, priests are becoming communists or Maoists."[377] A Spanish prelate remarked that the Church in Latin America was openly retreating from the position taken at Medellín.[378] Monseñor Alfonso López Trujillo repeatedly insisted that "Christian liberation need not inevitably be politicizing."[379] Changes occurred in the Pontifical Commission of Justice and Peace, and "those responsible for the Commission decided to forego the service of forty international experts."[380] In substance the Congregations were manifesting preconciliar tendencies. In Germany the progressive and critical lay journal *Publik* was closed. Meanwhile in the United States, Father Joseph Colonnese was dismissed as director of the Catholic International Cooperation Program (CICOP), where he had kept the North Americans informed of the reality of the poverty of Latin America that was resulting from U.S. policy. Bishop Lefebvre's movement was symptomatic of the tide of reaction against Council reform. This was the atmosphere in Latin America by the end of 1972.

(3) The Sucre assembly (November 15—23, 1972)

The Fourteenth Ordinary Assembly of CELAM was held in Sucre, Bolivia, during the period of November 15—23, 1972. The agenda consisted of four main issues: "the general restructuring of CELAM, the reelection of officers, the future of its specialized institutes as to their financing, and guidelines for pastoral practice."[381] The prediction was made and reported by the press that "after the Sucre Assembly, CELAM will run on a more conservative track since bishops in several countries have been questioning the activities and pastoral approaches in some of the CELAM departments. Bishops here [in Argentina] and in Colombia, among others, have not disguised their displeasure with initiatives taken by that organism."[382] Héctor Borrat, journalist and Christian intellectual, wrote,

Recent attacks on Segundo Galilea, the Pastoral Institute of Latin America (IPLA), and the Commission for Latin American Church History (CEHILA) was only a prelude to a final, all-out assault made during the CELAM Assembly in Sucre. It is more than a meeting; for the right wing it is the opportunity they have been waiting for and working towards to defeat the followers of Medellín. Will they, by electing new officers, succeed in effecting the shift that would turn Latin American bishops aside from the road opened up in 1968?[383]

These remarks, written before and during the Sucre Assembly, indicate the prevailing mood. Conservatives were indeed elected. López Trujillo became the Secretary General of CELAM, Bishop Luciano Duarte became President of the Department of Social Action, and Bishop Antonio Quarracino became President of the Department of the Laity. The shift was effected, and a new period in the history of CELAM and the Latin American Church had begun.

A *Memorandum* was signed by dozens of German theologians referring to the campaign against liberation theology initiated by conservatives as part of their program for Sucre. The Germans stated that "a driving force behind this campaign is Roger Vekemans," and "as far as the Latin American episcopate is concerned, the campaign against liberation theology is supported especially by the Colombian auxiliary bishops Alfonso López Trujillo and D. Castrillón." And finally, "in Germany Bishop Hengsbach of Essen is prominent in this campaign against liberation theology."[384]

Conservative theologians Weber, Rauscher, and Bossler sided with the "Church and Liberation" group in opposing Latin American liberation theology, which one of them referred to as "irrational obscurantism." In fact, these criticisms of the trends that began with Medellín, trends such as emphases on liberation and solidarity with the poor, actually benefited the national-security states, and they abetted State Department plans to reshape the physiognomy of Latin America through violent coups against liberation movements. The Church remained blind and deaf to the many horrors committed in the name of "Western Christian civilization."

The Chileans Galat and Ordóñez were typical of the growing reactionary spirit:

Material poverty cannot be confused with spiritual poverty. People may be poor in economic goods without being poor in spirit, or one can deify money and covet wealth one does not possess. Still one can be rich in material things and be truly *'anawim* or poor in spirit.[385]

Thus when a worker asks for more wages or when a peasant demands his land back from the landowner who has stolen it, he is coveting another's wealth and is doomed to fail. On the other hand, the wealthy landlord who feels liberated because of his millions is really poor in spirit. The gospel is now inverted — standing on its head — emptied of its real content and refilled with a dependent, capitalist ideology. Since 1972 the Church has had the choice of either condoning or opposing capitalistic designs on Latin America. In the Sucre Assembly, by opposing liberation theology and rebuking the Pastoral Institute, which produced saints and martyrs such as Rutilio Grande, the Latin American Church as a whole has muted its voice of protest on the international level, if not on the national and local levels.

2. The Ecclesial Situation from Sucre to Puebla (1973–1979)

During the last five years the Church has suffered from a veritable reign of terror. It has provided more martyrs to Christian communities and to the heavenly Jerusalem than in the almost five centuries of its existence. Through its members who work with the poor the Church has authenticated its witness to the gospel as the people of God and deepened in the understanding of the gospel's implications. Despite the pain, blood, and death, this half-decade has been a glorious period in the history of Latin American Christianity.

(1) The Church in militaristic states (Brazil, Argentina, Chile, Peru, El Salvador)

As an indication of the situation existing in repressive states, mention should first be made of the imprisonment in Riobamba, Ecuador, of thirteen Latin American and four

Mexican-American bishops on August 12, 1976. They were returning from a conference in Brazil on base communities and had come to Ecuador to discuss the situation of the Church in Latin America. One bishop exclaimed, "If this can happen to us, what happens to peasants, workers, and Indians when they are arrested?"[386]

The "Brazilian model" of development suffered a setback in Brazil itself as well as elsewhere in Latin America because of the oil shortage and the monetary crisis in the capitalistic countries. Foreign debt rose in Brazil to three and a half billion dollars in 1974. President Giesel allowed more freedom since he needed better press, and the Church quickly took advantage of this relaxation by providing courageous leadership to the people and by standing up to the national-security state. The Brazilian Church did not forget its martyrs but held them up as examples of the gospel. The deaths of Fathers Henrique Pereira Neto, Rodolfo Lunkenbein, João Bosco Penido Burnier, and many others indicated the Church's break with the neo-Christendom model. Many took part in this renewal: Cardinal Paulo Evaristo Arns of São Paulo supported the urban student and workers' front, Bishop Pedro Casaldáliga allied himself with the peasants of the Northeast, Bishop Tomás Balduino stood openly with the Indians, and Bishop Bliz Fernández coordinated thousands of base communities. Bishop Hélder Câmara continued his prophetic denunciations of the widespread injustices, and Bishop Aloisio Lorscheider became president of CELAM. Bishop Ivo Lorscheider directed the National Conference of Brazilian Bishops in establishing a new pattern of relations with the government and the dominating classes. Two documents issued on May 6, 1973 — "I Have Heard the Cry of My People" by the bishops of the Northeast and "The Margination of the People, Cry of the Churches" by the bishops of Central and Western Brazil — described the Church's new position. The latter pastoral declared, "Only people of the countryside and the cities, in unity and in labor, in faith and hope, can be the Church of Christ, ... this Church which struggles for liberation. And it is only to the extent that we venture into the waters of the Gospel that we become the people-Church, the people of God."[387]

Yet there is ambiguity in the Brazilian Church despite the fact that it follows the popular Church model and is freer from the national-security state and closer to the oppressed than elsewhere in Latin America. The ambiguity stems from the fact that the Church receives its support not only from the lower and middle classes, but also from the national bourgeois. Thus Church leaders speak of a "national" liberation but always within the confines of a capitalistic economic system. Is this attitude not just another Latin American populism?

In Argentina the situation has become more distressing since 1973 and especially after Perón's death in 1974. Given the amount of dependency and repression under López Rega during Isabel Perón's regime, the military coup of March 26, 1976, led to no basic changes.

A violent bloody repression of the people, among them many Christians, has characterized the period. Father Carlos Mugica was assassinated in the doorway of his little slum church on May 11, 1974, and Bishop Enrique Angelelli of Rioja was murdered August 4, 1976. The reason for the martyrdom of the Argentine people is to be found in an economy dependent upon North American capitalism, now directed by the government minister Martínez de Roz who defines Argentina as an agricultural producer and exporter of goods. As the buying power of earnings decreases allowing more profits to foreign transnational capital, the social pressure on the class-conscious workers increases, and institutional force or violence immediately represses any attempt by the workers to mobilize. Even more regrettable, the bishops still follow a neo-

Christendom model, and they remain allied to the state and the upper classes in spite of the crisis that exists among the upper class and the suffering endured by the lower classes. The hierarchy condemns the guerillas as the source of all evils and are oblivious to the fact that they are the product of previous and continued social and historical injustice. It is not hard to see why the Argentine episcopal delegation assumed the stance it did in Puebla or why it was considered by most observers and participants to be the most conservative group present.

In Chile the bloody coup of September 11, 1973, violently ended the only socialism ever established by a free democratic election. The repression that followed was unparalleled in all of Latin America. A veritable "massacre theology" has guided the military, many of whom claim to be Christians.[388] Two days after the coup the Chilean hierarchy issued an unfortunate statement entitled "Christian Faith and Political Action," which condemned the Christians for the Socialism movement at the very time when many of those Christians were being killed, jailed, tortured, or exiled. The document was influenced by Christian Democracy, ever dear to many of the Chilean hierarchy. The bishops were then obligated to condemn Allende's Popular Unity in particular and Marxism in general in order to gain some autonomy from the new dictatorship.[389] Some of the bishops, such as Tagle of Valparaíso, Fresno of La Serena, Vicuña of Puerto Montt, and Valdés of Osorno, publicly supported the military Junta, but others such as Camu, the episcopal secretary, and Hourton, Ariztía, González, and Piñera were more restrained. Cardinal Silva Henríquez held to a middle position, which displeased the new government a great deal since it needed and sought his support. But the Cardinal refrained from criticizing openly the Junta. The Cooperation Committee for Peace, directed by Bishop Ariztía in the name of the episcopacy, and the Lutheran Bishop Helmut Frenz, along with Father Salas, SJ, became irritating to the regime. After great pressure the Committee was dissolved and another body, the Vicarate of Solidarity, was formed. These institutions are a sign that the Church maintained a relative independence from the totalitarian state. But the Chilean Church desires its independence because it looks forward to a triumph of Christian Democracy over the dictatorship and because of its commitment to the poor. The same is true in Brazil, El Salvador, and Bolivia. In any criticism leveled against the Chilean regime the hierarchy has not moved beyond the traditional commitment to a "new Christendom." Thus the members of the old Popular Unity have changed their mind on the historical function of the Church in Latin American society.

In Peru the situation never degenerated to the atrocious level that was characteristic of Chile or El Salvador. Yet since 1975 the government has tended more and more toward a fascist dependent authoritarianism. The Forty-second Episcopal Assembly (January 1973) represented a weak attempt to promote the popular Church model: "The Church's liberating mission is the efficacious announcement of the Gospel. It means hope for all men, especially those who suffer injustice, for the poor and the oppressed."[390]

Peru suffered particularly from the crisis of capitalism, mainly because of the rigorous monetary policy of the International Monetary Fund, which served the interests of international finance. Velasco Alvarado had to submit to North American demands after his reformist revolution suffered a setback, and the people were repressed when they protested their suffering. The popular Church, even though it was a minority, was active in these struggles of the people. The hierarchy came under pressure from the State but declared: "We renew our commitment and fidelity at a time when the Medellín tradition is in danger of being forgotten."[391] Some Peruvian bishops, theologians, and laypeople were to take a progressive stand in Puebla.

In El Salvador, as in Nicaragua and Honduras, the military dictatorship became more repressive, and the condition of the people progressively worsened. The Episcopal Secretariate of Central America presided over by Bishop Obando Bravo, who incidentally was not chosen to attend the CELAM meeting in Puebla, stated on June 24, 1977: "We deeply regret that in order to silence the socially committed who are faithful to Christ and to the Gospel, the easy expedient is used of calling them communists, subversives, followers of exotic doctrines, ... all in flagrant violation of human rights."[392]

Peasants were shot and killed in 1974 at San Francisco Chinamequita, La Cayetana, Tres Calles, Santa Bárbara, and in the main square of San Salvador, as well as in many other places. Archbishop Chávez exclaimed, "Here coffee consumes men," referring to the exploitation of laborers by landlords. Father Rutilio Grande, pastor in Aguilares, was murdered on March 12, 1977. He is a symbol of this period in El Salvador's history, but he was not the only martyr. The priests Alfonso Navarro, Barrera Motto, and Octavio Ortiz were also killed on May 11 and November 28 of the same year, and on January 20 of the following year. Many laypersons died with them: for example, along with Father Ortiz the army murdered David Caballero, age 14; Angel Morales, age 22; Roberto Orellana, age 15; and Jorge Gómez, age 22.[393]

Monseñor Oscar Romero was named Archbishop on February 22, 1977, and at once manifested a courage rarely seen in the Church in defense of his people against the military regime and its paramilitary forces. The bishops declared on March 5, 1977, "This situation is one of collective injustice and institutionalized violence."[394] Even so the contradictions should not be overlooked. On the day of Father Grande's funeral, when Bishop Romero was asking the procession to proceed slowly toward soldiers blocking their way with bayonets, Bishop Pedro Aparicio was defending the government and criticizing his priests and laity in the meeting of the Synod in Rome. But in El Salvador both the model of neo-Christendom and that of the popular Church are operative. Bishop Romero has said that "the Church is being forced back to the time of the catacombs." Indeed the primitive Church could not appeal to the state for pastoral aid nor ally itself with the upper classes. Neither can the Church in El Salvador.

(2) The Church under formal bourgeois democracies (Colombia, Mexico)

In Colombia the military has recently increased its influence on the civilian government, but the military power and control is not as evident there as it is in Uruguay. In accordance with the national agreement between the Colombian Conservative and Liberal parties, the office of president passed from Misael Pastrana to Alfonso López in 1974, and to Julio Turbay in 1978. The Church faithfully followed the guidelines of neo-Christendom and continued to legitimate the system. Only since 1978 has the Church become somewhat critical.

Polarization within the Church, however, has sharpened. Father Domingo Laín died in a guerrilla action with the National Liberation Army (ELN) in 1974, but on June 26, 1975, the Cardinal was awarded the Order of Antonio Nariño by the military during the declaration of a state of siege and was made an honorary general in the Colombian army in June 1976. The most condemnatory document of the decade was issued by the Colombian bishops: "Christian Identity in Action for Justice," November 21, 1976, which named and denounced persons, journals, and movements. Some believe that it was an essay preliminary to the Working Paper for the Puebla meeting. In "Christian Identity" the bishops attributed the many problems in the Colombian Church to the young priests and others who though working with the poor were being influenced by "outside forces."[395] Are Colombian priests and theologians really so naive? Or does the real problem lie with foreigners who refuse to recognize structural injustice in the capitalist system as the cause of so much popular unrest and of the commitment of priests and laypeople to the poor?

Two Church models are obviously in conflict in Colombia. While most bishops maintain the perspective of neo-Christendom, some priests and religious have begun to implement the model of the popular Church. And even the hierarchy appears somewhat uneasy with its alliance with the upper classes. If the government becomes a military, national-security type dictatorship, many churchmen will support it. Colombia is less likely to become a more popular social democracy. At any rate, no easy future lies ahead for the Church, and the people receive no clear witness regarding the poor nor a commitment to their cause.

In Mexico the situation is quite different. The bishops' message on "Christian Commitment and Social and Political Choices," October 18, 1973, was surprisingly forthright.[396] Unfortunately, however, nothing else resulted, primarily because of lack of concern for the situation of the workers and peasants. The only real conflict between the Church and State was over the obligatory use of textbooks provided without cost to all schools, including the Catholic schools, many of which educate children of the bourgeoisie. The controversy has subsided, and the texts are only in partial use in private schools.

The rapid construction of the new Basilica of Our Lady of Guadalupe with government aid and under the tutelage of the largest banks in Mexico was viewed by many as a tacit reconciliation between Church and State but by others as the co-opting of the popular Virgin by the upper classes. Many diocesan and religious priests were in trouble with their bishops, and this intraecclesial infighting again revealed the existence of two models of the Church. Currently there exists an unconstitutional but undeniable understanding between Church and State according to the typical neo-Christendom model. The popular Church is, however, springing up in thousands of communities and parishes in poor urban barrios and in the rural areas. The murder of Father Rodolfo Aguilar on March 21, 1977 is an example of another kind of Christian testimony in Mexico today. Some churchmen hope to effect their witness through the power of the State, while others are determined to announce a gospel of poverty and simplicity to the poor and oppressed.

(3) The Church in a socialist society (Cuba)

The Church in Cuba is understandably in a difficult situation. Following Batista, the idol of neo-Christendom, the Church found it hard to abandon class preferences and accept living in a socialist country. By 1973, however, it had faced up to the real situation but still had trouble adjusting. Direct relations were established between the Cuban bishops and the Holy See when in March 1974 Bishop Agostino Casaroli visited the island. Cesare Zacchi became the first papal nuncio, having been named toward the end of the year, and was succeeded in 1975 by Monseñor Mario Tagliaferri as pronuncio. This contact has been mostly diplomatic and political, not pastoral or theological. Since Rome is its only input, the Cuban Church was and is still cut off from communication and cooperation with the rest of the Church, even from Latin American liberation theology and the popular Church.

The Cuban Church is too insecure to adopt socialism and too weak to criticize it. An example of its anemia can be seen in the one-sidedness in the new Cuban constitution as related to religion. The Church knows it must first contribute something to the revolution before it has the right to make demands. In the opinion of "the president of the Cuban Episcopal Conference, José Domínguez, Bishop of Matanzas, justice will come to Cuba after the economic and diplomatic blockade has been lifted."[397] The Church did condemn the attack on a Cuban airliner on November 9, 1976.[398]

The Church in Cuba, however, still does not play any strategic role in the Latin American Church as a whole, nor is it functioning as a popular Church. Unlike any other ecclesiastical body on the continent, it has the ideal conditions to embody the popular Church model by working independently with the people in their revolutionary process. But it has not done this. The task demands much moral courage and commitment to utter poverty, and a faith in the future. For if the Church looks back, it will turn into a pillar of salt.

3. The Situation in Puebla (1979)

(1) The sociopolitical context

When five men were caught in the Watergate building the night of June 17, 1972, a scandal began that ultimately ended the political career of President Richard Nixon. The ensuing moral crisis, together with the defeat in Vietnam and the economic troubles of the capitalist system, created an atmosphere of confusion in the United States. For this reason the Rockefeller interests together with members of the Bilderberg group founded the Trilateral Commission in 1973, claiming that "the international order prevailing since the Second World War" was "no longer adequate to deal with the new conditions."[399] An ideology for a new imperialism was formulated: "Although the initial problems of international character have disappeared, the prevailing feature of the present situation is the constant expansion and readjustment of *interdependence*; the control of this interdependence has become essential for world order."[400]

The Trilateral Commission "invented" Jimmy Carter and put him in power in 1975. At the time, Latin America was almost totally controlled by military dictatorships, for they were necessary to provide police security for transnational expansion after the failure of CEPAL developmentalism. But these military governments in a burst of hyper-nationalism plunged their countries into such poverty that they were no longer a viable international market. Trilateral Developmentalism (a new form of capitalist expansion for controlling a new unavoidable crisis) had clear ideas about some aspects of Latin America's future.

As far as politics were concerned, social democracies were to be strengthened. Balanguer was prevented from succeeding himself as president in the Dominican Republic and was forced to respect democratic rules. In June 1978 he stepped aside for the election of Antonio Guzmán. Pereda Asbún in Bolivia was defeated in 1979 by a more nationalistic government calling for new elections. In Peru the International Monetary Fund changed the rules of the game for the first time in March 1979, and the American Popular Revolutionary Alliance (APRA) won a relative majority. Elections were promised in Ecuador. In Nicaragua attempts were made to substitute a social democracy for Somoza whose regime finally collapsed in July of the same year. Representatives of Christian Democracy in Chile began to speak out for the first time since 1973. Even Uruguay was thought to be stable enough for a return to democracy.

In Brazil the opposition to the military asserted itself more, and the U.S. State Department defended all this as a part of its program for human rights.

From the economic viewpoint, the capitalist system may be entering a new phase of expansion through the creation of wider national markets. This plan is seen as a respite, if only temporary, from its troubles. Jimmy Carter said during his electoral campaign in Chicago in March 1976: "We should replace [Kissinger's] policy of the balance of power with one of world order."

(2) The Church context

The history of the Third Bishops' Conference in Puebla may be said to have begun in 1973. Early in that year it was reported that "observers have noted statements made by Bishop López Trujillo, the new Secretary General of CELAM, in Río de Janeiro at the beginning of this year to mean there may be no Third Conference for the present."[401] During the same period there was talk about valid and invalid interpretations of Medellín. One Mexican bishop said: "The talk about Medellín is different from what really happened; if read carefully, Medellín commitments do not require the Church to side with the poor."[402] But a new ideological base had to be established in order to ignore Medellín.

On November 30, 1976, CELAM was charged with organizing the Third Bishops' Conference, the beginning of a long journey which would end February 13, 1979. The two-year period of preparation allowed the Church in Latin America — and later in Europe, North America, and even in Africa and Asia — to recognize the importance of the event. This preparatory period can be divided into four segments: (1) the convocation until the appearance of the Working Draft, November 1976 to November 1977; (2) the appearance of the Working Draft until the final countdown, November 1977 to September 1978; (3) the final countdown until the opening of the Conference, September 1978 to January 27, 1979; and (4) the Conference itself, January 27 to February 13, 1979. The third stage was unforeseen and was due to the deaths of Popes Paul VI and John Paul I (August 6 and September 29, 1978, respectively), and the election of John Paul II. If the delay had not occurred, allowing for the details of the organization to become public and be assessed, the results of the Conference might well have been different.

The Secretary General, Bishop López Trujillo, along with others, doubtless conceived a plan to give the meeting a conservative orientation, and they hoped that this direction would be maintained. During the first stage their intentions were not clear, but there were several indications. The document "Christian Identity" issued by Colombian bishops, November 1976, and the conclusions of a meeting of laypersons in Buenos Aires, July 2 – 8, 1977, revealed the prevailing motif, namely, that the change in Latin America from a rural society to an urban industrialized one would best follow the capitalistic pattern. Thus began the thread of Adriana. The "bases" began to organize when they discerned what was happening, and they awaited the publication of the Working Draft.

Their suspicions proved to be well-founded. The long, 1,159-paragraph text ran counter to the Medellín Conference, presupposed a developmentalistic, even trilateral, theoretical framework, and was quite restrained if not ambiguous in its condemnation of transnational firms, national-security regimes, and the violation of human rights. In January 1978 there began the most important counteroffensive in the history of Latin American theology. Not only did theologians take part, but also bishops, groups of bishops, priests, religious, base communities, peasants, and Indians. It was an unplanned, spontaneous act of repudiation of the Working Draft. Two brief alternative documents appeared, "Contributions to Reflection" by a team in Northeast Brazil led by Bishop Marcelo Pinto Carvalheira, and "Good News: Birth of the Church in Latin American People" by a group in Venezuela.

Also, important theologians, pastors, and lay Christians in Europe, North America, Africa, and Asia supported the direction initiated by the bishops in Medellín and cautioned against any deviation from it in Puebla, a unique experience for the prelates and the first of its kind in the history of the Latin American Church. The "Memorandum" by German theologians issued in November 1977 was the first of several to appear. Other French, Spanish, Italian, North American (including Chicano bishops), and Canadian theologians followed suit as did over seventy theologians from Asia and Africa meeting in Colombo, Sri Lanka, shortly before the Puebla meeting. The explanation for this worldwide reaction was that the decisions made in the Puebla Conference would affect, directly or indirectly, the orientation of the Church on other continents. Also, the Christian population is shifting toward Latin America. In 1975 America surpassed Europe in the number of Christians, and Latin America will soon contain over half of all the Catholics in the world.

The protests against the Working Draft produced results.[403] Cardinal Aloisio Lorscheider personally assumed responsibility for the writing of the document, but with ample collaboration. Still, no liberation theologians were allowed to participate in the official preparation of the text. It was as if Karl Rahner, Yves Congar, and other prominent European theologians had been excluded from the Second Vatican Council. Of course, certain reactionary factions did try to exclude them, but John XXIII staunchly and prophetically defended the openness and freedom of the European Church. No such statesmanship was evidenced in Latin America. But the delay in opening the Puebla meeting resulted in numerous leaks and disclosures about the additions and exclusions that took place during the preparations.

Confrontation was, therefore, inevitable in Puebla. The bishops were divided by class loyalties, different ideologies, and even national blocs. Some wanted the Conference to condemn their version of the "popular Church," liberation theology, the so-called parallel magisterium, and Marxist social analysis. Others supported the Church's experience in the base communities and identification with the poor, and espoused the denunciation of national-security regimes, transnational economic expansion, and the violation of human rights. The delegations from Argentina, Colombia, Mexico, and finally Venezuela formed a conservative bloc in Puebla. The Brazilian bishops and those from Peru, Central America, the Caribbean, and Ecuador, as well as others, defended the Church's commitments to the repressed people of the continent.

(3) The Third General Conference of Puebla (January 17 — February 13, 1979)[404]

The arrival of Pope John Paul II in Santo Domingo on January 25, two days prior to the beginning of the conference in Puebla, attracted worldwide attention. During his trip to and from Mexico the Pope gave over forty addresses, sometimes arousing heated commentaries and obliging the bishops to make a careful exegesis. Although officially excluded from the Conference, the liberation theologians were invited by several bishops as consultants, and their presence was felt at once. On the very afternoon of the first session, a sixteen-page commentary on the Pope's inaugural address was already available to the bishops.

In his speeches, the Pope gave no substantial support to the old idea of Christendom.

He said nothing to imply that the Church should be situated in political society, allied with the upper classes, or dependent on the state in its pastoral function. Naturally, the politicians and power brokers, the bankers and the Mexican bourgeoisie, were surprised and perhaps frightened by the Pope's popular appeal, and they interpreted his words as the neo-Christian model. Within a few days, however, it became clear that he was supporting neither capitalism nor condemning socialism, but rather demanding freedom for the Church and its mission under both systems. His meaning was not quickly grasped, but of the words that found their way into the final Puebla Document, those of John Paul II are the most pastoral passages and clearly express the support for the poor.

There will be no attempt in this summary to describe the events in Puebla day by day, to give the constituency and responsibility of each commission, to discuss the four distinct revisions of the Final Document, nor to mention the times of extreme tension — such as the publication of the letter of Monseñor Alfonso López Trujillo to Monseñor Luciano Méndez, a communication that caused something of a sensation and the authenticity of which has not been questioned. What we will attempt to give is a series of reflections on the final text of the Puebla Document, believing that it is possible to derive certain conclusions regarding the Document itself and at the same time make some observations regarding the development of the Conference.

The groups that attempted to condemn the popular Christian movements, the base communities, the "popular Church," the Latin American theology of liberation, and the so-called parallel magisterium failed in their objective and were completely defeated — at least in the Conference. Those who attempted to muffle the voice of the Latin American Church in order to avoid being made uncomfortable by its denunciations achieved their ends, because in the last analysis little was said at Puebla that was not later neutralized to a large extent by compromise. The Puebla Document was, therefore, distinct from that of Medellín. For even though there were many sections of the Medellín statement that lacked clarity, none was weak, insipid, or inarticulate. Furthermore, the real losers, namely, the popular groups, the base communities, the theologians of liberation and the prophetic bishops, took control of the situation and evidenced a faithfulness to the Church that enabled them to leave Medellín strengthened and encouraged. One can observe, therefore, that in the last analysis Medellín was the point of departure and inspiration, and Puebla can be regarded as a continuation. Puebla was not nearly so original as the Second Bishops' Conference, but it followed the same direction, which in itself is significant and to a certain degree was unexpected. The door remains open, therefore, for Christians to continue supporting the interests of the people, the poor, and the oppressed.

One should note, for example, certain selections from the Final Document. These of course are only brief passages indicative of what took place. The material of the 22 commissions together with the Inaugural Message is now divided in the following way:[405]

Message to the Latin American People.

First Section. The Pastoral Perspective on the Latin American Reality (Commission 1) (Par. 1 — 161).

Second Section. God's Purpose and the Latin American Reality (Par. 162 — 562).

Chapter 1. The Content of Evangelization (Commissions 2, 3, and 4) (Par. 165 — 339).

Chapter 2. What is Evangelization? (Commissions 5, 6, 7, and 8) (Par. 340 — 562).

Third Section. Evangelization in the Latin American Church: Communion and Participation (Par. 563 — 1127).

The Inaugural Message indicated the continuity already existing between Medellín and Puebla and clearly underlined the ecclesiastical responsibilities "to the People of God in Latin America." "People" (*pueblo*) is the most frequently used word in the whole Document, together with the phrase "the Latin American People" or the "People of God," both of which are characteristic of *Lumen Gentium* of Vatican II. The word "nation" is rarely used, and even less frequent is the word "state." Because love, love for the poorest of God's children, is the beginning of Christianity, the Conference opened with an act of repentance:

For all of our faults and limitations, we — even we pastors — beg forgiveness from God and from our fellow human beings in the faith and all of humanity. The values of our culture are being threatened. Basic human rights are being violated. We therefore invite everyone, without class distinction, to accept and to assume responsibility for the cause of the poor as if it were your own cause and the very cause of Christ himself. "I tell you solemnly, in so far as you did this to one of the least brothers of mine, you did it to me" (Mt. 25:40).[406]

One may observe that the bishops emphasize the *position* of class as taking up the cause of the oppressed, as over against every class *situation*, when they say "without class distinction." The Message concluded with a hymn as it were to the "civilization of love" — an expression of Paul VI — the civilization that stands as the ideal for all historical civilization, the eschatological utopia of a community without divisions or contradictions. This was essentially a Christian proposition within the utopian tradition of the prophets and of Jesus, which was raised as an objection against antiutopian Christians and reformists who pinned their hopes on overhauling the current systems: "God is present and living — in Jesus Christ the liberator — in the heart of Latin America."

In the introductory text, the triumphalism of the second revision allowed for a perspective somewhat more variegated:

Intrepid strugglers for justice, evangelists for peace such as Antonio de Montesinos, Bartolomé de las Casas, Juan de Zumárraga, Vasco de Quiroga, Juan del Valle, Julián Garcés, José de Anchieta, Manuel Nóbrega, and many others defended the Indians against the *encomenderos* and the conquistadores, even to the giving of their lives as did Bishop Antonio Valdivieso. (Par. 8.)

This is in reality a new perspective of our history. The often-repudiated Bartolomé de las Casas has now been consecrated, not only by Puebla, but earlier by the Pope himself. At last Father Bartolomé has been vindicated, and this was necessary before asking forgiveness for the Church's legitimating of the Conquest. And before recognizing the sin of the Conquest, it was possible to exalt the heroes and saints.

For the first time in history reference was made to the role of women in the life of the Church (Par. 9). Of course there are certain ambiguous passages and phrases such as "our radical Catholic substratum" (Par. 1). But when the current Latin American reality was discussed, the document clearly stated that "we discover that this poverty is not a transitory stage, but rather it is the result of economic, social, and political situations and structures which produce this state of poverty" (Par. 30). Also for the first time the indigenous peoples along with the "Afro-Americans" were said to be suffering the most abject poverty; they are the poorest of the poor (Par. 34). Their situation was described with new phrases that complemented those of Medellín, for example, "institutionalized injustice" (Par. 46).

Of course the terciary position, the economy of the free market, and "Marxist ideologies" were evident.[407] But the ideology of "national security" was repeatedly condemned (Par. 49), together with a warning against the "economic, technological, political, and cultural *dependency*" (Par. 66).[408]

The subjects of personal and social sin along with the mechanisms and structures that contribute to individual and collective evil were repeatedly referred to in very specific terms. "We should be aware that in the deepest of them [the roots of injustices] there exists the mystery of sin" (Par. 70). "The *causes* of this unjust situation are multiple, but the root of all of them is to be found in sin, not only personal and individual evil, but also the evil of the unjust structures themselves" (Par. 1258).[409] "The anguish, suffering, and frustration which have been caused — if we observe in the light of faith — by sin has personal as well as enormous social dimensions" (Par. 73). The bishops likewise called upon the Church to cease being a tool of the State or part of the political society, and to commit itself to the poor as part of civil society. "The Church should continually become more independent of the powers of the world in order to take advantage of the freedoms that exist which allow for the completion of her apostolic labor without interference" (Par. 144). The model to be followed was that of the Brazilian Church and not that of the Colombian or Argentine Church.

Such independence can only be achieved, however, by recognizing and emulating "the evangelical value of poverty which makes us vulnerable to all people of God" (Par. 8), and which allows us to commit ourselves to the dispossessed and disenfranchised sectors" of society (ibid.). The bishops condemned certain simplistic Christologies that have identified Christ as a revolutionary or political leader, as well as theoretical and hypothetical rereadings of the Gospels (Par. 178ff.). In this regard the theology of liberation is not only in agreement with but has functioned as the vanguard of this very position. Unfortunately, however, the "political function" of the prophetic and priestly work of Christ was not made clear. In view of this fact and because this section of the Final Document was rather superficial, the better features of Latin American Christology were not examined. Yet certain familiar themes were repeated such as "the liberation of the people from Egyptian slavery" (Par. 187) and the declaration of Christ in Luke 4:18, along with others, were noted — passages that have become central in the formulation of the Latin American theology of liberation (cf. Par. 190).

The bishops did not condemn the "popular Church" as certain theologians have done previously. The theme is taken up in Paragraph 263 in which the following observation is made:

The problem with the *popular Church* — which has arisen from the People or through the inspiration of the Holy Spirit — has various ramifications. If by the term "popular Church" one understands it to be the Church which is attempting to identify with the popular movements of the continent — as has always been intended by the theology of liberation and the experience of the Conference of Bishops — then it arose as a response of faith on the part of these groups to the Lord.

The "popular Church" now has the green light if it reproduces the incarnation in popular ways. It should be condemned, however, if it proposes to be a Church distinct from the official and institutional Church. But it has never been thus understood by those who are committed to the poor in Brazil, Peru, or Mexico. The assertion that the "popular Church" is schismatic is simply a false accusation made by those who really desired to undermine this "incarnation in popular ways." Paradoxically, it has been these accusers who have been condemned. As the saying goes, "They went out to shear, and they returned sheared."

The theology of liberation is also free to continue and to develop. In the third revision of the Document there appears the statement: "We rejoice also that evangelization is not benefiting those constructive aspects of a theological reflection on liberation such as that which emerged in Medellín."[410]

Although this phrase was eliminated from the final text of Par. 375, another statement remained that was equally positive:

The theologians [of Liberation] offered an important service to the Church: systematizing the doctrine and the directions of the magisterium in a synthesis of the broader context, translating it into a language adapted to the times, submitting to a new investigation the acts and the words revealed by God in order to apply them to new sociocultural situations. The judging of their authenticity and the regulation of their endeavors belong to the authority of the Church, to those who are repsonsible for not quenching the Spirit, but for testing all and retaining that which is good (cf. *Lumen Gentium* 12) (Par. 375).

This was not a condemnation, but rather the true consecration of the Latin American theology. Furthermore, Pope John Paul II in his sermon in Rome on Wednesday, February 21, 1979, declared: "We should call by its name whatever social injustice, whatever discrimination, whatever violence is inflicted on the body, spirit, or conscience of a human being. We should call by its name injustice, the exploitation of a person by another person, and the exploitation of a person by the state and the economic systems." Subsequently the Pontiff said,

The theology of liberation insists that human beings not only should be instructed in the word of God, but also it speaks of their social, political, and economic rights. The theology of liberation refers at times exclusively to situations in Latin America, but we should recognize the demands of a theology of liberation for the whole world.[411]

Some of us expected these words from the Pope. The news media, and especially the rightists outside and inside the Church, had misrepresented his thinking, for he has an extraordinary sensitivity for the poor and will understand sooner or later the profound spiritual pathos of our theology. Bishop Bartolomé Carrasco of Oaxaca, commenting on the visit of the Pope to the diocese of Oaxaca, said to us:

At a private dinner which took place in the seminary, only the bishops from the area and the papal group were present. I was sitting next to the Pope on his right. We were talking about the problems of the region, problems such as *caciquismo* (bossism), exploitation, and poverty. I sensed his feeling, what he was like as a person and as a brother. Later he asked me if I was content with my pastoral work. I replied that I was, but that the people were suffering a great deal.

At this time Bishop Carrasco became very emotional, his eyes filled with tears, and we all remained silent.

As the Pontiff was dressing for the celebration of the Holy Mass, Monseñor Samuel Ruíz, Bishop of San Cristóbal [one of the bishops absent at Puebla but who had been very much involved at Medellín] said to me that he would like to give a Bible in the Chol language to His Holiness. When Bishop Ruíz approached the Pontiff, I said to him, "The Bishop of San Cristóbal has come to present to you the first Bible translated into Chol." When the Mass ended, and we were about to leave, the Pope said, "The Bible, the Bible in the indigenous language — where is it?"[412]

The Pope said to the bishops, "This day in Oaxaca has been marvelous, and I will never forget it. I have been deeply moved because I have sensed a spiritual communion with the poor, with the Indians, with the peasants, with the simple people of God."[413] With time the Pope will continue to learn from the humble, poor, and oppressed people of Latin America.

The same can be said regarding the question of the "parallel magisterium" — which was not clearly defined, and remained an irrelevant question between parenthesis in Paragraph 687, but it precedes the statement on the obligation of the bishops to promote "collaboration between the theologians who exercise their specific gift within the Church." In a certain sense the bishops recognize that all is not ministry, and that the Spirit originates in the people of God charismatic acts — as innovative theology — that are not necessarily distinct from the episcopal ministry. This is not to say that the charismatic activity is invalid because it did not originate with the bishop. The text again confirmed the Latin American theology in its sound, relatively ecclesial autonomy.

The key text in the Final Document is the "preferential option for the poor." It speaks of the poor who lack "the most basic *material* goods" (Par. 1135).[414] It avoids speaking of "spiritual" poverty, and rather deals more adequately with "evangelical" or "Christian" poverty (Par. 1148– 1152). To the capitalistic world the bishops set forth the poverty of the prophets as a criticism: "In today's world, this poverty is a challenge to materialism and sets forth alternative solutions to the consumer society" (Par. 1152).

What are these alternatives for a society of consumers? The text does not say, but at least capitalism is rejected, and a hope for noncapitalistic historical alternatives is set forth. The question of alternatives is, of course, fundamental.

The text demonstrates a healthy *universalism* of the option for the poor: "The testimony of a poor Church can evangelize the wealthy whose hearts are fixed on riches" (Par. 1156) in the same way as it evangelizes the poor.

In short, this text follows most closely the direction begun in Medellín, which actually saved the whole Puebla Conference from irrelevancy. The text on "Peace" historically manifested in its formulation the lucidity and the love for the Church and the poor — as though it had been written by the father of the theology of liberation, Gustavo Gutiérrez, who was excluded from Puebla, the reasons for which we will not speculate on here, nor about those who were responsible. Gutiérrez was more influential than many of those who were present.

In the text of Commission 20 there is a stringent reference to the military (Par. 1247), a theme dear to the heart of one of the editors, but which in the last analysis moves beyond the Working Drafts.

The text of Commission 21 is also very forceful in stating that "there are obvious contradictions between the unjust social order and the demands of the Gospel" (Par. 1257), that the "broad hopes for development have not been realized" (Par. 1260), and it condemns the domination of the "rich nations over the poor nations" (Par. 1264), "the wealth and power of the multinational corporations" (Par. 1264), and the lamentable situation of "the isolated, the refugees, and the exiled" (Par. 1266). "In view of the sinful situation there arises the need for the Church to denounce evil objectively, valiantly, and evangelically" (Par. 1269).

One should not overlook the dozens of letters that bishops sent to their fellow ecclesiastics and Christian brothers who live under persecution and in constant danger. Bishops Santiago Benítez, Cándido Padín, Hélder Câmara, Fernando Aristía, Ovidio Pérez, Gerardo Flores, Paulo E. Arns, Moacyr Grechi, Jorge Manrique, Manuel Talamás, Adriano Hipólito, Luciano Metzinger, Luis Bambaren, Leonidas Proaño, Carlos Palmes, Luis Patiño, and many others wrote to Monseñor Oscar Romero:

We know that the Lord placed upon your shoulders the pastoral responsibility of the Archdiocese of San Salvador at the time in which the chastisement, the veritable persecution began. In the midst of all this, accused and defamed along with those who search for ways of justice, you have remained steadfast knowing that you have to obey God rather than men.[415]

These same bishops wrote also to Monseñor Manuel Salazar, Bishop of León, who was present in Puebla, but with the obvious intention of supporting the Archbishop of Managua, Monseñor Obando, another prelate who was absent:

In these days of togetherness here in Puebla we have heard the clamor of anguish and hope from the Nicaraguan people. We still remember with profound sadness and righteous indignation the suffering, the injuries, and the death of so many men, women, children, and humble, generous young people, many of whom were innocent victims, offerings to justice and liberty for all. But in the midst of this terrible pain and suffering resulting from the injustice and hurt which they have experienced, we take comfort in seeing you and others of the Nicaraguan Church manifesting such solidarity with your people as exemplary pastors who have not abandoned the sheep. We are reassured by the fact that you have denounced with prophetic valor the horrors inflicted on these same people as earlier Jesus and the prophets condemned such injustices. (Signed in Puebla, February 10, 1979.)

The fact is that the meeting in Puebla has not ended; it has only begun. And the effects will be determined by what results from the Conference. If the Christian community appropriates the good that has come from Puebla, the Church will be purified, and Puebla will be a new Medellín. We will be the ones who determine the impact of Puebla.

4. The "Letter of the Law" in the Puebla Text and the "Puebla-event"

Frequently the mere text itself — especially an ecclesiastical text — is confused with the totality of the ecclesial event that includes much more than the words of any official document. In this case the "Puebla event" is much more important and comprehensive than the Final Document. If one forgets this fact there is the tendency to elevate the Document to a place of undue significance and overlook the event that produced the document.

In reality one can say that the "Puebla-event" has only begun, as far as its long-

The "Puebla-event" (1973–1990?)

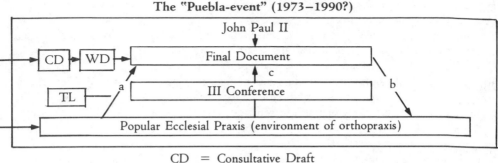

```
CD  = Consultative Draft
WD  = Working Draft
TL  = Theology of Liberation
```

term significance is concerned. The early antecedents began in 1973 when discussions first were held regarding the possibility of a Third Bishops' Conference. But the real impact of Puebla will only be seen during the decade of the 1980s. The same can be said of Medellín, which can be traced to 1959 with the beginning of the Second Vatican Council, but which continues even until today affecting the orientation of the Church. It is important, however, to understand that the Final Document, the product of the Third Conference (arrow *c*) is merely one moment and not the central feature of the whole "event."

The necessary point of reference of the ecclesial "event" is, in a positive or negative manner, the Latin American people, the Christian community, the popular ecclesial praxis. From this praxis emerged the discussion (arrow *a*), and the same "test" finally now reverts to praxis (arrow *b*). The "Puebla-event" was the product of the historical life of the popular ecclesial praxis — either for or against — but the praxis was always the point of reference.

It is for this reason that an analysis of the "text" of the Final Document can be made in two ways: an analysis of the "event" itself, that is, a thorough study of the document in order to understand, critique, and apply it; or an analysis of the Final Document as merely one segment in the historical process that has only begun.

If one follows this second alternative, the apparent contradictions in the text, rather than being stumbling blocks, will be signs of encouragement. The "text" then will become a *quarry* wherein one will know how to eliminate the inferior in popular ecclesial praxis. This popular praxis will serve as the underpinning of "discernment." It will be orthopraxis. This is not a Machiavellian misuse of the text nor an intentionally misrepresented rereading. On the contrary, it allows for the discriminate use of the better texts by the people of God and the utilization of these texts for the common good.

If this is accomplished, Puebla will then provide what the popular ecclesial praxis needs of her. When a peasant is jailed and in his defense says that the origin of his commitment is a text of Puebla, then the "Puebla-event" will be judged by those repressive groups as the cause of the subversion and as the reason for the popular emergency. This has been the historical importance of Medellín, not within the walls of the Medellín seminary, but in the thousands of ecclesial base communities, among the thousands of martyrs, in the torture chambers, and in the oppressive courts. Medellín became actualized, historical, and significant in the *popular ecclesial praxis*.

Many factors are woven into the "text" of Puebla: the innumerable meetings, the Consultative Document, the Working Document, the contribution of the Christian community, the words and intimations of the Pope, and many other important factors.

During the Puebla Conference itself, the theologians of liberation were also involved, and their voices — as the voice of the people — were heard. All the contradictions of the countries, of the classes that the Church in Latin America includes, are seen in open tension and are not resolved in the text. For some the Final Document of Puebla is a disaster, while for others it is a rich depository, a kind of mine containing an admixture of marble of superior and inferior quality, simple stone, dirt, and clay.

Since the conclusion of the Puebla Conference in February 1979, the most urgent need has been to initiate a "discernment" of what has taken place in order to formulate from the text itself the basis for a *valid discourse regarding popular ecclesial praxis* for the popular Church. Anthologies from the texts of Puebla should be published and distributed in order that the people can appropriate from the "event" what is theirs naturally even though perhaps it originated historically against the people, and even though some do not want it to be the people's. This popular "appropriation" of Puebla is the most pressing task before us.

In this respect the difference between Medellín and Puebla stems from the view that this question of popular *appropriation* from the "text" will constitute the irreversible "event" of Puebla. In Medellín the originators — CELAM of 1968 — and the conservatives surrendered the sessions as well as the texts to the more prophetic groups in the Church. Consequently there was hardly any necessity for a popular appropriation of Medellín. Medellín was born in the hearts of the oppressed.

This was not the case in Puebla, which was given birth by those who appear to have resisted the idea that the Third Conference be a popular Christian "event." The apparent intention was to bury Medellín and to consign to limbo many of the questions related to the Church committed to the poor. But this attempt failed. The "text" of Puebla, the *quarry-text*, contains many precious stones and an abundance of marble. We should avoid the historical mistake of allowing Puebla to be appropriated by the dominant classes, by the national-security governments, or by those elements in the Church that are not committed to the poor. It would be a crime to surrender the Puebla "text" for which so many in the Christian community have struggled and labored with their hundreds of meetings, demonstrations, writings, and sufferings. This "text" will not be willingly surrendered. The people have the right to the Puebla "text." They should constitute the historical reality.

It is for this reason that, assuming the responsibility of being members of the Church of Christ, we should equally exercise the right and the responsibility of "keeping the faith" with Puebla. The "realization" of the "Puebla-event" will be the first fruits in the daily lives of the Latin American Christian community. Let the Christian community, therefore, discover its role as leader. Let us understand which "discourse" of those contained in the "text" of the Final Document is consistent with our interests, with those of the poor in Christ, and with those of the popular Church.

Chapter XII

The Theological Meaning of Events Since 1962

We conclude this part with the following watchword from the gospel: "Follow me, and leave the dead to bury their dead" (Matt. 8:22). For ten years the Church has followed Jesus, and many have been occupied only with burying the dead. But as Antonio Machado says, "Traveler, there is no road, therefore make a road and walk," and little by little you will be able to follow the road that has been made. The evangelical watchword appears now to have been changed. We almost hear the Lord saying to us, "Stand erect, hold your heads high, because your liberation is near at hand" (Luke 12:28). Now it is not like it was a decade ago when the future advent was completely unforeseeable. Now the way is at least outlined, and we must *think* theologically if we are to specify thematically its *meaning*. Theologically, Latin America is being born at the time it is achieving its autonomy.

I. DIFFERENT DIALECTICAL MOMENTS AND THEIR CORRECT RELATION

In 1964 when I began writing about Latin American Catholicism from Germany, the interpretation at that time was limited. It has now been surpassed but not entirely negated, for many of the conclusions have been verified. Belonging, without knowing it, to a cultural, theological, or Europeanized Christian elite, my first interpretation contained a certain degree of alienation that now must be modified. Recognizing ourselves as part of a *dominated culture* (within a dialectic of domination) forces the theologian to examine critically his own situation and discover the level of his participation in the process of domination. In effect, the cultural elites (the same can be said of the political, economic, and religious elites) play a subordinate role of domination internally in the colonial countries, namely, that of domestication. They are unconsciously responsible for making their respective peoples a willing mass, resigned, passive in regard to the oppression, the injustice, and the hunger. The oligarchies benefit in part from the advantages of the North Atlantic powers — benefit economically, politically, and culturally. This class (even theologically) in the colonial countries is the noncritical intern of oppression. They "accommodate to the oppressor"[1] and are themselves the "sub-oppressors."[2] In the majority of cases they are the liberal-progressives or developmentalists. The alternative at all levels for them is the following: In order to achieve development (the ideal model) of the North Atlantic communities it is necessary to learn from them to overcome our political, economic, cultural, and Christian underdevelopment. Others, in contrast, fall into an equally false dialectic in which the colonies raise themselves by armed revolution in order to crush the empires and thereby take their place. This is the "infinite evil" about which Hegel spoke: the slave is now the master, the only master, the master who now has his own slave. Nothing has really changed. The situation is simply repeated.

The proper dialectic, however, is trinitarian, and the third moment is different. It is absolutely creatively new, unforeseen, and never a given. It is not the repetition or the inversion of "the Same," but rather the historical humanity.[3] The oppressor is not annihilated by the oppressed, but rather is humanized by the destruction of oppression itself and in the opening to the third liberating moment.

1. The Dominator-dominated Dialectic

The European-modern relation of domination began in the fifteenth century when the Portuguese conquered certain areas of North Africa. It is the colonial system upon which rests the European and North American culture in whose structure there is included the colony or the neocolony. The developed countries need as a part of their system the colonies that will continually be underdeveloped structurally if the relation between dominator and dominated is to continue. The suppression of the relation of domination makes the oppressed a new person and humanizes the dominator. It transforms one from an aspiring to "have more" into a "being more" person. Opulent society can never produce this type of humanism, which will necessarily be achieved when the oppressed peoples are able to suppress the relation of domination. The "new historical person" is not a slave who has become a master, rather the slave and the master become *brothers*. In this sense the process of liberation does not have as its correlative the "dependence" of the oppressed, but rather the "conversion" of the oppressed within the affluent society — which historically has only been achieved by the rebellion of the oppressed. For never will one who eats too much by his own decision begin to eat less while the one who has nothing to eat begins to move toward procuring his own food.

2. The Prophecy-people Dialectic

In the same way the prophetic-people dialectic within our "dependent" countries has produced many false alternatives, whereas the viable alternatives should be trinitarian. If Christianity is *elitist*,[4] it gives to the minorities the essential function of the process of development[5] or of progress[6] or of the integral conservation of the tradition — of the right-wing or traditionalist groups. Against this Europeanized elitism there has arisen recently a populism that, as seen in limited examples, appears to be inclined toward taking the Latin American masses spontaneously as the only authentic reality in a noncritical attitude that transforms the people into a myth. That is, populism *as a vice* "speaks much of the people, proposes symbols (in general people) who pretend to be representative in search of eliminating the elite-mass dialectic, because the populist leader or the common representative *of the people* assumes both representations."[7] Overcoming this false contradiction of elitism-populism can occur when the dialectical functions of the two moments of prophet-people correlation is fulfilled. On the one hand, the prophet — as did Jesus, the prophet of Galilee — should understand critically his own function for the people, and in view of his historical-popular role should discover his meaning. On the other hand, the people — Jesus was identified with the poor[8] — the oppressed people have interiorized in themselves the oppressor; and without a pedagogy of liberation which needs teachers, namely, the prophet, is not able to exorcise the culture of domination that maintains him as a slave. The people are not uncritically, purely authentic, nor is the prophet totally useless. The elite-mass dialectic comes now to constitute a new completeness that mutually overlaps: the people who, thanks to those who demonstrate the state of oppression, are constituted into a people moving toward authenticity (the Church of the poor). One should not think that the prophet (the consciously Christian group) realizes his destiny in contemplation or in solitary action, nor should one assume that the people have already within themselves alone the pure future authenticity. In Egypt, oppressed Israel was not in the Promised Land, and Moses was not a prophet while out in the desert guarding sheep. Moses became a prophet when he committed himself to the liberation of the oppressed people. The people became authentic when they left Egypt and moved into the Promised Land. The prophet demonstrated authenticity from within, not by imposing foreign "models," but by discovering historically the *already-given*, but germinally, the not-totally-yet given. Without prophets the people will sleep indefinitely in their oppression, their dependence, their inauthenticity mixed with a popular authenticity. Without a people the prophet is sectarianized, clearly mentally deranged — a person who is transformed into a suboppressor who solidifies the status quo, an antihuman relation of domination.

The question is not, therefore, whether the prophet will become the mass, or whether the opulent society will begin a process of nondevelopment — as some hippy groups pretend — or that the prophet will silence his voice and become nothing more than a poor individual — as certain contemplative European movements have become. Nor will all the people become prophets — which is the conscious ideal of liberal Christian progressivism, which points toward a "new Christendom" — or that the underdeveloped society will develop (developmentalism), or that a "learned" Jesus will cease to identify with the people as have certain professors of German theology. The question is whether the prophet will be a prophet in order to liberate the people. It is whether the relation of domination will cease in order that a new type of human being will be born. It is whether Jesus the prophet, the poor Church and the Church of the poor will signify the surpassing of the contradictions that are falsely absolutized and that immobilize the movement of sacred history, especially in Latin America.

3. The Past-present-future Dialectic

If in the oppressor-oppressed dialectic of the prophet-people that we studied at the level of temporality (with its three instances: past, present, and future) we could also see the gamut of attitudes, it could help us to interpret the Latin American actuality. In the first case, the oligarchic-elite of the right, integrist, defends the *past* of Christianity as an abstract ideal model. They have no critical awareness with respect to the relation of the empire-colony, and for this reason, without knowing it, their integrants are the suboppressors who desire by force, frequently military force, to impose the ideal model of Western Christian civilization on the people, but they fail to take into consideration the international dominator-oppressed structure, that of the "bourgeois North Atlantic" civilization. The integrist is a part of the inauthentic past.

The integrist of the static right has an ideology in the light of faith: the "theology of Christendom" — which we cannot analyze here although it would be of great benefit to do so. In the second case, the opposite of that just indicated is encountered in the attitude of the European liberal, the progressive developmentalist, and the orthodox Marxist. What is important for them is the *future*, but a future uprooted from an authentic past and lost in the many abstract types of utopia of liberalism, progressivism, orthodox Marxism, positivism, and reactionaryism. If integrism is a poor understanding of the "Father," this second position is also an inadequate presentation of the "incarnation," for it always falls into a dualism that separates it from the historical-people reality. The integrist accepts in part the Christian faith that rapidly degenerates into Docetism and humanism, which is not well grounded (positivism, liberalism, bourgeois or Marxist orthodoxy). All are "saving" elites of the masses, which in very little or in no way can be utilized. In fact they are noncritical with respect to the dominator-dominated dialectic. Even the orthodox Marxists do not understand the position of a developed country such as Russia. In the third case, the centrists, the majority of the people, are lost in an abstract present in that the popular "memory" is unable to discover a meaning that would permit the creation of a new future. The centrist is oppressed but does not know it because he has internalized the oppressor. His is an inadequate understanding of the "Holy Spirit," which although we all feel ourselves to be brothers, some are really slaves laboring next to free brothers. This oppressed people, people of Jesus and of the poor mystical Church, are the not-yet-altogether because they lack not only being awakened to their oppressed state, but also someone to stimulate them with what is exterior (the Other) in order to create a new historical stage.

The correct setting forth of the dialectic of the instances of temporality within those of domination and the elite-mass is that of the prophet-people: Moses-Israel and Jesus-Church; for Israel was not only a slave in Egypt but was already on the road to liberation through the desert, and remembering the past of servitude was understood by the future of the Promised Land. The prophet is one who understands *explicitly* (not necessarily thematically, because that would be theology) the meaning of the present open not abstractly but concretely to the historical past and future. None of the three is denied, and all of them are assumed synergically and simultaneously. The prophet has not received his understanding for his own perfection (Moses was a shepherd in the desert) but in order that his word — the creating *dabar* of Yahweh — might awaken the oppressed people, knowing that it could result in his death, for the prophet can be assassinated by the oppressing class that lives off of the slaves. Being a prophet is not child's play. It is violent work; it is subversive work; it is pedagogy; it is the language that explains the hidden meaning of history and that denounces, as a point of departure, the dialectic of domination. The enslaved masses, enslaved perpetually if they are without a prophet, are fertilized by the prophetic word (as the egg is fertilized by the sperm), move out of the abstract present, and understand, as a people now being born, the historic, the present, the concrete meaning of their state of oppression. The foresight of the prophet breaks first the opposition of domination. This is the moment not of reform nor of development, but of violence as the baby struggles to leave the womb. These are the birth-pangs, or, in sociopolitical language of today, it is revolution. The prophet then guides the people to their own future project. The prophet does not invent or construct a project: it is discovered in what is already authentic for the people, and it completely negates the inauthentic. It cultivates the not-yet but what will be for the oppressed. When this explicit existential understanding of the prophet is considered thematically we have the "theology of liberation." Both the "theology of Christendom," the past model, and European and utopian "progressive theology" are abstractions. The "theology of liberation" is *paschal*, historical, concrete, having in mind the fact of oppression. Faith, the popular existential mistaken understanding in which the authentic and inauthentic are mixed, fixes on an abstract present, that of "folk Catholicism," and is the point of departure in the Christian liberating process in Latin America. "Progressive theology," in contrast, joins or arranges in its "thematization" the existential faith of the progressive — which was a simple Latin American not yet alienated by his instruction. The "theology of Christendom" determines all of the process and is very much on the defensive, saving the human being by baptism, by a sacramentalism that is much akin to magic. The prophet understands *explicitly* what is implicitly the authentic part of the people's faith, that is, the prophet manifests an *existential* far-sightedness, indivisibly confounded with praxis, from that part which is constitutive. The "theology of liberation"—which derives from the "theology of revolution" its point of departure, from "political theology" its conditioning, from the "theology of hope" its future, and from the "theology of questioning" an outlook—attempts simply to arrange scientifically in a *thematic* fashion the concrete structure that is fulfilled in the prophet-people dialectic in its totality. Or, putting it another way, *it is all the traditional theology committed to a paschal movement from the perspective of the oppressed*. Paschal (*pesach*) is the "passage," the way through the desert of all human history, from the ontological sinfulness of man without salvation (original sin) to the irreversible salvation in Christ in the Kingdom (eschatological). The passage is achieved in every person, in every people, in every era, in all of human history. But the passage is fulfilled in a privileged way in certain *outstanding moments* of history: one of these could be the time through which Latin America is now passing, one when the complete eschatological liberation can be indicated, testified to, or manifested by the prophets to the people in the historical-concrete commitment to the political, economic, and cultural liberation of Latin America. Theology can never consider everything possible. It considers historically in each era those questions that are more easily clarified by concrete events. For this reason the Patristics revealed certain aspects, medieval and colonial Christendom others, and the new theology still others. In Latin America we should consider certain elements of Christian existence more thoroughly in order to explain the era that is about to begin. If this plateau is to be that of the liberation of Latin America, it is evident that an historical, concrete theology more adapted to reality should be forthcoming.

II. ON THE BIRTH OF LATIN AMERICAN THEOLOGY

The "birth" of Latin American theology occurred very recently. It resulted from the study in Europe by many Latin American seminary professors and theological teachers. Thus this first stage had the disadvantage of the relationship with continental thinkers, which led the Latin Americans to "repeat" as theology what they had studied in Europe, namely, an abstract theology. The second stage began when courses of study were organized under the unifying and universalizing direction of CELAM, which required the Latin American professors at least to be aware of all of their own continent. What began to appear was not a Latin American theology, but rather a Europeanized abstract theology that began its transition to the concrete by discovering the real level of what is Latin American. This transition was not primarily theological but sociological, at times even sociographical, one which at first could only take rudimentary steps. The importance of these sociological investigations, however, became increasingly evident: those of FERES under the direction of Houtart, of DESAL (The Center for Economic and Social Development of Latin America, 1961), and somewhat later of ILADES (Latin American Institute of Doctrine and Social Studies, 1961), these latter two in Santiago. The discovery of history indicated a new step— as this work also attempts the first synthetic steps. Immediately the pastoral began to demand a more comprehensive and profound attitude: ICLA (in the South in 1961 and in the North in 1966) opened new ways for the Latin American catechesis. The Latin American Institute of Pastoral Liturgy (1965) launched a series of studies and concrete investigation. OSLAM (Latin American Seminary Organization) organized courses for seminary professors, and finally ISPLA, the Institute which since 1968 has been known as IPLA (the Pastoral Institute of Latin America), had its first meeting January 10– 15, 1964, in Puerto Rico, a second meeting in Uruguay, July 6– 8, 1964, and a third meeting September 5– 8, 1964, in Ecuador. Then in 1965 courses of study were held in São Paulo directed by professors Segundo Galilea, José Comblin, and Alfonso Gregory. In 1966 an itinerant team composed of J. L. Segundo, Ivan Illich, Henri Bouillard, and Casiano Floristán was teaching in Riobamba, Ecuador, under the direction of Monseñor Proaño. In 1968 these courses were begun in Quito on a semestral basis. The average attendance in these studies has been between fifty and sixty persons. At the same time many other initiatives have been taken in this regard. For example, in Porto Alegre a theological seminar was held July 13– 29, 1964, led by professors Daniélou, Colombo, and Roguet with more than seventy leaders attending from all over Latin America. Then in April 1967 plans were made to have a continental congress in Mexico City on the theme "Faith and Development." By July 1968 the preparation was complete, and the congress was held on September 24– 28, 1969, with 24 bishops, 324 priests and religious, and 186 laypersons present. The methodology was very open and encouraged the participation of everyone. Along the same line but with a theological-scientific objective, a group of theologians and a few bishops met in Córdoba, Argentina, in November 1970. From the meeting emerged the idea, as also occurred in Mexico, of founding an Argentine association of theologians. By 1971 the association had more than 100 members. Yet all of these developments can be seen as no more than the second stage.

The third stage, that is, the "birth" of theology not "in" Latin America nor "with" sociographical Latin American themes, but a "Latin American" theology, will come only when the ontological moment, until now hidden, is realized — that is, when the political relations of human being to human being are seen in some of their possibilities as father-son, man-woman, brother-brother, or master-slave (the relation of dominator-dominated): the *political* relationship. The awareness of theology as pertaining to an *oppressed culture* was not immediate. *Before* theology there are the prophets who existentially begin the transition; theology comes later or *afterward*. Thus in Brazil a prophetic line is visible since 1964 against the bourgeois militarist State. Another prophetic line is seen in the transition from open condemnation to coexistence with and even the defense of socialism as a movement. This tends toward the rupture and the surpassing of the dialectic of domination, and also opposition to the question of violence which, rather than a total condemnation, becomes a just understanding. The same can be said in regard to agrarian reform, that is, the Church has been discovering critically the impossibility of ignoring this dialectic of dominator-oppressed, and little by little is beginning to see more clearly — as the Conservative was transformed into the Liberal in the Second Vatican Council, becoming first a developmentalist and afterward opening himself to a posture of liberation.[9] The relationship between the Church and the world was in part thought of from the perspective of the relation of man with nature (any man before nature as such — an abstract, economic relation). The discovery that came after Vatican II of the relation of person-to-person according to one's multiple possibilities is "the political," and, in our case, the dominator-dominated relationship. Latin America is in the position of the Third World: dominated and oppressed. The dialectical suppression of this opposition is the beginning of liberation.

The theme of liberation is biblical (for example, Exod. 3:7– 8: *lehatsiló*, and Luke 21:28: *apolytrosis*) throughout all Christian tradition. In the Tübingen School it was a preferred theme,[10] and for this reason is an essential moment in the Hegelian gnosis: *Befreiung* is the dialectical movement that denies all negations of the Being-here as the first determinant until concluding in the Absolute as the result (*Enciclopedia*, sec. 36). The Marxist inversion gives meaning to the "liberation of the proletariat." The FLN (National Liberation Front) in Algeria provided national anti-imperialistic meaning for "liberation," which was explicitly described by Frantz Fanon in his work *The Wretched of the Earth*. Herbert Marcuse, among others, deals with the question philosophically.[11] The term began to be used in 1964 but without an awareness of its political implications. Paulo Freire and his Brazilian MEB (Basic Educational Movement) utilized the method of liberation as a basic component: the conscientization as a correlative of liberation, that is, pedagogically it was a "liberating education" or an "education as the practice of freedom." When the "Message of the Bishops for the Third World" (1966) and Medellín (1968) employed the idea and term "liberation" in its political sense, that is, as liberation from the structures of neocolonial domination, the question was definitively set forth. A short time later the term began to appear in the Chilean episcopal documents and thereafter has been generally used.

Theology or *thematical thinking* developed later from the prophetic commitment, that is, from *existential praxis*. In October 1968, Gustavo Gutiérrez published his *La pastoral de la Iglesia en América latina* (*The Church Pastoral in Latin America*) in Montevideo in which, although it represented the fourth type of pastoral (not that of Christendom, "New Christendom," or even of the maturity of the faith, but "a prophetic pastoral"), he pointed out that "personal faith attempts to state clearly the situation of the masses in a salvific dialogue, and attempts to avoid ignoring the masses" (p. 28). There was not an explicit reference to the political, for this came a short time later when Gutiérrez wrote his "Hacia una teología de la liberación" ("Toward a Theology of Liberation") in 1969 for the "Documentation Service" of the JECI in Montevideo.[12] In this essay Gutiérrez severely criticized the "idea of development" and demonstrated the coexistence of the theological and political idea of "liberation." He cited the works of Falleto, Dos Santos, Sunkel, Arroyo, and Salazar Bondy who also had demonstrated the domination-dependency structure at various levels. Also, it was Gutiérrez who applied this idea to theology. One should not overlook, however, the team of the journal *Víspera* of Montevideo in which Héctor Borrat and Methol Ferré began to write in regard to this question in 1969 (cf., for example, No. 7) in which there was a political interpretation of the papal encyclical *Humanae Vitae*. The paradigmatic, theological essay of Methol Ferre entitled "Iglesia y sociedad opulenta. Una crítica a Suenens desde América latina" ("The Church and Opulent Society: A Critique of Suenens from Latin America") appeared in the December 1969 issue of *Víspera* (pp. 1– 24), together with a programatic introduction on "the struggle between two theologies," in which it was said "all theology implies in one way or another a politic," in fact, in the Catholic Church there is the "domination of the poor churches by the rich ones."

All of this led, still very timidly, to the "Symposium on the Theology of Liberation," which was held in Bogotá, March 6– 7, 1970, with nearly five hundred participants. The real question, however, was still not concretized. But in a later meeting in the same city on July 24 the matter became more specific.[13] Then in a meeting of Latin American theologians in Buenos Aires, August 3– 6, 1970, the "theology of liberation" was discussed in detail.[14]

Monseñor Pironio, Secretary General of CELAM, published two exegetical articles on the "theology of liberation,"[15] and in the declarations of the Maryknoll Fathers in

January 1971, the central text of Isaiah 61 was cited: "Our mission, as that of Christ, consists in giving the good news to the poor, proclaiming liberation to the oppressed." The question, therefore, was legitimized and would have to be dealt with.

It should be pointed out that the "theology of liberation" emphasizes *the political* in a way distinct from that of European "political theology."[16] In Europe the political in theology is essentially the consideration of the social aspects of dogma (following to a degree the line of *Catolicisme* of De Lubac) together with the critical-liberating dialectic on a *national* plane of the Church-world. "Political theology," nevertheless, has not perceived the meaning of the political as the dialectic of oppressor-oppressed at the *international* level nor the prophetic-critical-liberating function of theology with respect to the oppressed masses who are oppressed not only by the State but also by institutions. Furthermore, European "political theology" is abstract and not applicable to all peoples because "the political" is not concretized for any person. For this reason "political theology" becomes in practice the instrument whereby the oppressor continues his domination (*ouk-topos:* utopian) and never senses the kind of criticism that would motivate him to attempt to eliminate the dialectic of world domination. The "theology of liberation," however, radicalizes *the political* ontologically and becomes a theology of concrete, critical, subversive, real thinking.

III. THE DIALECTIC OF THE "INSIDE-OUTSIDE" OF THE CHURCH

The fundamental question, therefore, is how to develop an adequate ecclesiological formulation, because it is in history as in the Church that the economy of the Trinity is realized. In order to understand all the inadequate contradictions that develop with respect to the Church, it would be wise to add to the already indicated dialectical moments a new moment: the "inside-outside" of the Church. It may be said that one is *outside* the dining room and yet is still within the house itself — if inside the house is the scope of reference. In relation to the house as a whole, therefore, being in the bedroom is being inside and not outside the house. Between the inside and the outside there is a "frontier," but it fluctuates and depends on the limits of the field or "world" that is being considered. At any rate, the "outside" is a dialectical correlative of the "inside," and both are reconciled in an historical totality (finally eschatological), which explains what is included. The relationship between the "Church (within) — world (without)" is fluid, relative, and dialectical, and there will be the moment when the relation is identified: the "Church of the poor" as the scope where the mysterious and Christ-like grace "reigns" and saves all men of good will. In this case the "inside" is the totality of humanity in an historic era, and the "outside" is the future. There is always an "outside," an exteriority, an eschatological remainder, for never will mankind in history be a complete totality.[17] And it is this "outside," not only as future, but also as the incomprehensible mystery of the "Other" as liberty that is expressed in the demanding word "justice."[18] The implication of this is that all of the "inside" is transparent. But it is an "outside" in another respect. And even in the limited case of the most intimate personal structure, the human being is an "outside" in regard to the creative liberty that has been put within his being.

There is no level, therefore, in which the Church can say, "At last we are 'inside,'" because this "inside," as has been said, acts dialectically as an "outside" for a more intimate "inside." Besides, to understand this specialized dialectic in relation to the prophet-people (socio-temporal), we must have adequate hermeneutical tools.

The Church as a totality functions "prophetically" in respect to the world, that is, the people. One does not exist without the other; that is, there is no "inside" the

Church nor prophecy without an "outside" world, that is, without the people. If the world ceases being outside, the Church cannot be prophetic. Obviously, in this case we are speaking of the Church as a visible institution to which its members consciously belong. Every "inside" has, therefore, a means of "belonging." Every "outside" has a dialectical means of being "before," or "in the presence of." The visible Church itself acts as a people with respect to the bishops and presbyters. For the bishop (whose prophetic "inside" is the episcopal body into which he is incorporated), his prophetic function is realized on various levels of the people outside: in the priesthood, in the community of Christians, and in the world not belonging visibly to the Church as an institution but belonging to the universal Christian Church. The priesthood (the prophetic "inside" is the presbytery) fulfills its eschatological function in regard to the community of the faithful and to the world. The Christian (whose "inside" is the visible Church) fulfills his function with respect to the world. The world (whose "inside" is the totality of humanity mysteriously and secretly saved by Christ: "All men have sufficient grace to be saved") has its "outside," also: all that is lacking and growing in future history, the internal contradictions as negativity frustrating the actual possibilities, the mythical absolutization of that which is considered relative allowing for a continuation or further progress. The function of the Church with respect to the world as such is to open it continually to the "outside" in which it may move toward the Parousia. The world tends to be closed as a complete totality, and to deify its absolutized myths unduly. The political functions of faith and theology are simply to produce a critique that will liberate the world toward the "outside" of itself, which is always a new future historical human being. Europe, the United States, and Russia all tend to absolutize as universal and unique the state of things in the opulent, developed societies. Exteriority is thereby denied and the historical, eschatological dialectical process is halted. From the Third World, especially from Latin America, a fissure is seen, a new "outside": beyond the metaphysic of the subject — which Descartes inaugurated with his *cogito* and which culminated with Nietzsche in his *Will to Power* — as the basis of the dominator-dominated dialectic that opens the possibility of a human being to whom being-as-Other is self-imposed, not fixed as a dominator but demanding justice and calling others "Brother."

From this ontological structure we are now able to judge the historical attitudes adopted by the bishops, priests, and Christians in present-day Latin America. And what is more important, we are now able to know how to discern our own attitude in order that it will harmonize with the meaning and the *making* of history.

Thus the dialectic of the "visible Church-world" is established, but the perfect identity will never be realized until the Kingdom of God comes. In history the "Church-world" will be two moments, not contrary, but correlative.[19] The attempt to identify the "Church-world" is that of Christendom. And since there is no world, no "outside" of the Church, there is no prophecy, no mission, and the Church thereby loses its historical function. In effect, the historical function of the institutional or visible Church to which one consciously, voluntarily, and corporally belongs is the prophetic-world. The institutional Church does not have as its essential finality something basically "internal," the static salvation of its members, for example, who are merely a "part" of the Church. We know that "by the Church, mysteriously, all persons of good will are saved." No spiritual gift is received privately. Baptism, truthfully, is not received; rather it is by baptism that we are received into the Church in order to fulfill the prophetic mission of saving the world. The dialectic of the "outside-inside" can be seen, but we are never permitted to fix or finalize the "inside" by defining it as a mere closed "interiority." The visible Church as a community prophetically leads the people and the culture in which it is ministering toward the Parousia by criticizing, and by opening the doors that are closed, that alienate and frustrate people, cultures, and nations. Criticism is made at all levels: political, economic, cultural, spiritual, and religious. Without the visible Church, the historico-social catalyst, humanity proceeds without any bearings and is lost in fatal dead-end streets where the accumulation of sin makes impossible the maturation of history. By the visible and prophetic Church, humanity moves, even without knowing it, toward the Parousia. The visible prophetic community, the Church, has the essential function of saving humanity as an historical concrete totality. We have seen the Church fulfilling this function in Latin America. To the degree that the Church prophetically critiques the world — be it the bourgeois or socialistic state, be it a social class or any institution — it will fulfill its role or function. To the degree that it accepts the status quo for human reasons of false prudence, which is nothing more than immobility, astuteness, or cowardice, it will sin. It is the obligation of the historian-theologian to unmask this evil in the Church. In this critique of the visible Church before Latin American humanity as a whole, it is necessary to speak, to preach in season and out of season in regard to what is first and fundamental: the Latin American *world* is oppressed. And while the relations of domination-dominated on the part of the developed world continue, the liberation of the Latin American people will be declamatory but never real. This prophetic critique is violent because the oligarchy does not want to hear it. It is subversive in regard to the established unjust order. And it places the visible Church in the position of being prophet, the servant of Yahweh, martyred, jailed, and tortured as the propitiatory victim. All the persecutions, therefore, manifest that the institutional Church in Latin America has taken the authentic path that leads to the cross: of the preaching in Galilee to the city of Jerusalem, which kills the prophets.

In the same way we can judge the attitude of the bishops. The bishop is a prophet to his priests, his community, and to his world. This dialectic, as far as I know, has never been more powerfully expressed than the day when Dom Hélder Câmara took possession of the Archbishopric of Recife. As he put it, he was "a native of the Northeast speaking to other natives of the Northeast [the first dialectical sphere], with his eyes on Brazil [the second sphere], on Latin America [the third sphere], and on the world [the fourth sphere]. A human creature . . . a Christian . . . a bishop." And he added, "My door and my heart will be open to everyone." To the degree that Bishop Câmara has been able to realize an existential identification with the community of the poor (the world), given the difficulty in which his parishoners and priests live (it is supposed that he is the "first missionary" of his diocese and not a cloistered administrator in his palace), his prophetic function, his critical-liberating function, has been that of the Servant of Yahweh. He has of course been the object of great persecution on the part of the oligarchy that dominates (as the national suboppressor) the people unjustly. A bishop should not, however, be only a father to his priests; rather, he should also be their prophet going before them and saying, as Jesus said to his disciples, "Follow me." The "episcopal body" (the "inside" of the episcopacy) should become transparent, avoiding all forms of professional secrecy and unnecessary and unproductive authoritarianism in order to open itself and allow the "outside" to occupy the interior. The "pastor-flock" dialectic has its weaknesses, namely, when the pastors form a closed body it inevitably becomes mercenary.

The priests and the consecrated are the prophets of the Christian community and of the religious world. The priestly function is correlative to the community and to the world. When the world is ignored, the community becomes a useless ghetto. If, on the other hand, the community is ignored, the priest loses the support of his people and his prophetic efforts become nothing more than activism, social or political militancy. The priest fulfills his prophetic function in the community by guiding it toward the Parousia. He fulfills his function in the world by being a believer and a Christian. It is not surprising that when bishops fail to fulfill their prophetic role God stirs up the priests, and conflict is inevitable. If all were the visible Church as in Christendom, the priest would function only "inside." But in view of the fact that the "outside" is immense, the prophetic function in the world is more necessary than ever.

The same can be said of Christians in general, whose prophetic function "outside" presupposes a real, historical, human "inside" (the basic Christian communities) and not abstract, impersonal, traditional parochial communities. But apart from this insistence on the prophetic role in the world, in the oppressed Latin American world, the "inside" becomes, as we have already said, nothing more than a ghetto. The Christian does not need to present himself confessionally as a Christian in order to guide humanity toward the Parousia. Rather, the Christian must know effectively how to function critically, liberatingly, concretely, and historically, and without appearing to be Christian (working as a counter-witness, because to call oneself a Christian does not mean that one's praxis is really Christian) he fulfills his salvific function.

IV. A SOCIOPOLITICAL DIAGNOSIS OF THE PRESENT CHRISTIAN COMMITMENT

At a concrete level one may observe in the Latin American Catholic Church — and also in the Protestant churches — a phenomenon that indicates that the situation is changing and that a new process is beginning. The process has different moments, and in order to clarify our exposition we are including the following diagram as a point of reference.

The Different Christian Attitudes from 1960–1973

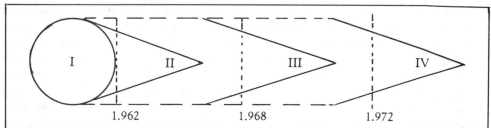

Level I is composed of those Christian groups who maintain an attitude that can be generalized as "preconciliar." These groups are comp ed of the simple people ancestrally committed to "folk Catholicism," or the extreme rightists who defend even yet the use of Latin in the liturgy or their prerogatives as the dominating class. There are Christian people, there are oligarchies, and there are ecclesiastical hierarchies in these groups. Christendom, or at least the "new Christendom," has survived with them. The present order is not questioned. Everything is as it was prior to 1962.

Level II is composed of Christians committed to development, who were referred to above as "progressives," a type now conciliar (since 1962, but principally since

1965), who were enthusiastically committed during the internal reform of the Church liturgically, biblically, theologically, and catechetically.

After Medellín, however, Church reform is seen as insufficient, and because of Medellín there has emerged since 1968 a third level composed of those who are committed to liberation, not only eschatologically, but also politically, economically and culturally, because of their insight into the reality of dependence. A result of Christian reflection on this level is the "theology of liberation." This is an advanced prophetic Christianity. The Latin American Bishops' Conference (CELAM) and the Protestant churches who are members of UNELAM all move along this line in an attempt at prophetic renewal.

Since the end of the decade of the 1960s, two new facts have become evident. On the one hand, among advanced prophetic groups, some have decidedly adopted new methods such as Marxism at the level of theoretical interpretation or the tactics of urban guerrillas as a practical revolutionary method. In this sense Cuba — and for a while Chile — provided arenas in which certain Catholic groups, among them organizations such as "Christians for Socialism" or the Protestant group ISAL (Church and Society in Latin America) succumbed to this temptation. These positions were generated as a reaction to the reorganization of traditionalists or right-wing groups that have been disorganized since the end of the Second Vatican Council — groups such as the "Short Courses in Christianity" — or by the presence of communities of *Opus Dei*. One must add that on the political level, the military takeovers of the governments in Uruguay, Bolivia, and Chile, along with the intensification of the work of the CIA, provide a clear indication of a return to the right in many Latin American countries.

All this produced *the return* of many groups — especially of CELAM since November 1972 in Sucre and of UNELAM the same year in Montevideo — toward the position prior to that of Medellín, that is, to Level II. This "step backward" lacks the inspiration of the "theology of liberation," which is regarded by many as "dangerous," and the self-censure and the open persecution at all levels of the Church against those committed to the third level, for those committed to this prophetic level (Level III) are said to be the extreme left (Level IV). This clearly orchestrated confusion permits the spread of a European type of progressivism, certainly superior to 1965 but reactionary in regard to 1973, well aware of its power, for it recognizes that it has the support of everyone on the first level, that is, of the right-wing traditionalists and the greater part of the leadership of the Christian institutions. The pastoral theological "modernization" of the progressive group, which does not criticize the status quo, serves traditionalism in defending its interest and has a certain amount of ideological structure which permits it to oppose strenuously the "theology of liberation."

Unfortunately, history sometimes seems to repeat itself. The extreme left, which disengages itself from the process or "drops out," as the political jargon puts it, plays into the hands of the extreme rightists, and the two extremes unite. This prompts us to raise the following questions: will European progressivism gain sufficient ecclesiastical power to make a pact with the extreme Catholic right, or can progressivism reconcile itself, at least as a negotiation tactic, to a popular, political, and Christian commitment for liberation? If Levels I and II unite, the immediate future will be extremely difficult for the prophet. If Levels II and III unite without losing contact with popular or "folk Catholicism," the "step backward" could be nothing more than a time lag and means of maturing whereby soon "two steps forward" can be made. This last hypothesis appears to be extremely unlikely, but not impossible. One should not be optimistic, but neither should one lose objectivity and hope.

V. THE TRINITARIAN UNITY OF CHRISTIAN LIBERATION

Two objections may be raised in regard to the exposition given here. In the first place, it would appear that an ecclesial attitude would invalidate all the others. For example, prophetism would invalidate progressivism or integrist traditionalism, prophetic violence would eliminate nonviolence, and to be a Christian would presuppose one — and only one — attitude. In the second place, it would seem that all the dialectical reciprocals or correlates appear to be bipolar, that is, with two terminals, which tends to simplify reality and above all to demand an infinite repetition without change. To these two objections, which in substance are really the same objection, we would respond as we began this chapter, presenting a tridimensional or trinitarian dialectic, and insisting that only the unity of the various moments in an ecclesial whole will prevent the historical movement from either closing or terminating.[20]

The dialectic between the developed countries, the oppressors, and the underdeveloped countries, the oppressed, has a third moment: the transformation into a fraternal, historical human being. The dialectic between prophet and people has as a third moment a "new people moving toward liberation," toward a new historical type of humanity, and eschatologically toward the Kingdom of God. The dialectic between the "traditional integrist," the "progressive," and the "extreme populist" will not be surpassed by a fourth position. Rather, it will be surpassed by the synergic unity and mutually constituted dialectic of prophet-people, which assumes the totality of the past and is open to the coming future in order to understand the meaning of the present. In the unity of the Church, the Father is not a father only (as in traditional paternalism). The Son has a real unity (not dualistic as in Progressivism) as a people who are indwelled by the fraternal Spirit (not the spirit of slavery or alienation). Historically and concretely these three human interecclesial groups can survive. Moreover, their continuation will produce a permanent correlation that will move everything. This will not prevent some from approximating more than others in their concrete experiences and through their attitudes the manifestation of the different dialectical moments which only in Christ are fulfilled in perfect unity and which heroically the saints approximated. And no one can say, "My position is adequate," although some positions will be more adequate than others to the degree that one approaches the limited, perfect, and historical case, namely, Jesus Christ. But one can, in contrast, sin against the dialogical unity by absolutizing a position or closing it to others, which impedes the realization of the effort or movement of *pericoresis* (the circumincession or interior movement of a totality in which the moments are mutually constituted in a unity).[21] All of this is well expressed in the prophet-people dialectic, both in the crossing of the desert and in the movement toward the liberation of *one* Church.

This brings us to the point of the last question. The *one* Church has one — and only one — tradition. This tradition is nothing more than the historical identity of the Church with itself through the centuries and the cultures. We use the phrase "historical identity" and not the immobile identity. For the traditionalist, tradition is a repository, integral, whose totality belongs to the past and which is necessary to preserve. Tradition is the impartial, eternal, absolute truth. For the progressive (the Europeanized or Marxist liberal) tradition serves only as it relates to a future situation, and truth tends to be converted into historical truth quite apart from the closed situation. Truth has a relation to an era, but it is hard to integrate it with the real, national, Latin American past. For the extreme populist, tradition is a "memory" of the people themselves, the customs of "folk Catholicism" that the people have maintained in their symbols and in their real *caudillos*. It is a present truth, theoretically indiscernible, and captured only in existential solidarity. The populist, in order to avoid the explicit *conciencialismo*[22] seen in the progressive, loses all sense of ecclesial revelation, because for him the truth should be mediated by the "popular conscience." Again the unitary overcoming of these different moments is explained by the prophetic understanding of truth as one historical and divine (and for this reason eternal) truth, but communicated by the divine economy always in specific situations. The truth, the manifestation of what something is (and it is revelation when it is the divine expression of the hidden being), always comes in the encounter of human personality with the historical world, with the actual situation. No one, not even God, is able to communicate absolutely without a remainder, without leaving an exteriority or a future for revelation and encounter. The living, ecclesial, historical tradition is not a static deposit. It is the historical revelation of the eternal God, the eternal truth to mankind in this world. This progressive revelation grows and becomes explicit in history. But the revelation cannot be completed in history; it would negate its very essence. The prophet understands the eternal in the historical-concrete revelation as a sign of God. He discovers the relation of the present with the past and the future. Because the truth or the revelation is historical, it is manifested as eternal eschatological Truth. If in Christ the manifestation was complete, then the total comprehension of this manifestation will be fulfilled only at the end of history and by the maturation realized by humanity in history and indicated by its prophets. The eternal Truth follows, therefore, manifesting itself historically in Latin America. To know how to discern the signs is essential so that we can know how to follow in the way that has just opened.

In the trinitarian unity of the Church each person should sincerely open himself or herself to dialogue and fraternal love illuminated by a prophetic understanding of the faith in the hope of the advent of a new person. A new historical human being beyond that of the relation of domination that oppresses all the underdeveloped peoples, beyond all historical humankind, is the final Kingdom of God. The struggle for liberation, the leaving behind the land of colonial servitude, is the hope of salvation. It signifies a new era. As a sign of God's grace it falls to us to be living at this time, and we are part of the adventure of seeing the dawn.

General Conclusions

It seems appropriate to indicate what should be the fundamental hypotheses with which one is able to interpret the history of the Church in Latin America. We know that in general as well as in particular there are many other judgments as to the best way to interpret this history and how to evaluate the reality of the Latin American Church. The history of the Church that we know, nevertheless, appears to be partial, and we do not propose to suggest theological and pastoral conclusions.

Some say that the current defects in the Church are the result of a superficial initial evangelization. But all evangelization is limited and is beset with unavoidable mistakes. As to the Spanish evangelization of Latin America one may first object to the use of the *tabula rasa* method at the level of the ethico-mythical nucleus, which really prevented an adequate understanding of Christianity from the point of view of the Indian World. One may respond, however, that the missionaries were attempting to avoid a syncretism, and, moreover, that the Indian cultures, even the Aztec and the Inca, had not reached the stage of social and spiritual development of the Roman, Hindu, or Chinese empires. On the other hand, with respect to the indigenous clergy — which was organized with great success in the Philippine Islands but not in Latin America — one can only say that this was a fundamental mistake of the Spanish missionary effort. With the pressure of the *Patronato* the Hispano-American society — which was a numerical minority in respect to the Indians — protected its primacy by not developing an Indian clergy. Thus, as a whole, the "new Christendom" of the colonial era was one of a kind and quite distinct from European medieval Christendom.

Others contend that the current state of the Church in Latin America is the result of the fact that the Church was organized too rapidly without allowing for time to evangelize the people thoroughly, or that it spread geographically to the limits of the Americas without taking root in the islands of the Caribbean or in Mexico. The fact was, of course, that the geographical expansion of the Church was one of the demands of the conquest. But likewise, the very purpose of the mission and the conquest was to civilize and convert, according to the judgment of the Spanish, all the centers of barbarism. Evidently the effort was exhausting, but it is doubtful that the methods employed for evangelization in either Africa or India would have produced a better result in Latin America, for in both Africa and India — working from the small ports or cities — the Christian missionaries never captured the heart of those continents and their respective cultures. The distance from Europe also demanded a Latin American episcopacy, an autonomous Church, and the complete conquest of the territory. All this weakened the evangelistic effort, but, nevertheless, one can observe in time the fact that from the efforts that began so heroically there are now the fruits of more than four and a half centuries.

Still others suggest that the problems in the Latin American Church are the result of a *minus valia* in the Spanish or Latin American people themselves. This suggestion of course, really confuses a race or a culture with a civilization. It is evident that the type of culture and temper of the Spaniards resulted in their losing control of the industrial world — on which the contemporary civilization is founded — and that they also lost the key to and the possibility of instruction, wealth, and comfort of material grandeur. But a poor illiterate Indian who lives "any old way" can be a sage, and a university graduate can be an ignoramus. "I bless you, Father, Lord of heaven and of earth, for hiding these things from the learned and the clever and revealing them to mere children" (Luke 10:21). "How happy are you who are poor: yours is the kingdom of God" (Luke 6:21).

The cause of the situation in the Latin America Church today is directly related to the Latin American civilization by the *Law of Incarnation*. The colonial structure of our culture, the Bourbon stagnation, the chaotic decadence of the nineteenth century, the systematic persecution by the Liberals purified but also impoverished and weakened the Church. Today it is impossible for the Church to continue to attempt to function as a Church of Christendom. It must now assume the attitude of a missionary Church.

Our Latin American Church is much poorer in power and goods today than it was in the colonial era, but it has encountered since the Second Vatican Council and Medellín the narrow way on which very few are traveling. Yet there are sufficient pilgrims that the way is being charted. "Traveler, there is no road. The road will be made by walking." The new stage, that is, after 1962, is full of mature hopes. It will be seen in the future histories as an agonizing period, as a time of struggle for the liberation of Latin America, Africa, and Asia, and as a time of discovery and formation of a new being. Latin America, nevertheless, had in its dependency upon Spain a special position: it was the only colonial Christendom, oppressed since that time by a new system devised in Europe. Because of this, today the Church leaves behind Christendom, modernity, and colonial servitude, and at least the unawareness of its dependency. Neither Africa nor Asia was ever Christian even though they were colonies. Latin America has therefore in world history and in the history of the Church a *sui generis* position. Europe, the United States, and Russia — all post-Christian and postmodern[1] — should look with special eyes at this area of the Third World, the only area that opposes it dialectically in its totality.

Latin America and its Church are awakening and hear more clearly the rich prophetic voice that creates the new; that which comes to move the people toward their historical and eschatological future, and that which appears to put into motion the dialectical movement of the countries which suffer from the neocolonial oppression of the North Atlantic empires. All of this is a "sign of the times" and of that beyond time. "Stand erect, hold your heads high, because your liberation is near at hand" (Luke 21:28).

Notes

NOTES FOR TRANSLATOR'S PREFACE

1. *Opresión-liberación* (Montevideo: Tierra Nueva, 1971), p. 31.
2. The title of his recent book (Philadelphia: The Westminster Press, 1978).

NOTES FOR CHAPTER I

1. See the final part of Appendix I for a fuller discussion of the methodological question.
2. This has been translated from the Spanish. Cf. Chilperic Edwards, *The Hammurabi Code: and the Sinaitic Legislation* (London: Watts & Co., 1921), p. 46: "... by my wisdom are they sheltered. That the strong may not oppress the weak; that the orphan and the widow may be counselled. ..." — Tr.
3. *Brevísima relación de la destrucción de las Indias* (Buenos Aires: EUDEBA, 1966), p. 36. For a synthesis of the historical perspective, cf. my *Ethics and the Theology of Liberation*, trans. Bernard F. McWilliams (Maryknoll, NY: Orbis Books, 1978); and for a philosophical perspective cf. my *Para una ética de la liberación latinoamericana*, 3 vols. (Buenos Aires: Siglo XXI, 1973–1974).
4. From the works of Alvaro Jara, Pierre Chaunu, and Oswald Sunkel.
5. *Nueva política comercial para el desarrollo* (México: Fondo de la Cultura Económica, 1966), p. 30. If there is added to these amounts "the deterioration of the relation of prices" (ibid., pp. 21ff.) between the raw materials and the manufactured products, then the so-called underdeveloped countries simply have been despoiled, expropriated, and robbed. From the report by CEPAL (UNESCO) there has emerged the socioeconomics of dependency elaborated in the works of Celso Furtado, Helio Jaguaribe, Fernando Enrique Cardoso, Enzo Faletto, Theotonio dos Santos, André Gunder Frank, and F. J. Hinkelammert in Latin America, of Samir Amin in Africa, and of Europeans such as Arghiri Emmanuel and Charles Bettleheim. Cf. the bibliography prepared by CEDIAL in *Desarrollo y revolución, Iglesia y liberación (Bibliografía)* (Bogotá, 1971-1973), Parts 1 and 2.
6. In the presidential elections in Argentina on September 23, 1973, Buenos Aires, the Federal Captial, gave the candidate of the workers, farmers, and marginalized people only 42% of the votes while the poorer provinces of the Northeast (Jujuy, Salta, Tucumán, Santiago del Estero, Catamarca, and la Rioja) more than 75%. The great capitals in Latin America — Mexico City, Guatemala City, Bogotá, Lima, Buenos Aires, Santiago, and Caracas, as well as São Paulo — all manifest the phenomenon of internal *dependence*.
7. *Three Essays on the Theory of Sexuality*, trans. James Strachey (New York: Basic Books, 1962). *Drei Abhandlungen zur Sexualtheorie* 3:4; *Sigmund Freud Studienausgabe* 5 (Frankfurt: Fischer, 1972): 123. Freud's error consisted in confusing the "reality of masculine domination" in society with the "reality of sexuality."
8. *Encomenderos* (from *encomendar*, to entrust), for which there is no adequate English equivalent, were Spanish conquerors and colonists who by gaining favor with the king were awarded tracts of land in the New World along with being entrusted (*encomendados*) with the

Indians who lived on those lands. The *encomendero* was responsible for the physical and spiritual well-being of his charges and had the right to exact certain work from them. It was a system vulnerable to the exploitation of the Indians. Cf. Hubert Herring, *A History of Latin America* (New York: Alfred A. Knopf, 1968), p. 186. — Tr.

9. *Archivo General de Indias* (Sevilla), Audiencia de Guatemala 156.

10. Cf. my *Para una ética de la liberación* (1973), 1:137ff.

11. Domingo F. Sarmiento, *Facundo* (Buenos Aires: Losada, 1967), p. 51. *Life in the Argentine Republic in the Days of Tyrants: or Civilization and Barbarism*, trans. Mrs. Horace Mann (New York: Hafner Books, 1966), p. 42.

12. Such is the meaning of *Realität* for Martin Heidegger, *Being and Time*, trans. John Macquarrie and Edward Robinson (London: SCM Press, 1962), pp. 244–56.

13. An expression used by F. W. J. Schelling in *Einleitung in die Philosophie der Mythologie*, 24; *Werke*, ed. Schröter (München: Becksche, 1959) 5:748: *transmunden*, although not in the same sense. *Beyond* being and the world one encounters "the Lord of being" (*der Herr des Seins*), ibid.

14. Xavier Zubiri, *Sobre la esencia* (Madrid: Sociedad de ediciones, 1963), p. 395: "Reality is like something which belongs to you. It is something actualized in intelligence; it comes to us intellectually, as belonging to us *before* (*prius*) being present with us." In the same sense *Autrui* (the Other) for Emmanuel Levinas is the real beyond the Totality of being. Cf. Levinas, *Totality and Infinity*, trans. Alfonso Lingis (Pittsburgh: Duquesne Press, 1969). Cf. my *La dialéctica hegeliana* (Mendoza: Ser y tiempo, 1972), pp. 141ff.

15. *Civ. Dei* XV, 1. In the *City of God* Augustine posits two fundamental biblical categories: totalization, which is based on auto-erotic love (*libido*), and detotalization, which opens the future as an alternative love for the Other (*caritas*). Cf. my *Para una ética de la liberación latinoamericana* (1973) 2:13–52, 66–89.

16. In Hegel it is the negation of the Difference and the entity, which as far as he is concerned is the negation of *Sein an sich* or of the Totality as original and divine Identity. Our example, in contrast, attempts to negate the alienation of the Other (reducing being to entity), that is, affirming (saying Yes to) the Other as Dis-tinct. Cf. my *Para una ética de la liberatión* (1973), 1:118ff; 2:42–52, 89–127. It is, therefore, the negation of what is affirmed by Hegel from an Exteriority unknown by him.

17. Las Casas, *Brevísima relación* (1966), p. 33.

18. Cf. my report, "El ateísmo de los profetas y de Marx," presented during the *II Semana de teólogos argentinos* (Buenos Aires: Guadalupe, 1973), and "Historia de la fe cristiana y cambio social en América latina," in *América latina, dependencia y liberación* (Buenos Aires: G. Cambeiro, 1973), pp. 193ff. Here I set forth that the prophets always began their critique of the system of sin with a "criticism of the religion of idols and fetishes" of the system. Is Marx's criticism then of the fetish of money not profoundly Catholic and Christian? (*Captial*, ed. Friedrich Engels [New York: The Modern Library, 1906], pp. 634–644 [I, 24, 1]: "Das Geheimnis der ursprünglichen Akkumulation.") And is not the negation of theology (Hegelian) in order to affirm an anthropology of the Thou an example of orthodoxy (L. Feuerbach, *Principles of the Philosophy of the Future*, trans. Manfred H. Vogel [Indianapolis: Bobbs-Merrill, 1966]), if one remembers that Christ is the Other person and the mediator between humanity and God the Father Creator? We could say, therefore, that the Latin American "theology of liberation" is atheistic in regard to the conquering European Christendom. (Do not, however, confuse Christendom with Christianity.) Cf. my article, "From Secularization to Secularism: Science from the Renaissance to the Enlightenment," trans. Paul Burns, *Sacralization and Secularization*, ed. Roger Aubert, *Concilium* 47 (New York: Paulist Press, 1969):93–107.

19. Permit me this translation of *hoí ptokhoí tô pneúmati* (Matt. 5:3) in order to distinguish between the "poor" as exteriority (the meaning given in section 5) and the "poor in Spirit" as a prophet actively and consciously participating in liberation. Cf. my *El humanismo semita*

(Buenos Aires: EUDEBA, 1969), especially the Appendix, "Universalismo y misión en los poemas del Siervo de Yahveh," pp. 127ff.

20. "He has pulled down princes from their thrones and exalted the lowly. The hungry he has filled with good things, the rich sent empty away" (Luke 1:52– 53). *Sub-vertere* in Latin means to put "below" what is "above" and vice versa.

21. Lev. 25:8– 12. The Hebrew noun *yobel* refers in the Old Testament (Exod. 19:13, 16; Lev. 25:9ff; Josh. 6:4– 6, 8, 13) to a piercing horn-blast, the instrument with which that sound is made, and by association, to such special occasions as the Jubilee-year announced by its sound.

22. "What is born of the *flesh* [Totality or system] is flesh; what is born of the *Spirit* [the Other, Otherness or Exteriority] is Spirit" (John 3:6).

23. *Je pense, donc je suis,* était si ferme et si assurée que toutes les plus extravagantes suppositions des sceptiques n'étaient pas capables de l'ébranler," *Discours de la Méthode,* ed. La Pléiade (Paris: Gallimard, 1953), 4:147– 48.

24. "Ich bin Ich. Das Ich ist schlechthin gesetzt" (*Grundlage der gesamten Wissenschaftslehre* [1794], ed. Medicus (Berlin:Meiner, 1956), 1:96. Cf. Johannes G. Fichte, *The Science of Knowledge,* trans A. E. Kroeger (Philadelphia: J. P. Lippincott, 1868), 1:96. One can still assert that "the essence of critical philosophy consists in the absolute position of an absolute and unconditioned I determined by nothing higher" (ibid., 1:119).

25. Cf. my works *La dialéctica hegeliana,* pp. 31– 121, and *Para una destrucción de la historia de la ética* (Mendoza: Ser y tiempo, 1972), pp. 75– 162.

26. Cf. my article "Crisis de la Iglesia latinoamericana y la situación del pensador cristiano en Argentina," *Stromata* (Buenos Aires, 1970), 1:3: "La comprensión existencial sobrenatural."

27. Cf. Heidegger, *Being and Time,* pp. 114– 23, 182– 95.

28. Cf. my *Para una ética de la liberación* (1973), 2:156– 74.

29. Exod. 3:1– 7. Cf. *Council of Trent,* Session VI, the Decree on Justification, chapter 6, where Saint Paul's words from Romans 10:17 are cited: ". . . fidem *ex auditu*" (Denzinger, 1963, m. 798; ed. Alberigo, p. 648).

30. This is discussed fully in my *Para una ética de la liberación* (1973), 1:42– 64, 118– 56.

31. For the relation between comprehension and praxis, see ibid., 1:65– 95, 128– 43. In my *Para una destrucción de la historia de la ética* (1973), I have discussed the same question in regard to Aristotle, Aquinas, Kant, and Scheler.

32. The theology of Karl Rahner is recognized as being part of a Heideggerian philosophy (with influences from Maréchal). Cf. Rahner, *Spirit in the World,* trans. William Dych (New York: Herder and Herder, 1968), or his *Hearers of the Word,* trans. Michael Richards (New York: Herder and Herder, 1969). It is on this basis that Eberhard Simons in his *Philosophie der Offenbarung Auseinandersetzung mit "Hörer des Wortes" von Karl Rahner* (Stuttgart: Kohlhammer, 1966), demonstrates how the *Mit-Sein* has not been clearly indicated in Rahner's thought even though he has said something about it (for example, we read in "Ueber die Einheit von Nächsten- und Gottesliebe," in *Theological Investigations,* trans. Cornelius Ernst (Baltimore: Helicon Press, 1961) 6:277ff., of "Nächstenliebe als sittliches Grundtun des Menschen"), as did Heidegger in *Being and Time,* pp. 153– 63. The point is not to speak casually of *the Other,* but to make the Other the very basis of theological discourse, and not only the divine but the human Other as well.

33. For a philosophical perspective, see the works of Levinas (above, n. 14), and of Michael Theunissen, *Der Andere* (Berlin: Gruyter, 1965), and chapter 3 of my work *Para una ética de la liberación* (1973), 1:97ff.

34. Yves Congar clearly indicates that the *locus theologicus* is everyday experience (". . . the history of the Church, in a certain sense, covers everything," "Church History as a Branch of Theology," trans. Jonathan Cavenagh, *Church History in Future Perspective,* ed. Roger Aubert; *Concilium* 57 [New York: Herder and Herder, 1970]:85), that is, revelation comes by means of historical exteriority: God is revealed *in* history. In the same sense Edward Schillebeeckx in his *Revelation and Theology* proposes "the word of God as a medium

of revelation," trans. N. D. Smith, 2 vols. (New York: Sheed and Ward, 1968), 1:33ff. In neither case, however, as in Schelling and Kierkegaard, is anthropological exteriority seen as a functional medium of divine revelation. I am not only stating that revelation through this medium is "possibly effected in the form of a human word" ("... auf die möglicherweise im menschlichen Wort") as K. Rahner states in his *Hearers of the Word* (1969), p. 155, but that it is the *poor* as the metaphysically Other who is the medium elected by God for his revelation. Moses, historically (and not mythically as in Exodus 3), heard the word of the Lord through the medium of the poor (Exod. 2:11– 15).

35. These categories are, for example, "flesh" (Totality), the "poor" (anthropological Otherness), God as "Creator-Redeemer," the "Word," the "Spirit" (alterable or different means from that of divine "face to face"), "service" (*Hadobah* or *diakonia*), etc. Cf. my *Ethics and the Theology of Liberation* (1978), 2:149– 77. The "category" is what is revealed in Christ as "constituent revelation." "What is interpreted" by these categories is the Christian *meaning* of the event, that is, the fruit of faith.

36. In *Liturgical Experience of Faith,* ed. Herman Schmidt and David Power, *Concilium* 82 (New York: Herder and Herder, 1973), in a discussion on faith, the Scriptures and poetry are treated, but nothing is said of the privileged place of faith in the Other: the *poor*; and apart from the poor, faith is nothing more than ideology and doctrine concealed anew.

37. Cf. my *Ethics and the Theology of Liberation* (1978), pp. 28– 46, and *Para una ética de la liberación latinoamericana* (1973), 2:107– 27, 156– 74.

38. Cf. my *El humanismo semita* (1969), pp. 75– 106.

39. Cf. my article, "Crisis de la Iglesia latinoamericana ..." (above, n. 26, 1:2): "Historicidad cristiana auténtica e inauténtica."

40. For the Latin American perspective see Hugo Assmann, *Theology for a Nomad Church,* trans. Paul Burns (Maryknoll, NY: Orbis Books, 1975), pp. 69– 71. A bibliography is available (also for the discussions in section 5 and 6) in *Desarrollo y revolución* 2 (CEDIAL):73– 95. This and the following theological line of thought are inspired in part by Latin American Christian praxis.

41. Cf. the bibliographical material, *Desarrollo y revelución* 2 (CEDIAL):31– 47.

42. The work of Johannes Baptist Metz is of particular significance. From his "Friede und Gerechtigkeit. Ueberlegungen zu einer 'politischen Theologie' " in *Civitas* 6 (1967):13ff., *Theology of the World,* trans. William Glen-Doepel (New York: Herder and Herder, 1969), and "El problema de una teología política" in *Concilium* 36 (1968):385ff., to his rather dull "Erlösung und Emanzipation" in *Stimmen der Zeit* 3 (1973):171ff., where he avoids the word "Befreiung" (revolution) for an equivocal meaning of *cross.* Is not the *cross* of the assassinated prophet the same as that of the *pain* of the oppressed "poor"?

43. The function of the Church as a liberating critic ("die kritisch-befreiende Funktion der Kirche," *Theology of the World* (1969), p. 117, is quite different if one is thinking of an international political critic (who demonstrates the unjust *accumulation* of the "center") and *social* critic (who demonstrates the domination exercised by the "oppressing classes"). What is lacking is the implementation that makes such a critic a *real* critic. Theology is essentially, primarily, and indivisibly ethical. Essentially it is a "political ethic."

44. Cf. Jürgen Moltmann, *Theology of Hope,* trans. James W. Leitch (New York: Harper & Row, 1967); his *Hope and Planning,* trans. Margaret Clarkson (London: SCM Press, 1971); and *Diskussion über die 'Theologie Hoffnung'* (München: Kaiser, 1967).

45. "... geschichtliche Veränderung des Lebens" ("... the historic transformation of life"), *Theology of Hope* (1967), p. 330. Moltmann suggests something such as a reactivated "professional ethic," but not as a subversive movement that criticizes the *totality* of the *system* and knows that a *historical* project of liberation should be implemented as a *sign* of the Kingdom.

46. Cf. Jules Girardi, *Christianisme, libération humaine et lutte des classes* (Paris: Ed. Cerf, 1972).

47. Cf. the general conclusions in my *De la dialéctica a la analéctica* (Salamanca: Sígueme, 1974).

48. Remember that Latin America is the only cultural continent that has been a colonial Christendom. Europe was a Christendom but not colonial, and the other colonial areas have not been Christendoms. This means that Latin America occupies a *unique* place in world history as well as in the history of the Church. From our *unique experience* it is imperative, therefore, that we develop a *distinct* theology if it is to be an authentic theology.

49. In Africa authors such as V. Mulago, A. Vanneste, Horst Burkle; the "Black theology" of James H. Cone, Archie Hargraves, Thomas W. Ogletree, Charles Wesley, and Eric Lincoln indicates the direction. Cf. Jan Peters, "Black Theology as a Sign of Hope," trans. Hubert Hoskins, *Dimensions of Spirituality,* ed. Christian Duquoc, *Concilium* 59 (New York: Herder and Herder, 1970):112−24; G. D. Fischer, "Theologie in Lateinamerika als 'Theologie der Befreiung'," in *Theologie und Glaube* (1971), pp. 161−78; R. Strunk, "Theologie und Revolution," in *Theologische Quartalschrift* I (Tübingen, 1973):44−53; and CEDIAL 2:58−72. Some European analyses, e.g., R. Vancourt, "Theologie de la liberation," in *Esprit et Vie* 28 (1972):433−40, 657−62, which assumes that liberation theology is inspired exclusively by a "Marxist method," are very one-sided.

50. Gustavo Gutiérrez asks in his brief *Hacia una teología de la liberación* (Montevideo: Servicio de Documentación, JECI, 1969) if, beyond a theology of development, a strict theology of liberation should not be formulated. A year earlier Rubém Alves in his *Religión: ¿opio o instrumento de liberación?* (Montevideo: Tierra Nueva, 1968) (ET: *A Theology of Human Hope* [Washington, D.C.: Corpus Books, 1969]) had already begun to move in this direction. Methol Ferré in his article "Iglesia y sociedad opulenta. Una crítica a Suenens desde América latina," in *Vispera* 12 (1969):1−24 stated that "there is already a struggle between two theologies" in that "all theology implies in one way or another a political perspective"; and, besides, in the Catholic Church itself "there is the domination of the poor local churches by the rich ones." Thus emerged *a new theological discourse.*

51. Cf. my *Para una ética de la liberación latinoamericana* (1973), 2:156−74. I would therefore define theology as "*a pedagogy* (because the theologian is a teacher and not a politician, nor is he occupying an erotic position), *analectical* (because the method is not merely epistemological nor dialectical) of the *historico-eschatological liberation.*" In regard to this definition see my *Ethics and the Theology of Liberation* (1978), pp. 149−77.

NOTES FOR CHAPTER II

1. Paul Ricoeur, *Freud and Philosophy,* trans. Denis Savage (New Haven: Yale University Press, 1970), p. 162.

2. Ibid.

3. Paul Ricoeur, *History and Truth,* trans. Charles A. Kelbley (Evanston: Northwestern University Press, 1965), p. 271.

4. Cf. "Chrétientés latino-américains," in *Esprit* (July 1965):3ff. (the inaugural of the *Semana Latinoamericana I,* Paris, 1964); *Hipótesis para una Historia de la Iglesia en América Latina* (Barcelona: Estela, 1967), chapters I, II, 1−2, and my course published for students, *Latinoamérica en la Historia Universal* (Universidad del Nordeste), §§ 2−5.

5. I am opposed to the view of Spengler (civilization as the decadence of culture) and of Toynbee (civilization as the "intelligible field of historical comprehension") in favor of the position of Arnold Gehlen, *Der Mensch* (Berlin: Athenäum, 1940) and Ricoeur in works cited above.

6. Cf. Heidegger, *Being and Time,* p. 99, the *Wozu* (the "towards which") or the means that is within our grasp.

7. It is the whole world of the "material vehicles" of Pitrim Sorokin in his *Las filosofías sociales de nuestra época de crisis* (Madrid: Aguilar, 1956), pp. 239ff.

8. Erich Rothacker, *Problemas de antropología cultural* (México: Fondo de Cultura Económica, 1957), p. 16.

9. Maurice Merleau-Ponty indicates this when he says that "the utilization of objects causes new cycles of behavior to emerge." *La estructura del comportamiento* (Buenos Aires: Hachette, 1957), p. 228.

10. "To enter into true intimacy with the evils of civilization will be very difficult. Diseases of the lungs do not always produce obvious lesions. . . . Civilization is this kind of sickness, and thus it is necessary that we [Hindus] be extremely prudent," *La civilización occidental* (Buenos Aires: Sur, 1959), p. 54. I do not agree with Gandhi's pessimism regarding civilization, but I believe that we can learn a great deal from his critical approach to technology.

11. In societies or groups the constituent elements of the *ethos* are exteriorized by social functions or institutions whose exercises are established in the community. Cf. Arnold Gehlen, *Urmensch und Spätkultur* (Frankfurt: Athenäum, 1964).

12. I do not agree with the distinction made by Max Scheler in his essay, "Etica," *Revista de Occidente* 1 (Buenos Aires, 1948):61ff., for the ends, the authentic ends of the will or individual propensity, are values.

13. Ricoeur uses the phrase, "le noyau ethico-mythique," "the ethico-mythical nucleus," *History and Truth*, p. 280. The Germans use the word "Kern."

14. Eduard Spranger, *Ensayos sobre la cultura* (Buenos Aires: Argos, 1947), p. 57.

15. Rothacker, op. cit., pp. 62–63.

16. Ricoeur, *History and Truth*, p. 284. He continues by saying that "the values of which we are speaking reside in the concrete attitudes toward life, insofar as they form a system and are not radically called into question by influential and responsible people. . . . It seems to me that if one wishes to attain the cultural nucleus, one has to cut through to that layer of images and symbols which make up the basic ideals of a nation" (pp. 279, 280).

17. In regard to life-styles, note the comments of Freyer, Spranger, and Rothacker, op. cit., as well as of Nicolai Hartmann, *Das Problem des geistigen Seins* (Berlin: Gruyter, 1933).

18. *Attitudes* can be referred to as the "deposited causes" of a culture, the *values* and symbols as the kingdom of "ends," the *life-style* as the "formal" constituent of the culture, and the cultural *works* as the material cause or the "medium" by which the culture is expressed and communicated. At the same time the cultural works represent the "effect" of the transitive operation.

19. Rothacker, op. cit., p. 29.

20. Cf. Miguel León-Portilla, "El pensamiento prehispánico," *Estudios de historia de la filosofía en México* (México: Universidad Nacional Autónoma de México, 1963), p. 44.

21. Max Scheler, *El saber y la cultura* (Santiago de Chile: Editorial Universitaria, 1960), p. 48.

22. Caracas: Universidad Central de Venezuela, 1959, pp. 21-22. One does not have to speak of the "preontological," as did Heidegger, but rather of the "prescientific" or "prephilosophical," as does Husserl — a point well made by Alphonse de Waelhens, *La Philosophie de Martin Heidegger* (Paris: B. Nauwelaerts, 1969). The cultured person is reflectively aware of the structures of daily life, life-styles, and values, as well as of works of art. All of these things are learned from one's origin and by one's own nature (from birth). It is not an elaborated system as such, either scientific or philosophical, but rather the accumulation of previous attitudes, those of the *Lebenswelt* of Husserl.

23. Spranger, op. cit., p. 69. Life-styles are transformed into social functions or institutions. Education then transmits and even procreates and reinforces them.

24. Cf. my article, "Iberoamérica en la Historia Universal," *Revista de Occidente* 25 (Madrid, 1965):85–95. "The new Latin American countries during the early stages of their independence were already aware that they were on the periphery of progress, on the periphery of the world which vigorously shunted them aside and which continually threatened

them with its inevitable expansion. This preoccupation is expressed in the writings of the Liberator, Simón Bolívar, and of other thinkers anxious about the structure of the recently emancipated nations — thinkers such as Sarmiento and Alberdi of Argentina, Bilbao and Lasterría of Chile, José María Luis Mora of Mexico along with many others. Face to face with the modern world the Latin American nations had to recognize the entities which would or would not permit them to become a part of the modern world as nations equally modern." *América Latina y el mundo* (Buenos Aires: Eudeba, 1965), p. 7. "This preoccupation has recently become the primary concern of our time in Latin America" (p. 9).

25. Cf. Mircea Eliade, *Traité d'Histoire des religions* (Paris: Payot, 1957), pp. 332ff.

26. In my course, *Historia de la Cultura*, I, op. cit., I deal in detail with this question, beginning in § 13 and following.

27. Consider, for example, the collection *Historia de las ideas en América* published by the Instituto Panamericano de Geografía e Historia and the Fondo de Cultura Económica (Tierra Firme). See especially the *Notes* and *Comentarios*. Every cultured person in Latin America should have this collection in his library. Included are the works of Arturo Ardao, *La Filosofía en el Uruguay en el siglo XX* (México: FCE, 1956); G. Francovich, *El pensamiento boliviano en el siglo XX* (México: FCE, 1956); Cruz Costa, *Esbozo de una historia de las ideas en el Brasil* (México: FCE, 1957); R. H. Valle, *Historia de las ideas contemporáneas en Centro-América* (México: FCE, 1960); V. Alba, *Las ideas sociales contemporáneas en México* (México: FCE, 1960); etc. All of these works were published by the Fondo de Cultura Economica in Mexico beginning in 1956. One could add to these the work of A. Salazar Bondy, *La filosofía en el Perú* (Washington: Unión Panamericana, 1960), and works such as that by Alfredo Poviña, *Nueva historia de la sociología latino-americana* (Universidad de Cordoba, 1959) — a book that also opens unknown panoramas on the level of the history of ideas — and Ricardo Donoso's *Las ideas políticas en Chile* (México: Fondo de Cultura Económica, 1946), to cite only two works which should be utilized in any serious study of the evolving intentional structures, and even more so in the study of Latin American sociology, philosophy, political science and literature in general as it was developed by many versatile personalities during our continent's history. Were not Echeverría, Sarmiento, or Lucas Alemán — all of these — sociologists, philosophers, political scientists, and historians — without being truly specialists in any of the fields we have mentioned?

28. One should examine the works in the history of religion such as Walter Krickeberg, *Die Religionen des alten Amerika* (Stuttgart: Kohlhammer, 1961), and for methodology the works of Friedrich Schmidt, Gerardus van der Leeuw, Mircea Eliade, Rudolf Otto, Wilhelm Dilthey, but within the phenomenological method proposed by Husserl and by Max Scheler.

29. "La symbolique du mal" (Paris: Aubier, 1960). This is the third section of Ricoeur's *La philosophie de la volonté*.

30. Cf. my work, *El humanismo semita* (1969).

31. There are general interpretative works that begin to indicate for us some hypotheses as to how we should proceed. For the most part, however, they lack a developed methodology of the philosophy of culture, and their investigation stops short of the desired goal. We should leave aside those works that deal primarily with the problems of Spain — from which have arisen too many Latin American reflections. I am referring not only to the writings of Ortega y Gasset and Julián Marías, but also those of Pedro Laín Entralgo, *España como problema* (Madrid: Aguilar, 1956), vols. I, II; Claudio Sánchez Albornoz, *España, un enigma histórico* (Buenos Aires: Sudamericana, 1956), vols. I, II, written in response to the work of Antonio de Castro, *La realidad histórica de España* (México: Editorial Porrua, 1954), and Ramiro de Maeztu, *Defensa de la Hispanidad* (Madrid: Fax, 1952). I would recommend instead books such as those of Leopoldo Zea, *La historia intelectual en Hispanoamérica*, in the series "Memorias del I Congreso de Historiadores de México" (México: TGSA, 1950), pp. 312-19, his *América en la historia* (México: Fondo de Cultura Económica, 1957), and *Dos etapas del pensamiento hispanoamericano* (México: El Colegio de México, 1949); Alberto Wagner de Reyna, *Destino y vocación de Iberoamérica* (Madrid: Cultura Hispanica, 1954), Pedro Enríquez

Ureña, *Historia de la cultura en la América Hispánica* (México: FCE, 1959) and his *Las corrientes literarias en la América Hispánica* (México: FCE, 1954). There are also the important works of E. Anderson-Imbert, *Historia de la literatura hispano-americana* (México: FCE, 1957); Herman Keyserling, *Meditaciones sudamericanas* (Santiago de Chile: L. Ballesteros, 1931); Alceu Amoroso Lima, *A Realidade Americana* (Río de Janeiro: Agir, 1954) and his "L'Amérique en fase de la culture universelle," *Panorama* 2 (August 1953):11 – 33; Víctor Haya de la Torre, *Espacio-Tiempo histórico* (Lima, 1948); Alberto Caturelli, *América bifronte* (Buenos Aires: Troquel, 1961), and his "La historia de la conciencia americana," *Diánoia* (México, 1957):56 – 77; Nimio de Anquín, "El ser visto desde América," *Humanitas* 3 (August 1955):13 – 27; Ernesto Mayz Vallenilla, *El problema de América* (Universidad de Caracas, 1959); Edmundo O'Gorman, *La invención de América* (México: FCE, 1958); José Ortega y Gasset, "La pampa . . . ," *Obras completas de José Ortega y Gasset* (Madrid: Revista de Occidente, 1957 – 1958), vol. 2; Antonio Gómez Robledo, *Idea y experiencia de América* (México: FCE, 1958); Abelardo Villegas, *Panorama de la filosofía iberoamericana actual* (Buenos Aires: Eudeba, 1963); Mariano Picón-Salas, *De La conquista a la independencia* (México: FCE, 1944); etc. See also the article by Ferrater Mora, "Filosofía americana," *Diccionario de Filosofía* (Buenos Aires: Sudamericana, 1958), pp. 518 – 23.

32. There are important works on the *ethos* of the time of the Spanish Conquest. See, for example, Lewis Hanke, *Colonisation et conscience chrétienne au XVIe siècle* (Paris: Plon, 1957), ET: *The Spanish Struggle for Justice in the Conquest of America* (Philadelphia: University of Pennsylvania Press, 1949), and Joseph Höffner, *Christentum und Menschenwürde* (Trier: Paulinus, 1947). There is, however, a scarcity of works on the ethos of the colonial era as well as on the period following political independence.

33. José Ortega y Gasset, *Una interpretación de la Historia Universal* (Madrid: Revista de Occidente, 1966), pp. 358, 359. An English translation by Mildred Adams is available, *An Interpretation of Universal History* (New York: Norton, 1973), but unfortunately it does not include this provocative appendix on "El hombre español" (pp. 335 – 59 of the Spanish edition) from which Dussel takes this quotation. — Tr.

34. *El problema de América* (1959), p. 41.

35. Ibid., p. 63. "In effect, does living expectantly [mean that] we cease to exist? Or does it mean on the contrary that we already exist . . . and our most intimate being consists of an essential and reiterated not-yet-always-being?" (ibid.) "To be temperate regarding the future, expectation maintains us in tense anticipation counting on that which is near and on nothing more. In view of the inexorability of the future's arrival, we know that we should be ready for anything, and in the same spirit, our being ready is pure expectation and nothing more" (p. 77).

36. A. Caturelli, *América bifronte*, (1961), pp. 41 – 42.

37. Ortega y Gasset, *Obras completas* 2:633, in the article on "La Pampa . . . promesas."

38. H. A. Murena, "Ser y no ser de la cultura latinoamericana," *Expresión del pensamiento contemporáneo* (Buenos Aires: Sur, 1965), p. 244. Murena has also written *El pecado original de América* (Buenos Aires: Sur, 1954), in which he says harshly that Latin America lacks its own culture, and that this lacking produces a state of cultural anxiety, which results in the collecting of an abnormal abundance of information regarding alien cultures (ibid., p. 252). He then describes "the great reaction during the years of 1910 and following (years of Rubén Darío, César Vallejo, Pablo Neruda, and Manuel Bandeira) which produced an abundance of counterpoint from which emerged the sound of what is truly American," especially in the works of Alfonso Reyes and Jorge Luis Borges.

39. Together with the works already cited one should be thoroughly familiar with the writing of José Vasconcelos, *La raza cósmica* (Buenos Aires: Calpe, 1948); Félix Schwartzmann, *El sentimiento de lo humano en América* (Santiago de Chile: Universidad de Filosfía, 1950 – 1953), vols. 1, 2; Víctor Massuh, *América como inteligencia y pasión* (México: Tezontle, 1955); Manuel Gonzalo Casas, "Bergson y el sentido de su influencia en América," *Humanitas*

7 (Dec. 1959):95– 108; Risieri Frondizi, "Is There an Ibero-American Philosophy?" *Philosophy and Phenomenological Research* 9 (Buffalo, March 1949); etc.

40. "The physical objects of culture" are not the same as "culture."

41. Europe and the West are not the same. When Zea speaks of "Europe on the margin of the West" (*América en la historia* [1957], pp. 155ff.), he is proposing an interesting distinction between "modernity," which Europe created (the European culture) from the time of the Renaissance and what was to be the "West," and previous and later Europe, which continues being the producer of contemporary culture (pp. 167ff.). Nevertheless, Zea fails to distinguish between civilization (i.e., the West, and this being the case, he should not speak of "western culture," pp. 158ff.) and culture. Western civilization is universal, while Europe continues to be the cradle of its own *culture.*

NOTES FOR PART 2

INTRODUCTION

1. R. Carbia, *La superchería en la historia del descubrimiento* (Buenos Aires: [no publisher given] 1929), *La historia del descubrimiento* (Buenos Aires, 1936), etc.

2. ". . . Romanos Pontifices praedecessores nostros concessorum versus dictas partes, cum quibusvis Sarracenis, et infidelibus de quibusque rebus, et bonis, ac victualibus emptiones, et venditiones, prout congruent facere; necnon quoscumque contractus inire, transigere, pasciaci, mercari, et negotiari, et merces quascumque ad ipsorum Sarracenorum, et infidelium loca, dummodo ferramenta, lignamina, funes, naves, seu armaturarum genera non essent, deferre, et ea dictis Sarracenis, et infidelibus vendere, omnia quoque alia, et singula in praemissis, etcirca ea opportuna vel necessaria facere, gerere, vel excercere" (*Aeterni Regis*, 8, 1. 1455) (*B. P. Port.*, 1:49). It is obvious that all of these privileges were given as a reward for the struggle against the "infidels," i.e., because of the Portuguese "Crusade" against Islam.

3. "Reservatus Regibus Portugalliae omnes Ecclesiae et beneficia ecclesiastica in terris a capitibus de Bojador et Nam usque ad Indos . . ." (*Dum fidei constantiam*, June 7, 1514, issued by Leo X, *B. P. Port.*, 1:98– 99; ". . . jus patronatus et praesentandi *personas* idoneas ad quaecumque ecclesiae et beneficia ecclesiastica . . . ut praefertur . . ." (ibid., p. 99).

4. ". . . ac pluriorum animarum salutem, orthodoxae quoque fidei propagationem et divini cultus augmentum" (*Romanus Pontifex*, ibid., p. 31).

5. ". . . ad Militiam et Ordines. . . . loca acquisita et acquirenda bujusmodi, nullius Diocesis existere" (*Inter caetera*, ibid., pp. 36– 37).

NOTES FOR CHAPTER IV

1. Cf. S. Cook W. Borah, *The Indian Population of Central Mexico, 1531 – 1610* (Berkeley: University of California Press, 1960), p. 48.

2. *La mita* was the institutionalization of the indigenous people by which the Spanish colonists were supposed to be regulated in their working of the Indians. — Tr.

3. Alexander von Humboldt, *Voyage aux régions équinoxiales du nouveau continent* 1 (Paris, 1804):594 ET: *Personal Narrative of Travels to the Equinoctial Regions of the New Continent*, trans. Tomasina Ross (New York: B. Blom, 1971), 3 vols. Humboldt once said to Simón Bolívar, "I believe that your country [Venezuela] is already mature, but I don't know any man who can take advantage of this fact." The explorer was speaking of the struggle for independence. Cf. Pedro Leturia, *Relaciones entre la Santa Sede e Hispanoamérica* 2 (Caracas: Sociedad Bolivariana de Venezuela, 1959):48

NOTES FOR CHAPTER V

1. Mariano Cuevas, *Historia antigua de México* 1 (México: Editorial Porrua, 1945):158— 78; A. López, "Los doce primeros apóstoles de México," Semana de Misiología 2 (Barcelona: Bib. Hispana Misiología, 1930):201— 26.

2. R. Ricard, *La conquête spirituelle*, p. 35.

3. Cf. my *Les évêques latinoaméricains, defenseurs et evangelisateurs de l'indien (1504 — 1620)* (Wiesbaden: Steiner, 1970), pp. 124— 38. The Spanish edition is *El episcopado hispanoamericano* 3 (Cuernavaca: CIDOC, 1969):74— 105.

4. Cf. the Spanish edition of the preceding work, *El episcopado hispanoamericano* 4 (1969):145— 316. This material is not included in the French edition published by Steiner.

5. *Archivo Vaticano, Ac. Canc.* 5, folio 178.

6. *Testamento del obispo de Chiapas*, given in Madrid (Atocha) in 1566. *Colección Doc. Inéd. para la hist. de México*, II, 511. The French, Germans, and English should not overlook the fact that the so-called Black Legend stemmed from the prophetic allegations of Bartolomé de Las Casas, who was himself a Spaniard. The Conquest of the Americas involved many great injustices, but it also produced some great saints. Sixteenth-century Spain deserves credit for both, just as England during the same period produced the Pilgrims and the Pirates such as Francis Drake, who was knighted for his thievery and pillaging of the Latin American cities of the Caribbean.

7. Letter written from León, Nicaragua, June 1, 1544. *Archivo general de Indias* (Sevilla), Audiencia de Guatemala 162.

8. Letter of July 20, 1544. Ibid.

9. Letter of September 20, 1545. Ibid.

10. Letter written by Licenciate Cerrato, Januuary 26, 1550. Ibid.

11. Letter of Valdivieso, July 20, 1544. Ibid.

12. Letter of May 9, 1545. Ibid.

13. Letter of 1547. Ibid. Valdivieso wrote in a letter of November 11, 1545: "The Bishop of Chiapas came to this province virtually fleeing from his parishoners to seek help in order to exercise his jurisdiction which he had not been permitted to do. Moreover, scandalous and disrespectful actions have occurred in his diocese all because of his efforts to liberate the Indians according to the law of God which they too deserve."

14. Letter from Valdivieso, 1547, Ibid.

15. Gil Gonzáles Dávila, *Teatro eclesiástico de la primitiva iglesia de las Indias Occidentales* 1 (Madrid: Diego Diazdela Carrera, 1655):235— 36.

16. *Archivo general de Indias* (Sevilla), Audiencia de Guatemala 164, letter of May 1, 1547, folio 1.

17. Ibid., folios 3— 13.

18. Ibid.

19. Letter of January 8, 1551. *Archivo general de Indias*, Audiencia de Quito 78.

20. Thus wrote the Secretary after visiting the entire diocese. "Informe," October 23, 1555. *Archivo general de Indias*, Audiencia de Quito 78. The Secretary also stated that "our bishop is more in danger from the Spaniards than from the Indians."

21. In regard to the synods, cf. my *Les évêques latinoaméricains* ... (1970), pp. 201ff.

22. Juan Friede, *Don Juan del Valle* (Segovia: Instituto Diego de Colmenares, 1952), p. 20. Valle had to enter France by way of the frontier of Laredo.

23. Letter of April 22, 1567, written from Popayán. *Archivo general de Indias*, Audiencia de Quito 78.

24. Ibid.

25. Juan del Valle, Letter of January 8, 1551. Ibid.

26. Francisco J. Hernáez, *Colección de bulas, breves, y otros documentos relativos a la iglesia de América y Filipinas* 2 (Brussels: Imprinta de A. Vromant, 1879):149.

27. Fernando Ocaranza, *Capítulos de la historia franciscana* 1 (México; 1933):23. Regarding the councils and synods, cf. my *Les évêques lationaméricains* ... (1970), pp. 162ff.

28. Hernáez, *Colección* I:54— 56; Francisco Antonio Lorenzana y Butrón, *Concilios provinciales primero, y segundo* ... 1 (México: En la imprinta de el superior gobierno, de el dr. J. A. de Hogel, 1769):1— 10; Cuevas, *Historia* 1:171ff.; Luke Wadding, *Annales Minorum seu trium ordinum a San Francisco institutorum* 16 (Romae: Rochi Bernabo, 1731— 1886):212; Juan de Torquemada, *Monarquía indiana* 1 (México, D. F.: Nicholas Rodrigo Franco, 1723):c. 16.

29. Lorenzana, *Concilios* 1:4. It is interesting to note how the 1769 edition of Lorenzana insisted that the teaching be in Spanish, a language that the missionaries never imposed on the Indians (cf. pp. 7— 8). Rome took certain measures, however, to impede baptism until all normal requirements were fulfilled. Cf the papal bull *Altitudo Divine Consilii* of Paul III in response to a letter sent to him by Bishop Julián Garcés of Tlaxcala. Cf. Hernáez, *Colección* 1:56— 62.

30. Zumárraga presided over the Council.

31. Johann Specker, *Die Missionsmethode in Spanisch-Amerika* (Schoneck-Beckenried, Schweiz: Administration der Neuen Zeitschrift fur Missionswissenschaft, 1953), p. 3. Cf. Fidel de Jesús Chauvet, *Fray Juan de Zumárraga* (México: Publicists B. de Silva, 1948), pp. 153ff., 331ff.

32. Joaquín García Icazbalceta, *Frey Juan de Zumárraga* (Buenos Aires: Espasa-Calpe Argentian, 1947), pp. 116ff., and Appendix 21, pp. 87ff. Cf. Lorenzana, op. cit., Appendices.

33. In the work published in 1947 on Zumárraga written by J. García Icazbalceta, the author states: "In baptizing the adults the ancient decrees were fulfilled and renewed as they were fulfilled and renewed by the conversion of Germany and England during the time of Pope Gregory and of the Emperors Charlemagne and Pepin, in view of the fact that we face the same type of situation as existed when those decrees were promulgated, and those who assented to these rites and ceremonies ... as during the pontificates of Siritio, Leo, Damaso, Gelasio, Ambrose, Augustine, and Hieronymus ... as now we offer them to many gentile adults who live wholesome and peaceful lives and who have believed and been converted and been baptized ... As the Manual instructs, there are two periods in the year for baptism, Pentecost and Holy Week, during which times the adults are to be baptized ... provided the bishop or minister certifies that the candidates have been perfectly instructed" (p. 119). "We are aware that in regard to the Holy Sacrament of Communion, there has been and is among the ministers of the Church some question as to whether after Confession the indigenous Christians should receive Communion, and that in these cases the priest or confessor must be the judge; but these ministers are uncertain as to whether they can or should deny the Sacrament to those simply because they are Indians and newly converted." (ibid., p. 131).

34. Ibid., p. 192. Cf. Specker, *Die Missionsmethode*, p. 35.

35. Lorenzana, *Concilios* 1:35— 144.

36. It was truly a change in the customs of the colonial society that they possessed something that existed for more than twenty years. It should be noted that Chapter 69 stipulated that when instructing the Indians, one should do so in their language. Consequently, it was necessary to have competent translators edit and correct the materials prepared in the indigenous languages. Chapter 73 refers to the Indian villages and to the necessity that they be legally organized: for the Indians to "be truly Christian and law abiding, rational people, it is necessary that they be assembled and confined (*reducidos*) to villages ...," ibid., pp. 147— 48.

37. Ibid., pp. 185— 208. Although the Church at times adopted some primitive rites, these were often modified considerably. "We command that the Indians not be permitted to have processions ... unless their Vicar or Minister is present" (cap. 11, p. 194). "For the conversion of the indigenous peoples, it is obligatory that we know their languages ... and all priests should be diligent in learning the dialects of their parishes" (cap. 19, p. 199). Attending the Council other than the Archbishop were the bishops of Chiapas, Tlaxcala, Yucatán, Nueva Galicia (Guadalajara), and Antequera (Oaxaca).

38. According to the Council, priests "in regionibus Indorum beneficia cum onere obti-

nentes in materna earumdem regionum lingua examinent, et quos repererint linguae huiusmodi ignaros, sex mensium spatio praefinito, ad discendas linguas compellant, admonentes eos quatenus elapso termino, si linguam huiusmodi non didicerint . . . ipso facto vacabit, et alteri de eo fiet previsio" (*De Doctrina Cura,* §V, I, pp. 139— 40). Regarding the seminaries — and in response to those who contended that the Latin American Church was anti-Tridentine — the Council declared: ". . . in singulis Diocesibus Collegium erigeretur, ubi pueri religiose educarentur, et omnibus Ecclesiasticis disciplinis imbuerentur, ita ut Collegium hoc Minis-trorum Dei perpetum esset Seminarium" (ibid., §II, p. 137). And restricting the privileges of the religious, the text declares: ". . . nisi ex urgenti causa, facultatem Episcopi non con-cedant" (ibid., §VI, p. 140); and "Parochos omnes, tam Seculares, quam Regulares haec Synodus . . ." (ibid., tit. II, *De officio Parochi,* I, p. 152). And regarding the dispensing of the Eucharist to the Indians, the Council commanded: ". . . eis (. . .) nullatenus Eucharistiam denegari patiantur . . ." (ibid., *De administratione,* III, p. 155). Texts of the Council, *Concilium Mexicanum Provinciale III,* II, 1— 328; Mansi, XXXIV (1902), 1015— 1228, and XXXVI bis, 317— 18 in the *Archiv. Vatic., Sectio Congr. Concilio,* Conc./Prov./Mex./A.D. 1585 (238 folios).

39. Cf. Rubén Vargas Ugarte, *Concilios Limenses (1551— 1772)* (Lima; 1951— 1954):3— 93.

40. Priests were ordered to baptize those adults among the Indians who requested baptism provided they had been catechized in their own language and could respond correctly to the questions therein (*Const.* 6 pp. 10— 11). Furthermore, *Constitution* 7 commanded that "no person should be baptized against his will" (p. 11). The Eucharist was to be administered only with the permission of the Prelate or Vicar. During this period the standards were more demanding in Peru than in Mexico, but in the second Council ". . . cum nullum absque causa possimus tam salutari cibo privare, monemus prefatos parochos, ut talibus sic despositis hoc sacramentum suo tempore ministrare non denegent" (*Const.* 58, p. 186).

41. The decisions of the Council of Trent were promulgated in Lima on October 28, 1565, and it is obvious that with the presence of several new bishops the program of evangelization was continuing from Panama (*Tierra Firme or Continentis*) to the River Plate area (Charcas) and Chile (*Sancti Iacobi et Imperialis*).

42. On the other hand ". . . doceant indos doctrinam quae eis a suo proprio episcopo tradetur" (*Const.* 2, p. 160); ". . . sacerdotes indorum curam agentes, eorum liguam addiscant . . . indorum linguam diligenter addiscant" (*Const.* 3, p. 161). The name given to the mis-sionaries was "*sacerdotes indorum,*" a beautiful and meaningful title. Regarding instruction to be given prior to baptism, (*Const.* 29), the 74th Constitution stated: "Sentit sancta Synodus, et ita servandum statuit, hoc noviter ad fidem conversos, *hoc tempore* non debere alique ordine initiari, neque in sollemni missarum celebratione . . .; et quam potuerint sollicitudine, tam pueros quam alios, hispane loqui edocere procurent" (pp. 192— 93). One notes herein the difference in the spirit of the prelates in Mexico and that of Toribio de Mogrovejo, in that there was a lamentable confusion in the Hispanic culture and civilization and the goals of the Church in her work of evangelization. What was at first a principle was slowly transformed into a means of social protection of the white minority from the Indian majority. And the Church unconsciously served to enforce the will of the Spanish colonial society.

43. Mansi, XXXIV bis (1913) col. 193— 258 and col. 807— 808, *Concilia Limana,* pp. 1— 125. The catechism of the Council can be examined in the *Biblioth.Nationale* in Paris, nat. res. D. 11171.

44. *Actio Prima,* Cf. Vargas Ugarte, *Concilios* 1:261.

45. "Nemo vero Indorum aut Aetiopum ad communionem recipiatur; nisi proprii parochi aut confessoris licentiam scripto sibi datam ostenderit" (ibid., cap. XXX, p. 274).

46. "In ordinibus minoribus conferendis . . . longe certe melius Dei Ecclesias et saluti Neophitorum consuliter paucitate electorum sacerdotum, quam multitudine imperitorum" (ibid., XXXIII, p. 278). The door was opened but the requirements were many and the possibilities were few for Indians to be accepted into the priesthood. In fact, the religious orders had internal standards and regulations that specifically prohibited the consecration to

the priesthood of either Indians or Negros. Cf., for example, the case of San Martín de Porres. Regarding the seminaries, Cap. XLIV, p. 282.

47. Actio III, cap. III, *De protectione et cura indorum:* "Nihil tes in harum Indicarum provincilis, quod Ecclesiae praesides ... curamque pro spirituali, et temporali eorum necessitate, prout ministros Christi decet, impendant. Et certe harum gentium mansuetudo et perpetuus serviendi labor et naturalis obedientia ... sed hodie quoque a pluribus designari, orat in Christo atque admonet omnes magistratus, et principes ut iis se benignos praebeant ... insolentiam frenent et catholicae majestatis fidei commissos et subditos liberos certe non servos agnoscant. Porro parochis ... non percurssores et tanquam filios, christianae charitatis sinu, Indos faveant et protent" (pp. 284 – 85).

48. *IV Conc. Provincial Limense* (1591), Vargas Ugarte, I, 377 – 88; *V Concilio* (1601), op. cit., I, 389 – 97. King Charles III convened the final Council in Lima in 1772 for the purpose of dealing with the question of the explusion of the Jesuits from his realm. But the Council did not discuss this matter; rather, it occupied itself with pastoral concerns. In the Conciliar texts matters related to the Indians were dealt with in the final chapter, *De privilegiis indorum,* occupying exactly six pages (of a total 137 pp.) even though at the time the Indians alone — not including the mestizos — comprised considerably more than half of the total population of Peru. It is evident that by the sixteenth century the missionary Church had become an institution of Hispanic-Creole, urbanized "Christianity" with virtually no regard for the Indian nor for the rural areas. The attitude should not, however, be exaggerated. In every chapter of the Council there was at least one reference to the Indians, but they were relegated to the lowest level of the social structure.

49. Archbishop Toribio organized diocesan councils in 1582 (29 decrees), 1584 (11 decrees), 1585 (93 decrees), 1586 (30 decrees), 1588 (30 decrees), 1590 (14 decrees), 1592 (30 decrees), and 1594 (48 decrees). The texts of these councils are found in *Lima limata* of 1673 or *Concilia Limana,* 1684. Cf. C. J. Sáenz Aguirre, *Collectio Maxima Conciliorum omnium Hisp. et Novi Orbis* (Rome, 1694).

50. Fernando de Armas Medina, *Cristianización del Perú* (Sevilla: G.E.H.A. 1953), pp. 344ff.

51. Ibid., pp. 348 – 49.

52. Ibid., p. 351.

53. Vicente de Sierra, *El sentido misional de la conquista de América* (Buenos Aires: Ediciones de Orientación Española, 1942), p. 171.

54. Felix Zubillaga, *La Florida, La mision jesuitica (1566 – 1572)* (Rome: Institutum Historicum, 1956), pp. 202ff. Jesuit missionaries had already been requested for Michoacán by Velasco de Quiroga, and for Peru by Andrés Hurtado de Mendoza, as well as for many other areas. Fathers Rogel and Villarreal began working in Calus and Tequesta as early as 1566, and the whole continent became a Jesuit mission field by 1568.

55. *Monumenta Peruana* 1 (1565 – 1575), edited by Antonio de Egaña (Rome: Apud "monumenta Historica Soc. Iesu," 1954).

56. Francisco J. Alegre, *Historia de la Provincia de la Compañia de Jesús de Nueva España* (Rome: Institum Historicum, 1956); Vol. I deals with the period of 1566 – 1596.

57. Roberto Levillier, *Gobernantes del Perú* 11 (Madrid: Sucesores de Rivadeneyra, 1921 – 1926):193 – 97.

58. A. G. G. Pérez, *El patronato Español en el virreynato del Perú,* (Tournai, 1937), p. 98.

59. S. Delacroix, "Le déclin des missions modernes," *Hist. Gen. des Missiones,* II, 363 – 90. The foundation of the *Society for the Propagation of the Gospel* in 1701 was not an indication of Protestant influence in Latin America during this period. Significant penetration of Latin America by Protestants has taken place during this present century although agents of the Bible societies (and later missionaries) began working in the River Plate area as early as the second decade of the nineteenth century.

60. R. Ricard, *La conquête spirituelle du Mexique:* "il est d'ailleurs assez frappant d'observer que ces populations restées à peu près purement païennes sont celles qui, par suite des obstacles géographiques, des dangers du climat ou de la difficulté de la langue, ont été à

peine touchées par l'évangélisation primitive ... Nous constatons une fois de plus que l'activité des réligieux du XVIe. siècle a fortement pesésur les destinées du Méxique" (pp. 330— 31). "Le XVIe. siècle a été la période capitale, la période où le Méxique s'est fait et dont le reste de son histoire n'a été que le développement presque inévitable" (p. 344). The same can be said of the other countries, although in some of them the above conditions prevailed more during the seventeenth and eighteenth centuries.

61. Delacroix, "Le déclin des missions modernes," pp. 371ff.

62. Chapter 6 of the *VI Concilio de Lima* (1772) stated that "bishops and others who have the obligation of educating the Indians so that they would be qualified for Sacred Orders ... should give particular attention to see that they are prepared in such a way that they acquire the qualities required by the Canons ...," Vargas Ugarte, op cit., p. 32. The success of the evangelistic efforts in the Philippines was due largely to the work of indigenous clergy. If Latin America had developed an indigenous clergy, it is possible that the evangelization of the Continent would now be complete.

63. Cf. the recent work of Gabriel Guarda, *Los laicos en la cristianización de América* (Santaigo de Chile: Ediciones Nueva Universidad, 1973), from which we have utilized the notes and to which we will repeatedly refer in dealing with this important theme.

64. Ibid., pp. 84ff. Guarda supports his affirmation with numerous estimates. It is interesting to note that the Psalms were the most frequently translated portion of the Old Testament while in the New Testament, in addition to the Gospels, the Apocalypse was favored. Commentaries were written in Latin and Spanish on the Song of Songs, the Prophets, Ecclesiastes, on the Pentateuch as a whole and on the individual books of Genesis, Exodus, Leviticus, etc. It is a mistake to assume, therefore, that Bible reading was not practiced during the period of colonial Christianity.

65. Ibid., pp. 92ff.

66. Ibid. Besides these works there were the viceregal liturgies and exercises, spiritual retreats, and fiestas honoring patron saints, together with other religious activities.

67. Ibid., p. 229. Cf. Bartolomé Valasco, "El alma cristiana del conquistador de América," *Missionalia Hispánica*, 22:282.

68. Raul Porras, "El Testamento de Pizarro," *Cuadernos de historia del Perú* 1 (1936):58.

NOTES FOR CHAPTER VI

1. "Relación de las cosas que sucedieron al P. Fr. Alonso Ponce," *CODOIN* 43 (1872):39— 43. Cf. my work *Para una historia del catolicismo popular en Argentina,* (Buenos Aires: Bonum, 1970), pp. 19ff.

2. Cf. the interesting discussion by Pedro Borges, *Métodos misionales en la cristianización de América* (Madrid: Consejo Superior de Investigaciones Científicas, Departamento de Misiología Española, 1960), pp. 58— 90.

3. Cristóbal de Molina, *Ritos y fábulas de los Inca* (Buenos Aires: Editorial Futuro, 1947). This work was first written c. 1572.

4. Juan de Tovar, *Historia de los índios mexicanos,* ed. T. Phillips (Middle Hill, England: Press of Sir Thomas Phillips, 1852).

5. José de Acosta, *De natvra Novi orbis libri dvo, et de promvlgatione evangelii apvd barbaros ...* (Salamanticae: Apud Guillelmum Foquel, 1589).

6. Bernardino Sahagún, *Historia general de las cosas de Nueva España,* 3 vols. (México: Editorial Alfa, 1955).

7. Ricard, *La conquête spirituelle,* pp. 55ff.

8. Ibid., p. 330.

9. Julio Iménez Rueda, *Herejías y supersticiones en la Nueva España* (México: Imprenta Universitaria, 1946), pp. 2, 19.

10. José Carlos Mariátegui, *Siete ensayos de interpretación de la realidad Peruana* (Lima: Biblioteca "Amauta," 1928), p. 127. Luis Eduardo Valcárcel maintains the same idea in his *Ruta cultural del Perú* (México: Fondo de Cultura Económica, 1945), p. 184.

11. George Kubler, "The Quechua in the Colonial World," *Handbook of South American Indians*, ed. Julian H. Steward, 2 (Washington: U. S. Government Printing Office, 1945):596—97.

12. José Vasconcelos, "El cisma permanente," *El Colegio Nacional Alfonso Reyes* (México; 1956), p. 210, proposes an idealist solution, viz., that the Indians would have voluntarily had a radical change of soul. This position, however, is socioculturally impossible — as are the others — as I have attempted to demonstrate.

13. Borges, *Métodos misionales en la cristianización de América*, pp. 521ff.

14. William S. Robertson, *La vida de Miranda*, tr. Julio E. Payro (Buenos Aires: Ediciones Anaconda, 1947), p. 57. The original English work was *The Life of Miranda*, 2 vols. (Chapel Hill: University of North Carolina Press, 1929).

NOTES FOR CHAPTER VII

1. Pedro Calmón, *Historia de civilização brasileira* (São Paulo: Companhia editora nacional, 1940), p. 189.

2. R. H. Valle, *Historia de las ideas contemporáneas en Centro-América*, p. 265.

3. V. Alba, *Las ideas contemporáneas de México* (1960), p. 20.

4. Cf. my *Para una historia del catolicismo popular en Argentina*, (1970), chapter 1: "Folk Catholicism in the Mediterranean Church"; chapter II: "The Amerindian Folk Religiosity"; chapter 3: "Hispanic and Latin American Folk Catholicism."

5. O. Di Lullo, *Cancionero popular de Santiago del Estero* (Buenos Aires: UNT, Baiocco, 1940), p. 92.

6. J. A. Carrizo, *Cancionero popular de Salta* (Buenos Aires: UNT, Baiocco, 1933), pp. 698—99.

7. J. A. Carrizo, *Cancionero popular de Jujuy* (Tucumán: UNT, Violetto, 1934), p. cv.

NOTES FOR CHAPTER VIII

1. Cited by Rubén Vargas Ugarte, *El episcopado en los tiempos de la emancipación sudamericana (1809—1830)* (Buenos Aires: Impr. de Amorrortu, 1932), p. 84.

2. Leandro Tormo, *La historia de la Iglesia en América Latina* 3 (Friburgo, Suiza: Centro Internacional de Investigaciones sociales de FERES, 1962):36.

3. Ibid., p. 17.

4. Ibid., p. 75.

5. Cf. Leturia, *Relaciones entre la Santa sede e Hispanoamérica*, Vol. 2, a primary source replete with profound insights and suggestive of new directions for research.

6. The official Spanish text is cited by Leturia, ibid., 2:110—113. This English translation is from J. Lloyd Mecham, *Church and State in Latin America* (Chapel Hill: The University of North Carolina Press, 1966), p. 64. — Tr.

7. Leturia, ibid., 2:235.

8. Ibid., pp. 241ff.

9. Ibid., p. 266

10. Ibid., pp. 265—71.

11. Ibid., p. 291.

12. The prolonged opposition of Rome had with time inclined the Spanish Americans

toward schism as is evident in "La Constitución civil del clero" ("The Civil Constitution of the Clergy") proposed by Miranda, the ideas and the writings of Dominique de Pradt, which advocated the naming for each country Patriarchs who would have the power to constitute the episcopacies independently of Rome, together with the machinations of the independentist cleric José Matías Delgado in El Salvador. Cf. Mecham, op. cit., p. 311, and the *ASV* (Secret Vatican Archives, Secrt. di Stato, 281, 1825— 1850, 3: "Scisma accaduto nella diocesi di Guatemala"). Only the position of Bolívar spared the Latin American Church the possible eventualities of this transcendental moment in her history. The Bishop of Charcas was named at this time, and he proceeded to reorganize the Church in Bolivia.

13. Leturia, op. cit., p. 314.

14. Ibid., p. 375.

15. G. F. Dominique de Pradt, *Concordat de l'Amérique avec Rome* (Paris: Bechet Aine, 1827), p. 265, citing Tormo, 3:145.

16. For a minimum bibliography on the *Chicanos* or Mexican Americans (or simply the "hispanic groups," for many are descendents of the Spanish in New Mexico and do not accept these designations) see Wayne Moquin and Charles Van Doren (eds.), *A Documentary History of the Mexican Americans* (New York: Praeger, 1971), Matthew Meier and Feliciano Rivera, *The Chicanos: A History of Mexican Americans* (New York: Hill and Wang, 1972), and Rodolfo Acuna, *Occupied America: The Chicano's Struggle toward Liberation* (San Francisco: Canfield Press, 1972).

17. Tormo, op. cit., p. 145.

18. The name "mazorca," i.e., an ear of corn, was a symbol of unity for the henchmen of Rosas whose opponents insisted that it should have been spelled *más horca,* that is, "more gallows" or hangings. Cf. Herring, *A History of Latin America*, p. 707.—Tr.

19. Vargas Ugarte, *El episcopado en el tiempo de la emancipación* (1832), p. 340.

20. Cf. Delacroix, *Le déclin des missions moderne*, 3:27ff.

21. Octavio Paz, *The Labyrinth of Solitude,* ed. Lysander Kemp (New York: Grove Press, 1962), pp. 125— 26. (Translation is from original.—Tr.)

22. Regarding Puerto Rico, cf. F. Ribes Tovar, *Handbook of the Puerto Rican Community* (New York: Plus Ultra, 1970); Lawrence R. Chenault, *Puerto Rican Migrants in New York City* (New York: Russell and Russell, 1970); Oscar Lewis, *A Study in Slum Culture* (New York: Random House, 1968); M. Maldonado, *A Socio-historic interpretation* (New York: Random House, 1972); and Juan Silen, *We, the Puerto Rican People,* trans. Cedrick Belfrange (New York: Monthly Review Press, 1971).

23. These groups appeared more akin to those of the Italian left (as in the case of Fanfani), and not to the German CDU or the French MPR. Cf. René L. Echáiz, *Evolución histórica de los partidos chilenos* (Santiago: Prensas de la Editorial Ercilla, 1939); Alberto Edwards, *Bosquejo histórico de los partidos políticos chilenos* (Santiago: Ediciones Ercilla, 1936); Carlos R. Melo, *Los partidos políticos argentinos* (Córdoba: Universidad Nacional de Córdoba, 1964); and Juliot Fabregat, *Los partidos políticos en la legislación Uruguaya* (Montevideo: Organizacion Taquigráfica Medina, 1949).

24. Federico Debuyst, *La Población en América Latina* (Friburgo, Suiza: Oficina Internacional de Investigaciones Sociales de FERES, 1961), pp. 68, 157.

25. Cf. *Acta et decreta Concilii plenarii Americae latinae,* (Rome: ex Typ. Vaticana, 1900); and Pablo Correa León, *El Concilio plenario Latinoamericano de 1899* (Bogotá: Imprenta San Pío X, n.d.), pp. 1— 24. There is no serious study available on the historical work of this council nor on its theological significance. Pablo C. León says: "One should note, nevertheless, the great abundance of Latin American sources and the presence of others as important as the already mentioned Lima Councils of the 16th century; it was the result perhaps of the absence of Latin American canonists in the group of conciliar consultants" (p. 10). But the truth is that such "Latin American canonists" did not exist in that era nor do they exist today, because the Latin American Church as well as the whole culture and civilization of this continent has turned toward Europe and rejected itself without even being aware of it.

(This was understandable in the nineteenth century, but much less so in the twentieth. Nonetheless, this is what is happening.) For any change to come it would be necessary for European educational institutions to provide scholarships to Latin Americans on the condition that they study problems that are distinctly related to their own culture.

26. Fr. Houtart, "Présent et avenir de la collégialité épiscopale," *Eglise Vivante* 14 (Jan. 1962):27–37; Karl Rahner, "Ueber Bischofskonferenzen," *Stimmen der Zeit* (July 1963):267–83 (cf. the small bibliography); and F. Fransen, "Die Bischofskonferenzen," *Orientierung* 27 (October 1963):119–23.

27. This generation of precursors existed in every country in Latin America, and they were dedicated to preserving the intellectual development of the population and emerging in the historical moment as the evolution allowed. Unfortunately, however, there does not exist today a single work that deals with this renaissance of Latin American Catholic thought in its entirety, even though this stage acts as a stimulator and promoter of the more important developments of the immediate future. Consider, for example, Antonio Castro (1867–1925) in Uruguay.

28. "Les Universités Catholiques en Amérique Latine," *Rythmes du Monde* 9 (April 1961):211.

29. A history of Latin American Catholic Action does not exist even though it has been an integral element in the history of the contemporary Church and one of the most important factors in the evolution of the civilization of the continent.

30. Cited in *Visión cristiana de la Revolución en América Latina* (Santiago: Centro Bellarmino, 1963, as a special edition of the periodical *Mensaje*, 115, 1963), an outstanding publication that has greatly assisted the social renovation, at least on the level of social theory.

31. J. Goldsack, President of the Confederation (CLASC), "Le syndicalisme chrétien," *Rythmes du Monde* 9 (April 1961):133–34.

32. Ibid., p. 137. The President of the *Confédération internationale des syndicats chrétiens* (CISC), with whom I spoke personally in The Hague in 1964, stated: "I am completely optimistic regarding the future of Latin American Christian syndicalism. The leaders are truly heroes." The directors of Christian institutions in Latin America commonly work during the day and give their evenings and weekends to labors of faith. This fact is totally unknown in Europe and in most of Latin America.

33. In this sense we are in complete accord with the author of the article.

34. The lack of Indian clergy is a well-known fact. But one should distinguish between autochthonous or native clergy (not only the Indians but also the Creoles, i.e., Hispanics born in America) and Indian clergy. There was an abundance of native (Creole) but not Indian clergy — which was very unfortunate considering the role of comparable clergy in the evanglization of the Philippines.

35. Don Maur Matthei, OSB, Las Condes (Chile), "Monastères et vie contemplative en Amérique Latine," *Rythmes du Monde* as cited in *Visión cristiana de la Revolución en América Latina* (1963), p. 149.

36. Víctor Sánchez Aguilera, *El pasado de Osorno* (Osorno, Chile: Impr. Cervantes, 1948), p. 28.

37. Cf. *Conferencia General del Episcopado Latinoamericano, Conclusiones, pro manuscrito* (Rome: Poliglotta Vaticana, 1956); *Conclusiones de la primera reunión celebrada en Bogotá, 5–15 de noviembre de 1956* (Suplemento del Boletín) (Bogotá, 1957); "II Consiglio Episcopale Latinoamericano," (CELAM) *La Civilta Cattolica* 2 (1957):160–175; *Conclusiones de la segunda reunión celebrada en Fómeque (Colombia), 10–17 de noviembre de 1957* (Bogotá, 1957); *Discours de SS. Jean XXIII au CELAM*, in *L'Osservatore Romano* (ed. franc.), Nov. 28, 1958, no. 467, p. 1; *EL CELAM es erigido en persona moral Colegial plena*, in *Sacra Congregatio Consistorialis*, Prot. N. 447–56, Marcellus Car. Mimmi, June 10, 1958.

38. *Conferencia General ...* (1956), pp. 89–111.

39. *Ad Ecclesiam Christi* (Letra apostolica), *AAS* 47 (June 29, 1955):539–44.

40. There were meetings in 1960, 1963, 1966, and 1968. Cf. *Directorio católico latinoamericano* (Bogotá: CELAM, 1968), p. 46.

41. These organizations are no longer Catholic nor confessional, and they are given here for information purposes. There has been organized also a political type of institution that has no connection whatsoever with the Church, namely, *La Oficina Latinoamericana de Partidos Demócratas cristianos* (which met in Strasbourg in 1963, with 147 delegates present).

42. For additional information and location of these institutions, cf. *Bilan du Monde*, 1:385ff.

43. Ibid., p. 391.

NOTES FOR CHAPTER IX

1. I have discussed this theme in my "Universalismo y Misión en los poemas del Siervo de Yahweh," *Ciencia y Fe* (Buenos Aires, 1965).

2. F. Debuyst, *La Población en América Latina*, p. 182.

3. Berta Corredor and Sergio Torres, *Transformación en el Mundo rural latinoamericano* (Bogotá: Oficina Internacional de Investigaciones Sociales de FERES, 1961); and F. Houtart, "La pastorale rurale," *Rythmes du Monde* 2−3 (1961):105ff.

4. P. V. Frías, "La solution actuelle du catholicisme en Argentine," ibid., p. 223.

5. The number of members in Catholic Action in 1959 was only 58,893, and can be explained by the fact that many who were members had become involved in syndicalism or political and public life in the country — despite the fact that in Argentina the adult generation was generally very conservative in their Catholicism and consequently unsure as to how to respond to new situations.

6. Juan L. Segundo, "L'Avenir du Christianisme en Amérique Latine," *Lettre* 54 (Paris, 1963):7−12. In 1971 the issue was presented in a more contemporary and less divisive manner.

7. W. Promper, "Statisques du clergé en Amérique Latine," *Aux Amis de l'Amérique Latine* (Louvain, May 1961), pp. 140−41.

8. The statistic of 41,088 Protestant pastors in 1961 possibly should be questioned in view of the supposed increase of 13,596 pastors in Brazil in only four years. The data seem to suggest either careless research or an error in reporting.

9. In Venezuela, for example, there were 630 priests in 1944 and 1,218 in 1960, which signifies a notable increase in the number of clergy. (On a scale of 100 for 1950, the 85 priests in 1944 increased to 165, while the population of 85.9 increased to 131.9. But the 33.1 statistic representing the increase in priests was actually insufficient to make up for the overall deficiency.) Isidoro Alonso-Orid, *La Iglesia en Venezuela y Ecuador* (Friburgo, Suiza: Oficina Internacional de Investigaciones Sociales de FERES, 1962).

10. Cf. the article by A. Souques, "Le signe de l'humanité de Dieu aujourd'hui," *Lettre* 65 (1964):25ff.

11. "Die Religion ist der Seufzer der bedrängten Kreatur ... Sie ist das *Opium* des Volks," from Marx's "Zur Kritik der Hegelschen Rechtsphilosophie," *Die Frühschriften* (Stuttgart: A. Kroner, 1953), p. 208.

NOTES FOR CHAPTER X

1. Celso Furtado, *La economía latinoamericana desde la conquista ibérica hasta la revolución cubana* (Santiago: Editorial Universitaria, 1969), p. 58.

2. Ibid., p. 111.

3. Ibid., p. 165.

4. Tulio Halperin Donghi, *Historia contemporánea de América latina* (Madrid: Alianza Editorial, 1969), p. 448.

5. Cf. J. William Fulbright, "Dimensions of Security," Epilogue of *American Militarism 1970*, ed. E. Knoll (New York: Viking Press, 1969), pp. 132–42; John J. Johnson, *The Military and Society in Latin America* (Stanford: Stanford University Press, 1964); and Rogelio García Lupo, *Contra la ocupación extranjera* (Buenos Aires: Editorial Sudestada, 1968).

6. Cf. the text in *Mensaje* 185 (Santiago, Chile, December 1969):396.

7. Cf. Alain Gheerbrant, *The Rebel Church in Latin America*, trans. Rosemary Sheed (Baltimore: Penguin Books, 1974), p. 207.

8. *Archivo general de Indias* (Sevilla), Audiencia de Quito 78.

9. Cf. my work "América latina y conciencia cristiana," *Cuadernos* 8 (Quito: IPLA, 1970):27. Also my "Iberoamérica en la historia universal," *Revista de Occidente* 25 (1965):85–95.

10. Cf. the discussion in *Mensaje* (Santiago) 139 (1965):13–16, which deals with the question of Latin American integration.

11. Cited by Abelardo Ramos, *Historia de la Nación latinoamericana* (Buenos Aires: Peña Lillo, 1968), p. 344.

12. Furtado, op. cit., p. 232.

13. The concentric circles are: the human genus, the European, the American, and the Latin American. The last two are taken as negative aspects "in the course of life."

14. Villegas, *Panorama de la filosofía iberoamericana actual*, p. 75–76.

15. Ricoeur, *History and Truth*, p. 271.

16. México: Siglo veintiuno, 1968, p. 121.

17. Ibid., p. 125.

18. Ibid., p. 132. Cf. Leopoldo Zea, *La filosofía americana como filosofía sin más* (México: Siglo venintiuno, 1969).

19. A. Methol Ferré, "Ciencia y filosofía en América latina," *Víspera* 15 (1970):3–16.

NOTES FOR CHAPTER XI

1. Cf. *Conciliorum Oecumenicorum Decreta* (Rome: Ed. Alberigo), pp. 610ff.

2. Cf. Leturia, *Relaciones entre la Santa Sede e Hispanoamérica*, 1:90.

3. Mariano Cuevas, *Documentos inéditos del siglo XVI para la Historia de México* (México: Editorial Porrua, 1975), p. 80.

4. Cf. *Alt-Katholisches Jahrbuch* (1966), p. 48. Cited by H. Bojorge, "A los cien años del Vaticano I," *Víspera* 12 (1970):8.

5. Monseñor Agusto Salinas Fuenzalida published a pastoral letter in Chile on Vatican II. Cf. *La revista católica* [Santiago] 993 (1962):3503–3509.

6. Published in *Política y Espíritu* [Santiago] (Aug.–Sept. 1966), pp. 42–51.

7. The Argentine episcopacy met in Pilar in 1964, for example, to prepare for the third session of the Council. Some of the more significant contributions by Latin American prelates were those of Méndez Arceo of Cuernavaca on the question of Church and state, Kremerer of Posadas on the diaconate, and Henríquez of Venezuela. Also noteworthy was the participation of the Argentine Methodist leader José Míguez Bonino who was an official observer.

8. Yves Congar, *Informations catholiques internationales* (Paris) 194 (1963):3. Hereafter cited as *ICI* with the Latin American counterpart being designated as *ICI* (México).

9. "The Pastoral Constitution on the Church in the World" (*Gaudium et Spes*) no. 5, *The Documents of Vatican II*, ed. Walter M. Abbott (New York: Guild Press, 1966), p. 204.

10. "La Acción Pastoral en América Latina," *Concilio Vaticano II* (Bogotá: Editorial Paulinas, 1966), p. 638.

11. The declaration has been widely circulated. It was signed by nine bishops from Brazil and one from Colombia. "A Letter to the Peoples of the Third World," August 15, 1967. The document is reproduced by the Peruvian Bishops' Commission for Social Action, *Between Honesty and Hope*, trans. John Drury (Maryknoll, NY: Maryknoll Publications, 1970), pp. 3–12. — Tr.

12. "Conclusiones de la primera reunión celebrada en Bogotá," CELAM, Nov. 5–15, 1956 (Bogotá, 1957). The ideal of a "new Christendom" can be seen in the emphasis given to the "defense of the faith," the necessity to establish Catholic universities, etc.

13. "Conclusiones de la segunda reunión celebrada en Fómeque, del 10 al 17 de noviembre de 1957" (Bogotá, 1957).

14. "Tercera reunión del CELAM. Conclusiones" (Vaticano: Tipográfica Vaticana, 1959).

15. "CELAM. Cuarta reunión. Conclusiones" (Bogotá, 1959).

16. "CELAM. Quinta reunión. Conclusiones" (Bogotá, 1961).

17. "CELAM. Sexta reunión. Conclusiones" (Bogotá, 1962).

18. Note the paper of the Secretary of the Brazilian Episcopacy presented and published in the *Boletín informativo* of CELAM (no. 49, 1962) on "La presencia de la Iglesia ante los problemas económico-sociales de la familia en América latina."

19. Declarations were published in *Criterio* (Buenos Aires, May 13, 1965):335.

20. "Presencia activa de la Iglesia en el desarrollo y en la integración de América latina," *Criterio* (March 23, 1967):190–91.

21. Cf. the eulogy given by Marcos McGarth on the occasion of Larraín's death in *Criterio* (June 14, 1966):494.

22. Cf., for example, "Desarrollo: éxito o fracaso en América latina"; and in *Víspera* 1 (May 1967):30–37, the article by Monseñor Marcos McGrath, "Los fundamentos teológicos de la presencia activa de la Iglesia en el desarrollo socio-económico de América latina"; and the commentary on the meeting in Mar del Plata in *Criterio* (June 22, 1967):432ff.

23. In regard to the Medellín Conference, other than news releases and articles in the well-known religious periodicals such as *Criterio*, *Víspera*, *Mensaje*, and *Sic*, and the bulletins from publication offices such as *Noticias Aliadas*, CIDOC, and LADOC, see also: Gheerbrant, *The Rebel Church in Latin America*, René Laurentin, *L'Amérique latine a l'heure de l'enfantement* (Paris: Seuil, 1968); Henry Fesquet, *Une Eglise en état de péché mortel* (Paris: Grasset, 1968); and the collection of documents published under the title *Iglesia latinoamericana ¿Protesta or profecía?* (Buenos Aires: Ed. Búsqueda, 1969), hereafter cited as *IL ¿PP?* The final documents of the Medellín Conference were published in English under the auspices of the Latin American Episcopal Council (CELAM) and entitled *The Church in the Present-Day Transformation of Latin America in the Light of the Council* (Bogotá: General Secretariat of CELAM, 1970), vol. 2, hereafter cited as *Medellín Conclusions*. (All quotations are from this official English text. — Tr.)

24. José Comblin, "Las Notas," *Marcha* 17 (1968):47–57. Available in English in Gheerbrant, op. cit., pp. 222–45.

25. Padim's text, "The Doctrine of National Security in the Light of the Gospel," is included in the collection published by Gheerbrant, ibid., pp. 201–20, and clearly evidences the prevailing militarist ideology of the Brazilian government.

26. Héctor Borrat in the "Introducción" of *Marcha* 17 (1968):5, an issue which deals with the theme of Medellín and the New Church. In this same issue are numerous letters from various entities sent to the Pope and the bishops who were to meet in Medellín.

27. *Medellín Conclusions*, p. 252.

28. Ibid., p. 259.

29. Ibid., p. 265.

30. Ibid., p. 23.

31. Ibid., p. 32.

32. Ibid., p. 33.

33. Hélder Câmara, *Spiral of Violence*, trans. Della Couling (Denville, NJ, 1971), pp. 29– 30. Dom Hélder writes: "If there is some corner of the world which has remained peaceful, but with a peace based on injustices — the peace of a swamp with rotten matter fermenting in its depths — we may be sure that that peace is false" (p. 33).

34. *Medellín Conclusions*, p. 58.

35. Ibid., p. 59.

36. Ibid., pp. 72– 75, 78.

37. Ibid., p. 90.

38. Ibid., pp. 99, 100.

39. Ibid., p. 168. This section deals with the "basic Christian communities."

40. There are also conclusions regarding the "Religious," the "Poverty of the Church," and "Joint Pastoral Planning" in which reference is made to the "basic Christian communities" (No. 10). Finally, there are some conclusions regarding the "Mass Media," without which, it is said, "the progress of the Latin American people and the necessary transformation of the continent will not be realized" (p. 242).

41. In this twelfth meeting it was agreed to increase the number of members of CELAM from 22 to 57 by including the presidents of the national conferences and the presiding bishops and secretaries of the various departments. Thereafter CELAM began to speak with much greater authority.

42. Monseñor Plaza, Bishop of La Plata, issued a pastoral on October 7, 1968, entitled "The Latin American Social Reality and the Medellín Conclusions," a copy of which appeared in *Criterio* (November 14, 1968):834– 38.

43. The *Synod of Santiago* had its first session September 8– 18, 1968, and a second session in September of 1969. Of the 400 persons participating at least 43% were laypersons.

44. Medellín is cited in Point IV. Cf. *Criterio* (November 28, 1968):880.

45. Buenos Aires: Ediciones Paulinas, 1969.

46. Some sixty-nine priests, religious, and laypersons met with the episcopacy August 19– 20, 1969. The nature of the discussion was not merely episcopal, but also represented an ecclesial reflection. Cf. *Criterio* (1969):792.

47. Cf. the declarations of Monseñor Proaño during the meeting of the Ecuadorian episcopacy, June 16– 22, 1969, at which time the sacerdotal crisis was discussed. See also the statment by Bishop Pironio, "Medellín a Year Later," published in *El Tiempo* (Bogotá), August 18, 1969.

48. "Herodianism," a term initially used by Toynbee, is usually employed by Latin American Christians to designate the national suboppressive oligarquies who, though they lack popular support, enjoy the backing of the "international imperialism of money." Cf. *Mensaje* 123 (1963):493, and *Vispera* 6 (July 1968):86.

49. Freire's principal works are *Pedagogy of the Oppressed*, trans. Myra Bergman Ramos (New York: Seabury Press, 1970), and *Education for Critical Consciousness*, trans. Myra Bergman Ramos (New York: Seabury Press, 1973).

50. Cf. *Anuario Iberoamericano* (Río de Janeiro, April 30, 1963), pp. 161– 64.

51. Cf. *Revista Da Conferencia dos religiosos do Brasil* (*CRB*), March 1964, pp. 129– 136; and Jean Toulat, *Espérance en Amérique du Sud* (Paris: Perrin, 1965), pp. 229ff.

52. Cf. José de Broucker, *Dom Hélder Câmara*, trans. Herma Briffault (Maryknoll, NY: Orbis Books, 1970), p. 154.

53. In *Marcha* 9 (January 1968):6.

54. Published in the *Revista Da Conferencia dos religiosos do Brasil* (July 1964):403– 405.

55. Cf. *Ecclesia* (Madrid, August 1, 1964):13– 14.

56. Cf. *IL ¿PP?*, p. 174.

57. Cf. *Mensaje* (March April 1965):133– 38.

58. Cf. "Evolución de las relaciones entre la Iglesia y el Estado en Brasil," in *Noticias da Igreja Universal* (São Paulo, February 15, 1968).46– 47.

59. Cf. *ICI* (México, September 7, 1966):30.

60. The student delegates entered the convent for Mass on July 30 and 31 and were not distinguished from other worshippers. They left the convent the same way.

61. Cf. *ICI* (1967):302.

62. Cf. *Marcha* 17 (1968):13– 20.

63. Cf. *Mensaje* (Madrid, October 1968):14– 15.

64. Cf. *IL ¿PP?*, pp. 178– 92.

65. En *Mensaje* 184 (Santiago, November 1969):568.

66. Cf. *Mensaje* 189 (June 1970):237ff.

67. Cf. Norberto Habegger, "Apuntes para una historia," *Los católicos posconciliares en la Argentina* (Buenos Aires: Galerna, 1970), pp. 91– 202. The book is dedicated to Father Pereira Neto and Juan C. Loureiro.

68. Cf. *Criterio* (July 26, 1962):543– 46.

69. "Editorial," ibid. (May 28, 1964).

70. Cf. *IL ¿PP?*, pp. 97– 103. Regarding the events that we have described prior to 1969, see the collection of documents published under the title *Los católicos posconciliares en la Argentina* (1970), especially documents 1– 60.

71. Cf. "La pastoral sobre Tierra Nueva" of December 8, 1966, ibid., pp. 287– 91.

72. Ibid., pp. 274– 79.

73. Ibid., p. 186. Priests, syndicalists, and laypersons demonstrated in the streets but were repressed by the police.

74. Subsequently I will describe the more significant priestly conflicts.

75. *Los católicos posconciliares en la Argentina* (1970), pp. 394– 96.

76. Cf. *Criterio*, extraordinary edition (November 1969):890– 94. Bishop Nevares' reflection was published in Neuquén on November 11, 1969.

77. *Criterio* (April 9, 1970):222– 23.

78. Regarding this issue cf. *Sacerdotes para el Tercer Mundo* (Buenos Aires: Movimiento de los Sacerdotes para el Tercer Mundo, 1970), pp. 116ff. Cf. the declaration of the Argentine episcopacy and the reply of the Movement in *Polémica en la Iglesia* (Buenos Aires: Búesqueda, 1970). These declarations were made public August 12, 1970. See also "Declaration of the Argentine Bishops' Permanent Committee," *LADOC* 10 (December 1970) I, 42 b.

79. Gera-Rodríguez Melgarejo, "Apuntes para una interpretación de la Iglesia Argentina," *Víspera* 15 (February 1970):86ff.

80. Cf. *ICI* 323 (1968).

81. Cf. *IL ¿PP?*, pp. 288– 99, and *Marcha* 17 (1968):21– 25.

82. Cf. *IL ¿PP?*, p. 324.

83. Cf. *ICI* 192 (1963):8. Cf. "Declaration of the Paraguayan Bishops," *LADOC* 13 (February 1971), I, 52 b.

84. Cf. *IL ¿PP?*, p. 283. Cf. "It is Calumny," *LADOC* 9 (November 1970), I, 39 b.

85. Cf. *Cuadernos para el diálogo* (Madrid, November 1969):39– 40.

86. "Paraguay: un grito en la noche," *Mensaje* 189 (December 1969):620.

87. Cf. *ICI* 183 (1962):12. Cf. "Haiti: A Church in Crisis," *LADOC* 13 (February 1971), I, 51.

88. Cf. *Le nouveau monde* (Port au Prince, August 18, 1969).

89. Cf. *IL ¿PP?*, pp. 359– 66. See also William L. Wipfler, *The Churches of the Dominican Republic in the Light of History*. Sondeos No. 11 (Cuernavaca: Centro Intercultural de Documentación, CIDOC, 1966), pp. 101– 13.

90. *ICI* 370 (1970):14– 15.

91. *IL ¿PP?*, p. 347.

92. *Marcha* 17 (September 1968):21.

93. Aldo Büntig, "La Iglesia en Cuba. Hacia una nueva frontera," *Revista del CIAS* 193 (Buenos Aires, 1970):21. I have relied heavily on this article for the discussion of the Church

in Cuba. Cf. "The Church in Cuba: Toward a New Frontier," LADOC 13 (February 1971), I, 54 a.

94. *Criterio* (March 26, 1959):235 – 36.

95. *La voz de Cuba* (Havana, 1961), p. 97.

96. Büntig, op. cit., p. 18.

97. Gheerbrant, op. cit., p. 269.

98. *ICI* 309 (1968):17. Monseñor Aacchi contended that Castro is ethically but not ideologically a Christian. Cf. Büntig regarding "the new man" in Castro, op. cit., pp. 25 – 28.

99. Büntig, ibid., pp. 50 – 53.

100. Ibid., p. 30.

101. Ibid., p. 55.

102. Ibid., p. 58.

103. Cf. *Ecclesia* (December 31, 1960):15 – 16.

104. *ICI* 178 (1962):26.

105. *Ecclesia* (first semester 1962):395.

106. *Anuario IB* (Madrid, 1962):153 – 61.

107. *ICI* (December 15, 1967):39 – 40.

108. Ibid., 307 (1968):14.

109. Cf. *Ecclesia* (June 7, 1969):23 – 24.

110. *Mensaje* 181 (August 1969):385.

111. Alba, *Le mouvement ouvrier* . . . (1953), pp. 117ff.

112. *Víspera* 5 (April 1968):44 – 45.

113. Cf. *Mensaje* (November 1962):577 – 87.

114. Cf. *La Voz* (Santiago, August 10, 1962):10.

115. Cf. *Sic* (Caracas, June 1966):257 and (July – August 1966):314 – 49.

116. *ICI* 360 (1970):12.

117. Cf. the work of Conrado Eggers Lan, Professor in the National University in Buenos Aires, *Violencia y estructuras* (Buenos Aires: Búsqueda, 1970), pp. 22 – 108, for a discussion of the types of violence; also the work of Hélder Câmara previously cited, *Spiral of Violence*.

118. Bogotá: Ediciones Tercer Mundo, 1962.

119. Cf. *Anuario IB* 1 (Madrid, 1962):162.

120. *Camilo Torres*, Sondeos (Cuernavaca: CIDOC, 1966), pp. 113 – 78, and Germán Guzmán Campos, *Camilo Torres*, trans. John D. Ring (New York: Sheed and Ward, 1969).

121. *Camilo Torres*, CIDOC (1966), p. 174.

122. *El Vespertino* (Bogotá, January 7, 1966).

123. This document may be found in the collection by CIDOC cited above, *Camilo Torres* (1966).

124. Ibid., p. 65.

125. Ibid., pp. 85 – 86. This quotation is from "Un sacerdote en la universidad" ("A Priest in the University") and originally appeared in *El Catolicismo* (Bogotá, June 28, 1962). Because of the continual student conflicts and street demonstrations, the students proposed Father Camilo Torres for the position of Rector of the National University. Cardinal Concha, who allied himself with the government of Alberto Lleras, ordered Torres to resign his professorship. Camilo later wrote that the Cardinal explicitly warned him that he, the Cardinal, did not want the Church nor Camilo to be involved in the problem. Camilo obeyed Concha who, nevertheless, showed no awareness of the fact that to fail to be involved was in effect a tacit support for the antipopular government. No one can wash his hands as did Pilate, because such attempts are always culpable acts in themselves. "My prelate," wrote Camilo, "who had the whole responsibility, felt that I should withdraw" (ibid., p. 87). History, however, always points to those responsible for the turn of events, and it is entirely possible that if Camilo Torres had become Rector of the University, he would not have later become a guerrilla.

126. Ibid., pp. 286 – 87, citing a letter written on June 24, 1965, to Cardinal Concha. In

the letter Camilo asked to be "reduced to lay status." It should be noted that after he had been obliged to give up his professorship, he was prohibited from lecturing, speaking, or even writing — restrictions which he said led him to conclude that "the current structures of the Church" made it impossible for him "to continue serving as a priest" (ibid., p. 285).

127. Ibid., p. 286.

128. Ibid., p. 224.

129. Ibid., p. 249.

130. Ibid., p. 186.

131. Ibid., pp. 330– 31.

132. Cited by Norberto Habegger, "La Iglesia en la historia de Colombia," *Marcha* 2 (January 1968):116.

133. Cited by Walter J. Broderick, *Camilo Torres* (New York: Doubleday, 1975), p. 248.

134. Habegger, "La Iglesia en la historia de Colombia," p. 118.

135. Gregorio Selser, "Conflicto de la Iglesia de Colombia," *Política internacional* 81 (Buenos Aires, November 1966).

136. *Camilo Torres,* CIDOC (1966), pp. 224– 45.

137. The Spanish priest Domingo Laín was expelled from Colombia in 1969, but he later returned and joined the rural guerrilla movement. Cf. *ICI* 356 (1970):11– 12. "Priestly consecration demands absolute self sacrifice in order that all people may live. Violence is neither atheistic nor Christian" (ibid).

138. *Archivo general de Indias* (Sevilla), Audiencia de Charcas, 313.

139. Cf. "Bolivia, revolución o contrarevolución," *Víspera* 19– 20 (October– December 1970):10– 22. For the declarations from Bolivia see *IL ¿PP?,* pp. 145– 50.

140. Ernesto "Ché" Guevarra, *The Diary of "Ché" Guevarra,* ed. Rovert Scheer (New York: Bantam Books, 1968), p. 25.

141. *Criterio* (September 28, 1967):699.

142. *ICI* 249 (1965):33.

143. Ibid., 301 (1967):16.

144. On January 12, 1971, afer the attempted rightist coup failed, General Torres declared: "Fellow workers, this government will not vacillate. I do not know if it will be through socialism, and I do not know if it will be through revolutionary nationalism, but we will move toward achieving prosperity for the Bolivian people." Reported by the United Press International.

145. Cf. Methol Ferré, "La revolución verde oliva, Debray y la OLAS," *Víspera* (October 1967):17– 39. See also Rubén Vázquez Díaz, *Bolivia a la hora del Ché* (México: Siglo XXI, 1969).

146. G. Fournial-R. Labarre, *De Monroe à Johnson* (Paris: Ed. Sociales, 1966), p. 117.

147. Cf. *Víspera* 5 (1968):56– 57.

148. Ibid.

149. Ibid., p. 52. Note the response regarding the "Theology of Violence" in which the exceptions stipulated by Paul VI are applied in nearly all the Latin American countries.

150. Gheerbrant, op. cit., p. 279 n. See also Thomas and Marjorie Melville, *Whose Heaven, Whose Earth?* (New York: Alfred A. Knopf, 1971), p. 280.

151. *ICI* 356 (1970):16 Cf. "Organized Torture in Brazil," *IDOC-International,* North American Edition, 5 (June 13, 1970):2– 19.

152. A discussion of what constitutes coercive violence can be found in *ICI* (March 1, 1970):16– 17. Sister Borges de Silveira wrote to the Ministry of Justice on December 17, 1969, accusing the police of the treatment herein described.

153. Cf. *IDOC-International* 28 (July 15– August 1, 1970):65ff.

154. *Osservatore Romano,* December 17, 1961, p. 2.

155. *ICI* 160 (1962):15.

156. *IL ¿PP?,* pp. 166– 67.

157. Besides the declarations cited in the text, see those of the Ecuadorian episcopacy

regarding "reform without Castroism" (*Ecclesia,* second semester 1961):1155; the "Pastoral Letter of the Peruvian Episcopacy Regarding Current Social and Political Activity" (CELAM, June—July 1963):245—55; Bishop Enrique Bolaños of Costa Rica on "Charity Should Support Development," *Eco Católico* (June 2, 1968); and Monseñor Román Arrieta, also of Costa Rica, on "La violencia, solución para Latinoamérica?" *Trípode* (Caracas, March 1969):20; and the XII Meeting of CELAM in Sâo Paulo, which issued the declaration through Monseñor Pironio: ". . . we condemn the utilization of national and foreign resources for the purchase of arms." *Noticias Aliadas y Criterio* (1969), p. 924.

158. Cf. *Informativo CIDOC* 70—211; and "Una revolución del mundo por el camino de no-violencia," *Iglesia viva* 15—18 (Spain):257. In the twelfth Assembly of the CNBB, May 27, 1970, the Brazilian bishops issued a strong statement regarding violence and torture. See "Documento pastoral de Brasilia," NADOC (Perú), pp. 154—70.

159. Cf. my work *El humanismo semita* (1969), pp. 35, 46.

160. Other texts are in Luke 16:16 and Acts 2:2; 5:26; 21:35; and 27:41.

161. Eggers Lan, op. cit., proposes the idea but does not suggest all of the possible conclusions, pp. 32ff.

162. *Medellín Conclusions,* pp. 79—80.

163. *Víspera* 5 (1968):55.

164. Title of the book by Paulo Freire (1970).

165. Roger Bastide, *Las Américas negras* (Madrid: Alianza Editorial, 1969), p. 13. See especially his bibliography, pp. 207ff.

166. Ibid., p. 15.

167. Rodolfo González, *I am Joaquín/Yo soy Joaquín* (New York: Bantam Books, 1972), pp. 6—7. The work of Armando B. Rendon, *Chicano Manifesto: The History and Aspirations of the Second Largest Minority in America* (New York: Collier Books, 1971) indicates a new awareness on the part of Mexican and Spanish Americans.

168. Cf. *ICI* (1962):10—15.

169. Cf. *Ecclesia* (May 15, 1962):16—18.

170. Cf. Fabio Da Silveira, *Frei, el Kerensky chileno* (Buenos Aires: Ed. Cruzada, 1968), Plinio Correa de Oliveira, *Transfondo ideológico inadvertido y diálogo* (Buenos Aires: Ad. Cruzada, 1966); and by the same author, *Revolución y contrarevolución* (Buenos Aires: Ed. TFP, 1970).

171. Cf. C. Beccar Varela (hijo), et. al., *El nacionalismo, una incógnita en constante evolución* (Buenos Aires: Ed. TFP, 1970), especially pp. 239—40.

172. Number 187 (March 1970):100.

173. "Communis omnium possessio." Thomas Aquinas, *Summa Theologico,* I-II, q. 94, a. 5, ad. 3.

174. "Distinctio possessionum." Ibid.

175. Cf. Santiago Ramírez, *El derecho de gentes* (Madrid: Studium, 1955), especially p. 192. The moral school of Rome, whose vocabulary no longer is evident in papal encyclicals, has forgotten the Thomist doctrine of *ius gentium,* which is seen in modern doctrinal statements. Cf. Ramírez, pp. 189—90, n. 575.

176. For example, Saint Basil of Cesarea, *In Hexam. Hom. VII (Patr. Migne, Graeca,* XXIX, col. 147).

177. "Per modum determinationis." Thomas Aquinas, *In X Ethic. Arist. ad Nicom. expositio,* L. V, lect. 12, n. 1023.

178. "In extreme necessitate omnia sunt communia." (Cf. the thesis defended in the Gregoriana by Gilles Couvreur, *Les pauvres ont-ils des droits?*, Univ. Grego. Roma, 1961.) In Aquinas, see II-II, q. 66, a. 3, c.; ibid., a. 7, c. Huguccio in his *Summa ad. prc. Decr.* (APP. 2, pp. 190—91) where he says: "Iure naturali omnia sunt communia, id est tempore necessitatis indigentibus communicanda."

179. Cf. *Mensaje* (Madrid, June 1959):3.

180. *Rythmes du Monde* 4 (Paris, 1961):212—22.

181. Cf. *Criterio* (November 8, 1962):824—27; (and November 22, 1962):866—870.

182. Ibid. (November 1962):870. Regarding agrarian reform, cf. Jaques Chonchol, "La reforma agraria," *Mensaje* 123 (Santiago):563—71, agent of the agrarian reform in the Church, the Christian Democrats, and in the Allende government.

183. Cf. Guillermo Leuta, "Aspectos de la Iglesia chilena," *Marcha* 9 (1968):80—85.

184. By 1965 Cardinal Silva Henríquez had already declared: "A just agrarian reform is indispensable." *Criterio* (January 27, 1966):71.

185. Cf. *IL ¿PP?*, pp. 333—38.

186. *ICI* 356 (1970):12.

187. *Anuario IB* (April 23, 1963):147—152.

188. *Noticias Católicas* (Buenos Aires, December 4, 1963).

189. *Anuario IB* (March 1970):10.

190. Cf. my *Les évêques hispano-américains* (1970), pp. 1—30 (*El episcopada hispanoameri-cano*, 1:27—82.)

191. Cf. *ICI* 366 (1970):18.

192. *Concilio Vaticano II* (Bogotá: Ediciones Paulinas, 1966), p. 622.

193. Ibid., p. 624.

194. *The Documents of Vatican II*, p. 405.

195. Ibid., p. 408.

196. Ibid., p. 585.

197. Ibid., p. 590.

198. Ibid., p. 612.

199. Ibid., p. 624.

200. Ibid., pp. 199—200.

201. *Medellín Conclusions*, pp. 80—81.

202. *Mensaje* 194 (Santiago, November 1970):536.

203. Broucker, *Dom Hélder Câmera*, p. 136.

204. Ibid., p. 137.

205. Ibid., pp. 148—49.

206. Ibid., p. 152.

207. Ibid.

208. Ibid., p. 154.

209. Ibid., p. 80.

210. Ibid., p. 56.

211. Ibid., p. 75.

212. Ibid., p. 84. Dom Hélder included remarks about the mini-imperialism of Brazil in regard to Paraguay and Bolivia.

213. Ibid., p. 45. From an address given at the Instituto de Investigaciones de la realidad brasileña, June 21, 1967.

214. Ibid., pp. 50, 51.

215. Ibid., p. 82.

216. Ibid., p. 107.

217. Ibid.

218. Ibid. Dom Hélder should have said "dialectical" rather than "Marxist," but he is a pastor, not a philosopher.

219. Ibid., p. 88. From an address given in Río, June 19, 1967.

220. Ibid., p. 90. From an address given at the inauguration of the Instituto de Teología de Recife, March 7, 1968.

221. Ibid., p. 91. From an address on "Science and Faith in the Twentieth Century" given at the Escuela Politécnica of Campina Grande, Brazil, December 17, 1966.

222. Ibid., pp. 45—46. From an address given at the Instituto de Investigaciones de la realidad brasileña, June 21, 1967.

223. Ibid., p. 106.

224. From an address given in Paris, April 25, 1968. Cf. *ICI* (May 15, 1968), and *Between Honesty and Hope*, pp. 54ff. Cf. also José Cayuela, *Hélder Câmara, Brasil ¿un Vietnam católico?* (Barcelona: Ed. Pomaire, 1969).

225. *ICI* 315 (1968). Father Pedro Arrupe, the Jesuit General, met at this time, May 6– 14, 1968, with members of the Order, and the decision was reached that the Jesuits in Brazil would leave aside educational work and become agents of integration and social action.

226. *Consudec* (March 20, 1964).

227. Cf. the declarations of May 1, 1965, regarding the Labor Day fiesta in *AC* (Buenos Aires, June 1965):187– 94.

228. Cf. *Criterio* (February 26, 1970):111.

229. "The faithfulness of the bishop to the Christian message is not rooted solely in his own personal faith." From a declaration published in *Crónica* (Buenos Aires, January 6, 1971):5.

230. *ICI* 269 (1966):11.

231. *IL ¿PP?*, p. 346.

232. *ICI* 171 (1962):10.

233. Ibid. 358 (1970).

234. Cf. "Iglesia de pueblo o secta de escogidos?" *Ecclesia* (February 14, 1970):15– 17.

235. Dom Hélder Câmara at the time when he "took possession" of the archdiocese of Recife, April 12, 1964.

236. *Medellín Conclusions*, Priests, no. 2, p. 173.

237. In the Vatican Council II "Decree on the Ministry and Life of Priests" (*Presbyterorum ordinis*), note the frequency of the word "difficult": the "ever-increasing difficulty" of tasks assigned to priests (no. 1), "priestly preaching is often very difficult in the circumstances of the modern world" (no. 4), "the difficulties which priests experience in the circumstances of contemporary life" (no. 22) in relation to the concrete particularities of "our present age" (no. 7), and the difficulties in today's world" (no. 14). *The Documents of Vatican II* (1966).

238. From the Preface of the "Decree on the Ministry and Life of Priests," p. 532.

239. Ibid., no. 6, pp. 544– 45.

240. *Medellín Conclusions*, Priests, no. 9 b, p. 1.

241. Ibid., nos. 17, 18, p. 179. (Dussel reverses the order. — Tr.)

242. Ibid., no. 19, pp. 179– 80. Italics are mine.

243. Ibid., no. 2, p. 173.

244. *ICI* 336 (1969). Cf. Ivan Illich, "Metamorphose du clerc," *Esprit* 10 (1967).

245. The publication on the *Polémica en la Iglesia* (1970) carries the heading of the text from Saint Paul: "I hear that when you all come together as a community, there are separate factions among you ..." (1 Cor. 11:18).

246. "Principales coincidencias de la reunión de Quilmes," June 28, 1965, *IL ¿PP?*, p. 98.

247. Ibid., pp. 98– 103. This document was severely censured by Cardinal Antonio Caggiano.

248. Ibid., p. 99. In Medellín, an "indirect" relation was discussed.

249. Ibid., p. 99.

250. Ibid., p. 100.

251. Ibid., p. 101. It would be very difficult to discuss in a few words the sacerdotal issue in Latin America.

252. Ibid., p. 102.

253. Habegger, "Apuntes ...," *Los católicos posconciliares* (1970), p. 159.

254. Ibid., p. 160.

255. Ibid.

256. *ICI* 259 (1966):12.

257. Cf. "La Iglesia en la calle," in the journal *Juan* (May 24, 1967).

258. *Los católicos posconciliares*, pp. 274– 79.

259. Ibid., p. 183.

260. Ibid., p. 185.

261. *ICI* 359 (1970):17— 19. Cf. "Sacerdotes de Neuquén" in a work already cited, *Sacerdotes para el Tercer Mundo* (1970), pp. 108— 12.

262. Cf. Domingo A. Bresci, "Argentina: Priests for the Third World," *IDOC-International* (North American edition) 15 (December 12, 1970):58— 96, and *Sacerdotes para el Tercer Mundo*. The letter sent by this group had some one thousand signatures of Latin American priests. *IL ¿PP?*, pp. 74— 78.

263. Cf. Gheerbrant, "Letter to the Latin American Bishops Assembled at Medellín," written from Buenos Aires. June 20, 1968, *The Rebel Church*, pp. 163-167.

264. "A Letter to the People of the Third World," *Between Honesty and Hope*, p. 5.

265. Cf. *Sacerdotes para el Tercer Mundo* for the declarations of priests in Reconquista, Corrientes, the Capital, Tucumán, San Juan, Nordeste, Santa Fe, 9 de Julio, Rosario, Mendoza, La Rioja, Neuquén, etc., regarding internal questions, strikes, the political situation, the kidnapping of General Aramburu, and the detention of Father Carbone.

266. Cf. the document signed in Córdoba, October 3— 4, 1970, *Polémica en la Iglesia*, pp. 41— 123. Also the commentary of Manuel Ossa in *Mensaje* 193 (October 1970):494— 95; "Recent Events and What to Do Now," *LADOC* 10 (December 1970), I, 426; and "Notes for an Interpretation of the Argentine Church," *LADOC* 10 (December 1970), I. 42 c.

267. *ICI* 205 (1963):34.

268. Ibid. 264 (1965):29— 31.

269. Broucker, op. cit., pp. 42— 43.

270. *ICI* 282 (1967):9.

271. *Il ¿PP?*, p. 178.

272. Ibid., p. 190. Cf. the discussion on celebacy, p. 192.

273. Ibid., p. 192.

274. Cf. Monseñor Brandâo Vilela, "Los sacerdotes extranjeros en América latina," *Mensaje* (Madrid, April 1968):9.

275. *ICI* 344 (1969):8.

276. Cf. *Mensaje* 186 (Santiago, 1970):26, and Dom Hélder Câmara, "El asesinato del Padre Henrique Pereira Neto," *CELAM* (Bogotá, June 1969):10.

277. Buenaventura Pelegrí, "Meditación ante el cadáver del Padre Antonio Henrique," *Víspera* 12 (September 1969):3.

278. Gheerbrant, op. cit., pp. 328— 354, for the testimony of Fathers Alipio de Freitas and Lage Pessoa, two heroes among many. See also the declaration of the priests in Fortaleza regarding the arrest of the Capuchin priest, Geraldo Bonfim. *IL ¿PP?*, pp. 193— 95.

279. *IL ¿PP?*, pp. 225— 235. For the first "Golconda Declaration," see *LADOC* 2 (June 1970):9.

280. Ibid., p. 227.

281. Ibid., pp. 229— 31.

282. Ibid., pp. 231— 34.

283. *ICI* 339 (1969):33.

284. Ibid. 356 (1970):16.

285. Cf. *IDOC-International* 22 (April 15, 1970), and *Between Honesty and Hope*.

286. *ICI* 224 (1964):38.

287. *IL ¿PP?*, p. 295.

288. Ibid., p. 296.

289. Ibid.

290. Ibid., p. 314.

291. The declaration of twenty-one priests in Arequipa, March 1969, regarding the marriage of Bishop Mario Cornejo and the attitude of the priests of Trujillo indicates the maturity of the Peruvian clergy (ibid., pp. 327— 31). The priests in Trujillo, incidentally, openly challenged their bishop, Carlos Jurgens Byrne.

292. *ICI* 277 (1966):9. In contrast, 220 missionaries in Chile were "dealt with" when the

meaning of their presence in the country was questioned (*IL ¿PP?* , pp. 198— 209). "This incident is indicative of the fact that rather than being on a dead end street the Church in Latin America has the historic opportunity to ordain married men, and could thereby clarify the mission of celibate priests who, because of their preparation, would be more disposed to itinerant service" (p. 106).

293.*Criterio* (November 28, 1969):678.

294. More detailed information was not available. Cf. *ICI* 353 (1970):14.

295. Ibid. 292 (1967):13.

296. Cf. my article, "From Secularization to Secularism" (1969), pp. 93— 119.

297. Cf. René Laurentin, *Flashes sur l'Amérique latine* (Paris: Éditions du Seuil, 1968), pp. 23— 28, 110— 39, along with the letter from Méndez Arceo and the commentary by Segundo Gaililea.

298. *IL ¿PP?*, p. 272. The priest Manuel Alzate, who was suspended *a divinis* for having criticized the episcopacy, gave some consideration to beginning a new priestly movement. Meanwhile in Cuernavaca, twelve priests did a study of the accomplishments of Mexico's Institutional Revolutionary Party (PRI) during its forty years of governing the country. Cf. *IDOC-International* 3 (August 1, 1969).

299. Río Piedras, Puerto Rico: Ed. Isla, 1968.

300. Ibid., pp. 18— 19. Explicit criticism always relates specifically to the Church. Monseñor Parrilla has said many things that only a few have had the courage to say.

301. Ibid., p. 101.

302. Ibid., p. 123. The bishops should read what is said about them (pp. 165— 216). "Today, the clergy, so marginalized in Canon Law, as they were marginalized in Vatican Council II [?], and in the hearts of many bishops — so much so that they declare the opposite to be the case — ask the same question to their pastors: "My hierarchical Church, sleepest thou?" (p. 265), reminding one of the question of Jesus in Gethsemane to his disciples.

303. Cf. *IL ¿PP?*, pp. 265— 268.

304. Ibid., pp. 273— 74 (May 1968).

305. Ibid.. pp. 238— 39.

306. Cf. Francisco Bravo, *The Parish of San Miguelito* (Cuernavaca: CIDOC, 1966).

307. Cf. *Boletín-CELAM* (Bogotá, April 1970):3, for the television address of Monseñor Marcos McGrath criticizing Medrano's expulsion.

308. *ICI* 364 (1970):16.

309. *Informe, CIDOC.* pp. 67— 170.

310. *IL ¿PP?*, pp. 245— 49.

311. These statements were very courageous regarding the problems with COMIBOL (October 6, 1965). Other statements on the Church in the process of transformation were issued in February 1968, and still others regarding the proposed reforms in May 1968 (ibid., pp. 145— 64).

312. *Criterio*, November 13, 1969, contained a vigorous denunciation.

313. *IL ¿PP?*, p. 284.

314. Ibid., p. 380.

315. Lage, "The Church and the Revolutionary Movement in Brazil," Gheerbrant, op. cit., pp. 335— 54.

316. "Boletín" of DEVOC (Department of Vocations of CELAM, 1970).

317. *ICI* 231 (1964):15.

318. Cf. *IDOC-International* 4 (June 15, 1969).

319. *ICI* 357 (1978):17.

320. "Estudio sociográfico de los religiosos y las religiosas en América latina," *Perspectivas* (Bogotá: CLAR, 1971), p. 26.

321. Ibid., p. 26.

322. Ibid., p. 27.

323. *Boletín de la CLAR* III, 1 (1965):1. For a minimum bibliography on this subject, consult the CLAR bulletin number I, 1 of January 1963, and also the *Colección CLAR:* 1. *La Renovación y adaptación de la vida religiosa en América latina* (5ª ed., 1971), which at the time included more than twelve volumes; and 2. *Perspectivas* which began with *La pobreza evangélica hoy* (1971), plus two other volumes in the series published the same year. See also the Vatican Council II "Decree on the Appropriate Renewal of the Religious Life" (*Perfectae caritatis*) approved during the fourth period of the Council (October 28, 1965), *The Documents of Vatican II,* pp. 187– 96; and Section 12 on the "Religious," *Medellín Conclusions,* pp. 187– 96, together with *Misión del religioso en América latina, Colección CLAR* 5 (Bogotá, 1971):19ff.

324. Vatican Council II "Decree on the Appropriate Renewal of the Religious Life" (*Perfectae caritatis*) no. 2, *The Documents of Vatican II,* pp. 468– 469.

325. *Boletín de CLAR* VI, 8 (1968):8.

326. Ibid. VI, 9– 10 (1968). The document "Misión del religioso en América latina" appears in this issue and was later published as a booklet in the *Colección CLAR,* No. 5.

327. Section 12, no. 3, on the "Religious," *Medellín Conclusions,* p. 188.

328. Ibid., nos. 10– 11, pp. 190, 191.

329. Ibid., no. 12, p. 191.

330. "La vida religiosa en América latina," *Colección CLAR,* no. 8 (Bogotá: CLAR, 1970), p. 23.

331. Ibid., p. 30.

332. Ibid., p. 11. Cf. in this book from the *Colección CLAR* No. 8, the conclusion of the III Conferencia latinoamericana de provinciales de los hermanos de las escuelas cristianas, the conclusions of the 1st Latin American Meeting of Salesian Inspectors, and the "Carta de los superiores provinciales de la Compañía de Jesús que trabajan en América latina." In this last source note the comment that "the Company of Jesus which labors in Latin America desires to dedicate more members to these works, and continually attempt to promote responsibility on the part of the people themselves for assuming a leading role in their own liberation" (ibid., p. 72).

333. *Boletín de CLAR* VII, 9 (1969):1– 2. See also my address on "La liberación de la mujer en la Iglesia," CIDAL (Cuernavaca) III, 3 (1972):36– 44, where I state: "The erotic man-woman relationship and the relation of actual physical maternity are consecrated in order to achieve the pedagogical and political level of maximum freedom according to the prophetic demand of the faith" (p. 43). From June 27 to July 3, 1971, there was a meeting in Bogotá on the "Problems of feminine religious life in Latin America." Cf. *Boletín de CLAR* IX, 7 (1971):1.

334. Ibid. VII (March 1970):4– 5.

335. Cf. the Vatican Council II "Decree on the Apostolate of the Laity" (*Apostolicam actuositatem*), *The Documents of Vatican II,* pp. 489– 521; and Section 10, "Lay Movements," of the *Medellín Conclusions,* pp. 163– 70, which were approved after much difficulty and debate. CELAM has a Department of the Lay Apostolate, which met in the *VI Semana interamericana de AC* in Buenos Aires, October 7– 9, 1966, under the presidency of Monseñor Dammert Bellido. The conclusions of these meetings were "severe" regarding the hierarchy of the Church.

336. Cf. *ICI* 285 (1967):7, declarations that were made during the period of January 27– 31, 1967.

337. *Los católicos posconciliares* (1970), pp. 269– 270.

338. Ibid., p. 159. Cf. *ICI* 263 (1966):8.

339. *ICI* 306 (1968).

340. Ibid. 329 (1970):11.

341. Ibid. 353– 54 (1970).

342. Ibid. 359 (1970):19.

343. Ibid. 241 (1965):23.

344. *Directorio,* CELAM, 1968, p. 43.

345. *ICI* 285—86 (1967).

346. Gheerbrant, op. cit., p. 73.

347. Ibid., pp. 74, 75.

348. "A Lay Critique of the Medellín Draft," *Between Honesty and Hope*, pp. 193—200. The clarity of the above statement is not as evident in the conversations of Cerro Alegre (Cañete, Perú), March 6—9, 1962, in the "Meeting for Reflection," although it did open new areas for consideration, e.g., the statement "the Marxists precipitate revolution from outside (of Latin America), while Christians promote it from within" (p. 33).

349. Cf. *Mensaje* (August 1967):362—63.

350. Cf. *Christus* (México, October 1967):946—49, and (January—June 1969):8—11.

351. *El Catolicismo* (Bogotá, March 19, 1967).

352. Ibid. (November 10, 1968):21.

353. See for example the "Carta pastoral sobre la misión general" of Monseñor Emilio Tagle Covarrubias, Archbishop of Valparaíso in *La revista católica* (Santiago, May—August 1963):3843—47.

354. "The Dogmatic Constitution on the Church" (*Lumen Gentium*), nos. 8—14, *The Documents of Vatican II*, pp. 22—23.

355. "Joint Pastoral Planning," no. 10, *Medellín Conclusions*, p. 226.

356. Cf. Laurentin, *L'Amérique latine a l'heure de l'enfantement* (1968), p. 112. Cf. pp. 52ff., 61ff., 69ff., 101ff., 169ff.; and José Marins, *La comunidad eclesial de base* (Buenos Aires: Ed. Bonum, 1971); and Antonio Alonso, *Comunidades eclesiales de base* (Salamanca: Sígueme, 1970).

357. Cf. the excellent interpretation of A. Methol Ferré, et al., "La DC ante su crisis," *Víspera* 3 (November 1969):39—80.

358. From an immense bibliography on the subject one may consult the following: *Juventud y cristianismo en América latina*, the final document of the seminary sponsored by the "Departamento de Educación del CELAM" (Bogotá, May 18—24, 1969); the *Documento de Buga*, the final document of the seminar of educational experts sponsored by the "Departamento de Educación del CELAM" (Buga, Colombia, February 12—18, 1967), *IL ¿PP?*, pp. 41—59. In regard to the Buga meeting see *Víspera* 5 (1968):69—77; "Introducción a la metodología de los movimientos apostólicos universitarios," MIEC-JECI, Servicio de documentación series 1, documents 17—18 (October 1969); *Iglesia-Universidad*, Centro "Conflicto y replanteamiento en la universidad católica del Peru," *Víspera* 6 (1968):39.

359. Cf. *Víspera* 4 (January 1968):69—88.

360. Ibid., p. 70.

361. *Iglesia-Universidad* (1968), p. 74, and as recently expressed by C. Aguilar, pp. 26—28. Cf. Rudolph Atcon, "La universidad latinoamericana," *Revista Eco* (Bogotá, May 1963):37—39.

362. Freire declares: "It is only the oppressed who, by freeing themselves, can free their oppressors. The latter, as an oppressive class, can free neither others nor themselves." *Pedagogy of the Oppressed*, p. 42.

363. *Verbum* (Río, May—June 1964):61—66.

364. *ICI* 288 (1967):19.

365. In the "Declaration on Christian Education" (*Gravissimum Educationis*), no. 10, *Documents of Vatican II*, pp. 648—49.

366. "Education," *Medellín Conclusions*, pp. 97—106.

367. *IL ¿PP?*, p. 54. Cf. "Catholic Universities in Latin America," *LADOC* 13 (February 1971), I, 53.

368. *IL ¿PP?*, p. 55. This document was approved by the CELAM and the Roman Congregation of Universities and Seminaries. Cf. *Víspera* 1 (Paris, 1967), and *Los cristianos en la universidad* (Bogotá: Departamento de Educación del CELAM, 1967).

369. *IL ¿PP?*, pp. 47—58.

370. Cf. *Esprit* 7—8 (1965):138—39, for the declaration.

371. Cf. *México: Iglesia y movimiento estudiantil,* series 3, document 11 (Montevideo: Servicio de documentación de MIEC-JECI, 1969), and in *CIDOC* 69 – 122.

372. *ACM* (México, October 15, 1968):4 – 7.

373. Habegger, "Apuntes . . . ," *Los católicos posconciliares en Argentina,* p. 194. Cf. H. Aguila, "Los cambios no bastan," *Confirmado* (Buenos Aires: June 12, 1969).

374. *ICI* 349 (1969):17.

375. Cf. the address of Dom Hélder, "La universidad en América latina," April 19, 1969. *CIDOC* 69 – 147, pp. 1 – 7.

376. *Evangelii Nuntiandi,* p. 30.

377. *Excelsior* (7 Oct. 1977), p. 2.

378. Ibid.

379. *Excelsior* (8 Oct. 1977), p. 3.

380. *ICI* 388 (1971):17.

381. *ICI* 428 (1973):12.

382. *La Nación* (Buenos Aires), 15 Nov. 1972, p. 9.

383. *Marcha* 1620 (1972):20.

384. *Uno más uno,* Spanish text (Mexico City, 26 Dec. 1977), p. 3.

385. *Liberación de la liberación* (Bogotá: Paulinos, 1976), p. 38.

386. R. Roncagliolo and F. Reyes Matta, *Iglesia, prensa y militares* (Mexico City: ILET, 1978), p. 91.

387. *Brasil ¿milagro-engaño?* (Lima: CEP, 1973), p. 110.

388. Cf. F. Hinkelammert, *Ideología del sometimiento* (San José, Costa Rica: EDUCA, 1977), pp. 41ff.

389. Cf. Gilberto Giménez, "El golpe militar y la condenación de cristianos por el socialismo," *Contacto* 1 – 2 (1975):12 – 115.

390. *Praxis de los padres,* p. 170.

391. Ibid., p. 847.

392. Ibid., p. 858.

393. *Excelsior* (20 March 1979), p. 9.

394. *Praxis de los padres,* p. 967.

395. "Christian Identity in Action for Justice," 21 Nov. 1976, No. 17.

396. *Documentos colectivos del episcopado mexicano* (Mexico City: Paulinas, 1977), pp. 313 – 69.

397. *Noticias Aliadas* (20 Nov. 1975), p. 9, n. 43.

398. *Boletín CELAM* 113 (1977):14 – 15.

399. R. Cooper, K. Kaiser, and M. Kosaka, "Towards a Renovated International System," draft report presented in Tokyo (9 – 11 Jan. 1977), *Estados Unidos* (Mexico City: CIDE, 1978), p. 94.

400. Ibid., p. 91.

401. *Noticias Aliadas* 26 (1973):2ff.

402. *Proceso* 86 (Mexico City, 26 June 1978):13.

403. For details see my forthcoming work, *De Medellín a Puebla (1968 – 1979),* 490 pages.

404. See my article "Crónica de Puebla," *Christus,* March – April 1979.

405. The paragraph numbers herein cited are from the first edition of the Final Document published following the conclusion of the III Conferencia General del Episcopado Latinoamericano, *Puebla: La Evangelización en el Presente y en el futuro de América Latina* (Consejo Episcopal Latinoamericano – CELAM, 1979). The text has apparently gone through several revisions, for the paragraph numbers in the copy of the Spanish text I have utilized are not those which Prof. Dussel cites in his comments. Furthermore, I understand that the forthcoming English edition of the Final Document will also be distinct from the Spanish. – Tr.

406. Text in off-set, p. VIII.

407. See paragraphs 47, 50 of *Puebla;* the key text is found in paragraphs 542 – 546. Reference is made to the question of Marxism in an ambiguous manner, and "the risk" is

seen (Par. 545) in ideologization. In reality there is no concrete condemnation, but it is rather very abstract and general. But this should be relative in the light of formulations such as: "The fear of Marxism prohibits many from facing the oppressive reality of liberal capitalism" (Par. 92).

408. Italics mine.
409. Italics mine.
410. Text of 3d Edition, Commission 6, Par. 16, p. 4.
411. *Uno más uno,* 22 February 1979, p. 11.
412. *CENCOS* (July 1979) p. 10.
413. Ibid.
414. Italics mine.
415. Manuscript letter, pp. 1 – 2, with signatures.

NOTES FOR CHAPTER XII

1. Freire, *Pedagogy of the Oppressed,* p. 28.
2. Ibid.
3. Levinas, op. cit., in the French edition, *Totalité et infini* (Den Haag: Nijoff, 1961), pp. 269 – 70: "Dieu sortant de son éternité pour créer. ... Mais dès lors, autrui, par sa signification, antérieure à mon initiative ressemble à Dieu. ... Un principe perce tout ce vertige et tout ce tremblement, quand le visage se présente et reclame justice."
4. Various works have tended toward this position, such as the original and important writings of Juan Luis Segundo, *Función de la Iglesia en la realidad rioplatense* (Montevideo: Barreiro y Ramos, 1962), *La cristiandad, ¿una utopia?*, (Montevideo: CCC, 1964), 2 vols., in which Segundo states: "Christianity is therefore a profound call to the minority impulse, free and personal, of all human beings" (2:92); and *Teología abierta para el laico adulto* (Buenos Aires: Lohle, 1968), especially his discussion "De la sociedad a la teología."
5. Cf., for example, José Comblin, *Christianismo y desarrollo* (Quito: IPLA, 1970). This outstanding Belgian theologian who has lived for many years in Latin America had not yet participated in the dialogue on the theology of liberation.
6. A certain liberal progressivism gives equal preponderance to the elite: the model of post-Christendom is that of *a* person aware, free, and convinced of the rightness of a democratic, liberal, secular pluralism. The "model" is the North Atlantic society. The *Criterio* group, made up primarily of theologians from various theological faculties, began to be critical of this model.
7. Hugo Assmann, *Teología de la liberación* (Montevideo: JECI, 1970), pp. 44 – 45.
8. In 1959 – 1961, while in Israel, I discussed this question with Paul Gautheir, which he later presented in written form in his *Les pauvres, Jésus et l'Eglise* (Paris: Ed. Universitaires, 1962). Cf. Benoît Dumas, "Los dos rostros de la Iglesia," *Víspera* 17, and in *Parole et Mission* 51 (Paris, 1970):293 – 304.
9. The developmental stage (other than in the work already cited) is presented in F. Houtart and O. Vetrano, *Hacia una teología del desarrollo* (Buenos Aires: Libros latinoamericanos, 1969), or V. Cosmâo, *Signification et théologie du développement* (París: IRFED, 1967). The next stage is discussed by Hugo Assmann, "Die Situation der unterentwickelt gehaltenen Länder als Ort einer Theologie der Revolution," *Diskussion zur "Theologie der Revolution"* (München: Chr. Kaiser, 1969), pp. 218 – 48.
10. Cf. Paul Asveld, *La pénsee religieuse du jeune Hegel. Liberté et aliénation,* (Louvain: Univ. Louvain, 1953); Adrien Peperzak, *Le jeune Hegel et la vision moral du monde* (The Hague: Nijhoff, 1960); Georg Lukács, *Der junge Hegel und die Probleme der kapitalistischen Gesellschaft* (Berlin: Aufbau, 1954).
11. Cf., for example, Marcuse, "Liberation from the Affluent Society," *To Free a Gen-*

eration, ed. David Cooper (New York: Collier Books, 1968), pp. 175–192; and his *An Essay on Liberation* (Boston: Beacon Press, 1969). Paul Sartre deals with the question in the "Preface" of Frantz Fanon's *The Wretched of the Earth,* trans. Constance Farrington (New York: Grove Press, 1966).

12. Virtually the same paper appeared in mimeographed form in Lima in 1970, and was subsequently published and distributed as "Apuntes para una teología de la liberación" (66 pp.), and as "Notes for a Theology of Liberation," *Theological Studies* 31 (June 1970):243–61.

13. Papers of the conferences were published as *Liberación. Opción de la Iglesia en la década del 70:* and *Aportes para la liberación* (Bogotá: Editorial Presencia, 1970), 2 vols. Cf. L. Gera, *La Iglesia debe comprometerese en lo político* (Montevideo: Servicio de Documentacion del JECI. 1970).

14. The Brazilian Protestant theologian Rubem Alves has written several essays on the subject including: "El pueblo de Dios y la liberación del hombre," *Fichas de ISAL* III, 26 (1970):7–12, and his book *Religión: ¿opio o instrumento de liberación?* (Montevideo: Tierra Nueva, 1968).

15. In *Criterio* 1607–1608 (November 1970):783–90.

16. J. B. Metz in *Diskussion zur "politischen Theologie"* (München Mantz: Kaiser-Grünewal, 1969), pp. 267ff. and the bibliography of W. Darschin, *ibid.,* pp. 302–17.

17. Cf. my *Para una ética de la liberación,* §§ 4–6, regarding historical comprehension and the dialectic of being. See also my *La dialéctica hegeliana* (1972), chapter 4.

18. Levinas, op. cit.

19. "Church" and "world" are used and misused without logical and ontological knowledge of the "contradiction" (*Widerspruch* in German). Hegel prefers to use "opposition," following the tradition of Fichte and Schelling. But "opposition" or the "Church vs. world" terminology has no relation to the "contradiction" in Aristotelian logic. For this reason, in Spanish and English, to maintain the correct meaning, it is better to use the idea of "correlation."

20. Cf. Juan Scannone, "La situación actual de la Iglesia argentina y la imagen de Dios Trino y Uno," *Estudios* (Buenos Aires, October 1970):20–23.

21. "Circumincession" is the theological doctrine emphasizing the reciprocal existence (i.e., in each other) of the three Persons of the Trinity. — Tr.

22. *Conciencialismo* signifies the giving of an inordinate importance to individual or personal awareness, in contrast to indiscriminate or uncritical popular experience.

NOTES FOR THE CONCLUSION

1. I have dealt with the question of overcoming the difficulties of modernity in an address later published and entitled, "Crisis de la Iglesia latinoamericana y situación del pensador cristiano en Argentina," *Stromata* (1970), pp. 277–336. I have not dealt with the metaphysical issue in the article (as it was already clearly present in the Spanish conquistador and philosophically expressed by Descartes in his *ego cogito*); but the metaphysical is the fundamental factor in the dialectic of the dominator-dominated. The overcoming of the difficulties of modernity on the ontological level is equally the condition of and conditioned by the overcoming of the dialectic of oppression on the international political level. This issue I have discussed in other works, e.g., *Para una ética de la liberación latinoamericana* (1973), 3 vols.

Appendices

Appendix I

Reflections on Methodology for a History of the Church in Latin America

An exposition by Professor Doctor Enrique D. Dussel, President of the Commission for Latin American Church History, given on January 3, 1973, in the meeting room of the Ecuadorian Episcopal Conference.

Your Excellency, Secretary General of CELAM, Monseñor Alfonso Trujillo; Your Excellency, Auxiliary Bishop of Quito, Monseñor Antonio González; esteemed Director of IPLA, Presbiter Segundo Galilea; colleagues of the Commission; and invited Consultive Members. I trust that you will interpret these words as reflections that are not intended to exclude other points of view. My explicit purpose is to propose some programmatical or hypothetical aids and material for our dialogue during this day of work together. For this reason I have entitled my remarks, "*A*" history of the Church and not "*The*" history of the Church, for only God himself has the complete, accurate, and unique understanding of the history which will finally be revealed to us at the Judgment and which we now anticipate analogically by faith.

My exposition will be in three parts: anthropological-historical, theological, and epistemological reflections. I want to begin with an outline of the fundamental question that we face, and avoid repeating the common equivocation among historians of the Church in Latin America.

"Methodology" suggests to us — as a composite word of Greek origin, a *lógos* or thinking regarding method (from *meta* + *hodos* way), that is, thinking about the procedure or process for attaining an objective, a mode of inquiry employing a systematic procedure or technique — a way of doing something. Methodology is, therefore, a reflection on the procedure one utilizes. It is one thing to follow an habitual method and quite another thing to reflect carefully on the method one follows. .

In these reflections, I will propose a certain method by which I will describe a history of the Church in Latin America. The subject will be approached by actual and not abstract historians, and these historians will discover the theme in order to express it, that is, in order to begin to write history. But in order to describe the subject one must discover the *meaning* of the ecclesial events. The discovery of the meaning will be attained by putting oneself within a certain horizon of comprehension in a way that it becomes impossible to give a description which is not at the same time a discovery of the meaning. And this description will always be an *interpretation*. For the Christian to discover the meaning of the something within a horizon of comprehension is to uncover something by faith which at the same time has been established by revelation.

If the Christian historian is to interpret an event, it is inevitable that he do so in the light of faith. The revealed faith may or may not be made clear by a theology. But in science this clarification is necessary. The historical-scientific interpretation should set forth clearly the norms or categories of faith illuminated by theology in order to know how to interpret the ecclesial event.

Historical-scientific interpretation is a part of this unique theology as the *methodical* Christian interpretation of the history of the Christian people.

I. ANTHROPOLOGIC-HISTORICAL REFLECTIONS ON LATIN AMERICAN CULTURE

What is the *meaning* of Latin America in universal history?

The historian is one who charts a course from history and gives a scientific expression to what has happened. Yet, the historian is always *in* a world, and this is his problem. Before becoming a man of science, the historian already has a certain horizon of understanding of what has happened.

From his daily horizon the historian begins to study the subject or the historical event. An historical event can only be expressed, however, after discovering the meaning of the event. The historian, therefore, is always in danger of lapsing into an ingenuousness, especially when he believes that he is about to give an *objective* and scientific interpretation for all times. The truth is, the historian will only objectify the biases he has always held and continually holds.

The horizon of daily comprehension of one who studies history is that which gives meaning to what is studied. The fundamental horizon of comprehension is the common horizon of the historian, the everyday horizon of the historian. If we are Latin Americans, Latin America then constitutes our everyday horizon of understanding. But if we are also part of an intellectual elite formulated in Europe, our horizon of understanding will be of that world. The *meaning* of the event which is the object of our study lies always within a certain horizon. And one must recognize this horizon in order to describe the meaning of the event in question.

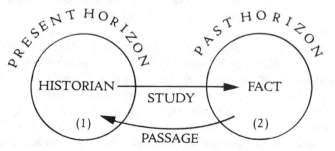

To this one must add that the event, the object of study, is not only "present" in the sense that it is occurring *now*, but also in the sense that it is a *past* event. But to say that an event is past signifies that it "*was*-in-a-world" that now "is not."

The historian lives in his *world* (1). Meanwhile, the theme or subject of his study is in *its world* (2). It was a fact that "*was*-in-a-world" but no longer is. To illustrate, let us take an example. Today, when one walks up to the Acropolis in Athens and enters the Parthenon, he sees no longer a real and sacred temple, but rather a tourist site. But for those in the Greek world, to enter the Parthenon was to enter a holy place, a place dedicated to the worship of the gods. The Parthenon "*was*-in-a-world," but this "world" no long exists. The reconstruction or historical description should, therefore, begin by recreating the horizon of comprehension of a world in which the past event made "sense" for that world. When we encounter such an event from within the horizon of our present world, we must consider with care the "passage" that formulates *from* that horizon which "was" (the past world of this event) to our horizon where the "fact" is, in such a way that the past event will have a new "meaning," "our" meaning, a meaning distinct from that which it had in the past world.

There are two ways in which one can approach the past. The first is to approach it ingenuously. The other is to approach it critically. The ingenuous approach is that which objectifies in the past a present meaning of the events. The critical approach is that which attempts to recreate the conditions that made possible the past historical event. Let me illustrate the difference with the following example. Ingenuously one can applaud and regard as heroes Simón Bolívar and San Martín. But critically, if we see San Martín in his historical context, we will recognize that he led a rebellion against his fellow Spanish soldiers who were for the most part "royalists," and that he was considered by them to be a "traitor." San Martín disobeyed the Spanish laws, "the Laws of the Indies" (before which he was a lawbreaker), and he risked the possibility of being condemned by the Pope who had issued the Bull *Etsi Longissimo*, January 30, 1816, which condemned the struggle for independence. San Martín's acts placed his Christian conscience in a state of culpability. Nowadays it is easy to applaud those heroes, but it is quite another thing to understand *critically* the historical conditions that produced them. It is even more difficult to imitate them today.

A *critical* interpretation presupposes taking into account the multiple aspects and conditionings of all kinds that historians in general, and even more so the historians of the Church, tend to ignore. This is precisely the problem of the *hermeneutic* or question of *interpretation*. To illustrate the magnitude of this problem, let me propose as a second example an interpretation of the "Latin American fact" in universal history. I am, of course, aware that mine is merely one possible "interpretation" among others. In our contemporary world how can we describe the "meaning" of Latin American culture in universal history? Darcy Ribeiro has attempted an outline in which Latin America has a "place" in his history. Toynbee, Spengler, Sorokin, and Weber have — as Leopoldo Zea said — left Latin America "outside of history."

But Latin America has a *unique* place in universal history, and therefore the Latin American Church also has a *unique* place in the history of the universal Church.

1. *The first stage*, Latin American prehistory, is found in our great neolithic civilizations, the history of the Maya-Aztec and Inca, and to a lesser degree of the Chibcha. Our prehistory is related to universal prehistory by way of the Pacific.

If we begin our historical description with Mesopotamia or with Egypt, India, or China in the fourth millennium before Christ, then we will be describing history much earlier than the great Maya-Aztec or Inca cultures, both of which developed during the first millennium after Christ. The Maya-Aztec of Mexico, the Inca of Peru, and the Chibcha in the Magdalena and Cauca valleys were the cultures of "nuclear America," leaving aside the areas of the tropical agriculturalists and the nomads of the plains and pampas of both North and South America.

Latin America entered neolithic universal history with the migration that began in the Euro-Asiatic continent, transversing the Pacific and arriving in America, and it would be entirely inexplicable to deal with the prehistory of Latin America and ignore the neolithic history of the Polynesians or the paleolithic history of the Euro-Asiatics and the Africans from whom the original American people developed not too many milennia ago. This would be the first stage of our history.

2. *The second stage*, if it is to be understood, must also recover the history of the

eastern Mediterranean region, In order to know who Columbus is, we must complete our description. An understanding of Latin American history demands that Latin Americans comprehend all of universal history. And only after comprehending universal and Latin American history can we ask ourselves the meaning of the history of the Church. Thus, in order to know who Columbus is, one must begin with the Mesopotamian and Egyptian cultures as well as those of the Anatolic and the Cretan cultures. We must understand in particular the history of the Indo-European invasions. For the Indo-Europeans invaded southern Europe, coming from the areas north of the Black and Caspian seas, and in a relatively short time they dominated the great cultures of the "half Moon" and Indo-Europeanized the areas of the Roman Empire, the Persian Empire, the Hindu kingdom, and even the Chinese Empire so influenced by the "Tao."

3. *The third stage* resulted from the great Semitic migrations. The Semites, from whom emerged Christianity, had another perspective of the world, and therefore another perspective of history. A few centuries after the beginning of Christianity, the whole of the Roman Empire had been Christianized. Later the Persian world was "Islamized," and Muslims eventually arrived as far East as India. Thus one can assert that there has been a kind of "Semitization" of the neolithic cultic world which earlier had been "Indo-Europeanized." And from this process there emerged two great Christendoms: the Latin and the Byzantine-Russian. Both of them — the Latin and the Greek — dominated the world later referred to as European and in which Spain was a single province. All of these events are a part of our *protohistory,* and we must understand well the Christendom of our historical origins. From A.D. 330, the year that Constantinople was founded, until the day that Columbus sailed for America — the same year that the Spanish were able to reconquer Granada and expel the Arab Moors — the history of the two Christendoms was completed.

To understand this process is to understand who is Columbus, who are the majority of the missionaries, and who are the majority of our first bishops, that is, to understand the history of the *Patronato.* Latin America and the Latin American Church are incomprehensible without understanding this history.

4. *The fourth stage* can be called protohistory. I would begin our history with the day in which the most western of the West — Spain — and the most eastern of the East — the Indians (the Indians were Asiatics) — encountered each other in what was the process of conquest and evangelization, the great process of aculturation. In 1492 the history of Latin America began not as "the-father-Spain" nor "the-mother-India," but rather as a child which was neither Indian nor European, but something completely distinct.

From this history Latin America soon emerged. Byzantium was a world, an *ecumene,* as was Russia (the "third Rome"), Latin Europe, the Arabs, the Hindus, and the Chinese. Together they comprised six coexistent ecumenes. But the Aztecs and the Incas were also ecumenes. In all there were in the fifteenth century eight ecumenes. Each of them believed itself to be the only ecumene and contended that outside their horizons lived infidels and barbarians.

But in the sixteenth century one ecumene conquered all the others, and the first to be oppressed was America. Latin America was to carry in its essence the new historical European oppressive moment. Europe, in the center, would bypass the Arab world and arrive in Asia. Soon it would touch America by way of the Pacific. From the sixteenth to the twentieth centuries, a new world structure developed: the eight ecumenes were reduced to one, and the "center" of this ecumene was first Europe, then the United States and Russia — after which one could add Japan, Canada, and Australia.

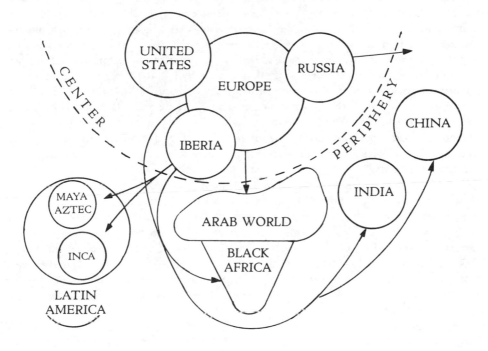

Europe thus conquered the Orient, weakened the Arab world, and conquered and colonized Africa and America. There developed, therefore, a "center" and a "periphery." Europe constituted the center and created the periphery, and the center would have as one pole of expansion Russia—for Russia expanded through Siberia to the Pacific on the East during the sixteenth century—and Spain and Portugal as the other pole of expansion via the Atlantic. In the twentieth century—following the Second World War—the center would be constituted by the United States, Europe, and Russia. Historically, Latin America remained with Black Africa, Islam, India, China, and Southeast Asia as peripheral cultures, dependent upon the central macroculture. Latin America remained as a part of the periphery, yet as the *only* underdeveloped part of post-Christendom. For the other peripheral cultures were dominated by Islam, animism, Hinduism, the Maoist revolution, and Buddhism in Southeast Asia. This is to say that during the period following World War II, Latin America was the only dependent area in Christendom, the only colonial Christendom. Neither Latin nor Byzantine Christendom could be said to have been dependent.

This interpretive outline, therefore, attempts to respond to the question: what is the meaning of Latin American culture in universal history? Now we are ready to pose the second question.

II. THEOLOGICAL REFLECTIONS ON THE HISTORY OF THE CHURCH IN LATIN AMERICA

What is the meaning of the history of the Church in Latin America? What function does the Church have in the history of this continent? We are ill-prepared to respond regarding the function of a single part, such as the meaning of the history of the Latin American Church, until we have established the meaning of the whole. But the fact is, an answer for the "whole" of our culture does not exist, because an adequate history of Latin American culture does not exist except for the programmatic studies written by Darcy Ribeiro as we mentioned above. It is possible, however, that if we ask ourselves how to write a history of the Church we will at the same time advance the question of how to give an exposition of a history of Latin America in a critical way.

There is a world, in the sense indicated above, where the pre-Christian or non-Christian historian is situated. And this world, in the light of faith, acquires a new "meaning." In the pre-Christian world of the Roman Empire there was money, and from the Roman horizon of understanding the money had a certain value. But upon becoming a Christian, the Roman had another horizon of understanding opened to him, and the same money acquired a new significance, another value, because in changing his horizon of understanding the *meaning* of all intraworldly entities changed. One can say ontologically that faith is a *new world* in the sense that a new horizon of understanding opens. This existential faith, because it is living, occurs every day. It constitutes the day-by-day world, even though it is invaded from outside of this world. This exteriority is the *Word* that reveals as "light" certain questions which earlier were impossible to resolve and in some cases were even unrecognized. This illumination or exteriority is a "cone of light" that is projected upon the world and that gives the world a new meaning.

The Word of God is like a "cone of light" that illuminates in such a way that all that is intraworldly changes meaning. Faith signifies believing the Word of the Other (the Revealer, God), and it is the Word which both clarifies the new horizon of understanding and uncovers a new meaning of all that is taking place.

How can one define, therefore, revelation? What is it that reveals the revealing Word? Revelation is the manifestation of the *Christly fact* ("reality") uncovered by means of interpretive norms. God reveals these norms, coordinates, or categories that allow us to discover what we have seen but see now with a *new* meaning. Moses, for example, was living in the desert, and he knew that his fellow Hebrews were slaves in Egypt. This was an historical fact. But the day came when God revealed to Moses that it was possible to bring the Hebrews out of Egypt, and Moses discovered a *new* meaning, namely, rather than being "natural" slaves they were transformed into "historical" slaves. From continuing to live as slaves they were transformed in the eyes of faith into beings who could possibly be freed from their Egyptian prison. The revelation consisted in gaining a different understanding of the same historical fact. And this new *interpretation* came through the light of faith, through seeing a *new* meaning of reality. Revelation, therefore, has interpretive norms that permit us to discover the "meaning" of events. This is fundamental for the Church historian, for one who is a Christian and who proposes to interpret the same historical phenomena in a way distinct from the non-Christian. The same document, for example, will have a different meaning in the eyes of the Christian scientific historian, because his interpretive norms are different.

What are these norms? In the tradition of the Old and of the New Testament one can observe several essential interpretive categories; for example, the word *basar* in Hebrew (*sárx* in Greek and *flesh* in English). A second fundamental category is that of *ruaj (pneúma* in Greek and *spirit* in English). When the "Spirit" (which is the divine otherness) inhabits the "flesh" (that is, the human *totality* or the creature, which is able to close itself by sin or open itself to the divine gift) the "Word" (*dabár* in

Hebrew, and *logos* in Greek) assumes humanity. Here I am speaking strictly of the "in-carnation."

These revealed categories were utilized early by the prophets and by Christ himself in his theological teaching and preaching. One must be able to discover these categories explicitly in order to know how to use them later in historical interpretation. Beginning with the category of "flesh" — which contemporary thinking calls "Totality" — and "Spirit" (or "Otherness") comes everything else. When the "flesh" is closed to the "Spirit," it sins.

When the "flesh" killed Abel, Cain was transformed into Adam the sinner, because Abel was the Other, the brother; and when Cain killed him, he was left alone. Cain, being alone, declared himself to be God, and in declaring himself to be God, Cain was repeating the sin of Adam. He denied God the Creator and became a fetish worshipper. When the history of the Church is totalized — and it was totalized in the time of *Christendom* as a culture — then Christianity is confused with that culture. When the Church identifies itself with a culture it is unable to hear the voice of the poor (the Other) by which the Spirit speaks, and therefore in these eras it falls into sin. These times are when Christians become closed as an earthly institution and are unable to observe clearly the presence of God in the poor who reveal injustice. The Church can even play at being the Church, and by not serving the poor it can be a part of those who dominate the poor.

Another interpretive norm is faith, and for this reason that which in Hebrew is called *habodáh* (*diakonía* in Greek, the act of the *doûlos,* and *service* in English or simply *work*) is both biblical and evangelical. Jesus indicated that it is characteristic of the "world" that those who have power oppress the weak, but that his followers are characterized by "serving" the poor and the weak. The category of *service* (which is more than *praxis* in that it indicates the gratitude of one who serves the other as other and not because of "necessity") refers to the action of the "Servant of Yahweh." It is liberating action (Isaiah 61:1ff.). It is when the "flesh" is resurrected by "Spirit" to new life and is both opened to the poor and serves the poor effectively. Thus the "worship" of the temple is divine "service" (*habodáh*), and "service" (*habodáh*) to the poor is the worship rendered to Jesus who identified with the poor (Matthew 25:11ff.). This service effects "release from prison" (God said to Moses, "*I ehitsaló,*" that is, "Bring them out," "Liberate them") for the slave. And this idea of liberation is truly biblical and Christian (cf. Exodus 3). When the "flesh" is closed, it becomes of necessity the dominator of the poor. Now we move closer to the essential category for the history of the Church. For if the Church is only relating a history of itself as an earthly institution — and it does this well in triumphalist histories — it can be a history of its alliance with the dominating powers. Meanwhile, if the gestures of solidarity with the poor are studied together with service to the poor, a strictly evangelical norm will be indicated.

There are many other categories that could be mentioned, but these are indicative of those which can be utilized from the Christian faith.

From this perspective one can ask, "What is the Church?" The Church is a *prophetic-institution* in the sense that it is an institution *in* the world fulfilling an eschatological and prophetic task in order to move history forward from the poor. There are cultures that turn in upon themselves as totalities such as the Roman Empire. The Church, committing itself to the poor who are always the dominated, pushes the process toward the future, and in this case toward the Holy Roman Empire. And from the Holy Roman Empire the Church formulated Europe. When the "flesh" turns in upon itself as a totality or sin, the Church from the poor pushes history eschatologically toward Christ who comes, who lives as future although already present. If a system turns in upon itself as a complete totality, it fossilizes. The Church in the history of the people comes to remind them that their ultimate destiny is beyond all historical kingdoms. The Church is an institution, but it is a prophetic institution. The Church is in the world, and because of this it can be allied with the dominators or with the poor. One is reminded of the parable of the seeds. There are seeds that fall in poor soil and other seeds that fall in good soil. Those that fall in good soil can germinate and grow. Both categories of seed can, however, represent the Church, and grace is operative in both. But it is the Church of the "poor," the Church of the "just," that allows the seed to grow.

The Church is an institution in the world, and at the same time it serves as the exteriority of the Word, as "outside" of the world criticizing culture and all totality in order to move history toward the Parousia.

Consider the following incidents in Latin American history and ask, "Which is the more important? Was it the founding of the Archbishopric of Santo Domingo, Concepción de la Vega, and Puerto Rico, or the preaching of Antonio de Montesinos on that Sunday of Advent in 1511? Which ecclesiastical fact is more relevant?" We know that the episcopal institution is fundamental, but the prophetic announcement of Montesinos is also essential. It is necessary, however, to attempt to discover the meaning of the events in the light of the categories of the Christian faith.

III. REFLECTIONS ON THE EPISTEMOLOGICAL PROTOCOL OF CHURCH HISTORY AS AN HISTORICAL SCIENCE

Only now are we ready to deal with the third subject of this exposition: the epistemological protocol of history, or the history of the Church as a science. At what level are we going to deal with the question? We know that historical science follows a system of investigation called the "historical method." Also, we are aware of the "external criticism" of historical documents (there is also "internal criticism") by which the historian studies ancient writings and inscriptions. These questions regarding any document are asked: Is it authentic or a forgery? What is the date? How was it preserved, discovered, and passed on to us? Along with history are the auxiliary sciences such as sociology, economics, law, psychology, and philosophy. These auxiliary sciences have not been utilized adequately in the writing of the history of the Church in Latin America. But this is not the basic problem. Let us leave aside the fact that the historian of the Church is "an historian," simply because he has acquired the use of the scientific method — if not in the universities, then by the extensive studies of historical documents (many of the Church historians are neither licentiates nor doctors in history, but after thirty or forty years of historical investigation they have become competent historians). The historical method can be perfected not only through university studies, but also by the constant and diligent investigation into the authenticity of historical documentation.

All methods, however, have their limitations, including all of the human sciences. This fact presents a twofold problem.

First, it is impossible in all sciences to attain *total* objectivity. What do we mean by total "objectivity"? The truth is, we have a contradiction in terms, because the historian always views an historical event from one point of view (1) — his object (a). If another historian views the same object from another point of view (2), obviously he will see it differently (b).

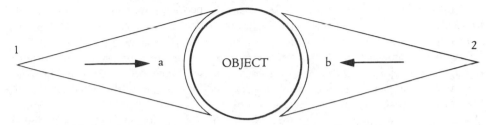

This would indicate that objectivity regarding the object from *1* is not pure or total, but rather limited and localized. Some would say that this is "relativism." We should clarify, however, what we mean by "relative." If by relative we mean that a human being is finite and is limited to his historical situation, then our position would be one of "relativism." But if by relative we mean to say that there is no manner of truth — which is patently false — then what we are saying is not relativistic because we affirm truth. Furthermore, everything can be considered from a perspective that not only is relative, but also that is absolute for everyone situated or localized *in the same sense*. Everything can be viewed from various perspectives and thereby suggest diverse "meanings" of the object (the meaning from perspective *a* is not the same as from *b*). Pure "objectivity," however, signifies analyzing an object from *all* points of view, which means not to analyze it as an object at all. Only the divine creative intelligence can attain this kind of objectivity. *Pure* "objectivity" does not exist. What does exist is situated objectivity.

Second, nonsubjectivity is also impossible. When one regards a description as *objective*, he is classifying the statement as being exempt from all subjective participation. But this is impossible for reasons already stated. All human consideration of any particular subject will be affected by *subjective* historical, sociological, and economic conditionings. And to assume that a description is objective is something quite distinct.

This is not to say that a description should not be subjective, nor that objectivity is *pure*, but that there has to be a methodical access of subjectivity to objectivity. Subjectivity can be nonmethodical, that is, it can attack an object from various perspectives, opinionated or vulgar. One can say out of ignorance, for example, that something is from the eighteenth century when in fact it is from the sixteenth. One makes this mistake because the movement is not methodical toward the object. But even the scientist is unable to leave aside completely his subjectivity, and his methodical subjectivity will be in one way or another a subjectivity. Those who pretend that this subjectivity should not exist, and that objectivity should be absolute or pure — and only then is a description — are saying something very dangerous since they naively objectify a political, economic, or social option, assuming that it is valid for everyone. This is precisely what has happened in the history of the Latin American Church.

To historicize objectivity and to historicize subjectivity is to be able to agree on the historicity of an object. It is to take into consideration all the conditionings that this can signify. *Methodical* subjectivity is called by Ricoeur "transcendental subjectivity" in the sense that it *transcends* more common, opinionated subjectivity and knows how to manage the subject scientifically. But even transcendental subjectivity is an interpretation of the "fact" from *a certain point of view*, which is not the only point of view. The recognition of this truth is very important in the study of the history of the Church, because one cannot write a history from all points of view nor for all Christians, since this would imply that the history has been written by God himself. For God is the only one who has a pure objective perspective of history as it really is. There is, therefore, the following difficulty: if one desires to write a noncommitted history, what he will write will be in fact an anecdotal history which in the last analysis will support the status quo. On the other hand, an historical non-Christian subjectivity will also interpret the same facts and their meaning from a concrete existential horizon, not in the light of faith, and will discover *another* "meaning." Likewise, a methodical historical Christian subjectivity will discover still a *different* "meaning" in the same events, not because the non-Christian interpretation constitutes scientific history while a Christian interpretation is an ideological history. Rather, it is because the horizons of comprehension are different. The truth is that each is an interpretation from a certain perspective and with a certain commitment. To say that an historian is not a Christian is not to say that he is not committed. He can be a liberal, a Marxist, a Buddhist, or a capitalist. He is commited, and he interprets a fact and gives it a certain *meaning* according to his commitment.

All of this is directly related to our proposed history of the Church in Latin America. For what is called the science of the history of the Church is epistemologically situated in a strictly *scientific* framework, because the method utilized is scientific. Those who write this history will be recognized as historians because of their descriptive works of historical facts. But this will be an intrinsically theological work because, in their methodical interpretation, these historians will be clearly aware of the Christian categories they are using in the description of the historical facts. One cannot first describe an historical fact and then proceed to interpret it, for the description is already an interpretation. The study of an authentic document can be "utilized" in various ways. Why, for example, does one historian extract the first paragraphs of a letter while another selects two paragraphs from the heart of the letter, and a third chooses two closing paragraphs? And why when selecting the same paragraphs does one historian ascribe one meaning while the other ascribes a second meaning? The reason is that each historian is interpreting the letter, even when he first reads it, as an important document selected from the thousands studied. Is the description, therefore, *purely* "objective"? No, the description is an interpretation resulting from the historical method utilized *a priori,* giving rise to many different explanations. The document will be verified by both the Christian and the non-Christian in regard to its authenticity. But each one will extract a different *meaning* because the horizon of interpretation of each is different.

A methodical interpretation of the history of the Church is an intrinsic art in theology if our understanding of art is that which is commonly accepted today. If theology is understood to be a syllogistic dogmatic (*more graecorum*), then the history of the Church will not be a part of theology. For that dogmatic has left the history of the Church outside of its constitution. In the Old and New Testaments and in the early Church fathers, history was a constituent part of theological reflection. If the theological categories utilized are not clearly determined, then the interpretation will be commonplace or even anti-Christian, because one can unconsciously use certain interpretive categories of a particular historical school of thought which is not Christian. The fact is that some histories of the Church are anti-Christian in their interpretation of the facts. For this reason it is necessary to know the Christian interpretive norms of day-to-day events or facts.

What can happen with the interpretation of the Christian historian? Our Church historians can be objective, *de hecho,* ingenuously, and their cultural and political option or bias can be held naturally, eternally, as valid for everyone. But they can forget or overlook the fact that an historian is in *his* world and that his world conditions his interpretation. One can incorrectly assume that by being an interpretation according to the historical scientific method, his interpretation is pure and not affected by any *a priori* option. But it is easy to note his choice simply by looking at what he has written. For usually his history is of the "great," of those called "the best" (*aristós* in Greek), that is, an aristocratic history. What about a history of the poor? Where is the history of the Indians, of the mulattoes, of the mestizos? What about the history of the oppressed Latin American people? Is it about to be written? Why? Because the choice is made; it is already made. Historians have described a certain kind of Christianity and have left aside the other. The documental maneuvering was at times methodically established, given the fact that the selection of documents was partial. Some were utilized at one level, but other levels were ignored. And the interpretation given was from a certain bias that was assumed to be unbiased. This was and is doubly dangerous. The description can be scientific because the scientific method is used. But at the same time the interpretation can be from an a-critical perspective. An a-critical interpretation has been purged of that which is "Christian," because the Christian faith always functions critically regarding an event. Thus an a-critical description, even though it is scientific, is in reality secular and makes Church history a secular exercise in the sense that it lacks the criticism of Christianity that prophetically interprets secular historical events.

Furthermore, history is almost always written from the perspective of the elite culture, which is culturally dependent. We have been educated in universities and seminaries in Europe or under European influence, and all of this has given us a certain perspective of reality. And even though we write "scientific" descriptions (this is considered a given), our interpretation is terribly defective.

The following is a suggested typology of positions in which one finds certain Church historians in Latin America.

1. Some give an anecdotal description — and all description is interpretation — of the period of colonial Christendom. Nearly all of the chronicles and the accounts of our colonial history until the nineteenth century are anecdotal descriptions, and they describe events from the Spanish perspective. Today there are many historians who are beginning to work from the *perspective of the defeated,* that is, from that of the Indians. To them reality appears distinct. The first description is basically documental and serves to relate the facts, even though strictly speaking it is not an historical or scientific account.

2. Some histories are written as a liberal, anticonservative description. These were especially prevalent in the nineteenth century when, beginning about 1850, liberalism erupted. History is thus transformed until today (and this is the history that is taught in our educational institutions in almost all Latin American countries) and is an ideological instrument of the education of the people. History, upon achieving a self-interpretation of a culture, permits one to say when the country began who were the "good guys" and who were the "bad guys." Our oligarchies, our liberals, wrote (almost "invented") a history in order to explain the beginning of their glorious acts. Liberal states objectify in their histories their day-to-day naive attitudes as an ideological struggle.

3. Some have written a "revisionist" description, traditional, antiliberal, and *apologetic*. Many of our Church historians are not exempt from this ideological position. Theirs is also a struggle that is not basically scientific. To put it another way, this attitude — that of the "revisionist" — is, however, more "scientific" or documented than those above, not leaving aside the commitment, and for this reason is no less ideological. We could say they are "scientistic" in the sense that they are opposed to the liberals

by the force of their documents and deny that there is any commitment. They pretend, therefore, that their "scientific," methodically written history is true, a real and not an interpretive description, without recognizing that sooner or later the scientific method is an interpretation that can be ideological, and for this reason it is concealing rather than revealing. Some historians of the Latin American Church can be thus classified because they believe that they have approached the thousands of documents scientifically and have not been biased in their interpretation, that their description is "*purely* objective," and that they have therefore discovered reality. The position that generally denies the "black legend" is Hispanic. Ferdinand and Charles V have been so maligned that historians now deal with them in such a way as to overlook the fact that they were less then perfect. They also tend to forget the contribution of Bartolomé de las Casas who, according to Menéndez Pidal, was paranoid. In regard to this third position, it is very difficult to be dispassionate because we are too close to the antiliberal struggle.

4. One possible option or choice for writing a history of the Church in Latin America is the *explicitly Christian critical approach,* which utilizes all of the appropriate values of the traditional positions. It is necessary to recover the contributions of the apologetic or Hispanic position that characterized the notable studies of the colonial era. Yet, at the same time, it is necessary to recognize the contribution of the liberals and not depreciate what many of them have done for the present constitution of our nations. Also, we should remember the indigenous position. The *critical* attitude, therefore, utilizes the best from all of these positions, but the critical Christian attitude, the attitude that keeps in mind which ones can be the essential criteria, determines whether the interpretation will be unequivocally Christian.

If a team of scientists proposes to write a history of the Church they should constitute themselves into a coherent body in order to give unity to their work. They should determine the norms that will allow them to describe the beginning and the development of the Latin American Church in a coherent and unified manner. When we consider one of the important European histories, such as the history of the Church by Fliche-Martin, which is a history of the Universal Church written by French historians, we see the Church from the perspective of a French historical school. This school manifests a unity of perspectives. But it appears that such a Latin American Christian school of history does not exist. It is quite possible that there are historians, scientists, who maintain the same point or a similar point of view who could become a team and in time also constitute a school. We will achieve this in one way or another, and if we do not, what we will produce as historians will be the contradictory juxta-positioning of interpretations which, rather than revealing the beginning and the de-velopment of the Church, will result in contradictory descriptions without meaning. Here is the difficulty.

The difficulty also arises from the fact that no one can write an *official* interpre-tation. The Church does not have an official interpretation, or if it does it is only the Holy Scripture, the Pontifical or episcopal declarations, and lastly the final Judgment of God. Any history that one attempts to write should be a serious and scientific interpretation of the history of the Church written by Christian historians who nec-essarily opt for certain criteria.

In reference to the revealed criteria of historical interpretation there is one absolutely essential principle, and for history it can transform itself into a revealer of its strictly Christian character. One can make the following statement: outside of the present totality, outside of an organized system (the "flesh") the *poor* are unsheltered and defenseless. But the poor are Jesus. In the Gospel of Matthew it is very clear that one who gives food to the hungry is in fact giving food to Jesus (chapter 25). Therefore, a theological reflection regarding the identification of Jesus with the poor is one of the present goals — perhaps the most important — of contemporary Latin American theology. The poor are poor because they are of no intrinsic value to the system. If value in the system is medieval honor, then the poor have no value. If the supreme operational value of the system is money, the poor have none. If in the future society the system has technology as the supreme value, the poor will be those without technology. The poor are the exterior or *outside* of that which is considered of value in the totality (the "flesh"). For to be exterior is to be *outside,* to be in the *future* — and because the poor are in the future — interpolating eschatologically the system. The poor are Jesus in that his word, his interpolative word reveals God to us today. He who sees Jesus in the poor and serves him is the only one who can be saved. It appears that this should be the essential *criterion* of our history. It would be a history that raises questions regarding whatever problem and whatever description, questions such as: What relation does this have with the poor? When we study, for example, the encounter of Columbus with the Indian, what should we ask ourselves? Who is the more significant, Columbus or the Indian? The Indian as "the poor" should be the one who interests us the most. And when we discover how Columbus acted in regard to the Indian, we are in a position to judge the "Columbus" fact. Many times we have interpreted the historical facts by inverting them. We have acclaimed Pizarro a hero, for example, while at the same time we have ignored the Indians.

We should remember that the "poor" are not poor only economically and politically or in an economic-political sense. The fact is that biblically the poor (*anabím*) is essentially the "servant of Yahweh," the one who opens the "Word" and who gives himself unto death in the service of God. We are speaking of the prophet. But also, the poor are those who receive the service of the prophet. In the parable of the Samaritan, Jesus teaches us that the Samaritan is poor (in the fullest and most perfect sense), but also "the poor" is the assaulted and abandoned one on the road. Thus *the poor* are "the poor ones" in the real, economic, and cultural sense, not that they are merely alienated by the system, but are in reality exterior to the system and aware that they are not a part of "this world"; and those who struggle in their behalf are the prophets, the *anabím,* the "Servant of Yahweh."

Conclusion. In the only history — secular history for those pre-Christians, and the history of salvation for the Christians in the light of faith, the Church signifies a distinct reality. For this reason the history of the Church is an interpretive account of the messianic function fulfilled by the institution founded in the only history, the history of the world in the light of faith. To discover the messianic function of the Church in the world is theology, the only theology, in its moment of historical and progressive description.

Quito, Ecuador, January 3, 1973.
An unwritten address that has been preserved and translated in the oral style despite the fact that it shows a certain awkwardness of syntax.

Appendix II

A Hypothesis for a History of Theology in Latin America

I. INTRODUCTION

In this brief essay I want to propose a few hypotheses that can facilitate the writing—in the future and as a team in CEHILA—of a larger work on the history of theology in Latin America. We will never develop an understanding of our theological past until we have such a work. It is not absolutely essential for the constitution of a new theology, but it is essential for any definitive maturing of our theology. For this reason, each day that passes makes more necessary a theological reconstruction, but not one less interpretative.

On the other hand, it should be pointed out that one could write the history of theology *from theology itself*, namely, by allowing theology to be the point of departure, and by looking into the internal development of theology as an abstract *whole* subsisting in itself. One would follow this logical process to the epistemological limits of theological reflection. We could demonstrate, therefore, the evolution of the phenomenom in Latin America from the sixteenth to the twentieth centuries. In this way, perhaps, the theology of Bartholomé de Las Casas or of José de Acosta would appear to be less technical or less "serious" in comparison to subsequent theology, the academic and university theology of the professors of Mexico or Lima.

But if we include dialectically the theological *whole* as a *part* of the totality of Christian existence, and even non-Christian existence, in the Christianity of the West Indies, and if we move from an abstract description of theology in itself toward the concrete level of theology conditioned by the nontheological (the real within which theology plays a practical role as theory), then our interpretation changes meaning, and the theology of Las Casas, though less academic, sophisticated, or articulated in his writings, is more authentic (because it denounces the fundamental contradictions and injustices of his day), while subsequent theology is imitative—hiding the injustices—ideological, and abstract.

Methodologically, then, it is necessary to place theology *within* the totality of existence in which it derives meaning, be it *within* the national or international geopolitical arena, or the life of the social classes, or the affected motivations to which it corresponds. An ideological-historical analysis could thereby produce some unexpected results. This analysis, however, is nothing more than a simple introduction to the problem, that is, it is merely a hypothesis for the task.

I hope that what I wrote in the *Encuentro del Escorial*, published in 1972 in Spanish by Sígueme Publishing House and in French by Cerf, will be kept in mind, since there I proposed a hypothesis for interpreting the *history of faith* in Latin America, while here I am dealing with a *history of theology*—a secondary and reflective level which has

306

to consider its point of departure: theology as a part of the everyday prophetic existential Christian faith.

II. IDEOLOGY AND THE HISTORY OF THEOLOGY

The context of the history of theology in Latin America is the history of theology of the new "center," originally that of the Mediterranean and Europe, and subsequently that of the United States (since Russia contributes very little today to theological thought). The context of the biography of the son is the biography of the father. This does not mean that the son's context is the same as the father's, but on the contrary, that the son's is only a reflection of the father's context. Latin American theology is a product of European theology, but it is different. It is another theology. It sprouted from the same tradition, but in a different setting, namely, in a "peripheral" world within the modern mercantile era and later in a monopolistic empire. Theology in a colonial or neocolonial world can refract momentarily the theology of the "center," but in its creative moments it will produce a new theology which will rise up against the more developed traditional theology. It is in this context of imitative ideological refraction or creativity that assents to a different reality in our Latin American world, that the history of theology in our dependent continent will be developed. Let us consider the question in parts.

1. The Ideological Constitution of Theology[1]

The concept of ideology can be seen by its opposite: nonideological revelation. If there is an expression that allows the eruption of the exteriority of all the constituted ideological system, it is the proto-word, the exclamation or interjection of pain, that immediate consequence of perceived trauma. The "Ouch!" or painful scream resulting from a blow, a wound, or an accident indicates immediately not *something* but rather *somebody*. One who hears the cry of pain is astonished because the scream interrupts his commonplace and integrated world. The sound, the noise, produces a mental image of an absent-present somebody in pain. The hearer does not know as yet *what kind* of pain it is, nor the reason for the outcry. But the hearer will be disturbed until he knows who is crying out and why. *What* that cry says is secondary; the fundamental issue is the cry itself; one who is *somebody* is saying something. It is not what is said, but rather the saying itself, the person who cries out, who is important — that exteriority which calls out for help. Nevertheless, to cry "Help!" is already a word, a part of a language, of a culture. The scream or the cry for help is perhaps the most remote indicator of the ideological: "I . . . have heard their *cry* by reason of their taskmasters" (Exodus 3:7). "And Jesus cried with *a loud voice,* and gave up the ghost" (Mark 15:37). It is the limit of human and divine revelation. It is putting oneself outside of the system, questioning it — when the pain is produced by sin, namely, by injustice and domination over the Other, it is the pain of Job, not merely physical pain, although this may also be involved.

The cry of pain such as "I am hungry!" requires an urgent answer, an answer that issues from a sense of responsibility: to be responsible for the one who is crying out in his or her pain. It is this responsibility that exemplifies authentic religion and worship,[2] and the trauma that one suffers for the Other who cries out is the *Glory of the Infinite* in the system. "I am hungry!" is the revelation that the gastric juices which are causing discomfort in the stomach, the acid that produces the pain, is the appetite, the "desire" to eat. This carnal, corporal, and material desire is the basis of the desire for the Kingdom of Heaven in its most fundamental meaning: it is the dissatisfaction that demands to be satisfied. When the hunger of people is habitual, hunger stemming from poverty, it is from *this* that nonideological words arise. It is the carnality or basic materialism that Jesus places as the supreme criteria of the Judgment: "I was hungry, and you gave me meat" (Matthew 25:35).

The "Ouch!" of the first pain, the "I am hungry!" are already articulated in a language, a social class, a people, in a moment of history and refer to the *Reality* or exteriority of every constituted system. They cannot be ideological expressions. They are political or primary words, words that inaugurate a new totality of language and of conceptual formulations of meaning.

In effect, it is only the provoking of the constitution of a new system that satisfies the insatisfaction of the poor of the old system, the starting point for the liberation of language. But just when the cry has been heard and is formulated, just when a new system is intended to be organized and a model is developed, just when the mediations for its realization are conceived, and much more when the system has been built, a new structured totality takes the place of the old one. Inside every system or totality of concepts, the words are structured by their role in the totality itself. But since the system is dominated by a few, by certain classes or groups, the projects of these groups are imposed on the whole system. From that very moment the conceptualization and the language of the dominating group is mingled with the "reality" of things and with the language itself. The concept and the word that expresses it establish on one hand the action of all members of the system, and at the same time it hides not only the internal contradictions of the system, but also and primarily the *exteriority of the poor*.[3] It is in that moment that the formulation (the concept, the word: the *idea*) becomes an *ideology*: a representation that for all practical purposes hides the reality.[4] There is, therefore, a dialectic between discovering and concealing, between theory and praxis.

When Jesus says that "they know not what they do" (Luke 23:34), he explicitly and clearly shows that twofold dialectic between discovering ("knowing" is seeing) and concealing (they know "not"), between theory ("knowing" is theory) and praxis ("doing" is praxis). On the one hand it is an authentic theological reflection on ideology, although in a single instance, since the torture of Jesus has unquestionable political significance, having been delivered by his government and national priesthood to the Roman authorities. Knowing not what they were doing is like saying that the interpretation of the praxis fails to discover its true meaning. Surely the soldiers knew what they are doing to a certain point: they were executing a political prisoner. The true meaning is, nevertheless, concealed, that is, the ultimate meaning of the praxis. This is precisely the practical function of ideology: it provides some knowledge for undergirding action, but at the same time it conceals the fundamental level of its ultimate or actual meaning. Thus, Jesus introduced us to the critique of ideology.

Ideology therefore serves a practical-interpretative function. This may be illustrated by a Latin American example first on the level of common interpretation, then on the level of the theological formulation.

The conquest of America, which began with its discovery in 1492, is not only a simple fact, it is also a historico-political fact. With Spain and Portugal, Europe began its dominating expansion over the peripheral world. Holland, England, and France followed. Spain since 1493 has theoretically "justified" the conquest. Pope Alexander VI issued the Bull *Inter coetera* in 1493 favoring the Roman Catholic kings of Spain by allowing them to evangelize these lands and bring them under their domain. Thus, in the *Recapitualation of Laws of the Indies Kingdoms* (1681), the first law of the first section of the first book declares that the Lordship[5] of the king of Spain over the new kingdoms is due to the obligation that the king has incurred with the Holy See to indoctrinate the Indians in the Roman Catholic faith. The conquering praxis is thereby "justified" by a theoretical basis — the papal bull. The whole juridical structure of the sixteenth century was obviously a type of *ideology*. Behind respectable principles was hidden the real *meaning* of the conquering praxis. The concealed meaning was the reality of the European domination of the Indian who was reduced to the most horrendous slavery. Death, theft, torture (that was the real fruit of the conquering praxis) was concealed by a false ideological interpretation, namely, evangelization. Papal bulls served the same ideological function in the quotidian conscience of the conqueror as the doctrine of *Manifest Destiny* in the mind of Sam Houston who occupied Texas and later separated it from Mexico in 1846. All the empires have reasons (void of reason) that permit them to establish their dominion over others. But their reasons are ideological-existentialist at the quotidian concrete level.

The quotidian ideological level is raised to the level of scientific ideology (as can be seen in some theological examples) in that science itself accepts certain judgments as principles (but with historico-cultural evidence), and experiences a moment of unavoidable ingenuity (science cannot by definition demonstrate its principles; that is to say, the principles of science are not scientific. It has been recognized since the time of Aristotle that they are the object of the dialectic).[6] It is in this way that the ideology supporting the praxis of the conquest is raised by Juan Ginés de Sepúlveda (1490— 1573) and by Francisco de Vitoria (1486— 1546) to the level of theology. To Ginés the conquest of America and war against the Indians was justified. The "cause of the just war (*iusti belli causa*) by natural and divine right (*iure naturali et divino*) is the rebellion of the less gifted who were born to serve and their rejection of the dominion of their masters; if they cannot be subdued by other means, then war is justified" — according to the *Democrates alter*.[7] It is evident that Ginés attributes this to Aristotle — in his ideological text on slavery in Greece in Book I of *Politica* — and also to the medieval authors, even to Thomas Aquinas in the *iustum dominativum* that the feudal lords had over the servants,[8] and to other contemporary professors like Juan Mayor (1469— 1550) in Paris who thought that in America "the people live like animals (*bestialiter*); therefore the first one that conquers them will rightly reign over them, because they are by nature servants (*quia natura sunt servi*)."[9] For this reason even in the best of situations the Indian was considered "crude," a "child" who must be civilized, a being with little intelligence and governed by instincts and "little inclined to celibacy" according to a missionary.

Even Vitoria himself, the eminent professor of Salamanca and author of *De Indis* (1537), pointed out in his *De iure belli* (1538) that the conquest of the Indians could not be justified on the basis of their having a different religion, nor because of the rights of the king, nor to preach the gospel, nor because of a pontifical concession, nor to oppose any sin *contra natura* that the indigenous American people committed. But Vitoria concluded that the conquest is justified when the missionary is hindered from proclaiming freely the gospel ("libere annuntient Evangelium" as Vitoria explains in his *Relectio de indis, quarta conclusio*). Thus the missionary can, "in order to avoid scandal preach to them even against their wills ... and accept war or declare it." By the *iniuria accepta* the eminent theologian justified the conquest. "From this conclusion it may also clearly be deduced that, for the same reason, if it is not possible to provide [the Indians] with religion any other way, then it is licit for the Spaniards to occupy their lands and territories and to establish for them new masters and to divest them of their former gods, and *do whatever else* [sic.] that is permitted by the right of war as in every righteous war" (Ibid.). One can see therefore that even this progressive European theologian — without doubt the most advanced of his period, since on other levels he valiantly defended the Indian — could not avoid theological formulations.

Finally, we conclude that the ideology of the dominant classes or of the oppressor nations is concealing, whereas the formulations of the oppressed classes or of the prophets of such groups is critically revealing. It is the articulation of meaning that comes out from the cry of the poor.

2. The Ideological Conditioning or the Theology of the "Center"

Ideology justifies, then, the praxis, hiding at the same time the ultimate meaning of praxis itself, allowing the one who commits the injustice to continue with a "clear conscience." Ideology is the formulation (existential or scientific) of the mediations of the project of the system without revealing itself to be a *system of domination*. What is concealed is the domination at certain levels. Because of this, it is possible to indicate the ideological sense of theology when one discovers the type of domination that it hides. This is to say that one can attempt to indicate the conditioning which inclines theological reflection in a certain concealing direction, in the direction that benefits or justifies the praxis of the group, class, nation, or culture that serves as the theoretical foundation. We can illustrate this by showing the conditioning that has constituted some of the theological levels ideologically of the history of the Mediterranean — European theology (which is the frame of reference of Latin American theology as it developed in the sixteenth century).[10]

During the New Testament era, Christians were oppressed as a group (Palestine was a distant Roman colony) and also as a social class (those first baptized were a despised class and without political and social influence, thus the ideological-concealing function of the first Christian formulations were minimal. One can observe in Paul some *machismo* (in regard to the problem of women) or the noncritical acceptance at the socio-political level of the institution of slavery (in his Letter to Philemon).[11] If at some point, nevertheless, the gospel is accepted, it is precisely because of its critical-de-ideological character, especially in those few formulations that can be attributed without doubt to Jesus of Nazareth. Later some inclinations toward "escapism" from the political reality can be seen in the texts of some of the primitive Judeo-Christian apocalyptic writers, such as the revelations of the Shepherd of Hermas. But even in these the reflections are hardly ideological.

The apologist Fathers, on the contrary, when they began to utilize Hellenistic categories, accepted certain ideological-concealing elements. Nevertheless, the politico-religious critique of those Christians who faced the dominating culture of the Empire was magnificent[12] (and for that reason de-ideologizing). There were also frontal attacks against all the ideologized values of imperialism by recently baptized thinkers who felt that they were Greeks and Christians at the same time.[13] It is doubtful that we have ever had critics of the prevailing imperial culture as competent as those of the early Christian centuries.

Criticism of the empire continued either against paganism, against the Hellenistic or Roman culture, or against the vices in the cities. Even in the theologians deeply influenced by Greek philosophy such as Clement of Alexandria, Origen, or Irenaeus of Lyon, the developing theology allowed for the discovering of the contradictions in the *system*. One should note that by being Christian communities they were considered by Rome as dissident groups, "fifth columnists" who were sabotaging the ruling culture, and for this reason they were frequently persecuted. Persecution in fact demonstrated that Christian theology was substantively critical or prophetic. Christians were persecuted because they challenged the "fundamentals" of the system, its values, and its gods. Theology had, then, a critical-prophetic function that was equally manifested at the political level. The Empire, in defending itself by political repression against Christians, actually revealed that Christianity was fulfilling its liberating mission, theologically de-ideologizing.

A crucially important step in comprehending Christian theology as ideology occurred when Constantine was crowned emperor (324), and also in the Council of Nicea (325). The most glorious century of patristic theology (A.D. 325–425) also constitutes the beginning of the formation of theology as ideology. (We are not saying that theology thereby lost its value. Rather, we are simply indicating that the ideological aspect of theology increased; it became more determinative). The Greek Patristics (Athanasius, Basil, and from Gregory to John of Damascus) and the Latin Fathers (from Ambrose and Augustine to Isidore of Seville), some of them under the authority of the Emperior and others under the Papacy, accepted the existence of the Empire not only as "natural," but also — especially in the Latin world — the Empire was virtually equated with the *civitas Dei* (by replacing the content of Augustine's *civitas Dei*). The *Christianitas* came to be identified with Christianity. Theology accepted too many imperial, social, cultural, linguistic, and sexual structures as essential ingredients of Christianity. Thus theology, with the platonic or neoplatonic method, came to justify the political and social domination of the early centuries of Byzantine and Latin Christianity. The displacement of the method (from the historico-existential in the biblical thought to the epistemical or apodictical, to which were added anthropological and ontological dualism) pushed theology into many ideological blind alleys. A detailed study is therefore necessary. It is evident that an aristocratic and imperialistic Christianity, constituted in its various levels of ecclesiastical decision making by the most powerful and influential classes, more and more instrumentalized Christianity to solidify its power. We want to point out again — and this applies to all of this appendix — that instrumentalization does not invalidate the theological effort; it simply limits it. (It is commonly recognized that every theology is only a remote analogy of the "science of God" in which God himself will participate as *visio* only in the fulfilled Kingdom). Ideological moments in every theology indicate that it is unavoidably an *historical*, conditioned, and limited reflection.

The theology of the Greek Patristics pressed on until the end (1453) without changing fundamentally during the centuries (although it grew continually, as was clearly demonstrated by the exiles in Italy during the fourth century). Latins, on the other hand, thanks to the Franks, generated a new theological process. The Venerable Bede (672–735) originated a process that developed in the Holy Roman Empire (whose *sacredness* justified Christianity: the political ideological moment of essential importance concealed the imperialistic and social domination of the oppressed kingdoms and of the feudal serfs). The classical era of the *Primera Escolástica* (early Scholasticism) followed the Fourth Lateran Council of 1215. The golden age of Latin Christianity and of Scholasticism (1215–1315) was that of Abelard, Bonaventure, Thomas, and Duns Scotus. The Plantonic or Augustinian method was modified by the discovery of Aristotle's *Organon,* which was derived from the Arabs via Spain (Toledo). Behind this apparatus — indeed much more precise with its substantialistic categories and employed with remarkable cleverness and with very well developed logic — a theology fundamentally a-historical, ideologically concealed innumerable contradictions from an

overbearing *machismo* — domination of women[14] — to the class struggle, to the opposition between classes (the citizen was the *simpliciter politicum iustim,* that is, only the
feudal lord)[15] or the clash of kingdoms — since no theologian questioned the right of
the emperor over the other kings, or, in other situations, of the Pope over the emperor
and other kings. An ideological analysis of this theology, so valuable and important
on the one hand, done socio-psychoanalytically or economico-politically, *avoiding extreme ingenuities,* will produce great results in the future. It will show us in a better way
the genius of those theologians and the unavoidable limitations of their conditioning.
They were men and not gods.

The same can be said of later Scholasticism — the classical age during the time of
the Council of Trent (1545– 1563), that is, from 1530 to 1630, under the influence
of Vitoria, Bañez, Soto, Suárez, Molina, and Juan de Santo Tomás — publicized by
Silvestre de la Ferrara y Cayetano — first in Salamanca and then through the whole
Hispanic Empire, resplendent in its Aristotelian-Thomistic commentaries, and already
moving in the *via moderna,* which subsequently provided the basis of the Cartesian
ontology as well as that of Wolff — followed by the Franciscan Schools in England
from which proceeded philosophical empiricism. We see then that Patristic theology
flourished in the Byzantine Empire and the Papacy together with its dependent kingdoms
in Africa, Gaul, and Spain. And if early Scholasticism needed the power of the Franks,
later Scholasticism was dependent on Charles V, Emperor of Spain, the Low Countries,
and Germany. Its ideological moment is evident. Yet one sees little or nothing of this
theology in the newly discovered and exploited colonies. There is no reference to the
serious problem of poverty in Spain — counterpart of conquered America. Trent was
concerned only with the Germanic problem and ignored the enormous possibilities that
Africa, Asia, and America portended for Europe. Modern Christianity, Catholic Christianity, turned in upon itself in Europe and developed a unique blindness to the
exteriority of other cultures, countries, and peoples. It is for this reason that the *Third
Scholastic,* which flourished after the First Vatican Council (1869– 1870) in Latino-
Catholic Europe — although one must recognize the many German theologians such
as Kleugten (d. 1893) — was wedded to the Encyclical on the necessity of beginning
all studies with Thomas Aquinas. Catholicism, which reluctantly abandoned imperial
and later monarchical and feudal theses, slowly accepted and subsequently justified
passionately liberal democracy and, surreptitiously, bourgeois capitalism — which is
always being *reformed.* When one reads today the writings of Mercier, Garriguod
Lagrange, or Maritain, leaving aside the fact that they have contributed greatly to the
reformulation of Catholicism, it is evident that an important ideological moment is
concealed at the socio-political level. Reyes Mate has demonstrated this fact in several
ways.[16]

On the other hand, the tradition that we may refer to as German theology — which
opened the way for Protestant theology was its French, Swiss, Dutch, and English
components — which has developed since the sixteenth century, that is, since the Reformation, does not avoid concealing the contradictions of its epoch. Luther himself
faced the withering criticism of Thomas Münzer who spoke out in defense of the
impoverished peasants of the feudal world in crisis. This tradition with Augustinian
origins and with Franciscan and even Thomastic influences (e.g., Melanchthon), subsequently felt the full impact of Wolffian rationalism, of Kant, of the *Aufklärung,* and
of idealism (especially that of the Hegelian right), although it was not the only tradition
affected (one need only remember the example of the fervently anti-Hegelian Schleier-
macher). The Catholic world of Moehler (d. 1838), which was formed in Tübingen,

continued in this direction. Together with a mediating neo-Kantianism, phenomenology, and Heideggerian ontology, we have a Bultmann or a Rahner (completely different theological positions which, nevertheless, develop from Heidegger), together with the socio-political critique of the Frankfurt School to Metz, from the position of Ernst Bloch to Jürgen Moltmann. Earlier, what was called the "nouvelle theologie" of prewar France, with the discovery of the history of theology, such as the kerygmatic theologies, the demythologizing, existentialist, political, and utopian theologies, all of them — and even their prolongations in the United States with the "death of God" movement, etc. — stem from the center of Europe, particularly during and following World War II. Like the Second Vatican Council (1962– 1965), and the highest levels of the World Council of Churches, all of this theology thrives in an optimum of a reconstructed Europe, the Europe of the "German miracle," during the time when the North American Empire displaced the British Empire overseas (the "Empire" later had to come "hat in hand" to the door of the European Common Market in order to be accepted as one of its members). The method of this theology is now existentialist, ontological, and even dialectical. Hegelian influence has continually increased since the bicentennial commemoration of his birth (1770– 1970).

At any rate, all this theology manifests significant ideological moments: one of them being the ingenuous idea that they represent the "center" of the world (from a cultural, political, and economical point of view. Even though Europe depends on the United States, it enjoys over the latter a recognized humanistic-cultural, though not a scientific-technical, "superiority.") At the same time, this theology has not yet taken seriously its class conditioning: the theologian is not only the product of an aristocratic class (the university), he also represents a dominating nation (which in various ways oppresses its colonies with its capitalistic and monopolistic industrialism). Furthermore, the "point of departure" of its theological reflection has never been questioned. If its point of departure were a praxis of liberating the oppressed (which is the origin of the non-ideological word and the criticism of all ideology), then its theology would have to explain its organic compromise with the economic and political system it represents. These issues are, however, not even recognized by this theology of the "center" (not only for social, but also for geopolitical reasons. Liberation theology is conversely a theology of the economically poor classes and of the politically dependent, neocolonial, and "peripheral" nations). The proposals of this theology remain within the confines of the "center," and for this reason are "ideologized," that is, they conceal the principal contradiction of our time, namely, the "center-periphery" system — and with it falsify the relations between the classes of the "center." It becomes, therefore, a theology that conceals and thereby justifies the domination of the poor peoples of the world.

From this we can conclude that theology, when denoting the reflection of a non-theological faith of the oppressed, that is, when it is the methodical expression of those who do not control the system, possesses all its anti-ideological and critico-prophetic faculties. To the degree that theology expresses a nontheological faith of the dominating groups or nations, and having lost in part its prophetic dimension (at least to the degree that it represents a system of domination), theology ideologizes itself. It is for this reason that in the United States and Europe (the latter is the "center" while being relatively dependent on the former) even the radical or democratic socialist movements can only be reformist, but without ever dialoguing seriously with those of the "periphery" who actually questioned the system itself.[17] It is easy to speak of freedom for one who in some way exercises power. An example can be seen in the imposition of an economic "liberalism" on its new colonies by England during the latter decades of the eighteenth century. England demanded "freedom" to sell its products to the nonindustrialized countries, ignoring the fact that in London during the early years of that same century they publicly hanged those who purchased any French product. The "protectionism" of the emerging English industry was exercised over the "peripheral" countries. Freedom means not only the possibility of choosing among several options; it means possessing the power or at least the possibility to make a choice. Before having the freedom to choose (between this or that possibility) between the liberalism or socialism of the "center," it is necessary to establish a justice that will permit having something to choose — justice will allow the oppressed to eat, to clothe themselves, to read, to make decisions). The fundamental human liberty is *the right to live*, rather than the freedom to decide to live *in this* or *in that way*. Justice or socio-political liberation is that which makes possible the freedom to choose: "Tempore necessitatis omnia sunt comunia," declared Huguccio. It is evident that there are times when it is necessary for everyone to cooperate in a disciplined way, even in spite of the aristocratic egoism of the old dominant classes (which are the only ones that "have" and that "choose" this or that), to produce or manufacture goods that will permit everyone to live as humans.

During the construction of the *new* order, "freedom" as the supreme value, which is itself an example of a reactionary ideology since it destroys the unity of discipline, creates divisions and in the name of pluralism makes impossible any real change. There will come times of diversity and freedom of choice, but the child cannot be killed until he is born.

III. THE PERIODIFICATION OF THE HISTORY OF THEOLOGY IN LATIN AMERICA

In previous writings we have proposed a periodification of the history of the Church in Latin America. It would be a history of a nontheological faith becoming praxis. We now propose as a hypothesis a given periodification which can open the way in an area in which — as far as I know — there is no writing. *The History of Catholic Theology* by Grabmann[18] makes some suggestions regarding theology in Hispanoamerica. But as usual — and we Latin Americans are accustomed to this — we are really *left out of history*. How can we describe the development of our theology? What are the most important periods? What is the meaning of each one of them?

1. The First Epoch: Prophetic Theology Confronting the Conquest and Evangelization (since 1511)

The discovery of America by the Spaniards and Portuguese initiated a geopolitical revolution without precedent in world history. The eastern Mediterranean, which was the "center" of history from the time the Cretans lost their primacy, was replaced by the North Atlantic (beginning in the sixteenth century until today). On the other hand, ten times more silver and five times more gold than there was previously in existence were taken back to the Mediterranean and Europe in the sixteenth century alone — all of it from the mines exploited with the blood of the Indians. This is the origin of the colonial *plus valia* (surplus in value), the accumulated capital that was essential for the developing industrial revolution. A world was collapsing; Europe, surrounded by the Turks and Arabs, became open to the whole world. It was a time of utopias, of novelties, and of discoveries. In Spain, Cisneros began the first reformation and edited the first critical commentaries on the Old and New Testaments — all toward the end of the fifteenth century, more than a generation before Erasmus.

In 1492 the Catholic kings sponsored the last medieval crusade against the remaining Arab kingdom in Europe, in the process recapturing Granada.

Papal bulls since 1493, as we have already noted, justified religiously the conquest of America. But the discovery of America had no apparent influence on the Council of Trent. The proposal by Cardinal Jiménez de Cisneros to occupy the Indies without guns was ignored, and the Spanish conquest was therefore violent, even as were the subsequent conquests by the Dutch, English, French, and Germans (the latter in twentieth-century Africa). The Spanish conquest, however, produced a small handful of prophets, outstanding Christian missionaries who valiantly — and often at great risk to themselves — defended the Indians.[19] We will mention just one of them.

Other than a Franciscan layman, it was Antonio de Montesinos, OP (d. 1545) who in 1511, by order of his superior, Pedro de Córdoba, OP (1460– 1525), uttered the first critico-prophetic cry in America. On that 30th of November, the cleric Bartolomé de Las Casas (1474– 1566) listened intently to Montesinos' sermon defending the Indians against the Spanish "encomenderos." It was not until 1514, however, that Las Casas took up the cause of justice. Prior to that time

clergyman Bartolomé was extremely busy and very diligent in making money like everyone else. He sent Indians from his parcel of land to extract gold from the mines and to sow his fields, taking advantage of them as much as he could. But on the day of the Feast of Pentecost he began to consider Ecclesiasticus 34:18– 20: "The sacrifice of an offering unjustly acquired is a mockery; the gifts of impious men are unacceptable. The Most High takes no pleasure in offerings from the godless, multiplying sacrifices will not gain his pardon for sin. Offering sacrifice from the property of the poor is as bad as slaughtering a son before his father's very eyes." Thus began, I would say, Las Casas' misery.[20]

This prophetic conversion of a thinker who later would be as prolific in writings as he was profound and practical in his conclusions, could be considered the birth of the Latin American *theology of liberation*. Bartolomé himself wrote in his Testament (1564) — fifty years later — that "God in His mercy chose me as his minister not because of any merit of mine, to try to return to the people whom we call Indians, the true owners and possessors, those kingdoms and lands, because of the grievances, wrongdoings and damage never before equaled, seen, or heard which they suffered from us Spaniards against all reason and justice, and to return them to their *pristine liberty* from whence they have been unjustly despoiled, and *to liberate them* from the violent death that they are still suffering."[21]

Bartolomé de Las Casas, like José de Acosta, SJ (1539– 1600) in Peru, Bernardino de Sahagún, OFM (d. 1510) in Mexico, as well as others, were — or at least were among — the theologians of the first generation after the conquest who faced the reality of their time with less ideological bias than their companions of conquest and evangelization. Consider the following text and the clarity with which Las Casas exposed the principal contradiction of his era and the ideological blindness of his contemporaries:

God will unleash against Spain his anger and wrath because *all of us* have communicated and participated more than a little in the bloody and stolen riches [of the Americas] so usurped and wrongly acquired, and with so much waste and death of those people, that even the greatest penitence cannot undo, a penitence which I fear will never come because of *the blindness* [here is the fruit of ideology!] that God because of our greater and lesser sins and especially in those who presume to be and who are regarded as wise and who rule the world, because of their sins, even this *obscurity of understanding* [here is another indication of ideological concealing!] so recently, that since sixty years ago they began scandalously to steal, kill, and exterminate these peoples: and *until now no one has noticed* these scandals and injustices of our holy faith, these robberies, ravages, deaths, enslavements, usurpations of states and other's properties, and finally the widespread devastations and depopulations *resulting from the enormous sin and injustice.*[22]

For our "theologian of liberation" the socio-political sin was the moment of conquest. The praxis was the "sin and enormous injustice," but "until now no one has noticed it" (seen it) because of the "blindness" and the "dullness of understanding." That is to say, the real *meaning* of the praxis is not recognized: and we are dealing therefore with an ideology that conceals from everyone the real nature of things, from adults and children as well as from the wise and powerful.

Bartolomé opposed not only Juan Ginés de Sepúlveda (the theologian who justified as natural the slavery of the Indian), but also Las Casas went far beyond the progressive Vitoria. Bartolomé recognized that war against the Indians could be justified if they were a barbarian, absolutely uncivilized people given to irrational and vicious actions. But the fact is that the Indians were not guilty of any of these deficiencies. For "of the universal and infinite number of people of *every gender* created by God [the Indians] were the most simple, without malice and duplicity, very obedient and faithful in every way to their natural lords and to the Christians whom they served. [They were the] most humble, patient, peaceful and quiet — devoid of quarrelsomeness and boistrousness — of all the people in the world."[23] Bartolomé had an incalculable appreciation for the Indians, the poor, and the oppressed. For him the war of conquest was absolutely unjustified. There was *no reason* to attempt to use force against the Indians, and all that had been stolen from them through the conquest, and apportionments of the land and the *encomiendas* should be restored to them, or those who participated in "it would not be saved."[24] Moreover, Bartolomé declared that "all persons from every place in the Indies where we have entered *have an acquired right* of making *a just war* and exterminating us from the face of the earth, and this right will be theirs until the day of judgement."[25] Bartolomé then defended the war of liberation by the Indians against the Europeans not only in his time, but also until the present. Thus he endorsed theologically the rebellion of valiant Tupac Amaru (1746– 1782) in Peru or of Fidel Castro in 1959 in Cuba — in the same Cuba of Bartolomé's prophetic conversion.

Las Casas' theological treatises, e.g., *De único modo (The Only Way);* his *Historia de la Indias (History of the Indies),* an apocalyptic-prophetic, not historic, treatise; the *Apologética historia sumaria (Summary of Apologetic History),* a treatise on the pre-Christian religiosity; a large quantity of pamphlets, articles, memorials, defenses, his *Brevísima relación de la destrucción de las Indias (A Brief Report on the Destruction of the Indies);* the *Dieciséis remedios para la reformación de las Indias (Sixteen Remedies for the Reformation of the Indies);* the *Argumentum Apologiae (An Apologetic Argument); Los tesoros del Perú (The Treasure of Peru);* etc. — all of these are a part of the praxis of a great Christian. Conqueror, priest, patron, litigator before kings and courts and councils, organizer of agriculture experiments, missions, and communities, a novice, student, writer, polemicist, defender, and attorney before tribunals: in the sixteenth century he sailed the Atlantic more than ten times. From his praxis of defending and attempting to liberate the Indian he developed and published his militant theology, a *totally political theology,* as Juan Friede demonstrates.[26] But it is also an *historical,*[27] *concrete*[28] theology with *anthropological meaning,*[29] and is *intentionally practical.*[30]

This was *nonacademic* or preuniversity theology — not because it was against learning, but as a matter of fact it was developed before there were such places of study in Latin America, and also because it was born in the heat of the battle and not as the product of the more or less artificial exigences of life in a professor's cloister.

This *critico-prophetic theology* was *missionary*, formed men of action, clarified the rules, and uncovered structural and personal sins. All of this anticipated by four hundred years the present experience of creative theology in Latin America. Of necessity, the first theological effort on our continent should be well studied in order to discover the first model developed on this side of the Atlantic from the exercise of authentic reflection on Christian praxis in a colonial, "peripheral" situation. Las Casas foresaw to some extent the beginnings of European imperialistic domination. He passed judgment on the beginning of the oppressive worldwide expansion of the "center," condemned in its totality the system that was being organized, regarding as "unjust and tyrannical *all* that was being done against these Indians in the West Indies."[31]

This was the theology elaborated and supported by the action of hundreds of missionaries during the first period of our Latin American Church, before the organization of a Christendom of the Indies.

2. Second Epoch: The Theology of Colonial Christianity (1533–1808)

On June 3, 1533, university courses in theology were begun by Professor Francisco Cervantes de Salazar, Professor of Rhetoric and Elocution in Mexico City. This academic beginning in theology, in an institution which granted degrees like those of the universities of Alcalá and Salamanca, was the formal initiation of a tradition which lasted two and a half centuries. In 1538 the Dominicans opened their cloister in Santo Domingo and began to offer the first classes in theology for their students. Then on July 1, 1548, the Dominicans organized the same classes in Lima. Somewhat earlier, in Tiripetío (Mechoacán), Mexico, the renowned Augustinian Alonso de la Veracruz began teaching theology. Then on September 21, 1551, Phillip II issued a royal decree supported by a papal bull, and the universities of Lima and Mexico were founded. On January 25, 1553, the Rector and Dean *del Cabildo*, Juan Negrete, led a procession through the streets of El Reloj and of La Moneda in Mexico City, beginning in this way university life in America. Among the first professors were Pedro de la Peña, OP in *Prima*, Alonso de la Veracruz, OSA in scripture, Pedro Morenos in Canon Law, Juan de García in Arts, Bartolomé Frias in Law, and Blas de Bustamante in Grammar and Rhetoric.[32] The course of study was for four years. On September 19, 1580, there began an obligatory class in the Nahua language in Mexico City and in Quechua and Aymara languages in Lima. By 1630 there were 500 pupils enrolled in Mexico, the majority studying theology, while there were only ten students in civil law and fourteen in medicine. By 1755, 1,162 students had been granted doctoral degrees by the university in Mexico.

By the royal decree of Phillip IV on May 26, 1622, and the papal bull of Gregory XV on July 9 of the following year, the secondary schools were founded — each with the authority to grant degrees — as far away as Manila in the Philippines, Cuba, and also in Mérida, Puebla, and San Luís de Potosí in Mexico, in Guatemala, Panama, Caracas, Santa Fé de Bogotá and Popayán in New Granada (Colombia), in Cuzco, Huamanga, and Quito, in Charcas (which in 1798 was elevated to the level of a university, as were Lima and Mexico), in Córdoba, Argentina, and Santiago, Chile. To these should be added many tridentine seminaries where theology was taught, schools such as the famous Palafoxiano School in Puebla, which was founded in 1641, together with those in Guadalajara and Oaxaca. Also, beginning in 1578 the Jesuit schools were authorized to grant degrees.

The young student in seventeenth-century Lima began his year of study on or about October 19 and concluded it approximately on July 31. His first course was from 8:15 until 9:15 a.m., followed by fifteen minutes of recitation. The second course was from 9:30 to 10:30 a.m., followed by recitation. From 2:00 until 2:30 p.m., he studied Quechua, followed by an hour of class on moral theology or Scripture. On Saturdays there were "sabatinas" (exercises) or the defense of theses. There were monthly debating sessions to prepare the students for the annual debates. The *Segunda Escolástica* (Second Scholastic) prevailed without question: Aristotle's *Logic*, in theology the *Summa* of Aquinas together with the various Dominican, Jesuit, and Franciscan interpretations.

Mexico shined in this "golden century" (the sixteenth); Lima in the seventeenth-century baroque culture, and Chuquisaca or Charcas in the eighteenth century of Jesuit humanism (at least until 1767 when they were expelled from Latin America). The following represent some sixteenth-century examples. One should not forget that Antonio Rubio (1548– 1615) was the author of *Lógica Mexicana* (Mexican Logic) (a German edition was published in Cologne in 1605, and there were other translations as well), which was used as a textbook in Alcalá. Rubio, professor in Mexico and in Córdoba del Tucumán, [33] provided a logical formation from which a student moved on to theology with the possibility of hearing, for example, Alonso de la Veracruz (1504– 1584), a prolific author in his own right. Among his writings were a *Commentary on the Book of Sentences,* another on the Epistles of Paul, a *Relectio de libris canonicis,* and even a *Relectio de dominio in infideles et iusto bello.* [34] Veracruz, like many others, was one of the first missionaries. He ministered in the indigenous town of Tripetío and eventually became the Prior of Tacámbaro in 1545. He later went to the Convent of "The Great Atotonilco" among the Otomi Indians and was elected Mexican Provincial in 1548, at a time when he was carrying tremendous academic responsibility.

If we consider the content of this theology in relation to the events of the time, we can quickly discover its ideological conditioning. This last theologian denied that the king had the right to dominate the Indians, but Veracruz believed that the Pope had *indirect power* over the Indians in order to evangelize them, and this right could be granted to kings. Therefore it was perfectly just, reasoned Veracruz, to deprive the Aztec king Montezuma of his power in order to civilize and Christianize his barbarian people. Against Bishop Montufar, Veracruz insisted that the Indians should not be forced to pay high taxes, but he did allow for the system of *encomienda.* One can see, therefore, that all the theology of Christendom in the West Indies was at best *reformist,* that is, it obscured the contradictions and injustices that the "Las Casian" group had condemned.

There was also the colleague of Veracruz, Pedro de la Peña, OP (d. 1583), admired as professor of the *Prima,* but who later abandoned his professorship to become a missionary in Verapaz (1563– 1565), and even later the renowned Bishop of Quito (1565– 1583) and author of commentaries on the *Summa.* We must also mention Bartolomé de Ledesma, OP (d. 1604), author of the well-known treatise *De iure et iustitia* and of the *Sumario de los siete sacramentos,* both works commissioned by the Bishop of Mexico, Pedro de Ortigosa, SJ (1537– 1626), who wrote *De natura theologiae, De essentia Dei,* as well as commentaries on the *Segunda Segundae;* Andrés de Valencia, SJ (1582– 1645), who edited the *Tractatus de Incarnatione;* the prolific author Juan de Ledesma (1576– 1636) who wrote some sixteen volumes, only one of which is extant, *De Deo uno:* and Pedro de Pavia, OP (d. 1589), author of *De sacrosanto sacramento eucharistae.* The list would be even longer if we included from this same century the names and works of Estéban de Salazar, OSA, Andrés de Tordehumos, OSA, Juan de Gaona, OFM, Bernandor de Bazan, OP, Francisco de Osuna, OFM, Pedro de la Concepción, Carmelite, and Juan López Agurto de la Mata, as well as many others.

If we take now as an example the university of Chuquisaca in the eighteenth century, we could read what a Jesuit provincial recommended to his religious: "Study, therefore, metaphysics, but immerse yourselves immediately into general physics which will teach all of you the harmonious composition of the universe and will provide you the basis to refute effectively Rousseau's *Emilio,* Voltaire's philosophical *Dictionary,* Holbach's *System of Nature,* Marechal's *Examination of Religion;* and Montesquieu's *Persian Letters,* as well as works of other monsters of impiety, aborted by unbelievers during this century."[35] Thomas Falkner, once a student of Newton, taught classes in Córdoba del Tucumán in 1763 and began his mathematics classes teaching Leibniz, Wolff, Newton, Locke, Cassandi, and Descartes. From mathematics his students passed to theology. In Chile, for example, the Jesuits had libraries with up to twenty thousand volumes, "the majority of scientific and literary works circulating in Europe until the middle of the eighteenth century."[36] Domingo Muriel (1734–1795) was well versed in the Scriptures, the decisions of Church councils, ecclesiastical history, as well as civil, ecclesiastical, and municipal law of Spain and the Indies. He was likewise proficient in Spanish, French, Italian, Greek, Latin, and Hebrew.[37]

This theology, nonetheless, imitated that of the Second Scholastic, and for that reason was doubly ideological because it was already widespread in Europe and simply repeated itself in America, thereby concealing not only the injustices of the old continent but also those of the new. Nevertheless, a documented history of our theology would show many critical and de-ideologized aspects, such as the theoretical treatment of the types of Guaraní property written by Father Muriel while he was teaching in the University of Córdoba del Tucumán. Muriel's was an outstanding work distinct from anything known thus far, one that promoted the organization of the famous Jesuit *reducciones* (reductions) of Paraguay,[38] a socialist type of experiment wherein property was held in common by the producers of work — an experiment that had repercussions in eighteenth-century France as a kind of protohistory that would later be called "utopian socialism" because of the influence that it had on people such as Meslier, Mably, or Morelli. Common property was not denied by Muriel or any colonial theologian, but his study contained an anticipated critique of bourgeoise property in the name of an agricultural or archaic society.

Portugal, through its famous University of Coimbra, had enormous influence on Brazil; but in contrast to Spain, the Portuguese had no interest in founding either universities or many secondary schools. Theological life in Brazil was nevertheless vigorous, although equally imitative. In the Lusitanian colony, the Jesuit presence was much greater than in Hispanic America; and even before the time of Antonio de Vieira (1608–1698), Jesuits were a part of the conscience of the Church in colonial Brazil.[39] On the other hand, because Brazil had no war for national emancipation, and Pedro I, King of Portugal, broke away from the mother country and inaugurated the Brazilian Empire and ruled until 1831, the crisis that devastated and isolated Spanish America was not so evident in Brazil. Furthermore, the new waves of foreign influence that so affected most of the other Latin American nations were not felt in Brazil.

3. The Third Epoch: Practical-political Theology of the Creole Oligarchies during the Neocolonial Emancipation (since 1808)

In approximately 1760 there began in Hispanic America the dissemination of information about and the study of the new interpretations of traditional theology and of the growing influences of the Enlightenment, especially of the French school. The occupation of Spain by Napoleon (1808) threw the colonies — guided by their creole oligarchies — against the Hispanic bureaucracy with its viceroys, judges, and the great majority of bishops, into the struggle for liberation from the metropolis. As a part of the liberation praxis, the oligarchical class — composed of priests and other clergymen, professors, religious, and university laypersons — began to formulate a theological "justification" for the revolution against Spain. Their theology was born, therefore, amidst the ruins of the theology of Christendom, a reflection formulated outside the universities; in fact, it became nonacademic, as during the early days of the Conquest. It was a theology articulated in the pulpits,[40] in the call to arms,[41] in the constituting assemblies — as in Tucumán where sixteen priests formed the absolute majority of the twenty-four representatives elected by the provinces in 1816 — in the texts of the new constitutions — such as the one of Quito written by the director of the theological seminary there, a constitution which, when it was proclaimed in 1809, was accompanied by the singing of the *Salve Regina* — in the multiple proclamations, and in hundreds of articles written in the revolutionary newspapers. The noise of war together with the socio-political, administrative, and economic changes produced a chaotic disorganization that included the closing of universities, secondary school, and seminaries; professors enlisting in the armies; and libraries being burned or otherwise left to ruin. No new books were imported from Europe; no more missionaries or teachers arrived. Seminarians and students abandoned their studies. The system of Royal Patronage disappeared, and theology was no longer supported by the state. The Holy Office of the Inquisition ceased attempting to stop the flow of every new kind of ideological influence. It is no wonder, then, that in this pandemonium and anarchy the Second Scholastic receded, and there appeared an apocalyptical enlightenment and eclectic currents of thought.

If the theology of Christendom was imitative, the theology of this era recovered some of the initial creativity of the theology in America. The learned principles (in Thomism and Saurecianism) were utilized to justify the liberation praxis of the creole oligarchy. This stage should be studied carefully in the writing of a history of Latin American theology. It represented a new nonacademic, practical, and *political* moment of theological reflection beginning with a faith committed to a process of liberation, and for this reason it was de-ideologized. The dominating class in the colonies (the Hispanic bureaucracies) were subjected to analysis and criticism by a practical theology developed by the creole oligarchies (not yet by the oppressed classes as has happened in the twentieth century). It is not surprising, then, that Manuel Belgrano (1770– 1820), a graduate in law from Salamanca and native of the Río de la Plata region, himself a General in the army of liberation, published in London in 1812 a commentary of four volumes by Father Lagunze, a Chilean Jesuit, on the Revelation of John: *El Reino del Mesías en gloria y majestad (The Kingdom of the Messiah in Glory and Majesty)*, a work that emphasized in its messianism the meaning of the future in a politico-eschatological movement. Nor is it strange that in the same year Las Casas' *La destrucción de las Indias* was republished in Bogotá to support the same liberating process.[42]

The superficiality of this theology, when compared with "serious" academic works, does not diminish its importance, even though it was aborted in part primarily because it lacked the time and conditions for its consolidation. Moreover, it quickly deteriorated into a reflection that justified the new order of things and, therefore, lost its critical revolutionary direction. But this was not the reason it failed to fulfill its historical function, because in fact it mobilized the people against Spain — since the creole oligarchy without the theological support of the Church could never have completed the liberating process.

4. The Fourth Epoch: The Neocolonial Conservative Theology on the Defense (1831–1930)

The dates of this period come from Rome's acceptance of the neocolonial liberation, as evidenced by Pope Gregory XVI's encyclical *Sollicitudo Ecclesiarum* (1831) and the political crisis of the neocolonial oligarchy or the somewhat later economic crisis of dependent liberalism of the "center" in 1929. During this long century theology moved from being a mere reflection of the theology of a colonial Christendom and of the euphoria of the two decades following 1809, *to confine itself* to a conservative, provincial, traditional position, always behind in regard to what was happening, at least until the middle of the nineteenth century. Positivism—which became known in Brazil through the book by M. Lemos entitled *Compte, Philosophie positive* (1874), in Mexico through the writings of Gabino Barreda, and in Argentina due to P. Scalabrini—was criticized by conservative theologians. But these studies of positivism are not without merit— works such as those by Mamerto Esquiú (1826– 1883) in Argentina, and slightly later those by Jacinto Ríos (1842– 1892). The situation changed somewhat with the "romanization" that began slowly with the foundation in 1859 of the *Colegio Pio Latinoamericano* (Latin American Pius College) in Rome, an event which coincided with the emergence of the elites of anticlerical neocolonial liberalism. They appeared in Colombia in 1849, in Mexico with Juárez in 1857, and in Brazil with the Republic in 1889. A larger group of thinkers, theologians, and bishops[43] began to espouse this liberal position toward the end of the century. The group later became known in political circles as "Christian Democracy." It is interesting to observe how Mariano Soler (1846– 1908), the first Archbishop of Montevideo and one of the first students of the Latin American Pius College in Rome and who presided the opening session of the Latin American Plenary Council (1899), criticized Darwinism, Protestantism, rationalism, irreligious propaganda, etc., in his book *El catolicismo, la civilización y el progreso* (1878)[44] (*Catholicism, Civilization, and Progress*). He employed progressive, liberal terminology and categories (with a bibliography of the era in French, English, and Italian) but couched in a fundamentally conservative and traditional agrarian posture. There was manifested a distrust of the bourgeois and of the nascent technological Anglo– North American culture that was beginning to emerge as a monopolistic empire. But the basis for the suspicion stemmed from the Latin Continental European and Latin American conservative agricultural tradition. Nevertheless, during the early part of the nineteenth century, beginning first with a small number of "liberal Catholics," there began a move away from this European– Latin American conservatism to a more progressive theological position adopted by members of the middle class who were allied with the upper echelons of the oligarchy.

Rome's influence grew, especially in Italy, and the theologians of Vatican Council I began to exert direct influence on Latin America, primarily because of the increased number of theology students who went to Rome. Since the end of the nineteenth century only Chile has sent a few seminarians to countries other than Italy. The Third Scholastic became present in all centers of theological teaching. The Catholic University of Chile was founded in 1869 and became the most important theological center of Latin America until well into the twentieth century.

Since 1850 the Protestant presence in Latin America has grown, whereas before it was sporadic and insignificant. Presbyterians began their work in Colombia in 1856, in Brazil in 1859, and in Mexico in 1872. Methodists began in Brazil and Uruguay in 1835. Their work in Uruguay produced little results and therefore ceased. It was begun anew in 1876. Baptists arrived in Argentina in 1881. Protestants did not begin to unite their forces until the Congress of Panama in 1916, and they failed to produce anything significant theologically until recently with the work of theologians such as Rubem Alves and José Míguez Bonino.

5. The Fifth Epoch: The Theology of the "New Christendom" (1930–1962)

During this period there occurred the transition away from *traditional theology* reflecting the thinking of the proprietary classes, the *integrista*, (whose enemies were bourgeoise liberalism, communism, Protestantism, and the "modern times" in general) who were committed to the *theology of development* that was reformist in nature. They accepted a bourgeoise *ethos*, but unfortunately one of a dependent capitalism, for in the majority of our nations the economy does not reach the level of capitalism. Most Latin American countries are nothing more than neocolonies exporting the raw materials, but without a truly national bourgeoise.

The crisis of 1929, resulting from the collapse of North American capitalism, profoundly affected the "periphery," especially Latin America. In some of the countries, such as Argentina, Uruguay, and Chile, together with the southern section of Brazil between Río de Janeiro and São Paulo, and in Mexico, the crisis incited a reaction of increased industrialization in order to limit imports, a movement that grew significantly during World War II. At the same time, however, there appeared a number of popular social movements (the first of which was the Mexican Revolution of 1910, which subsequently was cleverly orchestrated by the bourgeoise of that country) that made it impossible for the neocolonial bourgeoise to continue their domination. There followed the rise of the military classes in practically every country, first functioning in the name of the land owners and later on behalf of an ambiguous unity between the national bourgeoise and the working classes. This brought about the end of the militant, lay (following the French inspiration of Litreé), Positivist (since the time of Compte), anticlerical (although morally Christian) liberalism. On the other hand, there was an openness to and even a seeking of support from the traditional, conservative Catholic Church. This allowed for the celebration of gigantic Eucharistic Congresses, but principally it set the stage for the beginning of the movement known as *Catholic Action* and other similar institutions that were products of the theological theorizing of the "New Christendom."

In 1928 two priests — Caggiano, who would later become the Cardinal of Buenos Aires, and Miranda, who would be named the Cardinal of Mexico — went to Rome to study the organization of *Catholic Action*. Then, beginning in 1929, the movement slowly became institutionalized in all of Latin America. The theology of Catholic Action clearly distinguished between the "temporal" and the "spiritual." Laymen were said to be responsible for the temporal, the worldly, the material, and the political, while the priests were the "spiritual overseers," the vicars of the Kingdom of Christ. The function of Christians, of the militant, was to fulfill their "apostleship." This "sending" or mission was defined as "participation in the hierarchical apostleship of the Church," understanding that the hierarchy meant the priests and the bishops. In this way the ministries and the sacrament of orders virtually suppressed the significance of the charisms and the sacrament of baptism. Laymen could participate in political parties of "Christian inspiration," and thus there arose in Chile in 1936 the group known as the "Falange" (the Phalanx), which separated from the youth movement of the Conservative Party. Following World War II, and because of the Italian association, the "Falange" was called "Christian Democracy," prospering mainly between 1950 and 1970. Laymen could also participate in labor unions of "Christian inspiration," and thus was organized CLASC, the Latin American Confederation of Christian Unions, which for the most part were nothing more than movements for reform. Catholic laypersons were also encouraged to teach in "Christian schools." The task was seen, therefore, to be that of reconverting Latin America into a coalition of Catholic nations because the Kingdom of Christ required the recognition of the Catholic religion as the predominant and official faith of all the nations. The Church dreamed, therefore, of recovering through the work of militant laypersons the measure of power it had lost during the nineteenth century with the crisis of Christendom.

The *theology of the "New Christendom"* was not academic but militant, not directly political but rather dualistic in the sense of being temporal-spiritual. The State and the Church should, it was thought, be perfect societies each acting in its own sphere in a nonconflictual way. It was not until 1950 that the *theology of development* emerged, which represented the stage in which Christians — or at least some of them — began to participate in the bourgeoise project of expansion and development. Nevertheless, it is quite evident that no one was aware of the class problem or of the *dependence* of the Latin American continent on the economic, political, and military power of the United States. The Third Scholastic received the help of theologians such as Jacques Maritain and Emmanuel Mounier, and with them a particular interpretation of reality was rejuvenated.

Theologians began to organize other than in Italy, and the most progressive of them began studying in France, the country of the Pastoral, of catechetical, liturgical, and spiritual experiences, and of the "working priests." The "social doctrine" of the Church permitted many of these priests to work with laboring classes and with marginal groups.

During this period theological faculties or centers were initiated in many universities such as the Javeriana in Bogotá (founded in 1937), the Catholic University in Lima (1942), the Bolivarian in Medellín (1945), the Catholic Universities of São Paulo and Río de Janeiro (1947), of Porto Alegre (1950), of Campinas and Quito (1956), of Buenos Aires (1961), and many others later. Theology "a la Europe" thereby had an academic environment in which it could continue to grow while waiting for a creative moment.

Ecclesial praxis was also growing. Catholic Action, founded in Argentina and Chile in 1931, in Uruguay in 1934, in Costa Rica and Peru in 1935, in Bolivia in 1938, and eventually in all of Latin America, increased the *intensity* of the "social struggle." Groups such as *Human Economy*, inspired by Lebret, or the *Centro Belarmino* in Santiago, Chile, continued to make people aware of the prevailing social conditions. The same can be said of the Centers of Social and Religious Investigations which were begun in Buenos Aires, Bogotá, and Mexico City, centers that maintained a certain sociographic perspective (I am not saying sociological, much less economic-political) of the Latin American reality.

No less important was the foundation of CELAM (the Latin American Conference of Bishops) in Río in 1955, through the inspiration of Monseñor Larraín, a move that permitted the coordination of all of the apostolic movements and that played a significant role in the formation of the militant theologians of the following era. The same can be said of the organization of CLAR (the Latin American Confederation of

Religious) in 1958, as well as other movements of various types in the universities, theological seminaries, Catholic Action, and Catholic labor unions.

Furthermore, the bases of the biblical movement were established. Protestants with the *Bible Societies* and Catholics through their seminars, magazines, and new editions of the Bible began to pave the way for a spiritual renewal.

Nevertheless, one can say that even after World War II theological thought in Latin America was essentially a reproduction and application of European theology and was virtually devoid of any historical or contemporary knowledge of the Latin American reality.

6. The Sixth Epoch: The Latin American Theology of Liberation (since 1962)

This last period has three clearly discernible stages: the first from the beginning of the Second Vatican Council to Medellín (1962– 1968), a time of preparation and of development theology; the second (from 1968 to 1972), a time for the formulation of the *theology of liberation,* characterized by an attitude of euphoria despite the fact that there were clear indications that the road to freedom was fraught with difficulties; the third (which was initiated in Sucre in 1972 among Catholics with the restructuring of CELAM and among Protestants with their UNELAM), a time of maturing, of persecution, of becoming aware of the *long* process of liberation, of the awareness that we are now exiles in captivity. From the deepening of the Exodus we can restudy and rethink Second Isaiah and other books composed by and about the prisoners in Babylon. This era is a time of passing from the *theology of development* to the *theology of liberation.*

Nevertheless, we should not deceive ourselves. As Luís Alberto Gómez de Sousa declared during the First Latin American Theological Encounter (Mexico City, August 1975), within the process of a dependent capitalism there presently coexists as unequals a reflection of the classes tied to agriculture, the theology of development (a reflection of the bourgeoise classes and of the small bourgeoise), and the theology of liberation (which expresses the faith of emergent classes: the workers and peasants, marginalized and somewhat radicalized sectors of our society). It is for this reason that the theological confrontation in Latin America is not between traditional theology and the theology of liberation, but between a "progressive theology of development (inspired by the best of contemporary European thinking) and the theology of liberation." The criticism that the theology of liberation frequently voices against the best of European theology (either political theology or the theology of hope) is in reality addressed to those among us who use these European theologies to discredit a *valid and critical* theology in Latin America (which cannot be adapted by reformist European theology, which serves the world of the "center," but which is very ambiguous and idealogical for the "periphery"). The theology of liberation demands that European theologians consider the repercussions of their proposals for the "periphery," because there are in Latin America reformists who can be reactionary, antirevolutionary, or at least allied with the openly traditionalist theologies (such as *Opus Dei*).

The *theology of liberation* was not the result of spontaneous generation. It has a recent history, a history that goes back to Bartolomé de Las Casas in the sixteenth century. Among the youth movements (young people are still free to challenge the system!) were the *specialized* Catholic Action groups (JUC, JEC, JOC) of the last period of the "New Christendom." They began to discover the responsibility of being a lay Christian and the demands of political commitment. Within the middle classes composed of the smaller and somewhat larger bourgeoise, the workers, and peasant leaders, many were radicalized — in Brazil for example in the 1950s — because they refused any alliance with the industrial bourgeoise and the land-owning oligarchy. Many were students who were unwilling to accept the fact that they did not naturally belong to the oppressed classes. For this reason the students rejected their class, passed from reformism to revolution, frequently adopting not the anticommunism of the right but the communism of the extreme left (the Communist parties were for the most part reactionary), and at times fell into a naive romanticism because of their lack of political realism. Their attitude was basically zealot, and theirs was a kind of zealotry characterized by a utopianism and heroism that was neither practical nor operative — as can be seen in the case of Camilo Torres in Colombia (d. February 16, 1966), or the "Teoponte" guerrillas in Bolivia.[45] Confronting a general pessimism, Torres and the "Teopontes" voluntarily attempted to do everything simultaneously. It is not strange that the armed groups of the Peronist left in Argentina (the *Montoneros*) were founded by former leaders of the JUC, or that the MIR in Chile attracted the majority of the so-called Group of Eighty priests. Nevertheless, the *theology of liberation* is not the product of these single-issue groups, guerrillas, nor of *extreme* leftists. On the contrary, it is theological reflection based on a much more profound analysis of reality, a reflection that stems from the persecution and martyrdom of the Latin American christs, hundreds of whom have given their lives for their faith in concrete political situations, murdered by parapolitical forces, by the police, by the army, or by groups linked to the CIA or its henchmen (the soldiers of Pilate!).

A. Time of preparation (1962 — 1968)

The theology of development was based on the mythical process of the "development" of the underdeveloped peoples by means of the technical help and the capital of the powers of the "center" (principally the United States and Europe). This development reached its maximum expression with Kennedy's "Alliance for Progress." The *theology of development*[46] reflected the faith that partial social, political, and economic reforms would suffice. It had a "functionalist" spirituality: the "state's grace" would help it to fulfill its duty and provide a "good example." It was a spirituality that was updated with the latest thought from Europe. It attempted to be "incarnate" in the world (without having discovered the conflict existing in such a "world" — a world considered *a priori* to be good). What happened, however, was that the world was that of the bourgeoise, and the inherent conflict was not seen because the Christian had been educated inside the ecclesial bourgeoise culture.

The Second Vatican Council was held within the cultural process of central Europe and the peaceful coexistence between the United States, Europe, and Russia (which climaxed with the Helsinki Accords). Within this process the participation of Latin Americans can be considered theologically nonexistent. This is understandable, given the immaturity of theological reflection in Latin America since the beginning of the century.

The Bishop of Talca, Manuel Larraín, was elected President of CELAM in 1963 — a position that he held until his accidental death in 1966. This movement culminated with the Second General Conference of the Latin American Episcopacy held in Medellín in August 1968. Medellín represented the climax of the period of preparation. Its vocabulary was, however, developmentalist. It spoke of "human promotion," "development," "liberation," "international tensions and external neocolonialism," the "growing distortion of international commerce," "the flight of capital," and of the "international monopolies and imperialism of money." Medellín was the result of a long process.

Since the end of World War II, groups of young seminarians studied in France and later in Austria and Germany. Some of them studied in the United States. At the beginning they simply "repeated" what they had learned. But little by little as a result of certain organisms such as FERES,[47] founded by Houtart, or DESAL[48] by Vekemans in 1961 — although both were from Belgium, they would subsequently follow very different ways — the Latin American reality began to be described. In 1961, ILADES[49] was founded in Santiago, Chile. Religious sociology gave way to general sociology and then to the pastoral. ICLA[50] was founded in 1961 in the South and in the North in 1966. There followed the Latin American Insitute of Pastoral Liturgy (1965), then OSLAM,[51] which offered courses for seminary professors, and IPLA[52] — which opened its doors in Quito in 1968 and trained more than 500 pastoralists — began its itinerant activities in January 1964 under the inspiration of Monseñor Proaño and of a group of activist theologians. This period of the theology of development culminated in a congress held in Mexico City, September 24 — 28, 1969, under the theme "Faith and Development."

Their Latin American contacts, the need to present a theology to the participants from all the Latin American countries (from Mexico and the Caribbean to Brazil and the Andean Zone and the Southern Cone) prevented the theologians from "repeating" merely what they had learned in Europe. They had to adapt their discourses to the Latin American reality and deal with the agonizing problems of poverty and injustice that the continent was confronting.

The Latin American theologians of this period were, among others, Juan Luís Segundo[53] and José Comblín — who, although Belgian, lived and worked in Latin America for more than twenty years.[54] Comblín's L'echec de l'Action catholique (1959) was written from his experience in Brazil. It was the first and only authorized critique of the theology of the "New Christendom." At the same time, and in another sector — and as a passage to the later stage — a *theology of revolution*[55] was promulgated in ecumenical circles in which some Latin American theologians participated.[56]

B. The Formulation of the Theology of Liberation (1968 — 1972)

A long process had been incubating in Latin America. In 1959 a group of guerrillas defeated the dictator Fulgencio Batista in Cuba. Fidel Castro and "Che" Guevara became world and Latin American symbols. Liberation movements began to be organized everywhere. In Chile, with Allende's Popular Unity, the process manifested a new vitality (1970). The return of Perón to Argentina and the proposals for liberation by the popular movement there (1972 — 1973) engendered new hope. The organization of a movement for the liberation of the whole continent seemed possible. CELAM in turn promoted its Institutes. There followed seminars for bishops, priests, and laypersons. The "Christian Base Community" movement grew in number and influence. Priests for liberation multiplied — the most important were "Priests for the Third World" in Argentina, the "Group of Eighty" in Chile, and the ONIS in Peru. University students became politically committed to the socialist cause.

It was in the midst of these events, in approximately 1964, that an epistemological division occurred at the level of human sciences: the socio-economy of development was transformed into a theory of liberation, the result of a diagnosis that proposed the "theory of dependence."[57] The theory may be summarized as follows: it is impossible to develop the undeveloped countries because their undevelopment is due to the systematic exploitation by the countries of the "center." The "periphery" — as Raul Presbisch, UNESCO economist, had declared in 1964 in the first meeting of UNC-TAD — must consistently sell its raw materials for less while the manufactured products of the "center" are sold for consistently higher prices. The disequilibrium is structural, and it is growing. There followed the sociology of liberation and with it a new economy.[58]

It is not strange, then, that in 1968 Latin American theology began to reflect these socio-economic insights; thus there was born the "theology of liberation." Gustavo Gutiérrez, adviser to the student movements in Peru, raised the question: "Will it be a theology of development or a theology of liberation?"[59] Richard Shaull asked the same question at an ecumenical level,[60] as did the Brazilian Protestant leader Rubem Alves,[61] and the Argentine populist Lucio Gera in his opposition to the theology of secularization.[62] From the praxis of liberation there followed critiques of the theologies of revolution, of the "death of God," and of secularization. Hugo Assmann set forth the differences between the theology of liberation and European political theology and the theology of hope.[63] Since approximately 1970—1971, the theology of liberation has tended to coalesce as it received historical and philosophical support.[64] The meeting in Escorial, Spain, in July 1972,[65] was the first occasion when those participating in the movement could engage in face-to-face theological dialogue. Among those attending were José Míguez Bonino[66] who had for years been a leading Latin American participant in the World Council of Churches, Juan C. Scannone of Argentina,[67] the editors of Víspera (published in Montevideo), Héctor Borrat and Methol Ferre,[68] and representatives of the "Service of Documentation" of MIEC in Lima. Various theological journals such as Stromata (Bueno Aires), Teología y Vida (Santiago), Christus (Mexico), Pastoral Popular, Revista brasileira de Teología (Petrópolis), Sic (Caracas), Diálogo (Panama), etc., began publishing essays and editorials committed to liberation. This was the stage of euphoria initiated by Dom Hélder Câmara, Archbishop of Olinda-Recife, who with sixteen other bishops of the "periphery" declared in a document published in Témoignage Chrétien (Paris, July 31, 1966) that the "people of the Third World constitute the proletariat of the present world." This perspective was ratified by Monseñor Eduardo Pironio, then Secretary of CELAM, when in a meeting in New York he stated that "our mission, like Christ's, consists of bringing the good news to the poor, of proclaiming liberation to the oppressed" (Maryknoll, 1971).[69]

These events represented the theological reflection of those who were thinking of the *concrete* political commitment of Christians in their geopolitical situation of being the "periphery," and of the social responsibility of the "organic intellectual" of the oppressed classes (in this case the theologian), and of the participants in whole or in part who were risking involvement in the liberation of those classes. They were not looking for a fight. The "fight" is the fruit of sin. It is begun by the oppressor (the sinner) and is endured by the oppressed.

C. The "Captivity" and the "Exile" as Stages of Liberation (1972 —   )

The theology of liberation, which was preponderantly inspired by the positive efforts for liberation (such as Moses coming out of Egypt), soon discovered the hard reality from the praxis of "captivity" and of "exile." The present writer was obliged to flee his country and is writing now as one in actual, concrete exile. It is not difficult to understand why such a subject was proposed by Brazilian theologian Leonardo Boff.[70] The liberator Christ is the "suffering servant."[71]

The shadow of repression and imperial domination covered virtually the whole continent (with the exception of an island in the Caribbean). Liberation groups have meanwhile redefined themselves facing persecution from the outside (the police state) and from the inside (that of the Church itself), and the *theology of liberation* is beginning its maturation in the cross.

In view of the failure of the "Alliance for Progress," the United States changed its policies with respect to Latin America. For this reason the CIA, for example, opposed Allende's Popular Unity Party in Chile in 1963, the year that William Rogers was named U.S. Secretary of Latin American Affairs and delivered ten million dollars to a Belgian priest to help further the cause of Christian Democracy.[72] In 1964 there was a military overthrow of the government in Brazil under the theoretical and practical guidance of Golbery, establishing in effect a model that would be followed by military officers in carrying out coups in Uruguay (1971), Bolivia (1972), and Chile (1973). Many of these officers had been trained in the United States or in the Panama Canal Zone. The "Rockefeller Report" (1969)[73] reiterated the hard line by stating that the "security of the Western Hemisphere" (of the United States) makes it necessary to aid the military governments of Latin America — even though they are dictatorial (which they were never called) — because they functioned as defenders of the order and values of our "western Christian civilization." Among these defenders of Christian civilization are the presidents of Brazil, the Uruguayan military dictators, Banzer, and Pinochet. The North American Empire no longer speaks of liberty or of democracy in its neocolonies. It now speaks of "order" and "security," trusting in its "god" ("In God We Trust"), which more and more appears to be Mars, the god of war, the one founded on the victory of the oppressors. It is evident that the political imprudence of the single issue or guerrilla groups allowed the armies to be transformed into occupation forces favoring the Empire. Certain segments of the Church supported this action and sacralized this line of the "extreme right." It is important to note that these efforts were also assisted by the "progressives," reformists, and postconciliar theologians of development who were inspired by the best of European theology. All of these have been critical of the theology of liberation, and they continually formulate new projects, some of them supported by German Catholic entities, for their criticism. The argument is simple: the theology of liberation is allied with the "extreme left" (which is untrue) and with the guerrilla groups. Later, liberation theology was criticized as being the strategical Marxist-Christian support for such violent groups.[74]

The meetings in Bogotá in November 1973,[75] and in Toledo in 1974,[76] for example, were designed to counteract the theology of liberation, but were only partially successful. On the other hand, after the meeting in Sucre (November 1972), it was decided to close the Institutes of the Pastoral in Quito, of Liturgy in Medellín, and of Catechesis in Manizales in order to reorganize them into a single institution — from which Comblín, this writer, and others were excluded — with a new orientation. In Belgium the old Institute *Lumen Vitae*, where several Latin Americans were participating, was closed, and slowly everywhere institutes, seminars, and groups committed to the theology of liberation were canceled or suppressed.

Between the left and the right — in the "center" — some theological movements that we may call "populist" were functioning — especially in Argentina due to the euphoria accompanying the return of Perón — movements that since 1974 were understandably ambiguous in their position. Developments, however, prompted them to define more precisely their idea of "the people" and to understand better the distinction between reformist and revolutionary positions. A confrontation ensued, as we have said, between the progressives "a la Europe" and the proponents of the theology of liberation — a confrontation that was clearly visible in the meetings sponsored by CELAM in Bogotá in November 1973 and in Lima in September 1975.[77]

Meanwhile, the theology of liberation continued to mature amid persecution, and the number of its adherents increased. Expelled from their positions (e.g., Comblín in Brazil and Assmann in Chile), persecuted sometimes by those of their own Church, they grew in number and quality. Then there emerged spokesmen such as Ignacio Ellacuría and Jon Sobrino in El Salvador,[78] Luís del Valle in Mexico,[79] Virgilio Elizondo among the Chicanos in the United States,[80] Raul Vidales in Lima,[81] Rafael Avila in Colombia,[82] Ronaldo Muñoz in Chile,[83] and Alejandro Cussiánovich in Peru.[84]

The theology of liberation began to take more seriously its role in the popular movements of liberation and has been unable to avoid solidarity with these movements in their struggles, particularly with the martyrs of the Latin American Church: Antonio Pereira Neto, murdered in Brazil (1969); Héctor Gallego, disappeared in Panama (1971); Carlos Mugica, shot to death in Argentina (1974); and Ivan Betancourt, murdered in Honduras (1975).[85]

"Christians for Socialism," who held their organizational meeting in Chile in 1972, now represent a world movement. In their second meeting in Quebec they evidenced a real maturation, more precision in their interpretative categories, and a respectable distancing from their Chilean position. Latin American theology is, therefore, making a significant contributuion to Christian theology.[86]

The *I Encuentro Latinoamericano de teología* (First Latin American Theological Encounter) held in Mexico in August 1975[87] brought a halt to liberation theology's moving to a new stage of development by producing a clear confrontation between positions that were preponderantly North American and "functionalist," and which were virtually ignoring our concrete Latin American reality. One week later, however, the *Theology in the Americas* meeting held in Detroit made possible the first contact between several Latin and North American theologians — the latter group composed of representatives of Black, feminine, and Chicano theology, together with other critics of the system. In addition to these developments there was the added possibility of future dialogues with African and Asian theologians. The theology of liberation thus opened the debate to the whole world.[88]

We can, therefore, assert that the theology of liberation discovered the *political time* of captivity, of prudence, and of patience. But if it is to avoid being transformed into reformism, it will be necessary to move toward the single strategic goal of liberation.

IV. Conclusions

We have been able to see that in the history of Latin American theology there have been three creative periods. *The initial one* dealt with the conquest and the evangelization of the continent. It produced a prophetic, political, and extrauniversity theology. *The second one* dealt with the process of the neocolonial national liberation movements at the beginning of the nineteenth century. It produced a practical, political, and non-academic theology. *The third stage* dealt with the process of popular, national liberation against monopolistic, capitalistic imperialism. It produced the theology of liberation, likewise prophetic, political, and nonacademic. These theologies unite the people — the Indian, the creole or the proletariate, the peasant, the marginalized emerging groups, and revolutionaries — who think of *militancy* when they link their faith and the praxis of liberation. For this reason the theology of liberation could begin by using European theologians and categories. But it is in fact another theology because of its point of departure, its theological production of militancy, and its final goal. That is to say, it is a different theology because of its method.

The method of the theology of liberation is not merely functionalistic, taking "science" as a prototype, accepting as givens the components of the *contemporary* system without questioning radically the system as such. This would be the method of Lonergan who has his followers in Latin America, especially in the North. This would not be a radically critical theology.

Nevertheless, a mere dialectical method following the tradition begun by Hegel and carried on by the Frankfurt School and by Bloch himself moves from the given system and opens itself to future possibilities for the same system. But in reality this method is really reformist — at best it is the democratic socialism of the "center," composed of people who are as afraid of an oil embargo as are their compatriots in the Christian Democractic parties — because an oil crisis could bring an end to the domination by the "center."

What they fail to see is that the dialectical theology of the "center," that is, the meaning of theology *in* Europe, changes dialectically when applied to the "periphery." The theology which in Europe is radically critical of its own structures is nothing more than reformist and even counterrevolutionary in the "periphery," for it proposes to change things only in Europe. It strives only for an intranational, not an international revolution. It absolutizes its nation as a whole and in turn abstracts the rest of the world. This theology, therefore, is valid only for the European *partial*-whole, but not the the *total*-whole of the present world.

The method employed by the theology of liberation has as its point of departure the conduct of the people of the "periphery," of the laborers and peasants who still suffer because social and economic achievements of the "center" (a strike of Ford, Volkswagen, or Citroen workers means a rise in the price of the manufactured product that will be purchased by the worker in the "periphery"). On the other hand, the method of theological production itself is not essentially academic but takes on meaning at the "basic-base" as reflection on the experiences of Christians committed to the real process of liberation. It is reflection on *the militancy* of a movement that is ecclesial and political. For the theologian it means the risk of *orthopraxis*. Its method is more than dialectical (I prefer to call it *analectical*) or universally dialectical in that it knows how to pose the question of the *externalization of the culture* of the "periphery" and of the popular groups. It proposes not only a *technical* revolution, but also a *cultural* revolution by affirming the values of the people and of the oppressed classes.

Furthermore, the theology of liberation uses primarily the measurements of the social *critical* sciences, or as Fals Borda puts it, those tools of the social sciences of liberation.[89] Economics and sociology (from its "theory of dependency" situated at the proper level), geopolitics, political science, and Latin American history are aware of the "theoretical rupture" that proposes to use as a point of departure an individual from the oppressed and nonimperialistic culture, and they discover the "ideological scientificism" of the sciences of the "center." Furthermore, since 1970, the philosophical relation between the social sciences and theology has become increasingly clear. Thus a *philosophy of liberation* becomes a hermeneutical necessity.[90]

At any rate, the *written works* of the theology of liberation as works *in themselves,* as an "abstract whole," can — because of their language — use authors and ideas of European inspiration. As *parts* of a Latin American *whole* they make sense. If I take, for example, Gutiérrez' *Theology of Liberation* and do not understand that it is a book written in Gutiérrez' spare time, when he is free from his responsibilities as prophet and inspirer of a large number of priestly works, of various Christian base movements, as professor in the university, and participant in politics, actions that absorb all his time — if I do not understand that it is a tactical book, where he says what is possible to say and where everything cannot be said, where he includes a bibliography for the scholar's benefit — but is unnecessary for the "base" if the work is not seen as the fruit of *political* language itself, then the real Latin American meaning of the book is missed. One should not forget that political language, as that of the Councils, is not valued for what is said as much as for against whom it is said, why, and to whom it is written. The theology of liberation is essentially Latin American for the simple reason that only a Latin American or one who makes the effort to live together with others in the world can *fully* understand its meaning. For this reason theologians in Latin America are persecuted by the police, the security services, and even by ecclesiastical leaders. If the *real* evidence of its newness were not evident, Latin Americans could continue producing academic theological treatises and "the Prince of this World" would not disturb them.

For this reason, the criticism of theology can follow one of two alternatives:

ALTERNATIVE 1   Abstract Criticism
Theology *a* criticizes →theology *b*

In this case "theology *a*" criticizes "theology *b*" as one *part* criticizes another *part* of the same system, or as a *whole* criticizes another *whole*, both of which are independent of the total system. In both examples, if the *parts* or the *wholes* are homogeneous and not in conflict, then the criticism is abstract because it does not take into account the conditions or factors that could produce conflict and heterogeneity in these two examples.

ALTERNATIVE 2   Concrete or Historical Criticism
Theology *a* → is part of the "European" *whole* or of the "center"
Theology *b* → is part of the "peripheral" *whole* which is worldwide because it embraces the "center"

Only in this case can "theology *a*," aware of its European presuppositions, now analyze itself and "theology *b*," being aware also of the presuppositions of this different theology ("theology *b*"). Otherwise, the criticism is not concrete and historical but rather ideological because it confines "theology *a*" to the narrow horizons of its own world, and from the "center" it pretends to be able to interpret all of what is happening in the world. Thus it becomes doubly ideological, first because it ignores or forgets its own presuppositions, and in the second place because it assumes that the presuppositions of the rest of the world are the same as its own. If these two demands are fulfilled, then the criticism will be constructive and can help to advance the worldwide study of theology. (Note, I did not say "universally.")

The *point* of departure for European theology — even the most progressive theology — is the university or the pastoral praxis of the churches. The *point* of departure of the theology of liberation is the "militancy" of the theologians who are as parts of the Christian *movements* involved (even unto death) in the real, political, economic, cultural process of Latin America. The language of the theology of liberation is unintelligible without a knowledge of the hermeneutic of those Latin American movements.[91]

We know that Marx was born in Trier, Germany, but we also know that Theotonio dos Santos, Faletto, Cardoso, Fals Borda, Darcy Ribeiro, and many others were born in Latin America, thus redefining the part of the "center" from the theoretical rupture

that implanted all that had been said before as a *part* of a new *totality* where the
language acquired an essential, qualitative newness. This is the way the theology of
liberation applies an ideological interpretation to the same theology, to the praxis
situated within the respective classes, and to the nations within the "center" and the
"periphery." Thus theology is freed from the Mediterranean patristics, from European
medieval thought, and from the confines of the European— North American community to be open to the whole world for the first time in the history of Christianity.
The point of departure for liberation theology is Africa, Asia, and Latin America, the
oppressed classes, the discriminated races, the abused women, the dominated children,
the despised aged. It is de-ideologized theology because it hears the cries of the
oppressed, but with an awareness that only in *the Kingdom* will we know clearly what
we have done.

V. AN ABBREVIATED CHRONOLOGY FOR *A HISTORY OF THEOLOGY IN LATIN AMERICA*

1. Prophetic theology versus the conquest and evangelization (1511-— 1577)
   1511 Preaching of Antonio de Montesino in Santo Domingo.
   1514 Conversion of Bartolomé de Las Casas in Cuba.
   1527 Bartolomé begins his *Historia de las Indias*.
   1541 Bartolomé publishes his *Brevísima relación de la destrucción de la Indias*.
   1577 José de Acosta writes his *De procuranda indorum salute*.

2. The theology of Colonial Christendom (1533— 1808)
   1553 The University of Mexico opens, as well as San Marcos University in
        Lima.
   1553— 1563 Pedro de la Peña serves as Professor of the *Prima*.
   1605 Antonio Rubio writes his *Lógica Mexicana*.
   1622— 1625 A large number of secondary schools of theology are founded.
   1776 Domingo Muriel writes his *Fasti novi orbis*.

3. Practical-political theology versus the neocolonial emancipation (1808)
   1808 Lagunza's *El Reino del Mesías en gloria y majestad* is published.
   1809— 1812 Preaching by Hidalgo, Morelos, and many others in favor of
             national liberation.
   1813 The *Destrucción de las Indias* is reprinted in Bogotá.

4. Conservative neocolonial theology on the defensive (1831— 1931)
   1859 Colegio Pío Latinoamericano is founded in Rome.
   1867 The school of theology in the University of Mexico is suppressed.
   1869 The Catholic University of Santiago, Chile, opens.
   1878 Mariano Soler writes *El catolicismo, la civilización y el progreso* in Montevideo.
   1899 Latin American Plenary Council meets in Rome and issues what may be
        called a "Romanized" theology.
   1916 Meeting of American Protestant churches in Panama.

5. Theology of the "New Christendom" (1930— 1962)
   1931 Catholic Action founded in Argentina.
   1937 Founding of the Javeriana University in Bogotá.
   1947 Catholic Universities of Río and São Paulo founded.
   1955 CELAM organized in Río de Janeiro.
   1960 Catholic Universities in Buenos Aires and Córdoba are founded.

6. Latin American theology of liberation (1962—)

1962 — 1965 Participation of Latin American theologians in the Second Vatican Council.

1968 Second General Conference of CELAM in Medellín.

1969 Congress on "Faith and Development" in Mexico.

1970 Various meetings on the "theology of liberation" in Bogotá, Buenos Aires, Mexico City, Oruro, Bolivia, etc.

1971 Gustavo Gutiérrez publishes his *Teología de la liberación*.

1972 Meeting in Escorial on "Faith and Social Change in Latin America."

1973 Persecution of Christians involved in the process of liberation in Chile.

1975 First Latin American Encounter of Theology in Mexico, and the Theology in the Americas meeting in Detroit.

1976 *I Encuentro de los teólogos del Tercer Mundo* in Dar es Salaam, Tanzania.

1977 *II Encuentro de los teólogos del Tercer Mundo* in Accra, Ghana.

1977 Meeting in Mexico of various theologians of liberation with European and North American theologians (Assmann, Vidales, Dussel, Concha, *et al.*, with Moltmann, Cox, Cone, *et al.*).

1978 Meeting in San José, Costa Rica, of social scientists and theologians of liberation.

Notes for Appendix II

1. Cf. the brief bibliography in Kurt Lenk, *Ideologie, Ideologiekritik und Wissensoziologie* (Berlin: H. Luchterhand, 1971), pp. 429–450.

2. Cf. Chapter X, "La arqueológica," of my work *Para una ética de la liberación latinoamericana* (Buenos Aires: Siglo Veintiuno, 1975).

3. Cf. E. Dussel, "Domination-Liberation," *The Mystical and Political Dimension of the Christian Faith*, ed. Claude Geffré and Gustavo Gutiérrez in *Concilium* 96 (New York: Herder and Herder, 1974): 34–56.

4. In this work I will use the term "ideology" in a very limited sense, not as the total expression of a human class or group, but only *when it conceals* reality with its contradictions and basic conflicts.

5. "God our Lord, by his infinite mercy and goodness has given to us without merits a great part in *the Lordship* of this world," declared the King of Spain in the *Recopitulación* I, I, 1.

6. Cf. Aristotle, *Topica* I, 2, 101a, 26b; and Dussel, *Método para una Filosofía de la Liberación* (Salamanca: Ediciones Sígueme, 1974), pp. 17ff.

7. Cited by Venancio Carro, *La teología y los Teólogos juristas españoles ante la conquista de América* (Madrid: Talleres Gráficos Marsiega, 1944), p. 593. Cf. Juan Ginés Sepúlveda, *Opera* (Madrid: Real Academia de la Historia, 1780), I-IV, and especially his *Tratado sobre las justas causas de la guerra contra los índios* (Mexico: Fondo de Cultura Económica, 1941). See also Juan Solórzano Pereira, *De indiarum iure* (Iugduni, 1672), I-II, and Silvio A. Zavala, *La filosofía política de la conquista de América* (Mexico: Fondo de Cultura Económica, 1947). Lewis Hanke, Giménez Fernández, and Hoffner have written extensively on the theological-political controversies regarding the conquest. Sepúlveda insisted that to hunt the Indians like animals was suitable and justified, for hunting as an art "is practiced not only against beasts, but also against those who have been born to obey but refuse to serve. Such a war is by nature just." *Democrates alter*, cited by Carro, *La teología y los teólogos juristas españoles ante la conquista de América*, p. 595.

8. *Summa theologiae*, II-II, q. 57, art. 4.

9. J. Major, *In secundam sententiarum*, dist, XLIV, q. 3 (Paris, 1510).

10. What I have said in regard to the development of European theological thought is only indicative, the purpose being to provide the participants in the *Encuentro* (Meeting) with a ready frame of reference for the development of Latin American theology. For this reason no specific biliographical references are included. Furthermore, it would be helpful for Europeans to write a history of theology as a phenomenon that contains ideological stages.

11. The ideological-historical stage or period in no way invalidates the nature of revelation, for revelation consists of critical-eschatological eventualities that develop their potential in their own times. It was revelation that inspired the antislavery activity of the Jesuit teacher Ramírez and his disciple Pedro Claver, SJ in Cartagena during the early years of the seventeenth century. It is also revelation that inspires the *antimachismo* of the Christian feminist movements of our day. The question of revelation and ideology, however, remains.

12. Christianity originally was composed of the oppressed peoples and groups of the Roman Empire, as can be seen in the text of Tatian in his "Address to the Greeks": "But

with us there is no desire of vainglory nor do we indulge in a variety of opinions. . . . Not only do the rich among us pursue our philosophy, but the poor enjoy instruction gratuitously; for the things which come from God surpass the requital of worldly gifts" (chap. 32). *The Anti-Nicene Fathers* (Grand Rapids: Wm. B. Eerdmans, n.d.), Vol. II.

13. Artistides in his *Apology* attacked the very fundamentals of the Empire and Greek culture. His attitude was subversive when he declared: "Those who believe that the sky is God are wrong. . . . Those who believe that the earth is Goddess are wrong. . . . Those who believe that water is God are in error" (pp. 119–21).

14. *Summa theologiae*, I-II, q. 81, art. 5:" . . . quod principium activum in generatione est a patre, materiam autem mater ministrat . . . si, Adam non pecante, Eva pecasset, filii originale peccatum *non* contraherent." Woman gives only *matter*; it is the male who gives *being* to the son.

15. *Summa theologiae*, II-II, q. 57. art. 4.

16. Reyes Mate, *El ateísmo, un problema político* (Salamanca: Ediciones Sígueme, 1973).

17. We observed in a recent meeting of "Theology in the Americas" in Detroit, August 1975, that this was true of Black theology, e.g., James Cone, *Black Theology and Black Power* (New York: Seabury Press, 1969); *God of the Oppressed* (New York: Seabury Press, 1975); Benjamin A. Reist, *Theology in Red, White, and Black* (Philadelphia: Westminster Press, 1975); and feminist theology, e.g., Rosemary Ruether, *Liberation Theology* (New York: Paulist Press, 1972). No distinction is made between the center and the periphery on an international level. The liberation movement is promoted among these groups, but within the borders of their individual nations, which are in themselves as the center oppressors of other nations on the periphery. These groups may even include the oppressed countries in their project, but they fail to be aware of or criticize imperialism. This center-periphery contradiction distinguishes therefore *Black theology* in the United States from *Black theology* in Africa — in that the former struggles against oppressive racism but ignores economic-political oppression on an international level. The same can be said of the feminist movements of the "center" in relation to those of the periphery — as was evident in the World Congress of Women which met in Mexico City, July 1975, where the feminist movements of Viet Nam, Cuba, and Latin America openly criticized the apolitical and exclusively sexist feminism of the North American women specifically. If the theological movements of the "center" do not take into account the reality of imperialism, they will inevitably evolve into a dangerous revisionist reformism.

18. Martin Grabmann, *Die geschichte der katholischen theologie* (Frieburg: Herder & Co., 1933). Dussel cites the Spanish edition, *Historia de la teología católica*, trans. David Gutiérrez (Madrid: Espasa-Calpe, 1940), pp. 350ff.

19. Cf. my work, *El episcopado hispanoamericano, Institución defensora del indio 3* (1504–1620)¡ 6-147 (Cuernavaca: CIDOC, 1969).

20. *Historia de las Indias*, libro III, cap. 79 (Madrid: BAE, tomo II, 1961, p. 356). Cf. the synopsis of the life and bibliography of Las Casas in my article in the *Encyclopaedia Britannica*, 1974 edition.

21. *Obras escogidas*, V, 539.

22. Ibid.

23. *Brevísima relación de la destrucción de las Indias*, V, 136. The text continues stressing the qualities of the Indians: "Also they are extremely poor and powerless or want little of this world's goods. . . . They are clean and unpreoccupied, quick to understand, very capable and ready to accept every good doctrine; they are very apt to receive our holy faith. . . . These [are] tame sheep endowed with the aforementioned qualities by their Creator and Maker" (p. 136 a–b). Such descriptions are frequent in Bartolomé: the Indians are "so docile, patient, and humble" (*Apologética historia*, Argumento, III, 3). Remember that this immense work, the *Apologética*, is a respectful tribute by Las Casas to the Indian, a tribute in which he describes with sympathy their world, their culture, their beliefs. The same idealization appears also in the *Historia de las Indias*, I, cap. 40: "We Christians stopped to

observe the Indians ... how evident their meekness, simplicity, and trust in a people they had *never known*. . . . They are by nature kind, simple, humble, meek, passive, and virtuous in inclination, talented, prompt, yes very inclined to receive our holy faith" (I, 142 a — b); ". . . they are *a toto genere* by nature very meek people, very humble, extremely poor, defenseless or without arms, very simple" *Historia de las Indias*, Prólogo, I, 13b).

24. Cf. the full text in the *Memorial al Consejo de Indias* (1565), presented with commentary in the edition of J. B. Lassege, *La larga marcha de Las Casas* (Lima: CEP [Centro de Estudios y Publicaciones], 1974), p. 387.

25. Lassege, ibid.

26. *Bartolomé de Las Casas: precursor del anticolonialismo* (Mexico: Siglo Veintiuno, 1974).

27. It is important to note that as Las Casas wrote his enormous *Historia de las Indias,* José de Acosta published his *Historia natural y moral de las Indias* (Cf. the edition published in Madrid, 1894, 2 vols.). See also the work of León Lopetequi, *El padre José de Acosta* (Madrid, 1942).

28. This theology is explicit in letters, discussions, controversies, "memorials," apologies, and sermons. Though the literary style is impressive, the works were not written for university audiences.

29. Las Casas' *Apologética historia sumaria* is as significant as his *Historia*. José de Acosta's *De procuranda indorum salute* (Salamanca, 1589) is, as the previous work, an anthropological study. The great Bernardino de Sahagún collected materials for what would be his *Historia de las cosas de Nueva España* (Mexico: Ed. Pedro Robredo, 1938), I-V, which was the first study of world anthropology in a contemporary sense.

30. This theology influenced the thinking of laypersons, missionaries, and bishops, and helped shape laws, e.g., the "Leyes Nuevas" of 1542 which eliminated the system of *encomienda,* as well as inspiring other reforms.

31. *Historia de las Indias*, III, 79, p. 357.

32. For the theology of colonial Christianity, see the histories of the churches by nations (e.g., *Cuevas* for Mexico, *Groot* for Colombia, *Vargas* for Ecuador, *Vargas Ugarte* for Peru, *Cotapos* for Chile, *Bruno* for Argentina, etc.) See my *Historia de la Iglesia en América latina* (Barcelona: Editorial Nova Terra, 1974), pp. 433 — 459; *Para una historia de la Iglesia en América latina* (Barcelona: CEHILA, 1975); for Mexico only: José Gallegos Rocafull, *El pensamiento mexicano en los siglos XVII y XVIII* (Mexico: Centro de Estudios Filosóficos, 1951, Bibl. pp. 397 — 414); *Bibliotheca Missionum* (Münster, 1916 — 1938), I-XI; J. García Icazbalceta, *Bibliografía mexicana del siglo XVI* (Mexico: Andrade y Morales, 1886); Julio Jiménez Rueda, *Herejías y supersticiones en la Nueva España (los hereodoxos en México)* (Mexico: Imprenta Universitaria, 1946); Cristóbal B. Plaza y Jaen, *Crónica de la real pontificia universidad de México* (Mexico: Talleres gráficos del Museo Nacional, 1931); Oswaldo Robles, *Filósofos mexicanos del siglo XVI* (México: Librería de M. Porrúa, 1950) (where there is found material for our subject); and the work of Julio Jiménez Rueda, *Historia jurídica de la universidad de México* (Mexico: Facultad de Filosofía y Letras, 1955). See also Félix Osores, *Historia de todos los colegios de la ciudad de México desde la conquista hasta 1760* (Mexico: Talleres Gráficos, 1929). Among the colonial theologians one should not forget Juan Palafox y Mendoza, *Obras* (Madrid: Impresa de G. Ramírez, 1762), I-XVII. The works of Guillermo Furlong Cárdiff, e.g., *Nacimiento y desarrollo de la filosofía en el Río de la Plata, 1536-1810* (Bueno Aires: G. Kraft, 1952). His works on the thought in Río de la Plata, for example, help to fill a vacuum in that area of Latin America. Works like those of Pedro Henríquez Ureña, *Historia de la cultura de América hispánica* (Mexico: Fondo de Cultura Económica, 1947) serve as contextual reference. Nevertheless, we must admit that there is no work on the history of theology in Latin America, although the materials are minimally sufficient to provide an idea of the whole.

33. Cf. the work of Walter Redmond, *Bibliography of the Philosophy in the Iberian Colonies of America* (The Hague: Nijhoff, 1972), on the existent bibliography in Latin American colonial philosophy, which indicates the importance of these writings.

34. Cf. Ernest Burrus, "Alonso de la Veracruz. Defense of the American Indians," *The Haythrop Journal* 4 (July 1963):225 – 53; and Redmon, *Bibliography of the Philosophy in the Iberian Colonies of America*, notes 781 – 83. See also Bienvenido Junquera, "El maestro Alonso de la Veracruz," *Archivo augustiniano* 18 (1935).

35. Cited by Cárdiff, op cit., p. 617.

36. F. A. Encina, *Historia de Chile* (Santiago: Editorial Nacimiento, 1930), V, 550 – 95.

37. Cf. Javier Miranda, *Vida del venerable sacerdote Don Domingo Muriel* (Córdoba, 1916). Muriel's best-known works are *Fasti novi orbis* (Venice, 1776), *Rudimenta juris naturae et gentium* (Venice, 1791), and *Collectanea dogmatica de seculo XVIII* (Venice, 1792).

38. Guillermo Furlong Cárdiff's is the most complete work on the Paraguayan *reducciones*.

39. Cf. my work on Vieira, *América latina, dependencia y liberación* (Buenos Aires: F. García, 1973), pp. 52ff. This kind of messianism is traditional in Brazil even until today. Cf. M. I. Pereira de Queiroz, *Historia y etnología de los movimientos mesiánicos* (Mexico: Siglo Veintiuno, 1969).

40. Cf. Agustín Churruca, "El pensamiento de Morelos. Una ideología liberadora," *Christus* 477 (1975):13ff.; and 478 (1975):10ff, in which he illustrates the difference between creative, oppressive, and decadent Spain. "The aggressive affirmations of the Mexican liberator do not refer to Spain, which we Mexicans love and which was personified in Las Casas, Vasco de Quiroga, and many others. They are directed against that entity incarnated by the limited personality of Godoy, and haughtily and arrogantly trampled upon by Napolean and Botella" (p. 15).

41. It should not be forgotten that without the intervention of the "lower clergy," emancipation from Spain would have been impossible. It was the priest Miguel Hidalgo y Costilla (1753 – 1811), former director of the seminary in Morelia, who sounded the call to arms on September 15, 1810. He led the liberation forces until he was condemned for heresy by the University of Mexico and shot in 1811.

42. The historian Roberto Tisnés describes this edition in his work. For a description of the apocalyptic movement, cf. Horacio Cerutti, "América en las utopías del renacimiento," *Hacia una filosofía de la liberación*, ed. Osvaldo Ardiles, et al. (Buenos Aires: Editorial Bonum, 1973), pp. 53ff.

43. The crisis was real. Julio Jiménez Rueda in his *Historia jurídica de la universidad de México* says that Mora indicated in 1830 that it was necessary "to suppress an exhorbitant number of professorships of theology which had gone year after year without a single student" (pp. 152 – 53). In 1834 the whole program for teaching theology was changed: "the *prima* in theology became theological authorities, Scripture continued by its name, and vespers became ecclesiastical history" (p. 160). Little by little theology was abandoned in the national university forever. In 1857 the Theological Library became a part of the National Library, and in 1867 the School of Theology was definitively eliminated. "Catholic liberalism" was born in this kind of environment. Cf. Néstor T. Auza, *Católicos y liberales en la generación del ochenta* (Cuernavaca: Centro Intercultural de Documentación, 1966), 2 vols.

44. Cf. José María Vidal, *El primer arzobispo de Montevideo, Dr. Mariano Soler*, which contains a list of more than one hundred writings of this theologian. For information on the Plenary Council of 1899, cf. Pablo Correa León, *El concilio plenario latinoamericano* (Bogotá, n.d.) and Felipe Cejudo Vega, *El primer concilio plenario de América Latina* (Ottawa: University of Ottawa, 1948).

45. Cf. Hugo Assmann, *Teoponte: una experiencia guerrillera* (Oruro, Bolivia: Centro "Desarrollo Integral," 1971). The leader of this group was Néstor Paz, poet, physician, and Catholic seminarian who was killed October 8, 1970, at the age of 25.

46. Cf. François Houtart and Vincente Vertrano, *Hacia una teología del desarrollo* (Buenos Aires: Latinoamérica Libros, 1967); Víctor Cosmao, *Signification et théologie du développement* (Paris, 1967); Hugo Assmann, "Die situation der unterentwickelt gehaltenen Länder als Ort einer Theologie der Revolution," *Diskussion zur "Theologie der Revolution,"* Ernst Feil and Rudolf Weth, eds. (Munchen: Chr. Kaiser, 1969). The "theology of revolution" had already broken with the "theology of development" and represents a transition to the "theology of

liberation." Cf. Rubem Alves, "Apuntes para una teología del desarrollo," *Cristianismo y Sociedad* 21 (1969).

47. *Federación Internacional de Estudios de Sociología Religiosa* (International Federation of Religious Sociological Studies).

48. *Centro para el Desarrollo Económico y Social de América Latina*. This Center for Economic and Social Development of Latin America was inspired in part by the Christian Democracy movement in Chile. It moved in 1970 to Caracas and from there to Bogotá, where it now publishes the journal *Tierra Nueva*. In the first edition, April 1972, the first article was written by Alfonso López Trujillo, "La liberación y las liberaciones" (pp. 5–26), in which he says, "Everything which is not revolution (presumably violent) is catalogued as developmentalism, a useless and deceitful attempt." The theology of liberation is identified with extreme and even guerrilla positions and is distinguished from liberation despite the human and political contradictions. In the issue of July 1975, p. 27, n. 16, we are accused of using an ideological hermeneutical method with respect to theology (A. López Trujillo, "El compromiso político del sacerdote") without acknowledging the fact that the subject is proposed by Christ himself (Luke 23:34). Thus begins the criticism of the theology of liberation.

49. *Instituto latinoamericano de doctrinas y estudios sociales* (Latin American Institute of Doctrines and Social Studies), founded by Jesuits proceeding from *Action populaire* (Paris), such as the French Father Bigo, now in Bogotá, but does not support the theology of liberation.

50. *Instituto de Catequesis de latinoamérica* (Catechetical Institute of Latin America).

51. Organization of Seminaries in Latin America.

52. *Instituto Pastoral de América Latina*, which has done a commendable work of conscientization, publication, and seminars. It has been severely criticized by the more conservative groups.

53. Segundo was born in 1925 and is the author of *Berdiaeff. Une réflexion chrétienne sur la personne* (Paris: Aubier, 1963), *La Cristiandad; ¿una utopía?* (Montevideo: Cursos de Complementación Cristiana, 1964), 2 vols.; "L'avenir du christianisme en Amérique latine," *Lettre* (Paris) 54 (1963):7–12; and earlier *Función de la Iglesia en la realidad rioplatense* (Montevideo: Barreiro y Ramos, 1962); and later his five volumes: *A Theology for Artisans of a New Humanity* (Maryknoll: Orbis Books, 1973–1974). Two of his recent works are *De la sociedad a la teología* (Buenos Aires: Ed. Carlos Lohlé, 1970), and *The Liberation of Theology* (Maryknoll: Orbis Books, 1976).

54. Comblín was born in Belgium in 1923 but has lived and worked in Latin America since 1957. Among his writings are *Théologie de la Paix* (Paris: Editions universitaires, 1960–1963), 2 vols.; *Théologie de la ville* (Paris: Editions universitaires, 1968); *Le Christ dans l'Apocalypse* (Paris: Desclée, 1965); *Teología do desenvolvimiento* (Belo Horizonte, 1968); *Théologie de la revolution* (Paris: Editions universitaires, 1970–1974), 2 vols. Only in volume 2 does Comblín adopt some of the theses of the theology of liberation.

55. Cf. the bibliography on the subject in *Desarrollo y revolución* in the bibliography published by CEDIAL (Bogotá, 1974), pp. 73–95, and Hugo Assmann, "Caracterização de una teología de revolução," *Ponto Homen* 4 (1968):6–58. The question arose in part because of the meeting of "Church and Society" sponsored by the World Council of Churches in Geneva in 1966. Richard Shaull was a major contributor, together with several Latin American participants.

56. It should be noted that the "theology of liberation" will show that the "theology of revolution" is merely the application of certain themes from moral theology to the revolutionary situation; it is like giving it the "green light." It is not a complete reexposition of the theory, but rather more a manifestation of "opportunism."

57. The most creative group in regard to this doctrine was Brazilian, first Alberto G. Ramos, *La reducción sociológica* (Río de Janeiro: Instituto Superior de Estudios Brasileiras, 1958), followed by Helio Jaguaribe, Cándido Mendes, Alvaro Vieira Pintos, and others who

worked with the ISEB (The Brazilian Institute of Social Studies). To this group one should add Celso Furtado, Teotonio dos Santos, and others. The theory of dependency was formulated between 1968 and 1970, the period when most of the writing on the subject was published. Cf. the bibliography prepared by CEDIAL as well as the final bibliography in *Fe y cambio social en América Latina* (Salamanca, 1973).

58. Cf. the writings of the African economist Samir Amin, e.g., *L'accumulation a l'échelle mondiale* (Dakar: IFAN, 1970), which, following the "Latin American theory of dependence," suggests it as a hypothesis applicable worldwide.

59. Gutiérrez was born in 1928. Among his works are: *Líneas pastorales de la iglesia en América latina* (Lima: Editorial Universitaria, 1970); *A Theology of Liberation*, trans. Caridad Inda and John Eagleson (Maryknoll: Orbis Books, 1973), as well as a great number of articles in various journals.

60. In his brief work, "Consideraciones teológicas sobre la liberación del hombre," in *IDOC* (Bogotá) 43 (1968); and in "La liberación humana desde una perspectiva teológica," *Mensaje* 168 (1968):175–79.

61. Alves was born in 1933. Cf. his "El protestantismo como una forma de colonialismo," *Perspectivas de Diálogo* 38 (1968):242–48; *A Theology of Human Hope* (Washington, D.C.: Corpus Books, 1969); and *Tomorrow's Child* (New York: Harper and Row, 1972).

62. Among his other works are *La iglesia debe comprometerse en lo político* (Montevideo: JECI, 1970); "La misión de la Iglesia y del presbítero a la luz de la teología de la liberación," *Pasos* 8 (1972):21. He was the chief editor for *Sacerdotes para el Tercer Mundo: historia, documentos, reflexión* (Buenos Aires: Editorial del Movimiento, 1970), and coauthored with Rodríguez Melgarejo, "Apuntes para una interpretación de la iglesia en Argentina," *Víspera* 4 (1970):59–88. See also Aldo Büntig (b. 1931), *El Catolicismo popular en Argentina* (Buenos Aires, 1973).

63. Assmann was born in 1933. Cf. a bibliography in *Fe y cambio social en América Latina* (Salamanca: Ediciones Sígueme, 1973), p. 403. Assmann's most important work is *Teología desde la praxis de la liberación* (Salamanca: Ediciones Sígueme, 1973), in a revised English edition *Theology for a Nomad Church*, trans. Paul Burns (Maryknoll: Orbis Books, 1975). Together with Gutiérrez, Assmann is the most original thinker of the movement.

64. I was born in 1934. The first edition of my *Historia de la Iglesia en América Latina* was published in 1969, now in its third Spanish edition. See also my *Para una ética de la liberación latinoamericana* (Buenos Aires: Siglo Veintiuno, 1973), 2 vols. (Volumes 3 and 4 will be published shortly); *History and the Theology of Liberation* (Maryknoll: Orbis Books); and *Ethics and the Theology of Liberation* (Maryknoll: Orbis Books).

65. The papers of the meeting were published as *Fe y cambio social en América Latina* (1973). There were other meetings following the theme of liberation (once the break with development began). The meeting "Fe y desarrollo" in Mexico City, November 24–28, 1969, Sociedad Teológica Mexicana, *Memoria del primer congreso nacional de teología: Fe y Desarrollo* (Mexico, 1970), 2 vols., was one of the last under the theme of the "theology of development." On March 6–7, 1970, there was an international symposium which produced *Liberación: opción de la iglesia en la década del 70* (Bogotá: Editorial Presencia, 1970). ISAL brought together some twenty theologians in Bueno Aires, August 3–6, 1970. The papers were published in *Fichas de ISAL* 26 (1970) and in *Cristianismo y Sociedad* 23–24 (1970). The Second Meeting of the "theology of liberation" papers were published in the bulletin "Teología de la liberación" (Bogotá, 1970); another meeting was held in Juárez, Mexico, October 16–18, 1970, "Seminario de la teología liberación," the papers of which were mimeographed and are available from IDOC, Via S. Maria dell'Anima 20, 00186, Rome. There was a course of study on "the theology of liberation" in Oruro, Bolivia, December 2–19, 1970. We still remember the academic week of August 1971 on the "Dialéctica de la liberación latinoamérica," published in *Stromata* (Buenos Aires) 1 and 2 (1971), emphasizing the "philosophy of liberation." Cf. *Hacia una filosofía de la liberación latinoamericana* (1971) with contributions from authors such as Osvaldo Ardiles, Horacio Cerutti, Julio de Zan,

Enrique Dussel, Anibal Fornari, Daniel Guillot, and Juan C. Scannone. Since 1971, there have been an increasing number of meetings on "the theology of liberation." In Europe it is still not understood that liberation theology is not the fruit of university dialogue, but is the result of an ecclesial and politically-based movement that is supported by thousands of religious, priests, and laypersons in multiple situations. In the "dialogue" the theology of liberation is not intratheological, but emerges from historical *praxis*. As Rosino Gibellini de Brescia states, "There is no ecclesial movement of the theology of hope nor of political theology. . . . The European may read a book on the theology of liberation and conceptually understand the examples . . . *but he does not understand that it is a movement of the Church*" (*Christus* [Mexico] 479 [1975]:9).

66. Míguez was born in 1924. Cf. "La theologie protestante latinoamericaine aujourd'hui," *IDOC International* 9 (1969):77– 94; "Neuvas perspectivas teológicas," *Pueblo oprimido* (Montevideo, 1972); and *Doing Theology in a Revolutionary Situation* (Philadelphia: Fortress Press, 1974).

67. Scannone was born in 1931. Cf. his "Hacia una dialéctica de la liberación," *Stromata* 17 (1971):23– 60; "El actual desafío planteado al lenguaje teológico latinoamerica de liberación," *CIAS* (Buenos Aires) 211 (1972):5– 20; and "Ontología del proceso auténticamente liberador," *Panorama de la teología latinamericana* (Salamanca: SELADOC, 1975).

68. The outstanding articles of Ferre are: "Iglesia y sociedad opulenta. Una crítica a Suenens desde América latina," *Víspera* 12 (1969):1ff.; and the defense, for political reasons in the Third World, of the encyclical *Humanae vitae* in *Víspera* 17 (1970):26– 31; and "Hacia una teología de la liberación," *Marcha* (Montevideo) 1527 (1971):1– 15.

69. Cf. Eduardo Pironio, "Teología de la liberación," in *Criterio* (Buenos Aires) 1607– 1608 (1970).

70. Boff was born in 1938. Among his works are *Jesús Cristo libertador*, 4th ed. (Petropolis: Vozes, 1974); *Vida para Além de Morte*, 3rd ed. (Petropolis: Editoria Vozes, 1974); *O destino do homen e do mundo*, 3rd ed. (Petropolis: Editoria Vozes, 1974); and *A vida religiosa e a Igreja no processo de liberação* (Petropolis: Editoria Vozes, 1975). Also he was one of the collaborators in the *Concilium* series, "Salvation in Jesus Christ and the Process of Liberation," *The Mystical and Political Dimension of the Christian Faith*, ed. Claude Geffré and Gustavo Gutiérrez 96 (New York: Herder & Herder):78– 91.

71. This subject, nevertheless, has long been an object of contemporary Latin American reflection. Cf. my work, *El humanismo semita* (Buenos Aires: Editorial Universitaria, 1969), appendix "La misión en los poemas del Siervo de Yahweh." That Christ, the Servant of Jehovah, suffered, was crucified, and persecuted *politically*, has a very concrete significance in Latin America. The oppressed people — oppressed socially, politically, and economically for five centuries by the European or North American empires, and by the national oligarchies — for centuries have identified with the bleeding Christs of our baroque and colonial churches. He is the people's Christ, despised by the theologians of secularization and by our oppressive oligarchies.

72. It appears that Father Roger Vekemans received ten million dollars from the CIA in order to campaign against Allende's Popular Unity Party. Cf. the declarations of Father James Vizzard in *The Washington Star* (July 23, 1975), p. 1.

73. Cf. the text in *Mensaje* 185 (1969):396ff., and *The Rockefeller Report on the Americas* (Chicago, 1969).

74. This kind of argument has been used against the theology of liberation. Cf. Assmann, *Teología desde la praxis de liberación* (1973), pp. 238ff.

75. The papers of this meeting were published under the title *Liberación: diálogos en el CELAM* (Bogotá: CELAM, 1974) in which the article by Buenaventura Kloppenburg, "Las tentaciones de la teología de la liberación," pp. 401– 15, is significant because it discusses all of the attacks against liberation theology. Jorge Mejía in his "La liberación, aspectos bíblicos," criticizes liberation theology on the basis of exegesis (pp. 271– 307), and Monseñor

López Trujillo, "Las teologías de la liberación en América Latina," (pp. 27– 67), distinguishes between the "good" and the "bad" (Marxist) theologies of liberation.

76. Published under the title *Teología de la liberación. Conversaciones de Toledo* (Burgos, 1974), with contributions from Jiménez Urresti, Yves Congar, López Trujillo, et al., and they declared that there are "as many theologies as there are authors," and speak of "the integral and universal liberation of all of humanity" (pp. 295ff.). There appears to be no awareness of the existent confliction in a sinful situation, e.g., the domination of one nation by another nation (imperialism), of the class by another class, etc. Their "universalism" hides the contradictions of sin.

77. The theme of the meeting was "Social Conflict in Latin America and Christian Commitment," September 6– 13, 1975, in Lima. There was not a single theologian of liberation among the speakers. On the new direction taken by CELAM since 1972, see F. Houtart, "Le Conseil episcopal d'Amerique Latine accentue son changement," *ICI* (Paris) 481 (1975):10– 24.

78. Among the works of Ellacuría is "Posibilidad, necesidad y sentido de una teología latinoamericana," *Christus* (Mexico) 471 (1975):12– 16, and 472 (1975):17– 23. Ellacuría is an outstanding philosopher, and we can rightly expect a major contribution from him as from Sobrino, who has just published an important work, "La muerte de Cristo," following the liberation theme.

79. Valle is the author of various articles in *Christus* and is a leader in the "Sacerdotes para el pueblo" ("Priests for the People"), now referred to as the "Iglesia solidaria" ("Solidarity Church") in Mexico.

80. Elizondo's first theological-pastoral book will be published in the editorial section of *The Sunday Visitor*. He is founder and director of the Mexican-American Cultural Center in San Antonio, Texas, and the first "Chicano" theologian.

81. Cf. *La Iglesia latinoamericana y la política después de Medellín* (Bogotá: Departamento de Pastoral, CELAM, 1972). Vidales has written numerous articles in *Servir*, *Christus*, and *Contacto* (Mexico). He has just published an analysis on the theology of language of Gilberto Giménez, "El golpe militar y la condenación de Cristianos para el socialismo," *Contacto* 1 and 2 (1975):12– 115.

82. Avila is a Colombian lay theologian and author of various works.

83. Muñoz was born in 1933. His most well-known book is *Nueva conciencia de la Iglesia en América latina* (Santiago: Ediciones Nueva Universidad, 1973).

84. Cussiánovich, *Nos ha liberado* (Lima: Centro de Estudios y Publicaciones, 1972), was written for the "bases" to teach them to think in terms of liberation.

85. In regard to the recent Latin American martyrs, cf. *Scarboro Missions* (Ontario, June 1975). Among them are Carlos Mugica (Argentine priest, age 44), Maurice Lefebvre (priest, assassinated in Bolivia, age 49), Henrique Pereira (Brazilian priest, age 28), Tito de Alencar (priest who was tortured in Brazil and died "tormented" in France, age 29), Juan Alsina (died in Chile in September 1973, age 31), Héctor Gallego (Colombian priest who disappeared in Panama, age 28), and Ivan Betancourt (doctor in letters from the Buenaventura University in Bogotá). Betancourt was born July 28, 1940, and was martyred near Jutigalpa in the diocese of Olancho, June 23, 1975. All were aware that they were giving their lives for Christ the Liberator, and they are as much saints of our Church as were the martyrs of the Mediterranean during the first three centuries.

86. The meeting was held April 23– 30, 1972. The document was published in *Signos de liberación* (Lima: CEP, 1973), "I Encuentro latinoamericano de cristianos por el socialismo," ("The First Latin American Meeting of Christians for Socialism"), pp. 238– 43; more widely with all of the documents by Editorial Siglo XXI (Buenos Aires, 1974). Cf. Gonzalo Arroyo, "Católicos de izquierda en América latina," *Mensaje* 191 (1970):369– 72.

87. Materials from the meeting will be published in Mexico. The impact in Mexico is evaluated in articles by Vicente Leñero, "Teología de la liberación," *Excelsior* (Mexico), and reproduced in *Christus* 479 (1975):62– 70.

88. This meeting, August 18– 25, began to rectify the disencounter with Black theology — as seen in Freire, Assmann, Bodipo, and Cone, *A Symposium on Black Theology and the Latin American Theology of Liberation* (Salamanca: Ediciones Sígueme, 1974), the result of a meeting sponsored by the World Council of Churches, "A Symposium on Black Theology and Latin American Theology of Liberation" — since there was a productive dialogue between the Latin American, Black, feminists, and Chicano theologians. The discussion centered on the main contradictions: "center-periphery," and "United States (Empire) and Latin America (Neocolony)."

89. Orlando Fals Borda, *Ciencia propia y colonialismo intelectual* (Mexico: Editorial Nuestro Tiempo, 1970), especially "¿Es posible una sociología de la liberación?" pp. 22– 32.

90. *Revista de filosofía latinoamericana. Liberación y cultura* (Bueno Aires), in which liberation philosophers are collaborating. Editorial Bonum (Buenos Aires) has published various works by these philosophers. Of special importance is the work by Ricaurte Soler, *Clase y Nación en Hispanoamérica, Siglo XIX* (Panama: Ediciones de la Revista Tareas, 1975).

91. Some of these aspects were indicated by Hugo Assmann, "Iglesia y proyecto histórico," *Teología, Iglesia, y Política* (Madrid, 1973), pp. 137– 58.

Appendix III

A Brief Lexicon of Latin American and Technical Terms Used

Civilization. A new instrumental system.

Christian Institutions. In theology, institutions that theologically are without divine origin but serve in various stages in history for the realization of the mission of the Church. They may be Christian schools, private confessionals, Christian trade unions, confessional political parties, and also such entities as Catholic Action and parish administration. (Cf. Y. Frisque, *Lettre* 61 – 62 [Paris, 1963]: 31 – 39.)

Chtónic (Chthón). The earth, the combined earthly gods as related to the cult of life itself, i.e., fecundity: *Tierra Mater* (Mother Earth) and the Moon.

Civilization, secular and pluralistic. The system of instruments/tools and life-style of the political community, separate and free from all religious society. The self-awareness of the natural community. The insistence that every religious, ideological, and political group should be tolerant of others, especially of minorities. Freedom of worship is, therefore, the basis of the free acceptance of faith. Religious faith comes by free choice and conversion, not as a result of social pressure.

Criollo (from criar, to grow or to rear). A child born in the Americas of European parents. One born in the country and one who knows the secrets of the *tierra adentro* (the hinterland).

El Plata, Río de la Plata, platense. The geographical area contiguous to the River Plate (*Plata*), i.e., Argentina, Uruguay, and Paraguay. Should not be confused with La Plata (Charcas in Bolivia) or with the new city, La Plata, located near Buenos Aires.

Encomienda. The system of agricultural exploitation (as the mining exploitation was called *la mita*) by a Spanish conquistador or colonist to whom a group of Indians was entrusted. In return for the protection and religious instruction they were to receive from the Spanish *encomendero,* the Indians were required to work the Spaniard's land and perform domestic chores. The system was ready-made for abuse, and the Indians in many cases became virtual slaves.

Ethico-mythical nucleus. This provocative expression is from the French philosopher Paul Ricoeur of the Sorbonne. Cf. *Esprit* (Paris, October 1961): 447, in which he states that the "Noyau ethico-mythique" is the intentional foundation of a "world."

Ethos (from Greek). Signifies the customs, the virtues, and the attitudes of a people.

Gaucho. An inhabitant of the Latin American pampas. A descendant of the Spanish *vaquero* (cowboy), especially from the area of Estremadura, Spain.

Huaca. The graves of the Quechua Indians. *Huacal* is the "portable closet made of rods or sticks used for the purpose of transport." In the religious sense the *huaca* is the soul, spirit, or demon of a place, clan, or family. The Indians hold a *huaca* in awe and oftentimes utilize it is worship.

Llanero. The gauchos of Venezuela and Colombia, inhabitants of the Plains.

Nahuatl. Indian tribes who lived in southern Mexico and Central America. They were a Sonoran racial type and a language family of the *Uto-Aztec.* The *Toltecs, Chichimecs, Mexicas,* and *Aztecs* were all Nahuatls. The language used after the founding of the Aztec Empire was *Nahuatl,* and it became the language learned and used by the missionaries, especially by B. Sahagún.

New Christendom. A colonial type that was the politico-religious structure of the colonial Hispanic Empire, and it should be distinguished from medieval European Christendom and from the *New Christendom* proposed by Jacques Maritain.

New Spain. The geographical area comprising present-day Central America and the western United States including California, Arizona, New Mexico, Colorado, and Texas.

New Granada. The geographical area composed of present-day Venezuela, Colombia, and Ecuador.

Pampa. Signifies in the Quechua language the flat, level areas of the countryside. It is that virtually treeless plains area of meridional America.

Patronato. The juridical-religious system by which the Kings of Spain (and Portugal) enjoyed the right to select and present bishops, propose and divide dioceses and parishes, collect tithes, construct convents, church buildings, etc. It included also the right to create missions and send missionaries. In substance, the *Patronato* gave to the King the control of the Church in the Spanish colonies.

Popular Catholicism. The religiosity of the oppressed people in colonial Christendom.

Pueblos. In northern Mexico there were various Indian communities which were called "pueblos." But in this work the word is used in a sense analogous to *doctrinas* or *reducciones* (reservations in North America), viz., the Indian parishes that included the simple Christian communities in Indian villages created by the conquistadores.

Quechua. The primitive language of the inhabitants of the Cuzco area of Peru, which was imposed as the lingua franca on the subjects of the Inca Empire. It is possible that the Incas were linguistically related to the *Aymará* who occupied the Andean area south of Cuzco, i.e., those of the *Tiahuanaco* culture of Bolivia and Peru.

Reductions (from *reductus: plebis Romanae in urbem, Liv.* 2, 33, 11). From the earliest times of the Spanish conquest — and as the result of the inspiration of Vasco de Quiroga and Bartolomé de Las Casas — the gathering of and unifying of the Indians was considered humane and the only effective means of civilizing and evangelizing them. From this questionable assumption there developed slowly a method that was epitomized in the *reducciones guaraníticas* of Paraguay, which became the prototype for the Spanish of Indian society.

Sertâo (Portuguese). Signifies in Brazil the hinterlands or backlands of the country. The Portuguese settled in Brazil primarily along the eastern coast and subsequently in the Amazon Valley. The hinterlands continued to hold for the Brazilians a certain mystique and signified difficulty, infinitude, sublimity, and something absolutely distinct.

Tabula rasa. The missionary method that ignored the significance of the language, the rites, the customs, and the culture of an indigenous people in an attempt to evangelize them. One cannot say with absolute certainty that this method was used in

Latin America, but it is true that the missionaries failed to gain a profound understanding of the indigenous people and their culture. Yet one must recognize that the circumstances of time and distance acted as formidable impediments to the missionary efforts.

Tarasca. The generic language of the frontier inhabitants of western Mexico, people who were indomitable warriors and who lived in the present-day state of Michoacán.

Tierra adentro. Signifies in Latin America the inlands or geographical areas of a country sparsely settled or uninhabited. Also the phrase represents the depth or prehispanic era of the Creole "world." It can also signify the innate understanding and knowledge of the simple, traditional, autochthonous people.

Tupí. Generic name of the Brazilian Indians and their language, i.e., those who lived in the central and northeast areas of the country.

Uránico (Uranus). Heaven, the gods of the heaven, especially the Creator and the Sun. The religious system of the nonspecialized rural peoples.

LOCATION OF THE CULTURAL GROUPS
OF AGRICULTURALISTS, CULTIVATORS, AND NOMADS

THE PROGRESS OF THE MOVEMENT OF CONQUEST AND
EVANGELIZATION

THE PROGRESS OF THE CONQUEST
AND EVANGELIZATION OF BRAZIL

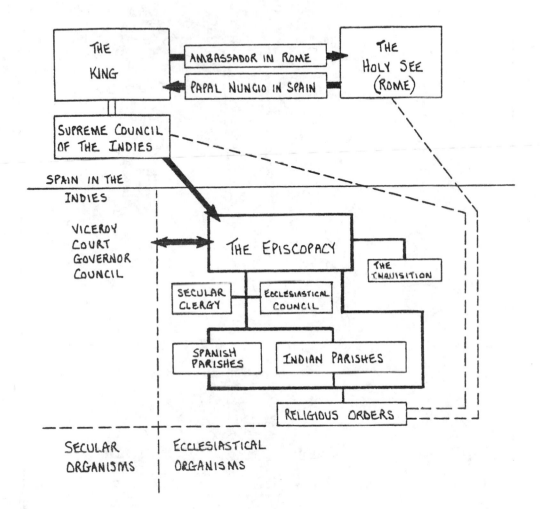

THE STATE-CHURCH SYSTEM OF GOVERNMENT IN COLONIAL
HISPANIC AMERICA

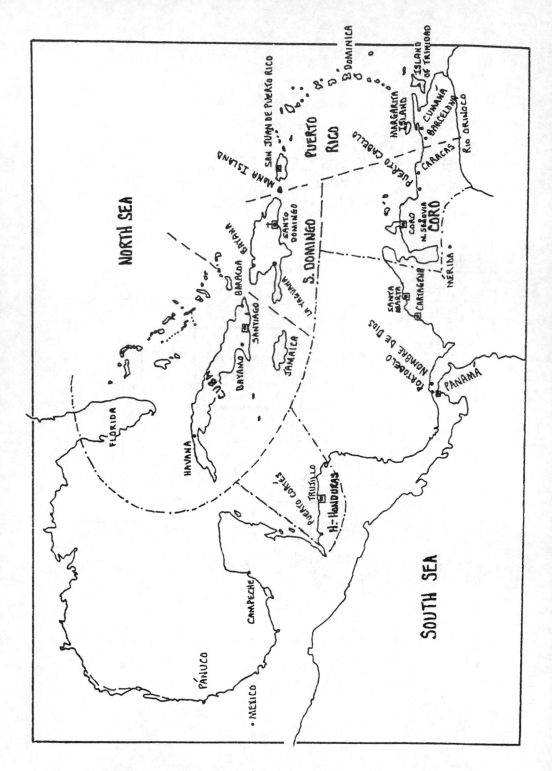

MAP OF THE DIOCESES OF THE ARCHDIOCESE OF SANTO
DOMINGO (1564)

KEY: 1 = Boundaries of the dioceses.
2 = Boundaries of the archdiocese.

– – –	1
–·–··–	2

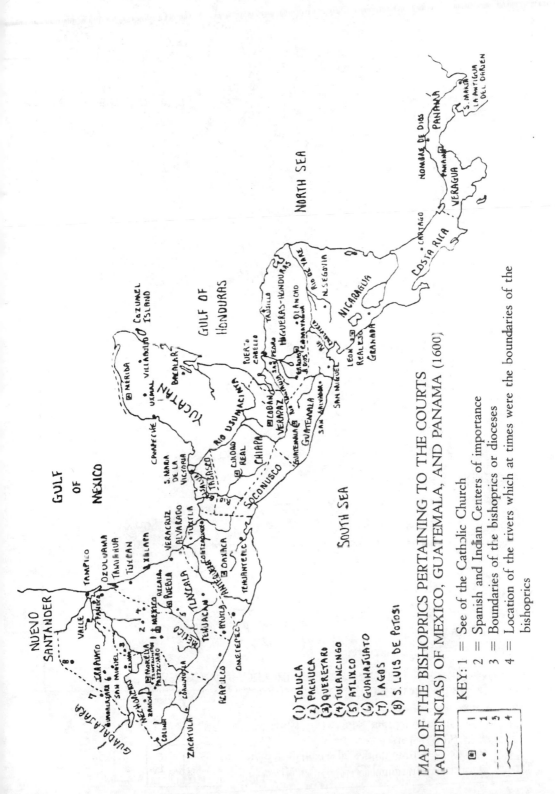

MAP OF THE BISHOPRICS PERTAINING TO THE COURTS
(AUDIENCIAS) OF MEXICO, GUATEMALA, AND PANAMA (1600)

KEY: 1 = See of the Catholic Church
2 = Spanish and Indian Centers of importance
3 = Boundaries of the bishoprics or dioceses
4 = Location of the rivers which at times were the boundaries of the
     bishoprics

(1) TOLUCA
(2) PACHUCA
(3) QUERETARO
(4) TULANCINGO
(5) ATLIXCO
(6) GUANAJUATO
(7) LAGOS
(8) S. LUIS DE POTOSI

MAP OF THE DIOCESES OF THE ARCHDIOCESE OF SANTA FE
AND THE DIOCESE OF QUITO (1620)

KEY: 1 = Borders of the dioceses
2 = Mountain Ranges
3 = Rivers
4 = Communities of Spanish and Indians
5 = Episcopal Sees

1 CASTROVIRREYNA
2 HUANCAVELICA
3 AYACUCHO
4 HUANTA
5 ACÓM
6 PAMPAS
7 VILCAS
8 LUCANAS
9 ANDAHUAYLAS
10 CUZCO
11 ABANCAY
12 URUBAMBA
13 PAUCARTAMBO
14 JULIACA
15 LAMPA
16 PUNO

MAP OF THE DIOCESES OF THE COURT (AUDIENCIA) OF LIMA
(1620)

MAP OF THE DIOCESES AND ARCHDIOCESE OF LA PLATA (1620)

Key: 1 = Borders of the dioceses
2 = Regions of the *reducciones*
3 = Bishoprics
4 = Archbishopric

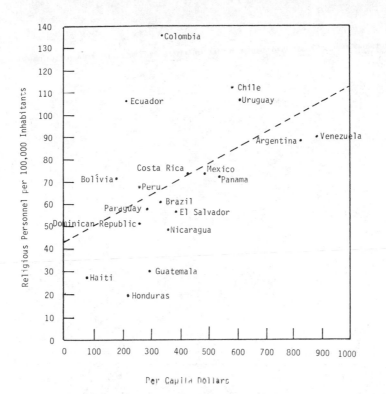

RESOURCES OF THE LATIN AMERICAN CHURCHES INCLUDING
RELIGIOUS PERSONNEL AND THE PER CAPITA INCOME (Source:
Memorandum of the Rand Corporation, 1969)

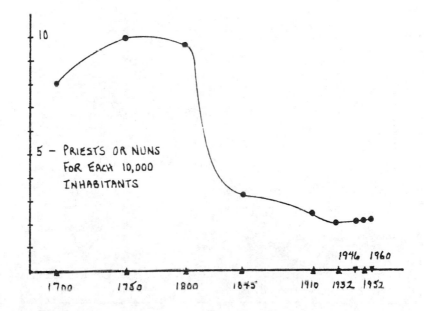

PROPORTIONAL DEVELOPMENT OF THE NUMBER OF RELIGIOUS
IN BRAZIL

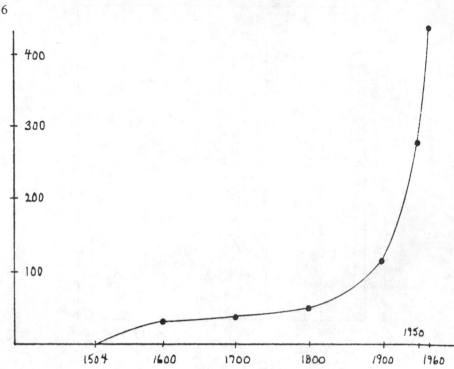

NUMBER OF DIOCESES AND MISSION TERRITORIES IN LATIN
AMERICA (1504-1960)

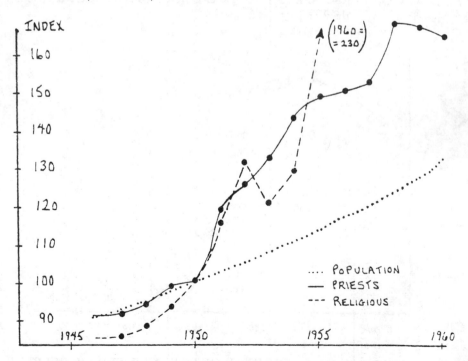

GROWTH OF POPULATION, PRIESTS, AND RELIGIOUS IN
VENEZUELA

THE NEW ORGANIZATION OF CELAM IN 1968

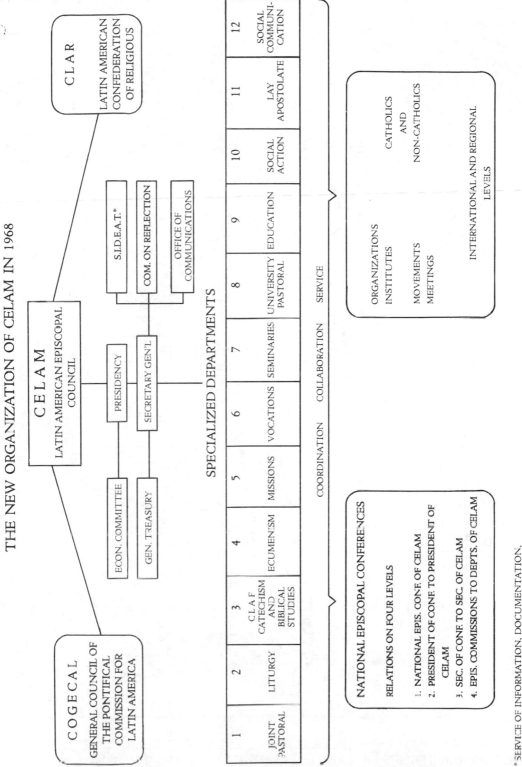

COGECAL
GENERAL COUNCIL OF THE PONTIFICAL COMMISSION FOR LATIN AMERICA

CLAR
LATIN AMERICAN CONFEDERATION OF RELIGIOUS

CELAM
LATIN AMERICAN EPISCOPAL COUNCIL

ECON. COMMITTEE

GEN. TREASURY

PRESIDENCY

SECRETARY GEN'L

S.I.D.E.A.T.*

COM. ON REFLECTION

OFFICE OF COMMUNICATIONS

SPECIALIZED DEPARTMENTS

1	2	3	4	5	6	7	8	9	10	11	12
JOINT PASTORAL	LITURGY	C L A F CATECHISM AND BIBLICAL STUDIES	ECUMENISM	MISSIONS	VOCATIONS	SEMINARIES	UNIVERSITY PASTORAL	EDUCATION	SOCIAL ACTION	LAY APOSTOLATE	SOCIAL COMMUNI-CATION

COORDINATION COLLABORATION SERVICE

NATIONAL EPISCOPAL CONFERENCES

RELATIONS ON FOUR LEVELS

1. NATIONAL EPIS. CONF. OF CELAM
2. PRESIDENT OF CONF. TO PRESIDENT OF CELAM
3. SEC. OF CONF. TO SEC. OF CELAM
4. EPIS. COMMISSIONS TO DEPTS. OF CELAM

ORGANIZATIONS
INSTITUTES

MOVEMENTS
MEETINGS

CATHOLICS
AND
NON-CATHOLICS

INTERNATIONAL AND REGIONAL LEVELS

*SERVICE OF INFORMATION, DOCUMENTATION, STATISTICS, AND TECHNICAL ASSISTANCE

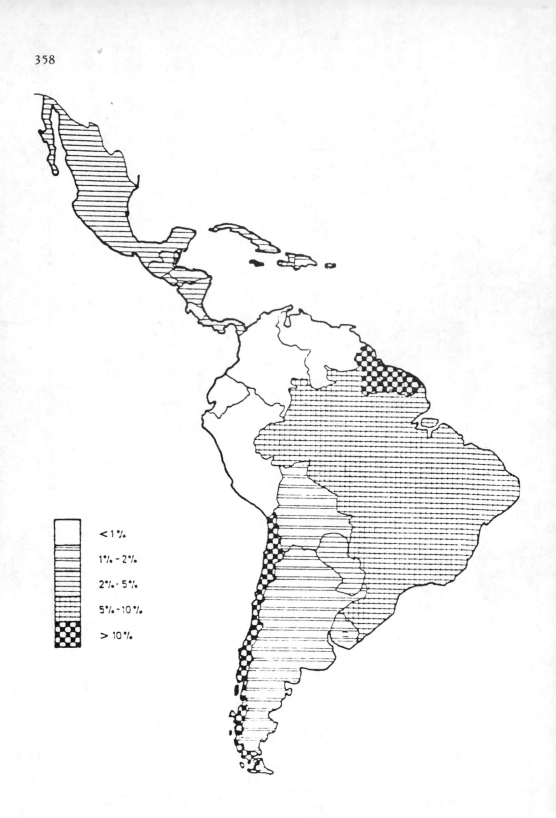

PERCENTAGES OF PROTESTANTS IN LATIN AMERICA (1961)

NATIONS	1916	1925	1938	1949	1952	1957	1961
Argentina	6,850	11,341	38,293	229,056	251,856	364,369	414,323
Bolivia	247	153	4,176	14,211	16,805	29,373	46,663
Brazil	50,297	101,454	241,128	1,657,524	1,600,958	1,755,929	4,071,643
Chile	6,293	11,591	99,460	264,667	370,016	370,428	834,839
Colombia	384	3,404	2,981	25,655	27,386	45,405	92,728
Costa Rica		1,019	1,663	7,771	8,475	10,998	22,902
Panamá		1,005	2,823	22,050	20,189	29,189	57,691
Honduras		10,708	16,515	30,453	29,179	37,666	(37,666)
Guatemala	18,564	10,455	21,740	76,248	75,845	142,465	149,081
Nicaragua		1,727	2,026	17,611	27,758	22,221	34,488
El Salvador		5,170	17,306	32,771	52,146	47,722	41,778
Cuba	25,031	15,942	36,184	96,460	100,582	215,723	264,927
Dominican Republic		8,897	29,005	126,334	193,078	313,279	327,140
Haití	12,044	13,068	14,934	26,094	27,146	22,828	43,765
Ecuador	59	158	546	2,503	3,777	4,888	11,499
Paraguay	321	321	350	15,741	9,264	22,839	36,560
Perú	1,962	4,568	12,212	27,421	69,930	72,789	94,033
Puerto Rico	16,178	13,384	29,122	130,984	136,885	147,411	174,707
México	30,842	32,499	55,652	265,148	334,756	910,951	897,227
Uruguay	1,311	1,321	4,534	20,586	15,666	10,459	42,594
Venezuela	144	1,819	1,913	13,639	13,775	17,776	26,042
LATIN AMERICA	170,527	239,773	632,563	3,171,930	3,380,291	4,230,413	7,710,412

NUMBER OF PROTESTANT FAITHFUL IN LATIN AMERICA (1961)

NUMBER OF PLACES OF WORSHIP AND MINISTRY OF THE PROTESTANT COMMUNITIES IN LATIN AMERICA (1961)*

NATIONS	PLACES OF WORSHIP				FOREIGN MINISTERS				NATIONAL MINISTERS			
	1949	1952	1957	1961	1949	1952	1957	1961	1949	1952	1957	1961
Argentina	955	1,046	1,593	2,067	391	468	680	500	371	618	844	1,703
Bolivia	116	173	323	444	286	233	527	426	129	218	208	637
Brazil	6,122	7,633	10,893	20,990	776	1,903	992	1,428	1,422	3,992	6,950	20,546
Chile	435	566	1,022	2,490	216	301	288	312	308	221	351	654
Colombia	640	799	555	1,618	336	241	297	466	380	224	266	838
Costa Rica	145	145	191	290	97	70	112	164	23	90	109	278
El Salvador	112	441	393	1,144	38	48	54	23	92	128	145	624
Nicaragua	244	262	297	(297)	64	65	65	(65)	473	160	238	(278)
Guatemala	947	837	1,084	1,553	108	119	194	99	139	252	395	598
Honduras	270	271	364	438	104	85	133	157	127	180	202	242
Panamá	240	263	365	358	100	40	278	255	107	213	137	327
Cuba	677	1,066	1,265	1,416	168	348	254	225	578	704	840	1,367
Haití	115	1,609	1,996	2,418	64	506	523	185	455	516	880	1,325
Dominican Republic	730	341	270	611	77	139	135	131	101	171	276	284
Ecuador	112	66	128	186	104	134	208	265	57	92	54	135
Paraguay	84	67	94	270	78	63	113	185	83	55	57	597
Perú	1,247	710	779	1,178	265	254	447	733	377	537	261	842
Puerto Rico	1,278	1,048	1,114	934	131	96	118	120	442	471	420	433
México	1,815	1,938	2,457	3,515	216	342	551	431	1,302	1,408	1,385	2,521
Uruguay	76	73	92	243	45	56	79	80	55	67	89	191
Venezuela	160	189	310	360	157	197	317	291	139	198	192	167
LATIN AMERICA	16,409	9,543	25,565	42,420	821	5,708	6,361	6,541	7,150	10,515	14,299	34,547

*This table was prepared for my work El Protestantismo en America Latina, Feres, II, 16-17.

DATE DUE

OCT 1 '86			
AUG 24 '88			

DEMCO 38-297